Divine Violence
and the Character *of* God

Divine Violence
and the Character *of* God

CLAUDE F. MARIOTTINI

Foreword by Scot McKnight

WIPF & STOCK · Eugene, Oregon

DIVINE VIOLENCE AND THE CHARACTER OF GOD

Copyright © 2022 Claude F. Mariottini. All rights reserved. Except for brief quotations in critical publications or reviews, no part of this book may be reproduced in any manner without prior written permission from the publisher. Write: Permissions, Wipf and Stock Publishers, 199 W. 8th Ave., Suite 3, Eugene, OR 97401.

Wipf & Stock
An Imprint of Wipf and Stock Publishers
199 W. 8th Ave., Suite 3
Eugene, OR 97401

www.wipfandstock.com

PAPERBACK ISBN: 978-1-6667-3212-2
HARDCOVER ISBN: 978-1-6667-2545-2
EBOOK ISBN: 978-1-6667-2546-9

JANUARY 7, 2022

In Memory of

Terence E. Fretheim

A scholar and a teacher

who spent his academic years teaching people

what kind of God God is

Contents

Foreword by Scot McKnight | ix

Acknowledgments | xi

Abbreviations | xiv

Introduction | xv

PART 1: THE CHARACTER OF GOD

1. The God of the Old Testament | 3
2. Divine Violence in the Old Testament | 16
3. Understanding Divine Violence | 35
4. Dealing With Divine Violence | 49
5. Divine Violence and the Suffering of God | 57
6. Divine Violence and Divine Pathos | 68
7. The Character of God | 83

PART 2: THE JUSTICE OF GOD

8. Divine Justice | 101
9. The Problem of Idolatry | 113
10. "The Day I Settle Accounts" | 128
11. The Case of the Twelve Spies | 136
12. The Alien Work of God | 148
13. The Genocidal God | 156

| 14 | THE PRACTICE OF RIPPING OPEN PREGNANT WOMEN | 171
| 15 | THE CANNIBAL MOTHERS | 180
| 16 | THE RIGHTEOUS JUDGE AND THE FATE OF SODOM | 197
| 17 | YAHWEH REJECTS VIOLENCE | 210
| 18 | THE NONVIOLENT CONQUEST OF CANAAN | 226
| 19 | THE CONQUEST OF CANAAN | 242

PART 3: GOD RECONCILING THE WORLD

| 20 | GOD RECONCILING THE WORLD BY HIMSELF | 271
| 21 | GOD RECONCILING THE WORLD THROUGH ISRAEL | 289
| 22 | GOD RECONCILING THE WORLD THROUGH RESTORED ISRAEL | 310
| 23 | GOD RECONCILING THE WORLD THROUGH RENEWED ISRAEL | 331
| 24 | THE WARRIOR GOD AND HIS DEATH ON THE CROSS | 350

POSTSCRIPT | 372

Bibliography | 379

Index of Authors | 399

Index of Subjects | 405

Index of Scripture | 423

Foreword

IN 212 BCE THE CHINESE EMPEROR, Qin Shi Huang, decreed the burning of all books and with them 460 scholars were buried alive. This is one way, cancel culture at the ultimate level, to deal with what someone fears or does not like.[1] Many have dealt with the "God of the Old Testament" in a similar manner, thinking, *that stuff is so violent, God is a God of love, therefore, that stuff can't be from God. Ignore it, or silence it, or alter it, or delete it.* As Hitler's German Christians did to the Jewishness of the Bible. Marcion was the original at this gimmick.

The Old Testament, or what John Goldingay calls the "First" Testament, speaks out of and into shifting generations in the ancient Near East, manifesting the revealing God as well as the context for those revelations. That context at times poses problems for sensitive Bible-reading Jews and Christians. At least that context has posed one unavoidable and career-long problem.

As I was growing into to a Christoform peace ethic I was challenged by the Old Testament stories of violence and a species of violence, war. Are those wars not *Bloody, Brutal, and Barbaric?* Justification of such brutalities was impossible for me. I wanted an explanation. As a young adult growing up in the Vietnam era in a church thoroughly unpolitical and yet committed to patriotic ideals like military service, I had no equipment to use for the barbarities found in the Old Testament. When in college, Dietrich Bonhoeffer's Christoform hermeneutic began to penetrate the marrow of my bones. I pondered in unconscious and unexplored momentary glimpses what to do with the violence. The old explanation that they were sinners, pagans, and destined for God's judgment lost its credibility. The other old explanation that this is reality and I need to suck it up didn't square with the kingdom vision of Jesus. These

---

1. The story found in Morson and Schapiro, *Minds Wide Shut*, 198–99.

war texts suddenly became one of my most challenging problems. The first book I read on this topic was by Peter Craigie, *The Problem of War in the Old Testament*. It seemed to settle my conscience but not for long, so over the next forty years I have read a number of books and essays on the topic, the two most recent of which are Greg Boyd's *The Crucifixion of the Warrior God* and Webb and Oeste's *Blood, Brutal, and Barbaric?*[2] both of which provide light by drawing attention to the hermeneutics of a Christian approach to war in the Bible.

No book has ever completely resolved the shocks I get when reading some of the violence texts, but each of these and others have helped me. Including the book in your hands by my friend and colleague, Claude Mariottini. All I want is for my co-strugglers-with-these-texts to face the texts squarely, admit the realities of the violence, and think about it in a Christian and moral manner. The challenge for all of us is square the violence with the vision of Jesus in the Sermon on the Mount or in his moral summons to cruciformity or Christoformity. How, I ask, do we square *harem* warfare with a Jesus who called us to love our enemies into neighbors, with a Jesus who made a paradigm of his life by submitting to violence, and to a Jesus who calls us to follow him? John Collins, in his provocative study of the Bible and "biblical values," said "The advice of Jesus to turn the other cheek stands in flat contradiction to the prevailing wisdom in the Old Testament" but that "Oddly, most Christians, through the centuries, have not been bothered by this contradiction."[3] Mariottini has been bothered, both by the texts and some recent attempts to resolve, and I believe his solution helps us immensely. This book deserves to be read slowly.

The violence of the Old Testament is in front of us but so is the cross, a cross on which God absorbed and ended the violence so that we might be transformed from nationalisms and violence into peacemakers in the mode of Jesus. Peter Craigie said it well: "Over and over again, Christians have forgotten that God the Warrior became the Crucified God."[4] This book will help you remember.

Scot McKnight
Professor of New Testament
Northern Seminary

2. Boyd, *Crucifixion of the Warrior God*; Webb and Oeste, *Bloody, Brutal, and Barbaric?*

3. Collins, *What Are Biblical Values?*, 147–48.

4. Craigie, *Problem of War*, 99–100.

Acknowledgments

THE ISSUE OF DIVINE VIOLENCE has been a topic of debate in the first two decades of the twenty-first century among scholars, college and seminary students, pastors and lay people, believers and non-believers. There are many reasons for this interest in divine violence. One reason is the rise of secularism and atheism in our society. The rejection of religion leads to the criticism of the God of the Bible.

Another reason is the practical rejection of the Old Testament by many pastors and church members. Some church members believe that Christians do not need to read the Old Testament anymore because the Old Testament has been superseded by the New Testament. This rejection of the Old Testament has created a group of people who could be classified as twenty-first-century Marcionites.

The Marcionites were a heretical group that followed the teachings of a man named Marcion in the second century. Marcion and his followers rejected the Old Testament and taught that the God of the Old Testament was a tyrant. Marcionites believed that the wrathful God of the Old Testament was not the loving and all-forgiving God of the New Testament. They believed that Jesus Christ was not the Son of the God of the Old Testament, but the Son of the good God, who was different from the God of the Old Testament. The present work seeks to present a different picture of the God rejected by Marcion.

Another reason for the interest in divine violence is because many people want to know what kind of God the God of the Old Testament is. During my tenure at Northern Seminary, I taught a course titled "Old Testament Theology: The God of the Old Testament" in which I taught my students how to gain a better understanding of the God of the Old Testament. In the process, I developed a model for understanding divine violence in the Old Testament, a model that I will share in the following chapters.

I would like to thank the hundreds of students who attended my classes on the God of the Old Testament. They had to read and write about difficult issues dealing with the nature and character of God. As a result, students wrote papers that allowed them to gain a better understanding of the character of God. Among the many excellent papers written for this course, I would like to emphasize three of them. Ming Zhang wrote on the "Repentance of God";[5] Vanu Kantayya wrote on "The God of the Old Testament and the God of the New Testament";[6] and Jean Sharp wrote on "The Character of God as Seen Through the Liturgical Credo of Exodus 34:6–7."[7] Many of my former students will recognize in this book many of the issues we discussed in class.

My friend and former colleague Scot McKnight graciously gave me his five books mentioned in the bibliography. Scot has been an encourager and helped me with some of the New Testament content. At the time of my retirement, Scot spoke memorable words on behalf of the faculty and also dedicated his commentary on Colossians to me.[8] I am grateful for his friendship.

I would like to thank Bill Shiell, president of Northern Seminary, for the appointment of Emeritus Professor of Old Testament and for allowing me to have an office at the seminary where most of the research for the book was done. I also want to thank the staff of the Northern Seminary Library, Blake Walter, Colleen Luna, and Janeane Forrest for requesting books and articles from other libraries. They were always ready to help me find material not available in our library.

I would like to thank my wife Donna, my editor for the past fifty years. Since the day we graduated from college and seminary, Donna has used her theological education to offer helpful input into all my writings. I owe her my eternal gratitude.

---

5. The paper is available at https://claudemariottini.com/2014/09/17/studies-on-the-repentance-of-god/.

6. The paper is available at https://claudemariottini.com/2014/07/16/studies-on-the-god-of-the-old-testament/.

7. The paper is available at https://claudemariottini.com/2021/01/14/the-character-of-god/.

8. McKnight, *Letter to the Colossians*.

This book is dedicated to the late Terence E. Fretheim who through his books and articles showed to his readers what kind of God God is.[9]

Claude F. Mariottini
Emeritus Professor of Old Testament
Northern Baptist Seminary

---

9. Chan and Strawn, *What Kind of God?*

Abbreviations

ANET	*Ancient Near Eastern Texts Relating to the Old Testament.* Edited by J. B. Pritchard. 3rd ed. Princeton: Princeton University Press, 1969.
BBE	The Bible in Basic English
BCE	Before the Common Era
BDB	Brown, F., S. R. Driver, and C. A. Briggs. *Hebrew and English Lexicon of the Old Testament.* Oxford: Clarendon, 1907.
CJB	The Complete Jewish Bible
ESV	English Standard Version
GWN	God's Word to the Nations
HALOT	Kohler, L. W. Baumgartner, and J. J. Stamm. *Hebrew and Aramaic Lexicon of the Old Testament.* 4 vols. Leiden: Brill, 1994–99.
HCSB	Holman Christian Standard Bible
KJV	King James Version
LXX	Septuagint
NAB	New American Bible
NEB	New English Bible
NET	New English Translation
NIV	New International Version
NJB	New Jerusalem Bible
NKJ	New King James Version
NLT	New Living Translation
NRSV	New Revised Standard Version
RSV	Revised Standard Version
TNK	Jewish Publication Society Tanak

Introduction

MOST PROBLEMS CHRISTIANS AND NON-CHRISTIANS have with the God of the Old Testament are because of the violence Yahweh uses in dealing with individuals and with nations. Yahweh is seen as an angry God, a God of wrath, a God who destroys the world with a flood, a God who incinerates Sodom, a city full of women and children, and a God who commands the extermination of the Canaanites.

Many people compare Yahweh, the God of the Old Testament, with the God Jesus revealed on the cross, a God of love and a God who rejects violence. These negative portraits of Yahweh trouble many Christians who live by the teachings of Jesus and who believe that Jesus taught that Christians should be nonviolent. People outside the church and the new atheists only know the angry and wrathful God of the Bible. To many of them, the God of the Old Testament is a violent God, a savage God who approves genocide and who forces mothers to eat their children.[10]

When people read the Bible, they read it with a fixed idea about God. God is either a God of love or a savage God who is always angry. Christians read the Bible selectively. They read the Sermon on the Mount, the parables of Jesus, and meditate on Jesus' love for sinners and his acceptance of people who were rejected by his society. They also emphasize how Jesus forgave those who killed him and urged his disciples to love their enemies. When they read the Old Testament, they read the book of Psalms, Proverbs, and a few of the prophetic oracles. When non-Christians and atheists read the Bible, they read it to know more about the annihilation of the Canaanites, the violent acts of God, and to find out how many people Yahweh killed during a fit of anger.

---

10. Berlin, *Lamentations*, 76 explains the sentiment of the author of Lamentations by saying that the "God who slaughters his people is no less cannibal than the mothers who eat their children."

There is another side to Yahweh that his critics seldom mention. Contrary to the image that people attribute to Yahweh, Yahweh presents himself as a God who is merciful and gracious, a God who is slow to anger, a God who abounds in love and faithfulness, and a God who forgives iniquities, transgressions, and sins (Exod 34:6–7). This work focuses on this character of God which he revealed to Moses on Mount Sinai.

My aim is to have a dialogue with the advocates of a nonviolent God. The advocates of a nonviolent God present a view of Yahweh, the Warrior God of the Old Testament, which contradicts what Yahweh says about himself when he revealed his true character to Moses. They emphasize texts that deal with God's wrath, his involvement with the slaughter of men, women, and children, and other acts of violence. They believe that the true nature of God was revealed in the death of Jesus on the cross. They emphasize that Jesus taught a message of nonviolence, a message exhorting his disciples to love their enemies. They believe that texts depicting a violent God do not represent the true God, the God of the New Testament.

In my study of the true nature and character of the God of the Old Testament, I focus on God's work of reconciliation. Paul says that "God was in Christ, reconciling the world unto himself (2 Cor 5:19). I contend that God was in the work of reconciliation from the beginning, from the day the first man and the first woman rebelled against him.

The book is divided into three sections. Section 1 deals with the problem of divine violence. Section 2 deals with the issue of divine justice. Section 3 deals with God's work of reconciliation. Each chapter is dependent on the previous chapter for the proper understanding of the nature and character of God. This is deliberate because it is necessary to emphasize how the revelation of Yahweh's character is the basis for the implementation of divine justice and the reconciliation of the world.

The last chapter, chapter 24, brings the argument to a conclusion. The chapter, "The Warrior God and His Death on the Cross," explains the reason the Warrior God had to die on the cross. Chapter 24 will explain the argument developed in chapters 1–23, that is, that God's intent is to reestablish the relationship with humanity that was broken because of sin and rebellion. The Postscript makes an application of the whole argument, how the death of the Warrior God on the cross has an implication for Christians and the church today.

Some people may argue that this project is a defense of God. My intent is not to defend God but to see how and why God acted the way he did and to understand the reason for divine violence in the Old Testament. Yahweh did use violence in his work of reconciliation. However, the use of violence was necessary when everything else failed. Israel provoked God to anger but they did so to their own harm (Jer 25:6–7). When God brought judgment upon his people, he did so with tears in his eyes. When God had to punish nations, he lamented their suffering and suffered with them.

In the end, I hope to show that Yahweh, the Divine Warrior, is not "a diabolic violent warrior god," but "a God merciful and gracious, slow to anger, and abounding in steadfast love and faithfulness."

PART 1

The Character of God

1

The God of the Old Testament

PEOPLE TODAY LIVE IN A postmodern society that eschews all kinds of violence and rejects the idea of a wrathful and violent God who uses violence against his own people in pursuit of divine justice. According to Whybray, the God of the Old Testament is a God who "turns against his own people" without cause because "there is a demonic or vicious side to his nature."[1] People who read the Bible have strong reactions to the many texts in the Old Testament that depict Yahweh acting violently by commanding his people to kill men, women, and children, by exacting vengeance against his enemies, by exercising retributive punishment, and by bringing severe judgment upon people who fail to obey his commandments. Even the people of Israel, at times, questioned the justice of Yahweh and the severe ways he dealt with the nation and with individuals. As Crenshaw puts it, "the problem is not so much the justification of God in the face of actual suffering as it is the reconciling of evil with the knowledge that God intends salvation for mankind."[2]

THE PROBLEM OF DIVINE VIOLENCE

In recent years many books and articles have been published dealing with the problem of divine violence in the Old Testament. One focus of these studies is to understand and explain the many texts in the Old Testament

1. Whybray, "'Shall Not the Judge," 1.
2. Crenshaw, "Popular Questioning," 380.

which attribute violence to Yahweh, the God of the Old Testament.³ C. S. Cowles, in his article "The Case for Radical Discontinuity,"⁴ asked the following question: "How do we harmonize the warrior God of Israel with the God of love incarnate in Jesus? How can we reconcile God's instructions to 'utterly destroy' the Canaanites in the Old Testament with Jesus's command to 'love your enemies' in the New Testament?"⁵ One problem with Cowles's interpretation of the violence in the Old Testament is his assertion that what the New Testament says about God is more important than what the Old Testament says about God. Cowles believes that what Jesus said about God is the way Christians should view God. To Cowles, the Old Testament reveals a God of wrath, but Jesus reveals a God that is a God of love and peace.

Cowles believes that Jesus presents an accurate revelation of the true God of the Bible. According to him, Christians should not believe what the Old Testament teaches about God in general, but what Jesus teaches about God in particular. Cowles wrote: "The God portrayed in the Old Testament was full of fury against sinners, but the God incarnate in Jesus is not."⁶ One reason for Cowles's critical view of the God of the Old Testament is his low view of the authority of the Old Testament. Cowles believes that the Old Testament distorts the true character of God. He said that many of the events of the Old Testament do not reflect the true nature of God, that is, what Moses and Joshua commanded the people to

---

3. Although there is much debate and disagreement on the use of the divine name, throughout this work, I will be using the name Yahweh to designate the God who revealed himself to Israel, "I am Yahweh, that is my name" (Isa 42:8 NJB). As Brettler, "Hebrew Bible," 26 explains, "The Israelite God was named YHWH, perhaps pronounced Yahweh." Brettler goes on to say that many English translations of the Bible "render YHWH as LORD; this is not quite correct, since YHWH, unlike LORD, is a proper name." The reason for the use of the divine name Yahweh is because, as Goldingay, *Biblical Theology*, 19–20 notes, "in the modern world one cannot assume that people who use the word God mean by it the being or the kind of being that the Scriptures speak of." He writes, "In connection with the First Testament, it is one reason for continuing to use the name Yahweh rather than replacing it by an ordinary word for 'the Lord' or 'God.' It is as Yahweh that God is the one who created the cosmos, is ultimately sovereign over everything in the heavens and on the earth, has been revealingly, persistently and self-sacrificially involved with Israel in a way that embodies love but also toughness, is committed to bringing Israel and the world to their destiny in the acknowledgment of him, has embodied himself in Jesus, makes himself known in the Holy Spirit and will be God to eternity as he was God from eternity."

4. Cowles, "Radical Discontinuity," 13–44.
5. Cowles, "Radical Discontinuity," 14.
6. Cowles, "Radical Discontinuity," 28.

do "are incompatible with the nature and character of God as disclosed in Jesus."[7]

Cowles's argument focuses on God's command to Moses and to Joshua to conquer the Canaanites and "devote them to complete destruction" (Deut 7:2). Cowles said that the God of the New Testament, a God of mercy and grace, would never order the Israelites to commit "genocide" and destroy the seven Canaanite nations, including men, women, and children. The God of the Old Testament fights as a warrior for Israel and Jesus in the New Testament tells his disciples to love their enemies. God's behavior in the Old Testament may seem different from his behavior in the New Testament, for the God of war becomes the God of love. To Cowles, this difference in God's behavior forces the reader of the Bible to harmonize these two supposedly irreconcilable perspectives of God.

Cowles has a low view of the relevance of the Old Testament for the proper understanding of God. If we accept Cowles's view that Moses and Joshua misunderstood God's purpose for the conquest, then how can people trust what the rest of the Bible says about God? Most Christians believe in the inspiration and the authority of the Bible, and that includes the Old Testament. When Christians proclaim the authority of the Scriptures, they also acknowledge that the writings of the Bible are a work of human authors, containing different literary forms, a work that reflects the attitude and cultural context of the people who wrote those books that form the Hebrew Bible.

The authority of the Bible implies that the Bible reveals the character and nature of the true God and that readers can trust what it says about God. In short, Christians accept the authority of the Bible because they trust the God who revealed himself in the history of ancient Israel. Jesus speaks of a God who is a God of judgment as well as a God of mercy. It is in his mercy that God keeps reaching out to men and women, even when they rebel against him. It is in his righteousness that the God of the Bible, the same God who is the God of the Old Testament and the God of the New Testament, is spoken of as the righteous judge who will bring judgment upon wicked people.

Eric Seibert[8] seeks to address some of the passages where God's behavior seemingly contradicts other passages in the Bible where God is presented as a loving and forgiving God. Seibert believes that it is

---

7. Cowles, "Radical Discontinuity," 42.
8. Seibert, *Disturbing Divine Behavior*; Seibert, *Violence of Scripture*.

impossible to reconcile (what he believes to be) these irreconcilable views of God and that these disturbing actions of God cannot be defended. According to Seibert, the issue of divine behavior becomes very important when people begin to study the Old Testament and are confronted with some of the things God said and did. Many people who read the Old Testament, even those who are Christians and believe in God, are surprised and horrified at some aspects of God's behavior and how he commanded the people of Israel to slaughter the Canaanites and kill all the people who lived in their cities.

Seibert says that the problem of divine behavior in the Old Testament is one of those issues that has caused believers and nonbelievers to question whether the God of the Old Testament is a good or an evil God. The Bible presents many of the actions of God that have raised moral and theological issues in the mind of readers. Some of these troubling images of God bewilder readers of the Bible. They struggle with these disturbing images of God and some even question whether the God who revealed himself to Israel and the God who was manifested in the person of Jesus Christ are the same God or whether this God is a God of love and mercy.

There is no doubt that some of the things God asked his people to do appear to be evil and unfair. How could God ask Abraham to kill his beloved son Isaac when God gave that son to Abraham in his old age and then promised Abraham that through Isaac and his descendants a great nation would emerge to bless all the families of the earth? How could God order Joshua and the Israelites to conquer the land of Canaan and in the process destroy many cities and exterminate entire populations, including men, women, and children, young and old? How could God order Saul to attack the Amalekites and then order him to "utterly destroy all that they have; do not spare them, but kill both man and woman, child and infant, ox and sheep, camel and donkey" (1 Sam 15:3)?

If the God of the Old Testament waged war, the God who revealed himself in Christ told his followers to love their enemies. If the God of the Old Testament commanded entire nations to be destroyed, the God who revealed himself in Christ told his followers to turn the other cheek, to forgive, and not to kill. The issue Seibert raises in his book is whether the God of the Old Testament is different from the God of the New Testament.

These are questions with which most readers of the Bible struggle. And in response to this disturbing divine behavior, some people lose faith in God and become atheists and critics of the God of the Bible. Others become like Marcion, who rejected the God of the Old Testament in favor of the God of Jesus. Marcion believed that the Old Testament was the gospel of an alien God. These neo-Marcionites reject the God of the Old Testament to become followers of the God of the New Testament.

Those who believe that the God of the Old Testament and the God of the New Testament are the one and same God, seek ways of understanding God's actions and make an attempt at demonstrating that this so-called disturbing divine behavior is not inconsistent with what the Old Testament says about God as a gracious and merciful God. Can Christians accept the God of the Old Testament and his actions and still believe that he is a merciful and gracious God?

Seibert's solution to the problem of disturbing divine behavior is not acceptable. To say that some of the things God commanded the people of Israel to do never happened, destroys the historical underpinnings of the Bible. To say that the God of the text and the real God are different is to minimize the fact that all that we know about God is found in the text. In the same vein, most of the solutions proposed by Seibert are unacceptable.

According to Cowles and Seibert, what Jesus reveals about the character of God is what matters. To Cowles and Seibert, if what Jesus said about God contradicts what the Old Testament says about God, then what Jesus said is what actually reflects the real character of the God of the Old Testament. The character of God presented in Cowles's and Seibert's argument is contrary to the character of God revealed in the Old Testament. According to them, the God whom Jesus revealed is nonviolent, a God who is kind to sinners, a God who does not judge people because he is a God of love. Jesus revealed a God who offers mercy to sinners but promised judgment to the unrepentant sinner. God in his mercy reaches out to humanity in love, but Jesus also emphasized the judgment to come. The God portrayed in the New Testament is the same God revealed in the Old Testament, a God who offers mercy and promises judgment.

The character of God is revealed in his relationship with Israel in the Old Testament. In dealing with Israel, God offers both mercy and judgment. In an act of redemption, God brought Israel out of Egypt into the land God promised Abraham to give to his descendants. In an act of judgment, God removed Israel from that land when they rebelled against him. When seen from a biblical perspective, there is no difference between the God revealed in Jesus from the God revealed in the Old Testament. In his nature, God is nonviolent. It is not God's "purpose that anyone should be destroyed, but that everyone should turn from his sins" (2 Pet 3:9), but the fact remains that the consequence of sin is death (Rom 6:23). God acts violently when it becomes necessary for him to act as a judge. The God of the Old Testament is love but he is also a righteous judge. Thus, making a distinction between the God of the Old Testament and the God of the New Testament, describes God in ways that are not only inaccurate, but also antithetical to God's true nature.

In his book, *The Crucifixion of the Warrior God*,[9] Gregory Boyd deals with the problem of divine violence in the Old Testament. One focus of his study is his effort to understand and explain the many texts in the Old Testament which attribute violence to Yahweh, the God of the Old Testament. To Boyd, the violent portrayals of God in the Old Testament must be reinterpreted in light of the full revelation of God in Christ and his death on the cross. Boyd says that the Old Testament portrays God as a wrathful and jealous God, who orders the slaughter of men, women, and children. In contrast, Jesus teaches a nonviolent message in which he calls his disciples to love their enemies. Boyd says that as he was writing his book, he came to the conclusion that attempts to defend texts in the Old Testament that portray Yahweh acting violently were futile. To mitigate divine violence is difficult because the texts clearly show that Yahweh, at times, acts violently against individuals and nations. However, to reinterpret violent texts as Boyd does (see chapter 3), creates a false impression that Yahweh does not act violently when dealing with the problem of sin, violence, and evil.

Boyd studies acts of divine violence in light of the cross. Boyd emphasizes that texts depicting a violent God are not accurate representations of God. These texts show that God is willing to allow fallen and culturally conditioned sinners to do to him what they did to Christ on the cross. Boyd wrote, "portraits of God commanding or engaging in violence were literary crucifixes, mirroring the sin of God's people that God humbly stooped to bear."[10]

The purpose of the present work is to look at divine violence in light of the character of God revealed to Moses on Mount Sinai.[11] In the

---

9. Boyd, *Crucifixion of the Warrior God*.

10. Boyd, *Crucifixion of the Warrior God*, 548.

11. This study on divine violence will dialogue primarily with the works of Cowles, Seibert, and Boyd since they have provided a more detailed criticism of divine violence in the Old Testament. The works of Creach, Lamb, and Copan listed below also deal with the problem of divine violence, but their approach is more irenic.

chapters below, I will be dialoguing with the views presented by Cowles, Seibert, and Boyd. Boyd has presented a more comprehensive view of divine violence in the Old Testament. Thus, many of the problems he raises and the views he proposes will be discussed in more detail throughout this study. The study of divine violence will conclude with a brief introduction to Jesus's ministry and how the death of the incarnate God on the cross provides the true answer to the problem of divine violence in the Old Testament.

UNDERSTANDING DIVINE VIOLENCE

The problem of divine violence in the Old Testament is a topic that has generated a vast amount of literature.[12] People everywhere are trying to understand or explain why God allows or commands brutal acts against nations and acts of violence against innocent people. I believe there are two important theological approaches that must be used if one seeks a better understanding of divine violence in the Old Testament. First, it is Boyd's fundamental principle enunciated in the title of his book, that is, that Yahweh, the Warrior God of the Old Testament, died on the cross. The proper understanding of the crucifixion of the Warrior God, as Boyd titled his book, has much to teach about the work of Yahweh in the world and why that work finds its culmination on the cross (I will discuss the crucifixion of the Warrior God in chapter 24).

The second theological approach that helps readers of the Old Testament understand the problem of divine violence is relational theology. Throughout the Old Testament Yahweh shows himself to be a relational God[13] and this aspect of the divine nature gives men and women freedom to make decisions that, at times, impugn Yahweh's reputation and inculpate him in acts that are contrary to his nature and character. In texts

---

12. The bibliography on divine violence has grown immensely in the last few years. The following works are cited most often in the discussion of divine violence: Cowles et al., *Show Them No Mercy*; Collins, *Does the Bible Justify Violence?*; Fretheim, "God and Violence in the Old Testament"; "Violence and the God of the Old Testament"; Brueggemann, *Divine Presence Amid Violence*; Seibert, *Disturbing Divine Behavior*; Seibert, "Recent Research on Divine Violence"; Copan, *Is God a Moral Monster?*; Lamb, *God Behaving Badly*; Creach, *Violence in Scripture*; Zehnder and Hagelia, *Encountering Violence in the Bible*; Copan and Flannagan, *Did God Really Command Genocide?*; Carroll R. and Wilgus, *Wrestling with the Violence of God*; Trimm, "Recent Research on Warfare in the Old Testament"; Boyd, *Crucifixion of the Warrior God*.

13. Fretheim, *God and World*. See also Fretheim, *God So Enters into Relationships*.

where violence is present, what Yahweh is trying to do in the world is dependent in many ways upon what men and women say and do. When readers read these texts, it becomes easy to fail to see that these acts are being perpetrated by free human agents. Then, instead of looking at human responsibility for these actions, readers see God at work in what is happening, or they blame God "when things go wrong" or for the act perpetrated by human agents.[14]

Many Christians are reluctant to adopt relational theology in their study of God's work in the world. They reject relational theology because their theological background does not allow them to look at what the text really says about God. As Patrick said, "Classical theism, with its understanding of God as an absolute being or will, made it impossible for God to be the character God is depicted to be in the Old Testament. The capacity of God to interact with God's creatures was sacrificed to divine immutability."[15] Jewish scholars have no problem in accepting a relational God who becomes vulnerable when dealing with his people. Christians who reject relational theology will struggle with some of the texts that portray a non-monarchical view of God, texts that "depict God as one who suffers, as one who has entered deeply into the human situation and made it his own."[16]

In the chapters that follow I will discuss several topics that are crucial in helping readers understand the problem of divine violence in the Old Testament. These topics, when applied together in the study of the texts that depict divine violence, provide a better understanding of the reasons God is acting violently.

The primary source for the knowledge about God is the Bible. The Old Testament does not provide a systematic doctrine of God. The God of the Old Testament is revealed in what he does and in what he says about himself. One book that most Christians have never heard of, but one that most Christians should read, is Gerald L. Schroeder's *God According to God*.[17] Schroeder has a PhD in physics and the earth sciences. He is a scientist who believes in God and who seeks to present an honest view of God as he is revealed in the Hebrew Bible.

---

14. Fretheim, "Divine Dependence upon the Human," 11.
15. Patrick, "How Should the Biblical Theologian Go," 364.
16. Fretheim, *Suffering of God*, xv.
17. Schroeder, *God According to God*.

In his book, Schroeder speaks about people's problem with the God of the Old Testament. He wrote:

> The problem so many people, believers as well as skeptics, have with God really isn't with God. It's with the stunted perception of the biblical God that we imbibe in our youthful years. As children we yearn for a larger-than-life figure who can guide and protect us. . . . So, we grow up retaining this childhood notion of an all-powerful, ever present, ever involved, never erring Creator. Unfortunately, this image of God fails when adults discover that the facts of life are often brutally at odds with this popular, though misguided, piece of wisdom. It's no wonder that atheists chortle at the naiveté of the idea of such a God.[18]

The major focus of this book will be on the character of the God of the Old Testament. The aim of this book is to address many of our preconceived views about Yahweh, the God of the Old Testament. The following chapters will focus on the character of God, paying particular attention to what I have called "the intergenerational punishment statement." The intergenerational punishment statement is found in Exod 34:7. Intergenerational refers to an issue or a problem affecting several generations. The intergenerational punishment statement in Exod 34:7 refers to Yahweh visiting the sins of the father over several generations: "yet by no means clearing the guilty, but visiting the iniquity of the parents upon the children and the children's children, to the third and the fourth generation" (Exod 34:7).[19] By dealing with preconceived ideas about the intergenerational punishment statement in Exod 34:7, the reader will know the true character of the God of the Old Testament, the God who also became human and lived among us.

YAHWEH, THE GOD OF THE OLD TESTAMENT

Christians believe in God, but most Christians do not know the God in whom they believe. This is most evident when it comes to the God of the Old Testament. The reason for this lack of knowledge of the God of the Bible is because most of our knowledge of God comes by word of mouth. People talk about God from the knowledge of what they have heard

---

18. Schroeder, *God According to God*, 5.

19. Unless otherwise noted, all scripture references are from NRSV. However, in many cases, when the divine name appears in the text, I will be using the NJB.

about God or from what they think about the kind of God God is or should be. A few Christians read theology books which provide a chapter on the doctrine of God, but few Christians spend much time studying what the Old Testament says about God. The Old Testament does not provide a systematic doctrine of God. The God of the Old Testament is known by what he does and by what he says about himself. The God of the Bible is the God of revelation. As Emil Brunner writes, "The God who is discovered through thought is always different from the God who reveals Himself through revelation. . . . The God of the Bible is absolutely the God of revelation."[20]

Richard Dawkins, the atheist who made his fame mocking religion, has one of the most unflattering views about the God of the Old Testament. He wrote, "The God of the Old Testament is arguably the most unpleasant character in all fiction; jealous and proud of it; a petty, unjust, unforgiving, control-freak; a vindictive, bloodthirsty ethnic cleanser, a misogynistic, homophobic, racist, infanticidal, genocidal, filicidal, pestilential, megalomaniacal, sadomasochistic, capriciously malevolent bully."[21]

The God presented by Boyd resembles the God that Dawkins describes because Boyd's true God is hiding behind a mask. In order to explain divine violence in the Old Testament, Boyd placed "a mask of ugliness" on God. This mask, unfortunately, hides the true nature of the merciful and gracious God. This masked God is a violent, genocidal God, a God who gave Israel a promise that God knew was destined to fail, a God who caused mothers to cannibalize their own children, a God who accomplished evil work through evil agents. This is what Boyd says about Yahweh, the God of the Old Testament: "On the cross, Jesus exposed this sinful god-in-our-own-image to be the blasphemous lie that it is. On the cross, the diabolic violent warrior god we have all-too-frequently pledged allegiance to has been forever repudiated and 'brought to nothing.'"[22] The God Boyd is describing, this masked God, is not the God who calls himself "a God merciful and gracious, slow to anger, and abounding in steadfast love and faithfulness" (Exod 34:6).

The answer to divine violence is found on the cross where Yahweh, the Warrior God of the Old Testament, died. Cowles, Seibert, and Boyd

---

20. Brunner, *Revelation and Reason*, 43.
21. Dawkins, *God Delusion*, 31.
22. Boyd, *Crucifixion of the Warrior God*, 1261.

say that the true character of God was revealed on the cross, but I contend that the true character of God was revealed in what Yahweh said about himself when he revealed his character and nature to Moses on Mount Sinai. Although the cross is the supreme revelation of God, the Warrior God who died on the cross is the same God who revealed himself to be the gracious and merciful God to the people of Israel.

After all, Yahweh, Israel's warrior who died on the cross, is none other than Jesus Christ himself. Jesus Christ is the embodiment of the God of the Old Testament. Jesus Christ is truly God and truly man. The fourth Gospel clearly identifies Jesus as Yahweh when John depicts Jesus as identifying himself with the "I Am" of Exod 3:14 (John 8:58). To paraphrase John, "In the beginning was the Word, the Word was God, and God became a human being and lived with us" (John 1:1, 14). As Brunner writes, "God revealed Himself truly and completely" when he became a man. Only a truly "Merciful and Loving God is capable of such a revelation."[23] Jesus said: "The Father and I are one" (John 10:30). In his article, "YHWH and Jesus in One Self-same Divine Self," MacDonald said that "Jesus is YHWH's visible conception of himself."[24]

Cowles, Seibert, and Boyd declare that the cross is the key that unlocks the true meaning of divine violence in the Old Testament. However, what Yahweh said about himself, the revelation of his true character and nature to Moses, is the only way we can truly understand Old Testament texts that display divine violence. The following chapters dealing with the nature and character of God will provide a small picture of how the statement on intergenerational punishment can shed some light on divine violence. The larger picture, the proper understanding of divine violence, will also be addressed in subsequent chapters. To summarize the content of this larger picture: "In Christ God was reconciling the world to himself" (2 Cor 5:19). But the fact is that God has been reconciling the world unto himself since Eden. The Old Testament is the story of God redeeming his fallen creation before Christ, a story that began in Eden and will end with the establishment of the new heaven and the new earth mentioned in the book of Revelation.

---

23. Brunner, *Revelation and Reason*, 236.
24. MacDonald, "YHWH and Jesus," 23.

THE REVELATION OF YAHWEH'S CHARACTER

In revealing what kind of God he was, Yahweh passed before Moses, and proclaimed, "Yahweh, Yahweh, a God merciful and gracious, slow to anger, and abounding in steadfast love and faithfulness, keeping steadfast love for the thousandth generation, forgiving iniquity and transgression and sin, yet by no means clearing the guilty, but visiting the iniquity of the parents upon the children and the children's children, to the third and the fourth generation" (Exod 34:6–7).

The revelation of Yahweh's character to Moses on Mount Sinai is "the normative conception of Yahweh" in the Old Testament. Boyd wrote, "A clear expression of the normative conception of Yahweh in the OT is Moses's confession that Yahweh is a 'compassionate and gracious God, slow to anger, abounding in love and faithfulness, maintaining love to thousands and forgiving wickedness, rebellion and sin' (Exod 34:6–7)."[25] However, in citing Yahweh's revelation of his nature and character to Moses, Boyd deliberately omitted the last clause of the confession which reads: "yet by no means clearing the guilty, but visiting the iniquity of the parents upon the children and the children's children, to the third and the fourth generation" (Exod 34:7).

The reason for omitting the intergenerational punishment statement found in Exod 34:7 is because Boyd, referring to the statement as it appears in Exod 20:5, said, "Ezekiel specifically taught that children are never punished for their parent's [sic] sin (Ezekiel 18). This insight arguably corrects the earlier Israelite conception of Yahweh 'punishing the children for the sin of the parents to the third and fourth generation (Exod 20:5).'"[26] Boyd's statement, that "Ezekiel specifically taught that children are never punished for their parent's [sic] sin (Ezekiel 18)" is a misunderstanding of Ezek 18. In his study of individual responsibility in the book of Ezekiel, Barnabas Lindars says that "Ezekiel makes no attempt to break out of the ideas of group solidarity common to the times in which he lived."[27] According to Lindars, if Ezekiel "is really denying that the sons suffer for the sins of the fathers, the tragic condition of the exiles ought not to have happened."[28] Rather, the prophet is denying the validity of the proverb in Ezek 18:2. The people used the proverb to say

---

25. Boyd, *Crucifixion of the Warrior God*, 282.
26. Boyd, *Crucifixion of the Warrior God*, 838n58.
27. Lindars, "Ezekiel and Individual Responsibility," 466.
28. Lindars, "Ezekiel and Individual Responsibility," 464.

that they were in exile because of their fathers' sins. Ezekiel declares that they are in exile not because of the sins of their fathers, but because of their own sins.

The intergenerational punishment statement appears in four texts in the Old Testament: Exod 20:5; 34:6–7; Num 14:18–19; and Deut 5:9–10. People writing about "the dark side of God"[29] and books dealing with divine violence in the Old Testament are horrified with the intergenerational punishment statement. They call it unjust, merciless, unfair, and unreasonable because God punishes innocent children for the wickedness of their fathers. However, in every one of these books and articles, no one has done a study of these four passages to see how the intergenerational punishment statement is applied in real-life situations. I believe that a detailed study of these four texts is important for anyone who seeks to know the true character of the God of the Old Testament and understand the problem of divine violence. In the chapters that follow, I will study these four passages and look at the historical context that serves to illustrate how these texts were applied to the people of Israel.

---

29. Nysse, "Dark Side of God," 437–46; Lloyd, "Sacred Violence," 184–99; Barton, "Dark Side of God," 122–34.

2

Divine Violence in the Old Testament

IN THE OLD TESTAMENT, YAHWEH is portrayed as one who speaks peace to his people: "Let me hear what God the LORD will speak, for he will speak peace to his people, to his faithful, to those who turn to him in their hearts" (Ps 85:8). "May the LORD give strength to his people! May the LORD bless his people with peace" (Ps 29:11).

CONTRADICTORY IMAGES OF YAHWEH

The word *šālōm*, "peace," appears 237 times in the Hebrew Bible. The word is used with a variety of meanings. In Ps 85:8 the word *šālōm* can mean well-being, the security and the salvation that Yahweh provides to his people.[1] In Ps 85:10, the word "peace" appears together with two words that also appear in Exod 34:6, steadfast love (*ḥesed*) and faithfulness (*ʾĕmet*): "Steadfast love and faithfulness will meet; righteousness and peace will kiss each other" (Ps 85:10). According to Zenger, the enduring significance of these words is that the world will only "be a world of God and human beings when the four entities of steadfast love, fidelity, justice, and peace encounter one another."[2] Although Yahweh is presented as a God who speaks peace, Yahweh is also presented in the Old Testament as a warrior God, "Yahweh is a warrior; Yahweh is his name" (Exod 15:3).

---

1. Stendebach, "*šālōm*," 15:41.
2. Hossfeld and Zenger, *Psalm 2*, 366.

Many people have trouble reconciling these contradictory images of Yahweh: Yahweh as a God of peace and Yahweh as a warrior God. Different texts in the Old Testament show different aspects of the character of Yahweh. Some texts reveal Yahweh as a warrior (Exod 15:3), others portray Yahweh as a savior (Ps 106:21). Some texts show Yahweh as a God who uses violence to combat violence (Gen 6–7), others show Yahweh as a God who saves people from violence (2 Sam 22:3). Although the people of Israel had different understandings of the nature of Yahweh, Yahweh always remained a gracious and merciful God, a God who does not change in his character (Mal 3:6), a God who remains the savior forever (Ps 102:27).

One of the major issues with violence in the Old Testament is that many people have used violent texts in the Old Testament to carry out violence in the name of God. Some authors, like Jan Assmann, believe that there is a link between monotheism and violence.[3] There is no escaping the fact that there is violence in the Old Testament, but the problem is that these violent texts become the primary texts used to describe the way God is conceived in the Old Testament. The violence used by the Israelites to conquer the land of Canaan should not be used as a validation for wars of conquest or as a support for genocidal practices. In order to avoid this misapplication of the violent texts of the Old Testament, the texts should be interpreted in their historical, social, and literary contexts.

When Yahweh made a covenant with Abraham, Yahweh promised to give his descendants the land of Canaan as an inheritance: "To your descendants I give this land, from the river of Egypt to the great river, the river Euphrates, the land of the Kenites, the Kenizzites, the Kadmonites, the Hittites, the Perizzites, the Rephaim, the Amorites, the Canaanites, the Girgashites, and the Jebusites" (Gen 15:18–21).

When Yahweh liberated Israel from their oppressive situation in Egypt, Yahweh told the people that he was about to fulfill the promise he made to Abraham to give them the land of Canaan as an inheritance: "Yahweh then said, 'I have indeed seen the misery of my people in Egypt. I have heard them crying for help on account of their taskmasters. Yes, I am well aware of their sufferings. And I have come down to rescue them from the clutches of the Egyptians and bring them up out of that country, to a country rich and broad, to a country flowing with milk and honey, to

---

3. Assmann, *Moses the Egyptian*.

the home of the Canaanites, the Hittites, the Amorites, the Perizzites, the Hivites and the Jebusites'" (Exod 3:7–8 NJB).

YAHWEH AND VIOLENCE

In order for Yahweh to give Israel the land of Canaan as an inheritance, Yahweh would have to remove all the inhabitants who were already living in the land centuries before Israel left Egypt. Israel was to take possession of the land of Canaan by means of military force. In the process thousands of people, men, women, and children, young and old, would have to be dispossessed of their land or killed in battle for Israel to have access to the land and establish themselves as a nation in the conquered land (the conquest of the land of Canaan will be discussed in detail in chapter 19).

The larger issue in the story of Joshua and the army of Israel taking possession of the land of Canaan is the legitimacy of killing the Canaanite population through a war of conquest and expansion. To the Canaanite population who lived in the land, Israel's war against them was unprovoked. Israel's war of aggression against women and children was to be conducted in the name of Yahweh.

Although Israel did not possess the kinds of weapons that later empires acquired and even though Israel's methods of warfare were not as sophisticated as the Egyptians', the Assyrians', and the Babylonians' were, the destructive force of Israel's army, the destruction of several cities, and the targeting of entire populations in the name of Yahweh, all throw into question the loving nature of Yahweh and his character as a gracious and merciful God. Texts that portray Yahweh engaged in violence seem to contradict texts in which Yahweh is portrayed as a merciful and gracious God, a God who is slow to anger, and a God who abounds in steadfast love (Exod 34:6). Is God's love compatible with violence? Can a loving and compassionate God use violence to deal with the problem of sin and violence in the world? The revelation of Yahweh on Mount Sinai shows that at times Yahweh must use violence in order to save his people (the exodus from Egypt), in order to deal with violence and wickedness (the flood), in order to deal with the moral order (the destruction of Sodom), and in order to deal with the sins of the nations (the oracles against the nations in Amos). As Belousek puts it, "if God's love does not necessarily save the innocent from suffering, then it need not save the wicked from death and could even destroy the wicked to avenge the innocent."[4]

In an age when the moral sensitiveness of the human race rejects war and violence, in an age when Christians everywhere follow Jesus Christ, the Prince of Peace, people ask whether the violence used by Israel in the name of God was justified. Christians who seek to live their lives in imitation of Christ and try to adhere to the Bible's teaching on peace, find these violent texts in Scripture to be offensive. In addition, the Bible's presentation of Yahweh, the God who sponsors and promotes violence, raises serious questions about the nature and character of God.

These portraits of Yahweh as a violent God have led many writers to use offensive language to describe the God of the Old Testament. Richard Dawkins has the most negative evaluation of the God of the Old Testament. Gregory Boyd called the God of the Old Testament "a sinful god-in-our-own-image, a blasphemous lie, and a diabolic violent warrior god."[5] R. N. Whybray called him "an immoral God" and a "malevolent deity."[6] Whybray also called Yahweh "a destroying God, a God of violence."[7] Walter Dietrich says that the God of the Old Testament is "gruesome."[8] In his study of Israel's testimony to Yahweh, Brueggemann described YHWH as "savage, odd, abusive, mean-spirited, wild, self-indulgent, unreliable, unstable, capricious, irascible, irrational, sulky, and more."[9] David Penchansky called Yahweh an insecure, irrational, vindictive, dangerous, malevolent, and abusive God.[10]

Schwager summarizes the problem of divine violence in the Old Testament. He wrote: "Approximately one thousand passages speak of Yahweh's blazing anger, of his punishment by death and destruction, and how like a consuming fire he passes judgment, takes revenge, and threatens annihilation."[11] Confronted with so much violence in the Old Testament, one must ask, "Why is there so much violence in the world?" The answer to this question is not easy to ascertain. The answer is to be

---

4. Belousek, "Nonviolent God," 60.
5. Boyd, *Crucifixion of the Warrior God*, 1261.
6. Whybray, "Immorality of God," 89–120.
7. Whybray, "'Shall Not the Judge," 7.
8. Dietrich, "Mark of Cain," 4.
9. Fretheim, "Some Reflections on Brueggemann's God," 33.
10. Penchansky, *What Rough Beast?*, 3.
11. Schwager, *Must There Be Scapegoats?*, 5.

found in the very nature of God's creational purpose for his creation. God created human beings with freedom to make independent decisions and in doing so God chose not to micro-manage human actions or micro-manage the life of the world. God established a relationship with humans and humans have been given genuine freedom to make choices, the choice to obey God and the choice to rebel against God, and God honors human decisions so much so that God limits himself in what he can do when humans choose to use violence to accomplish their goals. As Fretheim wrote, "Generally, God's relationship with the world is such that God is present on every occasion and active in every event, no matter how heroic or Hitlerian, and in every such moment God is at work on behalf of the best possible future for all creation, whether in judgment or salvation."[12]

That God is always and everywhere present, however, raises sharp issues regarding the violence of those "Hitlerian" events. God's involvement with his creation, at times, is the reason why God is blamed for events that happen in the world. It is those "Hitlerian" events that make people uncomfortable with the acts of God. Although these "Hitlerian" events are beyond human understanding, they are, as Fretheim puts it, God's work "on behalf of the best possible future for all creation, whether in judgment or salvation."

When God acts to save his people, he may use violence. When God comes in judgment of nations, as in the case of Sodom and Gomorrah, or of Israel, as in the case of the fall of Jerusalem, violent acts will occur, because God's agents for punishment, in this case the Babylonians, will use their own methods of warfare to conquer Jerusalem. When violence and brutality occur as the result of an invasion, it will be God who will be accused of causing women to eat their children, when in reality, it was the action of the Babylonian army that caused the severe famine in the city that forced some people to go to extremes in order to survive.

QUESTIONING GOD'S ACTS

The study of divine violence in the Old Testament has received much attention from scholars in the twenty-first century. One reason for this focus on the violent acts of God is the awareness that violent acts in the Old Testament by both God and humans have been used to justify wars

12. Fretheim, "To Say Something," 346.

and violence in the past and in the present. In addition, the rise of the peace movement and pacifism in the nineteenth and twentieth centuries served as a catalyst to reevaluate the actions of the God of the Old Testament in light of what is perceived to be the pacifism of Jesus and the message of the cross.

However, the questioning of God's violent action is not new. Several people in the Old Testament have questioned God's violent acts and have raised objections to God acting violently against the just and against the wicked. For instance, Abraham asked God whether he would punish a righteous person together with the wicked people who lived in Sodom: "Far be it from you to do such a thing, to slay the righteous with the wicked, so that the righteous fare as the wicked! Far be that from you! Shall not the Judge of all the earth do what is just?" (Gen 18:25). In response to Abraham's question, God replied that he was willing to save the city and not punish it: "Yahweh replied, 'If I find fifty upright people in the city of Sodom, I will spare the whole place because of them'" (Gen 18:26 NJB).

God told Moses that he was going to destroy Israel because of their rebellion, "Now let me alone, so that my wrath may burn hot against them and I may consume them" (Exod 32:10). Moses implored God not to punish the people, "Turn from your fierce wrath; change your mind and do not bring disaster on your people" (Exod 32:12). In response to Moses's prayer, "the LORD changed his mind about the disaster that he planned to bring on his people" (Exod 32:14). Another person who questioned God's action was the prophet Habakkuk. When the prophet complained about the violence present in Judah during his days, God answered Habakkuk's complaint by saying that he was bringing judgment upon the violence in Judah by using the Babylonians as his instrument of justice (Hab 1:1–6).[13]

YAHWEH, THE WARRIOR GOD

In the theophanies of God as a warrior, "God appears in order to help the people in time of need."[14] The idea of a warrior God who was always present with Israel, leading its army to victory, gave the people the confidence that Yahweh would protect them against their enemies. Thus, every battle was the Lord's battle, and every war was sacred because the people

---

13. Harris, "Laments of Habakkuk's Prophecy," 21–29.
14. Fretheim, *Suffering of God*, 80.

believed they were fighting the battles of Yahweh (1 Sam 25:28). The description of Yahweh as "a man of war" or as "a warrior" conjures the idea that Yahweh is a violent God, a God who fights against the enemies of his people by massacring all those who oppose Israel, "Yahweh will be at war with Amalek generation after generation" (Exod 17:16 NJB).

Yahweh is "the God of the armies of Israel" (1 Sam 17:45). As the commander of the armies of Israel, Yahweh is perceived as the one leading the army of Israel in battle. When David confronted Goliath, he said to the Philistine, "this whole assembly know that Yahweh does not give victory by means of sword and spear—for Yahweh is lord of the battle and he will deliver you into our power" (1 Sam 17:47 NJB). Israel experienced Yahweh as a warrior as it faced its enemies and because it was Yahweh who fought for Israel, the massacre of men, women and innocent children was attributed to him. David said that Yahweh would deliver Israel from the threat posed by Goliath, but when Goliath was defeated, he was killed by David with a stone and a sword: "David ran and stood over the Philistine; he grasped his sword, drew it out of its sheath, and killed him; then he cut off his head with it" (1 Sam 17:51). Yahweh received his title, "Yahweh is a warrior," in a triumph song celebrating Yahweh's victory over the army of Pharaoh (Exod 15:1–21), what Boyd calls one of the "famous acts of terror" in the Old Testament. Yahweh has been highly criticized for drowning the Egyptian army in the Sea of Reeds, but, as Weyde said, "this negative judgement on YHWH and YHWH's actions at the Sea of Reeds is not appropriate, for it fails to notice what is going on throughout the narrative."[15]

The popular perception is that Yahweh continues to be the divine warrior fighting for Israel throughout its history. However, the biblical evidence shows that Yahweh and his heavenly hosts fought with Israel to conquer the promised land and to secure the land against the Philistines. But, as Israel rebelled against Yahweh by becoming involved in the worship of other gods, the people still maintained the old view that Yahweh was a warrior fighting for them, "but YHWH did not fight on Israel's behalf; YHWH turned against Israel and mustered foreign armies" to fight against them.[16] The idea of Yahweh as a warrior disappears in the post exilic community. To the Chronicler, the wars of conquest belonged

---

15. Weyde, "Is God a Violent God?," 291.
16. Bloch-Smith, "Impact of Siege Warfare," 25.

to the distant past; Yahweh was not a man of war nor "a cruel warlord, but first and foremost God of the cultic community."[17]

THE NONVIOLENT GOD

The main objective of Seibert's and Boyd's books is to present the nonviolent portrait of the God of the Old Testament whom Jesus revealed on the cross. For this purpose, Boyd develops his Cruciform Hermeneutic which interprets the violent portraits of God from the perspective of the cross. Boyd wrote, "The claim I will be defending throughout this work is that there is a way of interpreting Scripture's violent portraits of God that not only resolves the moral challenges they pose but that also discloses how these portraits bear witness to God's nonviolent, self-sacrificial, enemy-loving character that was definitively revealed on Calvary."[18] According to Boyd, this nonviolent God desired to give the land of Canaan to Israel by nonviolently relocating the Canaanites (I will discuss the nonviolent conquest of Canaan in chapter 18). According to Boyd, the true character of the nonviolent God "is fully revealed in the crucified Christ."

Seibert's and Boyd's views represent the view espoused by Anabaptist theologians who developed their understanding of the character of the God of the Old Testament from the nonviolent teachings of Jesus. This nonviolent view of God is best seen in the formulation of J. Denny Weaver. Weaver said, "We believe God is fully revealed in the story of Jesus Christ, in his life, teaching, death and resurrection. Jesus rejected violence. If God is fully revealed in Jesus, then God also refuses to use or sanction violence. If God is fully revealed in Jesus, then God is nonviolent. We should cultivate nonviolent images of God."[19]

In his article "Nonviolent God: Critical Analysis of a Contemporary Argument," Darrin Belousek presents several reasons why the nonviolent God proposal runs contrary to the teaching of the Bible.[20] Belousek discusses the contemporary argument that the true God is nonviolent. According to Belousek, some scholars have made a distinction between the "textual God" and the "actual God." The textual God is the God of the Old Testament, a God of violence and a God of wrath. The actual God is the

---

17. Weyde, "Is God a Violent God?," 300.
18. Boyd, *Crucifixion of the Warrior God*, xxxiv.
19. Weaver, "Peace Church as Worship of God," 19.
20. Belousek, "Nonviolent God," 49–70.

God revealed by Jesus Christ, a God who is nonviolent, a God of *agape* love. Those who believe that the true God is nonviolent do so because they believe that Jesus revealed the true nature of God and because Jesus is nonviolent, therefore God is nonviolent.[21] This differentiation between the "textual God" and the "real God" is problematic. Since everything we know about God comes from the narratives found in the biblical text, then "the real God" is the God we conceive him to be, for we mold the God of the text into the kind of God we conceive the real God to be.

However, according to Belousek, since "God-in-Christ willed to renounce violence for the sake of redemption, it does not follow that God has renounced violence in all things. It thus appears that the 'nonviolent God' argument is premised on a false dichotomy: Jesus/God rejects violence either absolutely or not at all. The argument assumes that, because Jesus foregoes violence for himself and forbids violence to humans, God has simply rejected violence. It fails to consider that Jesus might forego violence for himself and forbid violence to humans while God nonetheless retains the prerogative as God."[22]

Belousek presents several arguments against the view that God is nonviolent. His main argument for the view that God is nonviolent is because it is "a confessional argument," an argument that is addressed to "an Anabaptist audience."[23] Another reason against the argument is because it "runs contrary to the biblical declaration that the right of vengeance belongs to God," a statement that appears in both the Old and New Testaments (Deut 32:35; Rom 12:19). Finally, Belousek says that the Bible does not say that God had promised never to use violence.[24]

Several texts in the Old Testament give witness that God does not want violence and death, but peace. When Gideon met Yahweh by the terebinth at Ophrah, "Gideon built an altar there to Yahweh and called it Yahweh [is] Peace" (Judg 6:24 NJB). Yahweh has established a covenant of peace with his people (Isa 54:10). Yahweh blesses his people with peace (Ps 29:11) and Yahweh delights to see his servant in peace (Ps 35:27). The prophets proclaim a day when the nations will live in peace. On that day, Yahweh will "judge between the nations" and the nations "shall beat their swords into plowshares, and their spears into pruning hooks; nation shall

---

21. Belousek, "Nonviolent God," 65.
22. Belousek, "Nonviolent God," 63.
23. Belousek, "Nonviolent God," 50.
24. Belousek, "Nonviolent God," 55.

not lift up sword against nation, neither shall they learn war any more" (Isa 2:1–4). Until then, violence will continue because there are people "who love to do violence" (Ps 11:5 NET).

VIOLENCE BEGETS VIOLENCE

Many texts in the Old Testament show that human violence begets divine violence. Yahweh announced to the people of Judah that they would be judged as their conduct deserved and that he would repay them for all their loathsome practices because their violence has risen to become the scourge of wickedness (Ezek 7:8–11). Because Judah was a country full of bloody executions and Jerusalem was a city full of deeds of violence, Yahweh was bringing "the cruelest of the nations" to vindicate the victims of violence (Ezek 7:23–24). The violence of Judah provoked Yahweh to anger (Ezek 8:17).

Because of the violence done to the people of Judah and to vindicate the innocent blood shed in Jerusalem, Yahweh was sending the Babylonians "a cruel and violent people" (Hab 1:6 NLT) to act as his agents of justice. The purpose of Yahweh's judgment on Judah was to insure that "the country and its population may be freed from the violence" of its leaders (Ezek 12:19). But when dealing with the people of Judah, the Babylonians "make their own laws and rules" (Hab 1:7 TNK). Jeremiah says that the Babylonians "are cruel and have no mercy" (Jer 6:23). This means that the Babylonians will be violent in battle, merciless and severe in their treatment of the people, dealing with the people of Judah according to their own war traditions. The violence of Judah begat the violence of the Babylonians.

One situation in which violence begets violence is the case of the avenger of blood, the *go' el haddām*. The avenger of blood was an individual who was responsible for avenging the murder of a member of his family or his clan by killing the person who had committed the murder. According to Sperling, the murderer

> could be killed with impunity by an avenger of blood unless he found asylum at an altar (Exod 21:13) or at a city of asylum. If, however, malice could be demonstrated, then it was permissible to remove the manslayer from the altar (Exod 21:14). If the killer had fled to a city of asylum, the elders of his native city were to

demand his extradition from the city of asylum and to turn him over to the avenger of blood for execution (Deut 19:12).[25]

In some societies, the avenger of blood would kill not only the person who had killed a member of his family, he also would kill the entire family of the murderer.

When people read the Old Testament, they associate much of the violence as acts of God. The people of ancient Israel associated natural calamities such as earthquakes, droughts, plagues, military invasions, and the brutality of wars with God's punishment for the sins of the nation or the sins of individuals.[26] Fretheim wrote,

> Prophetic literature is filled with violent speech and action, both human and divine. But let it be said immediately: if there were no human violence, there would be no divine violence. Gen 6:11–13 announces a pattern regarding divine and human violence that will persist throughout the canon: "I have determined to make an end of all flesh, for the earth is filled with violence because of them."[27]

THE VENGEANCE OF YAHWEH

The Hebrew word for violence is "ḥāmas." In the Hebrew Bible the verbal form of the word appears eight times and the noun appears sixty time. Both the verb and the noun "are virtually always used of sinful violence. Not surprisingly, therefore, God is never the agent involved in such behavior."[28] The first time the word ḥāmas is used in the Hebrew Bible is to introduce human violence (Gen 6:11, 13). All crimes described by the word ḥāmas "are directed ultimately against Yahweh and provoke his judgment."[29]

The word ḥāmas ("violence") is never applied to the actions of Yahweh except once. In Lam 2:6 the writer says that Yahweh acted violently in dealing with the people of Judah, "He has done violence to His temple"

---

25. Sperling, "Blood, Avenger of," 763.
26. Dell, "Amos and the Earthquake," 1–14.
27. Fretheim, "'I Was Only a Little Angry,'" 365.
28. Swart and Van Dam, "ḥms," 178.
29. Swart and Van Dam, "ḥms," 179.

(HCSB). All the violent acts of God in the Hebrew Bible are responses to the violation of the moral order set by God at the time of creation.

Divine violence occurs in response to human violence. Human violence "is the means whereby man as the image of God does as he pleases within the creation entrusted to him . . . corrupting, as is underlined with threefold repetition, the good creation of God."[30] Divine violence also occurs as a response to the violations of the demand of the covenant, "I will bring the sword upon you to avenge the breaking of the covenant" (Lev 26:25 NIV). When divine violence occurs in the life of Israel, either to save or to punish, God's action occurs within the context of the covenant and Israel's expectation to abide by the demands of the covenant.

In Ps 94:1 Yahweh appears as *ʾēl neqāmôt yhwh* "Yahweh the God of Vengeance." In his study of the vengeance of Yahweh, Mendenhall said when Yahweh acts in the world, that which is called the "vengeance of Yahweh" or divine violence "actually designates those events in human experience that were identified as the exercise of the sovereignty" of Yahweh as king and creator. It is Yahweh's sovereignty as creator that undergirds his authority and his legitimate power to act.[31]

Mendenhall says that of the seventy-eight occurrences of the word *nāqam* ("vengeance") in the Hebrew Bible, "fifty-one involve situations in which the actor is either Yahweh Himself, or an agency to which the power to act is specifically delegated in a specific situation. Thus, in over two thirds of the total occurrences, the root designates the exercise of divine imperium either directly or indirectly."[32]

Divine imperium may be directed against a foreign nation, against Israel, or against individuals. As Mendenhall explains, the concept of vengeance of Yahweh has do "with the use of power against the enemies of that power, *whether internal or external*" (emphasis his).[33] One example of the use of divine imperium is found in the Gibionites' effort to defend themselves against the Canaanite army. Because the Gibionites were allied with Israel through a covenant, they called on Joshua to deliver them. That call for help brought Joshua and the army of Israel to defend the Gibionites. With the help of Yahweh, the army of Israel defeated the Canaanites. On that day of battle "the nation took vengeance on their

---

30. Haag, "*chāmās*," 485.
31. Mendenhall, "'Vengeance' of Yahweh," 70.
32. Mendenhall, "'Vengeance' of Yahweh," 82–83.
33. Mendenhall, "'Vengeance' of Yahweh," 83.

enemies" because "the LORD fought for Israel" (Jos 10:13). Since the word *nāqam* ("vengeance") refers to the victory Yahweh gave to Israel, the verse means that "the nation defeated the enemies" because Yahweh fought for them.[34]

HOPE IN THE MIDST OF VIOLENCE

In those texts where divine punishment and divine violence occur, there is always an element of hope. In the midst of violence and punishment, grace and hope are present. In the story of humans' first sin, there was punishment, they were driven from the garden, but they did not die even though they were threatened with death (Gen 2:16–17). Rather, the grace of God was manifested when God provided clothes to cover their nakedness. When Cain violently killed his brother Abel, there was judgment: Cain was exiled from the fertile land (Gen 4:12). When Cain feared violence against him (Gen 4:13–14), the grace of God was manifested: God put a mark on Cain as a sign of divine protection.[35] When violence and "the wickedness of humankind was great in the earth, and that every inclination of the thoughts of their hearts was only evil continually" (Gen 6:5), God sent the flood as a judgment on the violence and wickedness of humanity but he also promised that he would not curse the earth again with another flood, even though humans' inclination for evil would continue (Gen 8:21). When humans challenged God by building a tower to reach heaven, there was judgment: humans were scattered throughout the earth. Although no sign of God's grace is visible, God's grace comes later, with the call of Abraham and his mission to be a blessing to all the nations (Gen 12:1–3).

When Yahweh, through Jeremiah, proclaimed his judgment upon the land of Judah, Yahweh promised that the destruction would not be complete: "The whole land will be ruined, though I will not destroy it completely" (Jer 4:27 NIV). When Yahweh announced that he would send the Babylonians to punish Judah for their rebellion and disobedience, Yahweh also mentioned the extent of the punishment:

> I am going to bring upon you a nation from far away, O house of Israel, says the LORD. It is an enduring nation, it is an ancient nation, a nation whose language you do not know, nor can you

---

34. Mendenhall, "'Vengeance' of Yahweh," 83.
35. Dietrich, "Mark of Cain," 3–11.

understand what they say. They shall eat up your harvest and your food; they shall eat up your sons and your daughters; they shall eat up your flocks and your herds; they shall eat up your vines and your fig trees; they shall destroy with the sword your fortified cities in which you trust. (Jer 5:15–17)

However, in the midst of violence there was hope. With the word of judgment came a promise: "But even in those days, says the LORD, I will not make a full end of you" (Jer 5:18). As Weyde wrote, "A just God would have destroyed his unfaithful people completely and without showing mercy. Justice and destruction, however, did not have the last word."[36]

From these texts we deduce that the violent God of the Old Testament is a God who by no means clears the guilty but is also a gracious and merciful God (Exod 34:6–7), a God who must exercise divine justice for the sake of the world, but also a God who shows his mercy. As Fretheim wrote, "That God would become involved in such human cruelties as war is finally not a matter of despair, but of hope. God does not simply give people up to violence. God chooses to become involved in violence in order to bring about good purposes; thereby God may prevent an even greater evil."[37] The God of the Old Testament is a God of justice. He judges people, at times using violence, but notwithstanding his use of violence, he never ceases being a gracious and merciful God, a God who wants to redeem Israel and the nations unto himself.

GOD'S ANGER

One important aspect of the character of the God of the Old Testament is that he is "slow to anger" (Exod 34:6). The expression "slow to anger" is an idiomatic translation of the Hebrew expression ʼ *erek* ʼ *appayim*, an expression which literally means "long nose."

> In Hebrew, the nose is associated with anger, apparently because when a person is angry, his or her face and nose may involuntarily redden and appear to "burn." . . . It is as if He takes a long, deep breath as He deals with sin and holds His anger in abeyance.[38]

---

36. Weyde, "Is God a Violent God?," 296.
37. Fretheim, "'I Was Only a Little Angry,'" 375.
38. Laney, "God's Self-Revelation," 45–46.

This aspect of the nature of God means that anger is not an integral part of the character of God since God is provoked to anger, "you have provoked me to anger" (1 Kgs 21:22). The fact that God is provoked to anger indicates that divine anger occurs within the context of human history and it is a strong reaction to violence or to the evil that people do. Berges says that "God's wrath is seen as a necessary instrument to prevent the earth and her inhabitants from falling into chaos and anarchy."[39] It takes human action or a specific situation to provoke God to be angry. According to Fretheim,

> God's anger is usually associated with God's judgment. . . . That God's anger is "provoked" (e.g., Jer 7:18; 8:19) reveals that God is moved by what people do and shows that anger is a divine response and not a divine attribute. God's anger is contingent; if there were no sin, there would be no divine anger.[40]

The anger of Yahweh is kindled against Israel when the people violate the demands of the covenant (Judg 2:20), they provoke him to anger when they follow other gods (Judg 2:12), and they provoke him to anger when they sin and do what is evil (2 Kgs 21:15).

The Old Testament teaches that God's anger is surpassed by his patience because God's anger is temporal: "his anger is but for a moment" (Ps 30:5), it only lasts for "a brief moment" (Isa 54:7). God often restrains his anger (Ps 78:38); for the sake of his name, he controls his anger (Isa 48:9), and eventually, the heat of his wrath comes to an end (Ezek 16:42). Sin, evil, and violence have consequences because God will not exonerate the guilty (Exod 34:7). A righteous God is angered by sin, by evil, and by violence. God is patient in judging sin and evil in the world, but God's patience is not an indication that the judgment has been rescinded. When God promised Abraham to give the land of Canaan to his descendants, he said they would not inherit it for four hundred years because the iniquity of the Canaanites had not yet reached its full extent (Gen 15:16). In describing God's ambivalence in executing judgment, Goldingay says. "The Scriptures do describe God as loving, compassionate, gracious and forgiving, though they also describe God as capable of being wrathful and as not inclined simply to ignore our wrongdoing. So, God acts in

---

39. Berges, "Violence of God," 26.
40. Fretheim, "'I Was Only a Little Angry,'" 373.

judgment, but the greater centrality of the first kind of characteristic in God means that he does so rather unwillingly."[41]

GOD'S REGRET

The flood story in Gen 6–8 reveals an important aspect of the character of God. When Yahweh saw the wickedness of humankind and their evil ways, "the LORD regretted that He had made man on earth, and His heart was saddened" (Gen 6:6 TNK). The divine anguish was provoked by human wickedness, by human sinfulness, and by human violence. The consequence of human sin and depravity was divine judgment that came in the form of a universal flood. When God brought judgment upon all living beings, "his heart was filled with pain" (Gen 6:6 NIV) because such a decision went against the basic character of his nature as God, a God who is "merciful and gracious" (Exod 34:6).

God had to bring judgment upon Israel because of their sins and rebellion, but judgment was not what God intended for the nation. When God brought judgment to his people through the Babylonians, God said, "I am sorry for the disaster that I have brought upon you" (Jer 42:10). These words reveal the true heart of God. God was sorry that he had to bring such a severe judgment upon the people of Israel. This does not mean that God regretted sending the judgment upon Israel. Jeremiah and Ezekiel affirm that the people deserved the judgment that came upon them. God was sorry about the pain and the suffering the people had to go through because the agents God had chosen to be his instrument of justice went beyond what God had designed them to do: "But I am very angry with the other nations that are now enjoying peace and security. I was only a little angry with my people, but the nations inflicted harm on them far beyond my intentions" (Zech 1:15 NLT).

Yahweh was greatly moved about the fate of Jerusalem (Zech 1:14) but he was also angry with the nations; they have provoked the anger of Yahweh because the nations had turned Yahweh's judgment on Judah to evil. The Babylonians were used as agents of God for the judgment of Judah, but they exceeded the severity of the punishment; they went too far in their cruelty and in their brutality against the civilian population of Jerusalem. Yahweh expresses a sense of regret because what he intended as a proper punishment of Judah had been turned into evil: "For a brief

---

41. Goldingay, *Biblical Theology*, 21.

moment I abandoned you, but with great compassion I will gather you. In overflowing wrath for a moment I hid my face from you" (Isa 54:7–8). "I was angry with my people, I profaned my heritage; I gave them into your hand, you showed them no mercy; on the aged you made your yoke exceedingly heavy" (Isa 47:6). These two oracles of judgment against Babylon were proclaimed "because of Babylon's improper exercise of power toward the object of Yahweh's anger, Israel."[42]

GOD'S RECONCILIATION OF THE WORLD

From the perspective of the life and ministry of Jesus and from the perspective of the cross, divine violence is hard for Christians to accept. However, I contend that divine violence, as hard as it for us to accept, must be understood in the context of God's work of reconciliation. "The crucifixion of Christ was itself an act of violence."[43] Our understanding of why God has to use violence in the world must be based on the assumption that what God does is for the benefit of creation and for the eventual salvation of all human beings. Thus, the God who was in Christ "reconciling the world to himself" (2 Cor 5:19), is a God of reconciliation.[44]

INTERPRETING BIBLICAL TEXTS

As we read the language of violence found in the biblical text, we must keep in mind "the metaphorical nature of the language used to describe the work of God in the world."[45] Israel's perception of what happened in their world was based on their social and cultural views about God. Their speech about God came out of their own personal experience with God. Thus, Christians today cannot read New Testament Christianity into what the writers of the Old Testament tried to communicate to the people to whom they were writing. Our worldview today is completely different from the worldview of the biblical writers.

Notwithstanding the reluctance of many interpreters today, the biblical text must, first of all, be interpreted from the perspective of the social and cultural background of the authors of the biblical text. As they

---

42. Petersen, *Haggai and Zechariah 1–8*, 154.
43. Busch, "God's Reconciliation of the World," 153.
44. Busch, "God's Reconciliation of the World," 151.
45. Weyde, "Is God a Violent God?," 299.

wrote, they were influenced by the historical and social situations that motivated them to write what they wrote. The biblical writers were influenced by their society and by the culture in which they grew up. Their writings reflect the cultural and religious thought of the world in which they lived. Before we look at the text from the perspective of the twenty-first century, we must look at the world in which the biblical writers lived and the audience to whom they were writing.

Another issue that affects the interpretation of the biblical text is the presuppositions that today's readers bring when reading and interpreting texts. No interpretation of the text is free of bias. However, it is important to remember that the world and the culture that today's readers bring to the text are different from the world and culture of the biblical writers and it is also different from the world and the culture of the people who first read what the biblical writers wrote.

The problem with the interpretation of the violent texts of the Old Testament is that interpreters look at these texts from a twenty-first century perspective, as Christians whose lives have been transformed by the message of Christ. Seibert and Boyd look at texts dealing with divine violence as Anabaptists whose religious heritage reads the Bible from a nonviolent perspective, and as a pacifist whose theology of obedience compels them to reject all kinds of violence, even the violence perpetrated by a God who acts violently in order to resist violence.[46]

The bias some writers bring to their reading of the Old Testament does not allow them to perceive the true nature and character of the God of the Old Testament as a God who judges and as a God who saves. By refusing to accept the fact that the God of the Old Testament is a God who by no means clears the guilty, these writers see the actions of the God who is a righteous judge, of the God who judges sin, rebellion, and violence to be the actions of a violent warrior God.

---

46. In his evaluation of Seibert's Anabaptist's views, Esau, "Disturbing Scholarly Behavior," 169, said that there are two types of Anabaptists. One group of Anabaptists advocates "nonviolence on the basis that Jesus taught this as the proper stance for followers of God who were to leave all retribution and vengeance to God (cf. Rom. 12:19)." The other group of Anabaptists believe that "followers of God should pursue nonviolence not simply because Jesus modeled and taught this while on earth but because nonviolence is and always has been the modus operandi of God." Esau concludes that "Seibert is an advocate of this second type of Anabaptism, and as a result, Old Testament images of Yahweh advocating and participating in violence are not only profoundly troubling but conflict with this core belief."

Because of the sins and rebellion of the people of Israel, Yahweh brought severe judgment upon the nation, but the suffering of the people brought great affliction to Yahweh. Although the book of Lamentations seems to imply that Yahweh was silent before the desperate situation of the people, Yahweh was aware of their anguish. By participating in the suffering of the people, Yahweh also suffered. He suffered with them and because of them. As Fretheim wrote, "Through such involvement, God takes into the divine self the violent effects of sinful human activities and thereby makes possible a non-violent future for God's people."[47]

---

47. Fretheim, "'I Was Only a Little Angry,'" 375.

3

Understanding Divine Violence

IN THIS CHAPTER I WILL discuss several issues that contribute to the proper understanding of divine violence in the Old Testament. In my view, the greatest contribution to the solution of the problem of divine violence is found in the title of Boyd's book. Boyd shows how the problem of divine violence can be solved and explained: with the crucifixion of the warrior God. In what follows, I will discuss several issues that are crucial for understanding divine violence in the Old Testament.

UNDERSTANDING DIVINE VIOLENCE: YAHWEH, THE DIVINE WARRIOR

The title of Boyd's book affirms that Yahweh, the warrior God of the Old Testament, died on the cross. To me, this is the most important statement in Boyd's book, a statement that helps us understand and deal with the problem of divine violence in the Old Testament. In the last chapter (chapter 24) I will focus on the crucifixion of the warrior God and how it relates to the problem of divine violence.

The expression "The Warrior God" comes from the title given to the God of Israel in Exod 15:3 at the time when the people of Israel left Egypt without fighting against their oppressors.[1] Pharaoh took six hundred picked chariots and all the other chariots of Egypt and his elite corps

---

1. On the Divine Warrior motif, see Miller, *Divine Warrior*; Longman, *God Is a Warrior*; Trimm, *YHWH Fights for Them!*; Carvalho, "Beauty of the Bloody God."

of officers and went in pursuit of the Israelites (Exod 14:7). The Israelites left Egypt defiantly, confident that their God would fight for them. Israel had no weapons and no army. A group of freed slaves was no match for the well-equipped and well-trained army of Pharaoh.[2] The people of Israel had to depend on Yahweh to save them from an imminent death. In order to save his people, Yahweh had to use violence. Fighting against the Egyptians was the only way by which the salvation of Israel could be accomplished. Yahweh used the forces of nature against the army of Pharaoh. Hundreds of Egyptian soldiers had to die in order for Yahweh to save the lives of thousands of men, women, and children. In their victory against the Egyptians, Israel celebrated Yahweh as a warrior because that was the first time Yahweh had fought on behalf of his people.

The Hebrew expression *yhwh ' iš milḥāmāh* is translated literally by the KJV as "The LORD is a man of war." The NRSV and several other English translations translate the same expression as "The LORD is a warrior." The NJB, using the divine name, translates Exod 15:3 as follows: "Yahweh is a warrior; Yahweh is his name."

The book of Exodus is not the only place in the Old Testament where Yahweh appears as a warrior. The post-exilic prophet known as Deutero-Isaiah describes Yahweh as *' iš milḥāmôt*, "Yahweh advances like a hero, like a warrior he rouses his fire" (Isa 42:13 NJB). Another translation translates this text as follows: "The Lord will go out as a man of war, he will be moved to wrath like a fighting-man" (Isa 42:13 BBE). Even the psalmist describes the God of Israel as *yhwh gibbôr milḥāmāh*, "Yahweh, a mighty man of war" (Ps 24:8).

According to the prophet Zephaniah, Yahweh is a warrior who gives victory to his people: "The LORD, your God, is in your midst, a warrior who gives victory (*gibbôr yôšiaʻu*); he will rejoice over you with gladness, he will renew you in his love; he will exult over you with loud singing" (Zeph 3:17). As a warrior, Yahweh commands the heavenly hosts, and he is the real leader of the armies of Israel. His deeds are written in "the Book of the Wars of Yahweh" (Num 21:14 NJB). The God of Israel is also known as Yahweh Sabaoth (1 Sam 1:3 NJB). The psalmist says that Yahweh Sabaoth is the God of Israel (Ps 59:5). Yahweh Sabaoth is a title translated in English as "the LORD of Hosts" or "the Lord of armies." Scholars disagree whether the reference is to the army of Israel or to the

---

2. Mariottini, "Egyptian Army," 46–49.

heavenly army or both.[3] The translators of the NLT believe that the title refers to the heavenly host. The NLT translates the title as "LORD of Heaven's Armies" (1 Sam 1:3 NLT).

The Old Testament teaches that the Israelite army fought in the battles, but the victory was generally given to the army by God. Before Israel engaged in battle against their enemies, the priest blessed the army. He would come forward and say to the troops: "Listen, Israel: today you are about to join battle with your enemies. Do not be faint hearted. Let there be no fear or trembling or alarm as you face them. Yahweh your God is marching with you, to fight your enemies for you and make you victorious" (Deut 20:3–4 NJB). In his study of the divine warrior in Israel, Miller wrote:

> The theme of the divine warrior constitutes a real problem area in biblical interpretation, especially as one seeks to move from biblical exegesis to theology and preaching, to proclamation of God and Jesus Christ. The picture of God as warrior forms the real *skandalon* of the Old Testament for modern man, including the Christian. As Christians we have a great deal of trouble with imagery and with the actual holy wars of the Israelites in which the enemy was supposed to be subjected to wholesale slaughter at the command of God. The picture does not jibe with the New Testament understanding of God as love.[4]

The imagery of God as a divine warrior has been misunderstood and misapplied by many who want to justify war and violence in the name of God. As Fretheim wrote, "By virtue of an imbalanced and incorrect interpretation, biblical metaphors for God—not least those from the OT which speak of God the Warrior—may have at least in part contributed to warmongering tendencies in human society, which have led to a perpetration of incomprehensible evil."[5]

The picture of Yahweh as a warrior who fights for Israel is a problem for many Christians because it contradicts the nonviolent revelation of God in Jesus Christ. However, it is the crucifixion of Jesus, the warrior God who became a human being, that explains Old Testament violent events. It is impossible to dismiss acts of divine violence in the Old Testament. The story of the flood, the drowning of the Egyptians in the Red

---

3. Miller, "God the Warrior," 39. See also Quine, "Host of Heaven and the Divine Army," 741–55.

4. Miller, "God the Warrior," 40–41.

5. Fretheim, *Suffering of God*, 15.

Sea, and the destruction of Sodom and Gomorrah are presented as acts of divine violence. Often, these acts of divine violence are judged by the moral values of the gospel or by the nonviolent teachings of Jesus. In the chapters to come, I will explore the reasons Yahweh acted the way he did and how the cross changed the way God carries out his work of reconciliation in the world.

UNDERSTANDING DIVINE VIOLENCE: GOD BECOMES HUMAN

The most amazing truth about the cross is that when God became a man and lived among us (John 1:1, 14), "God was in Christ, reconciling the world to himself, no longer counting people's sins against them" (2 Cor 5:19 NLT). Or, as another translation puts it, "God was in Christ making peace between the world and himself, not putting their sins to their account, and having given to us the preaching of this news of peace" (2 Cor 5:19 BBE). The translation of the Bible in Basic English (BBE) provides us with the best foundation to understand divine violence in the Old Testament by the three things Paul says about God. First, Paul says that the Warrior God of the Old Testament "was in Christ making peace between the world and himself." Second, the Warrior God of the Old Testament was treating human sins differently than in the past, "not putting their sins to their account." Third, the Warrior God of the Old Testament was teaching us through Christ how to do his work in the world, "having given to us the preaching of this news of peace."

Jesus was the embodiment of God. Jesus claimed to be God by identifying himself as the one bearing the divine name: "before Abraham was even born, I Am" (John 8:58 NLT). Even the Jewish leaders recognized that Jesus was claiming to be God. Jesus said:

> "I and the Father are one." Again, the Jews picked up stones to stone him, but Jesus said to them, "I have shown you many great miracles from the Father. For which of these do you stone me?" "We are not stoning you for any of these," replied the Jews, "but for blasphemy, because you, a mere man, claim to be God."
> (John 10:30–33)

Thomas called the resurrected Christ "My Lord and my God" (John 20:28). Paul refers to Jesus as "our great God and Savior, Jesus Christ" (Titus 2:13) and Peter described Jesus as "our God and Savior" (2 Pet 1:1).

The New Testament attributes to Jesus what the Old Testament attributed to Yahweh. The prophet Joel said: "All who call on the name of Yahweh will be saved" (Joel 3:5 NJB). Speaking about the salvific work of Christ, Paul said, "all who call on the name of the Lord will be saved" (Rom 10:13 NJB). In his article, "YHWH and Jesus in One Self-same Divine Self," MacDonald said that "Jesus is YHWH's visible conception of himself." In his identification of Jesus with Yahweh, MacDonald also said: "In the context of sameness according to soteriological self, the compassion of the real historical Jesus made tangible—made visible—during his earthly life can be understood as YHWH's compassion incarnate."[6] The God revealed in the gospel is Yahweh, the God of Israel.

The New Testament affirms that Jesus Christ is God. As Fretheim wrote, the writers of the New Testament "insist that in Jesus Christ we are in the fullest possible sense looking at the heart of God the Father, the God of the OT. The coming of God in Jesus Christ is indeed the coming of God in a quite concrete way in the entire life of a human being. That is the special force of the NT message: God, unsurpassably enfleshed in the human being, Jesus of Nazareth."[7]

It is this identification of Jesus with Yahweh that makes possible a better understanding of divine violence in the Old Testament.[8] MacDonald wrote: "One way of reading the New in terms of the Old Testament is to understand Jesus in terms of the identity of YHWH. . . . YHWH is a desisting, forbearing, merciful God who takes his own judgement on himself in the form of his son, Jesus of Nazareth."[9] Martin Hengel said: "God himself accepted death in the form of a crucified Jewish manual worker from Galilee."[10] "In Christ God was reconciling the world to himself" (2 Cor 5:19).

---

6. MacDonald, "YHWH and Jesus," 23.

7. Fretheim, *Suffering of God*, 4.

8. Ronning, "When YHWH Became Flesh." Ronning said that John 1:14 could be interpreted as saying "YHWH became flesh" because the gospel of John cites several passages in the Old Testament that portray Jesus speaking and acting as YHWH. See also Staples, "Jesus as YHWH," 1–19.

9. MacDonald, "YHWH and Jesus," 24.

10. Hengel, *Cross of the Son of God*, 181 (quoted by MacDonald, "YHWH and Jesus," 24).

UNDERSTANDING DIVINE VIOLENCE: GOD ACCOMMODATES TO THE CULTURAL SITUATION OF THE PEOPLE

The Old Testament teaches that God accommodates to the cultural situation of the people. It is in the context of God accommodating to the cultural situation of the people that the violence of Israel should be understood. The people of Israel lived in a very violent and brutal world. Nations and empires had to survive by the use of the sword and the might of their army. In the days of Abraham, four kings from the East attacked six nations in Canaan (Gen 14:1). They massacred the Canaanites, sacked their cities, and took many captives, including Lot, Abraham's nephew. At that time, the peaceful Abraham becomes a warrior and with 318 of his men fought against the kings of the East and routed them (Gen 14:15).

When the Israelites left Egypt, on their way to Canaan, the Amalekites attacked Israel. This attack was unprovoked and came at a time when Israel was very vulnerable: "how he [Amalek] attacked you on the way, when you were faint and weary, and struck down all who lagged behind you" (Deut 25:18). Israel was also attacked by Sihon, an Amorite king (Num 21:21–23) and by Og, king of Bashan (Num 21:33–34).

When Israel settled in the land of Canaan, Israel was oppressed by King Cushan-rishathaim of Aram-naharaim for eight years; by Eglon, king of Moab for eighteen years; by Jabin, king of Hazor for twenty years; by the Midianites, Amalekites, and Kedemites for forty years; by the Ammonites for eighteen years; and by the Philistines for forty years.

War is hell. When an atomic bomb fell on Hiroshima and another on Nagasaki, 146,000 people were killed in Hiroshima and 80,000 people were killed in Nagasaki. Peace comes at a cost: 226,000 people were killed in order to end a war that killed more than sixty million people or about 3 percent of the world population living at the time of the war.[11] No one can justify the carnage that happened in Hiroshima and Nagasaki, but how many million more people would have died if the war had continued for a few more years?

To Israel, war was a matter of survival. There is no doubt that in their war for survival, many brutalities occurred; no one should condone the violence, the brutality, and the atrocities that were committed by the Israelites. After all, they were BC people. We should not judge them from the perspective of Christian values that we all share because they were

---

11. "Atomic Bombings of Hiroshima and Nagasaki."

not Christians. The Israelites were not pacifists and they had not taken a pledge of nonviolence against their enemies. The problem with accommodation is that this issue cannot be pushed too far because when this happens, the God of the Old Testament becomes an unknown God, even an imaginary Yahweh. In his discussion of accommodation, Dale Patrick wrote: "What sort of 'metaphysical' existence does God have? From what has been said, it follows that nothing can be known of God's existence apart from the imaginary character, YHWH, depicted in the Scriptures. God is the Holy One who has condescended to meet us in Scripture. As John Calvin puts it, God has accommodated Himself to the human mind. The YHWH depicted in the Old Testament is this accommodation."[12]

UNDERSTANDING DIVINE VIOLENCE: GOD'S GOOD INTENTIONS MAY FAIL

An important contribution Boyd makes to the discussion of the violent God in the Old Testament is his statement that God's good intentions may fail. Chapter 20 of his book is titled "When God's Nonviolent Plans Fail: The Cruciform Interpretation of the Conquest Narrative." Boyd contends that God gave the people of Israel plans to conquer the land of Canaan without violence. God's first plan was to send hornets that would make the land so unpleasant that the indigenous population would be forced to relocate to a place outside of Canaan. The second plan of God was to have the land vomit the Canaanites by punishing the land and forcing the indigenous population to relocate elsewhere. The third plan was that God would bring the people to Canaan in the same way he brought them out of Egypt. The fourth plan for a nonviolent conquest of the land of Canaan was the appearance of the commander of the Lord's army to Joshua (Josh 5:13–15) indicating that the conquest of the land by violence was not God's idea. According to Boyd, God's plan for a nonviolent conquest of Canaan failed (in chapter 18 I will discuss God's first plan, the sending of the hornets, and God's fourth plan, the appearance of the Commander of the Lord's Army).

Yahweh has a plan to reconcile the world unto himself, "what I have planned will take place" (Isa 14:24 NJB). The ultimate goal of Yahweh's plan is the proclamation of his lordship over all the earth. This divine plan finds fulfillment in the last days, "Isaiah sets this saving act of Jahweh in

---

12. Patrick, "Debate with Terence Fretheim," 367.

the widest possible historical context, namely that of universal history."[13] The fulfillment of Yahweh's plan will include the salvation of a remnant, the coming of a ruler of justice and peace, and the establishment of his kingdom. Yahweh's plan, however, "is brought about through judgment on all that oppose his lordship." Thus, "it can be said that judgment and salvation are two sides of one and the same plan."[14]

The biblical text provides evidence that at times, God's plan for people and nations fails. This fact is crucial for the proper understanding of divine violence in the Old Testament. Many Christians are reluctant to accept the fact that God's good intentions fail because they have a preconceived idea about the way God acts in the world. There are several places in the Old Testament where God's intention for individuals failed because those individuals failed to obey God. I will cite two cases where God's intention for an individual failed because of the action of that individual.

The first example is God's intention for Saul. When the people of Israel asked Samuel to give them a king, God gave them Saul, the son of Kish, to be the first king of Israel. God's intention was to establish Saul's kingship forever. "Samuel said to Saul, 'You have acted like a fool. You have not obeyed the order which Yahweh your God gave you. Otherwise, Yahweh would have confirmed your sovereignty over Israel for ever. But now your sovereignty will not last" (1 Sam 13:13–14 NJB). Saul's kingship was conditional; it was based on the obedience of Saul and the people to the commandments of God (1 Sam 12:14–15). If they had obeyed, "Yahweh would have confirmed [Saul's] sovereignty over Israel for ever." Because Saul failed to obey God, God was unable to establish Saul's kingdom for ever as God intended to do.

The second example is the case of Jeroboam, the first king of the Northern Kingdom. After the death of Solomon, the monarchy was divided. Rehoboam, Solomon's son became king of Judah with its capital in Jerusalem and Jeroboam became king of the Northern Kingdom with its capital in Samaria. When Ahijah announced that Jeroboam would become king, Ahijah told Jeroboam what Yahweh intended for him: "If you will listen to all that I command you, walk in my ways, and do what is right in my sight by keeping my statutes and my commandments, as David my servant did, I will be with you, and will build you an enduring

---

13. Rad, *Old Testament Theology*, 2:162.
14. Jensen, "Yahweh's Plan," 445–46.

house, as I built for David, and I will give Israel to you" (1 Kgs 11:38). It was God's desire to build "an enduring house" for Jeroboam, but God's will for Jeroboam was not accomplished because Jeroboam established the worship of the golden calves in the kingdom and failed to walk in the ways of Yahweh.

When God's plan fails, the work of God in the world is compromised. God's work is the salvation of every person: "For I have no pleasure in the death of anyone, says the Lord GOD" (Ezek 18:32). Rather, the Lord wants people "to turn from their wicked ways and live" (Ezek 18:23). But when people refuse to turn to him, then God's intent to save people is not accomplished. God said, "Turn and live" (Ezek 18:32), but when people fail to turn, they do not live; they die, and often by violent means.

INTERPRETING DIVINE VIOLENCE

There are several problems with the way some interpreters seek to resolve the issue of divine violence in the Old Testament.

The Problem of Scripture

The biggest problem with the problem of divine violence in the Old Testament is the proper understanding of Scripture, primarily the Old Testament. To many, the New Testament reveals the true nonviolent character of God while the Old Testament portrays God in violent ways. The violent character of Yahweh contradicts what Jesus taught about God. The God of the Old Testament is a God who commanded the people of Israel to kill men, women, and children when they took possession of the land of Canaan. The God revealed in Jesus commands his followers to pray for their enemies and feed them when they are hungry.

According to Cowles, Seibert, and Boyd, the God Jesus revealed is a God who opposes violence and who commands his disciples to love their enemies. Old Testament texts in which Yahweh acts violently or commands his followers to act violently are evaluated and judged by the nonviolent teachings of Jesus. However, when the actions of people who lived thousands of years before Christ are evaluated in the light of the teachings of Christ and based upon the ethics of the Sermon of the

Mount, every action of Moses, Joshua, David, and many others will fail the test because they did not live and act as followers of Christ.

These writers emphasize that Jesus and the God revealed in Christ are nonviolent. However, this seems to contradict some of the evidence found in the New Testament. In his article "God and Violence in the Old Testament," Fretheim writes, "The Old Testament has a reputation: it is a book filled with violence, including the violence of God. The New Testament commonly avoids such a charge; but it, too, is filled with violent words and deeds, and Jesus and the God of the New Testament are complicit in this violence."[15] Aichele says that "Each of the synoptic gospels portrays Jesus as a violent man, one who contests violently with others."[16]

In his evaluation of the argument that the God of the Bible is nonviolent because Jesus taught nonviolence, Belousek writes,

> One can conclude with certainty that God is nonviolent because Jesus is nonviolent only if one gives absolute weight to the Gospel traditions of a healing, forgiving, non-resisting, non-retaliating Jesus and zero weight to the multiple traditions of a judging, punishing, destroying, and killing Jesus—an obviously biased weighing of the evidence. If one assigns a non-zero weight to the latter traditions of textual evidence, the upshot is that any argument inferring a nonviolent God from a nonviolent Jesus will be only as convincing as one's interpretation of the scriptural traditions of Jesus the divine judge.[17]

Divine Violence and the Anabaptist Tradition

Both Seibert and Boyd write their books and interpret divine violence in the Old Testament from an Anabaptist perspective. In fact, Boyd concedes the Anabaptist tradition "is the primary theological orientation out of which this book is written."[18] Anabaptists trace their origins to the Radical Reformation in sixteenth-century Europe. Anabaptists believe that the Bible is their only rule for faith and life. They also believe that the church should be separated from the state. Most Anabaptists are pacifists

---

15. Fretheim, "God and Violence," 18.
16. Aichele, "Jesus' Violence," 72.
17. Belousek, "Nonviolent God," 3.
18. Belousek, "Nonviolent God," 15.

who oppose war and violence. This opposition to war and violence is the prism by which Seibert and Boyd evaluate the God of the Old Testament.

Anabaptists have adopted a Christocentric hermeneutic by which they interpret texts dealing with divine violence. Anabaptists use Jesus, his life, his words, and his death on the cross to evaluate the actions of God in the Old Testament. Anabaptists believe that the cross reveals the nonviolent character of God. By reinterpreting texts portraying divine violence through kingdom ethics, most Anabaptists believe that the nonviolent, enemy-loving God revealed by Jesus is not the violent, genocidal God of the Old Testament.

Belousek says that the concept of a "nonviolent God" finds its home in Anabaptist circles. He writes, "The 'nonviolent God' argument, to be conclusive and convincing, requires more than the stated premises. At least, it presupposes a peace church hermeneutic."[19] Reimer says that the Mennonite view on violence and peace is "a minority position."[20]

Divine Violence and Pacifism

Both Seibert and Boyd look at the Old Testament from the perspective of pacifism. Pacifism has been practiced and emphasized within the Anabaptist tradition, which is the primary theological orientation that guides Seibert's and Boyd's reading of the many texts dealing with violence in the Old Testament.[21] As Boyd writes, "the centrality of nonviolence that most Anabaptists embraced caused them to discern a greater degree of tension between" the Old Testament and the New Testament. This tension was caused by violent acts of God and Jesus's kingdom ethics. Although he denies this fact, by employing Jesus's kingdom ethics in the interpretation of violence in the Old Testament, Boyd is "imputing modern moral sensibilities to ancient people."[22]

There is no doubt that pacifism clouds one's view of the God of the Old Testament. A pacifist interpretation of the Old Testament is anachronistic because it uses pacifism as the lens by which to view the ways Yahweh deals with the problems of sin, wickedness, and violence in the Old Testament. From a pacifist perspective, God should be the kind of

19. Belousek, "Nonviolent God," 6.
20. Reimer, "God Is Love but Not a Pacifist," 490.
21. Boyd, *Crucifixion of the Warrior God*, 15.
22. Boyd, *Crucifixion of the Warrior God*, 299.

God who never engages in violence.[23] If pacifism and kingdom ethics become the lens by which the Old Testament is interpreted, then almost every text in the Old Testament will be considered offensive because they will be contrary to the teachings of Jesus. Then, every text in which God takes action to deliver his people will be contrary to the pacifist's view of a non-violent view of God.

Reimer says that God is not a pacifist: "Some Mennonite theologians have implied that if we take Jesus to be the full revelation of God, and if we understand the gospel of Jesus essentially as the rejection of all violence, then it follows that God is a pacifist. This, in my view, has dire consequences. It implies that all violence . . . is ultimately meaningless and outside the providence of God. It also suggests that evil will not be punished and judged."[24]

Divine Violence and Marcionism

Reimer claims that because of their "strong commitment to non-resistance, Mennonites are always tempted by Marcionism, by separating the God of Jesus and the God of the Old Testament."[25] Although Boyd disagrees with Marcionites, he is sympathetic to their views. Boyd writes,

> though I disagree with them, I have to confess that I empathize with their shared impulse to dismiss these violent portraits. To be perfectly honest, I have a certain respect for Marcion and his followers who decided it was better to cast away the Old Testament than tarnish the image of the Father of Jesus Christ by mixing in traces of a warlike God. Given their mistaken belief that they had to choose between Jesus and the OT, I admire their bold choice. But it is this false either-or proposition that I strongly reject.[26]

---

23. Berges, "Violence of God," 23 says that the "image of a 'soft' and always loving God is part of the human wishful thinking and has to be qualified as idolatry."

24. Reimer, "God Is Love but Not a Pacifist," 491.

25. Reimer, "God Is Love but Not a Pacifist," 490.

26. Boyd, *Crucifixion of the Warrior God*, 344. Seibert, *Disturbing Divine Behavior*, 67 says that "we should not be too quick to judge Marcion and his followers." The reason is because "Marcion has become something of a 'poster child' representing the perils of questioning disturbing depictions of God or of suggesting that there are glaring contradictions between the ways God is portrayed in the Old and New Testament." Berges, "Violence of God," 40 says that the heretical splitting up of the positive and negative sides of God is a form of Marcionism. He wrote, "The heretical temptation to

The distinction between the God of the Old Testament and the God revealed in Jesus exhibits a tendency toward Marcionism, which, according to Belousek, is "a perennial problem in the Anabaptist tradition."[27] Marcion believed that the God of the Old Testament was a wrathful, violent, and malevolent god. He also believed that the wrathful Hebrew God was different than the all-forgiving God revealed by Jesus. Since Jesus reveals a nonviolent God, a God who is different from the diabolic violent warrior God, Marcion differentiated between the God of Jesus and the God of the Old Testament.

If we accept the truth that "in Christ God was reconciling the world to himself" (2 Cor 5:19) and if we believe that God's work of reconciliation began after the fall, then we must acknowledge that there is a continuity in the history of the God of the Old Testament and the God of the New Testament. As Paul said, there is only one Lord and one God (Eph 4:5–6) and this God is the same yesterday and today and forever (Heb 13:8).

THE BIBLICAL TEXT AND TODAY'S READERS

One issue that affects the interpretation of divine violence in the Old Testament is how contemporary readers interpret and evaluate what the biblical writers tried to communicate to their original audience. In interpreting the biblical text, today's readers must take into consideration the time and place in which the writers lived. This, at times, is very difficult to ascertain because the final form of the biblical text has gone through a complicated process of development. The biblical text we have today is the work of people who lived in the post-exilic time. However, the text is a compilation of ancient writings that incorporate ancient traditions and reflect the world out of which the traditions developed.

Another issue that affects the interpretation of the biblical text is the many presuppositions today's readers bring when reading and interpreting the text. No interpretation of the text is free of bias. However, it is important to remember that the world and the culture that today's readers bring into the text is different from the world and culture of the biblical writers and the world and culture of those people who first read what the

---

exorcize the dark sides of Jhwh, his wrath and negativity out of a Christian notion of God, hasn't lost any of its attraction since Marcion in the 2nd century C.E."

27. Belousek, "Nonviolent God," 65.

biblical writers wrote. The danger in interpreting the biblical text today is that we may explain the text from the perspective in which we live and from the bias that we bring to our reading of the text. The result may be that our interpretation may not reflect the original meaning and message of the text as it was intended by the biblical writer.

Today's readers believe that the Old Testament is the result of God revealing himself in the history of the people of Israel. Thus, the Old Testament was written to address the religious, social, and cultural life of a people whose life and practices were similar to the culture of many nations in the ancient Near East. Today's believing community read the Bible as sacred Scripture. They believe that the Bible is the inspired word of God, even though many Christians differ in their explanation of what it means for the text to be inspired and to be the word of God.

Cowles, Seibert, and Boyd interpret the Old Testament as Americans living in a country whose culture is completely different from the culture of the people who lived in the land of Canaan more than three thousand years ago. They interpret the Old Testament as Christians whose lives have been transformed by the gospel and whose religious values are completely different from the people who worshiped God in a tabernacle. Seibert and Boyd interpret the Old Testament as Anabaptists and as pacifists who reject all kinds of violence. Christians who are committed to nonviolence and who live by kingdom ethics found in the Sermon on the Mount and in the teaching of Jesus, cannot evaluate the people of Israel who lived in Old Testament times from a Christian perspective. Their view of God was culturally conditioned and pre-Christian.

4

Dealing With Divine Violence

MUCH OF DIVINE VIOLENCE IN the Old Testament comes in response to human violence. Yahweh uses violence in order to deal with human sinfulness and human violence. Yahweh uses violence to help maintain order in creation. The Old Testament portrays Yahweh as the creator of the universe and of human beings. He is also presented as the lawgiver and the righteous judge. The psalmist says that Yahweh "is a God who judges" (Ps 50:6 TNK). As creator and lawgiver, Yahweh is responsible for maintaining the moral laws that he established at the time he brought creation into being. Because Israel is his people, Yahweh has the right to command Israel to keep his covenant (Exod 19:5). Because Yahweh is the creator, he "is king over the nations" (Ps 47:8), he is exalted through all the earth (Ps 46:10); "the earth is full of the LORD's faithful care" (Ps 33:5 TNK). It is out of this context that one begins to understand and deal with the problem of divine violence.

CREATION THEOLOGY

The basic foundation to understand the issue of divine violence is creation theology. Creation theology is based on the "universalism of creaturality—there is only one God, the creator of heaven and earth, and he is the god of all nations and all people."[1] The Bible begins by introducing God as the creator of heavens and earth and of every human being. As

1. Assmann, *Invention of Religion*, 72.

the creator, "God stands in relationship with the world, and not only with Israel."[2] Yahweh is the God of every nation and the God of every person even though people may not know they are responsible to him.[3] Thus, God's work of redemption must be understood from the perspective of God's sovereignty over his creation.[4]

When God acts in the world, he acts through the moral order he established at creation.[5] Because God is the creator of every human being, the life of every individual is under the uncompromising claim of God. The moral laws that God established encompass every sphere of human life, therefore, every violation of the moral laws of God must be followed by its vindication. As Piper said, "No wrongdoer must get away with impunity."[6] God's justice in the world is done through direct intervention or through agents. God is the lawgiver; he upholds the moral order and no one can revoke the judgment when the moral order is violated (Amos 1:3).

Yahweh is the guardian of the moral order and he will act when this order is violated. In the Old Testament, when Israel violates the demands of the covenant, Yahweh acts.[7] When the nations violate the moral laws Yahweh has established, Yahweh acts. The actions of Yahweh dealing with sin and the violation of the moral order explain many of the texts where divine wrath and violence are present. As Fretheim writes, "God acts in and through the moral order. . . . The basic purpose of the moral order is that sin/evil not go unchecked and that God's good order of creation can be (re)established . . . that sins have consequences, including the sins of violence, is a working out of the moral order, and can be named the judgment of God."[8]

---

2. Maré, "Creation Theology," 693.

3. Yahweh chose Cyrus, bestowed titles of honor on him and gave him a mission, even though Cyrus did not know Yahweh, "For the sake of my servant Jacob, Israel, my chosen one, I have called you by name. I have given you a title of honor, although you don't know me" (Isa 45:4 GWN).

4. Maré, "Creation Theology," 693.

5. Berlejung, "Sin and Punishment," 278 says that "according to the Old Testament, the divine will is encoded in the creation."

6. Piper, "Vengeance and the Moral Order," 225.

7. Fretheim, "Character of God in Jeremiah," 213 says that God's wrath "is an effect that grows out of a violation of the moral order of God's creation."

8. Fretheim, "'I Was Only a Little Angry,'" 370.

THE REALITY AND THE CONSEQUENCES OF SIN

There are twenty-six words for sins in the Hebrew Bible. The confessional declaration in Exod 34:7 uses three of them: iniquity (*ʿāwōn*), transgression (*pešaʿ*), and sin (*ḥāṭāʾ*). These three words for sin are used in many different contexts, not as synonyms, but to describe "sin in its own way." According to Knierim, "where they are used together as a formula, they are 'intended to represent all other terms for sin.'"[9] Knierim says that *ḥṭʾ* is the comprehensive word for "sin" used in the Old Testament. For this reason, Old Testament writers prefer to use *ḥṭʾ* above all other words for "sin."[10]

The Old Testament refers to sin as human rebellion against the creator. Human rebellion against God results in a fundamental rupture in the human-divine relationship. Berlejung says that sin or moral evil "describes human intentions and actions that are qualified as evil, violent, wrong, or as vices and crimes. But passive aspects also are inherent, such as when a human being neglects or disregards divine orders. . . . Within this context, punishment is the divine or society's reaction to the sinner."[11]

What the Old Testament teaches about sin does not differ from the teachings of the New Testament. The Old Testament teaches that all individuals, men and women, are sinners. When Solomon dedicated the temple in Jerusalem, he asked Yahweh to be merciful to his people when they sinned against him: "When they sin against you—for there is no one who does not sin" (1 Kgs 8:46 NJB). The psalmist said, "no one living can be found guiltless at your tribunal" (Ps 143:2 NJB). Sin, however, could be forgiven by atonement and repentance, "What god can compare with you for pardoning guilt and for overlooking crime? He does not harbour anger for ever, since he delights in showing faithful love" (Mic 7:18 NJB).

In creation, Yahweh created a world in which human beings would live a moral order symbolized by the tree of good and evil: "And the LORD God commanded the man, 'You may freely eat of every tree of the garden; but of the tree of the knowledge of good and evil you shall not eat, for in the day that you eat of it you shall die'" (Gen 2:16–17). Human beings were given the freedom to accept God and reject evil and the devastation caused by sin. In Genesis sin is portrayed as disobedience and as a rejection of the limitations imposed upon humanity by the creator.

9. Knierim, "*ḥṭʾ* to miss," 544.
10. Knierim, "*ḥṭʾ* to miss," 548.
11. Berlejung, "Sin and Punishment," 272.

The consequence of sin is separation from God: "but your iniquities have made a separation between you and your God, and your sins have hidden his face from you so that he does not hear" (Isa 59:2 ESV). Another consequence of sin is death: "The person who sins shall die" (Ezek 18:20). The Bible does not specify how the evildoer and the sinner die. The death of the sinner can come in many ways, often by violence. When Yahweh brings judgment upon evildoers, he acts as a "righteous judge" for the judge of all the earth does what is right (Gen 18:25).

God does not want death for his creation; he wants them to live. However, in order for humans to live, they must repent from their sins and turn from their wickedness:

> Yet the house of Israel says, "The way of the Lord is unfair." O house of Israel, are my ways unfair? Is it not your ways that are unfair? Therefore I will judge you, O house of Israel, all of you according to your ways, says the Lord GOD. Repent and turn from all your transgressions; otherwise iniquity will be your ruin. Cast away from you all the transgressions that you have committed against me, and get yourselves a new heart and a new spirit! Why will you die, O house of Israel? For I have no pleasure in the death of anyone, says the Lord GOD. Turn, then, and live. (Ezek 18:29–32)

The people of Israel complained that Yahweh's judgment upon their sins and rebellions was unfair: "The way of the Lord is unfair." Their complaint is similar to people today who complain about the way God brings judgment upon sin and violence. Violence begets violence. As Fretheim writes, "Sometimes the Hebrew word *rā' â* refers to the evil/wickedness of the people, sometimes to the effects of their wickedness, commonly translated 'disaster.' In other words, the people's *rā' â* will issue in their *rā' â*."[12]

Since God uses nations as agents of his justice, these agents will use violence and barbaric methods to accomplish their goals.[13] Their goal is

---

12. Fretheim, "'I Was Only a Little Angry,'" 371.

13. Violence can be used for both judgment and salvation. As Fretheim, "'I Was Only a Little Angry,'" 371 writes, "The use of violence in the prophets is never an end in itself; it has a twofold purpose: judgment and salvation. So, for example, God uses the violence of the Persians under King Cyrus as judgment against the enslaving Babylonians as a means to bring salvation to the exiles (e.g., Isa 45:1–8; 47:1–15). In other words, God uses violence both to save Israel from the effects of other people's sins (cf. Israel in Egypt; Exod 15:1–3) and to save God's people from the effects of their own sins."

the enlargement of their empires and the pursuit of spoils of war. Yahweh used the Assyrians as his agents to bring judgment upon Israel for their sins, their iniquities, and their transgression. Assyria was the rod and the staff God used to judge his people.[14] In doing Yahweh's work, the Assyrians did all kinds of violence against the people of Israel and this violence was then attached to Yahweh. However, as Brueggemann writes, the violence assigned to Yahweh could also be considered counterviolence, "The violence undertaken by Yahweh as warrior is not characteristically a blind or unbridled violence. It is rather an act of force that aims to defend and give life. . . . It is likely that the violence assigned to Yahweh is to be understood as counterviolence, which functions primarily as a critical principle in order to undermine and destabilize other violence."[15]

Nineveh, the capital of the Assyrian empire, was known as "the city of bloody violence," a city made great by stolen goods, the booty of war that sustained the empire. In their wars of conquest, the Assyrians used horses and war chariots. Assyrian soldiers and their horsemen charged against the population, flashing their swords and their spears. The result was "piles of dead, heaps of corpses, dead bodies without end" (Nah 3:1–3).

God does not want to bring judgment upon people and nations. God's desire is the redemption of his creation. As a righteous judge, before sending his judgment, Yahweh warns people of the impending judgment, "To whom shall I speak and give warning, that they may hear? See, their ears are closed, they cannot listen. The word of the LORD is to them an object of scorn; they take no pleasure in it" (Jer 6:10). "God becomes righteous in the highest sense when He acts according to this inherent saving disposition. Righteousness becomes the action corresponding to the nature of the one true God."[16] In the Old Testament, through his many servants "God was reconciling the world to himself" (2 Cor 5:19), but when people refuse to repent and turn from their wickedness, God must act as a righteous judge.

---

14. Yahweh called the Assyrian king "the rod of my anger" (Isa 10:5). Childs, *Isaiah*, 353 said that the Assyrian king was Yahweh's agent "to carry out Yahweh's mission."

15. Brueggemann, *Theology of the Old Testament*, 244.

16. Davidson, *Theology of the Old Testament*, 212.

FREEDOM OF WILL

When God created human beings, he created them in his image and in his likeness and gave them dominion over every living thing that moves upon the earth (Gen 1:26–28). God also gave humans free will, which included the freedom to obey or disobey the will of the creator. In his discussion of human freedom in the world, Brueggemann writes, "Because Yahweh is genuinely interactive, on occasion human persons are emboldened to take the initiative with Yahweh, to insist on their right over against Yahweh, to address Yahweh in a voice of advocacy and insistence."[17] Then, using Job as a representative of all humans, Brueggemann writes, "Job is all of humanity gathered and mobilized against Yahweh, insistent on rights and entitlements that belong to responsible human creatures who have full membership in Yahweh's creation."[18]

Whybray believes that, at times, human beings are puppets in the hands of God. He writes, "It has, I think, to be accepted that human beings are sometimes treated by God as pawns or puppets—as beings whose lives and emotions are of no account for God, though in some cases they may be used as instruments serving some great and good purpose."[19] However, to be created in the image of God implies co-creatorhood. As Braaten explains, "the motif of created co-creator points clearly to the distinctiveness of humans as creatures with a high destiny, a destiny that is essential to the world if it is to bear the mark of its creator God."[20] To have free will means that humans have the freedom to make decisions, to implement those decisions, and be responsible for the decisions they make. When God established this relationship with humans, God had to impose some limitations upon himself. In delegating to human beings dominion of the created order, God gave power to human beings to act in the world.

This power means that human beings can act for good or for evil. It also means that they can achieve their goals by peaceful means or through violence. In order to honor the relationship established with human beings and in order to allow humans to become like God, knowing good and evil (Gen 3:22), God allowed humans to use their power of dominion to shape the life of the world: "In honoring this basic character of

---

17. Brueggemann, *Theology of the Old Testament*, 457.
18. Brueggemann, *Theology of the Old Testament*, 457.
19. Whybray, "'Shall Not the Judge,'" 16.
20. Braaten, *Christian Dogmatics*, 327.

the Creator-creature relationship, God chooses to exercise constraint and restraint in the exercise of power in the life of the world."[21] God's willingness to allow human beings to use these God-given powers in the world makes God vulnerable to criticism because when they use violence, that violence is attributed to God. When they kill, murder, commit atrocities and brutalities in the name of God, human action becomes God's action because he is accused of creating humans with the propensity for evil.[22]

The rupture of the relationship between God and human beings came when humans exercised their libertarian freedom and rebelled against God. Because of the freedom God gave to human beings, God cannot manipulate the will of individuals, otherwise they would not be free agents, with the liberty to choose whether to obey and love God or to reject him. The fact that "the inclination of the human heart is evil from youth" (Gen 8:21) demonstrates "humanity's incorrigible perversity" and the sinfulness of every human being. The flood story "reveals that Yahweh has to deal with human violence and human wickedness with violence. However, his will is not to destroy the world and punish human beings. The fact that Yahweh has to deal with 'humanity's incorrigible perversity' through human history shows that divine judgment is restrained by God's grace."[23] The fact that Israel openly rebelled against Yahweh even though they were singled out of all the families of the earth to be intimately known by God (Amos 3:2), shows that God cannot change the mind of free agents.

In order to deal with human violence and sinfulness, God works in the world redemptively, with the goal of reconciling the world unto himself. God seeks to redeem the world by himself (Gen 1–11), then through Israel, and finally through Christ: "God was in Christ, reconciling the world unto himself" (2 Cor 5:19). This freedom that God gives to people is a demonstration of the relational way God works with human beings. In his dealing with human beings, God sets before every person life and death, blessings and curses (Deut 30:19). They are free to choose and their choices will affect their lives and the societies in which they live. God wants them to choose life, "Choose life so that you and your descendants may live" (Deut 30:19), but because of their free will and their freedom to choose between good and evil, they choose evil and refuse to

21. Fretheim, "To Say Something," 347.

22. Brueggemann, "Warrior God," 31 asks, "What if we are made in the image of a God who struggles with violence?"

23. Goldingay, *Biblical Theology*, 26, 28.

choose good (Isa 7:15), they do what is evil in God's sight and choose to do what does not please God (Isa 66:4). Human rebellion against the will of God is the primary cause for human violence which in turn requires divine violence to contain human violence. Divine violence is provoked by human violence. God's relational way of dealing with human beings is the reason for some of the divine violence in the Old Testament for "this way of relating to people reveals a divine vulnerability, for God opens the divine self up to hurt should things go wrong. And things do go violently wrong, despite God's best efforts."[24]

---

24. Fretheim, "'I Was Only a Little Angry,'" 373.

5

Divine Violence and the Suffering of God

Few people today truly know Yahweh, the God of the Old Testament. Most Christians focus their study of Scriptures almost exclusively on the New Testament. For many, the God of the Old Testament is a violent God, a God of wrath, and an evil deity. Some people believe Yahweh to be the "destroyer, sinister, dangerous and unaccountably angered, as one who rejoices in destruction, ruins unexpectedly and craftily, who punishes without mercy, demands cruelty and creates evil."[1]

When describing Yahweh, the God of the Old Testament, most people emphasize divine violence, genocide, the killing of the Canaanites, maternal cannibalism, and other acts in which Yahweh seems to be acting contrary to his nature as a "compassionate and merciful God, patient, always faithful and ready to forgive" (Exod 34:6 GWN). They emphasize what they perceive to be the demonic in Yahweh. Consequently, the view of Yahweh as a compassionate God, a God who suffers with, for, and because of his people is foreign to many Christians. The reason for this lack of knowledge is due to the fact that many Christians have been influenced by Greek philosophy, a philosophy that led the leaders of the early church to adopt the doctrine of the impassibility of God.[2]

---

1. Volz, *Das Dämonische in Jahwe*, 9. Quoted in Heschel, *Prophets*, 2:83.
2. Kuyper, "Suffering and the Repentance of God," 257–77, offers a review of the early church's interpretation of the doctrine of divine impassibility.

THE SUFFERING OF GOD

The doctrine of the impassibility of God teaches that the God of the Bible is a perfect being who cannot be affected by outside events and thus cannot suffer, for suffering is a sign of imperfection. Jürgen Moltmann says that "a God who cannot suffer is poorer than any man. For a God who is incapable of suffering is a being who cannot be involved. Suffering and injustice do not affect him. And because he is so completely insensitive, he cannot be affected or shaken by anything. He cannot weep, for he has no tears. But the one who cannot suffer cannot love either. So, he is also a loveless being."[3] This view of God as a perfect being is not biblical, "The notion of a perfect Being is not of biblical origin. It is not the product of prophetic religion, but of Greek philosophy."[4] The God of the Old Testament is a God who chooses to identify himself with his people in their suffering. There are several passages in the Bible which reveal the pain of God for the sins and disobedience of his people. The God who in the New Testament suffered in the person of Christ is the same God who in the Old Testament suffered because of the sins of Israel and the nations. Several Old Testament texts give strong evidence that God experiences suffering. The suffering of God is portrayed in his words and actions. God's suffering for his people is consistent with his nature as a God who chooses to enter into the history of the world and establish a genuine relationship with people.

The God of the Old Testament is known primarily by his role as creator, savior, and redeemer, "I am Yahweh, your Savior, your Redeemer" (Isa 49:26). In these roles, God voluntarily limits himself to a gradual process of creation from the chaos of nothingness to the world in which we live. He is also the God who chooses to be patient with people who are arrogant, stubborn, and disobedient. The stubbornness and rebellion of Israel are summarized in the words of the Levite's prayer: "You warned them in order to turn them back to your law. Yet they acted presumptuously and did not obey your commandments, but sinned against your ordinances, by the observance of which a person shall live. They turned a stubborn shoulder and stiffened their neck and would not obey" (Neh 9:29).

The voluntary limiting of God sets the framework for the concept of God's suffering. Since the God of the Bible reveals himself to his people

---

3. Moltmann, *Crucified God*, 222.
4. Heschel, *Prophets*, 2:54.

in human form (Gen 18:1–2) and communicates directly with human beings, the people of Israel assumed that God had thought and will, and that he was capable of emotions, anger, and love. Throughout the Old Testament one can see that the moral evil of the world, the rebellion of human beings, and the disobedience of his people provoke God to anger (Deut 4:25; Judg 2:12) in the same way his love for them also moves him toward costly sacrifice (Joel 2:13; Hos 11:1–9). The God of the Bible is a God who carries the burden of his people, who knows the failure of his purpose for them, who sorrows over them with a love that prevails over wrath, and who suffers because of their affliction.

The suffering of God in the Old Testament anticipates the pain and the agony of the Suffering Servant of the New Testament. As Robinson puts it, "It is as if there were a cross unseen, standing on its undiscovered hill, far back in the ages, out of which were sounding always, just the same deep voice of suffering love and patience, that was heard by mortal ears from the sacred hill of Calvary."[5] These words express the nature of the God of the Old Testament, the very same loving, caring, hurting God who reveals himself in the person of Jesus Christ. Israel believed that God was present with the people in their suffering, that their God was a God who understood what the people were going through. Although Israel believed that God was the cause of their suffering, they also believed that God understood their suffering. Divine understanding for them presupposes suffering with them. The God who revealed himself to Israel could not be the personal God of his people without experiencing suffering. Those who do not experience suffering cannot sympathize with the pain and suffering of others (Heb 4:15; 5:8). God is a loving and compassionate God and it pains him to see humanity suffer.

According to Fretheim, there are two poles for understanding God in the Old Testament.[6] One is that God is a radically transcendent Lord who stands outside the world without acting in the world. This is what he calls the traditional view of God. The second is the organismic view, a view in which a greater continuity, that is, a greater intimacy between God and the world is discerned. In the organismic view there is a relationship of reciprocity. In other words, the world is not only affected by God, God is also affected by the world, both positively and negatively. God has chosen to be involved in the history of the world and to be

---

5. Robinson, *Suffering: Human and Divine*, 145.
6. Fretheim, *Suffering of God*, 35.

limited by it. Therefore, although God is unchangeable in his steadfast love and his salvific will for all creation, God does change in response to the interaction between himself and his creation.

For Israel to have understood God in any other way would have been incompatible with the revelation of God's character in their history. The people of Israel could not have understood a God who had complete freedom to act in the realm of history but who refused to do so because of a lack of compassion or desire. After all, they had experienced just the opposite in the exodus.

The belief in the genuine love of God for Israel necessitated, for them, a God who sympathized with his people, not merely superficially recognizing their condition, but actually participating with them in their sufferings. This is how Israel experienced God in Egypt: "God heard their groaning, and God remembered his covenant with Abraham, Isaac, and Jacob. God looked upon the Israelites, and God took notice of them" (Exod 2:24–25).

For God to have seen the affliction of his people, to have heard their cry, and to have known their suffering (Exod 3:7) required God taking their sorrows into his very being and allowing those sorrows to arouse feelings of compassion and to affect his being in his interactions with them. Thus, the suffering of God is basic for the proper understanding of the concept of relatedness or relationship which in the Old Testament derives from the concept of the covenant and the understanding of Israel as the chosen people of God. As Israel understood God, the idea of the suffering of God to some extent limited the concept of God's power. For the relationship between God and Israel to have integrity required God giving up some of his own power and freedom for the sake of the relationship.

THE SUFFERING GOD AND HIS PEOPLE

The God of the Old Testament is a God who chooses to identify himself with his people in their suffering. The view that God chooses to identify with Israel and enter their history raises an important question: does God suffer with his people? According to the Old Testament perspective, God cannot do otherwise. Yahweh is related to Israel through the covenant established at Sinai. Therefore, he is directly involved with Israel in their misfortunes and their failures.

In his book, *What Are They Saying About the Theology of Suffering*, Lucien Richard summarizes what biblical scholars and theologians have written on the biblical view of suffering. In his summary of Walter Brueggemann's view on the theology of the pain of God, Lucien wrote: "From within the covenantal relationship with God, Israel senses that its God is not only an enforcer and a legitimator of existing structures, but is also one who embraces Israel's pain."[7] By embracing the pain of his people, God's own self is transformed. God takes on the pain of Israel in his own person because of his compassion for them. Gerstenberger and Schrage wrote: "In the Old Testament . . . suffering can be regarded as a means of expiation. A deity has been injured through human misconduct. He becomes angry, strikes back, and brings disaster upon the culprit and his community. But because the deity in principle stands in a friendly, and even familiar, relationship to the sufferer, the suffering will soften the wrath of God. God cannot bear to see his own people in misery; his justifiable indignation is transformed into compassion."[8]

The God of the Old Testament saves and blesses Israel because of this covenantal relationship that is guaranteed by God's *ḥesed*, his faithful love for Israel. Because of this special relationship established with the nation, God is united with his people and participates in their life and their misery. This special relationship is affirmed in the Old Testament in the emotional language of human suffering. As a partner in this relationship, God assumes the function of not only Israel's God, but also her closest friend, a friend who takes upon himself part of the burden of his suffering friends (cf. John 15:13). The Old Testament writers describe God's response to Israel's sins and rebellions in words that already express within themselves an element of divine suffering. One example is the rebellion of Israel at the occasion of the building of the golden calf in Exod 32. At Sinai, Israel rebelled against God by being unfaithful to God and by violating the demands of the covenant which required exclusive allegiance to him. God's response to Israel's apostasy was one of indignation. God told Moses: "Now let me alone, so that my wrath may burn hot against them and I may consume them; and of you I will make a great nation" (Exod 32:10). Israel had entered into a relationship with Yahweh and now that relationship had been broken. God was affected by Israel's

---

7. Richard, *What Are They Saying*, 16.
8. Gerstenberger and Schrage, *Suffering*, 107.

disloyalty. God's words to Moses, "Let me alone," represent God's desire to suffer grief in isolation.

This language of divine suffering is designed to describe a faith which views God in terms of historical involvement and relatedness with his people. To Israel, God was not an impersonal being nor was he a God that was above and beyond the world. To the contrary, he was a God who was with them (Isa 7:14), the Holy One who lived among the people (Hos 11:9). "For what great nation has a god as near to them as the Lord our God is near to us whenever we call on him?" (Deut 4:7). This is the reason Israel ascribed personal characteristics to God, such as love, anger, anguish, patience, jealousy, and joy.

In addition, many other characteristics attributed to God reflect the fact that when God responds to human sin and rebellion, his response also contains the element of divine suffering. When God deals with humanity, God expresses a variety of reactions:

God is jealous: "Do not worship any other god, for the Lord, whose name is Jealous, is a jealous God" (Exod 34:14 NIV).

When God punishes, punishment is sometimes done out of a sense of injured honor: "Then my anger will cease and my wrath against them will subside, and I will be avenged. And when I have spent my wrath upon them, they will know that I the Lord have spoken in my zeal" (Ezek 5:13 NIV).

God becomes angry and enraged: "How long, O Lord? Will you be angry forever? How long will your jealousy burn like fire?" (Ps 79:5 NIV).

God is grieved by human sins: "The Lord was grieved that he had made man on the earth, and his heart was filled with pain" (Gen 6:6 NIV).

God changes his mind: "And the Lord changed his mind about the disaster that he planned to bring on his people" (Exod 32:14).

God is affected by the suffering of his people: "Whenever the Lord raised up judges for them, the Lord was with the judge, and he saved them from the hand of their enemies all the days of the judge; for the Lord was moved to pity by their groaning because of those who afflicted and oppressed them" (Judg 2:18 RSV).

God cries out like a person in pain: "The Lord goes forth like a soldier, like a warrior he stirs up his fury; he cries out, he shouts aloud, he shows himself mighty against his foes. For a long time I have held my peace, I have kept still and restrained myself; now I will cry out like a woman in labor, I will gasp and pant" (Isa 42:13–14).

Gerstenberger and Schrage wrote:

> All such affirmations in the Old Testament are deeply rooted in the emotional language of human suffering. "Pity" (e.g., Hos. 2:23) is a new turning toward a beloved person that is rooted in keen anxiety; "regret" (e.g., Gen. 6:6) is the painful concession to have failed in one's plan. Thus, for the Israelite God's suffering is, strange as it may sound, precisely like human suffering, a bitter experience that injures body and spirit . . . God's suffering results from the coinciding of human and divine action . . . His pain is the consequence of human misconduct.[9]

All these references which indicate that God enters into the sufferings of his people are affirmed by the statement of a prophet who spoke out of the experience of exile: "In all their distress he too was distressed. . . . In his love and mercy he redeemed them" (Isa 63:9 NIV). An implication of the prophetic words is that Yahweh can and does participate in the suffering of the world, not only as one who causes it, but also as one who is affected by it. The suffering of God in the Old Testament finds its finest expression in Hosea's description of God's heartbroken fatherly anguish over his prodigal child, Israel: "How can I give you up, Ephraim? How can I hand you over, Israel? How can I treat you like Admah? How can I make you like Zeboiim? My heart is changed within me; all my compassion is aroused" (Hos 11:8 NIV).

It is this picture of a suffering God who is intimately bound to his people which is the central focus of the Old Testament, not divine violence. This view of a God who suffers with, for, and because of his people is expressed throughout the Old Testament, especially in the messages of Isaiah, Hosea, and Jeremiah.

The God of the Old Testament is not absent from the world and is not detached from human affairs. Divine pathos refers to God's involvement in the word and his concern for human beings. It involves God's

---

9. Gerstenberger and Schrage, *Suffering*, 100.

concern for humanity and a divine vision for the world. According to Heschel, divine pathos is manifested in God's "love and anger, grief and joy, mercy and wrath."[10] God is intimately involved in the world and he chooses to enter into human history. God wills to be with humanity in bad as well as good times:

> The Lord said, "I have indeed seen the misery of my people in Egypt. I have heard them crying out because of their slave drivers, and I am concerned about their suffering. So I have come down to rescue them from the hand of the Egyptians and to bring them up out of that land into a good and spacious land, a land flowing with milk and honey." (Exod 3:7–8 NIV)

As a result of his involvement with his creation, God participates in the misery of humanity. His pain for the world is never the sympathetic view of the uninvolved onlooker, but it is the genuine pain of one who is directly affected by the suffering of those who suffer and who takes upon himself the burden of the people. As Fretheim wrote, "God is affected in many ways by what happens on earth."[11]

The opening speech in the book of Isaiah (Isa 1:2–9) deals not with the anger of God, but with the sorrow of God; it deals with the plight of a father who has been abandoned by his children. Isa 5:1–7 provides an additional example of the pain of God because of the rebellion of Israel. The "Song of the Vineyard" reveals the wonderment of God whose care for the vineyard has been of no avail: "What more could have been done for my vineyard than I have done for it?" (Isa 5:4). Here, God himself says that he is at a loss trying to explain the rebellion of his people. God's sorrow rather than the people's tragedy is the theme of this song. God's grief and disappointment are revealed in his being hurt at the thought of having to abandon his vineyard in which he had labored and placed so much hope for good things.

Thus, divine suffering is seen throughout the writings of the prophets and in many other passages of the Old Testament. God's suffering is seen in his disappointment with Israel:

> What wrong did your fathers find in me that they went far from me, and went after worthlessness, and became worthless? (Jer 2:5 RSV)

---

10. Heschel, *Prophets*, 2:263.
11. Fretheim, *Suffering of God*, 39.

> What shall I do with you, O Ephraim? What shall I do with you, O Judah? (Hos 6:4 RSV)
>
> My people, what have I done to you? How have I burdened you? Answer me. (Mic 6:3 NIV)
>
> Why do these people keep going along their self-destructive path, refusing to turn back, even though I have warned them? (Jer 8:5)

In trying to explain God's questions, Fretheim wrote, "These questions seem to imply a genuine loss on God's part as to what might explain the faithlessness of the people."[12] God's disappointment with his people gives occasion to these divine laments and expresses his pain at the rebellion of Israel. God suffers because of his love for Israel. He experiences pain because of their unfaithfulness. God's suffering teaches us an important lesson about God. Because God loves his people and desires their well-being, God identifies himself with their suffering. This identification of God with his people makes God vulnerable to being hurt, but it is this divine suffering that will motivate Israel to repent and turn to God.

DIVINE VIOLENCE AND DIVINE SUFFERING

It is unfortunate that those who are unhappy with and critical of divine violence do not recognize that Yahweh is provoked to anger, that the violence of God is a response to the violence of humans, that the human injustice is an affront to the God of justice, that Yahweh by no means clears the guilty person (Exod 34:7). Wrath and violence are not attributes of God.

The true character of God was revealed when he appeared to Moses and told him and the people of Israel what kind of God he was, "Yahweh, Yahweh, a God merciful and gracious, slow to anger, and abounding in steadfast love and faithfulness, keeping steadfast love for the thousandth generation, forgiving iniquity and transgression and sin, yet by no means clearing the guilty, but visiting the iniquity of the parents upon the children and the children's children, to the third and the fourth generation" (Exod 34:6–7).

Above all Yahweh is a merciful God. Yahweh is a gracious God. Yahweh is a God who is slow to anger. Yahweh is a God who abounds in

---

12. Fretheim, *Suffering of God*, 56.

steadfast love. Yahweh is a faithful God. Yahweh is a God who shows his love to thousands. Yahweh is a God who forgives iniquity. Yahweh is a God who forgives transgressions. Yahweh is a God who forgives sin. Only after all these merciful acts have failed, when people refuse to repent, when people refuse to turn from their wicked ways, only then Yahweh visits the guilty to bring them to account for their evil ways. God's visitation may be through an agent, by natural events, or by direct intervention. Judgment is God's last option. And when God exercises this last option, he does so with pain in his heart and tears in his eyes.

The people of Israel were the objects of God's love, "I have loved you with an everlasting love; therefore I have continued my faithfulness to you" (Jer 31:3). But the people of Israel did not remember the abundance of God's steadfast love but rebelled against him (Ps 106:7). Israel was not supposed to put Yahweh to the test (Deut 6:16), but they tested him ten times and did not obey his voice (Num 14:22). Israel promised to obey the demands of the covenant (Exod 19:8), but over and over they broke their promises (Jer 31:32). Through the prophets, Yahweh told the people to return and live (Ezek 18:32), but instead of choosing life, they chose death. The pain, the suffering, and all the agony associated with the siege of Jerusalem came because the people refused to repent. God did not want to punish the people. Yahweh said to the people in the temple, "if you truly amend your ways and your doings, if you truly act justly one with another, if you do not oppress the alien, the orphan, and the widow, or shed innocent blood in this place, and if you do not go after other gods to your own hurt" (Jer 7:5–6), I will change my mind and I will revoke the punishment. God can change his decision to punish the people if they repent and abandon their evil ways. "Jeremiah had to be taught that God is greater than his decisions."[13]

DIVINE SELF-ABASEMENT

Samuel Terrien discusses God's judgment of Israel in the context of divine self-abasement. According to Terrien, the prophets of Israel interpreted the hiddenness of God as a sign of his presence in judgment. The prophets also learned the full implication of divine righteousness, Yahweh must convict his people. Terrien writes, "Alienation revealed to the prophets an even deeper dimension of divinity: the creator of the universe and the

---

13. Heschel, *Prophets*, 1:66.

sovereign of the nations humbles himself for the sake of his own people. He suffers as he convicts. He wounds himself as he destroys."[14]

Terrien uses the capture of the ark of the covenant by the Philistines (1 Sam 4:1–11) to illustrate divine self-abasement and to explain God's self-imposed weakness. The psalmist describes the results of Israel's defeat at the time the Philistines captured the ark of the covenant, "When God heard, he was full of wrath, and he utterly rejected Israel. He abandoned his dwelling at Shiloh, the tent where he dwelt among mortals, and delivered his power to captivity, his glory to the hand of the foe" (Ps 78:59–61). Yahweh rejected Israel because Israel had rejected Yahweh. But the defeat of Israel brought humiliation to Yahweh. Terrien writes, "Presence in judgment meant absence in history, but the divine decision meant a divine humiliation. [Yahweh] voluntarily relinquished his royal magnificence to the power of the enemy."[15]

Because God is willing to make himself vulnerable in order to interact with his creation, God is also vulnerable to the whims of his people. Thus, as he relates to his people, God is prepared to be hurt by the ones he loves. In his love toward Israel, God's love can be spurned and as a consequence God may suffer because of the rebellion and the rejection of his people. Divine pathos is a reality in the Old Testament. Often, we encounter in the pages of the Old Testament a God who has been maligned and rejected by his people. The people of Israel abandoned the one they should love to follow the one who was no god. This rejection touched God deeply and as a result God was deeply hurt and lamented the ungrateful treatment of his people. Because of this rebellion and rejection, Yahweh brought judgment upon his people and the people suffered at the hands of their enemies. But even in their suffering God did not abandon his people. In the midst of their suffering, God chose to join his people and suffer with them. Although the people believed that they were alone, although they might believe that God had abandoned them, God was in their midst, suffering with them.

---

14. Terrien, *Elusive Presence*, 265.
15. Terrien, *Elusive Presence*, 265.

6

Divine Violence and Divine Pathos

IN THE PREVIOUS CHAPTER I discussed that when God uses violence to establish justice in the world, God is deeply affected by what he does. God suffered when he had to use violence to combat the violence present in the days of Noah. Yahweh used violence but at a cost, "his heart was filled with pain" (Gen 6:6 NIV). The present chapter deals with divine pathos. The Old Testament shows God's concern for his creation. Because God is concerned with the well-being of his creation, God is moved by what human beings do or fail to do. God is deeply affected by the people's rebellion and he is highly moved by the plight of the people. When the people suffer as a result of God's visitation, his compassion is seen in the tears God sheds for his people.

THE WEEPING GOD

One prophet who embodies the pathos of God is Jeremiah. Jeremiah was the embodiment of God to the people of Judah. The words of Jeremiah to Judah were the words of God to his people. The tears of Jeremiah were the tears of God as God expressed his grief over the apostasy of his people.[1] In his article, "The Tears of God in the Book of Jeremiah," David Bosworth said that in the book of Jeremiah, "YHWH weeps more often than Jeremiah does, and even Jeremiah's tears embody the tears of YHWH."

---

1. Roberts, "Motif of the Weeping God," 132–42; Scalise, "Way of Weeping," 415–22.

DIVINE VIOLENCE AND DIVINE PATHOS 69

He also said that while the prophet Jeremiah is known as "the weeping prophet," the focus of the book is on "the weeping God."[2]

Several passages in the book of Jeremiah deal with the tears of God for his people. God's anguish comes out of his love for his rebellious son: "Is not Israel still my son, my darling child? says the LORD. I often have to punish him, but I still love him. That's why I long for him and surely will have mercy on him" (Jer 31:20 NLT). It is God's love for Israel and the punishment that he must inflict on his people that gives rise to God's anguish, an anguish that brings God to tears.

> I will weep and wail for the mountains and take up a lament concerning the desert pastures. (Jer 9:10 NIV)

The versions differ in translating this text in Jeremiah. The Hebrew text reads: "I will take up weeping and wailing," with the "I" referring to God. This is the translation that was adopted by the NIV: "I will weep and wail for the mountains and take up a lament concerning the desert pastures." The NRSV follows the Septuagint, the Greek translation of the Old Testament. The NRSV reads: "Take up weeping and wailing for the mountains, and a lamentation for the pastures of the wilderness." The NRSV translation addresses the community, inviting the people to mourn for the land.[3] The reason the Septuagint changed the Hebrew text was to avoid the fact that the text presents God grieving and weeping over the devastation of the land caused by the Babylonian invasion. However, the Hebrew text must be followed here. The text shows God weeping and wailing over the devastation of the land. God weeps and wails because the land is laid waste, because the lowing of the cattle is not heard, and because the birds and the animals have fled and disappeared.

> Thus says the LORD of hosts: Consider, and call for the mourning women to come; send for the skilled women to come; let them quickly raise a dirge over us, so that our eyes may run down with tears, and our eyelids flow with water. (Jer 9:17–18)

In this text, God continues to express his grief which he mentioned in Jer 9:10. In Jer 9:10 God said that he "will weep and wail" for the devastation of the land and for the unfaithfulness of the people of Judah. In this present text, God says that he does not want to weep alone. He calls

---

2. Bosworth, "Tears of God," 24.

3. Fretheim, "Character of God," 212 believes that the NRSV translation may reflect an anti-anthropomorphic perspective of the translator.

for the mourning women to weep with him. In Judah, public lamentation was conducted by professional women who specialized in conducting community lament.[4] These professional mourners are commanded by God to raise a dirge so that *our eyes may run down with tears, and our eyelids flow with water*. Here God includes himself with the professional mourners weeping for the people. In his study of this text, Abraham Heschel emphasizes the pathos of God as God joins the women in lamenting for the people. Heschel wrote: "Does not the word of God mean: Cry for Israel and for Me? The voice of God calling upon the people to weep, lament, and mourn, for the calamities are about to descend upon them, is itself a voice of grief, a voice of weeping."[5] Then Yahweh instructed the women on what to say. Yahweh said:

> Hear, O women, the word of the LORD, and let your ears receive the word of his mouth; teach to your daughters a dirge, and each to her neighbor a lament. "Death has come up into our windows, it has entered our palaces, to cut off the children from the streets and the young men from the squares." Speak! Thus says the LORD: "Human corpses shall fall like dung upon the open field, like sheaves behind the reaper, and no one shall gather them." (Jer 9:20–22)

Yahweh weeps for his people because death will affect the whole population of Jerusalem, those living in the palace; men, women, and children who live in the city; and even the people who live in the villages of Judah. The devastation of Judah moves God to tears for his people. The coming of this devastation cannot be averted because of Judah's refusal to repent. The enemy, like a reaper, will cut down the people and pile the corpses "like sheaves."

> But if you do not listen I will weep in secret because of your pride; my eyes will weep bitterly, overflowing with tears, because the LORD's flock will be taken captive. (Jer 13:17 NIV)

Jeremiah has announced that devastation and exile are coming and the only way to avert the coming day of judgment was by repenting and by giving glory to Yahweh: "Give glory to the LORD your God before he brings darkness, and before your feet stumble on the mountains at twilight" (Jer 13:16). The focus of Jer 13:17, according to Fretheim, "is on the effect that the captivity of Israel will have on Jeremiah/God! That

---

4. Claassens, "Calling the Keeners," 63–77.
5. Heschel, *Prophets*, 1:113.

Israel is here named 'the Lord's flock' shows that the focus is not on the flock but on the shepherd, God. God is deeply affected by how Israel does or does not respond."[6] The anguish of the prophet is the anguish of God. In commenting on the anguish of the prophet as he contemplated the devastation of the nation, Heschel wrote: "When the catastrophe came, and the enemy mercilessly killed men, women, and children, the prophet must have discovered that the agony was greater than the heart could feel, that his grief was more than his soul could weep for."[7]

> You shall say to them this word: Let my eyes run down with tears night and day, and let them not cease, for the virgin daughter—my people—is struck down with a crushing blow, with a very grievous wound. (Jer 14:17)

Jeremiah 14:17 introduces another divine lament, "a lament that speaks of God's tear-filled eyes over what has happened to the people in these destructive events."[8] The statement in this verse is striking because, as Brueggemann wrote, the pathos of Jeremiah is the pathos of God.[9] The reason for God's grief is because of the attitude of the people. They have confessed their iniquities: "Although our iniquities testify against us, act, O LORD, for your name's sake; our apostasies indeed are many, and we have sinned against you" (Jer 14:7). However, God does not act because the people do not know the true character of God. The people said that God was absent, "like a stranger in the land" (Jer 14:8). They believed that God was unable to save because he was "someone confused, like a mighty warrior who cannot give help" (Jer 14:9).

In response to the people's action and rejection of him, God tells Jeremiah not to pray for the people: "The LORD said to me: Do not pray for the welfare of this people. Although they fast, I do not hear their cry" (Jer 14:11–12). Jeremiah blames the fate of the people on the prophets who are proclaiming a false message of salvation. Jeremiah said to God: "Ah, Lord GOD! Here are the prophets saying to them, 'You shall not see the sword, nor shall you have famine, but I will give you true peace in this place'" (Jer 14:13). In response to Jeremiah, God commands Jeremiah to send a message to the false prophets, a message in which God expresses his grief for the situation of the people. God told Jeremiah: "You shall say

---

6. Fretheim, *Jeremiah*, 209.
7. Heschel, *Prophets*, 1:121.
8. Fretheim, *Jeremiah*, 224.
9. Brueggemann, *Jeremiah 1–25*, 132.

to them this word: Let my eyes run down with tears night and day, and let them not cease, for the virgin daughter—my people—is struck down with a crushing blow, with a very grievous wound."

The coming judgment upon the people is the cause of God's grief, a grief so intense that the tears in his eyes are unending, just as they were in Jer 9:1. God's grief is because "my people" will be devastated, with a crushing blow, causing wounds that refuse to be healed. The expression "Let my eyes run down with tears" in Hebrew is a jussive and it carries the idea of something that is certain, something that is already occurring. The NET Bible has a better translation of this verse: "My eyes overflow with tears day and night without ceasing. For my people, my dear children, have suffered a crushing blow. They have suffered a serious wound."

Fretheim, in his commentary on Jeremiah, deals with the paradox of a God who judges and weeps. He wrote:

> The reason for this revelation of the divine emotions is to give readers a glimpse of the inner-divine side of wrath. The God who judges is also the God who weeps. This God is not punitive or uncaring with respect to what the people have had to endure. Such a portrayal of God is important in any interpretation of these events. Exilic readers of this material are reminded that this is the kind of God with whom they are related. This God is genuinely caught up in what has happened and mourns over the disasters experienced by this "virgin daughter," responding like any good parent would.[10]

Jeremiah 14:17 is the last text in the book of Jeremiah which mentions the tears of God. Israel refused to repent and turn to God. Jeremiah, more than any other prophet, called Israel to repent and turn to God. When they refused to repent, Yahweh told Jeremiah to stop praying for the people: "As for you, do not pray for this people, or lift up a cry or prayer on their behalf, for I will not listen when they call to me in the time of their trouble" (Jer 11:14).

The people's recalcitrant attitude and their rejection of God forced God to bring the judgment which he did not want to bring upon his people. The Lord told Jeremiah: "I have withdrawn my blessing, my love and my pity from this people, declares the LORD" (Jer 16:5). Bosworth wrote: "As a result of this withdrawal of love and compassion, YHWH no longer weeps for Israel and expects Jeremiah to stop weeping in order

---

10. Fretheim, *Jeremiah*, 224.

to manifest this divine detachment as he has previously manifested YHWH's care and concern."[11]

THE DIVINE PATHOS

The suffering of God for his people is clearly seen in the words and actions of Jeremiah. It is unfortunate that some Christians try to dismiss the tears of God in order to defend a theological position about the impassibility of God that clearly goes against what the Old Testament teaches about the nature and character of God.

Whenever God called a prophet to speak to Israel, God placed his words in the mouth of that prophet so that the prophet would speak words that was truly the words of God. Thus, when a prophet proclaimed God's message to the people, the words in the mouth of the prophet were the words of God to the people. The prophet was the embodiment of God to the people of Israel.

The best example of this ambiguity is Jer 8:18–9:3.[12] Scholars are divided on how to interpret this passage in Jeremiah. Some scholars believe that the speakers are Jeremiah and the people while others believe that there are three voices in the text: the voice of God, the voice of Jeremiah, and the voice of the people.

Scholars are even divided on how to structure the text. Jack Lundbom,[13] for instance, divides the text into three sections: 8:18–21; 8:22–9:2; 9:3–6. J. A. Thompson[14] divides the text into two sections: 8:18–9:1; 9:2–9. Scholars who believe that Jer 8:18–9:3 is a unit include Walter Brueggemann[15] and Kathleen O'Connor.[16]

The difference between those who accept the unity of the text and those who do not is due to a theological perspective on the nature of the God of the Old Testament. Bosworth wrote: "Broadly speaking, there appear to be two schools of thought: those who see God weeping in one or more of these verses, and those who deny that God weeps in any of them.

11. Bosworth, "Tears of God," 43.
12. The Hebrew Bible differs in the versification of the text as found in most English translations. Jer 9:1–3 in the NRSV is Jer 8:23—9:2 in the Hebrew Bible. All references to the text of Jeremiah follow the English translations.
13. Lundbom, *Jeremiah 1–20*.
14. Thompson, *Book of Jeremiah*.
15. Brueggemann, *Jeremiah 1–25*.
16. O'Connor, "Tears of God," 172–85.

K. O'Connor suspects that those who prefer that God not weep in any text are wed to an image of an invulnerable Almighty God."[17]

Bosworth writes that many Christians today believe in the impassibility (*apatheia*) of God, that is, "that God cannot be affected by something else or suffer in the broad sense, including experiencing emotion (*pathos*)."[18] Abraham Heschel, in his book *The Prophets*, has a remarkable study on the pathos of God in which he clearly shows that the God of the Bible experiences emotions and suffers with and because of his people. Heschel says that divine pathos is "a reaction to human history, an attitude called forth by man's conduct, a response, not a cause. . . . It is because God is the sources of justice that His pathos is ethical."[19]

Yahweh laments about the rebellion of the people,

> O that my head were a spring of water, and my eyes a fountain of tears, so that I might weep day and night for the slain of my poor people! O that I had in the desert a traveler's lodging place, that I might leave my people and go away from them! For they are all adulterers, a band of traitors. They bend their tongues like bows; they have grown strong in the land for falsehood, and not for truth; for they proceed from evil to evil, and they do not know me, says the LORD. (Jer 9:1–3)

The argument of those scholars who refuse to acknowledge that the tears in 9:1 belong to God is unconvincing. Generally, when the prophet announces the word of God, his oracle begins with "thus says the Lord." The conclusion of the oracle in verse 3 affirms that the speaker is Yahweh: "they do not know me, says the LORD." The expression "says the Lord" is not present in the Septuagint (LXX). Probably the omission of the expression was deliberate, due to reluctance of the translators to acknowledge a God who weeps.

In this text God has shed tears because he was highly touched by the situation of his people. Now that the tears have been exhausted, he wishes that his eyes were a fountain of tears that he might weep without interruption day and night for the people who have been killed by the army of Babylon. As Bosworth wrote: "Here, the speaker's grief is greater than the volume of tears his body can produce."[20] Or as Brueggemann wrote, "The

---

17. Bosworth, "Tears of God," 27–28.
18. Bosworth, "Tears of God," 26.
19. Heschel, *Prophets*, 2:5.
20. Bosworth, "Tears of God," 33.

hurt in the face of Judah's death requires and evokes more grief, more crying, and more tears than his body is capable of transmitting."[21]

Speaking about the pathos of God because of the suffering of the people, Brueggemann wrote: "With the formula attributing the poem to Yahweh, the pathos cannot belong only to Jeremiah. This is poetry that penetrates God's heart. The heart is marked by God's deep grief. God's anger is audible here, but it is largely subordinated to the hurt God experiences in the unnecessary death of God's people."[22]

Jeremiah describes God's hurt by saying that God wants to leave his people, "O that I had in the desert a traveler's lodging place, that I might leave my people and go away from them." Brueggemann wrote: "Now it is God . . . who yearns to leave, because the fickleness [of the people] is beyond bearing. This is not a God who loves eternally. There is only so much this God will tolerate. Now it is time to depart because the affronts and betrayals have become a burden too great for God."[23]

When one hears these words in the mouth of Jeremiah, one has to acknowledge that the pain of Jeremiah is the pain of God, that the tears of Jeremiah are the tears of God. God has been abandoned and betrayed by his people. The people of God have forgotten what God had done for them. They have been unfaithful and have removed themselves so far from God that God says, "they do not know me." According to O'Connor, it is this rebellion of Israel that brings grief to God and "provides the reasons for the tears of God and God's desire to escape to the wilderness." The unfaithfulness of Israel brings out "divine empathy, vulnerability, and profound sorrow. Grief overtakes anger, sympathy replaces fury."[24]

THE REPENTANCE OF GOD

Although many people reject the passibility of God, the passibility of God is based on biblical revelation.[25] If the God of the Old Testament revealed himself in Jesus Christ, then the God of the Bible is a God who

---

21. Brueggemann, *Jeremiah 1–25*, 90.
22. Brueggemann, *Jeremiah 1–25*, 87.
23. Brueggemann, *Jeremiah 1–25*, 90.
24. O'Connor, "Tears of God," 183.
25. Kuyper, "Suffering and the Repentance of God," 257–77 offers a review of the early church's interpretation of God's repentance and the issue of the passibility of God. Fretheim, "Repentance of God," 47–70 offers a comprehensive study of the repentance of God in the Old Testament. See also Moberly, "'God Is Not a Human,'" 112–23.

suffers and has emotions. In his book, *The Humanity of God*, Karl Barth said that the human characteristics of God are enthroned in heaven.[26]

The passibility of God is true to biblical revelation, not to theological dogmas based on Greek philosophy. Emil Brunner, in his discussion of the attributes of God, shows how Greek philosophy has affected and distorted our understanding of God.[27] Biblical teaching reveals God to be a personal God, a God who enters into a genuine relationship with the people of Israel. By establishing a covenant relationship with Israel, God gave the people real freedom to make decisions, even when those decisions could contradict what God intended for them.

In creation we see God as the Creator, a God who makes human beings in his own image. God gives genuine freedom to human beings to make real decisions, either to obey God or to go against his will. In this process of give and take, God chose to act in response to human choices. When humans obeyed God, he blessed them. When humans disobeyed, God acted as a righteous judge to bring his divine justice upon those who rebelled against his authority.

Kuyper says that it is because of this divine-human relationship, that "God responds to man's action within an ethical setting. Man's conduct is taken into account to make clear the moral integrity of God and to deal with man as a responsible moral being."[28] A good example of God's dealing with human beings is found in the story of the flood. When God saw how evil human beings had become on the earth and that their actions were continually evil, "The LORD was grieved that he had made man on the earth, and his heart was filled with pain" (Gen 6:6 NIV). God's pain was real, not imaginary.

This assessment of the human condition and the response of God is very revealing. While every inclination of the human heart was evil all the time, God's heart was broken, filled with pain. God was grieving for his creation, distressed because the bearers of his image had departed from the ideal he had established for them at creation.

The word for "grieving," *niham*, is used in the Hebrew Bible to describe both human and divine pain.[29] The rebellious attitude of Israel in the wilderness caused much pain and agony to God's heart: "How

---

26. Barth, *Humanity of God*.
27. Brunner, "Problem of the 'Divine Attributes,'" 241–47.
28. Kuyper, "Suffering and the Repentance of God," 275.
29. Parunak, "Semantic Survey of *niham*," 512–32.

often they rebelled against him in the wilderness and grieved him in the desert! They tested God again and again, and provoked the Holy One of Israel" (Ps 78:40–41). The people's rebellion against God was not just once, but again and again. Num 14:22 says that the people of Israel tested Yahweh ten times in the wilderness. Every time the people tested God, God was grieved again and again. Human sin and rebellion are the cause of God's suffering. "The grief of God is as current as the people's sin."[30]

The word *niḥam* is also used to reflect changes in God. The word is generally translated "repent": "And God saw their works, that they turned from their evil way; and God repented of the evil, that he had said that he would do unto them; and he did it not" (Jonah 3:10 KJV). More often, though, the word is translated as "regretting" or "changing one's mind." "I greatly regret that I have set up Saul as king" (1 Sam 15:11 NKJ). "The LORD was sorry that he had made humans on the earth, and he was heartbroken" (Gen 6:6 GWN). These different translations of the word *niḥam* express God's disappointment with human beings and his consternation that they had failed to achieve his purpose for them. The word *niḥam* also anticipates the suffering of God that was to be the result of the judgment he was bringing upon the world because of their rebellion.

Another passage that reflects the pain and suffering of God as a result of Israel's sins and rebellion is found in Exod 32–34 when Israel violated the demands of the covenant by fashioning a golden calf to worship while Moses was on Mount Sinai receiving the law from God. God's reaction to the apostasy of the people reflects another aspect of the nature of God. After calling Moses's attention to what the people had done, Yahweh said to Moses: "Now leave me alone so that my anger may burn against them and that I may destroy them" (Exod 32:10). God's disappointment with Israel was real. He had entered into a relationship with them so that the nation would accomplish God's work in the world. Israel had become God's special people, separated from the other nations to model a different type of life in the world.

The proper understanding of God's words to Moses indicate that God was planning to bring a severe judgment against the people. However, God's words also indicate that God expected Moses to intervene and pray on behalf of Israel. Thus, God wants to be left alone so that he can execute the punishment on his rebellious people. But Moses does

---

30. Fretheim, *Suffering of God*, 111.

not leave God alone. To the contrary, Moses spoke boldly, defending the people and asking for divine mercy for Israel. This dialogue between God and Moses demonstrates how seriously God values the relationship he had established with his people.

When it came to the future of Israel, God was not the only one who had a say in the matter. Moses argued with God and in a forceful way presented several reasons why God should not destroy the people. Moses's arguments on behalf of Israel moved God to change his mind about the punishment he had decreed to bring upon Israel: "And the LORD changed his mind about the disaster that he planned to bring on his people" (Exod 32:14 NRSV) or as the RSV translated: "And the LORD repented of the evil which he thought to do to his people." God's changing his mind is not a mere human way of describing what happened to God. To the contrary, the text speaks of a divine reversal taken because of Moses's intervention on behalf of Israel. In the Hebrew Bible, God never "repents" of sins. The word "repent" reflects God's decision to change his mind and reverse a decision made to bring judgment upon the people.

The word *niham* is translated "repent" thirty-eight times in the Bible. Most of the places where the word is translated "repentance," it refers to God's repentance, not human repentance. When the Bible says that God changes his mind or repents, it indicates that God's decision about judgment is not set in cement. God is open to a change in human conduct. When people change their ways or repent, that change also brings a change in how God will deal with them.

An example of this is found in God's words to Jeremiah. In the fourth year of Jehoiakim, king of Judah, God told Jeremiah to write down the words that he had proclaimed against Israel and Judah and read them in the temple as the people came to worship (Jer 36:1–7). Yahweh told Jeremiah: "Perhaps, when the house of Judah hears all the evil I have in mind to do to them, they will turn back each from his evil way, so that I may forgive their wickedness and their sin" (Jer 36:3 NAB). And Jeremiah spoke to Baruch: "Perhaps they will lay their supplication before the LORD and will all turn back from their evil way; for great is the fury of anger with which the LORD has threatened this people" (Jer 36:7 NAB). Twice the word "perhaps" is used in the same context. The use of the word "perhaps" by God and Jeremiah indicates that neither God nor Jeremiah knew how the reading of the scrolls would affect the people.

The shape of Judah's future was based on how the people would react to the reading of the scrolls. God's judgment upon Judah was coming, and it was coming rapidly. However, if the people would repent, God would change his mind and not bring the judgment. God had already said as much before: "Perhaps they will listen and turn back, each from his evil way, so that I may repent of the evil I have planned to inflict upon them for their evil deeds" (Jer 26:3 NAB). Writing on God's willingness not to punish Judah, Fretheim writes,

> The fundamental motivation of divine repentance is clear. God's desire is for life, not death. In fact, it may be said that God hopes that the announcements of judgment will *not* have to be fulfilled, so that God's salvific will can be realized. God's will is done, it would seem, when prophecies of judgment fail or, if deemed finally necessary, are stopped short of proceeding to their destructive end. In other words, God hopes to be able to reverse himself; God is open to change precisely in order that the people may experience salvation rather than judgment or final judgment.[31]

Israel is not the only nation that enjoys God's concern. Even in judgment, the compassion of Yahweh is present. When Yahweh brought the flood to deal with human violence and human wickedness, he did so with a grieving heart, "The LORD saw how great man's wickedness on the earth had become, and that every inclination of the thoughts of his heart was only evil all the time. The LORD was grieved that he had made man on the earth, and his heart was filled with pain" (Gen 6:5–6 NIV). God is "moved and affected by what happens in the world and reacts accordingly. Events and human actions arouse in Him joy or sorrow, pleasure or wrath. He is not conceived as judging the world in detachment."[32]

The grieving of God at the beginning of human history shows how human sin and wickedness and human violence (Gen 6:11) has a profound effect on God. God was grieved, his heart was filled with pain. For a God who is merciful and gracious, a God who is slow to anger, and a God who abounds in steadfast love (Exod 34:6), to send such a devastation upon the earth he created and destroy humans being he created in his image, was a painful decision, but a decision that had to be made for the sake of creation and for the sake of future generations of human beings. And because human sinfulness has not abated since the days of Noah, humans will continue to grieve God and divine suffering

---

31. Fretheim, "Repentance of God," 61.
32. Heschel, *Prophets*, 2:4.

will persist. In their sinful condition, human beings will provoke God to anger and when that happens, the longsuffering God will visit in justice and will requite them "according to their deeds and the work of their hands" (Jer 25:14).

Before Yahweh brought his judgment upon Sodom and Gomorrah, Yahweh came to see if what the people of Sodom had done was as bad as the outcry that has reached him (Gen 18:21). Yahweh gave Abraham an opportunity to intercede for Sodom and in his grace, he decided to answer Abraham's request and not to punish thousands of people for the sake of fifty righteous person. The amazing compassion of God was revealed once again when he decided to spare the whole city for the sake of only ten righteous people living in the city. The city was destroyed because Yahweh tests the mind and search the heart, and after doing that, he "gives to all according to their ways, according to the fruit of their doings" (Jer 17:10).

When Yahweh announced his judgment on Moab, he said, "I have broken Moab like a vessel that no one wants, says the LORD" (Jer 48:38). But when judgment came upon Moab, Yahweh was affected profoundly by the fate of the nation and by the suffering of the people,

> My heart cries out for Moab. (Isa 15:5)
>
> I weep with the weeping of Jazer. (Isa 16:9)
>
> My heart throbs like a harp for Moab. (Isa 16:11)

These texts show Yahweh weeping for what happened to Moab.

> That God is represented as mourning over the fate of non-Israelite peoples as well as Israelites demonstrates the breath of God's care and concern for the sufferers of the world, whoever they might be. Israel has no monopoly on God's empathy. All people everywhere have *experienced* the compassion (and the judgment) of God, even though they may not realize that fact.[33]

Judgment is the alien work of God (Isa 28:21) because it is contrary to his nature as a compassionate and merciful God (the alien work of God will be discussed in chapter 12). God is a righteous judge, but he is also a God who is angered by injustice. When God sees violence, wickedness, and injustice, God does not remain neutral; God acts out of concern for people and for the sake of the future of the world.

---

33. Fretheim, *Suffering of God*, 137.

THE EVIL OF INDIFFERENCE

When dealing with the problem of divine violence in the Old Testament, the tendency is either to reject the Old Testament or to take a Marcionite approach and vilify Yahweh by saying that the God of the Old Testament was not the God revealed by Jesus. Another way of dealing with the problem of divine violence is by humanizing God. Heschel talks about the humanization of God. The humanization of God means the creation of a God who acts the way humans act, the creation of a God in the image of humans. According to Heschel, such a process threatens our understanding of the ethical integrity of God's will. Heschel writes, "Humanization leads to the conception of God as the ally of the people. . . . The ideas of the divine anger shatters such a horrible complacency."[34]

God's judgment upon people and upon nations came because of evil and violence. "God in not indifferent to evil."[35] The people of Sodom were destroyed because of their evil. Peterson, using the Torah as his guide, says that the sins of Sodom include gang rape, oppression of the poor, inhospitality, transgression/wrongdoing against a person, adultery, incest, and homosexual acts.[36] Jones says that sins of the Canaanites include idolatry, incest, adultery, child sacrifice, homosexuality, and bestiality.[37]

Heschel speaks about the evil of indifference. He writes, "There is an evil which most of us condone and are even guilty of: indifference to evil. We remain neutral, impartial, and not easily moved by the wrong done unto other people. Indifference to evil is more insidious than evil itself; it is more universal, more contagious, more dangerous. A silent justification, it makes possible an evil eruption as an exception becoming the rule and being in turn accepted. . . .God is not indifferent to evil."[38]

There is violence in the Old Testament and lots of it. There is violence by humans and violence by God. We can easily understand human violence because every inclination of the thoughts of their hearts is always evil (Gen 6:5). It is hard to understand divine violence since the Old Testament affirms that Yahweh is a merciful and gracious God. Looking from a New Testament perspective, nonviolence should be the characteristic of the God of love whom Jesus revealed. Yahweh, the God

---

34. Heschel, *Prophets*, 2:55.
35. Heschel, *Prophets*, 2:64.
36. Peterson, "Sin of Sodom Revisited," 17–31.
37. Jones, "We Don't Hate Sin," 53–72.
38. Heschel, *Prophets*, 2:64.

of the Old Testament is the God of love whom Jesus revealed. Yahweh is a God who abounds in steadfast love (Exod 34:6), a God who continues to show his love to thousands of generations (Exod 34:7). And yet, Yahweh uses violence to combat violence, evil, and injustice in this world. Yahweh uses violence for the sake of creation, to establish his justice in the world.

Why does God need to use violence to accomplish his plan for creation? God knows why, but we do not. This is a great mystery, too deep for humans to fathom. Why does God use violence in the world? The answer to this question will have to wait until the day when the Warrior God of the Old Testament dies on the cross (chapter 24).

> The fierce anger of the LORD will not turn back until he has executed and accomplished the intents of his mind. In the latter days you will understand this. (Jer 30:24)

7

The Character of God

IN HIS ARTICLE ON DIVINE violence, Miroslav Volf wrote,

> There is no need to waste words here on showing that the God of the Bible is not, strictly speaking, a nonviolent God. Look wherever you want in the scriptures, in the Old or New Testament, in the teachings and practice of Jesus, in the epistles, or in the Book of Revelation, and you will invariably find a God who does not shy away from using violence.

Volf said that people who cannot accept the concept of divine violence tend to develop "an alternative picture of God."[1]

GOD'S REVELATION TO MOSES

Defenders of the nonviolent God believe that the true character of the God of the Old Testament was revealed in the death of Christ on the cross. On the cross God reveals what kind of God he is, a loving and merciful God, a God who takes upon himself human nature in order to reveal the purpose of his death, the reconciliation of the world: "God was in Christ reconciling the world to himself (2 Cor 5:19). In chapter 24 I will discuss in detail the reason for the death of the Warrior God on the cross.

There are two problems with this portrayal of divine violence in the Old Testament. First, thousands of years have elapsed between some of the violence attributed to God in the Old Testament and the teaching of

---

1. Volf, "Divine Violence?," 2.

Jesus in the New Testament. Over the years people's views about God changed and the way the people of Israel viewed God also changed. There is no difference between the God who appears in the book of Joshua and the God who appears in the book of Jonah. Second, the people of Israel also had problems with issues of divine violence. Abraham questioned God over the fate of Sodom (Gen 18:23–33) and Moses confronted God over his decision to destroy the people of Israel because of their apostasy (Exod 32:1–14).

The prophet Habakkuk was also not happy with the way Yahweh was planning to deal with violence in Judah. Habakkuk prayed, "How long, Yahweh, am I to cry for help while you will not listen; to cry, 'Violence!' in your ear while you will not save?" (Hab 1:2 NJB). The answer Yahweh gave the prophet was not what he expected. Yahweh told his prophet, "I am raising up the Babylonians, a cruel and violent people. They will march across the world and conquer other lands" (Hab 1:6 NLT). The prophet's dissatisfaction was because Yahweh was bringing the Babylonians to hold Judah accountable for its violent actions. The Babylonians were a ruthless and violent people, a nation that had plundered many nations, a nation that had caused much bloodshed, and a nation that used much violence against the countries and cities they conquered and against all the people who lived in them (Hab 2:8).

The people of Israel did not evaluate divine violence by the ethics of Jesus. The people of Israel evaluated divine violence by what God said about himself when he revealed the nature of his character to Moses on Mount Sinai (Exod 34:6–7). What God says about himself in Exod 34:6–7 has much to say about God's moral character. Boyd says that our knowledge of God should be anchored in the portrait of the crucified God because the Old Testament ascribes "sub-Christ-like activities and characteristics to God."[2] However, if Jesus is God then those characteristics are also characteristics about Jesus. The proper understanding of the nature and character of God and the problem of divine violence in the Old Testament must begin with what Yahweh says about himself and what led him to die on the cross. The best place to know about Yahweh's true character is his revelation to Moses on Mount Sinai and what he said about himself.

The revelation of Yahweh's character and nature came at a very crucial time in the life of Israel. The people had violated the demands of the

---

2. Boyd, *Crucifixion of the Warrior God*, 409.

covenant when they made an idol in the form of a bull and identified it with the God who had redeemed them from their oppression in Egypt: "This is your god, O Israel, who brought you out of the land of Egypt" (Exod 32:8 TNK). The building of the golden calf was a violation of the Second Commandment and this rebellious act required a severe punishment: "You shall not make for yourself an idol, whether in the form of anything that is in heaven above, or that is on the earth beneath, or that is in the water under the earth. You shall not bow down to them or worship them; for I the LORD your God am a jealous God, punishing children for the iniquity of parents, to the third and the fourth generation of those who reject me" (Exod 20:4–5).

As the people were celebrating a festival to Yahweh by offering burnt offerings before the idol, Yahweh told Moses that his wrath was burning hot against the people and that he was about to consume them. In response, Moses prayed to Yahweh and implored him not to destroy the people. In response to Moses's prayer, Yahweh "changed his mind" about the disaster that he was planning to bring upon his people (Exod 32:14).

YAHWEH, A MERCIFUL AND GRACIOUS GOD

The Old Testament is a book filled with violence, both human and divine. When discussing divine violence in the Old Testament, writers tend to focus on what they consider to be shocking examples of divine brutality such as the plagues against the Egyptians, the sufferings of the people of Egypt because of the actions of God, the death of the firstborn sons, the extermination of the Canaanites, the destruction of Sodom and Gomorrah, and several others.

Yahweh's revelation of his divine character to Moses came after the covenant between Yahweh and Israel was broken because of the people's idolatry. After Moses had declared the Decalogue to the people of Israel, he went up to Mount Sinai to meet with God to receive the statutes and commandments of the Lord. When the people saw that Moses was delayed on the mountain, they believed that he was dead. They immediately turned to Aaron and asked him to make a god for them and as a result the people worshiped a golden calf, which was a violation of the covenantal agreement between Yahweh and the people.

Moses understood that Yahweh was about to punish the people because of their idolatry and their violation of the covenant. Moses prayed and interceded on behalf of Israel, asking God to have mercy on the people. In response to Moses's prayer, "Yahweh changed his mind about the disaster that he planned to bring on his people" (Exod 32:14). When Yahweh assured Moses that he would go with the people in their journey to the land of Canaan, Moses asked Yahweh to show him his glory. In response, Yahweh said to Moses, "I will make all my goodness pass before you, and will proclaim before you the name, 'Yahweh'; and I will be gracious to whom I will be gracious, and will show mercy on whom I will show mercy" (Exod 33:19).

When Yahweh revealed himself to Moses on Mount Sinai, Yahweh told Moses what kind of God he was. On that occasion, Yahweh passed before Moses and proclaimed,

> Yahweh, Yahweh, a God merciful and gracious, slow to anger, and abounding in steadfast love and faithfulness, keeping steadfast love for the thousandth generation, forgiving iniquity and transgression and sin, yet by no means clearing the guilty, but visiting the iniquity of the parents upon the children and the children's children, to the third and the fourth generation. (Exod 34:6–7)[3]

What Yahweh says about himself is the basis for our understanding of who God is and what kind of God Yahweh is. In describing to Moses what kind of God he is, Yahweh stressed not only his mercy and compassion, his willingness to forgive iniquity and transgression and sin, but also his justice. As a just God, he does not leave the guilty unpunished. So significant was the revelation of these divine characteristics to Moses that these aspects of the divine character are mentioned on several other occasions in the Old Testament.[4] Allusions to the divine characteristics listed in Exod 34:6–7 appear throughout the Old Testament.[5]

---

3. Brueggemann, *Theology of the Old Testament*, 213–28, has provided a good exegesis of this text.

4. The expressions merciful, gracious, slow to anger, and abounding in steadfast love appear with some variations several times in the Old Testament: Exod 34:6; Pss 86:15; 103:8; 145:8; Joel 2:13; Jonah 4:2; Nah 1:2–3; Neh 9:17.

5. Allusions to the divine character appear in Exod 20:5–6; 22:27; 33:19; Num 14:18; Deut 4:31; 5:9–10; 7:9–10; 2 Chr 30:9; Neh 1:5; 9:31–32; Pss 78:38; 86:5; 99:8; 103:8; 111:4; 116:5; Isa 48:9; 54:7–8; 63:7; Jer 32:18; Dan 9:4; Mic 7:18; Nah 1:2–3.

YAHWEH'S TRUE CHARACTER AND NATURE

What Yahweh revealed to Moses was his true character and nature, "all his goodness," what kind of God he was. Yahweh revealed to Moses several aspects of his character, the basic aspects of the divine nature Moses and the people of Israel should know about their God.[6]

Yahweh is a merciful God

Yahweh told Moses that he was a merciful God. Mercy and compassion embody the nature and character of God. The Hebrew word *rāḥam* can be translated "to love deeply; to have mercy, to be compassionate." The word *rāḥam* and the word *ḥannûn* ("gracious") are often found together, emphasizing two aspects of the nature and character of Yahweh. The two words are only used in reference to God, with one exception.[7] The use of the two words is generally called the "compassion formula," a name derived from its use in intercessory prayers. The use of the two words is found often in prayers in the book of Psalms.[8]

The word *rāḥam* has its roots in the Hebrew word for "womb." The use of the word to describe the nature of God draws on motherly love as a metaphor for the understanding of divine compassion. Phyllis Trible suggests that the word carries the idea of "love as selfless participation in life. The womb protects and nourishes but does not possess and control. It yields its treasure in order that wholeness and well-being may happen."[9] In other contexts, the word indicates warmth, restoration, free gift, and liberty from sin. But foremost, *rāḥam* suggests God's unique favor to sinful people. This Hebrew word is frequently used of God to express his relationship with Israel. The word is used to express God's deep, tender love, his mercy, and forgiveness toward his people in the face of deserved judgment.

---

6. Wright, "Divine Name and the Divine Nature," 177–85.

7. The exception of *ḥannûn* being used to refer to an individual is found in Ps 112:4 where the word refers to the one who fears Yahweh.

8. Simian-Yofre, "'ēl raḥûm," 449.

9. Trible, *God and the Rhetoric of Sexuality*, 33.

Yahweh is a gracious God

Yahweh told Moses that he was a gracious God. The Hebrew word *ḥannûn* means "to be gracious, to have pity, to show favor." This word occurs thirteen times in the Hebrew Bible, eleven times in combination with the word *rāḥam*, the Hebrew word for "merciful, compassionate." The word carries the idea of an undeserved favor. A person finds kindness and mercy with Yahweh when one is looking for his goodness and generosity. Yahweh is a God whose purposes are good and whose justice is tempered with mercy.

In the Hebrew Bible all occurrences of the word *ḥannûn* refer to Yahweh. This word describes the gracious acts of Yahweh. This word shows a special aspect of the character of God, the capacity to act mercifully toward people in need. The word also carries the idea that grace and mercy are freely given without need of compensation. Yahweh gives his favor to people out of his inherent character as a gracious and merciful God. The notion that Yahweh freely gives his favor to human beings speaks of Yahweh's character as a God who provides, a God who cares, and a God who saves. Yahweh's grace is also related to Yahweh's righteousness since some passages which speak of him as a gracious God also speak of him judging evil.

Yahweh is a God who is slow to anger

Yahweh told Moses that he was a God who is slow to anger. The declaration that Yahweh is "slow to anger" is the English translation of a Hebrew idiomatic expression *'erek 'appayim* which literally means "long nose." In the Hebrew Bible, the nose is associated with anger. The expression, the "LORD became very angry" (Num 11:10) in Hebrew is "his nose became hot." The expression "the fierce anger of the LORD" (Num 25:4) in Hebrew is "the burning nose of Yahweh." The declaration that Yahweh is "slow to anger" indicates that Yahweh's patience exceeds divine anger and keeps it within boundaries. The statement that Yahweh is "slow to anger" appears several times together with the expression "abounding in steadfast love."[10] In the context of Exod 32–34, the anger of Yahweh was kindled because of the apostasy of Israel. When Yahweh saw that the people had abandoned him to worship the golden calf, Yahweh said

---

10. Exod 34:6; Num 14:18; Neh 9:17; Pss 86:15; 103:8; 145:8; Joel 2:13; Jonah 4:2.

to Moses, "Now let me alone, so that my wrath may burn hot against them and I may consume them" (Exod 32:10). Moses prayed for Israel and Yahweh's grace overcame the burning heat of his wrath.

Yahweh is a God who abounds in steadfast love

Yahweh told Moses that he was a God who abounds in steadfast love. The word translated as "steadfast love" in Hebrew is *ḥesed*. This word is difficult to translate into English because it is used in different contexts in the Hebrew Bible. The word *ḥesed* is the primary word used in the Hebrew Bible to express Yahweh's love for the people of Israel. When the Bible talks about Yahweh's *ḥesed*, the use of the word is based on the covenantal relationship God has established with Israel. The word *ḥesed* refers to the commitment that binds two parties to a relationship. In his study of the word *ḥesed*, Gordon Clark says that *ḥesed* is an "action performed, in the context of a deep and enduring commitment between two persons or parties."[11] Since faithfulness to a relationship is a character of God, God also expects his people to be as committed to the relationship as he is. When the word is applied to God, it refers to his faithfulness to the relationship. Thus, the word is best translated "faithfulness," "unfailing love," "loyalty." When the word is applied to human beings, it refers to the loyalty and commitment that people should bring to that relationship. In this case, a good translation of *ḥesed* should be "commitment," "loyalty." A strong relationship is built on commitment. Israel should be as loyal and committed to the covenant as God was. In the revelation of the divine self, the word *ḥesed* appears twice. The double use of the word *ḥesed* emphasizes that Yahweh's love is the basis by which he relates to people; all the works of Yahweh are based on his love. The association of *ḥesed* with divine mercy means that, when correctly interpreted, *ḥesed* in the Hebrew Bible corresponds to the word *agape* in the New Testament. As Goldingay puts it, "in substance, the distinctive New Testament word for love (*agape*) is equivalent to that First Testament word [*ḥesed*]."[12]

---

11. Clark, *Word "Hesed,"* 267.
12. Goldingay, *Biblical Theology*, 21.

Yahweh is a God who abounds in faithfulness

Yahweh told Moses that he was a God who abounds in faithfulness. The Hebrew word 'ĕmet means faithfulness, fidelity. When the word is applied to Yahweh, the word is used to express God's faithfulness and dependability. In addition to express the kind of God Yahweh is, the word also describes his works: "all his work is done in faithfulness" (Ps 33:4). The word "faithfulness" ('ĕmet) and the word "faithful love" (ḥesed) appear together thirteen times in the Old Testament.

The English word "amen" derives from the Hebrew word 'āman, a word which means "to be faithful," "to be reliable." Another word that derives from the word 'āman is the word 'ĕmet, a word which means "truth," "faithfulness." This word is also used to describe one aspect of God's character. In his explanation of this aspect of God's character, Freedman wrote, "The word 'ĕmet comes from the root 'āmēn (like our familiar amen) which has the meaning, to be firm, sure. Different aspects of this meaning can be recognized in the uses of the term: (1) faithfulness, that which is reliable, trustworthy; (2) constancy, that which does not change, but persists and abides; (3) truth, that which has substance and is real, in contrast with the false, which is nothing. The God of 'ĕmet is faithful, constant, and true: his word is sure, his actions are trustworthy, and his inner nature does not change."[13] In the Old Testament, Yahweh is called 'lōhê 'āmēn (Isa 65:16), "the God of Amen" or "the God Amen."

Yahweh is a God who keeps steadfast love for the thousandth generation

Yahweh told Moses that he was a God who keeps steadfast love for the thousandth generation. The Hebrew text says that Yahweh's ḥesed, his faithful love is freely given to thousands. This means that thousands of people experience God's love on a regular basis. The word "generations" does not appear in the Hebrew text, but it is implied. Yahweh's love is not limited. His love is given to many; he lavishes unfailing love to thousands of people. His love is eternal; he keeps his steadfast love for a thousand generations.

---

13. Freedman, "God Compassionate and Gracious," 13.

Yahweh is a God who forgives iniquity and transgression and sin

Yahweh told Moses that he was a God who forgives iniquity and transgression and sin. The Hebrew text uses three different words to express human sin. The Hebrew word ʿāwōn means "iniquity, guilt." The word refers to an action that deserves punishment. The word pešaʿ means "to rebel, to transgress, to revolt." The word is generally used to refer to a rebellion against God's authority. The word ḥāṭā' means "sin, to miss the way." The word is used to emphasize that people are missing the moral and spiritual standards God has established for them. These three words reflect the many ways human beings choose to rebel against Yahweh and turn away from establishing a relationship with him. The Hebrew word translated "forgive" is nāsā'. The word means "to lift up, to bear, to carry." When the word is applied to God forgiving sins, the word indicates that God forgives human sins by bearing the sins of the people upon himself. The bearing of the sins of the people is necessary to restore the broken relationship. This shows that Yahweh is committed to the process of reconciliation between himself and sinful humanity.

THE INTERGENERATIONAL PUNISHMENT STATEMENT

Yahweh is the gracious and merciful God who revealed himself to Moses on Mount Sinai. But, when people read the Bible and study the character and nature of Yahweh, they have a hard time understanding the reason God visits "the iniquity of the parents upon the children and the children's children, to the third and the fourth generation" (Exod 34:7). This statement about intergenerational punishment appears in four different texts in the Old Testament: Exod 20:5; 34:6–7; Num 14:18–19; Deut 5:9–10.

In citing God's revelation of his nature and character to Moses, Boyd deliberately omitted the last clause of the confession which reads: "yet by no means clearing the guilty, but visiting the iniquity of the parents upon the children and the children's children, to the third and the fourth generation" (Exod 34:7). Explaining the reason for his omission of the multi-generational punishment, Boyd wrote:

> Some readers may have noticed that I ended the quotation of Exod 34:6–7 without adding the final sentence about Yahweh not leaving the "guilty unpunished" and his punishing of "children for the sin of the parents to the third and fourth generation." I omitted this phrase not because of the contemporary

sentimental distaste for reflecting on the judgment of God, as this chapter will make abundantly clear. I rather omitted the last clause because, with one exception, this clause is omitted in all other references to this confession.[14]

By omitting the last clause of the confession, Boyd is engaging in what Brettler calls "grammatical violence in citing God's mercy (of Exod 34:6–7a) but omitting the promise of intergenerational punishment (of Exod 34:7b)."[15] According to Brettler, the purpose of the omission is to create "a 'kinder, gentler' God, with no mention of punishment."[16]

The question many Christians and non-Christians ask is how can a merciful and gracious God punish the sins of the fathers by punishing their children, grandchildren, and even their great-grandchildren?[17] To answer these questions, it becomes necessary to study the four texts that discuss the problem of intergenerational punishment: Exod 20:5; 34:6–7; Num 14:18–19; and Deut 5:9–10. The statement about intergenerational punishment in these four texts is almost identical, indicating that it was a conventionalized statement intended to express one aspect of divine justice. These four texts have gone through a long process of transmission. The study of these four texts in the next two chapters will follow the historical sequence as they appear in the canon. Such an approach will provide the proper background for the application of the statement and how it changed during the many centuries of the history of Israel.

Sakenfeld has shown that God's revelation of his character to Moses as a merciful and gracious God and as a God who does not clear the guilty (Exod 34:6–7) is the key to understanding the tension between Israel's "deserved destruction (for disobedience of covenant stipulations) and her ongoing existence as a community under Yahweh."[18] When studied in its historical, sociological, and theological contexts, the statement about intergenerational punishment will reveal that the God of the Old Testament is not an unjust God, a God whose wrath cannot be contained. Rather, a careful study of these texts reveals, as Rodney Duke

---

14. Boyd, *Crucifixion of the Warrior God*, 282n6.
15. Brettler, "God, Merciful and Compassionate," 24.
16. Brettler, "God, Merciful and Compassionate," 24.
17. Lane, *Compassionate, but Punishing God*.
18. Sakenfeld, "Problem of Divine Forgiveness," 317.

has expressed, "not the immorality of God, but the amazing faithfulness of God, a God who acts not only rationally and justly, but primarily mercifully."[19]

As late as the seventh century BCE, the prophet Nahum used the formula that speaks about Yahweh not clearing the guilty: "The LORD is slow to anger but great in power, and the LORD will by no means clear the guilty" (Nah 1:3). Another use of the statement on intergenerational punishment in the seventh century comes in the reaffirmation of the words of the Decalogue by the writers of the Deuteronomic History: "you shall not bow down to them or serve them; for I the LORD your God am a jealous God, visiting the iniquity of the fathers upon the children to the third and fourth generation of those who hate me" (Deut 5:9). Even Jeremiah, a prophet who ministered in the last days of the Southern Kingdom, knew Yahweh to be a God who visits the guilt of the fathers upon their children after them: "You show steadfast love to the thousandth generation, but repay the guilt of parents into the laps of their children after them, O great and mighty God whose name is the LORD of hosts" (Jer 32:18). In this text, Jeremiah links retribution of the guilt of the fathers on their sons.

In his study of trans-generational punishment in the Hebrew Bible, Wénin questions whether in the statement "punishing children for the iniquity of parents, to the third and the fourth generation" (Exod 20:5), punishment by violence or death is the first and only possible meaning.[20] Since the verb *pāqad* should be translated as "visit" and not as "punish," he says that it is possible that the statement may refer to a God who comes to see that the fathers' sin has consequences on the sons for several generations. Thus, a father may know in his lifetime what happens to his children because of his sin; this knowing constitutes his punishment. Wénin's view, however, does not reflect the true intent of the intergenerational punishment statement. Lindars believes that the punishment comes during the lifetime of the offender. He writes, "For whereas no limit is set on Yahweh's covenant-mercy, his wrath is restricted to the third and fourth generations. It means that the prolongation of divine punishment is limited to the generations who might be born within the lifetime of the offender."[21]

19. Duke, "'Visiting the Guilt of the Fathers,'" 347.
20. Wénin, "Dieu qui visite la faute des pères," 67–77.
21. Lindars, "Ezekiel and Individual Responsibility," 457.

GOD'S CHARACTER AND THE PROBLEM OF VIOLENCE

One way to better understand the character of God is by the way God interacts with his people and the experience of the people as they meet God in their daily lives. Throughout the Old Testament, the people's encounters with God display the truths about the character of God as revealed to Moses on Mount Sinai. The different aspects of God's character in Exod 34:6–7 are what the people call upon when they are worshiping God, when they are in trouble, when they are judged, and when they need help. These creedal statements are invoked in prayer and in celebration, in times of prosperity and in times of woes. These statements about God appear throughout the Old Testament. They guided the people of Israel in knowing and relating to their God. These same statements should guide people today in understanding the God of the Old Testament and the problem of divine violence.

What Yahweh said about himself and his character as a God is what he applies in his relationship with the people of Israel throughout its history. These are also the truths about God that guided the people of Israel and should guide people everywhere as they seek to deal with the problem of divine violence in the Old Testament. There are four important characteristics about God that should guide us in dealing with the problem of divine violence in the Old Testament.

First, the basic way by which Yahweh chooses to relate to people is with grace and mercy. Yahweh said that he is "a God merciful and gracious, slow to anger, and abounding in steadfast love and faithfulness, keeping steadfast love for the thousandth generation." Because Yahweh is a gracious and merciful God, he desires to be gracious and merciful to his people every day and in every situation. This was the affirmation of a person who was one of the recipients of the pain and suffering the people of Judah faced at the time the Babylonians conquered Jerusalem, "The steadfast love of the LORD never ceases, his mercies never come to an end; they are new every morning; great is your faithfulness" (Lam 3:22–23).[22] The experience of all Israel was expressed by a pious believer, "Yahweh your God is gracious and merciful, and will not turn away his face from you" (2 Chr 30:9). The psalmist was assured Yahweh's mercy

---

22. Boase, "Characterisation of God in Lamentations," 43, says that the sufferer in Lamentations experiences "the God of violence as one and the same God as the God of steadfast love and mercy."

would always be with him, "Surely goodness and mercy shall follow me all the days of my life" (Ps 23:6).

Second, because people have free will, sooner or later they will disobey God, they will rebel against him, and they will violate the moral order. When people fail to meet God's ideal, God is ready to show his grace to sinners. As Scot McKnight writes, "Disobedience by all humans creates the opportunity for the God of grace to show his love."[23] Yahweh is a God who forgives minor offenses, wrongdoing, disobedience, transgression, violence, iniquity, wickedness, all kinds of sins (Exod 34:7). But forgiveness requires repentance. "Repent and turn from all your transgressions; otherwise iniquity will be your ruin" (Ezek 18:30).

Yahweh spoke through Ezekiel and said, "if the wicked turn away from all their sins that they have committed and keep all my statutes and do what is lawful and right, they shall surely live; they shall not die" (Ezek 18:21). God's desire is for the sinner to live, but if they do not repent, they shall die. God does not want the death of sinners, "Have I any pleasure in the death of the wicked, says the Lord GOD, and not rather that they should turn from their ways and live?" (Ezek 18:23).

Third, Yahweh is a God of justice and a righteous judge, Yahweh by no means clears the guilty. God judges people according to their own doings. Yahweh told the people of Judah, "I the LORD test the mind and search the heart, to give to all according to their ways, according to the fruit of their doings" (Jer 17:10). The same message was given through Ezekiel, "I the LORD have spoken; the time is coming, I will act. I will not refrain, I will not spare, I will not relent. According to your ways and your doings I will judge you, says the Lord GOD" (Ezek 24:14).

Fourth, Yahweh is a God who holds people accountable for their sins, their wickedness, and their violence. Yahweh said, "But on the day I settle accounts, I will hold them accountable for their sin" (Exod 32:34 HCSB). God does not want to bring judgment upon the sinner; he wants them to live, but "If anyone does not repent, God will sharpen His sword" (Ps 7:12 HCSB). When the sword comes, some people repent and are delivered from the consequences of their sins. Others refuse to believe and pay the consequences of not repenting, "O LORD, . . . You have struck them, but they felt no anguish; you have consumed them, but they refused to take correction. They have made their faces harder than rock; they have refused to turn back" (Jer 5:3).

---

23. McKnight, *Reading Romans Backward*, 86.

EVALUATING GOD'S ACTIONS

What Yahweh says about himself provides all the information we need to know what kind of God Yahweh is. These statements about God provide the interpretative basis by which we should evaluate the actions of God.

God prefers to be always a gracious and merciful God, and he is. But people fail and sin against God. When that happens, God is always ready to forgive when they repent. When they refuse to repent, God deals with sins through agents, sometimes violent and brutal agents. Grace and mercy are always first. Judgment is God's last option; it only comes when people make their faces harder than rock and refuse to turn back.

When Yahweh is criticized for sending the flood, seldom is the pain Yahweh felt in his heart mentioned. When Yahweh is criticized for the death of three thousand people who violated the Second Commandment and celebrated an orgy in the name of God (Exod 32:6, 28), Yahweh is never remembered for sparing the whole nation (Exod 32:14). When Yahweh is criticized for destroying Sodom and Gomorrah, Yahweh is seldom remembered for his desire to save all the wicked people in the city for the sake of fifty righteous people there, even for the sake of forty, thirty, twenty, or even ten righteous people.

The people of Israel knew what kind of God Yahweh was. When the people of Israel experienced the ignominies of the destruction of their nation, the humiliation of going into exile, the scorn received from their enemies, and the pain and suffering produced by the siege of Jerusalem, the people of Judah still confessed the goodness of Yahweh:

> Gone is my glory, and all that I had hoped for from the LORD. The thought of my affliction and my homelessness is wormwood and gall! My soul continually thinks of it and is bowed down within me. But this I call to mind, and therefore I have hope: The steadfast love of the LORD never ceases, his mercies never come to an end; they are new every morning; great is your faithfulness. "The LORD is my portion," says my soul, "therefore I will hope in him." The LORD is good to those who wait for him, to the soul that seeks him. (Lam 3:18–25)[24]

---

24. Krašovec, "Source of Hope," 223–33. Krašovec says that even though the situation seems hopeless to the poet of Lamentations, he is deeply rooted in religious traditions of Israel, for "He is aware that ultimately, the Lord is not a God of wrath but of mercy" (230).

The revelation of Yahweh's character to Moses, which became Israel's confession about its God "has to do with what *kind* of God Yahweh has been, is, and will be. Yahweh is faithful, loving, gracious, and righteous; hence there is hope."[25] Because Yahweh is a God who continues to show his mercy and love to thousands of generations, people can always depend on the constancy of God: "God's salvific will is never diminished; God's righteousness is never compromised; God's faithfulness will never waver; God's steadfast love endures forever. God will be this kind of God whenever God is being God."[26]

---

25. Fretheim, "Authority of the Bible," 122.
26. Fretheim, "Authority of the Bible," 122.

PART 2

The Justice of God

8

Divine Justice

THIS CHAPTER WILL DEAL WITH the character of God and the issue of divine justice. The discussion will be based on God's revelation of himself to Moses on Mount Sinai. The specific focus of this chapter will be the intergenerational punishment statement in Exod 34:7, "yet by no means clearing the guilty, but visiting the iniquity of the parents upon the children and the children's children, to the third and the fourth generation." The concept of intergenerational punishment found in the Old Testament was also common in many societies of the ancient Near East, yet, "this specific term or limit of punishment is not found anywhere else in ancient Near Eastern literature."[1]

In dealing with the problem of divine violence one must also deal with the paradox that Yahweh is a merciful God and a God of justice. The Old Testament presents Yahweh as a "lover of justice" (Ps 99:4), as one who loves justice (Isa 61:8). Brueggemann says that Israel spoke wrongly about their God and compromised the distinctiveness of Yahweh by asking, "Where is the God of justice?" (Mal 2:17).[2]

The Old Testament presents Yahweh as a righteous judge, indicating that divine justice is a fundamental aspect of the character of God. According to the biblical writer, the right of vengeance belongs to Yahweh: "Vengeance is mine" (Deut 32:35). This same right was affirmed by Paul when he exhorts believers not to repay evil with evil, "Beloved, never

---

1. Littrell, "Origin of the Divine Punishment," 7–8.
2. Brueggemann, *Theology of the Old Testament*, 136–37.

avenge yourselves, but leave room for the wrath of God; for it is written, 'Vengeance is mine, I will repay, says the Lord'" (Rom 12:19). Belousek writes that this right of vengeance is empty if it does not contain an inherent right to violence. He wrote, "God's character is revealed by how God in sovereign freedom chooses to exercise that right of vengeance, whether punitively or mercifully, retributively or redemptively, violently or nonviolently. To know God's character, we must look to God's actions."[3]

One issue in the Old Testament that bothers many people, Christians and non-Christians alike, is the problem of intergenerational punishment. Is the punishment for sins of an individual passed down to his descendants? Does God punish children for the iniquity of their parents to the third and the fourth generation? Many people find this statement disturbing because they do not believe they should be responsible for something that their parents did.

The idea of intergenerational punishment was ingrained in the minds of many people who lived during Jesus's ministry. Once, when his disciples saw a man born blind, they asked Jesus, "Rabbi, who sinned, this man or his parents, that he was born blind?" (John 9:2). When asked by his disciples, "who sinned, this man or his parents," Jesus answered, "Neither this man nor his parents sinned" (John 9:3). Jesus's answer to his disciples should force us to reconsider the issue of intergenerational punishment.

THE SECOND COMMANDMENT

The disciples' view about intergenerational punishment was based on the words of the Second Commandment found in Exod 20:4–6, a commandment that forbids the worship of idols:

> You shall not make for yourself a graven image, or any likeness of anything that is in heaven above, or that is in the earth beneath, or that is in the water under the earth; you shall not bow down to them or serve them; for I the LORD your God am a jealous God, visiting the iniquity of the fathers upon the children to the third and the fourth generation of those who hate me, but showing steadfast love to thousands of those who love me and keep my commandments. (Exod 20:4–6 RSV)

---

3. Belousek, "Nonviolent God," 61.

Amie Littrell says that the retribution formula in Exod 20:5 "is an important theological expression of Yahweh's character."[4] Gregory Boyd makes reference to Exod 20:5 only once in his book. He wrote: "Ezekiel specifically taught that children are never punished for their parent's sin (Ezek 18). This insight arguably corrects the earlier Israelite conception of Yahweh 'punishing the children for the sin of the parents to the third and fourth generation' (Exod 20:5)."[5]

First, before I deal with the issue of intergenerational punishment, I need to make a few remarks about the Hebrew text of Exod 20:4–6. English translations differ on how they translate Exod 20:5. Below are a few examples:

New Revised Standard Version: "punishing children for the iniquity of parents, to the third and the fourth generation of those who reject me."

The Jewish Publication Society (TNK): "visiting the guilt of the parents upon the children, upon the third and upon the fourth generations of those who reject Me."

The NET Bible: "responding to the transgression of fathers by dealing with children to the third and fourth generations of those who reject me."

The New Jerusalem Bible: "I punish a parent's fault in the children, the grandchildren, and the great-grandchildren among those who hate me."

The New Living Bible: "I lay the sins of the parents upon their children; the entire family is affected—even children in the third and fourth generations of those who reject me."

The Septuagint: "recompensing the sins of the fathers upon the children, to the third and fourth generation to them that hate me."

Second, the word "generations" does not appear in the Hebrew text. All translations add the word "generations" based on the reading of Deut

---

4. Littrell, "Origin of the Divine Punishment," 7.
5. Boyd, *Crucifixion of the Warrior God*, 838.

7:9: "Know therefore that the LORD your God is God, the faithful God who maintains covenant loyalty with those who love him and keep his commandments, to a thousand generations." The only exception that I know that does not include the word "generations" is the New Jerusalem Bible: "I punish a parent's fault in the children, the grandchildren, and the great-grandchildren among those who hate me."

Most translations, as noted above, have problems with the Hebrew word *pāqad*. The basic meaning of the word *pāqad* is disputed, but both BDB and HALOT say that the basic meaning of the word is "to visit." Most translations emphasize the idea of punishment; however, the word is better understood when the concept of "visiting the sins" is used.

According to André, the Hebrew word *pāqad* has several meanings, however, one basic meaning of the word is to "examine closely," so that "the judgment or decision issuing from such examination is included."[6] André also says that in a large number of texts, the word *pāqad* "refers to the activity of the divine judge, generally in reference to the judge's decision."[7] For instance, in Exod 32:34, the word *pāqad* is used to refer to the day when Yahweh visits to pronounce his judgment: "in the day when I visit I will visit their sin upon them." The meaning of future visitation for the word *pāqad* is found in an oracle in Amos: "That in the day that I shall visit the transgressions of Israel upon him I will also visit the altars of Bethel: and the horns of the altar shall be cut off, and fall to the ground" (Amos 3:14 KJV). In a few texts, the word *pāqad* carries the idea of a punishment that is postponed to a distant future: "And there shall be no remnant of them: for I will bring evil upon the men of Anathoth, even *the year of their visitation* (Jer 11:23 KJV, emphasis added). The same idea of postponed judgement is found in Jer 8:12, "Were they ashamed when they had committed abomination? nay, they were not at all ashamed, neither could they blush: therefore shall they fall among them that fall; in the time of their visitation they shall be cast down, saith the LORD."

Third, the visiting of the sins of the fathers comes upon the third and the fourth generation of those who reject God. These words clearly imply that not all the descendants of an individual are punished for his sins. Thus, it is not all the children and the grandchildren of an individual who are punished, but only those who reject God or those who reject the demands of the covenant. As Brettler puts it, "Even while recalling

---

6. André, "*pāqad*," 51.
7. André, "*pāqad*," 57.

intergenerational punishment for four generations, both Exod 20 and 34 insist that God is much more gracious than reproving."[8] The expression "those who reject me" is not found in Exod 34:6–7 and in Num 14:18. The reason for its presence in the Second Commandment is because the statement deals with the breach of the covenant, that is, the rejection of Yahweh to follow other gods.

Fourth, the word "hate" means to dislike someone. In the context of the Second Commandment, to hate God is to reject him or to reject the covenant. As William Moran has shown, the languages of love and hate are words related to the covenant.[9] The two words carry the idea of choosing and rejecting. One example of this use is found in Malachi: "I have loved Jacob but I have hated Esau" (Mal 1:2–3). This means that God made a covenant with Jacob, but he did not make a covenant with Esau. In Exod 20:5, the Hebrew verb for hate is a participle, reflecting the idea of a continuous action. The use of the participle indicates that the act of rejecting God is something that continues over a period of time.

Fifth, Yahweh is presented as ʾēl qānāʾ, a jealous God. The word "jealous" is related to the covenant and refers to Yahweh's demands of exclusive allegiance from his people. According to Preuss, the jealousy of God refers to

> YHWH's desire for Israel to share his divine status with no one. Based on the special relationship that he has introduced historically to Israel, YHWH's jealousy is directed against Israel's apostasy to other gods. This jealousy is put in the form of a prohibition and the response of punishment. This evidence about YHWH's jealousy is closely connected to the understandings of his holiness ("jealous holiness"; cf. Josh. 24:19) and his love (cf. Deuteronomy).[10]

Deuteronomy 4:24 says that "Yahweh your God is a consuming fire, a jealous God." The biblical emphasis on divine jealousy is an affirmation that Yahwistic faith demanded the sole allegiance of his people.[11] Israel's worship of other gods was forbidden because apostasy was an affront to Yahweh: "you will worship no other god, since Yahweh's name is the Jealous One; he is a jealous God" (Exod 34:14 NJB). Yahweh's jealousy is a

---

8. Brettler, "God, Merciful and Compassionate," 245.
9. Moran, "Love of God in Deuteronomy," 77–87.
10. Preuss, *Old Testament Theology*, 1:241.
11. Routledge, *Old Testament Theology*, 111.

divine response to Israel's apostasy, "Nowhere in the Bible will you read that God is a jealous God except in connection with idolatry."[12]

GOD'S COVENANT WITH ISRAEL

Sixth, the statement about intergenerational punishment is given to Israel within the context of the covenant. The covenant between God and Israel establishes Israel as a unique nation in the world, a nation set apart to carry out God's mission in the world. Jan Assmann explains the nature of this distinction. He wrote: "With the covenant on Sinai, two new distinctions come into play, which likewise bear no relation to truth and falsehood. The first differentiates between outside and inside, belonging to the covenant and not belonging to it, exosphere and endosphere."[13] Assmann emphasizes that Yahweh made his covenant with Israel, the people whom he brought from Egypt and not with the world and the entire human race. Because Yahweh elected Israel to perform a special mission in the world and because Yahweh established a special relationship with Israel through the Sinai covenant, the world which God created is now divided into two groups, Israel and the nations. However, "It is important to emphasize that this distinction has nothing whatsoever to do with intolerance and violence. God cares for all peoples but he has something special in mind for Israel."[14]

The Second Commandment has to do with idolatry; Israel is forbidden to make idols and they are not allowed to bow down to them or worship them (Exod 20:4–5). In his article, "In Search of the Origins of Israelite Aniconism," S. I. Kang wrote,

> For a long time, aniconism has been presented as one of the most distinctive characteristics of the religion of ancient Israel. Aniconism refers to the absence or repudiation of divine images. Such a tradition was inconceivable to Israel's neighbours, where the care, feeding, and clothing of a deity, represented in the form of a divine statue, played a central role in national cults.[15]

---

12. Johnstone, *Exodus 20–40*, 30.
13. Assmann, *Invention of Religion*, 80.
14. Assmann, *Invention of Religion*, 80.
15. Kang, "Origins of Israelite Aniconism," 84.

INTERGENERATIONAL PUNISHMENT STATEMENT

The intergenerational punishment statement appears in four texts in the Old Testament: Exod 20:5; 34:6–7; Num 14:18–19; and Deut 5:9–10. The language of the intergenerational punishment statement in Deut 5:9–10 appears in the context of the prohibition against making images of Yahweh:

> I am Yahweh your God who brought you out of Egypt, out of the place of slave-labour. You will have no gods other than me. You must not make yourselves any image or any likeness of anything in heaven above or on earth beneath or in the waters under the earth; you must not bow down to these gods or serve them. For I, Yahweh your God, am a jealous God and I punish the parents' fault in the children, the grandchildren and the great-grandchildren, among those who hate me; but I show faithful love to thousands, to those who love me and keep my commandments. (Deut 5:6–10 NJB)

Deuteronomy 5:9–10

The intergenerational punishment statement in Deut 5:9 is the same as in Exod 20:5 because both statements appear in the context of God's covenant with Israel established on Mount Sinai. However, the Deuteronomic writer did change the language of what God said about himself in Exod 34:7. The version of the Decalogue that appears in Deut 5:6–21 differs from the version of the Decalogue that appears in Exod 20:1–17. The Deuteronomic historian changed the language of the Fourth Commandment (Exod 20:8–11; Deut 5:12–15). The Deuteronomic writer changed the reason why the people of Israel should rest on the seventh day. He changed the language of the Fifth Commandment (Exod 20:12; Deut 5:16) to emphasize the reasons children should honor father and mother. He also changed the language of the Tenth Commandment (Exod 20:17; Deut 5:21) to declare that a man's wife was not part of his property.

The Second Commandment forbids idolatry, the making of idols and the worship of idols. Worshiping other gods was a breach of the covenant and this violation would bring upon those who violated the demands of the covenant the curse included in the ratification of the commandments. In the case of idolatry, the punishment would be the visitation of Yahweh upon "the iniquity of the fathers upon the children to the third and fourth generation of those who hate me." The Deuteronomic writer reverses the order of the retribution language found in Exod 34:7. In the Exod 34:7 passage, the grace and mercy of Yahweh is stated first and then the language of retribution. In the Decalogue, both in Exodus and in Deuteronomy, the language of retribution comes first and then the language of grace and mercy.

Deuteronomic Revision

The revision of the Second Commandment by the Deuteronomic writer, according to Tigay, is an effort "to mitigate the doctrine of cross-generational punishment by God."[16] This view is based on the Deuteronomist's belief that God punishes only those who hate him: "Know therefore that the LORD your God is God; he is the faithful God, keeping his covenant of love to a thousand generations of those who love him and keep his commands. But those who hate him he will repay to their face by destruction; he will not be slow to repay to their face those who hate him" (Deut 7:9 NIV).

Weinfeld wrote that the Deuteronomic writer revised the concept of family solidarity. He wrote:

> one must admit that Deut 7:9–10 opposes collective retribution. . . . This may explain the additional phrases in the Decalogue, "those who hate me" or "those who love me and keep my commandments," which are missing in the parallels of Exod 34:6–7 and Num 14:18. These phrases look like explanatory glosses, which stress that God punishes only those of the sons who propagate the evil ways of their fathers.[17]

The judgment of Yahweh came upon the Northern Kingdom and upon the Southern Kingdom because the people had violated the demands of the covenant and had been involved in the cult of Baal and other gods. In the postexilic period, when Nehemiah looked at the condition of the people in exile, he recognized that the ancestors had violated the covenant. He said: "You have been just in all that has come upon us, for you have dealt faithfully and we have acted wickedly; our kings, our officials, our priests, and our ancestors have not kept your law or

---

16. Tigay, *Deuteronomy*, 437.
17. Weinfeld, *Deuteronomy 1–11*, 299.

heeded the commandments and the warnings that you gave them" (Neh 9:33–34).

The people who lived in the postexilic community often reminded each other that they too had followed in the sins of their ancestors. They recognized that God had acted justly because the reason for their suffering and for the exile in a foreign land was the violation of the covenant by the fathers. Ezra told the gathered community, "From the days of our fathers to this day we have been in great guilt; and for our iniquities we, our kings, and our priests have been given into the hand of the kings of the lands, to the sword, to captivity, to plundering, and to utter shame, as at this day" (Ezra 9:70). In his prayer, Ezra recognized that their exile was not only because of their fathers' iniquity, but it was also because of "our iniquities." The same sentiment was expressed by Daniel, "because for our sins, and for the iniquities of our fathers, Jerusalem and thy people have become a byword among all who are round about us" (Dan 9:16).

When fathers, kings, and priests violate the demands of the covenant they bring divine judgment upon themselves and this judgment affects children. Duke wrote, "The failure of the community leader was the failure of the whole community. The community shared in the responsibility and the guilt. Cultures with such corporate identities understood that there were cases in which innocent individuals inescapably suffered along with the guilty. That certainly must have been the case in the Babylonian exile; children below the age of accountability suffered the consequences met by their parents."[18]

The author of Deuteronomy repeats the words of the Decalogue as it was found in the tradition of Israel. But the writer tries to explain to the community of the seventh century who specifically receives the punishment for the sin of idolatry: "visiting the iniquity of the fathers upon the children to the third and fourth generation *of those who hate me* (emphasis added)" (Deut 5:9). The same expression also appears in the Decalogue found in the book of Exodus: "visiting the iniquity of the fathers upon the children to the third and the fourth generation *of those who hate me* (emphasis added)" (Exod 20:5).

The expression "of those who hate me" does not appear in the list of the divine attributes revealed to Moses on Mount Sinai. In his revelation to Moses, Yahweh said: "visiting the iniquity of the fathers upon the children and the children's children, to the third and the fourth generation"

---

18. Duke, "'Visiting the Guilt of the Fathers,'" 357.

(Exod 34:7). The expression "those who hate me" is also not found in Num 14:18 at the time Moses prayed on behalf of Israel. Thus, the intergenerational punishment statement in Exod 20:5 reflects a Deuteronomistic reinterpretation of the Decalogue to reflect the concerns of the seventh-century Judean community. This later development of the visitation formula indicates that the religious leaders of the Judean community of the seventh century were trying to explain that it is not the children who are visited for the sins of the father, but only the guilty person who is visited. This change in the Decalogue reflects a clear movement from collective responsibility to individual responsibility.

This reinterpretation of the words of the commandment is found in Deut 7:9–10:

> Know that Yahweh your God is God, the faithful God who keeps His gracious covenant loyalty for a thousand generations with those who love Him and keep His commands. But He directly pays back and destroys *those who hate Him* [emphasis added]. He will not hesitate to directly pay back *the one who hates Him* [emphasis added]." (Deut 7:9–10 HCSB)

THE DEUTERONOMIC THEOLOGY OF PUNISHMENT

The writer of Deuteronomy becomes specific about who receives the punishment. The Deuteronomic writer emphasizes that the punishment for the sin of idolatry is received only by "the one who hates Him." In analyzing the words of the Deuteronomist, it is important to notice the change from "those who hate Him" to "the one who hates Him." Thus, the writer is declaring that the transgenerational punishment is received only by those who specifically reject God. As Fishbane puts it, "As the Decalogue now reads, only those who hate or love the commandments will be punished or rewarded. Individual responsibility is now stressed; divine judgment is enacted on a person by person basis: sons will be punished or rewarded like their fathers *if* they continue the ways of their fathers" (emphasis his).[19] Fishbane calls this theological stress on individual responsibility "a presumptive misquote." He wrote, "With one stroke later tradition controverted the earlier revelation of divine attributes (Exod

---

19. Fishbane, "Revelation and Tradition," 353.

34:7), authenticating its novel viewpoint by means of a presumptive misquote."[20]

This change begins a movement in the Judean community of the seventh century that goes from collective punishment to individual punishment. This change anticipates Jeremiah and Ezekiel. Because the transgenerational punishment comes when people fail to obey the demands of the covenant, the writer of Deuteronomy urges the people to be diligent in obeying the commandment: "Therefore, observe diligently the commandment—the statutes, and the ordinances—that I am commanding you" (Deut 7:11).

The writer of Deuteronomy is also specific about the "thousands." While the Hebrew texts of Exod 20:5 and Deut 5:9 have only thousands (English translations add the word "generations"), the writer of Deuteronomy speaks of "a thousand generations" in Deut 7:9. By using the expression "a thousand generations" instead of "thousands," the writer is emphasizing God's mercy, that God is a faithful God, a God "who maintains covenant loyalty with those who love him and keep his commandments, to a thousand generations." According to the Deuteronomist, divine mercy prevails over divine justice.

The author of Deuteronomy, however, makes a difference between covenantal sins and criminal laws. Deut 24:16 says: "Parents shall not be put to death for their children, nor shall children be put to death for their parents; only for their own crimes may persons be put to death" (Deut 24:16). Although the word for "crimes" in verse 16 is the same as the Hebrew word for "sin," the context here implies that this law is part of the justice system of Israel. In criminal laws, a son could not be punished for the crimes of his father.

Lundbom emphasizes how this Deuteronomic law was designed to differentiate between covenantal sin and criminal sin. He wrote, "A distinction, nevertheless, has to be made between punishment meted out by God on the one hand and punishment by human judges on the other. God can and does carry out corporate and vicarious punishment, but human courts in Israel may not do likewise. The present law seeks then to limit the scope of punishment permissible in Israelite law courts: only the one who sins shall die."[21]

---

20. Fishbane, "Revelation and Tradition," 353.
21. Lundbom, *Deuteronomy*, 810.

This principle is expressed in 2 Kgs 14:5–6. After Amaziah became king of Judah and after his kingship was established, he put to death those who had assassinated his father, but

> he did not put to death the children of the assassins, in accordance with what is written in the Book of the Teaching of Moses, where the LORD commanded, "Parents shall not be put to death for children, nor children be put to death for parents; a person shall be put to death only for his own crime." (2 Kgs 14:5–6 TNK)

The Deuteronomic law decrees that only those who commit a crime should be punished. By sparing the children of the assassins, Amaziah was departing from the practice of blood revenge.[22]

Unfortunately, the NIV, the HSCB, and the ESV, among other English translations, say that each person "is to die for his own sins" (2 Kgs 14:6 NIV). These translations identify the statement in Deut 24:16 with covenant law as it appears in the Second Commandment. The law in Deut 24:16 does not refer to violation of the Second Commandment. The law is part of the legal system of Israel dealing with punishment for civil crimes.

---

22. Greengus, *Laws in the Bible*, 159.

9

The Problem of Idolatry

THE AUTHOR OF DEUTERONOMY IDENTIFIES the Ten Commandments with the covenant God established with Israel: "He declared to you his covenant, which he charged you to observe, that is, the ten commandments; and he wrote them on two stone tablets" (Deut 4:13). The two tablets of stone on which the Decalogue was written, was also known as the tablets of the covenant: "At the end of forty days and forty nights the LORD gave me the two stone tablets, the tablets of the covenant" (Deut 9:11). In the book of Deuteronomy, the Ten Commandments are known as the "Ten Words": "He revealed his covenant to you and commanded you to observe it, the Ten Words which he inscribed on two tablets of stone" (Deut 4:13 NJB). The reference to the Ten Words in Deut 4:13 indicates that by the time the book of Deuteronomy was written, the Decalogue was already a fixed formula. According to von Rad, the Ten Commandments were never spoken as laws: "In the Old Testament the Ten Commandments are never spoken as law: they are called only 'the Ten Words.'"[1]

SERVING OTHER GODS

The Hebrew Bible condemns idolatry and the worship of gods made of wood and stone.[2] Deuteronomy warns about the consequence of sin for

---

1. Rad, *Old Testament Theology*, 1:195.
2. In his discussion on how the Hebrew Bible condemns idolatry and the worship

a man or a woman, or a family or a tribe, whose heart turns away from Yahweh to serve other gods of the nations: "Yahweh will not pardon him. The wrath and jealousy of Yahweh will blaze against such a person" (Deut 29:19 NJB). Any Israelite who worships other gods and serves them rejects the covenant of Yahweh and will be visited by Yahweh in accordance with the stipulations written in the Second Commandment.[3] This person is guilty of idolatry for rejecting Yahweh and for rejecting the covenant. Explaining the fate of this individual, Lundbom wrote: "Yahweh is gracious and merciful, but will not clear the guilty" (Exod 34:6–7; cf. Deut 5:8–10). The idolater will take the full measure of the divine anger."[4] Because "the wages of sin is death" (Rom 6:23), on the day Yahweh will settle accounts, Yahweh will hold the guilty sinner accountable for his sin (Exod 32:34).

The writer of the book of Wisdom of Solomon believed the worship of idols was the cause of all evils, "For the worship of idols with no name is the beginning, cause, and end of every evil" (Wis 14:27 NJB). The book of Deuteronomy has much to say about idolatry. The Deuteronomic writer warns the people not to forget the covenant that Yahweh made with them. He warns them not to make for themselves an idol in the form of anything, since Yahweh has forbidden them to follow other gods (Deut 4:23). Deuteronomy also warns the people about the consequence of forgetting Yahweh to follow other gods: "If you do forget the LORD your God and follow other gods to serve and worship them, I solemnly warn you today that you shall surely perish" (Deut 8:19). The expression "other gods" occurs seventeen times in the book of Deuteronomy.

Patrick Miller explains the reason every Israelite should keep the Second Commandment. He wrote: "The Second Commandment concludes with an extended motivational clause giving a powerful reason

---

of gods made of wood and stone, Wyschogrod, "Jewish Perspective on Incarnation," 200, wrote, "Cheating, lying, stealing, oppressing the weak, the orphan and widow, are the offenses that, together, with idolatry, draw the bulk of prophetic condemnation. It is, in fact, questionable whether it is possible to speak of parallel offenses as if idolatry and injustice were separate transgressions. It is more than probable that the worship of other gods is the root problem, with injustice being an inevitable consequence of the abandonment of the God who demands Justice. If this is so, then the basic sin which is the root of all others is idolatry."

3. Janzen, "First Commandments of the Decalogue," 17, says that "The foundational texts for the Old Testaments imageless worship of God/Yahweh alone are, first of all, the first two commandments of the Decalogue."

4. Lundbom, *Deuteronomy*, 810.

why persons should obey this commandment, a rationalizing of the divine command that occurs in the following three commandments as well. The heart of the matter is the jealousy of God."[5]

One reason the making of images and the worship of other gods were forbidden in Israel was because Yahweh is a jealous God: "for you shall worship no other god, for the LORD, whose name is Jealous, is a jealous God" (Exod 34:14). According to von Rad, the statements about God being a jealous God in Exod 20:5, does not refer to the commandment prohibiting images, but it refers to the first commandment which requires Israel to worship only one God. Thus, Yahweh's jealousy, according to von Rad, "consists in the fact that he wills to be the only God for Israel, and that he is not disposed to share his claim for worship and love with any other divine power."[6]

THE DAY TO SETTLE ACCOUNTS

It is for this reason that the Second Commandment plays an important role in the theological argument of the Deuteronomist. Idolatry was a violation of the covenant. For this reason, the book of Deuteronomy could be considered a polemic against idolatry.[7] Throughout the book, the writer expresses his hostility toward the worship of other gods: "If you do forget the LORD your God and follow other gods to serve and worship them, I solemnly warn you today that you shall surely perish" (Deut 8:19).

The violation of the covenant brought consequences upon the whole community. For the community in the wilderness, after having put Yahweh to the test ten times (Num 14:22), the day to settle accounts had arrived: "on the day I settle accounts, I will hold them accountable for their sin" (Exod 32:34 HCSB). The community had violated the covenant by refusing to trust in God, so God held them accountable for their sin: God allowed that generation to live; their punishment was that they

---

5. Miller, *Ten Commandments*, 59.

6. Rad, *Old Testament Theology*, 1:208.

7. Milgrom, "Nature and Extent of Idolatry," 1–13. Milgrom says that "Datable biblical texts of the eighth century accuse Israel of idolatry 15 times in contrast to 166 accusations in the seventh century" (p. 1). Because of the proliferation of private religion in the seventh century, the reforms of Josiah arose in opposition to the idolatry prevalent in Judah. Milgrom also says that the book of Deuteronomy placed all idols in all their forms under total ban by declaring war on idolatry (p. 11).

would die in the wilderness without being able to enter the land of promise (Num 14:28–30). As for the children, they suffered the consequences of their parents' sins, "your children will wander in the wilderness forty years and suffer for your unfaithfulness" (Num 14:33 NET). However, God did not act violently against the innocent; only the guilty ones were punished with God's punishment, because God does not clear the guilty (Exod 34:7).

This pattern of divine visitation was repeated through the history of Israel. The people violated the covenant, God in his mercy allowed them to live and kept the covenant in order to maintain the relationship. But as God had said, "on the day I settle accounts, I will hold them accountable for their sin" (Exod 32:34 HCSB). Thus, when the community experienced wars of conquest, the Arameans, the Assyrians, and the Babylonians punished the community without pity, killing men, women, and children, young and old.

The Northern Kingdom went into exile because of their idolatry and their worship of false gods:

> The people of Israel did secretly against the LORD their God things that were not right. They built for themselves high places at all their towns . . . they set up for themselves pillars and Asherim on every high hill and under every green tree; they burned incense on all the high places, . . . they did wicked things, provoking the LORD to anger . . . they served idols . . . the LORD warned Israel. . . . Turn from your evil ways and keep my commandments and my statutes.
>
> But they would not listen, but were stubborn, as their fathers had been, who did not believe in the LORD their God. They despised his statutes, and his covenant that he made with their fathers. . . . they made for themselves molten images of two calves; and they made an Asherah, and worshiped all the host of heaven, and served Baal . . . they sold themselves to do evil in the sight of the LORD, provoking him to anger. Therefore the LORD was very angry with Israel. (2 Kgs 17:9–18)

For the people of the Northern Kingdom, after two hundred years of violating the covenant by serving other gods and by provoking Yahweh to anger, the day to settle accounts arrived in 722 BCE. After two centuries of being a patient and long-suffering God, Yahweh held the people accountable for their sins. And, as a result, the Assyrians came and took the people into exile.

For Judah, after almost 400 years of violating the covenant, the day to settle accounts also arrived and on that day, Yahweh held the people of Judah accountable for their sins. As a result, the people of the Southern Kingdom were taken into exile in Babylon in the midst of untold suffering caused by the long siege of Jerusalem.

Because of the fall of the Northern Kingdom and because the religious life of Judah prior to the reforms of Josiah, the book of Deuteronomy was written to warn the people of the Southern Kingdom of the perils of idolatry. But "Judah also did not keep the commandments of the LORD their God, but walked in the customs which Israel had introduced" (2 Kgs 17:19). As a result, Judah also had to face the ignominy of exile. In the exile of Israel and in the exile of Judah, the words of Yahweh were proven to be true: "on the day I settle accounts, I will hold them accountable for their sin" (Exod 32:34 HCSB).

THE DEUTERONOMIC INTERPRETATION

In his article, "The Reworking of the Principle of Transgenerational Punishment: Four Case Studies," Bernard Levinson calls the statement on the punishment for idolatry, "the injustice of the Decalogue's doctrine."[8] The reason Levinson calls the Decalogue doctrine "unjust" is because he associates the intergenerational punishment statement with the idea of retribution. He wrote: "The repudiated proverb [in Ezekiel 18:1–4] and the Decalogue doctrine share not only the notion of retribution vicariously transmitted from one generation to the next but also common terminology: the resonant language of fathers and children."[9]

The problem, as I see it, is the way Levinson translates Exod 20:5: "visiting the punishment for the iniquity of the fathers upon the sons."[10] The problem is that the expression "the punishment for" is not in the Hebrew text. Most translations translate *pōqēd ʿāwōn ʾābōt* (Exod 20:5) as "visiting the iniquity of the fathers" (Exod 20:5 RSV) or as "visiting the guilt of the parents" (Exod 20:5 TNK). Levinson, on the other hand, translates the words *pōqēd ʿāwōn* as "visiting the punishment for the iniquity."

---

8. Levinson, "Transgenerational Punishment," 60.
9. Levinson, "Transgenerational Punishment," 62.
10. Levinson, "Transgenerational Punishment," 58.

His translation is based on the view that the word *pōqēd* (Exod 20:5) should be translated as "punishment" as found in the NRSV: "punishing children for the iniquity of parents" (Exod 20:5 NRSV). The better translation for *pōqēd* is "to visit," as found in the ESV: "visiting the iniquity of the fathers." In his *Theology of the Old Testament* von Rad wrote, "retribution is not a new action which comes upon the person concerned from somewhere else; it is rather the last ripple of the act itself which attaches to its agent almost as something material. Hebrew in fact does not even have a word for punishment."[11]

The book of Deuteronomy provides the best way for understanding the transition from communal punishment to individual responsibility: "Know therefore that the LORD your God is God, the faithful God who keeps covenant and steadfast love with those who love him and keep his commandments, to a thousand generations, and requites to their face those who hate him, by destroying them; he will not be slack with him who hates him, he will requite him to his face" (Deut 7:9–10 RSV).

The expression, "and requites to their face those who hate him," may offer a clue to the Deuteronomic interpretation of intergenerational punishment in Deut 5:10. The TNK translates Deut 7:10, "but who instantly requites with destruction those who reject Him." Two other usages of the expression "upon the face of" in the Old Testament may clarify its meaning:

Haran died in the lifetime [upon the face of] of his father Terah. (Gen 11:28 TNK)

Eleazar and Ithamar served as priests in the lifetime of [upon the face of] their father Aaron. (Num 3:4 NRSV)

Thus, as Levinson proposes, the punishment comes upon the lifetime of the sinner or as the NRSV translates, "in their own person" (Deut 7:10). Levinson concludes that by emphasizing that the sinner's punishment comes in his lifetime, the author of Deuteronomy is declaring that transgenerational punishment does not cover several generations, but it applies only to the guilty person in his own time, or in his own lifetime.[12]

---

11. Rad, *Old Testament Theology*, 1:385.
12. Levinson, "Transgenerational Punishment," 77.

No other religion in the ancient Near East worshiped their gods without the aid of images; the aniconism of Israel was unique. This means that the intergenerational judgment applies only to Israel and not to the nations of the world because, as Assmann wrote, "God makes this covenant not with the world and the entire human race but with the children of Israel."[13] Thus, no one today should worry about intergenerational judgment because this is only applied to those who are bound to God by the covenant established on Mount Sinai. If intergenerational judgment applies only to Israel, then how was it enforced?

THE INTERGENERATIONAL PUNISHMENT STATEMENT

The most difficult aspect in the proper understanding of intergenerational punishment is how to interpret the phrase "the children to the third and the fourth generation."[14] One way of understanding the idea of generations is by taking it literally. If one generation is about twenty-five years, then the third generation would be seventy-five years and the fourth generation one hundred years. God's mercy lasts one thousand generations or twenty-five thousand years. Taking the phrase literally, the phrase means that God's grace lasts longer than his anger, that divine mercy trumps divine justice.[15] Thus, the numbers should be understood as a hyperbole to indicate that God's mercy lasts forever while his anger lasts only for a brief time.

Carol Meyers believes that this hyperbolic language is used to emphasize obedience:

> We can only wonder if this is the language of hyperbole, meant to emphasize the importance of obeying this stricture, rather than an expression of belief that the innocent descendents of someone who disobeyed would have to pay the consequences. . . . Blessings will come to the "thousandth generation" (20:6) of those whose love for God means that they obey all God's teachings. Such blessings will last, in a sense, forever.[16]

---

13. Assmann, *Invention of Religion*, 80.

14. Janzen, "First Commandments of the Decalogue," 18–19 writes, "Idolatry cannot be isolated; it affects future generations (Exod. 20:5), but God's 'steadfast love' reaches many times further than God's wrath (Exod. 20:6)."

15. Fernández, "El castigo de los hijos," 420.

16. Meyers, *Exodus*, 172.

Some people interpret the statement on intergenerational punishment by taking the whole statement literally, that is, that the divine punishment on the father's sins will last three or four successive generations. Thus, the sins of a father will affect his son (the second generation), his grandchildren (the third generation), and maybe even his great-grandchildren (the fourth generation). In this case it probably means that the whole family is living together as an extended family.[17] This is the way the New Jerusalem Bible interprets the statement: "I punish a parent's fault in the children, the grandchildren, and the great-grandchildren among those who hate me."

In his discussion of the punishment statement, Lindars concluded that the punishment for idolatry will come in the lifetime of the offender: "For whereas no limit is set for Yahweh's covenant-mercy, his wrath is restricted to the third and fourth generations. It means that the prolongation of divine punishment is limited to the generations who might be born within the lifetime of the offender."[18]

Another way of understanding the reason the punishment was extended to four generations would be to preserve the name of the father in Israel. If the whole family were to be killed together, then the name of the father would be eradicated from the memory of Israel (Deut 25:6). One good example of the need to preserve a name in Israel is the case of Absalom. In 2 Sam 18:18 Absalom set up a pillar in the Valley of the Kings because he had no son to invoke his name after his death: "Now Absalom in his lifetime had taken and set up for himself a pillar that is in the King's Valley, for he said, 'I have no son to keep my name in remembrance'; he called the pillar by his own name" (2 Sam 18:18). The pillar was not a burial place; it was a visible memorial to keep his name alive in Israel since he had no son to invoke his name after his death.[19]

THE GOLDEN CALF INCIDENT

The statement on intergenerational punishment must be understood in light of the covenant God made with Israel. Most people who criticize the statement on intergenerational punishment do so because they do not understand the nature of covenants as they existed in the world where

---

17. Lang, "Number Ten," 228–29.
18. Lindars, "Ezekiel and Individual Responsibility," 457.
19. Schmitt, "And Jacob Set Up a Pillar,'" 394.

Israel lived. The covenant between God and Israel was a suzerainty covenant that followed the form of international treaties between a king and a vassal. Although scholars disagree whether God's covenant with Israel follows a Hittite model or an Assyrian model, the result is the same, both parties were legally obligated to observe the demands of the covenant.

The covenant between Yahweh and Israel followed the deliverance of the people from the servitude in Egypt. The covenant was not with an individual but with the whole house of Israel. The corporate community, represented by the elders of Israel, agreed to keep the demands of the covenant as it was presented to them by Moses. The covenant was fully accepted by the people. They showed their willingness to abide by the demands of the covenant before and after the ratification of the covenant. By agreeing with the demands of the covenant, the people who came out of Egypt became the people of God and Yahweh became the God of Israel. The covenant was enforced with the blessings for obedience and the curses for disobedience as stated in Deut 27 and 28.

The first occasion when the statement on intergenerational punishment could be applied was at the time Israel built the golden calf. The story of the golden calf as presented in Exod 32–34 is a good example of how the God of the Old Testament lavished his mercy and steadfast love upon the people of Israel. The nature and character of God are displayed in the way God dealt with Israel's violation of the covenant and the worship of the golden calf. In his mercy, God makes his love known. God's mercy is his faithfulness and steadfast love at work.

Soon after the covenant between God and Israel was established, the people of Israel violated the demands of the second command because of the idolatry of the people of Israel. The story of Israel's idolatry is narrated in Exod 32 and its aftermath in Exod 33–34. After the ratification of the covenant, Moses goes up to Mount Sinai to meet with God.

While Moses was on the mountain in the presence of Yahweh, the people believed that Moses was dead because of his long delay in returning to them. When the people saw that Moses was delayed on the mountain, they believed that he would not return to them. The people approached Aaron and demanded that he make the image of a god who would lead them to the land of Canaan. Aaron yielded to their request and using the golden earrings that the women and children had brought from Egypt, he made an image of a young bull. The people proclaimed, "These are your gods, O Israel, who brought you up out of the land of Egypt" (Exod 32:4).

The making and the worship of the golden calf were a violation of the covenant relationship established between God and the people of Israel. By making an idol in the form of a god, the people had violated the first and the Second Commandments and had rejected Yahweh. Because of this violation of the covenant, Yahweh would impose the punishment: he would visit the guilt of the parents upon the children, upon the third and upon the fourth generations of those who had rejected him (Exod 20:5).

Yahweh said to Moses, "Go down at once! Your people, whom you brought up out of the land of Egypt, have acted perversely; they have been quick to turn aside from the way that I commanded them; they have cast for themselves an image of a calf, and have worshiped it and sacrificed to it, and said, 'These are your gods, O Israel, who brought you up out of the land of Egypt!' The LORD said to Moses, 'I have seen this people, how stiff-necked they are. Now let me alone, so that my wrath may burn hot against them and I may consume them'" (Exod 32:7–10).

Twice the text says that God was furious with the action of the people: "God told Moses: Now let me alone, so that my wrath may burn hot against them and I may consume them; and of you I will make a great nation" (Exod 32:10). Moses said to God: "O LORD, why does your wrath burn hot against your people" (Exod 32:11). Even Moses was angry at the betrayal of the people: "As soon as he came near the camp and saw the calf and the dancing, Moses' anger burned hot" (Exod 32:19).

"Let me alone, so that my wrath may burn hot against them and I may consume them." The people had provoked Yahweh to wrath by making an image and by worshiping and sacrificing to it. "Let me alone and I will consume them." These words alone could classify God as a violent God: "I will consume them." But the people knew the consequences of idolatry and the Lord had the right to do what he promised he would do. By consuming the people in his wrath, the first, second, third, and even the fourth generation would perish in this divine judgment.

Because Israel had rejected God by making an image of a god, now God was prepared to invoke the clause which stipulated the consequences for the violation of the Second Commandment. The second command reads as follows: "You shall not make for yourself an idol, whether in the form of anything that is in heaven above, or that is on the earth beneath, or that is in the water under the earth. You shall not bow down to them or worship them; for I the LORD your God am a jealous God, punishing children for the iniquity of parents, to the third and the fourth generation of those who reject me, but showing steadfast love to the thousandth generation of those who love me and keep my commandments" (Exod 20:4-6). Dozeman explains the consequences for the idolatry of Israel: "The command against idolatry in 20:4-6 is framed negatively and stated in terms of love or hate and of obedience or punishment. There is only one consequence for idolatry in the Decalogue."[20]

According to Freeman, the future of Israel revolves around the issue of divine justice and mercy,

> what is to govern the relationship between a righteous God and a sinful people? How may the requirements of just law be reconciled with the claims of absolute love? How can the righteousness of God be vindicated, without denying his grace and mercy? Or, how can God demonstrate affection and forgiveness without undermining the moral structure of the whole universe? Certainly if the "love" of God were not a central feature of the Old Testament these issues could not arise.[21]

MOSES INTERCEDES FOR ISRAEL

According to the words of the Second Commandment, the punishment for idolatry was severe. God was about to visit the covenant breakers and bring the consequences of their sins upon their children to the third and the fourth generation. As a result of the people's idolatry, God told Moses, "Now leave me alone so that my anger may burn against them and that I may destroy them. Then I will make you into a great nation" (Exod 32:10).

These words of God to Moses introduce several important issues about the future of Israel. First, the survival of Israel depends on Moses's work as an intercessor and how he deals with Yahweh. The implication of God's word to Moses, "leave me alone," "is that if Moses does not leave God alone, his wrath cannot burn hot . . . the implication is that God intends one thing but invites Moses to bring him to a place of repentance."[22] Commenting on Moses's contribution to God's decision, Fretheim wrote: "Moses could conceivably contribute something to the divine deliberation that might occasion a future for Israel other than

---

20. Dozeman, *Exodus*, 736.
21. Freedman, "God Compassionate and Gracious," 9.
22. Ellington, "Who Shall Lead Them Out?," 53.

wrath. The devastation of Israel by the divine wrath is thus conditional upon Moses's leaving God alone."[23]

Second, Moses prayed to pacify God and save Israel from God's wrath: "Moses tried to pacify Yahweh his God" (Exod 32:11 NJB). God takes his relationship with Moses seriously and accepts Moses input before the final decision is made. Fretheim explains the role Moses played in God's decision: "God here recognizes the relationship with Moses over having absolute free decision in the matter. The devastation of Israel by the divine wrath is thus conditioned upon Moses giving God leave to do so."[24]

Third, God told Moses, "I will make you into a great nation" (Exod 32:10). God's decision to begin a new nation with Moses and his descendants suggests, as Ellington puts it, "that God's plan is at least partially open. He will bring the descendants of Abraham into the land of promise, but it does not have to be these descendants."[25]

Fourth, by consuming Israel, God would break his promise to Abraham to bring his descendants to the land of Canaan. However, by promising Moses that he would make Moses and his descendants into a great nation, God would still do what he promised Abraham he would do. As Ellington puts it, "Seeking to persuade Moses to remain on the sidelines, Yahweh offers a face-saving solution to the problem that allows for the continuation of the promise made to Abraham. If Moses will remain silent, God can consume 'these people' and start over again, this time with Moses as a new Israel."[26]

Moses knew that God would consume the people because of their idolatry and because of their violation of the covenant. So, Moses interceded on behalf of Israel and asked God to have mercy upon his people. As a result of Moses's prayer, Yahweh repented or changed his mind about the disaster that he planned to bring upon his people (Exod 32:14). The remarkable statement that God repented is not the same as when humans repent of their sins. God's repentance refers to God's response to prayers, to repentance, or to human behavior.

By God's grace, Israel was allowed to live, but not without some cost to God. As Fretheim puts it, "It is clear that human sin has not been

---

23. Fretheim, "Repentance of God," 50.
24. Fretheim, *Exodus*, 284.
25. Ellington, "Who Shall Lead Them Out?," 54.
26. Ellington, "Who Shall Lead Them Out?," 54.

without cost for God, and that cost is due in significant part to the fact that God has chosen to bear the people's sins rather than deal with them on strictly legal terms. For God to assume such a burden, for God to continue to bear the brunt of Israel's rejection, meant continued life for the people. Thus, there is an explicit connection made between divine suffering and Israel's life; the former was necessary for the later to occur. God's suffering made Israel's life possible."[27]

By changing his mind about the punishment, God was saying to Moses that he was willing to bear upon himself the iniquity and transgression and sin of the people, but that he was not willing to clear the guilty. Moses's prayer saved Israel. As the psalmist puts it, "[Yahweh] would have destroyed [the people] had not Moses His chosen one confronted Him in the breach to avert His destructive wrath" (Ps 106:23 TNK).

In his important article on God's repentance, Fretheim wrote: "An appropriate emphasis on divine repentance, however, means that there must always be a reckoning with the effects of the continuing divine-human conversation when thinking about the future. God is ever about the business of making new decisions for new times and places in the light of that ongoing dialogue, which decisions are always in consonance with God's most basic purposes to bring salvation to all."[28]

But the judgment never came. When God told Moses, "leave me alone," God was inviting Moses to intercede on behalf of the people. God expected him to do so. As God said to Ezekiel about the destruction of Jerusalem: "I sought for anyone among them who would repair the wall and stand in the breach before me on behalf of the land, so that I would not destroy it; but I found no one. Therefore, I have poured out my indignation upon them; I have consumed them with the fire of my wrath; I have returned their conduct upon their heads" (Ezek 22:30–31).

The Lord told Ezekiel that he sought anyone to stand in the breach before him on behalf of the land, so that he would not destroy the land; but he found no one. So, Judah was invaded and as a result, thousands died, and thousands were taken into exile.

Now, because of the idolatry of Israel, the people were threatened with destruction. At the time when Israel deserved to be severely punished for its idolatry, for its violation of the covenant, and for its rejection of God, the punishment never came because the unforgiving, vindictive,

---

27. Fretheim, *Suffering of God*, 148.
28. Fretheim, "Repentance of God," 65.

immoral, diabolic violent warrior god removed his mask, the "mask of ugliness," and revealed the true nature of his character, that he is "a gracious God and merciful, slow to anger, and abounding in steadfast love, and ready to relent from punishing."

Moses stood in the breach before Yahweh on behalf of the people and as a result, the people who sinned, their children and grandchildren were not destroyed. Prayer is the most effective way of controlling divine anger. And so is repentance. As I will show in chapter 13 dealing with the destruction of Nineveh, Yahweh had threatened to totally destroy Nineveh. When the leaders of the city heard Jonah's message, they and all the people repented, and the destruction of the city was averted. When Jonah saw that Nineveh was not destroyed, he became angry. He explains his anger to God with these words: "for I knew that you are a gracious God and merciful, slow to anger, and abounding in steadfast love, and ready to relent from punishing" (Jonah 4:2). God was gracious and merciful toward Nineveh, and the city of blood, full of lies and violence (Nah 3:1) was spared.

The prophet Ezekiel said, "The person who sins is the one who will die" (Ezek 18:4 HCSB). The people of Israel sinned against God by breaking the covenant. They provoked Yahweh to anger by building an image of a strange god. As Yahweh had promised, he would punish the evildoers and their families. And Yahweh is faithful in fulfilling his promises. But Yahweh did not destroy the people who deserved to be punished because his mercy is greater than his anger. Even when the people deserved to be severely punished for their rebellion against Yahweh, Yahweh's *ḥesed*, his faithful love, triumphed over his anger and the people lived who deserved to die.

This demonstration of mercy and love does not belong to a vindictive, violent God. God responds to prayer and he accepts the repentance of his people, but even when they did not repent, God's mercy triumphed over his wrath, as the psalmist correctly observed: "he was merciful; he forgave their iniquities and did not destroy them. Time after time he restrained his anger and did not stir up his full wrath" (Ps 78:38 NIV). With these words the psalmist revealed the true nature and character of the God of the Old Testament.

CONCLUSION

Although many people are horrified by the statement on intergenerational punishment, because they perceive it to be cruel and unjust, the reality is that the statement says more about God's mercy than God's violence upon the innocent. As Duke puts it, "The contrast between judgement and mercy could hardly be more extreme. Whereas consequences of guilt could have an impact on one extended living family that breaks covenant with God, God's mercy and love, in great contrast, extend to the thousandth generation for those who keep covenant. Again, we find that our texts are not about a wrath-bearing, vengeful God, but about one who demonstrates covenantal faithfulness to the extreme."[29]

---

29. Duke, "'Visiting the Guilt of the Fathers,'" 353.

10

"The Day I Settle Accounts"

THIS CHAPTER CONTINUES THE STUDY on the character of God based on God's revelation of himself to Moses on Mount Sinai. The specific focus of this chapter is the intergenerational punishment statement in Exod 34:7, "yet by no means clearing the guilty, but visiting the iniquity of the parents upon the children and the children's children, to the third and the fourth generation."

THE GUILTY ONES PAY FOR THEIR SINS

Yahweh changed his mind about the terrible disaster he had threatened to bring upon his people because of their apostasy with the golden calf, however, he did not leave the guilty unpunished. Those who were involved in the worship of the golden calf were held accountable for their transgressions for God forgives iniquity and transgression and sin, yet God by no means clears those who are guilty (Exod 34:7).

When Moses came down from Mount Sinai, he

> stood at the gate of the camp and shouted, "Who is for Yahweh? To me!" And all the Levites rallied round him. He said to them, "Yahweh, God of Israel, says this, Buckle on your sword, each of you, and go up and down the camp from gate to gate, every man of you slaughtering brother, friend and neighbour." The Levites did as Moses said, and of the people about three thousand men perished that day. (Exod 32:26–28 NJB)

Boyd calls the death of the guilty people another example of divinely sanctioned violence with Moses. He wrote,

> Yahweh is depicted as ordering the massacre of multitudes of others through his servant Moses. For example, in response to the idolatry of the Israelites while he was on Mount Sinai, Moses reported that Yahweh told him to have each of the Levites "strap a sword to his side." They were to then "go back and forth through the camp from one end to the other, each killing his brother and friend and neighbor." The Levites did as Moses commanded, and the narrative reports that "about three thousand" people died that day (Exod 32:27–28). Moses congratulated the willingness of the Levites to slaughter "brothers, friends and neighbors," saying that this "set [them] apart to the Lord." In the view of the author of this narrative, this ruthless bloodshed of their kin apparently rendered these Levites holy and "blessed" (Exod 32:29).[1]

Boyd is more critical of Moses and God than of those rebellious Israelites who worshiped the image of the golden calf. Moses understood the gravity of what the people had done. This is the reason he offered his life as an atonement for the people's sin. God refused Moses's offer because he was not guilty of the sin of rebellion; he decided to punish those who had rejected him. Those rebellious Israelites who violated the first and the Second Commandments rejected God and deliberately rejected the demands of the covenant. They died because the time of visitation had arrived, "in the day when I visit I will visit their sin upon them" (Exod 32:34). They died because they sinned against God, "The person who sins shall die" (Ezek 18:20). They died because of their iniquity, "if the righteous turn from their righteousness and commit iniquity . . . they shall die for their sin" (Ezek 3:20). They died because God is a holy God whose eyes are too pure to behold evil, a God who cannot look on wickedness with favor (Hab 1:13).

Since all have sinned (1 Kgs 8:46; 2 Chr 8:46; Eccl 7:20), no one can stand in the presence of God apart from his grace and mercy. Since the worshipers of the golden calf rejected God, they sinned and died according to the stipulations of the Second Commandment. They could have died of natural causes or old age but dying of natural causes or old age would not communicate to the community the gravity of their sin. The justice of God was on trial. Since God uses agents to bring justice

---

1. Boyd, *Crucifixion of the Warrior God*, 310–11.

to rebellious people, God used human agents to carry out divine justice. God is a God of love but also a God of judgment. As Freedman expressed,

> The God who has chosen Israel in love, and delivered it from bondage, must nevertheless sit in judgment over his people. He must deal with sin and rebellion. He may be merciful and ready to forgive, but without repentance on their part, there can be no reconciliation. Responsibility, morality, and judgment cannot be separated from his love. They point to the apparent paradox of a God who can choose and reject, forgive and punish, save and condemn.[2]

But the whole nation was still guilty before God. On the next day, after the worshipers of the golden calf had died, Moses said to the people, "You have sinned a great sin. But now I will go up to Yahweh; perhaps I can make atonement for your sin" (Exod 32:30). So, Moses goes back to God and once again he prayed for the people with a bold prayer. Moses said to God: "But now, please forgive their sin—but if not, then blot me out of the book you have written" (Exod 32:32 NIV). Moses comes before God and identifies himself with his sinful people. He is willing to die with the people and offers his own life to spare the lives of people from the death they deserved. In his study of Moses's prayer, Widmer writes,

> when Moses asks to be erased from God's record, he appears to express a willingness to be cut off from his relationship with Yhwh and thus subjects himself to curse and eventual death . . . he is prepared to bear the divine wrath with the sinful and to die with them if Yhwh will not give them a second chance.[3]

GOD REVEALS HIS CHARACTER TO MOSES

But the punishment of Israel was not yet over. Although the lives of the people were spared, "Yhwh reserves the sovereign right to judge whoever sinned against Him and announces a day of judgment."[4] Yahweh told Moses: "Now go, lead the people to the place I told you about; see, My angel will go before you. But on the day I settle accounts, I will hold them accountable for their sin" (Exod 32:34 HCSB). Yahweh did not consume

---

2. Freedman, "God Compassionate and Gracious," 17.
3. Widmer, *Standing in the Breach*, 88–89.
4. Widmer, *Standing in the Breach*, 88–89.

the people and he did not take away Moses's life. Instead, Yahweh forgave the people and the punishment they deserved was delayed. Yahweh told Moses, "on the day I settle accounts, I will hold them accountable for their sin." The people were forgiven because of Moses, but eventually they would have to give an account to God for their sins.

Then Yahweh sent a plague on the people, because they had made the image of the calf and had proclaimed that it was the god who had brought them out of the land of Egypt (Exod 32:4). The plague was sent because the whole nation was guilty of celebrating a festival to an image whom they identified as their redeemer god.

> Yahweh said to Moses, "Say to the Israelites, You are a stiffnecked people; if for a single moment I should go up among you, I would consume you. So now take off your ornaments, and I will decide what to do to you." (Exod 33:5)

It is important to take literally what God told the people. He said to them, "I will decide what to do to you" (Exod 33:5). Yahweh had not yet decided what to do with the people who had rebelled against him. The future was open to God because his final decision would be based on what Moses and the people would do in the near future. Since the people had not yet made a decision, God could not decide what to do to Israel.

Since Yahweh had not yet decided what to do with Israel, Moses went back to God and told him, "if I have found favor in your sight, show me your ways" (Exod 33:13). Then Moses said, "Show me your glory" (Exod 33:14). In response, Yahweh said to Moses,

> I will do the very thing that you have asked; for you have found favor in my sight, and I know you by name. I will make all my goodness pass before you, and will proclaim before you the name, "Yahweh"; and I will be gracious to whom I will be gracious, and will show mercy on whom I will show mercy. (Exod: 33:17-19)

As a result, Yahweh revealed the true nature of his character to Moses:

> Yahweh, Yahweh, a God merciful and gracious, slow to anger, and abounding in steadfast love and faithfulness, keeping steadfast love for the thousandth generation, forgiving iniquity and transgression and sin, yet by no means clearing the guilty, but visiting the iniquity of the parents upon the children and the

children's children, to the third and the fourth generation (Exod 34:6–7).

This is what Yahweh says about himself: Yahweh is a merciful and gracious God, a God who is slow to anger and a God who abounds in steadfast love and faithfulness. Yahweh is a God who keeps steadfast love for the thousandth generation, a God who forgives iniquity and transgression and sin.

However, notwithstanding his nature as a merciful and gracious God, Yahweh is also a God who by no means clears the guilty. The punishment of the guilty person may be extended to the third and the fourth generation, but not always. All the people, with the exception of the ones who worshiped the golden calf, were not punished for their sin because Moses interceded for them. In the case of the Ninevites, the whole nation escaped divine punishment because they repented at the preaching of Jonah. The law says that the sinner must die, but the mercy of God allows them to live.

THE IDEA OF DELAYED PUNISHMENT

The statement of intergenerational punishment says that the punishment of God upon those who reject him may be postponed until the second, third, or fourth generation. The reason for this delay is, again, the mercy of God for the sinner. Yochanan Muffs wrote: "There is available to the righteous an inexhaustible fund of divine grace which they enjoy, as do their progeny after them for a thousand generations; But God also wants to treat the wicked in a kind fashion. God bears their sins but does not expunge it entirely."[5]

The Hebrew word for "forgive" is *nāsā'*. When the word *nāsā'* is used together with the words "sins" and "iniquities," the expression means "to load sin upon oneself," and "to (have to) bear (the punitive consequences of) one's guilt." God forgives the sins of Israel by bearing the people's sins upon himself. This bearing of sins is a demonstration of God's grace: "He bears the sin is an expression of grace. The punishment has been delayed, the people have been forgiven, but the forgiveness is not complete."[6]

---

5. Muffs, "Who Will Stand in the Breach?," 20.
6. Muffs, "Who Will Stand in the Breach?," 21.

The idea that God forgives the sinners but does not revoke the punishment is found in the book of Psalms. The psalmist said: "Yahweh our God, you answered them, you were a God of forgiveness to them, but punished them for their sins" (Ps 99:8 NJB). This text says three things about God:

"Yahweh our God, you answered them"—Yahweh is a God of mercy.

"Yahweh, you were a God of forgiveness to them"—Yahweh is a God who took upon himself the people's sins.

"Yahweh, you punished them for their sins"—Yahweh is a God who does not clear the guilty.

The concept of delayed punishment is clearly illustrated in the story of Ahab. Ahab was an evil king. The writer of Kings says the following about him: "Ahab son of Omri did evil in the sight of the LORD more than all who were before him" (1 Kgs 16:30). The prophet Elijah told Ahab that a severe punishment would come upon him and his house because of all his sins.

> When Ahab heard those words, he tore his clothes and put sackcloth over his bare flesh; he fasted, lay in the sackcloth, and went about dejectedly. Then the word of the LORD came to Elijah the Tishbite: "Have you seen how Ahab has humbled himself before me? Because he has humbled himself before me, I will not bring the disaster in his days; but in his son's days I will bring the disaster on his house." (1 Kgs 21:27–29)

The sins of Ahab were forgiven because he repented, however, as Muffs wrote, "The repentance saves the sinner. But the sin must still be paid for and expunged."[7]

Isaiah talks about deferred punishment: "For my name's sake I defer my anger, for the sake of my praise I restrain it for you, that I may not cut you off" (Isa 48:9 ESV). And so did the author of Ecclesiastes: "because the punishment decreed for an evil act is not promptly carried out; therefore people who plan to do evil are strengthened in their intentions" (Eccl 8:11 CJB).

---

7. Muffs, "Who Will Stand in the Breach?," 18.

The concept of deferred punishment is hard for people in the twenty-first century to accept. Muffs talks about modern sensibility: "One might ask how a human being could make peace with such Divine forgiveness. This whole procedure is the height of cruelty—it has nothing to do with mercy, at least according to modern sensibility. This merely goes to show how different the moral sensibilities of the ancients are from our own. Those wicked people whose punishment has been delayed because of their personal repentance or the merit of their fathers think that it is a good thing, even if their children bear the sins of their parents."[8]

THE WAGES OF SIN

In light of the punishment of those who sinned against God, one might ask, "was the punishment of the evil doers justified?" People criticize God as a violent God because he punished those who sinned against him. Society today has a low view of sin and practically no idea of the holiness of God. If people would believe that sin is a great offense against God, then there would be no problem in accepting the punishment of the evildoers in Exod 32:28, because, as the prophet Ezekiel said, "The person who sins is the one who will die" (Ezek 18:4 HCSB) or as the apostle Paul said, "the wages of sin is death" (Rom 6:23).

Jesus said:

> For God so loved the world that he gave his only Son, so that everyone who believes in him may not perish but may have eternal life. Indeed, God did not send the Son into the world to condemn the world, but in order that the world might be saved through him. Those who believe in him are not condemned; but those who do not believe are condemned already, because they have not believed in the name of the only Son of God. (John 3:16–18)

Jesus said that those who reject him "are condemned already." In the mind of some people, these are not words of love. For Jesus to say that people are condemned already because they do not believe could be considered by some an act of violence, but people who reject Jesus will die in their sins because God "by no means clears the guilty" unless they repent and believe. Jesus Christ, our God and Savior (2 Pet 1:1), said to some of the Jewish leaders, "if you do not believe that I am He, you will

---

8. Muffs, "Who Will Stand in the Breach?," 19.

die in your sins" (John 8:24 NJB). For Jesus to impose the death penalty for the act of unbelief could also be considered an act of violence.

But sin is sin and as Paul said, "the wages of sin is death" (Rom 6:23). The people who sinned against God by worshiping the golden calf died, just as Paul said that sinners die because they are sinners—"the wages of sin is death"—and because God "by no means clears the guilty" unless they come to repentance. It does not matter whether they die of natural causes, by the plague, by the hands of their enemies, or by the hand of members of the community who were set apart to execute divine judgment. The three thousand people died because they rejected God and because they were sinners: "the wages of sin is death."

CONCLUSION

We may evaluate the punishment of those who sinned against God by considering what Fretheim says about divine punishment:

> Moreover, God's extraordinary patience reveals the length to which God will go for the sake of the future of the relationship. In patience, God goes beyond justice again and again. Judgment is thus never simply a juristic matter, as if measured objectively in terms of an external ordinance. A relationship is at stake, not an agreement or a contract or a set of rules. The judgment that does fall may be in fact entail an "eye for an eye" correspondence, but that comes only on the far side of slowness to anger revealing a fundamental "lack of fairness" on God's part, if God's actions are measured in terms of a strict standard of justice. In terms of any straightforward legal thinking, God is too much lenient. But such corresponsive thought is important; for should judgment come, it will be seen to be absolute fair in terms of any human canon of accountability.[9]

People in the twenty-first century may not accept the way God deals with human sins because God by no means clears the guilty. As God said, "on the day I settle accounts, I will hold them accountable for their sin" (Exod 32:34). God's way of dealing with sins and iniquities is strange to modern sensibilities, but, as God said, "my thoughts are not your thoughts, neither are your ways my ways, declares the LORD" (Isa 55:8).

---

9. Fretheim, *Suffering of God*, 125.

11

The Case of the Twelve Spies

THIS CHAPTER CONTINUES THE STUDY of the character of God based on God's revelation of himself to Moses on Mount Sinai. The specific focus of this chapter continues to be the intergenerational punishment statement in Exod 34:7, "yet by no means clearing the guilty, but visiting the iniquity of the parents upon the children and the children's children, to the third and the fourth generation." This chapter deals with the case of the twelve spies and the intergenerational punishment statement in Num 14.

THE INTERGENERATIONAL PUNISHMENT STATEMENT IN NUMBERS 14

Numbers 14 is an important passage for the proper understanding of how the intergenerational punishment statement worked out in most cases in the history of Israel. In order to provide the foundation for the reasons of why the enforcement of the intergenerational punishment statement happened the way it happened, four passages from both the Old and New Testaments will serve as biblical background for the proper understanding of the enforcement of the intergenerational punishment statement.

The first passage is Jesus's words to the Jewish leaders: "I told you that you would die in your sins, for you will die in your sins unless you believe that I am he" (John 8:24). In John 8:58, Jesus identifies himself with God. When Jesus said, "before Abraham was, I am," he was identifying himself with the great I AM of Exod 3:14. Thus, the words of Jesus to the Jewish leaders were that whoever does not believe in God will die in their sins.

The second passage is Paul's declaration about humanity: "For the wages of sin is death" (Rom 6:23). The consequences of sin is death. This is the same message Ezekiel announced twice during his ministry, "The person who sins is the one who will die" (Ezek 18:4 HCSB) and "The person who sins shall die" (Ezek 18:20). Every person who sins will die because, as the Yahweh said, "for the treachery of which they are guilty and the sin they have committed, they shall die" (Ezek 18:24).

The third passage is Yahweh's words to Moses at the time the people of Israel made the image of the golden calf to worship. Yahweh told Moses that he was a God who "does not leave the guilty unpunished" (Exod 34:7). Yahweh may delay his visitation upon the sinner, but he will not exonerate the guilty person from his sins, unless that person repents.

The fourth passage is also Yahweh's words to Moses in response to Moses's intercession on behalf of Israel. When Yahweh forgave the people for making the golden calf, Yahweh told Moses, "Nevertheless, in the day when I visit, I will visit their sin upon them" (Exod 32:34). Or, as the HSCB puts it, "But on the day I settle accounts, I will hold them accountable for their sin" (Exod 32:34 HCSB). The story of the spies in Num 14 is a story of Yahweh's settling accounts with the people of Israel.

THE TWELVE SPIES

Numbers 14 deals with Moses sending twelve men to survey the land of Canaan, their report to the people, and the consequences of their reluctance to enter the land. Since this story is well known, I will provide only a summary of Num 13–14.

According to the text, it was Yahweh himself who proposed to Moses to send spies to reconnoiter the land of Canaan (Num 13:1). Moses selected twelve men, one each from their ancestral tribes; each one of them was a leader in Israel. These twelve men represented all the people of Israel. These men represented the whole community, thus, when they presented a negative report to the people, they were speaking on behalf of the whole nation.

They spent forty days scouting the land. At the end of forty days, they returned to the camp and brought a report to all Israel: "they brought back word to them and to all the congregation" (Num 13:26). However, their report was very negative:

> Yet the people who live in the land are strong, and the towns are fortified and very large; and besides, we saw the descendants of Anak there. The Amalekites live in the land of the Negeb; the Hittites, the Jebusites, and the Amorites live in the hill country; and the Canaanites live by the sea, and along the Jordan. . . . The land that we have gone through as spies is a land that devours its inhabitants; and all the people that we saw in it are of great size. There we saw the Nephilim (the Anakites come from the Nephilim); and to ourselves we seemed like grasshoppers, and so we seemed to them. (Num 13:28–33)

When the people heard the words of the spies, they raised a loud cry and the people wept that night. The people complained against Moses and Aaron and

> the whole congregation said to them, "would that we had died in the land of Egypt! Or would that we had died in this wilderness! Why is the LORD bringing us into this land to fall by the sword? Our wives and our little ones will become booty; would it not be better for us to go back to Egypt?" So they said to one another, "Let us choose a captain, and go back to Egypt." (Num 14:2–5)

By expressing their desire to return to Egypt, the people were rejecting what Yahweh had done in redeeming them from their slavery in Egypt and they were not trusting Yahweh's power to bring them to the land of promise. The people's attitude was, for all practical purposes, a revocation of the covenant and a rejection of their relationship which they had established with Yahweh on Mount Sinai. The people's propensity to want to return to Egypt was real. In Exod 13:17 Yahweh recognized that, when faced with a possible war against the Philistines, the people might express their desire to return to Egypt: "If the people face war, they may change their minds and return to Egypt" (Exod 13:17).

Joshua and Caleb were the only two spies who supported going into Canaan at that time. Faced with the rebellion of the people, Joshua told them, "do not rebel against Yahweh" (Num 14:9), but the people threatened to stone them. Then Yahweh appeared to Moses and said, "How long will this people despise me? And how long will they refuse to believe in me, in spite of all the signs that I have done among them?" (Num 14:10–11). Yahweh accused the people of rejecting him and refusing to believe in him. The people failed to believe that God would fight for them, deliver them from their enemies, and give them the land of Canaan as he had promise to Abraham. The problem with the people was that they lacked faith to believe that the same God who performed all those miraculous signs in Egypt could do the same as they prepared to face their enemies.

MOSES INTERCEDES ON BEHALF OF ISRAEL

After the people expressed their desire to return to Egypt, Yahweh said to Moses, "How long will this people despise me? And how long will they refuse to believe in me, in spite of all the signs that I have done among them?" (Num 14:11). The people of Israel sinned against Yahweh by despising him and by not believing that he was powerful to deliver them from the hands of their enemies.

Because of the people's unfaithfulness, once again Yahweh threatened to destroy Israel and create a new nation with Moses and his descendants (see Exod 32:10 and Deut 9:14). However, in this story of Israel's rebellion and a threat of punishment, not once does the writer mention divine wrath. Instead, twice Yahweh expresses his frustration with Israel with a language of lament, "How long" (Num 14:11), "How long" (Num 14:27). These two lament questions, according to Fretheim, express "divine wonderment over what has happened."[1] Fretheim explains the use of the "how long" questions by saying that they represent "a cry that contains two key elements: complaint with respect to something that is believed to have gone on long enough, and anguish over the abandonment and its seeming finality."[2]

In response to the rebellion of the people, Yahweh passed his judgment: "I will strike them with pestilence and disinherit them, and I will make of you [Moses] a nation greater and mightier than they" (Num 14:12). First, God said that he would "strike them with pestilence." The word pestilence refers to any kind plague or disease that causes human death or the death of animals (Exod 9:3; Num 11:33). Second, the Lord said that he would "disinherit them." In her study of Num 14, Sakenfeld said that "The contexts suggest that the action is regarded as tantamount to rejection of the whole covenant relationship, an action which Yahweh

---

1. Fretheim, *Suffering of God*, 122.
2. Fretheim, *Suffering of God*, 121.

must treat in judgment."³ This disowning of Israel means, according to Levine, that "Israel will no longer be God's inheritance."⁴ Third, the Lord said that he would make of Moses a great and powerful nation instead of Israel. This is the same promise God made to Moses at the time of the apostasy of the golden calf.

In Num 14:11, the question is followed by an announcement of judgment in verse 12. Yet that announcement is not irrevocable, as what follows in the dialogue between Yahweh and Moses reveals. As Fretheim puts it, "the question is a genuine question, intended to draw forth a positive response in leaders and people, so that the announced judgment may be forestalled."⁵

Carolyn Pressler says that the announcement of judgment was made by a spurned God who acts out of anguish.⁶ The divine threat to disinherit Israel and make of Moses a nation greater and mightier than Israel ((Num 14:12) would compromise the promise Yahweh made to Abraham that he would make "of you a great nation" (Gen 12:2).

YAHWEH FORGIVES ISRAEL

Yahweh consults Moses before announcing the judgment on Israel. Moses intercedes for Israel by appealing to Yahweh's reputation. Moses tells Yahweh that the Egyptians will hear what Yahweh has done to Israel and they will tell the Canaanites: "Egyptians will hear of it, for in your might you brought up this people from among them, and they will tell the inhabitants of this land" (Num 14:13–14). Thus, Yahweh's failure to bring the people to Canaan shows that Yahweh does not have the power to save his people. "The logic of Moses' argument here and in Exod 34:6–7," according to Milgrom, "is that God's reputation as a compassionate divine being, as well as a powerful one, will suffer if Israel perishes."⁷

Moses then appeals to the merciful character of Yahweh by repeating the divine attributes revealed to him on Mount Sinai:

> And now, therefore, let the power of the LORD be great in the way that you promised when you spoke, saying, "The LORD is

---

3. Sakenfeld, "Problem of Divine Forgiveness," 321.
4. Levine, *Numbers 1–20*, 110.
5. Fretheim, *Suffering of God*, 114.
6. Pressler, *Numbers*, 130.
7. Milgrom, *Numbers*, 366.

slow to anger, and abounding in steadfast love, forgiving iniquity and transgression, but by no means clearing the guilty, visiting the iniquity of the parents upon the children to the third and the fourth generation." Forgive the iniquity of this people according to the greatness of your steadfast love, just as you have pardoned this people, from Egypt even until now. (Num 14:17–19)[8]

Moses knew that the sin of the people was very great and that they did not deserve the mercy of Yahweh, thus Moses asked Yahweh to forgive his people according to his great *ḥesed*, "according to the greatness of your steadfast love." Moses's recognition that Yahweh visits "the iniquity of the parents upon the children to the third and the fourth generation" coupled with his declaration that Yahweh had forgiven the iniquities of the people "from Egypt even until now" (Num 14:19) is an affirmation that divine grace restrains divine justice so that the people are not punished because of their sins. Thus, the statement that Yahweh punishes the sin of the fathers on the children to the third and fourth generation "is not an expression of strict justice and total destruction, as it is usually understood."[9] The expression "just as you have pardoned this people from the time they left Egypt until now" (Num 14:19) emphasizes that in the many rebellions of Israel, Yahweh had not destroyed them, rather he had carried their sins "until the time He actually punishes them, in other words, until they die a natural death."[10]

The version of the divine attributes in Num 14 differs slightly from Exod 34. The version here is somewhat abbreviated and it is presented differently from Exodus The words "the LORD, a God merciful and gracious," "faithfulness," and "keeping steadfast love for the thousandth generation" in Exod 34:6–7 were omitted in Num 14:18. According to Scharbert, these words were obviously omitted on purpose. The words of the spies and the people's decision not to enter the land were a rejection of Yahweh, thus, these people were not among the "thousands" worthy of the promised divine grace. Thus, an appeal to Yahweh, the one "keeping

---

8. Pressler, *Numbers*, 129–30 says that the "words in verse 18 are a shortened form of a liturgical confession. Most fully expressed in Exod 34:6–7, the confession is among the central statements of Israel's understanding of its God. This can be seen in the way the formula functions in the Exodus passage, where it is linked to, or perhaps is even a full statement of, YHWH's name."
9. Muffs, "Who Will Stand in the Breach?," 21.
10. Muffs, "Who Will Stand in the Breach?," 22.

steadfast love for the thousandth generation" (Exod 34:7), would be out of place here.[11]

Once again, Moses acts as an intercessor for Israel before Yahweh, the same role he had during the crisis in Exod 32 after the golden calf incident. Here, as in Exod 32, Yahweh told Moses that he was planning to consume Israel for its apostasy and violation of the demands of the covenant. Moses appeals to Yahweh saying that the Egyptians will see how he destroyed the people in the wilderness and then they will tell the Canaanites that Yahweh was unable to deliver his people. Yahweh had proposed that Moses and his descendants would replace the people of Israel. In its place, Yahweh would make Moses and his descendants into a great nation (Exod 32:10; Num 14:12). Moses refused Yahweh's offer and again interceded on behalf of Israel and asked Yahweh to forgive the people according to his merciful nature and fulfill his promise to Abraham to bring the people to the land of promise.

Yahweh told Moses that he was planning to strike the people with pestilence and disown them (Num 14:12), but once again, because of Moses's prayer, Yahweh changed his mind. Yahweh said to Moses,

> I forgive them as you ask. But—as I live, and as the glory of Yahweh fills the whole world—of all these people who have seen my glory and the signs that I worked in Egypt and in the desert, who have put me to the test ten times already and not obeyed my voice, not one shall see the country which I promised to give their ancestors. Not one of those who have treated me contemptuously will see it. (Num 14:20–23 NJB)

Yahweh's decision did not change the divine plan to bring Israel to the promised land, but this action will be delayed. Yahweh will not allow the present generation, the generation of those who rebelled against him, to enter the land of promise. They will die in the wilderness. However, Yahweh will allow their children and grandchildren, all the people under the age of twenty to enter the land of Canaan: "And as for your little ones, who you thought would become booty, your children, who today do not yet know right from wrong, they shall enter there; to them I will give it, and they shall take possession of it" (Deut 1:39). Muffs calls attention to the idea of deferred punishment.[12] Concerning the survival of the community, Sakenfeld writes, "Forgiveness is announced and yet in the

---

11. Scharbert, "Formgeschichte und Exegese von Ex 34,6," 132.
12. Muffs, "Who Will Stand in the Breach?," 16–21.

same breath God announces the punishment of the rebels. It is essential to recognize that the real content of God's forgiveness here is in the non-destruction of the people, in the very continuation of his relationship to the community as his community. . . . Yahweh's willingness to maintain the covenant relationship is based solely in his great *ḥesed*, just as it has been from the time of the initiation of the relationship with the people in the Exodus."[13]

In response to Moses's prayer, Yahweh told Moses, "I do forgive, just as you have asked." The Hebrew word *sālaḥ* is used in the Old Testament to refer to Yahweh's pardoning and forgiving sinners. Yahweh told Moses that the people had tested him these ten times. Jesus said, "Do not put the Lord your God to the test" (Luke 4:12; cf. Deut 6:16) and yet, the people of Israel tested him ten times. Moses's prayer was effective, Yahweh forgave the sin of the people, but the people still had to bear the consequences of their sin. The consequence of sin is death: "the person who sins shall die" (Ezek 18:4).

THE JUDGMENT OF ISRAEL

Yahweh forgave the people; however, divine forgiveness came with one caveat. Yahweh told Moses,

> nevertheless—as I live, and as all the earth shall be filled with the glory of the LORD—none of the people who have seen my glory and the signs that I did in Egypt and in the wilderness, and yet have tested me these ten times and have not obeyed my voice, shall see the land that I swore to give to their ancestors; none of those who despised me shall see it. (Num 14:20–23)

One issue that is raised by some people about the intergenerational punishment statement in Exod 34:7 is whether Yahweh literally visits the sins of the fathers on the generations yet to be born. The punishment of the people in Num 14 provides important information about this question; Num 14 indicates that the answer is "no." In Numbers the whole community violated the covenant and for this reason, the whole community was held accountable for their rejection of Yahweh's gift of the land.

The expected consequence of the apostasy of Israel would be the destruction of the covenant community. However, because Moses prayed on behalf of the community, Yahweh answered Moses's prayer and of the

---

13. Sakenfeld, "Problem of Divine Forgiveness," 326.

twelve men who were sent to spy the land, Yahweh punished only ten men who had deceived the people: "the men who brought an unfavorable report about the land died by a plague before the LORD" (Num 14:37). They died because they sinned against Yahweh: "it is only the person who sins that shall die" (Ezek 18:4).

The parents and the adults who demanded that the people return to Egypt were forbidden to enter the land of Canaan because of their rejection of Yahweh and they died of natural causes in the wilderness. The people who died in the wilderness were the first, the second, and some people of the third generation. The people who were condemned to die in the desert were punished because they despised Yahweh and refused to believe in him (Num 14:11, 23). So egregious was the act of despising Yahweh that Sakenfeld said that it was "an act which *cannot* go unpunished, in that some divine response is required in terms of God's administration of worldly justice. The texts apparently assume that divine punishment is the inevitable consequence of 'despising' Yahweh. Once judgment is announced, there is no possibility of removing it."[14] The reason for this finality about the judgment is because despising Yahweh is the kind of sin for which there is no sacrifice that can conduce to expiation. The threat that Yahweh made to completely destroy the people of Israel (Num 14:12) did not happen. Yahweh answered Moses's prayer and the people survived. But, as Moses was aware, Yahweh by no means clears the guilty (Num 14:18), thus, the people who despised the Lord would not see the land (Num 14: 22–24, 30–32). Yahweh forgives sin and rebellion but there is always a consequence for sinning against Yahweh. Although the people experienced Yahweh's promise to keep the relationship with them, the judgment on the people for despising Yahweh remains a fact that could not be rescinded.

THE JUDGMENT OF THE CHILDREN

Caleb and Joshua, and the children of the second and third generation were not punished for the sins of the generation that came out of Egypt. The children under the age of twenty suffered because of the sins of their fathers: "And your children shall be shepherds in the wilderness for forty years, and shall suffer for your faithlessness, until the last of your dead bodies lies in the wilderness" (Num 14:33). These children, some of them

---

14. Sakenfeld, "Problem of Divine Forgiveness," 321.

belonged to the second generation, but most of them would be members of the third and the fourth generation. The children suffered because of the faithlessness of their parents, but they did not die in the wilderness. They, Joshua, and Caleb survived the forty years wandering in the desert. After a long journey in the wilderness, they entered the land of promise.

Concerning the judgment of the children, Fretheim wrote,

> One characteristic of communal judgment is that no clean distinction can be made between the righteous and the wicked. . . . Because life is so interrelated, the righteous and the innocent (e.g. children) are often caught up in the judgmental effects of other people's sins. In other words, they will undergo the experience of judgment in ways that are often devastating to their life and health."[15]

When Yahweh visited the fathers and the second generation for their sin, the visitation was not by violence; their death was not at the hands of their enemies nor at the hand of Yahweh. Rather, they were visited with natural death, the lot of every individual in this world. The third and the fourth generation did not die in the wilderness, but by God's mercy, they were allowed to live, even though they had to pay for the sins of their parents.

The statement of intergenerational punishment is as follows: "yet by no means clearing the guilty, but visiting the iniquity of the parents upon the children and the children's children, to the third and the fourth generation" (Exod 34:7). But here is how the statement of intergenerational punishment works in the three passages studied so far. In the case of Exod 20:5, the intergenerational punishment that appears in the Ten Commandments, the people who worshiped the golden calf were not killed because Moses interceded for them and they lived. The guilty people died, but the visitation upon the second, third, and fourth generation was averted because of Moses's prayer. Although the statement on intergenerational punishment does not appear in the book of Jonah, the visitation upon the Ninevites, upon the fathers and all generations, was averted because they all repented.

In the case of the spies, the guilty ones died because Yahweh does not clear the guilty, but the parents died of natural death and the children

---

15. Fretheim, "'I Was Only a Little Angry,'" 369. Berlejung, "Sin and Punishment," 279 said that "When sin and punishment are collective, there is the possibility that innocent individuals are part of that collective. The innocent can become collateral damage in such cases."

under the age of twenty survived, even though they had to live in the wilderness forty years because of the faithlessness of their parents.

In all three cases, there was no violence upon the children. In all three cases only the guilty ones were punishment, Yahweh did not act violently against the innocent; only the guilty ones were punished with some kind of punishment, because as Yahweh said, he by no means clears the guilty (Exod 34:7).

Most of the people who sinned against Yahweh survived because of Moses's prayer or because of their repentance. In all these cases, Yahweh showed himself to be "a God merciful and gracious, slow to anger, and abounding in steadfast love and faithfulness, keeping steadfast love for the thousandth generation, forgiving iniquity and transgression and sin."

However, because Yahweh does not clear the guilty, since "the wages of sin is death," some people died because they deliberately rejected Yahweh. But, when it comes to "visiting the iniquity of the parents upon the children and the children's children, to the third and the fourth generation," the intergenerational punishment as stated in Exod 20:5, 34:7, and Num 14:18 did not happen. As Fretheim puts, it, "God's anger, which threatens judgment, can be turned aside by human repentance (Joel 2:13) or intercession (Exod 32:9–14) or by God's own independent decision (Exod 4:14; Hos 11:8–9)."[16] The Deuteronomic writer emphasizes intergenerational punishment, however, when properly understood, the kings of Israel and Judah did not die because of the sins of their fathers, each king died for his own sin, a truth that Ezekiel emphasized to the people in exile (Ezek 18:4).

The violation of the covenant brought consequences upon the whole community; thus, when the community experienced war of conquests, the Arameans, the Assyrians, and the Babylonians punished the community without pity killing men, women, and children, young and old.

In the case of the twelve spies, where the community violated the covenant, Yahweh allowed the present generation to live; their punishment was that they would die in the wilderness without being able to enter the land of promise. This pattern was repeated through the history of Israel. The people violated the covenant, Yahweh in his mercy allowed them to live and he kept his covenant with them in order to maintain the relationship. But as Yahweh had said, when the day to settle accounts would arrive, eventually Yahweh would hold the people accountable for

---

16. Fretheim, "Reflections on the Wrath of God," 13.

their sins. For the people in the Northern Kingdom, after two hundred years of violating the covenant, the day to settle accounts arrived in 722 BCE. and at that time Yahweh held the people accountable for their sins. For the people of Judah, after almost four hundred years of violating the covenant, the day to settle accounts arrived in 587 BCE. and at that time Yahweh held the people accountable for their sins.

12

The Alien Work of God

For the LORD will rise up as on Mount Perazim, he will rage as in the valley of Gibeon; to do his deed—strange is his deed! and to work his work—alien is his work!

—Isa 28:21

THE HISTORICAL CONTEXT

Isaiah 28:21 speaks of the work of Yahweh as "strange" and "alien." Scholars are divided on the meaning of Isaiah's words because his statement is not very clear since he does not provide a definition of what he means by "strange" and "alien." One way of understanding what the prophet meant by these words is by studying the context of his oracle.[1]

Isaiah 28 is an oracle in which Isaiah emphatically declares Yahweh's judgment upon both Ephraim (the Northern Kingdom) and Judah (the Southern Kingdom) because of their many violations of the covenant. Scholars agree that this oracle is dated to the time of Hezekiah as he prepared to revolt against Sennacherib, king of Assyria (705–701 BCE). Isaiah 28:1–6 is an indictment against the Northern Kingdom, probably

---

1. Blenkinsopp, "Judah's Covenant with Death," 472–83.

a reference to the fall of Samaria and the end of the Northern Kingdom in 722 BCE.

Isaiah 28:7–22 is an indictment against the Southern Kingdom and an announcement of the imminent judgment against the nation. In verse 7, Isaiah accuses the priests and the prophets of being drunk with strong drink and blames them for the spiritual condition of the people. In 28:15 the prophet accuses the priests and prophets of making a "covenant with Death" and "an agreement with Sheol." The covenant with Death probably refers to Judah's alliance with Egypt as Judah prepared to face the Assyrian threat: "Alas for those who go down to Egypt for help and who rely on horses, who trust in chariots because they are many and in horsemen because they are very strong, but do not look to the Holy One of Israel or consult the LORD" (Isa 31:1).[2]

THE ALIEN WORK OF GOD

Scholars differ on the meaning of the "strange" and "alien" work of God, what von Rad calls the "dark reverse side of the work of Jahweh" because of the theological ambivalence this statement reveals about Yahweh: Yahweh is a God who judges and a God who saves.[3] John Bright believes that the alien work of God is that God was fighting against Israel. Bright wrote: "Yahweh was himself fighting against Jerusalem as David once did."[4]

Philips Long says that the alien work of God is a return of the holy war in which Yahweh fights against Israel. He wrote: "The prophetic proclamation of God's future is to be termed eschatological in the sense that the previous history of God with Israel reaches its end, an end in history, which Isaiah, for example, in the return to the old holy war, in which Yahweh now fights against Israel instead of for her (28:21)."[5]

In his reflection on Abraham Lincoln's Second Inaugural Address, the war between North and South, and the problem of evil, Walter Sundberg wrote,

---

2. Mastnjak, "Judah's Covenant with Assyria," 465 believes that Judah's covenant was made with Assyria and not with Egypt.
3. Rad, *Old Testament Theology*, 2:164.
4. Bright, *History of Israel*, 295.
5. Long, *Israel's Past in Present Research*, 538–39.

> God accomplishes his will in the kingdom of the world through the things of the world, even things as terrible and evil as the sword. *God causes this evil.* He wears it like a mask, behind which he does his harsh, alien work. "For the Lord will rise up [says the prophet Isaiah]—strange is his deed, and to work his work-alien is his work" (Isa 28:21).[6]

To Sundberg, the alien work of God is the evil God causes in the world through the evil actions of human beings.

In his discussion of Ps 30, a psalm in which the psalmist says that his distress was caused by God, Jacobson quotes Luther's view on the alien work of God. Jacobson wrote,

> Borrowing language from Isa. 28:21 (in which Isaiah announced God's judgment of Judah and cried, "strange is his work! . . . alien is his work!"), Martin Luther referred to this type of divine activity as God's "alien work." Luther wrote, "God's 'alien' works are these: to judge, to condemn, and to punish those who are impenitent and do not believe. God is compelled to resort to such 'alien' works and to call them His own because of our pride." . . . As Luther emphasized, God's alien work exists only for the purpose of accomplishing God's proper work, which is to save, bless, and be gracious.[7]

Albertz sees the alien work of God as a devastating judgment upon the nation and a rejection of what has been called "Zion theology," the view that God would protect Jerusalem from its enemies because the city was the location of God's temple. Albertz writes:

> Isaiah makes a similar correction to the Zion theology: the guarantee of salvation promised in it is only to the helpless who deliberately dispense with the safeguards of power politics, . . . not for the well armed city. The cultic presence of the God who is enthroned on Zion will even be dangerous for the present capital. . . . Thus in Isaiah's view Yahweh liberates himself from the ideological entanglements in which the Jerusalem theology of king and temple had involved him. In the onrush of historical events Isaiah sees a divine plan at work according to which Yahweh demonstrates his compelling majesty precisely

---

6. Sundberg, "'Evil' after 9/11," 204.
7. deClaisse-Walford et al., *Book of Psalms*, 187.

by systematically shattering any hybrid human political or military attempt at finding security.[8]

Halpern identifies the "strange" and "alien" work of God with God's wrath. He writes,

> not even the underworld is sturdy and wide enough to save Jerusalem's "rulers" from exposure to Yhwh's wrath. Though sepultured comfortably, in the very bosom of the earth, they will remain vulnerable. As in the valley of Gibeon (v. 21; Josh 10:11), Yhwh's hail will irresistibly demolish all their shelters. The "sweeping scourge" (cf. 2 Sam 5:20; Isa 28:21, "Mt. Perazim") will carry those hidden in the shelters to the ground-sweeping the fugitives from their beds-and they will be trampled.[9]

Eric Seibert does not discuss Isa 28:21 in his book *The Violence of Scripture*. In his review of the book, Richard Bowman wrote that Seibert "does not discuss Isa 28:21, which characterizes divine violence as the alien work of God. Perhaps this omission is a reflection of his personal commitment to theological peace traditions, which leads him to 'regard all forms of violence as inappropriate for Christians' (p. 6)."[10]

In his book *Crucifixion of the Warrior God*, Boyd quotes Isa 28:21 four times to speak about the judgment of God and the violent acts that God brings upon people. Boyd writes:

> Having spelled out in general terms the view of Scripture that will be assumed throughout this work, I turn now to the legitimacy, and even the necessity, of honestly questioning this very Scripture when it depicts God in ways that seem "strange" and "alien" to the way he has revealed himself to be in Jesus Christ (Isa 28:21).[11]

Boyd writes: "When Yahweh's covenant partners voice their questions and objections to his apparently 'strange' and 'alien' behavior, they are manifesting their confidence that their covenant relationship with God is solid enough to handle their expressed complaints, confusions, and even occasional accusations."[12] In every place where Boyd speaks about the "strange" and "alien" work of God, Boyd refers to violent acts of

---

8. Albertz, *History of Israelite Religion*, 168–69.
9. Halpern, "'Excremental Vision,'" 118.
10. Bowman, "Review of *The Violence of Scripture*," 211.
11. Boyd, *Crucifixion of the Warrior God*, 7.
12. Boyd, *Crucifixion of the Warrior God*, 13.

God in judging people. In the case of Abraham, the "strange" and "alien" work of God is God's plan to "to annihilate Sodom and Gomorrah." In Moses's case, the "strange" and "alien" work of God is God's plan to annihilate his covenant people.[13]

It is true that the statement about God's "strange" and "alien" work appears in an oracle of judgment, but the "strange" and "alien" work of God is a reference to something else besides judgment and wrath. Isaiah is saying that the judgment of Jerusalem is alien to God's nature. God's character and nature were revealed to Moses on Mount Sinai:

> The LORD passed before [Moses], and proclaimed, The LORD, the LORD, a God merciful and gracious, slow to anger, and abounding in steadfast love and faithfulness, keeping steadfast love for the thousandth generation, forgiving iniquity and transgression and sin. (Exod 34:6–7)

Or, as the New Jerusalem Bible, using the divine name, translates:

> Then Yahweh passed before him and called out, Yahweh, Yahweh, God of tenderness and compassion, slow to anger, rich in faithful love and constancy, maintaining his faithful love to thousands, forgiving fault, crime and sin. (Exod 34:6–7 NJB)

This declaration of the nature and character of God appears in several sections of the Old Testament. The frequency with which this aspect of God's nature appears throughout the Old Testament indicates that the people of Israel knew their God as a compassionate and gracious God. This is the reason Isaiah saw the coming devastating invasion by the Assyrian army as the "dark reverse side" of the character and nature of Yahweh. In describing this dark reverse side of Yahweh, Kinzer writes that the work of Yahweh

> is described as "strange" and "foreign" because Yahweh's predominant means of dealing with Israel throughout their history was one of mercy and longsuffering. The Lord's merciful nature and the persistent expression of his mercy toward Israel stayed his hand in judging the nation in such a climactic fashion as Isaiah predicted in his ministry. Thus, Isa 28:21 points to a shift in the approach of Yahweh with his people, so that his persistent mercy would temporarily yield to his strange work of climactic judgment.[14]

---

13. Boyd, *Crucifixion of the Warrior God*, 10.
14. Kinzer, "Strange and Foreign Work of Yahweh," iii–iv.

SEEKING MILITARY HELP

When Isaiah spoke about the "strange" and "alien" work of God, he was announcing the judgment of Yahweh upon Judah, but Isaiah also said that Yahweh did not want to punish Judah, Yahweh wanted to save Judah from the brutal consequences of the Assyrian invasion.

Isaiah said that the leaders of Judah went to Egypt seeking military help against the coming Assyrian invasion:

> Oh, rebellious children, says the LORD, who carry out a plan, but not mine; who make an alliance, but against my will, adding sin to sin; who set out to go down to Egypt without asking for my counsel, to take refuge in the protection of Pharaoh, and to seek shelter in the shadow of Egypt; Therefore the protection of Pharaoh shall become your shame, and the shelter in the shadow of Egypt your humiliation. (Isa 30:1–3)

According to Isaiah, the leaders of Judah "carry out a plan," but it was not Yahweh's plan for the nation. They made an alliance with Egypt against Yahweh's will. They went to Egypt for advice, but they never asked for Yahweh's word. They sought protection from Pharaoh instead of depending on Yahweh to deliver them. As a result of their political decision, they will be ashamed and humiliated by the Assyrians.

Yahweh wanted to help Judah in their struggle against Assyria, but the people refused: Yahweh said to them: "In returning and rest you shall be saved; in quietness and in trust shall be your strength. But you refused and said, 'No! We will flee upon horses'" (Isa 30:15–16).

The people refused, but Yahweh wanted to be gracious to Israel. Isaiah said: "Therefore the LORD waits to be gracious to you; therefore he will rise up to show mercy to you" (Isa 30:18). The words "gracious" (*ḥānan*) and "mercy" (*rāḥam*) are two words that are integral aspects of the character of Yahweh revealed to Moses on Mount Sinai (Exod 34:6).

JUDAH'S REBELLION

Again, Isaiah said that the people would rather trust in the horses of Egypt than in Yahweh's power to save. He said: "Alas for those who go down to Egypt for help and who rely on horses, who trust in chariots because they are many and in horsemen because they are very strong, but do not look to the Holy One of Israel or consult the LORD" (Isa 31:1).

Isaiah said that Yahweh wanted to save the nation: "Like birds hovering overhead, so the LORD of hosts will protect Jerusalem; he will protect and deliver it, he will spare and rescue it. Turn back to him whom you have deeply betrayed, O people of Israel" (Isa 31:5–6). Isaiah was insistent in proclaiming that Yahweh wants to save Judah, not punish or destroy the nation, "behind and within Yahweh's judgment was the divine will to deliver and renew."[15] The prophet declared that Yahweh would fight for Judah and Assyria would fall by the hands of Yahweh: "The Assyrians will be destroyed, but not by the swords of men. The sword of God will strike them, and they will panic and flee" (Isa 31:8 NLT).

The salvation of Jerusalem depended on the repentance of the people: "Turn back to him." The Hebrew word for "turn back" is *sārah*, a word that means turning from apostasy. Isaiah is saying that the people have abandoned Yahweh and have decided to depend on military might for their deliverance. Thus, Isaiah said that what Yahweh was about to do to Jerusalem was alien to his nature, because Yahweh is a merciful and gracious God and had been so throughout Israel's history. Many times and in many ways Yahweh had expressed his merciful nature to the people and on several occasions, Yahweh has been "slow to anger and abounding in steadfast love and faithfulness" to Israel.

In that same revelation at Sinai in which Yahweh revealed his nature, Yahweh said to Moses, "all the people among whom you live shall see the work of the LORD; for it is an awesome thing that I will do with you" (Exod 34:10). The use of the word "work" in Exod 34:10 and in Isa 28:21 and Isaiah's use of the words "gracious" and "mercy" in Isa 30:18 clearly indicate that Isaiah is referring to what Israel believed and confessed about Yahweh's character and nature.

CONCLUSION

In conclusion, Isaiah is saying that Yahweh will bring judgment upon Jerusalem, but that is not what he wants to do. Yahweh's desire is to save his people, but because of their rebellion and because of their refusal to repent, Yahweh has to bring judgment upon the city, even though judgment is alien to his nature as a God who is merciful and gracious. Yahweh wants to save Judah because he is a God who is slow to anger and is a God who is abounding in steadfast love and faithfulness. Yahweh does

---

15. Anderson, *Understanding the Old Testament*, 352.

not want to bring judgment upon Judah because he is a God who keeps steadfast love for the thousandth generation and because he is a God who forgives iniquity, transgression, and sin.

Isaiah says that the judgment of Jerusalem was the "strange" and "alien" work of God because divine judgment was contrary to the merciful and gracious nature of Yahweh. As Kelley said, "Judgment is the 'strange' and 'alien' work of God (Isa. 28:21); it is the dark side of his mercy and compassion."[16] The gracious and merciful nature of Yahweh is the reason the people of Israel were not destroyed in the wilderness. The gracious and merciful nature of Yahweh is the reason Judah would not suffer the indignities of an Assyrian invasion, if they only repented and turned back to Yahweh.

Yahweh did not want to annihilate Sodom and Gomorrah. His dialogue with Abraham clearly shows he wanted to spare the city. After the people of Israel made the golden calf, Yahweh practically asked Moses to intercede on behalf of Israel. Moses did and Yahweh spared the people. Yahweh did not want to bring judgment on Judah. Rather, Yahweh wanted to be gracious and spare the people from the atrocities of an Assyrian invasion. Yahweh is a God of justice (Isa 30:18). Those who wait upon him will be saved because Yahweh does not take pleasure in the death of the wicked: "As I live, says the Lord GOD, I have no pleasure in the death of the wicked, but that the wicked turn from their ways and live; turn back, turn back from your evil ways; for why will you die, O house of Israel?" (Ezek 33:11).

If Judah had turned back from their evil ways in the same way that the Ninevites did (Jonah 3:7–10), Judah would have avoided the Assyrian invasion and the people would have not suffered the indignities caused by Assyrian brutalities.

---

16. Kelley, "Prayers of Troubled Saints," 380.

13

The Genocidal God

IN HIS BOOK *OUR SAVAGE God*, Robert Zaehner speaks of Yahweh, the God of the Old Testament, as a God who "appears in a savage guise." According to Zaehner, Yahweh is the frenzied God who storms and rages throughout the Old Testament.[1] The savage God is the God who is vengeful, radical and repugnant.[2] The savage God is a God who is cruel and violent, unjust and harsh in his dealings with the Israelites and with people from other nations. The notion of the savagery of God arises when people are unable to reconcile the love of God with a God who is a righteous judge and with God's demands for righteousness and justice. The God of the Bible is a merciful and loving God, but he is also a God who requires justice from people.

According to some people, the savage God of the Bible is the God who arbitrarily demanded the destruction of entire cities and the killing of men, women, and children. The savage God is the God who allows drought, hurricanes, tornadoes, and other natural disasters to cause havoc to cities and to bring misery to thousands of people. If God is a merciful and loving God, how could this God allow the destruction of innocent people?

The reason people believe that the God of the Bible is a savage God is because God exercises divine justice when people fail to meet divine standards. As Yahweh declared to the prophet Jeremiah, "I am the LORD

1. Zaehner, *Our Savage God*, 232.
2. Zaehner, *Our Savage God*, 225.

who demonstrates unfailing love and who brings justice and righteousness to the earth, and I delight in these things" (Jer 9:24). As the psalmist expressed, Yahweh "loves uprightness and justice; the faithful love of Yahweh fills the earth" (Ps 33:5 NJB). God delights in justice and justice is what God demands from Israel and all nations.

The reality of divine justice does not mean that there is a standard of justice for Israel and one for the rest of the world. On the contrary, there is a single standard of justice for all. God's judgment falls not only upon Israel but also upon other nations when they fail to meet the moral standard set by God at creation.[3] In order to dispense justice, God intervenes in human history to redress injustice and restore the moral order of society.

When one considers the theme of justice in the Hebrew Bible, one encounters a different perspective from that which appears in the popular understanding of justice. Justice means a restoration of normalcy in society, a return to a condition where human rights are recognized.[4]

AMOS'S ORACLES AGAINST THE FOREIGN NATIONS

One good example of divine justice at work is found in the book of the prophet Amos. Amos proclaimed that since God was the sovereign Lord over all nations, his demand for justice was universal and that it applied to all. "All of mankind is considered the vassal of the Lord whose power, authority, and law embrace the entire world community of nations."[5] To Amos, God was not only the guarantor of Israelite laws, but also of the entire moral order. God's universal requirements applied to Israel and included the conventional norms of international behavior. Amos saw God's universal requirements as justice, and his judgment as a punishment for injustice against members of the human community.[6]

---

3. Via, *Divine Justice, Divine Judgment*. In his study of the judgment of nations, Via says that Amos's call for justice is based on God's justice, God's *mišpāt*. Amos's oracles against the foreign nations (Amos 1–2) reveal that all nations, including Israel and Judah, are accountable to God's demand for justice. When nations commit acts of injustice, their violation of the moral order has consequences. God intervenes to vindicate the victims of injustice.

4. Muis, "Human Rights and Divine Justice," 1–8.

5. Paul, *Amos*, 45.

6. Mills, "Divine Violence," 153–79; Carroll R., "I Will Send Fire," 113–32.

God's universal requirements demand right conduct of individuals and nations. God's righteousness is manifested not only in the judgments which he brings to individuals and nations, but also in his acts of mercy and salvation toward Israel and, eventually, towards all peoples.

In Amos's oracles against the foreign nations, we see divine justice at work.[7] Concerning the Arameans, God spoke through Amos and said: "The people of Damascus have sinned again and again, and I will not let them go unpunished! They beat down my people in Gilead as grain is threshed with iron sledges" (Amos 1:3 NLT). The principal transgression of the Aramean kingdom was the threshing of the people in Gilead with iron threshing-machines. When the Arameans conquered Israel, they crushed the prisoners to pieces with iron threshing-machines: "threshing one's enemies or their territories is a metaphor for savage conquest."[8] This act of cruelty against the people of Gilead reflects a barbarous war-practice that was prevalent in the ancient Near East. Since no one could bring Ben-Hadad to justice, God intervened and caused the invasion of Damascus by the Assyrians and the deportation of the Arameans to Kir (Amos 1:5; 2 Kgs 16:9).

Concerning the Philistines, God spoke through Amos and said: "The people of Gaza have sinned again and again, and I will not let them go unpunished! They sent whole villages into exile, selling them as slaves to Edom" (Amos 1:6 NLT). The captives of war mentioned here were sold as slaves by the Philistines to the Edomites, the archenemies of Israel. According to Amos, the captivity was so devastating that not a single captive remained. Entire villages were taken away and none of them ever returned to their land. Since there was no way the people taken as slaves could obtain redress in a court of law, God intervened, and the Philistines were threatened with divine retribution for having plundered the land and sold the captives as slaves. To vindicate the oppressed slaves, God promised that the king of Ashdod would be destroyed (Amos 1:8). The divine judgment came by the hands of Sargon, king of Assyria, and his army after Assyria conquered Ashdod (Isa 20:1).

Concerning the Phoenicians, God spoke through Amos and said: "The people of Tyre have sinned again and again, and I will not let them go unpunished! They broke their treaty of brotherhood with Israel, selling whole villages as slaves to Edom" (Amos 1:9 NLT). The people of Tyre are

---

7. On Amos's oracles against the foreign nations see Andersen and Freedman, *Amos*.

8. Kessler, "Crimes of the Nations," 211.

charged with selling people to Edom, but not by having conquered them. This implies that Tyre bought war prisoners from an enemy of Israel, and then sold them as slaves to Edom. Tyre was a nation known by its trade and commerce. Tyre also carried out an extensive slave business, including people from Israel. The prophet Joel said that Tyre "sold the people of Judah and Jerusalem to the Greeks, removing them far from their own border" (Joel 3:6). Tyre purchased prisoners from different nations and sold them as slaves to more nations than just Edom.[9]

Slaves have no one to fight for them and vindicate their cause. So, God intervened[10] and promised that the fortresses of Tyre would be destroyed. The prophet Isaiah announced the destruction of Tyre: "This message came to me concerning Tyre: Weep, O ships of Tarshish, for the harbor and houses of Tyre are gone! The rumors you heard in Cyprus are all true" (Isa 23:1). Whether the destruction was caused by the Assyrians or the Babylonians, Isaiah was clear on who brought the demise of Tyre: "Who has brought this disaster on Tyre, that great creator of kingdoms? Her traders were all princes, her merchants were nobles. The LORD of Heaven's Armies has done it to destroy your pride and bring low all earth's nobility" (Isa 23:8–9).

Concerning the Ammonites, God spoke through Amos and said: "The people of Ammon have sinned again and again, and I will not let them go unpunished! When they attacked Gilead to extend their borders, they ripped open pregnant women with their swords" (Amos 1:13 NLT). The ripping up of the women with child was one of the many atrocities that came as a result of the many wars in the ancient Near East (see 2 Kgs 8:12; 15:16). This cruel act was practiced by the Arameans, the Assyrians, the Ammonites, and even by an Israelite king. The Ammonites are singled out by Amos for the cruelty which they inflicted upon the Israelites during a time of war. Since these women, the victims of this atrocity, were powerless to defend themselves and bring justice to their cause, God intervened and as a punishment for this cruel act, the Ammonite capital was to be burned, and the king and his officials would go into exile (Jer 27:1–6).

---

9. Ezekiel said that Tyre obtained slaves by trading them for their merchandise: "Javan, Tubal, and Meshech were your clients; they exchanged slaves and bronze items for your merchandise" (Ezek 27:13 NET).

10. Kessler, "Crimes of the Nations," 206, says that the "author of Amos 1–2 sides with the victims and identifies the perspective of the victims with God's perspective."

Concerning the Moabites, God spoke through Amos and said: "The people of Moab have sinned again and again, and I will not let them go unpunished! They desecrated the bones of Edom's king, burning them to ashes" (Amos 2:1 NLT). According to Amos, the people of Moab opened the grave of one of the kings of Edom and burned his bones. The king's bones were burned so completely that the bones turned into ashes. This desecration of the dead king was unacceptable to God. Since the dead king was unable to defend himself, God intervened and promised to bring judgment upon Moab by the hands of Nebuchadnezzar, king of Babylon.

These examples show that the God of the Bible is not a savage God. He is a God of justice who vindicates the oppressed and who acts as the sovereign judge to bring justice to people and nations on behalf of victims of violence and brutality. God acts on behalf of nations other than Israel to bring justice upon evildoers. Thus, divine justice is the process by which God renders redress on behalf of those who are unable to act on their own behalf. Since God in his nature is righteous, God imposes righteous laws on his creatures and executes them righteously. Justice is not an optional product of his will, but an unchangeable principle of his very nature. As Creator, God requires his creatures to conform to his moral laws. When they fail to do so, God acts and justice is upheld. What people believe to be divine savagery is nothing but God's dealing with his accountable creatures according to the requirements of his laws.

DIVINE GENOCIDE

The advocates of a nonviolent God argue that Yahweh commanded the annihilation of the Canaanites. Cowles asks, "What could be more morally bankrupting and spiritually corrupting than slaughtering men, women, and children?"[11] Seibert believes that Yahweh sanctions genocide. He writes, "What kind of God commissions genocide?" . . . "Images of God sanctioning–and, at times, actively participating in–genocide are deeply disturbing since this kind of behavior is exceedingly difficult to justify."[12] To Seibert, the idea that God commissions genocide is one of the most

---

11. Cowles, "Case for Radical Discontinuity," 32.
12. Seibert, *Disturbing Divine Behavior*, 25, 32.

disturbing aspects of the Old Testament because "Jesus never speaks of God as one who commands genocide."[13]

Gregory Boyd deals extensively with the problem of genocide in his book. In chapter 19, titled "Defending Divine Genocide: The Inadequacy of Traditional Defenses of the Conquest Narrative," Boyd deals with the concept of *ḥērem*, calling it "genocidal.[14] According to Boyd, the genocidal portraits of God and the command to destroy the Canaanites reflect the fallen heart of Moses. Boyd wrote:

> Viewed through the lens of the cross, these genocidal portraits of God rather reflect the fallen heart and mind of Moses and of God's people as a whole at this point in history. At the same time, because Yahweh is a faithful God who bound himself in covenant with this fallen and untrustworthy group of people, he was willing to humble himself by stooping as far as was necessary to continue to remain in solidarity with his people.[15]

Boyd said that it was a culturally conditioned people who believed God ordered the extermination of a people group. He wrote, "so long as we believe that God might actually be capable of commanding genocide, thereby indicating that we do not fully trust the revelation of God on the cross, we will not be able to see how the genocidal portrait of God bears witness to the cross."[16] Boyd wrote, "the genocidal portrait of God that is found throughout the conquest narrative reflects the way God's fallen and culturally conditioned people imagined God and the way they believed Moses had heard from God. It does not reflect what God actually said or the way God actually is."[17]

It is unfortunate that in dealing with genocide in the conquest narratives,[18] Boyd failed to deal with Yahweh's genocidal intent to destroy Nineveh as narrated in the book of Jonah.[19] In fact, only once Boyd

---

13. Seibert, *Disturbing Divine Behavior*, 190.
14. Boyd, *Crucifixion of the Warrior God*, 920.
15. Boyd, *Crucifixion of the Warrior God*, 963.
16. Boyd, *Crucifixion of the Warrior God*, 921.
17. Boyd, *Crucifixion of the Warrior God*, 942.
18. I will address the issue of genocide in the conquest narratives in chapter 19.
19. Seibert, *Disturbing Divine Behavior*, 25–26, emphasizes the inequity in the way God treated the Ninevites and the Amalekites. He writes, "narratives depicting God as genocidal become increasingly challenging to understand when viewed in light of other biblical stories in which God appears ready and eager to forgive those who repent of their wicked ways. Consider how the Ninevites escape destruction after

mentions Jonah in his book, in a footnote on page 282 where he cites Jonah 4:2 in association with the reference to Exod 34:6–7 a text in which Yahweh reveals himself to Moses as a compassionate and gracious God.

Before I address Yahweh's intention to punish Nineveh and Jonah's anger against Yahweh because of what Yahweh decided to do to Nineveh, we need to know what kind of nation Assyria was.

THE CRUELTY OF ASSYRIA

The Assyrians were known for their cruelty and for the brutal ways they treated their war prisoners.[20] Assyrian monuments document the extent of their brutality and the cruel ways they treated conquered people. Prisoners of war were impaled, beheaded, dragged with fishhooks, blinded, tortured by being hung up by their hands or feet.

Pregnant women had their stomach opened and the fetus removed from their womb. When Hosea prophesied about the fall of the Northern Kingdom, he mentioned the brutality the Assyrians would bring to the people of Samaria. He said: "Samaria shall bear her guilt, because she has rebelled against her God; they shall fall by the sword, their little ones shall be dashed in pieces, and their pregnant women ripped open" (Hos 13:16).

During the days of the prophet Isaiah, God used the Assyrians as the rod of his anger to punish the people of Judah for their sins: "Ah, Assyria, the rod of my anger—the club in their hands is my fury" (Isa 10:5). Tucker wrote: "God's purpose to punish Israel, carried out by Assyria, is just, but Assyria's own purpose to plunder at will is lawless."[21]

Tiglath-pileser III bragged about the violence he inflicted upon the nations he conquered: "By my own powerful arm I have done this. With my own shrewd wisdom I planned it. I have broken down the defenses of nations and carried off their treasures. I have knocked down their kings like a bull" (Isa 10:13 NLT).

The Assyrians were well-known for the practice of deporting conquered people to other parts of the Assyrian empire. When Sargon

---

responding favorably to the preaching of Jonah (Jonah 3). Why don't the Amalekites enjoy the same opportunity of divine grace?"

20. Bleibtreu, "Grisly Assyrian Record," 52–61,75. Bleibtreu uses inscriptions and pictures in Assyrian monuments to detail how the Assyrian treated conquered peoples, their armies, and their rulers.

21. Tucker, "Isaiah," 713.

conquered Samaria in 722 BCE, he deported 27,290 inhabitants of the Northern Kingdom and resettled them to other parts of the Assyrian empire (2 Kgs 17:6).[22] Samaria was incorporated into the Assyrian empire and became a province of Assyria.

The prophet Nahum proclaimed the punishment of Nineveh for their atrocities. In fact, the whole book is an oracle concerning Nineveh (Nah 1:1). The prophet lamented the fate of the city: "What sorrow awaits Nineveh, the city of murder and lies! She is crammed with wealth and is never without victims" (Nah 3:1 NLT).

If any city deserved punishment, that city was Nineveh. In light of Nineveh's crimes against humanity, who could bring the nation to justice? No other nation could serve as a tribunal of justice and vindicate the victims of Assyrian brutality. No human king could sit as a judge of the atrocities committed by the Assyrians. The Old Testament presents Yahweh as the Lord of the nations and as such, all nations, including Assyria, are held accountable to him. Because of their atrocities, Yahweh was about to bring a severe judgment upon Assyria. Yahweh was about to judge the city for the ways the Assyrians dealt with people. Yahweh said: "'I am your enemy!' says the LORD of Heaven's Armies. 'Your chariots will soon go up in smoke. Your young men will be killed in battle. Never again will you plunder conquered nations. The voices of your proud messengers will be heard no more'" (Nah 2:13 NLT). Nahum believed that the fall of Nineveh was good news: "Look, there on the mountains, the feet of one who brings good news, who proclaims peace! Celebrate your festivals, O Judah, and fulfill your vows. No more will the wicked invade you; they will be completely destroyed" (Nah 1:15 NIV).

YAHWEH'S COMMAND TO JONAH

In order to address the many crimes of Assyria against its neighbors, Yahweh commissioned Jonah to go to Nineveh and proclaim his verdict upon the nation. According to Walker, the book of Jonah "reveals a prophet whose genocidal desire for the Ninevites destruction was so strong that if they lived, he preferred to die."[23] Yahweh's command to Jonah was very specific: "Go at once to Nineveh, that great city, and proclaim judgment upon it; for their wickedness has come before Me" (Jonah 1:2 TNK).

22. ANET, 284.
23. Walker, "Jonah's Genocidal and Suicidal Attitude," 7.

Yahweh's words about Nineveh are similar to his words against Sodom: "How great is the outcry against Sodom and Gomorrah and how very grave their sin" (Gen 18:20). In the case of Sodom, Yahweh sent two messengers to destroy the city because of its wickedness (Gen 19:13). In the case of Nineveh, Yahweh sent his servant Jonah to announce the coming judgment. Many prophets proclaimed oracles against foreign nations, but Jonah was sent to a foreign nation to proclaim in person the message Yahweh had for them.

The judgment of Nineveh was also announced by the prophet Zephaniah. According to Zephaniah, Yahweh "will stretch out his hand against the north, and destroy Assyria; and he will make Nineveh a desolation, a dry waste like the desert" (Zeph 2:13).

So, at the command of Yahweh, Jonah reluctantly went to Nineveh, entered the city, and proclaimed to the people of Nineveh: "Forty days from now Nineveh will be destroyed" (Jonah 3:4 NLT). Another translation puts it more bluntly: "In 40 days Nineveh will be demolished" (Jonah 3:4 HCSB).

I believe these two translations, "will be destroyed" and "will be demolished," do not reflect the intensity of the Niphal participle which implies an act that is already accomplished, that is, the verb refers to a city being overthrown and destroyed: "in forty days Nineveh will be no more." Jonah proclaimed the total destruction of Nineveh. The destruction of the city would include the death of all its citizens, men, women, children, and even the animals in it. The Assyrian leaders were guilty of crimes against humanity, of injustice, of violence, of mistreatment of prisoners of war, and of untold atrocities. They were guilty and Yahweh "does not leave the guilty unpunished" (Exod 34:7). In his commentary on Jonah, Nogalski said: "The prophet offers no call to repentance, no message of hope, and no plea for change . . . Jonah clearly did not preach to get the people to change their ways. Jonah wanted Yahweh to destroy Nineveh. He delivered this message in hope that the people would do nothing and that Yahweh would make good on the threat to destroy the city."[24]

---

24. Nogalski, *Book of the Twelve*, 439.

THE REPENTANCE OF THE NINEVITES

When the king and his servants heard the message Jonah was proclaiming, he ordered a time of mourning and repentance:

> And the people of Nineveh believed God; they proclaimed a fast, and everyone, great and small, put on sackcloth. When the news reached the king of Nineveh, he rose from his throne, removed his robe, covered himself with sackcloth, and sat in ashes. Then he had a proclamation made in Nineveh: "By the decree of the king and his nobles: No human being or animal, no herd or flock, shall taste anything. They shall not feed, nor shall they drink water. Human beings and animals shall be covered with sackcloth, and they shall cry mightily to God. All shall turn from their evil ways and from the violence that is in their hands. Who knows? God may relent and change his mind; he may turn from his fierce anger, so that we do not perish." (Jonah 3:5–9)

The speech of the king appeals to Yahweh's gracious nature, expressing the hope that Yahweh would respond to Nineveh's repentance. This action is a "hopeful expression that perhaps God will not bring about a threatened destruction."[25] When Yahweh saw that the people had repented and turned from their evil ways, Yahweh had mercy on the people of Nineveh, changed his mind, and spared the whole city: "When God saw what they did, how they turned from their evil ways, God changed his mind about the punishment He had planned to bring upon them, and did not carry it out" (Jonah 3:10). As Fretheim wrote: "The repentance of the Ninevites provides the necessary occasion for God's repentance."[26]

JONAH'S ANGER

When Jonah saw that Yahweh had changed his mind about the punishment that he had said he would bring upon the Assyrians, Jonah was enraged. The English translations do not present the full extent of Jonah's anger against Yahweh. The NRSV says, "this was very displeasing to Jonah, and he became angry" (Jonah 4:1). But Jonah was more than displeased with Yahweh. The Hebrew says: *wayyēraʿ ʾel-yônah rāʿah*

---

25. Dozeman, "Inner-Biblical Interpretation," 209.
26. Fretheim, "Jonah and Theodicy," 231.

gedôlah wayyiḥar lô (Jonah 4:1). Literally, this expression could be translated as follows: "And unto Jonah it was evil, a great evil, and he was angry."

Jonah was angry with Yahweh because Yahweh changed his mind and did not send his judgment on Nineveh. Jonah said to Yahweh: "Didn't I say before I left home that you would do this, LORD? That is why I ran away to Tarshish! I knew that you are a merciful and compassionate God, slow to get angry and filled with unfailing love. You are eager to turn back from destroying people" (Jonah 4:2 NLT).[27]

Jonah was very angry with Yahweh because he believed that the decision to spare the citizens of Nineveh was wrong and unfair. Jonah believed that what Yahweh had done, being merciful to the Assyrians and sparing them from the judgment he had proclaimed, was a great evil. Jonah was angry with Yahweh because the merciful and compassionate God who had been merciful and compassionate to Israel over and over again in the past now shows himself to be merciful and compassionate to the most despicable people in the world, a people who should be completely destroyed.

In explaining Jonah's anger, Fretheim wrote:

> Jonah's complaint concerns the leniency made available to the guilty. Nineveh had taken up the sword (more than any other known!) and should, if anyone should, perish by the sword. But now Nineveh, at whose very hand Jonah's Israel had suffered so mercilessly, was to be offered the chance to escape the guillotine. Israel, God's covenant people, had been destroyed, and now the destroyer was being offered life.[28]

YAHWEH'S RESPONSE TO JONAH

The last verse of the book shows the reason Yahweh did not send the judgment that Jonah had announced would come upon Nineveh. Yahweh told Jonah: "And should I not be concerned about Nineveh, that great city, in which there are more than one hundred and twenty thousand

---

27. According to Preuss, *Old Testament Theology*, 242, in Jonah 4:2, this "formula of grace" does not refer only to the "wicked Ninevites"; "the formula speaks about YHWH's behavior toward humanity."

28. Fretheim, "Jonah and Theodicy," 227.

persons who do not know their right hand from their left, and also many animals?" (Jonah 4:11).

According to Jonah 4:11, the population of Nineveh was more than one hundred and twenty thousand people. This statement indicates that Yahweh has a deep concern for people, that he does not want anyone to perish but that all come to repentance. The sparing of the sinners who lived in Nineveh shows God's compassion. Jonah had compassion for a simple plant, but Yahweh had greater compassion for the people and the animals living in Nineveh.

YAHWEH, THE MERCIFUL GOD

The date of the book of Jonah is a matter of debate among scholars. Conservative scholars identify the Jonah of the book with the prophet who prophesied in the days of Jeroboam II, who ruled in 786–746 BCE (2 Kgs 14:25). I agree with most scholars that the book is exilic or postexilic. The postexilic audience was aware of Assyria's brutalities. They were also aware that the Northern Kingdom had been conquered by the Assyrians and its inhabitants had been exiled to other parts of the Assyrian empire. However, the date of composition does not change what the book says about the nature and character of God.

According to the book of Jonah, Yahweh truly intended to punish Nineveh and destroy the city. If he had destroyed Nineveh, then all the people living in the city, men, women, and children, would have died. And if they had died, that would be considered genocide, but the book of Jonah emphasizes that God changed his mind about the judgment against Nineveh because the people repented of their evil ways: "When God saw what they had done and how they had put a stop to their evil ways, he changed his mind and did not carry out the destruction he had threatened" (Jonah 3:10 NLT).

Sinful people are condemned to die, "the wages of sin is death" (Rom 6:23), but Yahweh has "no pleasure in the death of anyone" (Ezek 18:32). Rather, Yahweh wants people "to turn from their wicked ways and live" (Ezek 18:23). The God of the Old Testament is a righteous God, a merciful and just God. The people of Nineveh should have received the punishment they deserved for their wickedness but because they repented and turned from their wicked ways, the grace of God prevailed over his wrath.[29] Fretheim wrote, "Because God's will is for the salvation of the whole world, God will repent of judgments upon the repentance of any people."

What Jonah in his anger failed to understand was that even in their wickedness, Assyria was a special people to God. The prophet Isaiah predicted that in the future, the blessings of Yahweh will be extended to Egypt and Assyria, the traditional archenemies of Israel, and they will worship Yahweh together: "The Assyrians shall join with the Egyptians and Egyptians with the Assyrians, and then the Egyptians together with the Assyrians shall serve the LORD" (Isa 19:23 TNK). Israel will join Egypt and Assyria and they will serve God and the three nations, once enemies who fought against each other, will be one before God, a blessing in the world: "On that day Israel will be the third with Egypt and Assyria, a blessing in the midst of the earth, whom the LORD of hosts has blessed, saying, 'Blessed be Egypt my people, and Assyria the work of my hands, and Israel my heritage'" (Isa 19:24–25).

Nineveh deserved the divine judgment because "The LORD is slow to anger but great in power, and the LORD will by no means clear the guilty." This was the message that Nahum proclaimed about Assyria (Nah 1:3). However, when God saw the sincere repentance of the Ninevites, his mercy prevailed against his wrath: "The LORD, the LORD, a God merciful and gracious, slow to anger, and abounding in steadfast love and faithfulness, keeping steadfast love for the thousandth generation, forgiving iniquity and transgression and sin" (Exod 34:6–7).

A BEACON OF HOPE

There are several lessons in the book of Jonah dealing with the issue of violence and genocide. First, it is clear that Jonah desired the total destruction of the Ninevites. Since the general definition of genocide is the destruction of a "national, ethnical, racial or religious group," Jonah's intention for the people of Nineveh was genocidal. The selection of Jonah, a prophet from the Northern Kingdom, to go to Nineveh is significant. Jonah was called to preach to the same nation that invaded and conquered his nation. Yahweh was compassionate to the people of Nineveh and forgave the city, notwithstanding Jonah's desire for its destruction. Yahweh's compassion is the reason that, according to Walker, the book of Jonah is a

---

29. Walker, "Jonah's Genocidal and Suicidal Attitude," 25.

beacon of hope because it shows that "there are canonical voices that balance the violence" found in the Old Testament. "Jonah functions canonically to direct God's people away from hatred and toward compassion."[30]

Second, concerning the judgment of the nations, Yahweh said, "At one moment I may declare concerning a nation or a kingdom, that I will pluck up and break down and destroy it, but if that nation, concerning which I have spoken, turns from its evil, I will change my mind about the disaster that I intended to bring on it" (Jer 18:7–8). The book of Jonah show that the mercy of God applies to nations other than Israel. Jonah 3 shows that Yahweh changed his mind about the judgment against Nineveh because the people repented.

In her study of God changing his mind, Tiemeyer says that "The message of the book of Jonah seems clear: when someone repents, then God will cancel his planned destruction and instead relent."[31] According to Tiemeyer, God changes his mind because of the prayers of intercessors, because people repent or change their ways, or because of God's overwhelming love. God takes no pleasure in the death of the wicked. Ezekiel declares that Yahweh wants life and not death for all people: "As I live, says the Lord GOD, I have no pleasure in the death of the wicked, but that the wicked turn from their ways and live" (Ezek 33:11).

Third, the book of Jonah reveals God's compassionate nature. Jonah proclaimed a message of complete destruction of Nineveh, but God did not destroy Nineveh as Jonah had proclaimed, for when God saw how the people repented, God changed his mind about his decision to punish the Ninevites. Gerhard von Rad says that "the salvation of the Ninevites was motivated by God's compassion, which was resulted from their acts of repentance, humility and national penitence in which even the domestic animals shared."[32] In his anger, Jonah explained to Yahweh the reason he did not want to come to Nineveh, "for I knew that you are a gracious God and merciful, slow to anger, and abounding in steadfast love, and ready to relent from punishing" (Jonah 4:2).

The words of Jonah's are a reference to Yahweh's revelation of his character to Moses on Mount Sinai (Exod 34:6–7). Yahweh was treating the people of Nineveh in the same way he dealt with Israel, as a merciful and gracious God. God's mercy is not bestowed on Israel only; his mercy

---

30. Walker, "Jonah's Genocidal and Suicidal Attitude," 25.

31. Tietmeyer, "When God Changes His Mind," 125.

32. Rad, *Old Testament Theology*, 2:290

is available to all, including the violent Assyrians. According to Fretheim, in forgiving the Ninevites, "God takes upon himself the evil of Nineveh and bears the weight of its violence, the pain of a thousand plundered cities, including Israel's. God chooses to suffer for Nineveh."[33]

---

33. Fretheim, "Jonah and Theodicy," 236–37.

14

The Practice of Ripping Open Pregnant Women

THE PROPHET HOSEA PROPHESIED IN the Northern Kingdom of Israel in the mid-eighth century, probably between 750–725 BCE. In his many years of prophetic activity, Hosea saw the rise of Assyria and the threat it posed to his nation. When Tiglath-pileser III ascended to the throne in 745 BCE, Assyria began a process of territorial expansion. Hosea prophesied during the Syro-Ephraimite war and probably ended his ministry at the time of the siege of Samaria, a siege that lasted three years.[1]

Hosea and the people of the ancient Near East were familiar with the brutal ways Assyria treated its prisoners of war. Peggy Day, in her study of siege warfare and mass deportation, speaks of the results of a protracted siege on women and girls. Day writes,

> women and girls were fully present in a city besieged by enemy forces. They too knew that an inimical army was just outside the city gate, readying assault ladders and siege engines, armed with battering rams to breach the walls, and perhaps tunneling under them as well. They too would come face to face with enemy combatants.[2]

The results of a protracted siege on women and girls were famine, cannibalism, and rape. Hosea describes one of the atrocities perpetrated

---

1. For a detailed introduction to the historical background of Hosea's ministry, see Dearman, *Book of Hosea*, 21–28.
2. Day, "'Until I Come and Take You Away,'" 522.

by Assyrian soldiers on the inhabitants of a captured city. Hosea wrote, "Samaria shall bear her guilt, because she has rebelled against her God; they shall fall by the sword, their little ones shall be dashed in pieces, and their pregnant women ripped open (Hos 13:16).

Hosea's statement "their little ones shall be dashed in pieces, and their pregnant women ripped open," has been highly misunderstood and misinterpreted. Elizabeth Anderson says that by condemning the people of Samaria that their pregnant women will be ripped open, God was showing an evil aspect of his moral character.[3] Maximillien de Lafayette says that because "God Yahweh decided to dash children and babies to the ground, and the pregnant women of Samaria to be ripped wide open," demonstrates that "the Bible God is against women for perpetuity."[4] People who support abortion use Hos 13:16 to show "that God approves [abortion] under some circumstances."[5] John Hartung misquotes Hos 13:16 by saying that the text describes "Israelites murdering the babies of their enemies."[6]

THE PRACTICE OF RIPPING OPEN PREGNANT WOMEN

Seibert does not mention the disembowelment of pregnant women in Hos 13:16 as a disturbing divine behavior. In his study of the "dark side of the Bible," Boyd discusses one of the most "horrific" acts of God, that of "God judging people by having unborn babies ripped out of their mother's [sic] wombs (Hos 13:16)."[7] Boyd quotes Hos 13:16 six times in the book to emphasize this dastard act of God. Boyd writes,

> because my goal is to be ruthlessly honest in my evaluation of this material, readers who stand within more conservative traditions should be forewarned that I cannot shy away from sometimes using words like "horrific," "macabre," and "revolting" when describing it. I am certainly not trying to be inflammatory or disrespectful in speaking this way. I simply cannot find a more polite way of describing, with integrity, portraits of

---

3. Anderson, "If God Is Dead," 336–37.
4. de Lafayette, *And as Written in the Bible.*
5. Pomeroy, *Paul Tillich*, 31.
6. Hartung, "Chastity, Fidelity and Conquest," 77–90.
7. Boyd, *Crucifixion of the Warrior God*, 146–47.

God doing things like causing fetuses to be ripped out of their mothers' wombs (Hos 13:16).[8]

THE SYRO-EPHRAIMITE WAR

Hosea ministered during the Syro-Ephraimite war and its aftermath. In announcing the coming of Assyria, Hosea proclaimed that when the Assyrians invaded Samaria, little children would be smashed to death and pregnant women would be disemboweled (Hos 13:16). These frightful words of Hosea were proclaimed in the context of the Syro-Ephraimite war in the eighth century BCE and the rise of Tiglath-pileser III. What follows is a summary of the events that serve as the background for Hosea's oracle.

Tiglath-pileser III was one of the most aggressive Assyrian kings in the long history of the nation. When Tiglath-pileser III came to the throne in 745 BCE, his desire was to enlarge the Assyrian empire and establish complete domination of the Middle East. His quest for domination brought Israel into the sphere of his influence. In order to establish his empire, Tiglath-pileser established a policy of permanent conquest. This means that each nation conquered by Assyria became a province of the empire. Each conquered nation had to pay an annual tribute to Assyria.

An administrative system of regional governors was set up by Assyria to rule over the provinces and each province had to provide for the needs of the Assyrian army in case of war: food, soldiers, and slaves. Each citizen of the provinces became an Assyrian citizen. Assyria reenforced these policies by instituting brutal reprisal in case of revolts. In case of revolt by the vassals, Assyria would punish them by inflicting much pain and suffering, including the mass deportation of a vast amount of people.

In order to prepare for war with Assyria, Pekah, king of Israel, and Rezin, king of Syria, formed an alliance in order to resist Tiglath-pileser. Acting in partnership, Pekah and Rezin turned their efforts to the south, to Judah, hoping to increase the strength, proximity, and size of their coalition. Ahaz (735–715 BCE), king of Judah, refused to join the alliance, so Pekah and Rezin invaded Judah. In desperation, Ahaz invited Tiglath-pileser to protect him, thus beginning a series of events that brought

---

8. Boyd, *Crucifixion of the Warrior God*, 290.

Assyria to Samaria, motivated the preaching of Hosea, and culminated with the deportation of the people of the Northern Kingdom.

THE WAR POLICIES OF ASSYRIA

No one likes war, but war is a reality that has existed in human society from the dawn of civilization. With no exception, one characteristic of wars is the extreme violence that goes on in the battlefield. Wars cause much anguish, disruption, destruction, and an untold number of lost lives.

In warfare, nations use different techniques to achieve their goal, which is victory against their enemies. In antiquity, as well as in modern times, nations develop policies of intimidation and terror in order to force submission by their opponents. These acts of uncontrolled violence strike fear in the hearts of those under siege.

Olmstead said that "War is after all nothing but war, a reversion to savagery."[9] In wars, soldiers cast aside their inhibition, their sense of humanity, and take the lives of men, women, and children. Their actions express the horrors of war and the paroxysms of violence that are present in conflicts between nations.

One of the most violent nations in antiquity was Assyria. In his article, "Cruelty and Military Refinements," De Backer presents a detailed catalogue of the brutal ways the Assyrians dealt with their prisoners of war.[10] Assyrian records and monuments preserve the evidence that they were a brutal and violent nation. Assyrian reliefs show prisoners being impaled, Assyrian soldiers flaying captured soldiers, beheadings, mutilation, and dismembering.

In wars some of the most vulnerable victims are the women and children.[11] In wars children were torn to pieces, babies were smashed to death,[12] and women were raped, brutalized, and mutilated (their breasts were cut off).[13] On one Assyrian monument, women and children are portrayed with their lifted arms, lamenting the violence and the destruction

---

9. Olmstead, *History of Assyria*, 646.
10. De Backer, "Cruelty and Military Refinements," 13–50.
11. Kruger, "Mothers and their Children," 100–115.
12. Dashing children to pieces is mentioned in Ps 137:9; 2 Kgs 8:12; Isa 13:16; Nah 3:10; Hos 10:14; 13:16.
13. Kern, *Ancient Siege Warfare*, 80.

of their city. Archaeologists have uncovered many mass graves in places where battles occurred, and one common feature of these mass graves was the presence of bones of women and children who were buried along with the men killed in battle.

THE DISEMBOWELMENT OF PREGNANT WOMEN

One of the most violent and brutal conducts in times of war was the Assyrian practice of ripping open pregnant women in order to expose their fetuses.[14] According to Dubovsky,[15] the purpose of the disembowelment of pregnant women was the Assyrian desire to "eliminate not only their actual enemies but also potential ones: those not yet born, who might seek to reclaim the land or orchestrate another revolt." It is also possible that the disembowelment of pregnant women was seen as an act of "revenge exerted by the winners for all the friendly losses which they had to deplore during the combat."[16] In his study of a graphic scene in one Assyrian relief, Dubovsky describes in detail how the act of disembowelment was done.[17]

Most scholars agree that the concept of "ripping open pregnant women" and the concept of "dashing in pieces the little ones" is not found in Assyrian war accounts. This practice is found in Assyrian reliefs celebrating victories in war. Some scholars believe that these claims of violence against women "are intended to serve propagandistic or ideological purposes."[18] According to Olmstead,[19] "These atrocities were committed by 'battle-crazy Assyrians.'"

The disembowelment of pregnant women is attested in only two reliefs. One relief comes from the time of Ashurbanipal. This relief depicts Assyrian troops ruthlessly ripping open a pregnant Arab woman. The relief shows an Assyrian soldier inserting his hands into the woman's belly. The second relief comes from the time of Tiglath-pileser I. Dubovsky concludes that since no extant Neo-Assyrian inscription mentions this

---

14. The practice of ripping pregnant women open is mentioned in 2 Kgs 15:16; Amos 1:13; Hos 13:16.
15. Dubovsky, "Ripping Open Pregnant Arab Women," 417.
16. De Backer, "Cruelty and Military Refinements," 44.
17. Dubovsky, "Ripping Open Pregnant Arab Women," 414.
18. Kruger, "Mothers and their Children," 106.
19. Olmstead, *History of Assyria*, 647.

kind of atrocious act, that the disembowelment of pregnant women was performed only in an extreme case and that such an act was justified as a divine punishment falling upon the enemies of Assyria for their egregious disloyalty.[20]

In his article, "'Ripping Open Pregnant Women' in Light of an Assyrian Analogue," Mordechai Cogan quotes an Assyrian poem, probably dated to the reign of Tiglath-pileser I (1114–1076 BCE), in which the poet praises the actions of the victorious king. One section of the poem, in which the poet relates the victory of the Assyrian king against his enemy, reads as follow:

> *He slits the wombs of pregnant women*
>
> *he blinds the infants*
>
> *He cuts the throats of their strong ones.*

In commenting on the words of the poet describing the acts of the victorious king, Cogan wrote: "Out of the entire catalogue of the horrors of war, he singled out the attack upon the defenseless women and children; and this in order to impress upon all that the cruelest of punishments awaits those who sin against Assyria's god."[21] This terrifying practice, the disembowelment of pregnant women, was a form of psychological warfare. It was Assyria's way to show their enemies the consequences of revolting against the empire. In case of rebellion by vassals, the Assyrians would bring reprisal by enforcing their rule with violence and brutality.

However, the biblical record shows that the practice of ripping open pregnant women was also the practice of war of other nations in the ancient Near East. When the prophet Elisha anointed Hazael to be the next king of Damascus, Elisha wept aloud when he saw how Hazael would cause violence and horror against the women of Israel. When Hazael saw the prophet weeping, he asked: "'Why does my lord weep?' [Elisha] answered, 'Because I know the evil that you will do to the people of Israel; you will set their fortresses on fire, you will kill their young men with the sword, dash in pieces their little ones, and rip up their pregnant women'" (2 Kgs 8:11–12).

In his oracle against the Ammonites, Amos said the Lord would punish them because of their violence against the women of Gilead: "Thus says the LORD: For three transgressions of the Ammonites, and

---

20. Dubovsky, "Ripping Open Pregnant Arab Women," 418.
21. Cogan, "Ripping Open Pregnant Women," 756.

for four, I will not revoke the punishment; because they have ripped open pregnant women in Gilead in order to enlarge their territory" (Amos 1:13).

In his oracle against Israel, the prophet Hosea pronounced a judgment against the Northern Kingdom. The judgment would be an Assyrian invasion that would bring untold terror and violence against the inhabitants of Samaria: "Samaria shall bear her guilt, because she has rebelled against her God; they shall fall by the sword, their little ones shall be dashed in pieces, and their pregnant women ripped open" (Hos 13:16).

In discussing this inhumane practice during siege warfare, Cogan wrote: "Acts of horror such as these, performed during the course of war, are documented throughout history, and no specific age or people can be pointed to as having had a patent on atrocity."[22] Cogan's words, that "no specific age or people can be pointed to as having had a patent on atrocity," can be seen in the fact that one king in Israel also committed such an atrocity.

The writer of the book of Kings says that Menahem, after he became king of Israel and a vassal of Tiglath-pileser, invaded Tappuah to punish them for not supporting him. Most texts read "Tiphsah" (2 Kgs 15:16 NIV), a city near the Euphrates River. However, the text should be read "Tappuah," a town located in the tribe of Ephraim (Josh 17:8).

During the invasion, "Menahem punished Tappuah, all the inhabitants of the town and of its whole district, because on his way from Tirzah they did not let him in. He punished them even to ripping open all the pregnant women" (2 Kgs 15:16 NAB).

In his description of Menahem's act, Josephus wrote:

> Menahem, the general of his army, . . . made himself king, he went thence, and came to the city Tiphsah; but the citizens that were in it shut their gates, and barred them against the king, and would not admit him; but in order to be avenged on them, he burnt the country round about it, and took the city by force, upon a siege; and being very much displeased at what the inhabitants of Tiphsah had done, he slew them all, and spared not so much as the infants, without omitting the utmost instances of cruelty and barbarity; for he used such severity upon his own countrymen, as would not be pardonable with regard to strangers who had been conquered by him. And after this manner

---

22. Cogan, "'Ripping Open Pregnant Women,'" 755.

it was that this Menahem continued to reign with cruelty and barbarity for ten years.[23]

Josephus was so appalled at the cruelty and barbarity Menahem used against his own countrymen that he said such a practice would be unforgivable even if it were done against foreign enemies.

AHAZ'S FATAL DECISION

It is wrong for Boyd to say that Yahweh vowed to rip open the womb of Israelite women or that Yahweh caused "fetuses to be ripped out of their mothers' wombs." The disembowelment of pregnant women was one of the many barbarities of war that the Assyrians (and other nations) had committed for centuries. When the Assyrian army came to Samaria and ripped open the womb of Israelite women to remove the fetuses, they did what they had been doing for hundreds of years. Ripping open pregnant women is an act of terror that soldiers in the ancient Near East committed in their wars of conquest. Cogan's words must be emphasized again, "no specific age or people can be pointed to as having had a patent on atrocity."[24]

When Pekah and Rezin besieged Judah, Yahweh offered Ahaz a way out of the conflict. Yahweh sent the prophet Isaiah with a message for Ahaz: "Tell him to stop worrying. Tell him he doesn't need to fear, . . . This invasion will never happen; it will never take place" (Isa 7:4, 7 NLT). Ahaz refused to accept Yahweh's offer. Instead, "King Ahaz sent messengers to King Tiglath-pileser of Assyria with this message: 'I am your servant and your vassal. Come up and rescue me from the attacking armies of Aram and Israel'" (2 Kgs 16:7 NLT). So, because of an unwise political decision by Ahaz, Tiglath-pileser came to fight against Israel. Thus, early in Hosea's ministry, "King Tiglath-pileser of Assyria came and captured Ijon, Abel-beth-maacah, Janoah, Kedesh, Hazor, Gilead, and Galilee, all the land of Naphtali; and he carried the people captive to Assyria" (2 Kgs 15:29). Hosea knew what the Assyrians would do when their army came to Samaria. It was common knowledge that the Assyrians were brutal in the treatment of their enemies.

It was not Yahweh who caused fetuses to be ripped out of the womb of Israelite mothers. Assyrian soldiers did to Israel what they had been

---

23. Josephus, *Ant.* 4.231–32.
24. Cogan, "'Ripping Open Pregnant Women,'" 756.

doing to other nations for centuries. The Syrians, the Ammonites, and other nations also ripped fetuses out of the womb of women they conquered, and yet, they were not motivated by Yahweh.

Ahaz's "no" to Yahweh in rejecting Yahweh's help could not be overturned. As Fretheim wrote, "The creature is given power to reject God, power to make the world other than what God desires for it."[25] If Ahaz had listened to Isaiah and relied on Yahweh to deliver him from his enemies, it is possible that the women of Samaria would never have had to suffer the indignities they suffered at the hands of Assyrian soldiers.

Assyria was the agent God used to chasten Israel for its apostasy, "Assyria, the rod of my anger," "the staff in their hands is my wrath" (Isa 10:5). Assyria, however, went beyond its intended mission. Yahweh said: "I send them against a godless nation. In my fury I order them against the people to take their belongings, loot them, and trample on them like mud in the streets. But that's not what they intend to do. Their minds don't work that way. Their purpose is to destroy and put an end to many nations" (Isa 10:7 GWN).

Although the Assyrians were acting as God's agents, they were responsible for the violence, the brutality, and the atrocities committed against the people of Israel. In Isaiah's oracle against Assyria, Yahweh begins with a lamentation, "Woe to Assyria" (Isa 10:5), announcing the judgment that will come to them, "I will punish the king of Assyria" (Isa 10:12 NIV) for what Assyria did to the people of the Northern Kingdom. God holds Assyria responsible for their cruelty, for their sadism, and for their violence against the people during the invasion of Samaria.

---

25. Fretheim, *Suffering of God*, 76.

15

The Cannibal Mothers

IN HER DISCUSSION OF THE cannibal mothers (2 Kgs 6:24–31), Frymer-Kensky wrote, "Child cannibalism is a symbol of utter moral collapse in the face of suffering so severe that ordinary ethical considerations cannot be sustained. Assyrian treaties threaten such a horrendous fate for those who break the agreement. A people who eat their children cannot long exist."[1]

One of the many consequences of siege war is famine.[2] Both Israel and Judah had to face the problem of prolonged siege and the pain and suffering the people had to endure. The book of Lamentations bears witness to what happened in Jerusalem during the siege of the city, a siege that lasted more than two years. By the end of the siege, the "famine became so severe in the city that there was no food for the people of the land" (2 Kgs 25:3). Little children were begging for food (Lam 4:4); people were dying because there was nothing left in the fields to eat (Lam 4:9). This extreme situation forced some mothers in Jerusalem to kill and eat their children in order to survive. Adele Berlin said that "The picture of women devouring their children is a particularly gruesome form of cannibalism signifying extreme famine; it is a reversal of the natural order in which women feed their children."[3]

---

1. Frymer-Kensky, *Reading the Women of the Bible*, 174.
2. On famine during the siege of a city, see Ephal, *City Besieged*, 57–64.
3. Berlin, *Lamentations*, 75.

Boyd says that when reading the Old Testament through the lens of the cross, the idea that God caused fetuses to be ripped out of their mothers' wombs (Hos 13:16) and that God caused parents to cannibalize their children (Lev 26:29, Jer 19:9, Lam 2:20) contradicts the revelation of the enemy-loving, nonviolent God revealed on the cross. He writes,

> if we accept that the God who is depicted as engaging in horrendous violence is supremely beautiful, logical consistency requires us to also accept that the biblical portraits of God smashing parents and children together, causing parents to cannibalize their children, and having fetuses ripped out of wombs would be less beautiful if they had depicted God refraining from this brutal activity.[4]

Boyd's "mental picture" of the God of the Old Testament is "of a God who was Christ-like to a degree but who was also capable of commanding merciless genocide and bringing about familial cannibalism."[5] The problem of maternal cannibalism must be understood in light of the problem of siege warfare.

THE IMPACT OF SIEGE WARFARE

In the Bible and in most cases in the ancient Near East, cannibalism was the result of extended siege warfare. Tigay said that, as a result of siege warfare, the horror of cannibalism has occurred throughout history.[6] Siege warfare as practiced by the Assyrians and the Babylonians caused untold suffering to the people under siege. The invasion of the Assyrian king Tiglath-pileser III against Israel and Judah in the eighth century BCE brought an immense devastation of the land. His policy of total conquest brought untold suffering to thousands of people. In their wars of expansion, the Assyrians used improved siege technology which contributed to the conquest and to the destruction of cities and untold suffering to thousands of people. According to Bloch-Smith, archaeological work provides evidence to the devastating results of Assyrian siege warfare in the cities and villages of Israel and Judah.[7] Maternal cannibalism was one

---

4. Boyd, *Crucifixion of the Warrior God*, 325.
5. Boyd, *Crucifixion of the Warrior God*, xxxi.
6. Tigay, *Deuteronomy*, 489–94.
7. Bloch-Smith, "Impact of Siege Warfare," 19–28. See also Machinist, "Assyria and Its Image," 719–37.

of the horrors of long-term siege war. According to Bloch-Smith, the extent of destruction left behind by the Assyrians reveals the impact of siege warfare. Most cities and villages in the Northern Kingdom were affected by the Assyrian invasion. Villages suffered major destruction and many people were deported.

Bloch-Smith writes,

> Mass graves excavated at Ashdod and Lachish containing the remains of besieged and conquered victims vividly illustrate the profound human toll of siege warfare. Most of the more than fifteen hundred individuals from Lachish, including large numbers of women and children, died with no obvious injuries and so likely succumbed to dehydration, starvation, or illness.[8]

Jeremy Smoak says that

> Assyrian sources indicate that one of the most devastating tactics that the Assyrian army employed during or following a siege was the destruction of agricultural support systems. Some studies have argued that the destruction of agriculture was used to punish a rebellious vassal of the empire. A close reading of these inscriptions suggests that the destruction of vegetation was directed toward rural populations who had fled to the cities for protection.[9]

Jeffrey R. Zorn, in his study of wars in antiquity and its effects on civilians in ancient Israel presents a vivid description of how a prolonged siege affected the population of a besieged city. He writes,

> During an invasion the size of a settlement's population could swell considerably as people who lived in unfortified or inadequately fortified nearby towns, villages and homesteads sought protection. A sudden and sustained increase in a settlement's population during a siege also led to a faster than normal depletion of the settlement's food reserves, which could not be replenished easily. The biblical authors were quite cognizant of the threat posed by famine, and used it, along with the threat of death by the sword and disease. . . . Food resources could be severely rationed, and items not typically part of the diet would have to be consumed, including dung and urine, foods that were less desirable or were normally fed to animals, and animal heads. One of the most horrific aspects of famine was that

---

8. Bloch-Smith, "Impact of Siege Warfare," 20.
9. Smoak, "Assyrian Siege Warfare," 83–84.

the settlement's population, even the elite segments, might be forced to resort to cannibalism, even the consumption of one's own children.[10]

A reference to cannibalism as a result of an Assyrian invasion is found in the message of Isaiah:

> Through the wrath of the LORD of hosts the land was burned, and the people became like fuel for the fire; no one spared another. They gorged on the right, but still were hungry, and they devoured on the left, but were not satisfied; they devoured the flesh of their own kindred; Manasseh devoured Ephraim, and Ephraim Manasseh, and together they were against Judah. For all this his anger has not turned away; his hand is stretched out still. (Isa 9:19–21)

Scholars differ whether the expression "they devoured the flesh of their own kindred," is a reference to cannibalism or to a war among two tribes: Manasseh devoured Ephraim, and Ephraim devoured Manasseh. Honeyman says that this statement is a euphemism for anthropophagy or cannibalism. This reference to the cannibalism of the Israelites reflects "the extreme hardship to which those who practiced it were reduced, it is referred to with revulsion and detestation."[11]

CANNIBALISM IN SAMARIA

During the Aramean siege of Samaria under Benhadad, there was a shortage of food and a severe famine in Samaria. According to Fritz, "The aim of the siege was to starve Samaria into submission."[12] The famine was so severe that two women agreed to eat their children to satisfy their hunger (2 Kgs 6:24–33).[13] On this issue, Boyd writes,

> While the Cruciform Hermeneutic would assess aspects of these judgments to reflect the pre-Christian perspective of the author—the depiction of Yahweh causing parents to cannibalize

10. Zorn, "War and Its Effects on Civilians," 83.
11. Honeyman, "Unnoticed Euphemism," 223.
12. Fritz, 1 & 2 Kings, 268.
13. On the cannibalism in Samaria during the Arameans siege, see Lasine, "Jehoram and the Cannibal Mothers," 27–53; Hens-Piazza, "Forms of Violence," 91–104; Lanner, "Cannibal Mothers and Me," 107–16; Matthews, "Taking Calculated Risks," 4–13; Garroway, "2 Kings 6:24–30," 53–70.

their children (v. 29), for example—I believe the motivation this passage ascribes to God when he sees he must judge people is a direct revelation.[14]

Unfortunately, cannibalism was the result of prolonged sieges. The Assyrian king Ashurbanipal, writing about his two-year siege of Babylon which ended in 648 BCE, said that "famine seized them; for in their hunger, they ate the flesh of their sons and daughters." Later he tells of a siege of King Uate' of Arabia and his army in the mountain stronghold of Hukkuruna, where "famine broke out among them and they ate the flesh of their children against their hunger."[15] In the case of the siege of Samaria, there is no statement that Yahweh caused the women to eat a child. The war between Benhadad and the king of Israel was political in nature and the result of this struggle between two nations was that famine caused two mothers to resort to extreme actions to satisfy their hunger. According to Boyd, having parents cannibalize their children is a literary portrait of God that reflects a pre-Christian, culturally conditioned understanding of the character of God.[16]

THE FALL OF JERUSALEM

The fall of Jerusalem, the destruction of the temple, and the deportation of the people of Judah to exile in Babylon did not come suddenly, without a warning. Prophets like Jeremiah, Ezekiel, and others had been warning the people of Judah that unless they repented and turned to God, the curses of the covenant would be invoked upon the nation and the people would be removed from the land which they had received as their inheritance.

The exile of Judah began when Nebuchadnezzar and his army arrived in Jerusalem. In 598 BCE Babylon advanced against Judah. Nebuchadnezzar's army came up to Jerusalem and besieged the city. During the siege Jehoiakim, king of Judah, died. Jehoiachin (his name appears as Jeconiah in 1 Chr 3:16 and Coniah in Jer 22:24), the son of Jehoiakim, was installed as king of Judah at the age of 18 (2 Kgs 24:8). According to the biblical text, Nebuchadnezzar himself came to Jerusalem while his servants were besieging the city (2 Kgs 24:11). According to the

---

14. Boyd, *Crucifixion of the Warrior God*, 791.
15. Keener and Walton, *Cultural Backgrounds Study Bible*.
16. Boyd, *Crucifixion of the Warrior God*, 651.

Babylonian Chronicle, Nebuchadnezzar entered Jerusalem on March 16, 597 BCE.[17] Jehoiachin, along with his mother and members of the royal family, his officers, advisors, and other government leaders surrendered to the king of Babylon.

At that time, the first deportation of Judah took place (597 BCE), according to 2 Kgs 24:12–16, ten thousand people were taken into exile, including the royal family, their servants, and the palace officials. In addition, another eight thousand professional people were also taken to Babylon. The second deportation of Judah took place in 587 BCE during the reign of Zedekiah, the last king of Judah. Zedekiah was a weak ruler who was unable to stand up against the anti-Babylonian forces in Judah and who was afraid of popular opinion. Probably incited by the prophets who were taken to Babylon and by the nobles who formed part of the anti-Babylonian forces in Judah, Zedekiah rebelled against Babylon.

In 588 BCE Nebuchadnezzar invaded Judah and Jerusalem was blockaded:

> In the ninth year of his [Zedekiah's] reign, in the tenth month, on the tenth day of the month, Nebuchadnezzar king of Babylon came with all his army against Jerusalem and laid siege to it. And they built siegeworks all around it. So, the city was besieged till the eleventh year of King Zedekiah. (2 Kgs 25:1–2)

In 587 BCE Jerusalem was captured and Zedekiah fled from the city, but he was captured, blinded, and deported to Babylon (2 Kgs 25:5–7). As a result of the long siege, a siege that lasted more than two years, the cities and villages of Judah were destroyed; suffering, hunger, and death affected everyone in Jerusalem. One tragic consequence of the long siege was the profound human toll caused by the siege; great hunger affected the population, especially a large number of women and children. Because of the long siege, the people of Jerusalem had to survive with unhealthy diets, poor sanitary conditions due to restricted water supplies, and with human excrement employed as fertilizer.[18]

The author of Lamentations describes his personal pain because of the agony the mothers of Jerusalem faced with the suffering of their children,

---

17. Horn, "Babylonian Chronicle," 21. According to the Babylonian Chronicle, Nebuchadnezzar entered Jerusalem in the seventh year of his reign, on the second day of the month of Adar (16 March, 597 BCE).

18. Bloch-Smith, "Impact of Siege Warfare," 21.

> My eyes are spent with weeping; my stomach churns; my bile is poured out on the ground because of the destruction of my people, because infants and babes faint in the streets of the city. They cry to their mothers, "Where is bread and wine?" as they faint like the wounded in the streets of the city, as their life is poured out on their mothers' bosom. (Lam 2:11–12)

According to Hendrik Bosman, the author of the book of Lamentations depicts Yahweh as the author of the misery experienced by the population of Jerusalem when the Babylonians destroyed the city. In addition, the writer of Lamentations also confronts Yahweh with the intense suffering of the people which he brought upon the population with the destruction of Jerusalem and charges him with the maternal cannibalism which was the result of the extreme punishment he inflicted upon the people.[19]

CANNIBALISM IN LAMENTATIONS

The book of Lamentations describes the horrors experienced by the covenant community in the aftermath of the siege of Jerusalem.[20] The despair of the people and the intense agony that followed the destruction of Jerusalem was poignantly expressed by the author of the book of Lamentations who protests what he perceives to be the injustice of Yahweh in causing so much pain and suffering by refusing to show mercy, by being silent during the tragedy that afflicted the people, by withdrawing his saving hands, by becoming the enemy of the people. The readers of Lamentations are given a vivid picture of the pain and the suffering faced by the covenant community during and after the Babylonian invasion of Jerusalem. The writer gives the reason for the incomprehensible tragedy that befell the nation: "The LORD gave full vent to his wrath; he poured out his hot anger, and he kindled a fire in Zion that consumed its foundations" (Lam 4:11).

The book of Lamentations introduces two female images. The book opens with of portrayal of the city of Jerusalem as a widow who has been shamed, rejected, and abandoned: "How lonely sits the city that was full of people! How like a widow has she become, she who was great among the nations! She who was a princess among the provinces has become a

---

19. Bosman, "Function of (Maternal) Cannibalism," 152–65.
20. Moore, "Human Suffering in Lamentations," 534–55; "Rhetoric of Lamentations," 1–17.

slave" (Lam 1:1). The image of the city as a widow is also meant to evoke a sense of desolation and loneliness, of pain and suffering, of horror and outrage. The book of Lamentations portrays the city of Jerusalem as a woman in the deepest state of desolation. The city now is left desolate, a city that once was full of people. Jerusalem is portrayed as a widow suffering and mourning for her children. The city that once was a great city receiving the homage of the nations is now but a vassal, paying tribute to its overlord. The portrayal of Jerusalem as a widow conveys the idea of mourning and abandonment, and it is meant to evoke pity from the reader. Pity is what Israel desires to receive from God, but the writer welcomes pity from anyone who will hear the people's cry: "Is it nothing to you, all you who pass by? Look and see if there is any sorrow like my sorrow, which was brought upon me, which the LORD inflicted on the day of his fierce anger" (Lam 1:12).

The second female image describes the suffering of Judean mothers. Berlin writes,

> The other female image in Lamentations, the maternal image, is used for the real mothers of Judah, who lose their maternal status by virtue of the fact that they cannot care for and nourish their children. Indeed, they become the antithesis of mothers— cannibals who eat their children instead of feeding them (2:12, 20; 4:10). For women, this is the worst suffering imaginable.[21]

The outrage of the women of Judah was to watch the death of their own children: "Should women eat their offspring, the children they have borne?" (Lam 2:20).[22] Another grisly detail of maternal cannibalism is found in Lam 4:10: "The hands of compassionate women have boiled their own children; they became their food in the destruction of my people."

The graphic picture of Jerusalem as a lonely widow provides a small glimpse of the great devastation that came upon the nation. Kings and people had built an impregnable city hoping to find protection behind its walls, trying to escape the judgment and the death proclaimed by the prophets, but not knowing that those mighty walls of protection were no protection at all against the God who had brought in the Babylonians as

---

21. Berlin, *Lamentations*, 9.

22. Hillers, "History and Poetry in Lamentations," 157, says that cannibalism is the result of prolonged starvation and it is an extreme act of human behavior.

his instrument of divine justice. No city is so impregnable that it might become immune to God's righteous judgment.

The ruins of the city and of the temple were also vivid reminders to the people who took a low view of human life. Jeremiah had warned the people: "For if you truly amend your ways and your deeds, if you truly execute justice one with another, if you do not oppress the sojourner, the fatherless, or the widow, or shed innocent blood in this place, and if you do not go after other gods to your own harm, then I will let you dwell in this place, in the land that I gave of old to your fathers forever" (Jer 7:5–7). The devastation of Judah was a visible demonstration of the great moral failure of the people who refused to respect the dignity of the poor and the other weak members of their society. The tears shed by the lonely widow were the tears of remorse for the people's violation of the covenant. Judah did not go into exile because of their faithfulness to God. Rather, the nation was driven into exile and hard servitude because of the people's disobedience to their God.

The writer of Lamentations again gives the reason for the catastrophe that came upon Jerusalem: "Because the LORD has afflicted her for the multitude of her transgressions." As a result, Jerusalem's children have gone away, captives before her enemies. Because of her rebellion, Zion's majesty has departed, her princes fled without strength before the pursuer (Lam 1:5–6). These words are very descriptive of the reason for Judah's exile. The punishment was from above, but the cause was from within. Israel had rebelled against their God. They had gone after other gods and now they are experiencing the consequences of that disobedience. Now, in their distress they cry out to God. Their lament is a cry for help and a plea for mercy, which they cannot find. It is for this reason that the people acknowledged that God has brought this devastation: "It was for the sins of her prophets and the iniquities of her priests, who shed the blood of the righteous in the midst of her" (Lam 4:13). With the destruction of Jerusalem and the exile of the people, the threat of the covenant curse had been invoked (Deut 28:47–57), and the righteousness of Yahweh had been vindicated.

Kathleen O'Connor says that notwithstanding the violence and the calamity that came upon the inhabitants of Jerusalem by the hands of the Babylonians, the violence against the people was the results of their refusal to repent. She writes, what I see in this shocking violent imagery is a provisional effort to make sense of the disaster, to hold onto God, to cling mightily to the Creator in the midst of destruction all around. . . . I see in God's violence a potent stammering toward meaning. . . . To tell of the fall of the nation as a result of God's punishment reframes the disaster. It defends God from charges of injustice and arbitrariness. It strives to persuade readers that God is innocent of cruelty, reluctant to punish, and required to do so because of Judah's sin. . . . If God is the enraged punisher, then the people bring on the punishment and force God to act.[23]

The book of Jeremiah says that Babylon was the agent God was using to punish Judah for its sins. Nebuchadnezzar is God's servant who will accomplish God's purpose: "I am going to send for . . . King Nebuchadrezzar of Babylon, my servant" (Jer 25:9). Then, Yahweh would bring judgment on Babylon: "Then after seventy years are completed, I will punish the king of Babylon and that nation, the land of the Chaldeans, for their iniquity, says the LORD, making the land an everlasting waste" (Jer 25:12). The reason for the punishment of Babylon was because God "was only a little angry" with Judah, but the Babylonians "made the disaster worse" (Zech 1:15). The words of the prophet explain the reason Yahweh was punishing the king of Babylon for their iniquity, because of the excessive violence the Babylonians used against the people of Judah. As Fretheim writes, "God's agents of judgment commonly exceed their mandate."[24] Ezekiel also considers the Babylonians instruments of God for judgment: "I will leave it to them to judge, and they will judge you by their own ordinances. I will let loose my jealousy against you, so that they shall deal with you in fury" (Ezek 23:25 NAB).

THE CURSES OF THE COVENANT

In response to the apostasy of Israel, Yahweh called on foreign armies to discipline Israel for its many violations of the covenant, "The king of Assyria carried the Israelites away to Assyria . . . because they did not obey the voice of the LORD their God but transgressed his covenant" (2 Kgs 18:11–12). In order to visit Judah for its violation of the demands of the covenant, Yahweh called Nebuchadnezzar, king of Babylon, as his agent to punish the rebellion of the nation: "[The Babylonians] . . . will come

23. O'Connor, "Reclaiming Jeremiah's Violence," 47.
24. Fretheim, "'I Was Only a Little Angry,'" 365.

against you with an alliance of nations and with weapons, chariots, and wagons. They will set themselves against you on every side with shields, bucklers, and helmets. I will delegate judgment to them, and they will judge you by their own standards" (Ezek 23:24 HCSB).

The book of Deuteronomy lists the consequences for the violation of the covenant. Among the curses that will come upon the rebellious nation will be the coming of a nation who will serve as the agent of divine justice:

> The LORD will bring a nation from far away, from the end of the earth, to swoop down on you like an eagle, a nation whose language you do not understand, a grim-faced nation showing no respect to the old or favor to the young. It shall consume the fruit of your livestock and the fruit of your ground until you are destroyed, leaving you neither grain, wine, and oil, nor the increase of your cattle and the issue of your flock, until it has made you perish. It shall besiege you in all your towns until your high and fortified walls, in which you trusted, come down throughout your land; it shall besiege you in all your towns throughout the land that the LORD your God has given you. In the desperate straits to which the enemy siege reduces you, you will eat the fruit of your womb, the flesh of your own sons and daughters whom the LORD your God has given you. (Deut 28:49–53)

The apocryphal book of Baruch says that the cannibalism that occurred during the fall of Jerusalem was the consequence of the violation of the demands of the covenant as God had warned the people through Moses: "So the Lord carried out the threat he spoke against us: against our judges who ruled Israel, and against our kings and our rulers and the people of Israel and Judah. Under the whole heaven there has not been done the like of what he has done in Jerusalem, in accordance with the threats that were written in the law of Moses. Some of us ate the flesh of their sons and others the flesh of their daughters" (Bar 2:1–3 NRSV).

The curse of maternal cannibalism is one of the consequences for the sins of the people: "In the desperate straits to which the enemy siege reduces you, you will eat the fruit of your womb, the flesh of your own sons and daughters." When Yahweh delegates the judgment of Israel by the hands of nations who act as his agents, these nations judge Israel "by their own standards." The standards the Babylonians used against their enemies were harsh, violent, barbaric, and at times, sadistic. The curses of the covenant are invoked against Israel when the people's disobedience and hostility against Yahweh remain unabated, "If . . . you do not obey me but walk in hostility against me, I will walk in hostile rage against you and I myself will also discipline you: You will eat the flesh of your sons and the flesh of your daughters" (Lev 26:27–29 NET). The hostility of the people against Yahweh would be punished by the coming of a foreign nation to punish Israel for its infidelity to Yahweh.

THE SINS OF JUDAH

The judgment on Judah occurred because of their rebellion against Yahweh and because of what they did at Topheth (see below). Before the invasion, Yahweh sent Jeremiah to Zedekiah, king of Judah, with a message of hope: "Thus says the LORD, the God of hosts, the God of Israel, If you will only surrender to the officials of the king of Babylon, then your life shall be spared, and this city shall not be burned with fire, and you and your house shall live. But if you do not surrender to the officials of the king of Babylon, then this city shall be handed over to the Chaldeans, and they shall burn it with fire, and you yourself shall not escape from their hand" (Jer 38:17–18).

Yahweh's message to Zedekiah was intended to save Jerusalem from destruction. If Zedekiah would surrender to the Babylonians, the city would not be burned, he and the population of the city would live, and everyone would be spared the horrors of a long siege, and mothers would not cannibalize their children. A refusal to surrender would bring much violence upon the city and its inhabitants would face all the paroxysms of war. On the other hand, a positive response by Zedekiah "would lessen God's association with violence."[25] Because of the king's refusal to listen to the voice of Yahweh and because of his refusal to surrender to Nebuchadnezzar, Jerusalem was judged by the Babylonian's "own standards" (Ezek 23:24): Jerusalem was devastated, thousands died, thousands were deported, mothers cannibalized their children, and Yahweh receives the blame for causing women to eat their children.

Why did Yahweh allow such horrible misery and destruction to come upon his chosen people? The answer given by the prophets was because of the wickedness of the people, "And I will punish him and his offspring and his servants for their iniquity" (Jer 36:31), and because they refused to repent, "they commit iniquity and are too weary to repent" (Jer

25. Fretheim, "'I Was Only a Little Angry,'" 367.

9:5). Yahweh is a merciful and gracious God, a God who is slow to anger, a God who forgives iniquity when the people repent and turn from their iniquities. But Yahweh is also a God who by no means clears the guilty, a God who acts justly when he visits the iniquity of the people upon themselves (Exod 34:6–7). Yahweh is a God who is slow to anger but he also said, ""My Spirit will not contend with humans forever" (6:3 NIV). Or as the New Jerusalem Bible translates, "My spirit cannot be indefinitely responsible for human beings" (Gen 6:3 NJB).

The judgment on Judah occurred because of their rebellion against Yahweh and because of what they did at Topheth.[26] At the Topheth the people of Judah were involved in the hideous practice of child sacrifice. The practice of child sacrifice was a ritual that was common in the cult of Molech, the god of the Ammonites.[27] The Topheth was the place in the Kidron Valley where these sacrifices were offered. In antiquity, many people believed that the sacrifice of human lives was the greatest gift one could offer to the gods. Many reasons motivated people to make a human sacrifice to the gods. Some of these reasons include the desire to please the gods, the request for a special favor, a desire to obtain better crops, or as an atonement for one's sins.

According to the narrative found in the book of Kings, Mesha, the king of Moab offered his son to Chemosh, his god, in order to obtain a victory against Israel: "When the king of Moab saw that the battle was going against him, . . . he took his firstborn son who was to succeed him, and offered him as a burnt offering on the wall" (2 Kgs 3:26–27).

People in ancient Israel believed in and practiced child sacrifice. The people's rhetorical question to Micah the prophet reflects a popular belief that child sacrifice was one way by which they could atone for their sins: "With what shall I come before the LORD, and bow myself before God on high? . . . Shall I give my firstborn for my transgression, the fruit of my body for the sin of my soul?" (Mic 6:6–7). Some of the kings of Judah sacrificed their children as an offering to pagan gods. Ahaz "made his son pass through fire, according to the abominable practices of the nations whom the LORD drove out before the people of Israel" (2 Kgs 16:3). Manasseh "made his son pass through fire" (2 Kgs 21:6). The practice of child sacrifice was forbidden in Israel: "No one shall be found among you

---

26. Dearman, "Topheth in Jerusalem," 59–71.
27. Day, *Molech: A God of Human Sacrifice*.

who makes a son or daughter pass through fire" (Deut 18:10).[28] Although some scholars believe that the expression "pass through fire" does not refer to human sacrifice, the biblical evidence clearly suggests that these two kings practiced child sacrifice because the Deuteronomic historian accused them of following the pagan practice of other nations.

In Jeremiah's temple sermon, Yahweh condemned the practice of child sacrifice: "they go on building the high place of Topheth, which is in the valley of the son of Hinnom, to burn their sons and their daughters in the fire" (Jer 7:31). Child sacrifice was abhorrent to God. Concerning child sacrifice, Yahweh said: "That is something I never commanded them to do! Indeed, it never even entered my mind to command such a thing" (Jer 7:31 NET). It is for this reason that Jeremiah prophesied that the Valley of Hinnom would become "the valley of Slaughter" (Jer 7:32), because in that place Yahweh would judge and punish those who engaged in child sacrifice.

Yahweh announced through Jeremiah: "And I will make them eat the flesh of their sons and the flesh of their daughters, and all shall eat the flesh of their neighbors in the siege, and in the distress with which their enemies and those who seek their life afflict them" (Jer 19:9). The Septuagint (LXX) has a different reading. Instead of reading "I will make them eat," the LXX reads "they shall eat": "And they shall eat the flesh of their sons, and the flesh of their daughters; and they shall eat every one the flesh of his neighbour in the blockade, and in the siege wherewith their enemies shall besiege them" (Jer 19:9). According to Lundbom, the Septuagint seeks to absolve Yahweh from being the cause of the cannibalism that occurred during the siege of Jerusalem. The Qumran text of Jeremiah (4QJerc) follows the reading of the Septuagint. According to Lundbom, the reading of the Masoretic Text is the more difficult and the original reading and must be preserved because the context describes the acts of Yahweh in judging Judah.[29]

THE JUDGMENT OF JUDAH

Once again, before God sent the Babylonians as his agents of judgment, Yahweh gave the people of Judah another opportunity to repent. Yahweh sent Jeremiah with an urgent message to the people of Judah:

28. Smith, "Note on Burning Babies," 477–79.
29. Lundbom, *Jeremiah 1–20*, 840.

> Thus said the LORD: Go and buy a potter's earthenware jug. Take with you some of the elders of the people and some of the senior priests, and go out to the valley of the son of Hinnom at the entry of the Potsherd Gate, and proclaim there the words that I tell you. You shall say: Hear the word of the LORD, O kings of Judah and inhabitants of Jerusalem. Thus says the LORD of hosts, the God of Israel: I am going to bring such disaster upon this place that the ears of everyone who hears of it will tingle. Because the people have forsaken me, and have profaned this place by making offerings in it to other gods whom neither they nor their ancestors nor the kings of Judah have known; and because they have filled this place with the blood of the innocent, and gone on building the high places of Baal to burn their children in the fire as burnt offerings to Baal, which I did not command or decree, nor did it enter my mind. (Jer 19:1–5)

Jeremiah went to the Topheth and broke the flask as Yahweh had commanded. When Jeremiah returned from the Topheth, he went to the temple, stood before the people and announced to them, "Thus says the LORD of hosts, the God of Israel: I am now bringing upon this city and upon all its towns all the disaster that I have pronounced against it, because they have stiffened their necks, refusing to hear my words" (Jer 19:15). The people had broken the covenant by sacrificing to foreign gods and by sacrificing their children to pagan gods. God gave them a chance to repent but they refused to repent. Yahweh wanted to avoid violence and the horrors of war, but the people rejected Yahweh's last offer of a nonviolent sentence of judgment. Because of the refusal to repent, Yahweh sent the Babylonians who would judge according to their own customs. And when the Babylonians came, Yahweh said, "I will make them eat the flesh of [your] sons and the flesh of [your] daughters" (Jer 19:9). The words of Yahweh, according to Lundbom, are similar to what the people do when they sacrifice their sons in the Topheth, that is, cannibalism is described in a similar way to child sacrifice.[30]

SACRIFICING CHILDREN

It is difficult for people today to understand the motive behind child sacrifice. To the modern mind, child sacrifice would be considered a barbaric ritual that should be unacceptable in any situation. People today

---

30. Lundbom, *Jeremiah 1–20*, 841–42.

would be unable to understand the need for child sacrifice or find any justification for this barbaric rite. However, child sacrifice, although a practice that is unacceptable today and would be considered a crime in almost any society in our civilized world, must be understood from the perspective of the social, cultural, and religious context of the people who believed that it was an acceptable religious practice.

Child sacrifice, when looked at from the perspective of the parent who was sacrificing his or her child to a god, was an act of pious faith. The sacrifice of children was considered to be a deep demonstration of faith that came out of deep religious conviction. The dedication of one's child to a god or goddess was accompanied by a solemn ritual that was performed at the Topheth, the sacred place where child sacrifice was performed. But the question that Boyd and others raise is relevant to Christians today, why would God punish children for the sins that their parents have committed?

In seeking to understand Yahweh's role in maternal cannibalism, it is important to take two important issue into consideration. First, Yahweh forgives iniquities, transgressions, and sins (Exod 34:7) when people repent and turn from their sinful ways. Yahweh is slow to anger, but when people do not turn from their wicked ways, Yahweh, as a righteous judge, does not declare the guilty guiltless. Everyone must give an account to God for their sins, "on the day I settle accounts, I will hold them accountable for their sin" (Exod 32:34 HCSB).

Second, in today's society it is not popular to say that people will be held accountable for their sins. For this reason, when Yahweh punishes Judah for their sins, we judge Yahweh and blame him for the atrocities that happened during the fall of Jerusalem. However, God works through agents and he allows his agents to judge and they judge by their own customs and traditions (Ezek 23:25 NAB). In judging Judah, God works through his servant Nebuchadnezzar and his army. The actions of the Babylonians become the actions of God. What the Babylonians do, God does. Since the siege of Jerusalem forced people to eat their children, the acts of God's agents become the acts of God. God is accused of doing what the Babylonians did. Concerning the use of agents, Fretheim writes,

> God does not (micro)manage the work of the agents, but exercises constraint and restraint in relating to them. This point is demonstrated by texts that show that God's agents may exceed the divine mandate, going beyond anything that God intended. See, e.g., Zech. 1.15, where God says: "I am extremely angry

with the nations that are at ease, for while I was only a little angry, they made the disaster worse." God was only "a little angry"! The nations exceeded God's will and their misuse of power complicated God's merciful activity on Israel's behalf.[31]

How about the children? The violence displayed in wars among nations, does not choose its victims. In wars, men, women, and children die. Both the guilty and the innocent become victims of human actions and human sinfulness. It is only when through Christ, God finishes reconciling the whole world unto himself (2 Cor 5:19) that human beings will beat their swords into plowshares, and their spears into pruning hooks and nations will not take up the sword against other nations, and they will no longer train for war. Until then, unfortunately, violence will continue.

---

31. Fretheim, "Violence and the God of the Old Testament," 121.

16

The Righteous Judge and the Fate of Sodom

THE STORY OF SODOM AND Gomorrah deals with the problem of human sin and divine judgment. God's judgment upon Sodom[1] came as a result of what Yahweh discovered when evaluating the cry of the people who lived in the city. As Fretheim explains, "Judgment is thereby shown to be responsive to specific human sinfulness, not a capricious divine act."[2]

COMMUNAL JUDGMENT

In the Old Testament, divine judgment is both individual and communal judgment. Ezekiel speaks about individual judgment: "it is only the person who sins that shall die" (Ezek 18:4). The reason for communal judgment is because God's judgment upon human sin affects individuals not directly related to the sins being judged by God. One of the consequences of communal judgment is that when judgment comes, both the wicked and the righteous become involved in the outcome. Duke wrote,

---

1. The destruction of Sodom involves two cities, Sodom and Gomorrah. Two other cities were also destroyed in the conflagration, Admah and Zeboiim (Deut 29:23). In this chapter I will mention only Sodom; however, Gomorrah should also be included whenever Sodom is mentioned. This follows a pattern that appears in the Hebrew Bible, where Sodom is mentioned thirty-nine times and Gomorrah is mentioned only nineteen times. A fifth city, Zoar (cf. Gen 14:8), was spared because Lot found refuge in Zoar (Gen 19:23).

2. Fretheim, "Divine Judgment and the Warming of the World," 22.

"crimes of nations, even when carried out by a few, may receive national consequences that cause innocent individuals to suffer. Not unexpectedly, neither Ezekiel nor Jeremiah ever state that the innocent will never suffer due to the sins of others."[3]

When communal judgment occurs, men, women, and children suffer because of the sins of others. Fretheim explains the consequences of communal judgment, "One characteristic of communal judgment is that no clean distinction can be made between the righteous and the wicked (hence Abraham's question in Gen 18:25). Because life is so interrelated, the righteous and the innocent (e.g. children) are often caught up in the judgmental effects of other people's sins. In other words, they will undergo the experience of judgment in ways that are often devastating to their life and health."[4] The destruction of Sodom and Gomorrah, the fall of Samaria, and the fall of Jerusalem are examples of communal judgment. When God uses Assyria to bring judgment upon the Northern Kingdom and when he uses Babylon as an agent of judgment against the Southern Kingdom, these nations become "the weapons of his wrath" (Jer 50:25).

Divine judgment is what von Rad calls the "dark reverse side of the work of Jahweh."[5] Judgment is the "dark reverse side" of Yahweh because Yahweh is a merciful and gracious God, a God who is slow to anger (Exod 34:6). Anger is not a divine attribute. Rather, the Old Testament says that Yahweh is provoked to anger by human sin, by unfaithfulness, and by rebellion against him. Yahweh said, "The children gather wood, the fathers kindle fire, and the women knead dough, to make cakes for the queen of heaven; and they pour out drink offerings to other gods, to provoke me to anger" (Jer 7:18). In his discussion of divine anger, Fretheim writes, "That the divine anger is provoked reveals several things about God. For one, God is affected by, moved by what people say and do. For another, anger is a divine response and not a divine attribute, as if anger were no different from, say, love. God's anger is contingent. If there were no sin, there would be no divine anger."[6]

Whether the sin of Sodom was inhospitality, the oppression of the poor, gang rape, or homosexuality, the judgment of the city came because

---

3. Duke, "'Visiting the Guilt of the Fathers,'" 362.
4. Fretheim, "'I Was Only a Little Angry,'" 369.
5. Rad, *Old Testament Theology*, 2:164.
6. Fretheim, "Divine Judgment and the Warming of the World," 26.

the citizens of Sodom violated the moral order that God had established at creation.

THE DESTRUCTION OF SODOM

Seibert has a problem with God's behavior when it comes to the appropriateness of punishing people's sin with death. He writes that events such as the flood and the destruction of Sodom and Gomorrah "imply that divine judgment results in the death of people of all ages, including infants and toddlers. It is hard to imagine how anyone could persuasively argue that babies have committed sins worthy of death."[7]

Gregory Boyd gives much attention in his book to the destruction of Sodom and Gomorrah.[8] The problem the destruction of Sodom and Gomorrah poses to Boyd "concerns the violent manner in which God is depicted as judging these cities. It is one thing to judge a people-group by allowing them to suffer the natural consequences of their own decisions and quite another to personally incinerate them."[9] One reason for his preoccupation with Sodom is because of "God's ferocious rain of fire that incinerated all the inhabitants of Sodom and Gomorrah." Another reason is because although Yahweh was willing to spare ten righteous persons, Boyd says that "it is difficult to understand how the infants and young children in these cities could not have been considered righteous enough to spare."[10]

Whybray believes that Yahweh announced to Abraham that he was going to destroy Sodom. Whybray writes, "it is quite clear that before Abraham addressed him, God intended to destroy the innocent in Sodom and Gomorrah indiscriminately together with the wicked."[11] But the text does not say that Yahweh told Abraham that he was going destroy Sodom.[12] Whybray's view is based on Yahweh's words in Gen 18:17: "Shall I hide from Abraham what I am about to do." This verse seems to suggest that Yahweh has already made the decision to destroy Sodom. Whybray

---

7. Seibert, *Disturbing Divine Behavior*, 75.

8. The word Sodom appears fifty times in the body and in the footnotes of Boyd's book.

9. Boyd, *Crucifixion of the Warrior God*, 1186.

10. Boyd, *Crucifixion of the Warrior God*, 318.

11. Whybray, "Immorality of God," 101.

12. Macdonald, "Listening to Abraham—Listening to Yhwh," 25–43.

also says that Abraham's first question, "Will you indeed sweep away the righteous with the wicked?" (Gen 18:23) indicates that Yahweh had already decided to destroy Sodom. However, verse 21 says that Yahweh had come down to see what was happening in Sodom before he made the final decision. By coming down to investigate what was happening in the city clearly indicates that the fate of Sodom had not yet been decided, for as Yahweh said, "and if not, I will know" (Gen 18:21).

Boyd offers a cruciform interpretation of the destruction of Sodom and Gomorrah. The cruciform interpretation of Yahweh's destruction of Sodom attributes the devastation to "Satan and other cosmic forces of evil."[13] These "cosmic forces of evil" are "anti-creational forces" which are "bent on destruction." Boyd writes that although God uses "human agents as his instruments of judgment, they are not able to account for portraits of God engaging in violence, such as when Yahweh is depicted as sending a worldwide flood or incinerating the cities of Sodom and Gomorrah."[14] Thus, when God uses the elements of nature as a weapon of judgment, they are cosmic forces of evil, anti-creational forces that are bent on destruction.

Boyd writes,

> in light of the cross, I submit that all canonical depictions of God using nature as a weapon of judgment (e.g., the flood, Sodom and Gomorrah) can be, and should be, understood to be occasions in which God, with a grieving but hopeful heart, withdrew his protective hand to allow anti-creational forces that are "bent on destruction" (Isa 51:13; cf. Hab 1:9) to bring about "the undoing of creation" in an individual, people-group, or geographical region.[15]

In order to support his view that these anti-creational forces are bent on destruction, Boyd cites Isa 51:13 and Hab 1:9. However, these two texts do not support Boyd's contention that these agents are cosmic forces of evil bent on destruction. The context for Isa 51:13 is Isa 51:12: "I, I am he who comforts you; why then are you afraid of a mere mortal who must die, a human being who fades like grass? You have forgotten the LORD, your Maker, who stretched out the heavens and laid the foundations of the earth. You fear continually all day long because of the fury

---

13. Boyd, *Crucifixion of the Warrior God*, 870.
14. Boyd, *Crucifixion of the Warrior God*, 1002.
15. Boyd, *Crucifixion of the Warrior God*, 1070–71.

of the oppressor, who is bent on destruction. But where is the fury of the oppressor?" (Isa 51:12–13). According to Isaiah the oppressor mentioned in verse 13 is "a mere mortal who must die, a human being who fades like grass." Those "bent on destruction" in Hab 1:9 are the Chaldeans (Hab 1:6), the nation God is using as his agent of judgment. Again, Boyd says that "Sodom and Gomorrah were destroyed not because of something God did (viz., sending down fire) but because of something God stopped doing."[16] Boyd's view contradicts what the text says, that the Lord did it and it came from heaven: "Then the LORD rained on Sodom and Gomorrah sulfur and fire from the LORD out of heaven" (Gen 19:24).

THE SINS OF SODOM

Sodom had a reputation of being a wicked city: "Now the people of Sodom were wicked, great sinners against the LORD" (Gen 13:13). According to Ezekiel, the sins of Sodom were mostly social sins: "This was the guilt of your sister Sodom: she and her daughters had pride, excess of food, and prosperous ease, but did not aid the poor and needy. They were haughty, and did abominable things before me" (Ezek 16:49–50). The narrative in Genesis says that the sin of Sodom was sexual immorality. The text says that the men of the city wanted to have intercourse with the two visitors: "all the men from every part of the city of Sodom—both young and old—surrounded [Lot's] house. They called to Lot, 'Where are the men who came to you tonight? Bring them out to us so that we can have sex with them'" (Gen 19:4–5 NIV). Peterson develops a list of the sins of Sodom by using the laws of the Torah. According to Peterson, the sins of Sodom include gang rape, oppression of the poor, inhospitality, transgression/wrongdoing against a person, adultery, incest, and homosexual acts. Whatever the sins of Sodom were, they were sins against God.[17]

A CRY FOR HELP

The context of Abraham's dialogue with Yahweh was the announcement of the birth of Isaac. When the two men who were with Yahweh got up to leave toward Sodom, Yahweh and Abraham remained behind. Yahweh said to himself: "'Shall I hide from Abraham what I am about to do, seeing

---

16. Boyd, *Crucifixion of the Warrior God*, 1188.
17. Peterson, "Sin of Sodom Revisited," 17–31.

that Abraham shall become a great and mighty nation, and all the nations of the earth shall be blessed in him?' No, for I have chosen him, that he may charge his children and his household after him to keep the way of the LORD by doing righteousness and justice; so that the LORD may bring about for Abraham what he has promised him" (Gen 18:17–19). By revealing his intentions to Abraham, Yahweh implicitly invites Abraham to intercede for divine mercy on behalf of Sodom.[18] Yahweh's resolve to tell Abraham about his intentions concerning Sodom was based on the promise he had made to Abraham that all nations would be blessed through him. Since Abraham would teach his descendants how to keep the way of the Lord by doing righteousness and justice, Yahweh uses this opportunity to teach him "the way of the Lord." As Widmer writes, "In order to become a blessing to all nations, Abraham and his descendants must learn to discern between justice and injustice in all its universal complexity."[19]

Yahweh said to Abraham, "How great is the outcry against Sodom and Gomorrah and how very grave their sin" (Gen 18:20). The outcry against Sodom motivated the action of God against the city. The Hebrew word for "outcry" is *ze' aqah*. The Hebrew word refers to a cry that is directed to God by someone asking for help in time of distress. In the Old Testament, the outcry of people generally refers to the cry of suffering by people who are oppressed like the enslaved Israelites in Egypt, "the cry of the people of Israel has come to me" (Exod 3:9). The outcry against Sodom that came before God may have been the cry of individuals needing some kind of help because of their oppression, or the cry of people suffering injustice, or it may refer to a cry from a disturbed heart because of the wickedness of the people. The wickedness of the people of Sodom was "very grave" but it remains unspecified. Yahweh comes down to investigate and know the true situation of Sodom before he reaches his final decision about the fate of the city. Yahweh needed to know firsthand whether the outcry against Sodom was valid: "I must go down and see whether they have done altogether according to the outcry that has come to me; and if not, I will know." As a result, Yahweh discovered that the men of Sodom, "both young and old, all the people without exception" (Gen 19:4 NJB) were involved in the wickedness of the city.

---

18. Widmer, *Standing in the Breach*, 34.
19. Widmer, *Standing in the Breach*, 34.

ABRAHAM'S INTERCESSION FOR SODOM

The destruction of Sodom must be understood from the perspective of what kind of God Yahweh says he is. Yahweh is a merciful and gracious God, a God who is slow to anger, a God who abounds in steadfast love and faithfulness, a God who forgives iniquity, transgression, and sin. The merciful character of Yahweh is revealed by the fact that Yahweh is willing to spare hundreds of wicked people for the sake of a few righteous non-Israelites who lived in Sodom. However, Yahweh is also a God who by no means clears the guilty (Exod 34:6–7). The fact that Yahweh is a merciful and gracious God and a God who judges and visits the iniquity of the parents upon the children (Exod 34:7) is one of the greatest paradoxes of the Old Testament. The psalmist says that Yahweh is "coming to judge the earth; he will judge the world with saving justice, and the nations with constancy" (Ps 96:13 NJB). Divine judgment is what Isaiah calls the "strange" and "alien" work of God (Isa 28:21). Because divine judgment goes against the merciful and gracious nature of Yahweh, von Rad calls divine judgment the "dark reverse side of the work of Jahweh."[20]

The biblical text provides several reasons for the judgment that came upon Sodom: "Then the LORD said, 'How great is the outcry against Sodom and Gomorrah and how very grave their sin! I must go down and see whether they have done altogether according to the outcry that has come to me; and if not, I will know" (Gen 18:20–21). When the outcry reached Yahweh, he determined to come down to personally ascertain whether the sins of the people were as serious and as evil as the outcry which had come to him, but if the people's sins were not as bad as they seemed from the outcry which had come to him, then he would know.

Crucial to the understanding of the destruction of Sodom is the prayer of Abraham on behalf of Sodom.[21] Abraham's prayer deals with the issue of God's justice. James Crenshaw says that Abraham's intercession for Sodom raised several issues in the mind of the biblical writer about Yahweh's justice. Crenshaw writes, "The Yahwist recognizes that there is more injustice in the death of a few innocent people than in the sparing of a guilty multitude; his question, however, is . . . 'What determines God's judgment on Sodom, the wickedness of the many or the

---

20. Rad, *Old Testament Theology*, 2:164.

21. Scholars differ on the theological interpretation of the text and its main teaching, cf. Ben Zvi, "Dialogue Between Abraham and Yhwh," 27–46.

innocence of the few?""[22] The biblical writer believes that because Yahweh is willing not to destroy the city, that a small number of innocent people could spare all the inhabitants of Sodom.

Abraham came near to Yahweh with an audacious request.[23] Abraham approached Yahweh to intercede for Sodom, appealing to Yahweh on behalf of the righteous people who lived in the city: "Will you indeed sweep away the righteous with the wicked?" (Gen 18:23) Abraham could not accept that the righteous and the wicked would be treated the same way: "Far be it from you to do such a thing, to slay the righteous with the wicked, so that the righteous fare as the wicked! Far be that from you! Shall not the Judge of all the earth do what is just?" (Gen 18:25). Whybray, however, believes that Abraham was concerned "about the morality of God's standard of justice."[24] Whybray believes that Abraham confronted Yahweh because he was on committing an injustice by destroying Sodom. He writes, "So Abraham, faced with Yahweh's stated intention here, appears as the bold antagonist, first accusing Yahweh of immorality and then proceeding to teach him how he should behave."[25]

The Hebrew word for "just" is *mišpāt*, a word that is generally translated as "judgment" or "justice." This means that when a case is brought before him, Yahweh, as a righteous judge, will make a decision or pass a sentence that is based on his character as a gracious and merciful God, as a God who forgives iniquity, transgression, and sin, but as a God who by no means clears the guilty (Exod 34:7). The Old Testament has much to say about Yahweh and justice: "Yahweh loves justice" (Ps 37:28 NJB). "Yahweh acts with uprightness, with justice to all who are oppressed" (Ps 103:6 NJB). When Solomon dedicated the temple in Jerusalem, in his prayer of dedication, Solomon asked Yahweh to judge the guilty and the innocent. He prayed, "If someone . . . comes . . . before your altar in this house, hear in heaven, and act, and judge your servants, condemning the guilty by bringing their conduct on their own head, and vindicating the righteous by rewarding them according to their righteousness" (1 Kgs 8:32).

---

22. Crenshaw, "Popular Questioning of the Justice of God," 385.

23. According to Bridge, "Audacious Request," 281–96, Abraham was not asking Yahweh to spare Sodom nor was he appealing for justice for the people in the city. Rather, Abraham's audacious request was for Yahweh to spare his nephew Lot at the time the city was destroyed.

24. Whybray, "Immorality of God," 120.

25. Whybray, "Immorality of God," 102.

The psalmist believed that as a judge, Yahweh would judge the nations with righteousness and with his truth, "he comes to judge the earth! He judges the world fairly, and the nations in accordance with his justice" (Ps 96:13 NET) but, as Brueggemann has said, Yahweh's justice is demanding, "As judge, Yahweh does indeed, in the rhetoric of Israel, enact justice, but it is a justice that is demanding, fierce, and uncompromising. Thus the 'judge of all the earth' (Gen 18:25) does justice by destroying Sodom."[26]

According to Abraham, the judge of all the earth should make a distinction between the righteous and the wicked; God should not punish the righteous with the wicked. In his argument against Marcion, Tertullian said that God, in his role as judge, must feel emotions such as offense and anger, and that he must punish evildoers. Tertullian said that God is good but "in order to be good in a divine manner, God must also be able to condemn. . . . God is not fully good unless He is the enemy of evil. . . . Judgment without punishment is irrelevant to morality and religion."[27]

Because of the wickedness of the people of Sodom, Yahweh was planning to destroy the whole city, all the people in it, including men, women, and children, the second, third, and in some cases even the fourth generation living in the city, but God is not an arbitrary judge. He consulted Abraham about what he was about to do, "the Lord GOD does nothing, without revealing his secret to his servants the prophets" (Amos 3:7).[28] Abraham prayed to God, the righteous judge, to do what was just. Abraham prayed: "Suppose there are fifty righteous within the city; will you then sweep away the place and not forgive it for the fifty righteous who are in it?" (Gen 18:24). Yahweh told Abraham, "If I find at Sodom fifty righteous in the city, I will forgive the whole place for their sake" (Gen 18:26). Abraham's prayer was effective; God changed his mind; because of Abraham's prayer, the Lord would spare the city for fifty righteous persons.

It is tragic that when speaking about the destruction of Sodom, people tend to emphasize the fact that the wrath of God was coming upon the city and that he would destroy Sodom, killing men, women, and children. However, people seldom emphasize that God in his mercy would

---

26. Brueggemann, *Theology of the Old Testament*, 248

27. Hallman, "Mutability of God," 377–78.

28. Although Abraham is not called a prophet before his dialogue with Yahweh, Yahweh himself calls Abraham "a prophet" (Gen 20:7).

spare the whole city and all the wicked people who lived in it for the sake of fifty righteous people. It is so much easier to emphasize the wrath of God in destroying the city than to emphasize the mercy of God in sparing the city because of fifty righteous people who lived there. While there were hundreds, maybe even thousands of wicked people in Sodom who deserved to be judged because of their wickedness, they would be spared judgment because of fifty righteous people. This shows again that God does not want to destroy people, but to save them: "Have I any pleasure in the death of the wicked, says the Lord GOD, and not rather that they should turn from their ways and live?" (Ezek 18:23). While thousands deserved to die, the lives of fifty righteous people were more important to God than the death of thousands of sinners, "For I have no pleasure in the death of anyone, says the Lord GOD" (Ezek 18:32).

Abraham realized that there were not fifty righteous people in Sodom. So, Abraham prayed for forty-five and once again Sodom would be spared destruction for the sake of forty-five righteous people in the city. But, alas, there were not forty-five righteous people in Sodom, so Abraham prayer for forty, and God would spare the whole city for the sake of forty. Abraham prayed for thirty and twenty and again God would spare the destruction of the city in answer to Abraham's prayer. Then, something amazing happened, Abraham prayed for ten righteous persons in the city: "'Oh do not let the Lord be angry if I speak just once more. Suppose ten are found there.' The Lord answered, 'For the sake of ten I will not destroy it'" (Gen 18:32).

Yahweh was willing to save the whole city and spare the lives of thousands of wicked people for the sake of ten righteous people who lived in Sodom. If God was willing to spare the city for the sake of fifty, that was a demonstration of God's mercy; the sparing of the city for the sake of ten people is a demonstration of the immense grace that God shows in dealing with people.[29] The willingness of Yahweh to forgive the whole city for the sake of ten righteous people reflects, as Fretheim puts it, "the extent to which God is willing, and indeed eager, to go in order to fulfill God's uncompromising will for the salvation of as many as possible."

By demonstrating his willingness to spare Sodom for the sake of ten righteous persons, Yahweh showed to Abraham what kind of God he was. As Hawk puts it, "Yahweh's back-and-forth with Abraham on the matter of Sodom and Gomorrah confirms that Yahweh undertakes serious

---

29. Fretheim, "Prayer in the Old Testament," 58.

deliberation about how to respond to threats. Yahweh does not inflict massive violence unless the threat has magnified to such an extent that destruction is the only foreseeable end."[30]

Although Yahweh was willing to save the city, the city was destroyed because Abraham stopped asking. As long as Abraham prayed asking God to have mercy on the city, God kept giving him what he asked for. Many people wonder why Abraham stopped at ten. What if Abraham had asked God to spare Sodom for the sake of one righteous person? God told Jeremiah that he would be willing to spare Jerusalem if Jeremiah could find one righteous person in the city: "Run to and fro through the streets of Jerusalem, look around and take note! Search its squares and see if you can find one person who acts justly and seeks truth—so that I may pardon Jerusalem" (Jer 5:1). God was willing not to destroy Sodom, but he did not find a reason to save the city because of the wickedness of the people since not even ten righteous people were in a city of thousands. Sodom was destroyed, but before the city was destroyed, God removed the few righteous people who were in the city.

YAHWEH'S RESPONSE TO ABRAHAM'S PRAYER

Abraham did not ask God to spare Sodom nor did he appeal to the mercy of God to spare the city. Abraham appealed to the mercy of God and asked God for full forgiveness for the city for the sake of the righteous. The reason Yahweh answered Abraham's prayer and gave an opportunity for Sodom to be spared was because Yahweh had not yet made a final determination on the fate of Sodom. He was willing to forgive the whole city for the sake of ten righteous individuals. As Widmer writes, "Preserving even a tiny number of innocent humans is more important to God's eyes than bringing deserved judgment on the guilty. Thus, this account underlines the biblical teaching that God's will to save clearly dominates over His will to punish."[31] Notwithstanding Abraham's intercession on behalf of Sodom and Yahweh's desire to spare the city, Sodom was destroyed and thousands of people died. Yahweh is a God who forgives ʽ*āwōn* "iniquity" (Exod 34:7) but he could not forgive the iniquity (ʽ *āwōn*) of Sodom (Gen 19:15 TNK) because the wickedness of the people had become so pervasive that it had touched every segment of the community.

30. Hawk, *Violence of the Biblical God*, 45.
31. Widmer, *Standing in the Breach*, 54.

Yahweh is a God who forgives iniquity (Exod 34:7). The Hebrew word *nāsā'*, "forgive" in English, carries the idea of "to bear, to carry." In explaining the meaning of Abraham's request, Widmer wrote,

> Abraham prays that God would "forgive" (NRSV), or perhaps the Hebrew *nāsā'* should be rendered with "bear" with the wicked, for the sake of the innocent, and not for the removal of the innocent few from the sphere of judgment. Thus, Abraham seems to imply that there is greater injustice in the death of the innocent than in the life of the wicked. By praying that God should "endure" (*nāsā'*) the wickedness of the majority for the sake of a minority of righteous, Abraham appeals no longer to justice, but to the mercy of God.[32]

Fretheim says that when God forgives, he takes the sins of the guilty person upon himself. He wrote, "God judges the world in and through the created moral order, acting within the interplay of human actions and their consequences, so that sin and evil do not go unchecked in the life of the creation. God saves the world by taking its suffering into the very heart of the divine life, bearing it there, and then wearing it in the form of a cross."[33]

As Yahweh responded to his requests, Abraham learned an important truth about the character of God, that is, that in dealing with wicked people, Yahweh is a gracious and merciful God. This truth about the character of God was revealed in its fulness to Moses at the time Israel rebelled against God and committed the sin of apostasy when they worshiped the image of the golden calf.

In explaining the reason for the destruction of Sodom, Sarna said, "The indictment of Sodom lies entirely in the moral realm." The story of Sodom and Gomorrah "assumes the existence of a universal moral law that God expects all humankind to follow. The idea that there is an inextricable connection between the social and moral behavior of a people and its ultimate fate is one of the pillars upon which the entire biblical interpretation of history stands."[34]

The New Testament uses Sodom and Gomorrah as an illustration of how God deals with ungodly people: "For if God . . . by turning the cities of Sodom and Gomorrah to ashes he condemned them to extinction and

---

32. Widmer, *Standing in the Breach*, 41.
33. Fretheim, "To Say Something," 350.
34. Sarna, *Genesis*, 132.

made them an example of what is coming to the ungodly . . . then the Lord knows how to rescue the godly from trial, and to keep the unrighteous under punishment until the day of judgment" (2 Pet 2:4–9).

In her discussion of Yahweh as a judge, Alyssa Walker writes, "Today, for the majority of people living in Western cultures the concept of a judgmental God is difficult. The biblical portrayals of God as judge are de-emphasized in favor of biblical portrayals of God as love. What is fascinating is that this squeamishness toward judgment is cultural." She writes that people who live in oppressive situations welcome the role of God as a judge: "Knowing that God judges brings hope to the oppressed—that their oppressors will not be allowed to persist in their evil ways forever. In order for God to love the oppressed, he must act as a judge to the oppressors."[35]

---

35. Walker, "Jonah's Genocidal and Suicidal Attitude," 10.

17

Yahweh Rejects Violence

JEHU'S OVERTHROW OF THE OMRIDE dynasty is a story filled with violence and brutality. Yahweh commanded the prophet Elijah to anoint Jehu in order to avenge the death of Naboth and the killing of Yahweh's prophets. Elisha and the sons of the prophets anointed Jehu as king of Israel. Immediately after his anointing Jehu embarked on a purge of the Omrides in order to eradicate the worship of Baal from the Northern Kingdom and reestablish the worship of Yahweh. So brutal and violent was the rebellion against the Omrides that Yahweh disapproved the actions of Jehu and declared that he would visit Jehu's family for the bloodshed of Jezreel. This chapter will study Jehu's actions and Yahweh's rejection of the violence and brutality Jehu used to overthrow Ahab's family.[1]

POLITICAL CONFUSION IN ISRAEL

When the United Kingdom divided after the death of Solomon, both Judah and Israel went their different ways. The Northern Kingdom (Israel) was plagued by internal instability. The Southern Kingdom (Judah) remained somewhat stable because the Davidic dynasty survived until the end of the Southern Kingdom. However, Israel's throne changed occupants many times, often by violence, in the first fifty years of its history.[2]

---

1. Some of the material on Jehu was adopted from my article "Jehu: His Leadership and Legacy," 51–55.

2. Jaruzelska, "Prophets and *coups d'état*," 19–31. According to Jaruzelska, there

The accession of Omri to the throne brought stability and prosperity to Israel.

Omri's rise to power was preceded by much political unrest in Israel (see 1 Kgs 16:8–22). Elah, the son of Baasha reigned two years in Israel (877–876 BCE). Elah was an incompetent king who did not have the support of his people. While the army of Israel was fighting against the Philistines (1 Kgs 16:16), Elah, "while drinking himself drunk" (1 Kgs 16:9), was killed by Zimri in the house of one of his officers. The death of Elah was seen as a judgment upon the house of Baasha, in accordance with the words of the prophet Jehu, the son of Hanani (1 Kgs 16:12–13).

Israel's next king, Zimri (876 BCE), was king of Israel for seven days. Zimri was the commander of half of the chariots of the army of Elah. Zimri killed the royal family and assumed the throne of Israel (1 Kgs 16:11–12). When the news of the death of the royal family reached the Israelite army, the troops on the field proclaimed their commander, Omri, as king of Israel. After the death of Zimri, Israel was divided between two pretenders to the throne, Omri and Tibni, the son of Ginath (1 Kgs 16:21–22). Nothing is known about Omri's family. The fact that Omri's family is not mentioned may indicate that he probably was a non-Israelite, who was serving the king as commander of the army.

THE REIGN OF OMRI

After he became king of Israel, Omri's first priority was the consolidation of his kingdom. One of Omri's major political decisions was to establish an alliance with Ethbaal, king of Tyre. This alliance was sealed by the marriage of Ahab, Omri's son, to Jezebel, the daughter of the king of Tyre (1 Kgs 16:31). The treaty with Tyre brought economic prosperity to Israel. The royal treasury enjoyed considerable prosperity because of its trade with Tyre. Many people in Israel benefitted from the active commerce between Israel and Phoenicia. Omri also made an alliance with Judah. This alliance was sealed by the marriage of Athaliah, the daughter of Ahab and Jezebel, to Jehoram, the son of Jehoshaphat (2 Kgs 8:18).[3]

---

were nine *coups d'état* in the Northern Kingdom.

3. Athaliah appears as the daughter of Ahab and Jezebel in 2 Kgs 8:18 and 2 Chr 21:6 and as the daughter of Omri in 2 Kgs 8:26 and 2 Chr 22:2. The NRSV says that Athaliah was the granddaughter of Omri.

Internally, Omri established a new capital for Israel (1 Kgs 16:24). Omri bought a site from Shemer to build his capital and named it Samaria (1 Kgs 16:24). Omri paid two talents of silver for Samaria. Thus, Samaria became royal property and Omri had total control over the city. Omri introduced a system of taxation to maintain the government. The economic condition in Israel created a class of rich people who controlled the means of production and the wealth of the nation. The situation of the poor became worse. In the days of the prophet Elisha, many poor people had to mortgage their land and sell their children and themselves to pay their debt and the taxes owed to the state and to creditors (see 2 Kgs 4:1). This economic hardship upon the poor people of Israel was caused by the system of taxation which became necessary in order to maintain a large military complex and to fund royal projects in Samaria and throughout the nation. The oppressive economic policies of the Omrides brought much dissatisfaction with the policies of Omri and Ahab and created a desire for change.

THE RELIGIOUS CRISIS IN ISRAEL

Jezebel was the daughter of Ethbaal, king of Tyre. Ethbaal was also a priest in the cult of Baal and the goddess Asherah. It is possible that Jezebel, as a king's daughter, was also "a high priestess of the chief local god, in this case, Baal Melqart."[4] Jezebel is called the *gĕbîrâ*, "the queen mother" (2 Kgs 10:13). The *gĕbîrâ* exerted some official position in the court of her son after the death of her husband, the king.[5]

The issue that forced the community to conspire against the house of Omri and Ahab was the religious crisis in Israel brought about by the missionary program established by Jezebel. After her marriage to Ahab, Jezebel came to live in Samaria. She maintained her identity as a worshiper of Baal. According to 1 Kgs 18:19, Jezebel tried to promote the worship of Baal in the Northern Kingdom by sponsoring four hundred fifty prophets of Baal and the four hundred prophets of Asherah. For this reason, Jezebel encountered much opposition from the prophets in

---

4. Yee, "Jezebel (Person)," 3:848–49.

5. Ackerman, "Queen Mother," 385. The queen mother also had some official responsibility in the religious life of Israel. One of these responsibilities was to promote the cult of the mother goddess Asherah. Scholars are divided whether the queen mother had religious duties in Israelite religion; cf. Ben-Barak, "Status and Right of the *Gĕbîrâ*," 23–34; Andreasen, "Role of the Queen Mother," 179–94.

Israel who saw her as a threat to the worship of Yahweh in the Northern Kingdom. In order to accommodate the religious needs of Jezebel, Ahab "erected an altar for Baal in the house of Baal, which he built in Samaria" (1 Kgs 16:32). Baal was the main god of the Canaanites. Baal was a storm and fertility god. Ahab also made an asherah pole (1 Kgs 16:33). The asherah pole was a wooden object made by the worshipers of Asherah as a symbol of the fertility goddess Asherah, the consort of Baal. The people of Israel were forbidden to make asherah poles: "Do not set up any wooden Asherah pole beside the altar you build to the LORD your God" (Deut 16:21 NIV). As part of her effort to establish Baal as the official religion of the land, Jezebel persecuted and killed many of the prophets and followers of Yahweh (1 Kgs 18:4). Jezebel's motivation to kill the prophets of Yahweh and replace them with the prophets of Baal was to eliminate those who could pose a threat to her religious reforms.

GOD'S REVELATION TO ELIJAH

Elijah the prophet was commissioned by Yahweh to confront Ahab and oppose the religious aspirations of Jezebel. Elijah began his ministry by proclaiming a three-year drought in the land. Since Baal was a storm god, Baal was held by his worshipers to be the god who controlled the rain (1 Kgs 17:1). The drought was a challenge to Jezebel and to the worshipers of Baal. The announcement of the drought intended to show that Yahweh was the true God and the one who controlled the rain. This challenge found its culmination in the confrontation between Elijah and the prophets of Baal on Mount Carmel.

In order to promote the religion of Israel, Elijah challenged the prophets of Baal to a contest on Mount Carmel (1 Kgs 18). Elijah called on the people to follow either Yahweh or Baal. When Yahweh powerfully demonstrated that he was able to answer the prayer of his prophet, the people recognized that Yahweh was the true God (1 Kgs 18:39).

When Elijah confronted the prophets of Baal on Mount Carmel, Yahweh gave Elijah a great victory against the four hundred prophets of Baal. At the request of Elijah, Yahweh had demonstrated his great power by consuming the sacrifice Elijah offered (1 Kgs 18:20–40). By his action, Elijah demonstrated that Yahweh was the only God of Israel. The inaction of Baal and the meaningless prayers of his prophets showed that Baal could not answer the prayers of his followers because Yahweh was the only true God. Everyone recognized that Elijah was Yahweh's prophet. This was Elijah's request when he prayed to Yahweh: "O LORD, God of Abraham, Isaac, and Israel, let it be known this day that you are God in Israel, that I am your servant, and that I have done all these things at your bidding" (1 Kgs 18:36).

Elijah's purpose in calling for this confrontation was to show the people of Israel that Yahweh was the true God. Elijah prayed: "Answer me, O LORD, answer me, so that this people may know that you, O LORD, are God" (1 Kgs 18:37). Yahweh answered Elijah's prayer by sending fire from heaven, thus vindicating Elijah's work as a prophet. Yahweh showed that he was a true God by giving Elijah a great victory. After the people proclaimed that Yahweh was the true God of Israel, Elijah killed the prophets of Baal (1 Kgs 18:40). Elijah followed the Deuteronomic teaching about false prophets (Deut 13:1–18) by putting the false prophets of Baal to death: "If prophets . . . appear among you and . . . say, 'Let us follow other gods' . . . those prophets . . . shall be put to death for having spoken treason against the LORD your God" (Deut 13:1–5).

When Jezebel heard what Elijah had done to the prophets of Baal, Jezebel threatened to kill Elijah the next day. Jezebel sent a messenger to Elijah with a severe message. She said: "So may the gods do to me, and more also, if I do not make your life like the life of one of them by this time tomorrow" (1 King 19:2). When Elijah heard about Jezebel's threat, he was greatly afraid. He became so depressed that "he got up and fled for his life" (1 Kgs 19:3). Elijah fled to hide himself on Mount Horeb (or Sinai).

Elijah came to Horeb (Sinai), the mountain of God to meet with Yahweh (1 Kgs 19:8). When God met Elijah on Mount Horeb, Yahweh asked his depressed prophet: "What are you doing here, Elijah?" (1 Kgs 19:9). Elijah said: "The Israelites have rejected your covenant, broken down your altars, and put your prophets to death with the sword. I am the only one left, and now they are trying to kill me too" (1 Kgs 19:10). To help Elijah, Yahweh revealed himself to him, "The LORD said, 'Go out and stand on the mountain in the presence of the LORD, for the LORD is about to pass by'" (1 Kgs 19:11).

On Horeb Yahweh gave Elijah a plan to overthrow the dynasty of Omri (19:15–18). "Then the LORD said to him, 'Go, return on your way to the wilderness of Damascus; when you arrive, you shall anoint Hazael as king over Aram. Also you shall anoint Jehu son of Nimshi as king over Israel; and you shall anoint Elisha son of Shaphat of Abel-meholah as prophet in your place. Whoever escapes from the sword of Hazael, Jehu shall kill; and whoever escapes from the sword of Jehu, Elisha shall kill'" (1 Kgs 19:15–17). The instruction Yahweh gave to Elijah was a political plan that would culminate with the overthrow of the dynasty of Omri in Israel.[6] Elijah returned to Israel to carry out Yahweh's wishes; he was only able to carry out the third of Yahweh's commands; it was left to Elisha to carry out the other two.

JEHU'S ANOINTING

Jehu, the son of Nimshi, was the tenth king of Israel and he reigned twenty-eight years (843–815 BCE). He came to the throne of the Northern Kingdom with prophetic approval in order to overthrow the dynasty of Omri. Jehu appears as the son of Nimshi in 1 Kgs 19:16 and 2 Kgs 9:20 and as the son of Jehoshaphat in 2 Kgs 9:2, 14.[7] It has been suggested that Nimshi was Jehu's grandfather. In his youth Jehu served as a chariot officer in Ahab's army. He was one of the two witnesses who heard the prophetic sentence against Ahab and his house (2 Kgs 9:25–26; see 1 Kgs 21:17–19, 28–29). The selection of Jehu to be king of Israel was made by Yahweh himself. Yahweh's will was revealed to Elijah and fulfilled by Elisha. Jehu became king of Israel at a crucial time in the life of the nation. The events that preceded his accession to the throne provide the proper background for understanding his anointing and the bloodshed that followed his coronation.

Jehu's conspiracy against the house of Ahab was supported by the prophet Elisha and it was initiated with Jehu's anointing by a member of the prophetic guild of which Elisha was the leader.[8] After the disappearance of Elijah, Elisha became the leader of the prophetic community. One of his first acts was to commission one of his servants to go to Jehu and anoint him king over Israel. Elisha called one of the members of the

---

6. Sweeney, *I & II Kings*, 233.

7. Baruchi-Unna, "Jehuites, Ahabites, and Omrides," 4, based on an Assyrian inscription, believes that Jehu was a member of Omri's family. She writes, "Jehu appears in the Bible as 'son of Jehoshaphat, son of Nimshi', and in the inscriptions of Shalmaneser III of Assyria he appears as 'son of Omri.' Taken together, this evidence suggests that Jehu was a descendant of Omri, apparently, of a family branch other than that of Ahab, and that his coup was an inner manoeuvre within the ruling family." This view, however, finds no biblical support.

8. Jaruzelska, "Les prophètes face aux usurpations," 165–87.

prophetic guild of which he was the leader and gave the young prophet a specific command. He was to take a flask of oil, go to Ramoth-gilead, and there in private, in the inner chamber, anoint Jehu king over Israel. After the anointing, the young prophet should leave immediately (2 Kgs 9:1–3). The anointing was to be done in secret. Since there was a king sitting on the throne of Israel, the act of anointing Jehu would be considered a treasonous act.

There is, however, a difference between what Elisha told the young prophet to do and what the young man did when he arrived at Ramoth-gilead to anoint Jehu. The anointing of Jehu took place while he was with the army at Ramoth Gilead in preparation for war with Hazael, king of Syria (2 Kgs 9:1–13). At that time Elisha gave orders to one of his servants to anoint Jehu as king. Elisha's messenger came to where Jehu was meeting with his officers; he took Jehu apart, poured oil on his head and anointed him king over Yahweh's people, over Israel (2 Kgs 9:6).

The statement that Jehu was anointed to be king over Yahweh's people serves to identify Israel as Yahweh's people, in contradistinction to those who worshiped Baal. Then, in the name of Elisha, the messenger gave Jehu the order to utterly destroy the house of Ahab in order to avenge on Jezebel the blood of the prophets whom Jezebel had killed. He was also told that he was supposed to kill Jezebel and leave her body unburied (2 Kgs 9:1–10). After the prophet left, Jehu declared to his fellow officers what had just happened. The officers hastily spread their garments for Jehu to stand on, blew the trumpets and proclaimed: "Jehu is king" (2 Kgs 9:11–13). Scholars are divided on whether the young prophet conveyed faithfully the message he received from Elisha or whether he expressed his own views by telling Jehu to exterminate the house of Ahab.[9]

Jehu was anointed in order to abolish the worship of Baal, to reestablish the worship of Yahweh, to terminate the political alliance with Tyre, and to eliminate the socioeconomic abuses against the poor people of Israel. Jehu failed to meet the expectations of Elisha. Jehu wiped out the worship of Baal from Israel,[10] at least during his reign (2 Kgs 10:28),

---

9. In describing the action of the nameless prophet, Moore, "Jehu's Coronation and Purge of Israel," 103, wrote, "We have no idea who this person is, and this is precisely the point. His anonymity is deliberate—thus our surprise when an entire 'oracle' comes out of his mouth. Elisha gives him one scripted line—'This is what Yahweh says: I anoint you king over Israel'—but this is not what he actually says. Instead, he commands Jehu to 'destroy the house of Ahab,' 'to avenge the blood of my servants the prophets.'"

10. King, "Did Jehu Destroy Baal," 309–32.

but soon after he became king, he had to submit to Shalmaneser III, king of Assyria. As an Assyrian vassal, Jehu had to pay heavy tribute and probably a "formal acknowledgment of Assyrian gods."[11]

JEHU'S VIOLENT PURGE

Jehu began to carry out his mission immediately. He set off, together with a group of his horsemen, to Jezreel, where Joram (also known as Jehoram), a grandson of Ahab, king of Israel, was recovering from a wound that he had received in battle (2 Kgs 9:17–24). When Joram was told that Jehu was driving his chariot "furiously," Joram sent messengers to Jehu, asking, "Is it peace?" When the messengers did not return, Joram, together with his cousin Ahaziah, king of Judah, went to meet Jehu. When Joram asked, "Is it peace?" Jehu responded by denouncing the sins of Jezebel. At this Joram cried: "It is treason, Ahaziah." When Joram turned to escape, Jehu drew his bow and shot Joram in the back and the arrow pierced his heart and Joram died on his chariot. Jehu commanded his aide Bidkar to take Joram's body and throw it in the field that belonged to Naboth. This action fulfilled the oracle of Elijah concerning the death of Ahab's house.

Jehu then proceeded to kill Ahaziah, king of Judah, the son of Athaliah (2 Kgs 9:27–29). When Ahaziah saw that Jehu had killed Joram, Ahaziah fled but Jehu's men caught up with him and wounded him (2 Kgs 9:27). Ahaziah once again escaped, but he died in Megiddo of his wounds. Ahaziah's body was taken to Jerusalem by his aides, where he was buried in the tomb of the kings.

After having killed Joram and Ahaziah, Jehu went to Jezreel to deal with Jezebel, the queen-mother. Jezebel, when told what had happened, prepared to meet her death with dignity: she painted her eyes, arranged her hair, and put on her royal garments. Her defiance in the face of death is seen in her insulting words to Jehu from the window of the royal residence: "Have you come in peace, you Zimri, murderer of your master?"[12] Jezebel's words refer to the murderous actions of Zimri who usurped the throne by killing the family of Baasha. Without an answer, Jehu asked some palace officials to throw Jezebel down from the window. When Jezebel's body hit the ground, her blood splattered on the wall and on the horses. Jehu drove his horses and his chariots over her body, and then, he

---

11. Gottwald, *Hebrew Bible*, 345.
12. Olyan, "Jehu as Zimri," 203–7.

entered the palace to eat. Later, when his men went to bury Jezebel, they only found her skull, her feet, and her hands. The rest of her body was eaten by dogs. When Jehu was told what had happened, he recollected the words of Yahweh to Elijah that dogs would eat the body of Jezebel in Jezreel (2 Kgs 9:36–37; see 1 Kgs 21:23).

Jehu continued the purge of Ahab's family by sending letters to guardians of the seventy sons and grandsons of Ahab who lived in Samaria. He asked them to select one of the descendants of Ahab, make him king and be prepared to fight and defend the kingdom. Terrified of the possible outcome of a resistance, the rulers of the cities and the guardians of the royal heirs submitted themselves to Jehu. Jehu then sent a second letter asking for the heads of Ahab's descendants. The city officials decapitated the descendants of Ahab, put their heads in baskets and sent them to Jehu at Jezreel. The heads were then piled up in two heaps and placed at the city gate until morning. The next day Jehu began to kill those associated with Ahab: "So Jehu killed everyone in Jezreel who remained of the house of Ahab, as well as all his chief men, his close friends, his priests, leaving him no survivors" (2 Kgs 10:11).

After eliminating the family of Ahab, Jehu set out to go to Samaria. On his way to Samaria, he met forty-two relatives of Ahaziah, all members of the royal house of Judah who were going to Jezreel to visit Jezebel and the members of her family. Jehu ordered his men to kill them. Jehu and his men, "with wanton brutality and for no apparent reason, slaughtered them all"[13] and placed their bodies in a cistern near Beth Eked (2 Kgs 10:12–14).

Before Jehu reached Samaria, he met Jehonadab, the son of Rechab. Jehonadab was the leader of the Rechabites, a group of people who remained faithful to the old traditions of the religion of Yahweh. Because of the Rechabites' commitment of loyalty to Yahweh, Jehu invited Jehonadab to join him in his quest to purify the religion of Yahweh, "Come with me, and see my zeal for the LORD" (2 Kgs 10:16).[14] Jehonadab accepted the invitation and together they went to Samaria to confront the worshipers of Baal. When Jehu arrived in Samaria, he killed all the relatives of Ahab who were living in Samaria.

Once in Samaria, Jehu proceeded to eliminate the worshipers of Baal. Pretending to be a follower of Baal, Jehu organized a great celebration for

---

13. Bright, *History of Israel*, 251.

14. For a discussion on Jehu's zeal for Yahweh and his violence, see Fretheim, *First and Second Kings*, 172–75.

Baal. Jehu invited the priests, the prophets, and the worshipers of Baal from throughout the land of Israel. When all the worshipers were inside the temple of Baal, Jehu gave orders to his soldiers, eighty of them, to kill all those related to the worship of Baal. Jehu's men butchered the worshipers of Baal. Bright calls the slaughter of the Baal worshipers "a purge of unspeakable brutality, beyond excuse from a moral point of view."[15] The temple of Baal was torn down, the sacred objects were destroyed, and Jehu desecrated the holy place by making the temple a latrine for common use. "Thus Jehu wiped out Baal from Israel" (2 Kgs 10:28).

Schulte says that Elisha was responsible for Jehu's violence, "By giving support to Jehu's anointing and the military takeover of the kingdom, Elisha himself contributed to Jehu's use of violence."[16] Yahweh initiated the fall of the Omride dynasty, but in the end, he did not approve the way Jehu carried it out.

GOD'S JUDGMENT ON JEHU

Boyd mentions Jehu twice in his footnotes, both times to emphasize that Hosea condemned the violence perpetrated by Jehu with the approval of Elisha. Boyd wrote, "Creach[17] also argues that Hos 1:4 provides a precedent for the denunciation of a famed prophet on the basis of the violence he participated in. Here the house of Jehu is cursed because of all the blood Jehu shed in his overthrow of Jezreel." Boyd goes on to say that "Elisha, apparently speaking on Yahweh's authority, supported this overthrow."[18]

The second mention of Jehu is a reference to Hosea condemning Elisha for Jehu's violence. Boyd wrote, "A precedent for rejecting the violent exploits of Elijah was arguably set by Hosea, who implicitly rebuked Elisha, Elijah's successor, for the brutally violent campaigns against Jezreel that were carried out by King Jehu, whom Elisha had helped put in office (Hos 1:4, cf. 2 Kgs 9–10)."[19]

---

15. Bright, *History of Israel*, 251.
16. Schulte, "End of the Omride Dynasty," 133–48.
17. Boyd is citing Creach, *Violence in Scripture*, 158.
18. Boyd, *Crucifixion of the Warrior God*, 82n159.
19. Boyd, *Crucifixion of the Warrior God*, 1224n75.

What Boyd failed to notice is that it is Yahweh who is condemning the violence of Jehu at Jezreel.[20] It is Yahweh who tells Hosea how to name his child, "Name him Jezreel." It is Yahweh who tells Hosea what he will do: "I will visit the blood of Jezreel." It is Yahweh who tells Hosea who will receive the divine visitation "upon the house of Jehu." It is Yahweh who tells Hosea when the visitation will occur, "in a little while." Jehu was commissioned by Elisha with the approval of Yahweh, but Yahweh condemns the atrocities committed by Jehu because the violence and the brutality Jehu used to accomplish his mission was beyond what he was commissioned to do.

Jehu's overthrow of the Omrides fulfilled the judgment which God had denounced by Elijah against the house of Ahab for the murder of Naboth and for the killing of the prophets of Yahweh. However, in executing God's judgment upon the Omrides, Jehu went beyond what was required of him. He was cruel and heartless toward the family of Ahab. Although he was acting as God's agent of retribution, Jehu acted out of personal ambition; he was only interested in the throne. Although Jehu was doing Yahweh's work, Yahweh rejected the violence, the atrocities, and the brutality he used against the house of Ahab and the worshipers of Baal.

Yahweh honored the work of Jehu by promising him that his dynasty would last four generations: "Because you have done well in accomplishing what is right in my eyes and have done to the house of Ahab all I had in mind to do, your descendants will sit on the throne of Israel to the fourth generation" (2 Kgs 10:30). Yet, because of Jehu's excessive shedding of blood, and the excessive violence in accomplishing his mission, Yahweh began to bring his judgment upon the house of Jehu and upon the kingdom of Israel: "In those days the LORD began to trim off parts of Israel. Hazael defeated them throughout the territory of Israel" (2 Kgs 10:32). The rest of Jehu's reign is occupied with his wars against Syria. He also had to deal with the loss of territory on the east side of the Jordan. In addition, Jehu became a vassal of Assyria, and had to present

---

20. Chisholm, "'Bloodshed of Jezreel,'" 429, does not believe that Hosea is condemning Jehu's action in Jezreel. He writes, "Interpreters typically understand Hos 1:4 as a promise that Yahweh would soon punish the house of Jehu for the massacre he had carried out at Jezreel against the house of Ahab. However, this interpretation collides with the account of Jehu's coup in 2 Kgs 9–10. Of various solutions that have been proposed for this problem, it is most likely that Hos 1:4 does not condemn Jehu's actions at Jezreel, but uses them as a paradigm for the judgment that would fall on the house of Jehu."

himself before Shalmaneser III, king of Assyria, with his tribute.[21] The indignity of this submission is that Shalmaneser calls Jehu "the son of Omri." However, the most profound word of judgment upon Jehu's selfish ambition and violent nature comes from Yahweh through the prophet Hosea. The indignity of Jehu paying a tribute to the king of Assyria to secure the throne that Yahweh had given to him demonstrates that in doing the work of God, one is responsible and accountable for the work done.

YAHWEH REJECTS JEHU'S VIOLENCE

Yahweh's condemnation of the violence perpetrated by Jehu when he massacred the house of Ahab comes through Hosea and his painful experience with Gomer. "The pain in the heart of the prophet became a parable of the anguish in the heart of God."[22] The story of Hosea's marriage to Gomer has been a source of endless debate. Yahweh called Hosea to take "a wife of whoredom and have children of whoredom" as a sign that the land had committed "great whoredom" by forsaking the Lord. In obedience to Yahweh, Hosea went and took Gomer to be his wife and she bore him three children: two sons and one daughter. Hosea's children were given symbolic names to reflect Yahweh's judgment upon Jehu for the senseless shedding of blood and upon the sins of the people of Israel. The names of Hosea's three children are prophetic messages from Yahweh to the people. The names represent signs of judgment upon Jehu's dynasty and against the nation.[23]

Hosea's first child was a son: "And the LORD said to him, 'Name him Jezreel; for in a little while I will punish the house of Jehu for the blood of Jezreel, and I will put an end to the kingdom of the house of Israel. On that day I will break the bow of Israel in the valley of Jezreel" (Hos 1:4–5). The sign of Jezreel represents the rejection of the house of Jehu.

Hosea's second child was a daughter: "[Gomer] conceived again and bore a daughter. Then the LORD said to him, 'Name her Lo-ruhamah'

---

21. Smith, "Sin of Jehu," 117, believes that the sin of Jehu which Hosea condemns was not the brutality Jehu used to overthrow the Omride dynasty. Rather, Smith says that Hosea criticized and condemned Jehu "because he made a covenant with Assyria . . . and did not trust solely in YHWH, instead relying upon foreign alliances." Smith says that for Hosea, Jezreel becomes "a rallying cry against ill-fated alliances with anyone other than YHWH" (128).

22. Limburg, *Hosea–Micah*, 10.

23. May, "Interpretation of the Names of Hosea's Children," 285–91.

[Not pitied], for I will no longer have pity on the house of Israel or forgive them. But I will have pity on the house of Judah, and I will save them by the LORD their God; I will not save them by bow, or by sword, or by war, or by horses, or by horsemen" (Hos 1:6–7). The sign of Lo-ruhamah represents the rejection of the nation.

Hosea's third child was also a boy: "When [Gomer] had weaned Lo-ruhamah, she conceived and bore a son. Then the LORD said, 'Name him Lo-ammi' [Not my people], for you are not my people and I am not your God" (Hos 1:8–9). The sign of Lo-ammi represents the rejection of the people.

THE SIGN OF JEZREEL

Yahweh told Hosea to name his firstborn son Jezreel. The name Jezreel means "God sows." Jezreel was also the place where Ahab's second residence was located (1 Kgs 21:1). Jezreel was where Jezebel orchestrated the murder of Naboth in the name of Ahab in order to take possession of his field, the field that Ahab wanted for himself (1 Kgs 21:2). Jezreel was the place where Jehu mercilessly slaughtered Ahab's family. By telling Hosea to name his firstborn son Jezreel, Yahweh was announcing that he was visiting the house of Jehu and vindicating the bloodshed of Jezreel.[24]

"I will punish the house of Jehu for the blood of Jezreel." The Hebrew word *pāqad* which is translated "punish" in most English translations, literally means "to visit." When the word is used in relation to God, it means that God will come and act to bless or to punish, for good or for ill. A better translation is "I will visit the blood of Jezreel upon the house of Jehu." English translations use different words to describe what happened in Jezreel: "massacre" (NIV), "bloodshed" (NJB), "murders" (NLT), "slaughter" (GWN). The shedding of blood brings guilt on the person shedding blood. There was bloodguilt on Saul and on his house because he put the Gibeonites to death (2 Sam 21:1). There was bloodguilt on Joab because he shed blood without cause (1 Kgs 2:31). In the case of Jehu, the visitation upon his house carries the idea of a reckoning for the violence committed against the Omrides. In Jezreel Jehu put an end to the Omride dynasty. Now Yahweh will put an end to Jehu's dynasty. The Omride dynasty came to an end by violence; the dynasty of Jehu will come to an end by violence. "Bloodshed gives birth to bloodshed. . . . Jezreel leads

---

24. Irvine, "Threat of Jezreel," 494–503.

to Jezreel."²⁵ Because of the violence committed in Jezreel, the name of Jezreel has been forever "linked with violence and mass murder."²⁶

The time of the visitation will be "in a little while." Once again God's mercy is manifested to his sinful people. Divine visitation will not come without giving the people a warning and an opportunity to repent, "Return, O Israel, to the LORD your God, for you have stumbled because of your iniquity" (Hos 14:1). The judgment on the house of Jehu has been pronounced, but the execution of the sentence will not occur until the fourth generation. This was the promise Yahweh gave to Jehu, "Your sons shall sit on the throne of Israel to the fourth generation" (2 Kgs 15:12).

The fourth generation is associated with the Second Commandment, "You shall not make for yourself an idol, whether in the form of anything that is in heaven above, or that is on the earth beneath, or that is in the water under the earth. You shall not bow down to them or worship them; for I the LORD your God am a jealous God, punishing children for the iniquity of parents, to the third and the fourth generation of those who reject me, but showing steadfast love to the thousandth generation of those who love me and keep my commandments" (Exod 20:4–6). The Second Commandment is also associated with the issue of intergenerational punishment.

The Second Commandment addresses the issue of idolatry, the making and the worship of idols. Israel was not allowed to worship idols. Those who violated the demands of the Second Commandment and worshiped idols would encounter the visitation of Yahweh to the third and fourth generation of the idolater. The family of Jehu would be visited because "Jehu was not careful to follow the law of the LORD the God of Israel with all his heart; he did not turn from the sins of Jeroboam, which he caused Israel to commit" (2 Kgs 10:31). The sins of Jeroboam were the two golden calves that he set up in Dan and Bethel (1 Kgs 12:28–30).

THE REJECTION OF JEHU

Elisha supported the overthrow of the Omrides primarily because of the religious reforms introduced by Ahab and Jezebel. However, according to Schulte, Elisha was deeply affected by the suffering of the people because of the economic conditions of the population due to the heavy taxation

25. Guenther, *Hosea, Amos*, 43.
26. Limburg, *Hosea–Micah*, 9.

imposed by Omri.²⁷ The stories about Elisha mention poverty (2 Kgs 6:5), lack of food (2 Kgs 4:38–42), and even debt slavery (2 Kgs 4:1–7). By living as members of a commune, these impoverished people dealt with their poverty by helping one another (2 Kgs 9:42–43).

Schulte believes that Elisha opposed the Omrides out of solidarity with the people. Elisha also realized that the community would be unable to support the growing number of people who were joining the community. The situation was so dire that a change in government became imperative, so Elisha "entered the political arena and felt that a new king would improve everything."²⁸ A change of dynasty would require removing the present king by violence. Schulte wrote, "For their part, the poor did not go to Samaria to demand equity and justice from the king. They relied on violence, on another king, to topple the old dynasty and pursue a domestically oriented political line. This was the mistake in their calculations, the mistake in Elisha's reckoning."²⁹ So, Elisha sent a prophet to anoint Jehu as Elijah had requested.

The overthrow of the Omrides and the selection of Jehu to become the new king did not improve the oppression of the poor in the Northern Kingdom as demonstrated by the preaching of Amos and Hosea.³⁰ Jehu assumed power in Israel because of the strong religious opposition to the policies of Ahab and Jezebel. He was able to establish a dynasty because he had the support of the prophetic community, of the army, and of the people.³¹

The sign of Jezreel reflects Hosea's attitude toward the bloody deeds of Jehu, "Hosea condemns the *coups d'état* of his times because of the use of violence."³² Hosea's oracle is also a declaration that Yahweh rejects the use of violence in the political life of his people. When Yahweh declared that Judah would be delivered, he said that Judah would be delivered without violence, "I shall take pity on the House of Judah and shall save them, not by bow or sword or force of arms, not by horses or horsemen, but by Yahweh their God" (Hos 1:7 NJB).

---

27. Schulte, "End of the Omride Dynasty," 140.
28. Schulte, "End of the Omride Dynasty," 141.
29. Schulte, "End of the Omride Dynasty," 146.
30. Ahlström called the anointing of Jehu "a prophet's mistake," cf. Ahlström, "King Jehu: A Prophet's Mistake," 47–69.
31. Schulte, "End of the Omride Dynasty," 137.
32. Jaruzelska, "Prophets and *coups d'état*," 30.

Although Jehu attained the throne of the Northern Kingdom with prophetic approval, the excess of violence Jehu used to deal with the family of Ahab did not gain divine support. Jaruzelska writes, "A comparative analysis of the description and interpretation of events by the editors of the book of Kings and Hosea's condemnation of legitimisation of violence in the attempts at taking power, illustrates the diversity of opinions expressed in the Bible on the same question."[33] Schulte says that Jehu ascended to the throne through much violence and bloodshed:

> Elisha gave Jehu the religious sanction for this. That the God of Israel was not to be used for such a political policy by a prophet such as Elisha is evident in the verdict conveyed through the prophet Hosea (1:4): Give him (i.e. your son) the name Jezreel, for soon I will requite the blood of Jezreel on the house of Jehu and bring the kingdom of Israel to an end.[34]

The violence Jehu used to exterminate the Omrides is a very good example of God working with a fallen and culturally conditioned individual. Throughout history God uses human agents, both nations and individuals, to do his work in the world, both to save and to judge. Whenever God selects an individual to do his work, God does not control that individual, thus, at times the actions of agents will go beyond what God designed them to do. The violence Jehu used against the family of Ahab, against the royal family of Judah, and against the worshipers of Baal was excessive and unacceptable, but because it was Yahweh who commanded his prophet to anoint Jehu, the violence of Jehu will be associated with God. In the end, Yahweh rejected Jehu's use of violence, but because Yahweh chose to work with Jehu, an agent who was violent, cruel, and savage in war, the violence of Jehu becomes the violence of God.

---

33. Jaruzelska, "Prophets and *coups d'état*," 30.
34. Schulte, "End of the Omride Dynasty," 146.

18

The Nonviolent Conquest of Canaan

THE CONQUEST OF THE LAND of Canaan by Joshua and by the army of Israel is a narrative filled with violence and cruelty. One of the most troublesome issues in the book of Joshua is the issue of Yahweh commanding the people of Israel to commit genocide. Boyd doubts that such a command reflects the true character of God as revealed on the cross. To deal with the problem of violence and genocide, Boyd offers a cruciform interpretation of the conquest of Canaan. He concludes that looking from the cross, "the use of violence to acquire the land of Canaan was not God's idea."[1] Boyd studies four passages dealing with the conquest of Canaan which he believes that in light of the cross, God never intended for Israel to use violence in their conquest of the land.

THE NONVIOLENT CONQUEST OF CANAAN

On God's intent to give the land to Israel without violence, Boyd writes, "the plan to gradually relocate the indigenous population of Canaan, whether by making the land pesky or by some other means, was contingent upon the Israelites trusting God rather than the sword."[2] Yahweh's plan for a nonviolent conquest of Canaan did not materialize because the people of Israel did not trust in God to deliver the land to them without violence. According to Boyd, "the macabre portraits of Yahweh" ordering

---

1. Boyd, *Crucifixion of the Warrior God*, 962.
2. Boyd, *Crucifixion of the Warrior God*, 968.

THE NONVIOLENT CONQUEST OF CANAAN 227

genocidal warfare was not God's plan for Israel. Rather, "these genocidal portraits of God reflect the fallen heart and mind of Moses and of God's people as a whole at this point in history."³

The first passage that shows God's intent to give the land to Israel without violence is found in Exod 23:20, a text in which Yahweh promises to send his angel who will bring the people to Canaan: "I am going to send an angel in front of you, to guard you on the way and to bring you to the place that I have prepared" (Exod 23:20). This promise also involves Yahweh's promise to send the hornets to force the people to relocate themselves outside the land of Canaan, "I will send the hornet ahead of you to drive the Hivites, Canaanites and Hittites out of your way" (Exod 23:28 NIV).

The second plan to give the land to Israel without violence was God's intent to make the land uninhabitable, thus forcing the Canaanites to migrate to another place. In Lev 18:24–25 "Yahweh announces a plan to relocate the indigenous population, whose sin, he says, had defiled this land, by punishing the land in such a way that it 'vomited out its inhabitants.'"⁴

Yahweh's third plan to give the land to Israel without violence was God "reassuring the Israelites through Moses, telling them that he would get them into the promised land the same way he got them out of Egypt."⁵

The fourth passage in which Yahweh reveals his intent to bring Israel to Canaan without violence is seen in the revelation of the commander of the army of Yahweh who appeared to Joshua before the conquest of Jericho and declared his neutrality concerning the taking of the city (Josh 5:13–15). Boyd writes, "The fact that this encounter takes place on the eve of the assault on Jericho in which every man, woman, and child (other than Rahab and her family) as well as every animal was put to death (Josh 6:17) renders this commander's neutrality all the more remarkable."⁶

In this chapter I will address only two of the passages Boyd says indicate Yahweh's plan for a nonviolent conquest of the land of Canaan: the sending of the hornets and the neutrality of the commander of Yahweh's army. It is not clear what the Bible means when it says that the land

---

3. Boyd, *Crucifixion of the Warrior God*, 963.
4. Boyd, *Crucifixion of the Warrior God*, 968.
5. Boyd, *Crucifixion of the Warrior God*, 969.
6. Boyd, *Crucifixion of the Warrior God*, 975.

vomited the Canaanites. Even Boyd believes that it is impossible to know how these words should be interpreted.[7] As for comparing the entrance into Canaan with the going out of Egypt, the comparison is not legitimate. There was much violence at the time Israel came out of Egypt: the plagues, the death of the firstborn, and the drowning of Pharaoh's army. It was the divine warrior who brought Israel out of Egypt and it will be the divine warrior who will bring Israel into the land of Canaan.

INSECTS AS WARFARE AGENTS

According to Boyd, Yahweh's intent was that Israel would conquer the land of Canaan without violence. The nonviolent conquest of Canaan would be accomplished by the use of insects.[8] Yahweh would send hornets against the indigenous population and make the land unpleasant to live in and thus force the Canaanites to relocate to a place outside of Canaan. However, "the reason God could not get the Israelites into the promised land in a nonviolent way was that Moses and the people he led were incapable and/or unwilling to completely trust God and thus incapable and/or unwilling to hear, let alone obey, God's plans to have them take possession of the land nonviolently. They rather placed their confidence in the sword."[9]

There are three passages in which the hornets are mentioned in association with the land of Canaan:

> Exod 23:28 (NIV): "I will send the hornet ahead of you to drive the Hivites, Canaanites and Hittites out of your way."

> Deut 7:20 (NIV): "Moreover, the LORD your God will send the hornet among them until even the survivors who hide from you have perished."

> Josh 24:12 (NIV): "I sent the hornet ahead of you, which drove them out before you—also the two Amorite kings. You did not do it with your own sword and bow."

---

7. Boyd, *Crucifixion of the Warrior God*, 968.

8. Nelson, *Deuteronomy*, 103–4 says that "Insects are sometimes a metaphor for attackers or invaders." Isaiah compares Egypt to a fly and Assyria to a bee: "On that day the LORD will whistle for the fly that is at the sources of the streams of Egypt, and for the bee that is in the land of Assyria" (Isa 7:18).

9. Boyd, *Crucifixion of the Warrior God*, 971.

According to Boyd, the nonviolent conquest of the land of Canaan would be accomplished by the use of insects as warfare agents against the Canaanites. In Exod 23:28, Yahweh promised that he would "send the hornet ahead of you to drive the Hivites, Canaanites and Hittites out of your way" (Exod 23:28 NIV). The same promise is also made in Deut 7:20. Boyd says that God's promise to send the hornet was fulfilled in Josh 24:12: "I sent the hornet ahead of you, which drove out before you the two kings of the Amorites; it was not by your sword or by your bow" (Josh 24:12). Thus, according to Boyd, Israel gained victory against Sihon and Og not by their sword or bow, that is, not by violence, but by the direct intervention of Yahweh.

The reference to the hornets in Deut 7:20 changes the intent of what the hornets would accomplish according to the book of Exodus. According to the book of Exodus the hornets would drive the Canaanites out of the land in a nonviolent way. According the Deuteronomy, the hornets would kill the Canaanites who had survived the army of Israel. Boyd said that in light of "God's earlier announced nonviolent use of hornets," the text in Deuteronomy "has now been reinterpreted in light of the Hebrews' culturally conditioned assumption that if Yahweh wants them to acquire Canaan, he must also want them to kill the indigenous population."[10]

There is, however, a problem with Boyd's view. In his study on the use of insects as warfare agents, Edward Neufeld says that commentators and translators differ on the actual meaning of the Hebrew word *ṣirʿah*. Some believe that the word "hornet" refers to a real hornet while others believe that the word "hornet" is used metaphorically.[11] For instance, the NRSV translates the word *ṣirʿah* as "pestilence" (Exod 23:28), the TNK as "plague" (Josh 24:12), the GWN as "panic" (Exod 23:28), and the NLT as "terror" (Exod 23:28).

In his study of insects as weapons of war, Jeffrey Lockwood wrote, "For thousands of years insects have been incorporated into human conflict, with the goals of inflicting pain, destroying food, and transmitting pathogens."[12] In antiquity, when fighting wars, soldiers used bees, hornets, wasps, or ants in order to inflict terror among the enemies and to drive them into the open where they could be defeated. Lockwood accepts the view that the *ṣirʿah* mentioned in the Old Testament were literal

---

10. Boyd, *Crucifixion of the Warrior God*, 972–73.
11. Neufeld, "Insects as Warfare Agents," 34.
12. Lockwood, "Insects as Weapons of War," 205.

hornets. He wrote, "Biblical accounts make clear that ancient people were aware that insects could be used as weapons to cause suffering in an enemy. Hornets were evidently used to dislodge entrenched opponents."[13] Neufeld believes that the three texts mentioning the hornets may reflect authentic tradition about the use of insects in warfare. He wrote, "these texts give a strong impression of illustrating an authentic tradition of the use of insects as warfare agents."[14] Oded Borowski identifies the hornet with Egypt. He writes, "It is possible that the hornet references to Egyptian military presence in Canaan before the Israelite takeover are to be associated with Merneptah's campaign in ca. 1220 B.C.E., celebrated in the 'Israel Stele.'"[15]

Entomologist Gene Kritsky, in his study on insects in the Bible, lists all the ninety-eight insects named in the Bible. In his list of biblical insects, the hornet is not listed. Kritsky says that "the translators working on the King James Version invented 'a whole glossary of new English words' for the Bible, including words dealing with insects."[16] New development in biblical scholarship has led to a reevaluation of how insects are named in the Bible. The King James Version lists 120 insects and other arthropods in the Bible. Using the Revised English Version of the Bible, Kritsky lists ninety-eight insects and other arthropods mentioned in the Bible. He accepts the view that the hornets of the KJV should be translated as "panic" or "terror."[17] In her commentary on Joshua, Beal says that "The limited occurrences of the 'hornet' makes its identity uncertain. Perhaps the best understanding is that it refers to terror, fear, or discouragement—all effectual agents for removing the inhabitants."[18]

Yahweh promised to send the hornet to defeat the people of the land. In Josh 24:12 Yahweh tells the people that he has fulfilled that promise. According to Josh 24:12, Israel was able to defeat Sihon, the Amorite king and Og, the king of Bashan because Yahweh sent "the hornet" ahead of Israel and the hornet drove out "the two kings of the Amorites."[19] Joshua said to all the people, "Thus says the LORD . . . I sent the hornet ahead of

13. Lockwood, "Insects as Weapons of War," 207.
14. Neufeld, "Insects as Warfare Agents," 36.
15. Borowski, "Identity of the Biblical sirʿâ," 317.
16. Kritsky, "Insects and Other Arthropods," 183–88.
17. Kritsky, "Insects and Other Arthropods," 183.
18. Beal, *Joshua*, 415.
19. Bartlett, "Sihon and Og, Kings of the Amorites," 257–77; Edelman, "Kings of the Amorites," 279–86.

you, which drove them out before you–also the two Amorite kings. You did not do it with your own sword and bow" (Josh 24:12 NIV).

According to Josh 24:12, the people of Israel did not defeat the Amorite kings "with your own sword and bow." However, according to Num 21:22–25, "Sihon gathered all his people together, and went out against Israel" and "Israel put him to the sword, and took possession of his land." According to Num 21:33–35, Yahweh told Moses "Do not be afraid of [Og] for I have given him into your hand, with all his people, and all his land. You shall do to him as you did to King Sihon of the Amorites, who ruled in Heshbon. So [Israel] killed him, his sons, and all his people, until there was no survivor left; and they took possession of his land." Thus, the "hornet" cannot be taken literally because what Boyd said would be a nonviolent conquest was accomplished with the sword and with much violence.

Since the defeat of the Amorite kings was done by the sword, the hornets mentioned in Exodus and Joshua should not be taken literally. The reason is, as Phetsanghane explains, "because there is not a word in the book of Joshua about the Canaanites being overcome and exterminated in any such way, but chiefly on account of Josh 24:12, where Joshua says that God sent the hornet before them, and drove out the two kings of the Amorites, referring thereby to their defeat and destruction by the Israelites through the miraculous interposition of God, and thus placing the figurative use of the term hornet beyond the possibility of doubt."[20]

THE COMMANDER OF THE LORD'S ARMY

According to Boyd, the appearance and the neutrality of the commander of the Lord's army to Joshua (Josh 5:13–15) was an indication that the conquest of the land of Canaan by violence was not God's idea. The commander of the army of Yahweh appeared to Joshua at the time Israel was preparing to battle against the king of Jericho and his soldiers.

The book of Joshua begins with the people of Israel making preparations to cross the Jordan River and to enter the land of Canaan. Joshua sent two spies into Jericho to bring back some information about the land. After a stay in the house of a woman named Rahab, the spies returned with their report. Joshua ordered the priests to take the Ark of the Covenant and carry it before the people as they crossed the Jordan River.

---

20. Phetsanghane, "What Is the הַצִּרְעָה," 175–94.

The presence of the Ark of the Covenant, a symbol of Yahweh's presence with the people, was a reminder that it was Yahweh who enabled them to cross the river.

After the people crossed the river, Joshua ordered that all male Israelites be circumcised as a dedication to Yahweh. After the men were circumcised and the time of healing had passed (Josh 5:8), the people of Israel celebrated the Passover in Gilgal. On the day after the Passover, "on that very day, they ate the produce of the land, unleavened cakes and parched grain. The manna ceased on the day they ate the produce of the land" (Josh 5:10–12).

As Joshua and the people of Israel made preparations to attack the city of Jericho, Joshua had an encounter with a man standing before him with a drawn sword in his hand who identified himself as the commander of the army of Yahweh. The narrative of this encounter is found in Josh 5:13–15:

> Once when Joshua was by Jericho, he looked up and saw a man standing before him with a drawn sword in his hand. Joshua went to him and said to him, "Are you one of us, or one of our adversaries?" He replied, "Neither; but as commander of the army of the LORD I have now come." And Joshua fell on his face to the earth and worshiped, and he said to him, "What do you command your servant, my lord?" The commander of the army of the LORD said to Joshua, "Remove the sandals from your feet, for the place where you stand is holy." And Joshua did so. (Josh 5:13–15)

Boyd makes four references to the words of the commander of the army of Yahweh in his book. The words of the commander of Yahweh's army are important to Boyd because the commander told Joshua that he was neutral about the war between Israel and Jericho. Boyd says that the words of the commander reflect "the Spirit of the cruciform God" telling Joshua that he was neutral in the conflict of Israel against Jericho.[21] Boyd quotes Douglas S. Earl[22] who said that "the commander's neutrality breaks down the 'us-them' categories that the intended audience of this book presumably embraced." Boyd goes on to say that the neutrality of the commander "serves as a reminder that while God must sometimes stoop to further his purposes by accommodating the 'us-them' mindset

---

21. Boyd, *Crucifixion of the Warrior God*, 745.
22. Earl, *Joshua Delusion?*

THE NONVIOLENT CONQUEST OF CANAAN   233

of his fallen people, God and his army transcend our fallen polarities, and his ideal is always for his people to transcend them as well."

According to Boyd, the war of conquest reflects Israel's willingness not to trust in God since war does not originate in the heart of God: "The Israelites were often too hard-hearted and spiritually dull to understand this. And yet, the heavenly missionary was not too proud to nevertheless continue to work in and through his fallen covenant people, bearing their sin, thereby taking on the ugly semblance of an ANE warrior deity in the inspired written witness to his faithful covenantal activity."[23]

In another section of his book, Boyd says that the commander's words provide "confirmation that the violence involved in the Israelite conquest was not Yahweh's idea." Boyd wrote,

> Given that Israel and all other ANE people assumed that earthly battles participated in battles among divine beings associated with each side, as we will discuss in the next chapter, discovering that the commander of Yahweh's army is neutral is surprising, to say the least. The fact that this encounter takes place on the eve of the assault on Jericho in which every man, woman, and child (other than Rahab and her family) as well as every animal was put to death (Josh 6:17) renders this commander's neutrality all the more remarkable.[24]

Boyd also believes that the words of the commander reveal that God intended for Israel to conquer the land of Canaan without violence. He wrote, "my primary reason for believing Yahweh was not firmly on the side of Israel's violent campaign is because the revelation of God on Calvary requires this as well as because of the above cited evidence that Yahweh had originally hoped his people would acquire this land nonviolently."[25] And again, "the revelation of God on the cross requires us to believe that God hoped to bring his people into this land without having them engage in violence, and as I have argued, this is confirmed by the . . . neutral stance of the commander of the Lord's army (Josh 5:13–15)."[26]

According to Boyd, the words of the commander prove that the violent conquest of Canaan was not Yahweh's idea. Boyd wrote,

---

23. Boyd, *Crucifixion of the Warrior God*, 746.
24. Boyd, *Crucifixion of the Warrior God*, 975.
25. Boyd, *Crucifixion of the Warrior God*, 976.
26. Boyd, *Crucifixion of the Warrior God*, 977–78.

the appearance of this neutral angelic commander can easily be understood to provide yet another confirming indication that the extremely violent conquest was not Yahweh's idea. How can we imagine the angelic commander of Yahweh's army remaining neutral if Yahweh was himself the mastermind behind the Israelite massacre, especially if, as some scholars argue, this commander is actually the 'angel of the Yahweh' who is a manifestation of Yahweh himself?[27]

Boyd also believes that the neutrality of the commander is a reflection of God's heart: "I find it much more reasonable, and certainly much more consistent with the character of God revealed on the cross, to see in this neutral commander a reflection of the Spirit of God breaking through the fallen and cultural conditioning of the author/redactors of this narrative to provide a direct revelation of God's heart."[28]

Boyd is highly dependent on Earl's interpretation of Josh 5:13–15. However, a careful exegesis of the biblical text in Josh 5:13–15 will show that the neutrality of the commander of the army of Yahweh in the war between Israel and Jericho is not as evident as Earl and Boyd claim.

In order to gain a better understanding of the words of the commander of the army, it becomes necessary to study four important things in the passage: (1) the identity of the commander; (2) the symbolism of the drawn sword; (3) the textual problem present in the text; and (4) the structure of the text.

The Identity of the Commander

The Commander of the Army is Michael. Early Christians identified the commander of the army of Yahweh with Michael. In Joshua, the Hebrew word for "commander" is *sar*. The word *sar* is translated in English as "prince, chief, captain, chief captain." Michael appears in Dan 10:21 as "your prince." In Dan 10:13 he appears as "one of the chief princes," and in Dan 12:1 he appears as "the great prince." The reference in Dan 8:11 is debated. The "Commander of heaven's army" (Dan 8:11 NLT) or "prince

---

27. Boyd, *Crucifixion of the Warrior God*, 976.
28. Boyd, *Crucifixion of the Warrior God*, 976.

of the host" (Dan 8:11 NRSV) has been identified with God[29] and with Michael.[30]

The Commander of the Army is Christ. Most old commentators believe that the commander of the army was the Second Person of the Trinity. Gangel believes that the man who identified himself as the commander of the Lord's army is a Christophany, that is, "a literal representation of Jesus on earth in a preincarnate form."[31] Payne believes that the commander of the Lord's army was a manifestation of Christ.[32]

The Commander of the Army is an Angel. The man who appeared to Joshua was a divine being. Since he identified himself as the commander of Yahweh's army and not as Yahweh or the Angel of the Lord, some people believe that he was an angel sent by God. The Targum of Jonathan identifies the commander of the army as "an angel sent from before the Lord."[33]

The Commander of the Army is the Angel of the Lord. Most scholars identify the commander of the army with the Angel of the Lord. Aubrey Johnson, in his study of *The One and the Many in the Israelite Conception of God*, has shown that in most references to the Angel of the Lord in the Old Testament, the Angel of the Lord is "indistinguishable from Yahweh Himself."[34] Routledge, in his *Old Testament Theology*, says that the Angel of the Lord "is the personal representative of God, who speaks for Yahweh and is, in many cases, identified with him."[35] However, Routledge does not cite Josh 5:14. Walther Eichrodt calls the Angel of the Lord "an almost hypostatic form of Yahweh's manifestation."[36] He seems to differentiate between the Angel of the Lord and Yahweh.[37] The Angel of the Lord is a hypostasis of Yahweh, that is, the Angel of the Lord is the persona Yahweh assumes to reveal himself to Israel. When Moses met God

---

29. Newsome, *Daniel*, 264.
30. LaCocque, *Daniel*, 162.
31. Gangel, *Joshua*, 95.
32. Payne, *Theology of the Older Testament*, 168.
33. Azuelos, "'Angel Sent From before the Lord,'" 163.
34. Johnson, *One and the Many*, 29.
35. Routledge, *Old Testament Theology*, 119.
36. Eichrodt, *Theology of the Old Testament*, 195.
37. Eichrodt, *Theology of the Old Testament*, 196.

on Mount Sinai the Angel of the Lord appeared to him in a flame of fire out of a bush, but when Moses turned aside to see why the bush was not burning up, it was Yahweh who spoke to him (Exod 3:3–4). The Angel of the Lord appeared to Gideon under the oak at Ophrah, but it was Yahweh who commissioned him to deliver Israel from the hand of the Midianites (Judg 6:11–18).

The Commander of the Army is Yahweh. The man who appears to Joshua as the commander of the army of Yahweh in Josh 5:14 did not say that he was the Angel of the Lord. Some scholars believe that the commander of the army of Yahweh is the Angel of the Lord and that the Angel of the Lord is Yahweh himself, however, this identification is not universal. Preuss believes that the commander of the army is different from Yahweh.[38] Von Rad does not believe that the commander of the army was God; he was an Elohim-being. He wrote: "When the Elohim-beings made their appearance upon the earth, they were so much in human form that often they were not immediately recognized as Elohim."[39] He cites Josh 5:13–14. I believe that the commander of Yahweh's army and the Angel of the Lord is one and the same person and that he is also Yahweh.

The Symbolism of the Drawn Sword

In my article, "Swords: Their Development and Use," I wrote that the sword was a weapon of war: "The Bible generally speaks of a sword in the context of war and personal combat. Weapons played an important part in the life of Israel since the nation had to spend much time fighting wars against its enemies, first against the Canaanites and eventually against other nations, especially the Arameans, the Assyrians, and the Babylonians."[40]

The drawn sword appears in two other places in the Old Testament. In Num 22:23, the Angel of the Lord confronts Balaam with a drawn sword. In 1 Chr 21:16, the Angel of the Lord confronts David with a drawn sword to punish him for taking a census of Israel.

---

38. Preuss, *Old Testament Theology*, 1:258.
39. Rad, *Old Testament Theology*, 1:146.
40. Mariottini, "Swords," 51.

The commander of the army of Yahweh appears before Joshua as a warrior prepared for battle. His drawn sword indicates that the war against Jericho was imminent. According to Nelson, the significance of the drawn sword is "to assure Joshua (and the reader) of impending victory and Yahweh's participation in the upcoming battle."[41] The warlike manifestation of the commander of the army indicates that the army of Yahweh is ready to join with the army of Israel against the army of Jericho. Israel will fight against its enemies, but not alone; they will fight with the help of the army of Yahweh. According to Miller, the revelation of the commander of the army of Yahweh to Joshua indicates that "the ensuing conquest was sacral and that Israel's army would be led by Yahweh's divine army."[42]

The Problem with the Text

When Joshua saw the man standing before him with a drawn sword in his hand, Joshua asked him, "Are you one of us, or one of our adversaries?" The man answered, "Neither; but as commander of the army of the LORD I have now come" (Josh 5:13–14). In the Hebrew text of Josh 5:14, the response of the commander uses the negative *lō'*, "not." This reading is the more difficult reading and should be preserved. However, the Septuagint and some Hebrew manuscripts ignore the negative denial of the commander of the army and read *lô*, "to him" because it expected the commander to give a positive answer. The Syriac translation drops the negation all together and only reads the commander's statement.

The Septuagint translates Josh 5:14 as follows: "And he said to him, I am now come, the chief captain of the host of the Lord." If one accepts the text of the Septuagint, then the neutrality of the commander of the army disappears. The only English translation (that I know of) that accepts the reading of the Septuagint is the NET Bible.

The NET Bible translates Josh 5:14 as follows: "He answered, 'Truly I am the commander of the Lord's army'" (Josh 5:14 NET). The NET Bible follows the proposal put forth by Alberto Soggin that the answer of the commander of the army is not negative, but emphatic. According to Soggin, the answer of the commander of the army in Hebrew uses an emphatic *lamed* to answer Joshua's first question with an emphatic positive

---

41. Nelson, *Joshua*, 81.
42. Miller, *Divine Warrior*, 131.

response. Thus, according to Soggin, the text should be translated as follows: "Certainly! Since I am the Captain of the army of Yahweh."[43] Again, if one accepts the emphatic *lamed* proposal, the neutrality of the commander of the army disappears.

The NIV translates Josh 5:14 as follows: "'Neither,' he replied, 'but as commander of the army of the Lord I have now come.'" Many English translations also use "neither" to introduce the commander's answer to Joshua's question. However, the "neither" translation is interpreting the words of the commander of the army because his words to Joshua are ambiguous. When Joshua asked the commander, "Are you for us or for our enemies?" (Josh 5:13 NIV), the commander of the army answered "No" (*lō'* in Hebrew). This is how the ESV translates the words of the commander: "And he said, 'No; but I am the commander of the army of the Lord. Now I have come.'" The reading of the ESV does not imply neutrality, but ambiguity. The NIV's use of the word "neither" implies that the commander of the army told Joshua that he was neutral in the conflict, the position that Boyd also defends. However, the "No" of the commander can be interpreted in different ways.

If one accepts chapter 6 as the context of what happened in chapter 5 (see the discussion below), then the commander's response to Joshua must be understood as affirmative to Joshua's first question ("Are you one of us?") and thus negative to his second question ("Are you one of our enemies?"). The commander of the army of Yahweh could not be against the army of Israel. Therefore, the "no" of the commander of the army must be in reference to Joshua's second question, "Are you for our enemies?" The commander's answers, "no." The commander of the army of Yahweh was not on the side of Israel's enemy.[44]

The Structure of the Text

The structure of Josh 5:13—6:27 has received much scrutiny from scholars. Many scholars, following the work of Wellhausen, separate the theophany in 5:13–15 from the narrative about the destruction of Jericho in 6:1–27. Some scholars believe that the theophany in 5:13–15 is related to a high place, either in Gilgal or Jericho. Others believe that the passage is truncated and that the commander's message to Joshua has been

---

43. Soggin, "Negation in Joshua 5,14," 220.
44. Soggin, *Joshua*, 77.

lost. Miller wrote: "The episode originally contained a longer message or conversation which has now been deleted by the 'collector' because of religious reasons. The remaining record indicates that there were directions about the nurture and care of the sanctuary."[45]

Recent scholarship has revisited Wellhausen's proposal and has opted for the unity of the narrative. Römer believes that the book of Joshua must be understood "as a literary and ideological construction in which the invention of the conquest of the land serves the theological agenda of the Deuteronomist."[46] To Römer, the book of Joshua follows Neo-Assyrian war ideologies warfare propaganda. However, Römer believes that Josh 6:2–5 is a continuation of the story of Joshua's encounter with the commander of the army of Yahweh.[47]

Dozeman, writing about the unity of Josh 5:13—6:5, wrote,

> The procession of the ark and the fall of Jericho in Joshua 5:13—6:27 may be separated into four unequal parts. The first section (5:13—6:5) establishes the mystical character of the story as an event of revelation, when the prince of the army of Yahweh encounters Joshua (5:13–15). The introduction shows that the imminent war against Jericho is intended to be a theophany of the divine warrior. The theme of holy war is clarified through a sequence of exchanges between Joshua and the prince of the army of Yahweh, in which Joshua becomes enlightened on the nature of holy war.[48]

Joshua asked the commander of the army, "What do you command your servant, my lord?" Joshua received two answers to his question. The first answer was "Remove the sandals from your feet, for the place where you stand is holy" (Josh 5:15). The second answer to his question, given to him by Yahweh himself, was instructions on how to wage war against Jericho through proper ritual procedures (6:1–5).[49]

45. Miller, *Divine Warrior*, 173.
46. Römer, "Joshua's Encounter," 51.
47. Römer, "Joshua's Encounter," 55.
48. Dozeman, *Joshua 1–12*, 323.
49. Pomeroy, "'As Commander of the Army of the LORD,'" 48, says that "A divine mandate to carry out warfare was an essential feature of Ancient Near Eastern war narrative as it provided ideological justification to the unnatural act of killing. Joshua is described as having divine authority to carry out battle. . . . the appearance of "the Commander of the army of YHWH" in a vision to Joshua in 5:13–15 admits to the divine sanction of war, as well as the explicit instructions given to Joshua by YHWH in Joshua 6:2–5."

Dozeman said that scholars often overlook the influence of the theophany of the commander of the army of Yahweh on the story of the conquest of Jericho in 6:1–27.[50] Since the commander of the army who appeared to Joshua is Yahweh, then the commander of the army was not neutral in the war between Israel and Jericho because it is the commander of the army, or Yahweh, who gave Joshua instructions on how to wage war against Jericho.

YAHWEH'S INSTRUCTIONS TO JOSHUA

The encounter between the commander of the army of Yahweh and Joshua "reveals that the heavenly armies have been mobilized to fight alongside Israel and endorses Joshua's leadership as the commander of Israel's army."[51] The expression "the army of Yahweh" appears only in Josh 5:14. However, the plural form, "the armies of Yahweh," appears in Exod 12:41 and it refers to the people of Israel as they departed from Egypt. In Exod 7:4, Yahweh calls Israel, "my armies, my people, the children of Israel." In 1 Sam 17:45 Yahweh is called "the God of the armies of Israel."

After his encounter with the commander of the army of Yahweh, Joshua receives instructions from Yahweh himself[52] on how to conduct the war against Jericho:

> The Lord said to Joshua, See, I have handed Jericho over to you, along with its king and soldiers. You shall march around the city, all the warriors circling the city once. Thus you shall do for six days, with seven priests bearing seven trumpets of rams' horns before the ark. On the seventh day you shall march around the city seven times, the priests blowing the trumpets. When they make a long blast with the ram's horn, as soon as you hear the sound of the trumpet, then all the people shall shout with a great shout; and the wall of the city will fall down flat, and all the people shall charge straight ahead. (Josh 6:2–5)

In this narrative, which serves as an introduction to the conquest of the land, the commander of the army of Yahweh meets with the commander of the army of Israel. The commander of the army of Yahweh came to give

---

50. Dozeman, *Joshua 1-12*, 323.

51. Hawk, *Joshua*, 83.

52. Wenham, "Deuteronomic Theology," 141, says "That Yahweh directs the war is brought out vividly by the vision of 'the commander of the Lord,' who appears to Joshua with a drawn sword in his hand (5:13–15)."

Joshua instructions on how to conquer the city of Jericho. This is the intent of chapter 6:2–5. In his instructions to Joshua, Yahweh told him that his battle would be with the king of Jericho and with his soldiers. Yahweh gives Joshua instruction for how to proceed against Jericho. Hawk explains the reason for the manifestation of the commander of the army: "The wars in Canaan will be initiated and conducted by YHWH's own purposes. Israel will occupy the land only because it is the beneficiary of divine choosing and faithfulness (cf. Deut 9:4–7)."[53]

As much as Boyd seeks to defend the neutrality of the commander of the army of Yahweh, the evidence is not there to support his views. The commander of the army appears to Joshua as a warrior, with a drawn sword ready for battle. Rather than being neutral in the conflict that is about to begin, the commander of the army has come to join and lead the army of Israel in the battle against Jericho.

The commander of the army is none other than Yahweh himself. Yahweh spoke to Joshua and gave him instruction on how to defeat the enemy and bring down the walls of Jericho. Yahweh's instructions to Joshua were very specific: "See, I have handed Jericho over to you, along with its king and soldiers" (Josh 6:2). The army of Israel was commanded to fight against the army of Jericho, against its king and soldiers. Nowhere in God's instructions to Joshua was Joshua commanded to kill men, women, and children.

But atrocities happened in the war against Jericho, and many innocent people died, as it happens in every war, past and present. This section was intended to deal only with the neutrality of the commander of the army of Yahweh. As for the violence that occurred in the conquest of Jericho and the problem of Israel's fight against the Canaanites, I will deal with this issue in the next chapter.

---

53. Hawk, *Joshua*, 85.

19

The Conquest of Canaan

IN HIS STUDY OF HOLY war in ancient Israel, Michael Walzer begins by expressing what many readers of the Bible feel when they read the book of Joshua. He wrote, "For the modern reader, the conquest of Canaan, with all its attendant slaughter, is the most problematic moment in the history of ancient Israel."[1]

When God called Abraham to leave his country and his ancestral family and go "to the land that I will show you" (Gen 12:1), that land, the land of Canaan, was already occupied, "At that time the Canaanites were in the land" (Gen 12:6). Among the many promises Yahweh gave to Abraham, the gift of the land was very important because the nation that would be born of Abraham needed a land to call its own. In order to fulfill his promise to Abraham, Yahweh had to remove the Canaanites to allow Israel to possess the land. The reason Yahweh favors Israel and not the Canaanites is because of the covenant he made with Abraham and with Israel. As Assmann writes, "God makes this covenant not with the world and the entire human race but with the children of Israel. . . . Through the covenant and divine election, the world splits into Israel and the nations. It is important to emphasize that this distinction has nothing whatsoever to do with intolerance and violence. God cares for all peoples, but he has something special in mind for Israel."[2]

---

1. Walzer, "Idea of Holy War," 215.
2. Assmann, *Invention of Religion*, 80.

The forced removal of the Canaanites poses a moral problem for people who reject violence.[3] The conquest of Canaan has been classified as genocide and ethnic cleansing. Richard Dawkins writes, "The ethnic cleansing begun in the time of Moses is brought to bloody fruition in the book of Joshua, a text remarkable for the bloodthirsty massacres it records and the xenophobic relish with which it does so."[4] Cowles and Seibert say that the genocidal murder of the Canaanites was commanded by Yahweh, "But as for the towns of these peoples that the LORD your God is giving you as an inheritance, you must not let anything that breathes remain alive. You shall annihilate them—the Hittites and the Amorites, the Canaanites and the Perizzites, the Hivites and the Jebusites—just as the LORD your God has commanded" (Deut 20:16–17). This is the reason Cowles calls Yahweh, the God of the Old Testament, "Yahweh, the genocidal warrior of the Old Testament"[5] and "a genocidal despot."[6] Seibert calls Yahweh the "genocidal general."[7]

GIVING THE LAND TO ISRAEL

Based on his crucicentric hermeneutics, Boyd believes that the conquest narrative must be read in light of the cross.[8] However, this approach creates a problem for modern interpreters because from the perspective of the cross, the violence used by Joshua and the army of Israel is unacceptable. The war of conquest was fought under the rules of engagement prevalent in the ancient Near East in the second millennium BCE but, from today's perspective, this way of fighting wars is not acceptable and should be rejected.

Boyd believes that the violence of the conquest was not God's plan. He writes,

> I contend that the macabre portraits of Yahweh uttering the *ḥērem* command to Moses and then helping his people carry it out . . . indicate that the genocidal warfare recounted in this narrative was not, in fact, God's plan. Viewed through the lens

---

3. Copan et al., *Holy War in the Bible*.
4. Dawkins, *God Delusion*, 247.
5. Cowles, "Response to Tremper Longman III," 193.
6. Cowles, "Response to Eugene H. Merrill," 99.
7. Seibert, *Disturbing Divine Behavior*, 32.
8. Boyd, *Crucifixion of the Warrior God*, 963.

of the cross, these genocidal portraits of God rather reflect the fallen heart and mind of Moses and of God's people as a whole at this point in history.[9]

God allows his people to act on his behalf and when they do, they will act as fallen and culturally conditioned people and will do the things that fallen and culturally conditioned people do. Since God does not force his will on people, God will not force the people of Israel to act contrary to their fallen and culturally conditioned lives in order to eliminate their violence and brutality.

Since Yahweh is faithful to his covenant, he had to give the land of Canaan to Israel as he promised to Abraham. Yahweh promised to give Israel a land so that they could become a great nation and fulfill its mission in the world. Giving land to a people was nothing new to Yahweh. According to the biblical text, Yahweh gave the city of Ar as a possession to the descendants of Lot (Deut 2:9). The former inhabitants of the city were the Emim, who were a large and numerous people (Deut 2:10). Yahweh gave to the Ammonites, the descendants of Lot, the land of Rephaim, a strong and numerous people. The Ammonites conquered the land, dispossessed the Rephaim and settled in their place (Deut 2:20–21). Yahweh gave the descendants of Esau the city of Seir. The descendants of Esau conquered the Horim, dispossessed them of their land, and settled in their place (Deut 2:22). According to the prophet Amos, Yahweh brought the Philistines from their original home of Caphtor and the Syrians from their original home in Kir (Amos 9:7).[10] Now Yahweh was bringing Israel from the land of Egypt to give them the land of Canaan.

THE REASON FOR EXPELLING THE CANAANITES

The biblical text presents several reasons for the expulsion of the Canaanites from the land. As Israel prepared to enter the land, Moses spoke to the new generation of Israelites and told them the reason Yahweh was giving them the land of Canaan: "It is not because of your righteousness or the uprightness of your heart that you are going in to occupy their land; but because of the wickedness of these nations the LORD your God is dispossessing them before you, in order to fulfill the promise that

---

9. Boyd, *Crucifixion of the Warrior God*, 963.
10. Brueggemann, "'Exodus' in the Plural," 15–34.

the LORD made on oath to your ancestors, to Abraham, to Isaac, and to Jacob" (Deut 9:5).

The first reason given by the biblical writer was because of Yahweh's love for Israel as his special people, "It was not because you were more numerous than any other people that the LORD set his heart on you and chose you—for you were the fewest of all peoples. It was because the LORD loved you" (Deut 7:7–8). Because of this special love for Israel, Yahweh redeemed them from the house of slavery in Egypt and brought them to the land he promised to Abraham.

The second reason was because Yahweh is a faithful God who keeps his promises, "the LORD your God is God, the faithful God who maintains covenant loyalty" (Deut 7:9). Yahweh made a covenant with Abraham and his descendants after him. Now that Israel was about to enter the land of Canaan, Yahweh shows his faithfulness as a God who is true to his promises and as a God "who maintains covenant loyalty" (Deut 7:9).

The third reason was because Yahweh is a God of justice. According to the biblical writer, the seven nations of the Canaanites were being dispossessed of their land because of their wickedness (Deut 9:5). In justifying the dispossession of the Canaanites, the biblical writer emphasizes the gracious mercy of Yahweh. He is the faithful God who maintains covenant loyalty to a thousand generations (Deut 7:9). But he is also a God "who repays in their own person those who reject him" (Deut 7:10). According to Craigie, Yahweh was dispossessing the Canaanites as an act of judgment, "the expelling of the Canaanites from Palestine was not to be understood as an arbitrary divine act, but as an act of judgment by a just God."[11]

Most information about Canaanite religion is drawn from the texts found at Ras Shamra, ancient Ugarit.[12] Hillers says that the Canaanites portrayed in Ugaritic literature are completely different from Canaanites found in the Old Testament. Hillers says that scholars have a negative view of the Canaanites because the Bible has a negative view of the Canaanites. According to Hillers, the sexual licentiousness in Canaanite temples, the practice of child-sacrifice, and the practice of sacred prostitution are not attested in the hundreds of texts found at Ras Shamra.[13] However, John

---

11. Craigie, *Book of Deuteronomy*, 193.

12. On Canaanite religion, see Hillers, "Analyzing the Abominable," 253–69; Gray, "Social Aspects of Canaanite Religion," 170–92.

13. Stager, in his article, "Child Sacrifice at Carthage," 31–51 has found evidence

246   PART 2: THE JUSTICE OF GOD

Day, in his study of Canaanite religion says that there is evidence that child sacrifice and sacred prostitution were practiced within the Canaanite world, "although we have no indications of it at Ugarit."[14]

THE INDIGENOUS POPULATION OF CANAAN

Yahweh's instruction to Moses about the indigenous population of Canaan came after Yahweh revealed the true nature of his character as a gracious and merciful God, a God who is slow to anger and who abounds in steadfast love (Exod 34:6). This revelation came after Israel worshiped the golden calf in violation of the commandment which forbade Israel from making idols to worship them (Exod 20:5).

Yahweh renews the covenant that had been broken because of the golden calf (Exod 32:1–6). As God promised to renew that covenant, Yahweh added instruction about the making of images and about the assimilation with Canaanite culture. Yahweh said to Moses,

> I hereby make a covenant. Before all your people I will perform marvels, such as have not been performed in all the earth or in any nation; and all the people among whom you live shall see the work of the LORD; for it is an awesome thing that I will do with you. Observe what I command you today. See, I will drive out before you the Amorites, the Canaanites, the Hittites, the Perizzites, the Hivites, and the Jebusites. Take care not to make a covenant with the inhabitants of the land to which you are going, or it will become a snare among you. You shall tear down their altars, break their pillars, and cut down their sacred poles (for you shall worship no other god, because the LORD, whose name is Jealous, is a jealous God). You shall not make a covenant with the inhabitants of the land, for when they prostitute themselves to their gods and sacrifice to their gods, someone among them will invite you, and you will eat of the sacrifice. And you will take wives from among their daughters for your sons, and

---

that the Phoenicians, a people of Canaanite ancestry, sacrificed children to Baal and Astarte, the divine couple. Stager says that the Phoenicians had Tophets in Carthage, Sicily, Sardinia, and Tunisia. In the Carthaginian Tophet, Stager estimates that it contained as many as twenty thousand urns with the remains of burned children. Stager says that although some scholars have dismissed the practice of child sacrifice in Israel, "the growing body of archaeological and epigraphic evidence, provided by the Carthaginians themselves, strongly suggests that the classical and Biblical writers knew what they were talking about."

14. Day, "Canaan, Religion of," 834.

their daughters who prostitute themselves to their gods will make your sons also prostitute themselves to their gods. (Exod 34:6–16)

Israel's propensity to disobey Yahweh and go after other gods and Israel's proclivities toward syncretism made it imperative that they separate themselves from the Canaanites after they enter the land. Israelite religion was strongly influenced by Canaanite religious practices. While Israel was still in the wilderness, "Israel yoked itself to the Baal of Peor" (Num 25:3).[15] After the death of Joshua, early in the period of the judges, a new generation of Israelites "did what was evil in the sight of the LORD and worshiped the Baals" (Judg 2:10–11). Gideon's father had an altar dedicated to Baal and an Asherah pole in his house (Judg 6:25).

Israel was forbidden to make a covenant with the inhabitants of the land, otherwise they "will become a snare among you." The intent of the word "snare" is not known. The Hebrew word was used for designating a trap to catch birds. The word is also used metaphorically to designate the danger of idolatry, "if you worship their gods, it will surely be a snare to you" (Exod 23:33). Once in Canaan, Israel was to break down Canaanite altars, smash their sacred stones, and cut down their Asherah poles.

In Ps 106 the psalmist describes in vivid details the deleterious Canaanite influence in the life of Israel. He says that the people of Israel "attached themselves to the Baal of Peor, and ate sacrifices offered to the dead" (v. 28), "they did not destroy the peoples, as the LORD commanded them" (v. 34), "they mingled with the nations and learned to do as they did" (v. 35), "they served their idols, which became a snare to them" (v. 36), "they sacrificed their sons and their daughters to the demons" (v. 37), "they poured out innocent blood, the blood of their sons and daughters, whom they sacrificed to the idols of Canaan" (v. 38), "they became unclean by their acts, and prostituted themselves in their doings" (v. 39).

In the postexilic period, the Jews still remembered the evil influence the Canaanites had in the religious and social life of their ancestors. The writer of The Wisdom of Solomon, an apocryphal book written in the second century BCE, expresses the negative feelings the Jews had toward

---

15. The incident at Baal Peor is mentioned in Josh 22:17; Hos 9:10; Ps 106:28. The prophet Hosea expresses Yahweh's disappointment with the apostasy of Israel at Baal-Peor: "Like grapes in the wilderness, I found Israel. Like the first fruit on the fig tree, in its first season, I saw your ancestors. But they came to Baal-peor, and consecrated themselves to a thing of shame, and became detestable like the thing they loved" (Hos 9:10); see Mendenhall, "Incident at Beth Baal Peor," 105–21.

the Canaanites: "Those who lived long ago in your holy land you hated for their detestable practices, their works of sorcery and unholy rites, their merciless slaughter of children, and their sacrificial feasting on human flesh and blood. These initiates from the midst of a heathen cult, these parents who murder helpless lives, you willed to destroy by the hands of our ancestors, so that the land most precious of all to you might receive a worthy colony of the servants of God" (Wis 12:3–7 NRSV).

Yahweh promised that he would "drive out" the Canaanites from the land. According to Crüsemann, the Hebrew verb *gāraš* "to drive out," when used in the qal stem, "is used almost exclusively as a designation for a divorced woman."[16] This expression seems to indicate that before Abraham, Yahweh had a relationship with the Canaanites. Crüsemann writes, "YHWH announces that he will cast out the Canaanite people, in other words, from an already presupposed union with him."[17] According to the biblical text, the worship of Yahweh began many years before Abraham. Crüsemann writes, "in the earliest times people called upon the name of YHWH [Gen 4:26], this means that all the people he created worshiped him as God, and that this changes with the misdeed of Ham, the 'father of Canaan in Gen 9:21ff."[18]

War was a fact of life in the ancient Near East.[19] As nations prospered, they grew by conquering other nations and becoming large empires. The reality of war is that, in wars, there is violence and killings. Soldiers committed brutalities and people suffered. In wars, combatants died and so did innocent civilians, men, women, and children, young and old. Israel's war of conquest was no different. The issue that causes problems for people today is that the command to kill women and children was given by God. Before I deal with the issue of God commanding the people to kill the Canaanites, I will discuss several issues that exacerbate the moral problem posed by the violence Israel used to conquer the land of Canaan.

---

16. Crüsemann, *Torah*, 127 (see Lev 21:7, 14; 22:13; Num 30:10; Ezek 44:22).

17. Crüsemann, *Torah*, 127.

18. Crüsemann, *Torah*, 127.

19. Craigie, "Yahweh Is a Man of Wars," 185 says that "War was for [the people of Israel] a natural—if unpleasant—part of the world in which they lived."

THE LANGUAGE OF CONQUEST

The word genocide has been used to describe the action of the army of Israel in conquering the land of Canaan. However, when properly defined, the word genocide does not represent what Israel did in taking possession of the land. One issue that contributes to the moral dilemma the conquest of Canaan poses to people today is the fact that translators of the Old Testament bring into an old text modern concepts of warfare. Wilma Bailey says that one issue which conditions the mind of readers to see genocide in the conquest narratives is the violent and militaristic language found in the translations of the book of Joshua. According to some translations, the army of Israel was composed of "men of war" (Josh 6:3 KJV). Some translations render the Hebrew expression as "soldiers" (Josh 6:3 NAB). Such a language evokes comparison with the military elite that fought with David (2 Sam 23:8–39) or with the Cherethites and the Pelethites (2 Sam 8:18), the professional soldiers who served as David's personal army. As Bailey said, "'Soldier' language envisions a trained military force; 'warriors' or 'men of battle' does not."[20]

Because of the rebellion of the people against Yahweh, they were in the wilderness thirty-eight years where an entire generation of Israelite warriors died (Deut 2:14–16). But as Nelson writes, "In light of the former generation's poor military record, one suspects that the appellation 'warriors' is ironic."[21] Joshua's army consisted of ordinary people, not professional soldiers. The army was composed of former slaves who had spent forty years in the wilderness. They were "armed men" (Josh 6:3 NIV), many of whom "had no experience of any war in Canaan" (Judg 3:1). Joshua's army had no horses nor chariots "for horses and chariots are tools of states and empires, necessary and paid for in order to guard the monopoly."[22] The Israelites also had primitive weapons. According to Josh 8:18 (NRSV), during the war against Ai, Joshua had a sword (a *kîdôn*) in his hand which Yahweh told him to stretch it out toward Ai. However, the Hebrew word *kîdôn* is translated "a javelin of bronze" (1 Sam 17:6 NRSV), the weapon used by Goliath.

Thomas Dozeman says that the *kîdôn* used by Joshua was a scimitar, "the curved sword that broadens out near the point, like the sickle sword. The curved sword was prominent in the second millennium but

---

20. Bailey, "Thoughts on Eric A. Seibert's *Disturbing Divine Behavior*," 165.
21. Nelson, *Deuteronomy*, 40.
22. Brueggemann, "Revelation and Violence," 293.

became obsolete and was replaced by the straight sword, after which time it became a symbol of power rather than an active weapon of war."[23] The Canaanites had professional soldiers and modern equipment of war in their army. The Canaanite alliance which fought against Joshua and his army came out "with all their troops, a great army, in number like the sand on the seashore, with very many horses and chariots" (Josh 11:4). Years later, when Israel was fighting wars against the Philistines, Saul's army was poorly equipped, "on the day of the battle neither sword nor spear was to be found in the possession of any of the people with Saul and Jonathan" (1 Sam 13:22). When Israel fought against the Canaanites, Yahweh helped Israel defeat Sisera, his army, and their nine hundred chariots of iron (Judg 4:15) by sending torrential rains which flooded the Kishon River (Judg 5:20–21). Israel's army was not equipped to fight against the superior army of the Canaanites. Israel needed the help of the Divine Warrior to conquer their enemies.

Another issue is the genocidal language used to translate what Yahweh would do to the Canaanites. Several Hebrew words are used to describe the actions Yahweh will take against the Canaanites. The word *gāraš* is translated "drive out" (Exod 23:31). The word *yāraš* is translated "dispossess" (Deut 2:21 NRS), "take possession" (Deut 11:31 NIV), and "occupy" (NRSV). The word *šālaḥ* is translated "cast out" (Lev 18:24 KJV). The word *hādap* is translated "thrust out" (Deut 6:19 NRSV) and "expell" (CJB). The word *šāmad* is translated "destroy" (Deut 7:23 NRSV), "defeat" (NRSV), "wiped out" (TNK), and "devastate" (Deut 9:3 HCSB). The word *'bād* is translated "destroy" (Deut 8:20 NRSV). The word *kānaʻ* is translated "subdue" (Deut 9:3 NRSV), "wipe out" (TNK), and "destroy" (NIV). The word *nāšal* is translated "to clear away" (Deut 7:1 NRS), "dislodge" (TNK), "drive out" (HCSB). The word *kārat* is translated "cut off" (Deut 12:29 NRSV), "cut down" (TNK), "annihilate" (HCSB), "remove" (NAB), "destroy (DRA), and "eliminate" (NET). The English translations of these Hebrew words are very misleading. A Hebrew word can have a genocidal meaning in one translation of the Bible and a less violent meaning in another translation.

When Yahweh established his covenant with Israel on Mount Sinai, Yahweh renewed his promise to Abraham that he would bring his people to the land of Canaan: "When my angel goes in front of you, and brings you to the Amorites, the Hittites, the Perizzites, the Canaanites,

---

23. Dozeman, *Joshua 1–12*, 370.

the Hivites, and the Jebusites, and I blot them out" (Exod 23:23). The Hebrew verb translated "I blot" is *kāḥad*. The English translations differ in the way they render this word: "I annihilate them" (TNK); "I will wipe them out" (NIV); "I will make an end of them" (CJB); "I will completely destroy them" (NAS); "I shall exterminate them" (NJB).

The translations listed above use the language of genocide; the Israelites are to annihilate the Canaanites. However, the word *kāḥad* is used once again in a text where the word "angel" appears: "The LORD sent an angel who annihilated every mighty warrior, commander, and officer in the army of the king of Assyria" (2 Chr 32:21 TNK). The writer of the book of Kings said that the angel killed one hundred eighty-five-thousand Assyrian soldiers (2 Kgs 19:35). The Chronicler said that the angel only killed the military leaders of the Assyrian army, "without whom any further action would be impossible."[24]

A second occurrence of the word *kāḥad* appears also in a context of judgment. Yahweh sent Moses to Pharaoh to warn him of another plague. Through Moses, Yahweh said to Pharaoh, "For by now I could have stretched out my hand and struck you and your people with pestilence, and you would have been cut off from the earth" (Exod 9:15). Unlike the previous plague that only killed livestock (Exod 9:3), Yahweh had not yet sent a plague that would take human life. When the hail came (Exod 9:23–24) the Egyptians were not spared, but they were not annihilated.

Thus, the use of *kāḥad* does not imply genocide because Egypt and Assyria survived, for God had other plans for both nations (Isa 19:18–25). Zehnder says that the use of *kāḥad*

> may best be understood as hinting to some supernatural blow that Yhwh is going to strike against the Canaanites to break their resistance. This includes a clear element of violence, but not necessarily on a genocidal scale, since both in the case of the Egyptians (potentially) and of the Assyrians (actually, according to the extended reports) the act did not entail the complete annihilation of the group affected by it.[25]

Yahweh was highly involved in the conquest of the land. Moses told the people, "The LORD your God will bring you to the land you're about to enter and take possession of. He will force many nations out of your way" (Deut 7:1 GWN). The Hebrew word *nāšal*, "he will force

24. Japhet, *I & II Chronicles*, 991.
25. Zehnder, "Annihilation of the Canaanites," 268.

out," is translated differently by the various English versions: "he clears away" (RSV), "he dislodges" (TNK), "he drives out" (NIV), "he will expel" (CJB), "shall have destroyed" (DRA). The English translations use language of annihilation, "have destroyed"; language of force, "He will force out"; and language of expulsion, "he drives out." The word *nāšal* appears in 2 Kgs 16:6: "At that time the king of Edom recovered Elath for Edom, and drove the Judeans from Elath; and the Edomites came to Elath, where they live to this day." In this context the word *nāšal* does not carry the idea of genocide. Such a use "proves that no notion of killing or extermination is part of its semantic range."[26] Zehnder concludes by saying that "The use of the word *nāšal* implies that the conquest of the land of Canaan will be accomplished with little violence."[27]

THE CONCEPT OF HOLY WAR

Another issue that creates a misunderstanding about the war of conquest is the use of the expression "holy war" to describe the wars in the book of Joshua. In his study of holy war in the Old Testament, Stephen Chapman says that it is not correct to call the war of conquest "holy war." He writes, "The Old Testament never once calls war 'holy.' The phrase 'holy war' nowhere appears; neither is the adjective 'holy' ever used attributively or substantively in reference to warfare or any battle."[28] The expression "holy war" is not biblical. The people of Israel did not distinguish between sacred and secular war.[29] The biblical text calls the wars in which Yahweh participates and helps Israel attain victory "Yahweh War." The expression "Yahweh War" appears in association with "the Book of the Wars of Yahweh" (Num 21:14).[30] The same expression appears also in 1 Sam 18:17 and 25:28. Gwilym Jones makes a distinction between holy war and Yahweh war.[31]

---

26. Zehnder, "Annihilation of the Canaanites," 269.
27. Zehnder, "Annihilation of the Canaanites," 269.
28. Chapman, "Martial Memory, Peaceable Vision," 47.
29. Gelston, "Wars of Israel," 325–31.
30. On the texts dealing with war in the Old Testament, see Webb and Oeste, *Bloody, Brutal, and Barbaric*.
31. Jones, "Holy War or Yahweh War?," 642–58.

The expression "holy war" became popular by Gerhard von Rad in his study of war in ancient Israel.[32] In his book, von Rad used the Greek concept of amphictyony to study the war of ancient Israel. He concluded that, in Israel, war was a cultic institution. In holy war, it is the people who fights for Yahweh. According to Römer, in the book of Joshua, Yahweh is presented "as a warrior-God who is the high chief of a people who are just as warlike as he is."[33]

In the wars of Israel, it was Yahweh who gave the victory to the people: "The horse is made ready for the day of battle, but the victory belongs to Yahweh" (Prov 21:31). Yahweh is a warrior who fights for Israel and delivers the nation from its enemies. On many occasions Yahweh intervenes in the wars of Israel by using the powers of nature and the heavenly bodies to deliver his people from the hands of their enemies.[34]

THE USE OF THE WORD *ḤĒREM*

Another issue that produces anxiety for people who oppose violence is the use of the word *ḥērem* in the conquest narrative. Walton and Walton say that when people read the book of Joshua, "what God and the Israelites are doing is often misunderstood because the Hebrew word *ḥērem* is commonly mistranslated."[35] English versions of the Bible differ on the way they translated the Hebrew word *ḥērem*. The translations use words such as "ban" (NIV), "devoted to destruction" (NRSV), "proscribed" (TNK), "utterly destroyed" (KJV), "permanently sets apart" (HCSB), "devoted things" (RSV), "vows as doomed" (NAB), and a few other related words.

Walton and Walton say that *ḥērem* may "often involve destruction, but 'destruction' is not the essential meaning of *ḥērem* because not everything that is *ḥērem* is destroyed."[36] They argue that the words "utterly annihilate" and "devote to destruction" are misleading translations of *ḥērem* because the words imply everything must be destroyed. They use the destruction of Jericho as an example. In Josh 6, the objects taken from the city are *ḥērem*, but the silver and gold, and vessels of bronze and

---

32. Rad, *Holy War*.
33. Römer, *Dark God*, 76.
34. Weinfeld, "Divine Intervention and War," 121–47.
35. Walton and Walton, *Lost World of the Israelite Conquest*, 167.
36. Walton and Walton, *Lost World of the Israelite Conquest*, 171.

iron could not be destroyed; they were "consecrated to Yahweh and put in his treasury" (Josh 6:19 NJB). They propose that the ḥērem refers "to the removal of something from human use."[37] The practice of the ḥērem is mostly confined to the conquest narrative; "the gradual absorption of the Canaanites, as subjugated peoples, into the Israelite population soon made the ḥērem obsolescent, and by the time of the monarchy, it is virtually a dead letter."[38]

The word ḥērem appears both in religious and military contexts. According to Younger, "85 percent of the occurrences of ḥērem are in warfare contexts."[39] When the word carries the idea of a vow made to Yahweh, the word carries a religious connotation, and as "part of the vocabulary of the sacred, it must be seen as integral to the worldview of ancient Israelite religion."[40] The first reference to ḥērem in the Old Testament appears in Exod 22:20. The text says that any person who sacrifices to any God beside Yahweh will be put to death, "Whoever sacrifices to any god, other than the LORD alone, shall be devoted to destruction." Another text that discusses a person under ḥērem is Lev 27:29, "No human beings who have been devoted to destruction can be ransomed; they shall be put to death." Although scholars differ concerning the person under ḥērem in this text, the text seems to be an explanation of Exod 22:20, that the person devoted to being put to death because of idolatry cannot be ransomed. In Lev 27:21 the word ḥērem appears in a religious context and does not carry the idea of violent destruction: "But when the field is released in the jubilee, it shall be holy to the LORD as a devoted field; it becomes the priest's holding."

The warfare use of ḥērem is found in Deut 7:2: "when the LORD your God gives them over to you and you defeat them, then you must utterly destroy them." The possession of the land of Canaan is the work of Yahweh: he brings Israel into the land, he clears away seven nations that inhabit the land, he gives the seven nations into Israel's hands. The work Israel must do is to defeat them and "utterly destroy them."[41] The idea of destroying the Canaanites also appears in Deut 7:16: "You shall destroy

---

37. Walton and Walton, *Lost World of the Israelite Conquest*, 170–72.
38. Lindars, "Ezekiel and Individual Responsibility," 455.
39. Younger, "Some Recent Discussion on the Ḥērem," 505.
40. Emery, "Ḥērem," 384.
41. Several of the cities Joshua and his army conquered and destroyed were under the ḥērem: Jericho (Josh 6:21); Ai (Josh 8:26); Makkedah (Josh 10:28); and Hazor (Josh 11:11).

all the peoples that the LORD your God delivers to you." Although the word *ḥērem* is not used (the word used is ' *ākal*, "devour"), this statement "cannot be interpreted in any other way than as aiming at the annihilation of the inhabitants of the cities that are in view, together with their livestock."[42]

In their dealing with the Canaanites, Israel must not make a covenant with them, they must not intermarry with them.[43] They also must "break down their altars, smash their pillars, hew down their sacred poles, and burn their idols with fire" (Deut 7:5). Israel had to place the inhabitants of Canaan under *ḥērem*, "But as for the towns of these peoples that the LORD your God is giving you as an inheritance, you must not let anything that breathes remain alive. You shall annihilate them" (Deut 20:16–17). It is clear that the use of *ḥērem* in this context implies that in their fight against the Canaanites Israel must put to death the inhabitants of the land. The issue, however, is how much killing occurred during the conquest of Canaan.

THE CONQUEST OF CANAAN

The book of Joshua describes how the tribes of Israel fought against the Canaanites to conquer the land Yahweh had promised to Abraham.[44] Boyd says that the people of Israel shared "the uniform ANE assumption that if a deity wants his people to acquire a certain parcel of land, he requires them to wage war against the indigenous population to get it."[45] But Paul recognized that it was the Lord who defeated the Canaanites and gave the land to Israel. Paul wrote, "After [God] had destroyed seven nations in the land of Canaan, he gave them their land as an inheritance" (Acts 13:16–19).

---

42. Zehnder, "Annihilation of the Canaanites," 272.

43. According to Jacob Milgrom, "Religious Conversion," 172, the people of Israel were allowed to marry people from outside of Canaan. The law of the *ḥērem* in Deuteronomy reflects the "fear that intermarriage with the Canaanites will lead to apostasy." The leaders of Israel were "alarmed not because Canaanites practice Israel's religion, but for the reverse reason: intermarriage with them will lead to the abandonment of Israel's religion."

44. The promise that Abraham and his descendants would receive the land of Canaan as an inheritance was given to Abraham six times: Gen 12:1–2; 13:15; 15:16, 18–20; 17:8; 22:17. The promise of land, fruitfulness, and blessing is also given to Isaac (Gen 26:3–4) and to Jacob (Gen 28:13–14; 35:12).

45. Boyd, *Crucifixion of the Warrior God*, 972.

When Israel fought against King Sihon, the Amorite king of Heshbon, Moses sent messengers to King Sihon with terms of peace (Deut 2:24–28). But King Sihon was not willing to allow Israel to cross his territory and because of that, Israel defeated him in battle (Deut 2:30). Joshua made a treaty of peace with the Gibeonites and allowed them to live and not be killed (Josh 9:15). With the exception of the Gibeonites, not a single city in Canaan tried to make peace with the Israelites. Because of their refusal, these cities and their kings were conquered by Israel (Josh 11:19 TNK).

The first two cities conquered by Joshua and his army were the cities of Jericho and the city of Ai. The site of ancient Jericho is located on the mound of Tell es-Sultan. The height of the mound is twenty-four meters (about seventy-nine feet) and the area is approximately four hectares (about ten acres).[46] Jeffrey Zorn says that when attempting to estimate the population size of an ancient city, scholars estimate that there were between two hundred to two hundred fifty inhabitants per hectare.[47] Thus, the population of Jericho would be about a thousand inhabitants. In times of war, the population of the city would grow because many people from the villages around the city would seek protection within the walls of the city.

The Iron Age I city of Ai, the modern et-Tell,[48] at the time when Israel entered the land of Canaan, was a small village. According to Joseph Callaway,[49] the village was only 2.75 acres in size, with a population estimated to be from one hundred fifty to three hundred persons. As for the people of Jericho, "the city and everything in it are set apart to the LORD for destruction" (Josh 6:17). All the people of Ai were put to the sword (Josh 8:25). Walton and Walton try to mitigate the fate of the people of Ai. They write, "'Putting them to the sword' is an alternative to their normal expected fate, which was slavery. They are being killed not for the purpose of making them dead but to remove them from use as slaves."[50]

Zorn, in his study of war and its effect on civilians wrote, "By the time the people of Israel began to emerge on the world scene, around

---

46. Holland, "Jericho (Place)," 723–40.

47. Zorn, "War and Its Effects on Civilians," 84.

48. Some scholars believe that et-Tell was not the actual site of Ai. They believe that the city of Ai was located at a different site, a place still unknown, see Allen, "Archaeology of Ai," 41–52.

49. Callaway, "Excavating Ai," 18–30.

50. Walton and Walton, *Lost World of the Israelite Conquest*, 173.

1200 BCE, organized warfare, with all of its attendant atrocities, had been in existence for well over two thousand years."[51] During a siege of the city, the civilian population, "including older men, children, and women, would often aid in the defense of the fortifications."[52] Civilians had to endure the brutality and the barbarism that came with defeat in war. The Assyrians and the Babylonian inflicted much pain and suffering on civilian populations as the archeological record shows. The biblical record indicates that the massacre of civilian populations was not done by the army of Israel.

The reason Yahweh was dispossessing the Canaanites was because of what the biblical writer calls "their abhorrent practices."[53] When God made a covenant with Abraham, he mentioned the destiny of the people of the land, "And [your descendants] shall come back here in the fourth generation; for the iniquity of the Amorites is not yet complete" (Gen 15:16). Moses told the new generation of Israelites who were about to enter the land of Canaan, "When the LORD your God thrusts them out before you, do not say to yourself, 'It is because of my righteousness that the LORD has brought me in to occupy this land'; it is rather because of the wickedness of these nations that the LORD is dispossessing them before you" (Deut 9:4). He also spoke about the practices of the Canaanites, "For whoever does these things is abhorrent to the LORD; it is because of such abhorrent practices that the LORD your God is driving them out before you" (Deut 18:12).

Most English Bibles translate the word ʻāwōn as "iniquity" (Gen 15:16). The NIV translates the Hebrew word as "sin." Walton and Walton disagree with the NIV. They believe that Gen 15:16 does not says that the Canaanites were committing sin. They write, "we are never shown any misdeeds of the Amorites, and we have no real basis for assuming that they did them based only on the presence of ʻāwōn."[54] They also believe that the word "Amorite" is not a synecdoche for the Canaanites. Rather, the word Amorite refers to Mamre the Amorite, brother of Eshcol (Gen 14:13), the ally of Abraham. They also do not believe that the word ʻāwōn

---

51. Zorn, "War and Its Effects on Civilians," 79.

52. Zorn, "War and Its Effects on Civilians," 80. Zorn mentions one example in the Old Testament: "In the biblical narrative this blurring of roles is exemplified in the story of the would-be king Abimelech, who was mortally wounded at Thebez by a millstone thrown by a woman from the wall during the attack on a tower."

53. Jones, "We Don't Hate Sin," 53–72.

54. Walton and Walton, *Lost World of the Israelite Conquest*, 50.

should be translated "sin" or "iniquity." They believe that ' *āwōn* means "a destiny of calamity." They translate Gen 15:16 as follows, "It won't be until after your lifetime is over that your family will return here because the destiny of destruction that has been decreed for your friends and allies has been and will continue to be deferred."[55]

Daniel Block, on the other hand, accepts the traditional interpretation of Gen 15:16 and declares that "the policy of *ḥērem* functions as a divinely ordained means of dealing with sin. The mandate to eliminate the Canaanites was driven by neither genocidal nor military considerations but by the eradication of evil and the prevention of evil from spreading to the new population. Although the Canaanites may not have been any more degenerate than other nations, this policy is rooted in the perception of the Canaanites as a wicked people."[56]

The Complete Conquest of Canaan

The word "genocide" was coined by a Polish Jewish lawyer Raphaël Lemkin in 1944 to describe Nazi policies against the Jews in World War II.[57] Genocide refers to the systematic extermination of an entire population or a national group. The conquest of Canaan has been called genocide because of the violence and brutality against in inhabitants of the land and the apparent annihilation of the Canaanites. The basis for classifying the conquest of Canaan as genocide is based on three texts from the book of Joshua where the author says that Joshua and the army of Israel conquered the whole land and killed all its inhabitants: Josh 10:40–43; 11:16–23; 21:43–45. Josh 10:40 says, "So Joshua defeated the whole land . . . he left no one remaining, but utterly destroyed all that breathed, as the LORD God of Israel commanded." Another text says, "So Joshua took all that land . . . For it was the LORD's doing to harden their hearts so that they would come against Israel in battle, in order that they might be utterly destroyed, and might receive no mercy, but be exterminated, just as the LORD had commanded Moses" (Josh 11:16, 20).

The message of these three texts seems to convey to the reader an erroneous idea that the people of Israel killed every Canaanite, since the Israelites had no mercy on the people and since Joshua and his army

---

55. Walton and Walton, *Lost World of the Israelite Conquest*, 60, 62.
56. Block, "How Can We Bless Yhwh?," 46.
57. Irvin-Erickson, *Raphaël Lemkin*.

"left no one remaining, but utterly destroyed all that breathed." However, the correct reading of these three texts and of the entire book of Joshua, together with the book of Judges, reveals that the term genocide cannot be applied to the conquest of Canaan. Kitchen shows the fallacy of calling the conquest of Canaan an act of genocide. He wrote,

> It is the careless reading of such verses as these, without a careful and close reading of the narratives proper, that has encouraged Old Testament scholars to read into the entire book *a whole myth of their own making*, to the effect that the book of Joshua presents a sweeping, total conquest *and occupation* of Canaan by Joshua, which can then be falsely pitted against the narratives in Judges.[58]

Kitchen uses Josh 10:20 to show the war rhetoric of these texts. Josh 10:20 says that when Israel fought against the coalition of five Canaanite kings, Joshua and the army of Israel slaughtered and completely crushed the enemy (NLT). The Canaanites were wiped out (ESV); Israel's army destroyed them (NJB). This is language of genocide. But the text also says that "those who had escaped alive took refuge in their fortresses" (Josh 10:20 NJB). Thus, the language of complete destruction is hyperbolic because not all were killed, many survived, even though biblical text seems to indicate that all the enemies had been killed in battle. Terence Clarke, in his study of the three texts that imply a complete conquest of Canaan, says that "the writer of Joshua does not assert that the Israelites killed all the people of the land or claim that they captured and occupied every city or parcel of land in Canaan."[59]

The Incomplete Conquest of Canaan

Although Josh 1–12 seems to indicate that Israel conquered the whole land and killed all its inhabitants in a short time, the book of Joshua indicates that the war of conquest took a long time and that the Canaanites were not exterminated from the land. Joshua fought against the Canaanite kings for many years (Josh 11:18). At the end of his life, much of the land of Canaan remained to be conquered, "Now Joshua was old and advanced in years; and the LORD said to him, You are old and advanced in years, and very much of the land still remains to be possessed" (Josh

---

58. Kitchen, *On the Reliability of the Old Testament*, 173–74.
59. Clarke, "Complete v. Incomplete Conquest," 91.

13:1). It is Yahweh himself who says that *"very much of the land still remains to be possessed"* (emphasis mine). After the author of Joshua says that "the LORD gave to Israel all the land" and that "not one of all their enemies had withstood them" (Josh 21:43–44), Joshua tells the assembled leaders of Israel that Yahweh will drive out those nations that remain (Josh 23:4–5), indicating that at the end of Joshua's life many of the Canaanite nations were still in the land.

The books of Joshua and Judges indicate that many Canaanites were not conquered; most of the Canaanite population remained in the land until the time of the monarchy. Israel was unable to conquer the Canaanites who lived in Beth-shean because they had chariots of iron (Josh 17:16). Israel was not able to drive out the Jebusites (Josh 15:63); they were not able to drive out the Canaanites who lived in Gezer (Josh 16:10). Manasseh was not able to drive out the Canaanites from its territory, so, "Canaanites continued to live in that land" (Josh 17:12).[60]

The book of Judges also indicates that at the end of the war of conquest many of the Canaanites were still living in the land. Ephraim did not drive out the Canaanites who lived in Gezer; Zebulun did not drive out the inhabitants of Kitron, or the inhabitants of Nahalol; Asher did not drive out the inhabitants of Acco; Naphtali did not drive out the inhabitants of Beth-shemesh; and the Danites could not conquer the Amorites (Judg 1:27–35).

The Conquest of Hazor

The conquest of Canaan was accomplished with much violence and much killing, some of them were civilians, men, women and children. When the army of Israel confronted the inhabitants of the land, they believed that Yahweh would fight for them and that he would be an enemy to Israel's enemies and a foe to Israel's foes (Exod 23:22). Modern readers of the book of Joshua are highly vexed by these texts of violence because, as Brueggemann puts it, "these texts of violence are at least an embarrassment, are morally repulsive, and are theologically problematic in the Bible not because they are violent but because this is violence either in the name of or at the hand of Yahweh."[61]

---

60. Weinfeld, *Promise of the Land*, 99–120.
61. Brueggemann, *Social Reading of the Old Testament*, 289.

Israel's conquest of Hazor presents a good overview of Israel's struggle to conquer the land.[62] The fight for Hazor came after Joshua and his army had defeated a coalition of five kings from southern Canaan who came together to attack the Gibeonites for making a peace treaty with Israel (Josh 9–10). When Jabin, king of Hazor, heard that the southern coalition was defeated by Israel, he formed a coalition of several city-states to fight against Israel.

The Canaanite coalition was large. It was composed of King Jabin of Hazor, King Jobab of Madon, the king of Shimron, the king of Achshaph, the kings who were in the northern hill country, the kings who were in the Arabah south of Chinneroth, the kings who were in the lowland, and the kings who were in Naphoth-dor on the west. The coalition also included the Canaanites in the east and the west, the Amorites, the Hittites, the Perizzites, the Jebusites, and the Hivites (Josh 11:1–3). When these kings came together, with all their troops, they were "a great army, in number like the sand on the seashore, with very many horses and chariots" (Josh 11:4).

The mention of horses and chariots in verse 4 is important in this context. This was Israel's first experience with horses and chariots in Canaan. When Israel left Egypt, they had to face "Pharaoh and all his army, his chariots, and his chariot drivers" (Exod 14:17). Now they face the horses and chariots of the Canaanite coalition. Israel had no horses and chariots for as Brueggemann explains, "horses and chariots are tools of states and empires, necessary and paid for in order to guard the monopoly."[63] Chariots of iron were powerful weapons in war, which caused Israel to fear because the horses and chariots reminded the people of how vulnerable they were as they prepared to battle.

As Israel prepares to battle, Yahweh speaks to Joshua to assure him about the threat posed by the Canaanites: "And the LORD said to Joshua, 'Do not be afraid of them, for tomorrow at this time I will hand over all of them, slain, to Israel; you shall hamstring their horses, and burn their chariots with fire'" (Josh 11:6). Yahweh encourages Joshua not to be afraid of the force of the Canaanite's army. When Yahweh instructed Moses about how to fight against the Canaanites, Yahweh told Moses, "When you go out to war against your enemies, and see horses and chariots, an

---

62. This section is indebted to Brueggemann's excellent article, "Revelation and Violence," 285–318. The article appears in the book listed in the previous note.

63. Brueggemann, *Social Reading of the Old Testament*, 293.

army larger than your own, you shall not be afraid of them; for the LORD your God is with you" (Deut 20:1).

Yahweh told Joshua that after they conquered their enemy they should "hamstring their horses, and burn their chariots with fire." Yahweh's words to Joshua are very important in attempting to understand the use of violence against the Canaanites. Brueggemann writes that in his speech to Joshua, "Yahweh undertakes no direct action. We should note that in this direct command, the only object of violence is horses and chariots, that is, weapons. There is nothing here about burning cities, killing kings or people, or seizing war booty."[64]

God's instruction to Joshua about the Canaanite coalition is similar to the instruction he gave to Joshua before the attack on Jericho. At that time, Yahweh said to Joshua, "I have handed Jericho over to you, along with its king and soldiers" (Josh 6:2). Again, there is no mention of burning cities, killing people, or seizing war booty.

In commanding Joshua to destroy the chariots of the Canaanites,

> Yahweh gave permission for Joshua and Israel to act for their justice and liberation against an oppressive adversary. This revelatory word of Yahweh, given directly without conduit or process, is only authorization for a liberating movement that is sure to be violent, but only violent against weapons.[65]

When Joshua and his army conquered Hazor, they put the city under *ḥērem*, "And they put to the sword all who were in it, utterly destroying them; there was no one left who breathed, and he burned Hazor with fire" (Josh 11:11).

The total destruction of the Canaanite cities was not included in Yahweh's authorization in verse 6. However, as Brueggemann writes, "The warrant for violence is grounded in verse 6. . . . Israel took that limited, disciplined warrant of Yahweh and went well beyond its intent or substance in its action.[66] Yahweh authorized the destruction of horses and chariots. Israel did much more to the Canaanites than Yahweh had authorized; they burned Hazor, killed the kings who opposed Israel, and killed people in the conquered cities. The reason Joshua and his army did more than Yahweh had commanded him is because Israel was fighting wars using military practices that were common in the ancient Near

---

64. Brueggemann, *Social Reading of the Old Testament*, 294.
65. Brueggemann, *Social Reading of the Old Testament*, 295.
66. Brueggemann, *Social Reading of the Old Testament*, 303.

East in the second-millennium BCE. Thus, the violence of Joshua and his army becomes the violence of Yahweh. Niehaus, in his study of warfare in Joshua, has shown that military practices in the book of Joshua were comparable to warfare in mid-second-millennium Ugarit, Assyria, and Babylon.[67] Brueggemann says that the "warrant for violence" against the Canaanites was made necessary for the sake of Israel's survival.[68]

THE SURVIVAL OF THE CANAANITES

After looking at the conquest narrative, it is clear that the label "genocide" and "ethnic cleansing" does not apply to what happened to the Canaanites during the war of conquest. The fact is that most of the Canaanite population remained in the land and were not killed. Those who were killed at the hands of the Israelite army died as the result of armed conflict. Wars result in many casualties, both combatants and civilians. Although it is impossible to estimate the number of people killed by the army of Israel, the fact is that the majority of Canaanites survived.

The survival of the Canaanites is attested by three important texts. They are important because they prove that there was no genocide of the Canaanites. Judges 3:5–7 lists six of the seven Canaanite nations that survived the war of conquest:

> So the Israelites lived among the Canaanites, the Hittites, the Amorites, the Perizzites, the Hivites, and the Jebusites; and they took their daughters as wives for themselves, and their own daughters they gave to their sons; and they worshiped their gods. The Israelites did what was evil in the sight of the LORD, forgetting the LORD their God, and worshiping the Baals and the Asherahs. (Judg 3:5–7)[69]

This statement reveals that most of the people living in these six Canaanite cities were not killed; most of them survived and as the leaders of Israel feared, the Israelites took the daughters of the Canaanites as wives and they worshiped their Gods. Milgrom said that if the Canaanites "had they been wiped out at the time of the conquest as God commanded to

---

67. Niehaus, "Joshua and Ancient Near Eastern Warfare," 37–50.
68. Brueggemann, *Social Reading of the Old Testament*, 303.
69. Only the Girgashites is missing from the list of seven nations that appears in Deut 7:1.

Moses (Deut 20:17) there would be no apostasy in Israel."⁷⁰ In the days of the judges, Israel was oppressed for twenty years by King Jabin of Canaan and Sisera, the commander of his army who had nine hundred chariots of iron (Judg 4:2–3).

A second text also indicates that the Canaanites survived the war of conquests. In the days of David, Joab took a census of Israel that also included the land of the Hittites and all the cities of the Hivites and Canaanites (2 Sam 24:6–7). A third text that reveals that most of the Canaanites survived comes from the days of Solomon: "All the people who were left of the Amorites, the Hittites, the Perizzites, the Hivites, and the Jebusites, who were not of the people of Israel—their descendants who were still left in the land, whom the Israelites were unable to destroy completely—these Solomon conscripted for slave labor, and so they are to this day" (1 Kgs 9:20–21). The number of the people conscripted by Solomon was one hundred fifty thousand.

Meredith Kline said that if the conquest of Canaan were to be adjudicated in a secular court of law or in a court of nations, "it would have to be condemned as an unprovoked aggression and, moreover, an aggression carried out in barbarous violation of the requirement to show all possible mercy even in the proper execution of justice."⁷¹ A secular court would not accept as valid the covenant God made with Abraham. It would not accept the argument that the iniquity of the Canaanites was under divine judgment, nor would it accept the words of Moses and Joshua as reliable testimony. From a human perspective, the conquest of Canaan would not be acceptable by any human standard. According to Kline, the only way to justify the conquest of Canaan and the killing of the Canaanites is to acknowledge that "the ordinary [ethical] standards were suspended."⁷² According to Kline, it is only when the ethical principles of the last Judgment is applied to the conquest of Canaan "that the divine promises and commands to Israel concerning Canaan and the Canaanites . . . can be justified."⁷³

---

70. Milgrom, "Religious Conversion and the Revolt Model," 172.

71. Kline, "Intrusion and the Decalogue," 15.

72. Kline, "Intrusion and the Decalogue," 15. Craigie, "Yahweh Is a Man of Wars," 186, writes, "In the Old Testament, if we were to expect to see God working only in what we might call an absolutely 'ethical' manner, we would in effect be denying the possibility of seeing Him work at all; the men with whom God meets and deals remain essentially sinful men."

73. Kline, "Intrusion and the Decalogue," 15–16.

In conclusion, there is no doubt that there is human and divine violence in the Old Testament. In the sinful world in which we live, it is impossible to eliminate human violence for "warfare and violence are necessary in extreme circumstances."[74] The Old Testament shows that human violence causes divine violence. Yahweh cannot allow evil to go unchecked in the world. According to the writer of the book of Ecclesiastes, wars will continue for the foreseeable future: "For everything there is a season, and a time for every matter under heaven: . . . a time for war, and a time for peace" (Eccl 3:8). Jesus said, "You will hear of wars and rumors of wars, but see to it that you are not alarmed. Such things must happen but the end is still to come" (Matt 24:6). The reason war exists is because "complete pacifism [is not] a realistic option at the present time."[75]

Yahweh said, "See now that I, even I, am he, and there is no god beside me; I kill and I make alive; I wound and I heal; and there is none that can deliver out of my hand" (Deut 32:39). Since the life of every individual is dependent upon Yahweh, he has power over life; in his hands are the power of life and death. Even Paul recognizes God's exclusive power over human life. Paul said, "If anyone destroys God's temple, God will destroy that person" (1 Cor 3:17).

It is this divine sovereignty over human life that allowed Yahweh to bring judgment upon the world though a flood to deal with human violence (Gen 6:11) and human wickedness (Gen 6:5). It is Yahweh's power to take life that allowed him, as a righteous judge, to bring his judgment upon Sodom because their sin was very grievous (Gen 18:20). It is because Yahweh has the power of life and death that he allowed Israel to act as his agents in taking human life during the conquest of Canaan.

From a Christian perspective violence should be rejected because as Christians, we should love our enemies and pray for those who persecute us (Matt 5:44). This Christian behavior would eliminate violence in the world. However, violence, killings, brutality, savagery will always be present in the world because those who cause these abhorrent acts do not live by the ethics of the kingdom.

As Christians, we should follow the advice of Paul, "If it is possible, so far as it depends on you, live peaceably with all . . . if your enemies are hungry, feed them; if they are thirsty, give them something to drink; for by doing this you will heap burning coals on their heads" (Rom 12:18,

---

74. Rowley, "Epistemology of Sacralized Violence," 64.
75. Rowley, "Epistemology of Sacralized Violence," 64.

20). But we live in a world full of evil people and "evil people do the evil things that are in them" (Matt 12:35 GWN). As Christians, we must not "be overcome by evil, but overcome evil with good" (Rom 12:21). When that fails, we must allow God to act, "Beloved, never avenge yourselves, but leave room for the wrath of God; for it is written, 'Vengeance is mine, I will repay, says the Lord'" (Rom 12:19).

"Leave room for the wrath of God." The wrath of God was manifested in the Old Testament because of human wickedness, because of violence, brutality, and savagery. To deal with human wickedness God acted alone or used agents to act on his behalf. Joshua and his army acted the way they did because they did not know the ethics of the kingdom of God.

L. Daniel Hawk says that the conquest narrative in the book of Joshua explains "modern narratives of conquest and colonialism."[76] The motif of God as founder of a nation and the notion of a people set apart for a unique work in the world found in the biblical narrative also form part of the "American national mythology." There is no doubt that many people, past and present, have used the conquest of Canaan and the killing of the Canaanites to justify religious violence, the confiscation of land, and the indiscriminate killing of native people.

The conquest of Canaan involved the killing of the kings of the city-states and the burning of their cities. In this war of conquest, many people died, both combatants and civilians. But Israel's war against the Canaanites was similar to the wars conducted by the Assyrians, the Babylonians, the Persians, the Greeks, and the Romans. The only difference was that Yahweh was fighting for and with Israel.

Hawk says that he interprets the book of Joshua by the social realities that define his context. He writes, "I write as a citizen of the United States, of Anglo-Saxon lineage, and as a Christian clergyman and seminary professor—important factors among many that shape my identity and the way I read the narratives."[77] When the conquest narrative is read from this perspective, the violence and the brutality used in subduing the Canaanites is not acceptable. To believe that God is a warrior God who fights for Israel also betrays the idea of a God who is known as "the Prince of Peace." However, when we accept the book of Joshua as Christian Scriptures, we also accept the kind of God Yahweh is revealed to be in the

---

76. Hawk, "Truth about Conquest," 129–40.
77. Hawk, "Truth about Conquest," 137.

book. Yahweh as a Warrior God was an integral part of the faith of Israel. However, the New Testament teaches how God relinquishes violence in order to accomplish his work in the world.

In chapter 24 I will study how Yahweh deals with the problem of divine violence and how he relinquishes violence in order to accomplish his work in the world.

PART 3

God Reconciling the World

20

God Reconciling the World By Himself

GENESIS 1–11 IS POPULARLY KNOWN as the Primeval History. In these chapters Yahweh is not dealing with Israel; Yahweh is dealing with humanity as a whole. The Primeval History is concerned with the beginning of the world, the creation of humanity, and how humanity's rebellion brought the world to the brink of destruction. This history is an explanation and an introduction to the creation of Israel. Yahweh, in a great demonstration of grace, chose Abraham, and eventually Israel, for the redemption of the human race from the sins which beset and destroy it. These stories focus on the sinfulness of humanity and their need for redemption. Men and women are sinners who rebelled against Yahweh their creator and, as a consequence of their rebellion, human culture is presented as a denial of the sovereignty of God. These stories provide a theological introduction to the history of Israel. Yahweh has chosen Israel as an instrument to fulfill his redemptive purpose.

THE SIN OF ADAM

After God made human beings and placed them in the garden of Eden, God gave Adam the following command: "You may freely eat of every tree of the garden; but of the tree of the knowledge of good and evil you shall not eat, for in the day that you eat of it you shall die" (Gen 2:16–17). When Adam told Eve of God's prohibition, he probably also told her that they were forbidden even to touch the fruit of the tree, for when the serpent enticed Eve to eat of the fruit of the tree, Eve said to the serpent: "God said, 'You shall not eat of the fruit of the tree that is in the middle of the garden, nor shall you touch it, or you shall die'" (Gen 3:3).

In response to Eve's reluctance to eat of the fruit, the serpent said to the woman: "You will not die; for God knows that when you eat of it your eyes will be opened, and you will be like God, knowing good and evil" (Gen 3:4–5). The serpent was right.[1] The serpent did not lie, for everything the serpent said to Eve happened. This is what happened: Eve touched the fruit (Gen 3:6) and nothing happened. Eve ate the fruit and gave it to Adam who was by her side (Gen 3:6) and neither of them died. Adam and Eve became like God, knowing good and evil. Yahweh himself said that, after Adam and Eve ate of the tree: "Then the LORD God said, 'See, the man has become like one of us, knowing good and evil'" (Gen 3:22).

If Adam and Eve did not die when they ate from the tree of the knowledge of good and evil, what then did God mean when he told Adam that "in the day that you eat of it you shall die?" The Hebrew construction of the verb in Gen 2:17 includes two forms of the verb *mût*, "to die": the infinitive absolute and the imperfect. In Hebrew, the infinitive absolute emphasizes an action when it immediately precedes the finite verb. Gesenius, in his *Hebrew Grammar* wrote: "The infinitive absolute used before the verb to strengthen the verbal idea, i. e. to emphasize in this way either the certainty (especially in the case to threats) or the forcibleness and completeness of an occurrence."[2] He translates *môṭ tāmûṭ* as "thou shalt surely die." Thus, the full implication of Yahweh's threat to Adam is clear: Adam must not eat from the tree of the knowledge of good and evil for the moment he would eat from it he would die. But Adam ate from the tree of knowledge of good and evil and he did not die. So, how must one understand Yahweh's prohibition in Gen 2:17?

One way to interpret the divine prohibition is to say that because one day with God is like a thousand years (2 Pet 3:8), then Adam died before "the Lord's day" was over. Another way of interpreting the prohibition is by taking the infinitive form of the verb and translating it as a verbal noun: "dying you shall die." Thus, Yahweh's threat means that if Adam ate from the tree of the knowledge of good and evil then, he would eventually die. The Septuagint translates 2:17 as "you shall die by death."

---

1. Moberly, "Did the Serpent Get It Right?," 1–27.
2. Gesenius, *Hebrew Grammer*, 113n.

Another interpretation is that if Adam disobeyed God's command, he would become mortal. However, this interpretation contradicts Genesis because the book seems to imply that humans were already mortal. The book of Genesis says that man would only live forever after eating from the tree of life: "Then the LORD God said, 'See, the man has become like one of us, knowing good and evil; and now, he might reach out his hand and take also from the tree of life, and eat, and live forever'" (Gen 3:22).

The divine threat should be taken literally, that Adam and Eve should have died on the day they violated the prohibition not to eat from the tree of the knowledge of good and evil. I disagree with Gordon Wenham's interpretation of this threat as "death before death." He wrote:

> If to be expelled from the camp of Israel [as lepers were] was to "die," expulsion from the garden was an even more drastic kind of death. In this sense they did die on the day they ate of the tree: they were no longer able to have daily conversation with God, enjoy his bounteous provision, and eat of the tree of life; instead they had to toil for food, suffer, and eventually return to the dust from which they were taken.[3]

The reason the divine threat was not fulfilled was because the grace of God intervened and the penalty was not carried out. Probably the best commentary on this verse is found in 2 Pet 3:9: "The Lord is not slow in keeping his word, as he seems to some, but he is waiting in mercy for you, not desiring the destruction of any, but that all may be turned from their evil ways." This was the same position taken by John Skinner. According to Skinner, the simple explanation for why the punishment was not carried out "is that God, having regard to the circumstances of the temptation, changed His purpose and modified the penalty."[4]

Westermann also intimates a change in God's decision to carry out the punishment. He wrote: "After the man and the woman have eaten from the tree, a new situation arises in which God acts differently from the way he had indicated." God's failure to carry out the punishment "shows that God's dealing with his creatures cannot be pinned down, not even by what God has said previously."[5]

The reason Adam and Eve did not die was because of the nature and character of God, that God is a compassionate God who is gracious

---

3. Wenham, *Genesis 1–15*, 74.
4. Skinner, *Genesis*, 67.
5. Westermann, *Genesis 1–11*, 225.

to whom he wants to be gracious and who shows mercy on whom he wants to show mercy (Exod 33:19). As Yahweh said to Moses at the time he had decided to consume Israel because of their great sin (Exod 32:10): "The LORD, the LORD, a God merciful and gracious, slow to anger, and abounding in steadfast love and faithfulness, keeping steadfast love for thousands, forgiving iniquity and transgression and sin" (Exod 34:6–7).

It is the compassionate grace of God that is revealed in the first eleven chapters of Genesis. God's desire is to reconcile human beings unto himself. God gave humans the freedom to choose between good and evil. In their free will, humans chose to disobey God but instead of punishing them, God showed his grace in the midst of their sinfulness. The grace of God is seen in the story of Cain and Noah. The sin of Adam affected the whole creation and produced a violent world. As Jørstad writes, the violent world of Gen 1–11 has affected the whole creation showing "that the world does mirror our destructive behavior and that violence echoes across generations, place, and times, replicating itself."[6] Human violence, culminated with a universal flood that destroyed all humans, except Noah and his family. From Adam to the flood, God was unable to reconcile the world unto himself because of human sin and violence.

CAIN AND ABEL

The story of Cain and Abel is found in Gen 4. According to the narrative in Genesis, Abel was a keeper of sheep and Cain a tiller of the ground (Gen 4:2). The story of the struggle between the two brothers is placed in the context of the conflict between two occupations, the conflict between shepherds and farmers that was so common in antiquity. In the course of time both brothers brought offerings to Yahweh. The text does not explain how or when the brothers became aware that they needed to bring an offering to God. Since Cain was a farmer, he brought an offering of the fruit of the ground, Since Abel was a shepherd, he brought of the firstlings of his flock. Both types of offerings were acceptable by God. A farmer would bring an offering from the produce of the ground and a shepherd would bring from the firstlings of his flock.

However, for some unknown reason (maybe because of Cain's attitude?) Yahweh rejected Cain's offering, but accepted the offering of his brother Abel. The killing of animals, which many people today consider

---

6. Jørstad, "Ground That Opened Its Mouth," 715.

to be an act of violence, was a reality in many societies of the ancient world, a reality which cannot be denied. When Abel killed a sheep to offer as an offering to God, Abel was not criticized for killing a sheep from his flock. Even Yahweh himself killed an animal to clothe Adam and Eve (Gen 3:21). Cain became very angry and made plans to kill his brother. While they were in the fields, Cain killed his brother and buried him. The murder of Abel by a violent action which his brother committed against him demonstrates how the initial intent of God for humans and for his creation had been affected by an act of violence. But Yahweh confronted Cain about the death of his brother:

> And the LORD said, "What have you done? Listen; your brother's blood is crying out to me from the ground! And now you are cursed from the ground, which has opened its mouth to receive your brother's blood from your hand. When you till the ground, it will no longer yield to you its strength; you will be a fugitive and a wanderer on the earth." (Gen 4:10–12)

Because the life of human beings is precious to God, God demands the life of any person who kills another person (Gen 9:5). For his crime, Cain was punished with a curse. He was banished from the fertile land that was the original home of his parents (Gen 2:5). It is possible that God's words to Cain may indicate that he was banished from the land where his brother was buried. It is out of this sense of desperation that Cain cries out to Yahweh in prayer. "Cain said to the LORD, 'My punishment is greater than I can bear! Today you have driven me away from the soil, and I shall be hidden from your face; I shall be a fugitive and a wanderer on the earth, and anyone who meets me may kill me'" (Gen 4:13–14).

This is the first prayer recorded in the Bible. It was the prayer of a murderer recognizing the immensity of his sin. The expression "My punishment is greater than I can bear" implies that Cain was aware of the consequence of what he had done and the penalty he must pay for his sin. He had committed a crime that demanded punishment. This prayer of Cain is an appeal to Yahweh. Cain's words to Yahweh may not have the fixed structure of other prayers in the Old Testament. Not all prayers in the Bible have a fixed structure. There are different types of prayer. As Miller wrote: "There are also occasions when the prayer itself is not recorded in the text, but some indication is given of God's positive response."⁷ Cain's crying out to Yahweh is the prayer of a desperate sinner in need of divine mercy.

There is no reference to a holy place to which Cain came to make his appeal to God. Cain's prayer was not the prayer of a righteous man. The book of Proverbs declares that the prayers of a righteous person delights Yahweh: "The sacrifice of the wicked is an abomination to the LORD, but the prayer of the upright is his delight" (Prov 15:8). Cain was not a righteous person and yet Cain's prayer was the cry of a sinner to God asking for mercy. The prophet Isaiah said that when people committing violence and unrighteousness pray to Yahweh, Yahweh will not listen to their prayers: "When you stretch out your hands, I will hide my eyes from you; even though you make many prayers, I will not listen; your hands are full of blood" (Isa 1:15). When the people Isaiah mentioned in his oracle raised their hands in prayer to God, they revealed their sins because their hands were "full of blood." We do not know whether or not Cain stretched out his hands when he cried out to God, but Cain's hands were full of blood because he had killed his brother Abel.

Yahweh knew that Cain's hands were filled with blood, but when Cain prayed to Yahweh, Yahweh heard his prayer and as a result, Cain experienced the mercy of God and his life was spared. When Cain prayed to Yahweh, Yahweh answered his prayer. "Then the LORD said to him, 'Not so! Whoever kills Cain will suffer a sevenfold vengeance.' And the LORD put a mark on Cain, so that no one who came upon him would kill him" (Gen 4:15). Why was Cain's prayer heard? Because his cry to God was an agonizing cry for mercy. He was asking a merciful God to have mercy upon him because his sentence was greater that he could bear. Cain asked God to be merciful to him because in his situation, God was the only one who could help him.

There is a difference between the prayers of the people in Isaiah's time and Cain's prayer. The people in Isaiah's time were arrogant people who believed they could continue in their sins without punishment, that they could continue oppressing and exploiting people and at the same time come in prayer to God to find mercy and forgiveness. Cain, on the other hand, recognized the immensity of his crime and the overwhelming judgment that came upon him for taking the life of his brother. Cain recognized that his punishment was too harsh and in desperation, he cried to Yahweh for mercy. It was Cain's recognition of his sin and the

---

7. Miller, *They Cried to the Lord*, 139.

magnitude of his punishment that led him to cry to Yahweh. It is also this that sets him apart from the people in Isaiah's days and made his prayer different from their prayers.

Cain's prayer demonstrates that there is mercy for the sinner. As a killer, living away from the presence of Yahweh and away from divine protection, Cain feared retribution from an avenger of blood, one seeking to avenge the murder of Abel. Yahweh assured Cain that he would be protected from blood vengeance by putting a mark (or sign) on Cain to indicate that he was under Yahweh's protection. The nature of this sign is unknown. Scholars have made various suggestions to identify the nature of the sign, but none of them has found wide acceptance. Whatever the nature of the sign, the sign meant that Cain was under Yahweh's protection and anyone who tried to kill him would be severely punished.

In his commentary of Genesis, Derek Kidner wrote the following about Cain's prayer: "God's concern for the innocent is matched only by His care for the sinner. Even the querulous prayer of Cain had contained a germ of entreaty; God's answering pledge, together with His mark or sign—not of stigma but of safe-conduct—is almost a covenant, making Him virtually Cain's goel or protector. It is the utmost that mercy can do for the unrepentant."[8] Although Yahweh punished Cain for killing his brother, Yahweh put a mark on Cain to protect him from the violence that others could inflict on him. There is a mystery in God's mercy. Although God heard Cain's prayer and although Cain was assured of God's protection, the burden of Cain's punishment was not revoked. Cain must live with the consequences of his crime. Cain was protected from the avengers of blood, but his punishment was not revoked.

Because of his action against his brother, Cain must live away from the presence of the Lord, as a wanderer and a fugitive on earth. Cain's prayer was heard by God and the sinner received divine mercy, and yet the punishment remained because the sinner never repented. As Leon Kass wrote: "Moved more by dread than by reverence, Cain does not draw the most pious conclusion. Reassured but only temporarily, Cain sets out on his travels."[9] The first prayer mentioned in the Bible was not prayed by a righteous person who deserved to find a hearing with God. Cain was an angry man, jealous of Abel, a killer of his brother. Yet, he prayed to Yahweh and Yahweh answered his prayer. The prayer of Cain

---

8. Kidner, *Genesis*, 76.
9. Kass, *Beginning of Wisdom*, 144.

reveals the true nature and character of God. The God of the Old Testament is a merciful and gracious God, a God who is slow to anger, and a God who forgives iniquity, and transgression and sin. It is because of the gracious nature of God that Cain did not die.

THE VIOLENCE OF LAMECH

The creation stories in Gen 1 and 2 and the creation of the first human beings introduce an ideal for marriage that portrays heterosexual and monogamous marriage as the will of God for his creation. This design continues to be the ideal throughout the Bible, even though many deviations from this norm are found within the narratives of the Old Testament. The apparent reality of monogamous marriages is seen in the many stories of couples in the Old Testament. From these examples and many others, it is clear that most marriages in Israel were monogamous. In fact, when one looks at the history of Israel narrated in the books of Samuel and Kings, a history which covers a period of about five hundred years, one does not find a single example of bigamy among common people, with the exception of the case of Elkanah, Samuel's father, who had two wives (Sam 1:1–2). In ancient Israel, polygamy became popular in the days of the judges and in the period of the monarchy and it was generally practiced by the rich and powerful.

The first case of bigamy in the Old Testament appears in the genealogy of the sons of Cain, when Lamech took two women to be his wives: "And Lamech took two wives. The name of the one was Adah, and the name of the other Zillah. Adah bore Jabal; he was the father of those who dwell in tents and have livestock. His brother's name was Jubal; he was the father of all those who play the lyre and pipe. Zillah also bore Tubal-cain; he was the forger of all instruments of bronze and iron. The sister of Tubal-cain was Naamah. Lamech said to his wives: "Adah and Zillah, hear my voice; you wives of Lamech, listen to what I say: I have killed a man for wounding me, a young man for striking me. If Cain's revenge is sevenfold, then Lamech's is seventy-sevenfold" (Gen 4:19–24). Lamech used Yahweh's protective statement for Cain as an excuse to justify his violence.

According to the writer of the book of Genesis, Lamech was the first bigamist and the first polygamist of the Bible. Lamech's words in which he boasted to his two wives that he killed a man for wounding him, indicates that his two wives were alive and that they were contemporary rather than successive wives. The text describing Lamech's bigamy shows how human activity, including marriage, is affected by sin. Nevertheless, the fact that the statement in Gen 2:24 pictures the ideal relationship between a man and a woman, it is evident that the author regards monogamy as the norm and that Lamech's bigamy reflected one aspect of man's decline from the creator's pattern for human life. The biblical text presents a very negative view of Lamech, a view that may show an ugly aspect of Lamech's moral character. Lamech not only violated God's design for monogamous marriage by taking two wives, but he was also a violent man who killed a young man for striking him. Thus, the writer of Genesis presents Lamech as a violent and vengeful man and a murderer, just like his ancestor Cain. "Violence, brought into the world by Cain, increases and becomes ever more senseless."[10] John Goldingay wrote that in Lamech we find "A machismo that reveals itself in classic forms, in the finding of identity and significance in the number of women you possess and the number of men you overwhelm."[11]

In the genealogy of the sons of Cain, Lamech is the seventh generation from Adam. This contrasts with Enoch who was the seventh generation from Adam in the genealogy of Seth, thus, the narrator is emphasizing and contrasting the seventh generation from Adam. The narrative of Genesis presents a distinction between the descendants of Cain and the descendants of Seth. The genealogy of Cain represents the line of those people who rebelled against God while the line of Seth represents those people who called the name of Yahweh in worship (Gen 4:26).

It seems that the intent of the writer in listing the two contrasting genealogies and emphasizing the seventh generation of each genealogy, was to condemn Lamech's bigamy and his violence. To the writer of Genesis, Lamech and his family symbolizes a godless culture that is marked by self-aggrandizement and human irrationality that culminates in violence, vengeance, and murder. Lamech also represents the progressive development of the consequences of sin. His polygamous marriage and killing represent the downward moral degeneration of human beings, a moral descent that began with the sin of Adam and Eve, Cain's murder of Abel, and polygamy and the killing committed by Lamech. At the end of the story of Lamech there is no sign of God's grace toward Lamech

---

10. Cotter, *Genesis*, 44.
11. Goldingay, *Old Testament Theology*, 1:155.

and his violence. Lamech, the seventh generation of Cain, violated the moral order by committing murder, thus rebelling against God by killing a human being created in the image of God (Gen 9:6). The grace of God is seen in Enoch, the seventh in the generation of Seth, a man who walked with God and was no more because God took him (Gen 5:24).

THE FLOOD

The Sons of God

The text dealing with sons of God in Gen 6:1–4 is difficult to interpret because scholars disagree on the identification of the sons of God and the daughters of men. Since the editor of Genesis introduced these two groups of people without identifying them, it is left to the reader of Genesis to decide the interpretation of this enigmatic passage.

Several theories have been developed by interpreters for identifying the people involved in this story. The first possibility is that the sons of God were the descendants of Seth and the daughters of men were the descendants of Cain. Thus, the problem mentioned in this passage is the marriage of the godly descendants of Seth and the ungodly descendants of Cain. Another view, developed by Meredith Kline, proposes that the sons of God were dynastic rulers and the daughters of men were the women in their royal harem.[12] This view proposes that the sin of the kings was polygamy. A popular view proposes that the sons of God were angels and the daughters of men were mortal women. This view emphasizes the marriage between angelic beings and humans in violation of God's order.

The view that the sons of God were angels is developed in the book of First Enoch, an apocryphal book that contains the account of the fall of a group of angels called "The Watchers." The story in Enoch is similar to the story in Genesis. The Watchers are angels who had intercourse with women and as a result, they gave birth to evil men, giants, whose violence brought desolation to the earth. The intermingling between divine beings with mortal women finds support in passages such as 1 Pet 3:19–20, where the writer speaks of spirits in prison who disobeyed in the days of Noah; in 2 Pet 2:4–6, where the writer speaks of God not sparing the angels who sinned and not sparing the ancient world when he brought the flood on its ungodly people, but protecting Noah and his

---

12. Kline, "Divine Kingship and Genesis 6:1–4," 63–78.

family. From this perspective, God sent the flood in order to deal with this intermingling between divine beings and mortal women.

The *Nephilim*

Questions about the identification of the *Nephilim* abound. Most scholars derive the word *Nephilim* from the Hebrew verb *nāpal*, which means "fallen ones." Thus, some scholars view the *Nephilim* as the ones fallen from heaven, that is, divine beings or angels. Others have identified the *Nephilim* with robbers and people who preyed upon individuals, violent men who fell upon their victims. A more difficult problem is posed by the relationship between the *Nephilim* of Gen 6:4 and the "sons of God" and "the daughters of men" of Gen 6:2. Genesis 6:1–4 does not clearly say whether the *Nephilim* were the offspring of the marriage between the sons of God and the daughters of men. The text, however, identifies the *Nephilim* with the *gibbōrim*, "the heroes that were of old, warriors of renown" (Gen 6:4). These warriors were probably men trained for war, probably the same people filling the earth with violence (Gen 6:11).

The Reason for the Flood

The events that preceded the flood are the proper context to understand Yahweh's covenant with Noah and the earth. The reason for the flood was the sinful condition of human beings. The Bible gives two reasons for the flood: violence and evil. The first reason was the wickedness of human beings: "The LORD saw that the wickedness of humankind was great in the earth, and that every inclination of the thoughts of their hearts was only evil continually" (Gen 6:5). The second reason was violence and corruption: "Now the earth was corrupt in God's sight, and the earth was filled with violence" (Gen 6:11). In Hebrew, the word for "violence" designates an antisocial behavior and the use of brutal force. It is often translated by the word "oppression." The people who oppose Yahweh are using violence to kill other human beings. The Hebrew word *šāhat*, "corruption," occurs in the context of divine judgment, primarily when people are rebelling against Yahweh. "Those corrupting the world and practicing violence stand in opposition to Yhwh, his paths, and his nature."[13] Human violence has no place in God's creation. However, in

---

13. Strong, "Israel as a Testimony to Yhwh's Power," 99.

order to stop human violence, Yahweh had to act violently by sending the flood in order to curb human violence: "if there were no human violence, there would be no divine violence."[14]

God and the Flood

Human sinfulness had a profound effect on God. God's heart was wounded and filled with pain: "The LORD was grieved that he had made man on the earth, and his heart was filled with pain" (Gen 6:6 NIV). Some Christians use the word "anthropomorphism" to describe God's reaction to human sin. However, the concept of anthropomorphism does not explain the plain meaning of the text and misinterprets the true character of God. The characterization of God's feelings as anthropomorphism is an attempt at denying the reality of divine passability. The consequence of human sin was divine judgment: "So the LORD said, 'I will blot out from the earth the human beings I have created–people together with animals and creeping things and birds of the air, for I am sorry that I have made them'" (Gen 6:7). Since God's judgment upon sinful humanity would "blot out from the earth" the human beings God had created, God decided to give human beings a second chance. This second chance or God's recreation would occur through God's covenant with Noah and with "every living creature of all flesh" (Gen 9:15).

GOD'S COVENANT WITH NOAH

God's covenant with Noah shows God's grace toward creation. In his discussion of God's covenant with Noah and the disruption of God's relationship with humanity, John Goldingay writes, "the natural relationship that came about by creation has been devastated by human rebellion against God and by God's destroying the world. A fresh relationship therefore needs to be established through God's covenant."[15] This covenant is God's commitment to protect and maintain his creation. God's covenant with Noah also shows God's mercy toward human beings. Although the flood brought judgment upon all flesh, in his mercy God preserved a remnant with whom he would begin the process of recreation.

---

14. Fretheim, "'I Was Only a Little Angry,'" 365.
15. Goldingay, "Covenant, OT and NT," 1:768.

Although a covenant in general is an agreement between two parties, in God's covenant with Noah, it is God who takes the initiative in establishing the covenant: "I now establish my covenant" (Gen 9:9). Since God takes the initiative in establishing his covenant with Noah, it is God who sets the conditions required for the establishment of the covenant. Since in this type of covenant God is the party in the superior position, God binds himself to the obligations of the covenant for the benefit of the party in the inferior position. As Nahum Sarna wrote: "This covenant is strictly an act of divine grace, for it involves no corresponding obligations or participation on the part of man. God binds Himself unconditionally to maintain His pledge to all humanity."[16] This means that even when human beings do not keep the stipulations of the covenant, God will keep his pledge to humanity.

The recipients of the covenant are Noah, his descendants, all future human beings, and every living creature: "I am establishing my covenant with you and with your descendants after you and with every living creature that was with you—the birds, the livestock and all the wild animals, all those that came out of the ark with you—every living creature on earth" (Gen 9:9–10). The obligation to which God binds himself for the sake of creation is God's promise never again to judge the world through another flood: "I establish my covenant with you, that never again shall all flesh be cut off by the waters of a flood, and never again shall there be a flood to destroy the earth" (Gen 9:11).

The Stipulations of the Covenant

After Noah and his family came out of the ark, "God blessed Noah and his sons, and said to them, 'Be fruitful and multiply, and fill the earth'" (Gen 9:1). God's command to Noah to repopulate the earth is similar to God's words to Adam. Although Noah was a righteous man and although God desires humanity to live in covenantal relationship with him, God is aware that the sinful nature of human beings, which brought about the flood, is the same sinful nature with which God is beginning his new creation: "Yahweh . . . said to himself, 'Never again will I curse the earth because of human beings, because their heart contrives evil from their infancy. Never again will I strike down every living thing as I have done'" (Gen 8:21 NJB).

---

16. Sarna, *Understanding Genesis*, 57.

God's covenant with Noah contains three obligations imposed upon human beings: Human beings must abstain from eating blood, they are forbidden to commit murder, and capital punishment is imposed upon those who take human life. Since violence prevailed before the flood, in this new beginning, human beings are forbidden to commit murder. "Whoever sheds the blood of a human, by a human shall that person's blood be shed; for in his own image God made humankind" (Gen 9:6). This prohibition in the covenant obligates humans to have respect for all human life. Murder is a disrespect for human life and since humans are created in the image of God, murder is a destruction of the image of God. In his discussion of Gen 9:6, Fretheim wrote: "Murder means that human beings, who carry the divine image, would be in danger of no longer perpetuating themselves, the divine image, into the future.... That is one of the primary forms of evil manifest in the world: the killing of human beings, which is the killing of an image of God."[17]

In his article "Divine Creation and Human Procreation: Reflections on Genesis in the Light of Genesis," David Heyed said that murder is "a diminution of God's image." He wrote, "Taking the life of an individual entails the non-life of all his potential descendants, the destruction of life to an almost infinitive degree (in Abel's case, exactly half of all potential human beings)." Thus, the killing of an unborn person is the loss of life of "future contingent lives" when that unborn person is killed.[18] From God's perspective, the unborn is a human being that has not yet been outside of a mother's womb, but the unborn is a person with whom God can interact. God said to the prophet Jeremiah, "Before I formed you in the womb, I knew you. Before you were born, I set you apart for my holy purpose. I appointed you to be a prophet to the nations" (Jer 1:5). Anyone who takes a life shows disrespect for God, the creator of life. In addition, the murderer must be punished. "Whoever sheds the blood of a human, by a human shall that person's blood be shed" (Gen 9:6). The sentence of death upon the murderer is a reminder to all people that human life is precious to God. Human violence brought about divine judgment against humanity. Human violence against another human being will bring divine judgment upon the murderer. In this case, divine judgment has been delegated to a human authority, who "is the servant of God to execute wrath on the wrongdoer" (Rom 13:4).

---

17. Fretheim, *God and World*, 51.
18. Heyed, "Divine Creation and Human Procreation," 65–66.

The Sign of the Covenant

God's promise is sealed with the sign of the covenant: "God said, This is the sign of the covenant . . . I have set my bow in the clouds, and it shall be a sign of the covenant between me and the earth" (Gen 9:12–13). God confirms his covenant with Noah and the earth by displaying the bow in the cloud. "The rainbow that appears in the clouds after the rain, and has the shape of a bow, will henceforth not be a sign that God is acting as a warrior."[19] The bow serves as a visible reminder of the everlasting nature of the agreement God established with humanity. The bow speaks to the universality of God's covenant with Noah. It also represents God's guarantee that the world would not be destroyed with another flood and God's promise never again to interrupt his purpose and plans for creation: "As long as the earth endures, seedtime and harvest, cold and heat, summer and winter, day and night, shall not cease" (Gen 8:22).

The Duration of the Covenant

"When the bow is in the clouds, I will see it and remember the everlasting covenant between God and every living creature of all flesh that is on the earth" (Gen 9:16). The implication of God's promise is that his covenant with Noah will last an indefinite period of time, that is, "as long as the earth remains" (Gen 8:22). Through God's covenant with Noah, human beings are assured that creation will maintain its regularity and that the world will not experience another destruction by a flood. Although "the wickedness of humankind" is still great in the earth (Gen 6:5), God's covenant with Noah assures humanity that the waters of chaos will never disrupt creation again.

THE TABLE OF NATIONS

The Table of Nations listed in Gen 10 divides the nations and countries into three main groups. Although scholars differ on the structure, meaning, and historicity of the interlink between the nations, the intention of

---

19. Goldingay, "Covenant, OT and NT," 768.

the Table of Nations is to emphasize that these pre-Abrahamic nations are descendants from the three sons of Noah: "These three were the sons of Noah; and from these the whole earth was peopled" (Gen 9:19).[20]

THE TOWER OF BABEL

After the flood, the people had one language and they settled in the land of Shinar. In the land of Shinar, the people began to build a tower "with its top in the heavens." The purpose of the project was because they desired to make a name for themselves so that they would not "be scattered abroad upon the face of the whole earth" (Gen 11:4). The precise nature of their endeavor is not clear. The expression "with its top in the heavens" means an effort to reach up to heaven and communicate with or challenge Yahweh. The people feared being "scattered abroad upon the face of the whole earth" but what they feared happened. In response to their decision, Yahweh acts against them by confusing the language and by forcing the community to scatter. Human arrogance brought God's judgment upon the people, but now there was no violence and no one died.

Twice the text says that Yahweh came down to see what the people were doing and to pronounce the divine judgment upon their project (Gen 11:5, 7). This shows that Yahweh acts from within his creation. God's decision was for the sake of creation. In making their decision to remain in the land of Shinar, the people were rejecting God's command to "fill the earth" (Gen 1:28).

With the story of the Tower of Babel, the Primeval History comes to an end, what Kidner calls, "its fruitless climax."[21] Throughout this section of the book of Genesis, we see human arrogance, defiance, and rebellion against God. Human sin brought divine judgment, but each time judgment took place, the grace of God was manifested. When Adam and Eve sinned against God, God made garments to cover their nakedness. When Cain killed his brother, God put a mark of protection on him. When the world was destroyed by the flood, God placed a bow in the clouds to assure humanity that the earth would never again be destroyed by a flood. The Primeval History ends with what people feared the most, being scattered across the earth. The Primeval History reveals the story of humans rebelling against God and God judging human sin

---

20. Oded, "Table of Nations," 14.
21. Kidner, *Genesis*, 109.

and rebellion. However, in the midst of judgment, the grace of God is always manifested.

THE GRACE OF YAHWEH

The Primeval History shows how the very good world that God had created (Gen 1:31) was gradually deteriorating. The evil and violence that began with the killing of Abel had not abated. The final narrative of the Primeval History is the story of the Tower of Babel. The people's decision to build the tower and remain in the place where they were living was a denial of the divine command to fill the earth. With the scattering of the people, God was unable to reconcile the world unto himself. Because the world is now populated by many nations, the work of reconciling the world unto himself became more imperative for God. So, God chose one man and through him, one nation to be his agent of reconciliation. The call of Abraham must be read in the context of the people who built a tower that reached the heavens and their scattering throughout the world.

In his covenant with Noah, God promised not to destroy humankind again (Gen 9:11). This promise imposed a limit on what God could do to humanity. With the rebellion of human beings at the Tower of Babel, God could not respond by destroying humanity again, so, instead of punishing them, God changed his approach in dealing with human beings. With the call of Abraham, "it is clear that . . . God has developed another plan" to redeem the world unto himself.[22] The background of Abraham is given in the genealogy of Shem in Gen 11:10–26 and in the genealogy Terah in Gen 11:27–32. When Abraham was called to leave the house of his father and come to Canaan, the world in which he lived was filled with the many nations that had spread all over the world (Gen 10:32). Some of these nations were in existence thousands of years before Abraham left Ur with his father. When Abraham came to Canaan, "the Canaanites were in the land" (Gen 12:6). The divine speech at the end of the story of the Tower of Babel connects the story of the call of Abraham to the story of the Tower of Babel. Before God called Abraham, "the nations spread abroad on the earth after the flood" (Gen 10:32). In his desire to redeem the world unto himself, God called Abraham so that, through him, all the nations on earth would be blessed (Gen 12:3).[23]

---

22. Strong, "Israel as a Testimony to Yhwh's Power," 103.
23. God's promise to Abraham is repeated in Gen 18:18; 22:18; 26:4; 28:14.

The apostle Paul says that the call of Abraham was God's plan to reconcile all the families of the earth unto himself. Paul wrote, "And it was because scripture foresaw that God would give saving justice to the gentiles through faith, that it announced the future gospel to Abraham in the words: All nations will be blessed in you" (Gal 3:8 NJB). God was unable to finish the work of reconciliation that he began in Eden. Now, he calls Abraham and announces "the future gospel" to him so that through his descendants the scattered nations of the world might be reconciled to God. The Primeval History presents a story of human sin and alienation from God. It also presents the work of reconciliation by a gracious and merciful God.

21

God Reconciling the World Through Israel

IN HIS ARTICLE, "ISRAEL AS a Testimony to Yhwh's Power: The Priests' Definition of Israel," John Strong defines the mission and destiny of Israel in the world as follows: "The Hebrew Bible insists that ancient Israel was forged on the anvil of history for a singular purpose: to be an enduring witness among the world's nations to the beneficent sovereignty and providence of the God who had fashioned it."[1]

God's covenant with Israel, also known as the Mosaic Covenant, is based on God's call and promises made to Abraham. God's covenant with Abraham established the basis for the birth of a nation to be known as Israel. From a canonical perspective, the call of Abraham and God's covenant with him follow the events that happened after God's covenant with Noah. Throughout the first eleven chapters of Genesis, the text deals with the problem of human sin and its universal progression. The Primeval History in Gen 1–11 reveals God's effort to deal with the problem of sin. Up to this point, God has been dealing with human beings on a universal basis, doing the work of reconciliation by himself. But God's work of reconciliation met with resistance, a resistance that brought divine judgment in the days of Noah.

God's covenant with Noah and the earth initiated a new beginning in God's plan to redeem sinful humanity. God promised that human beings would never again be destroyed by a flood. And God gave the

---

1. Strong, "Israel as a Testimony to Yhwh's Power," 89.

rainbow as an everlasting sign of his promise. However, after the flood, human rebellion took the form of a challenge to God's plan that human beings populate the earth (Gen 11:4). The Tower of Babel becomes a symbol of human rebellion against God. This rebellion again brought divine judgment upon the human race and people were scattered across the face of the entire earth (Gen 11:9). The call of Abraham introduces a new phase in God's story of redemption. God's promises to Abraham, promises sealed by God's covenant with him, become the foundation for Israel's mission in the world. Through Israel, God was reconciling the world unto himself.

THE CALL OF ABRAHAM

Before there was a people called Israel, there was Abraham. God called Abraham from a pagan background to be the father of a people who would become the bearers of God's message of salvation to the world. The Bible declares that Abraham's family came out of an idolatrous background: "Joshua said to all the people, 'Thus says the LORD, the God of Israel: Long ago your ancestors—Terah and his sons Abraham and Nahor—lived beyond the Euphrates and served other gods'" (Josh 24:2). Abraham and his family came out of polytheism. As worshipers of other gods, Abraham received a direct revelation from Yahweh. When God called Abraham and told him to leave his country, his family, and his father's house, God promised that he would give him a land in which he and his descendants would settle and become a great nation. The promise that Yahweh would give Abraham and his descendants the land of Canaan is one of the major themes of the Pentateuch.[2] The promise of the giving of the land was made to Abraham and renewed to Isaac and Jacob.

GOD'S PROMISES TO ABRAHAM

When God called Abraham, God made several promises to him. These promises must be understood in the context of God's purpose for his creation. Because human beings failed to fulfill God's purpose for their lives (Gen 6:5–7), God called Abraham to become the father of a people who would then do God's work of reconciliation in the world (Exod 19:5–6). On Israel's role in God's redemptive purpose, Fretheim writes, "God's

---

2. Yahweh called Abraham "my friend" (Isa 41:8).

redemptive purpose in and through Israel presupposes the reality of the world as a creation of God and the world in the need of reconciliation; God's activity in the history of Israel is for the sake of the world."[3]

The first promise God made to Abraham was the promise of the land: "Go from your country and your kindred and your father's house to the land that I will show you" (Gen 12:1). The second promise was that Abraham would become a great nation: "I will make of you a great nation" (Gen 12:2). The third promise was the promise of God's blessing: "I will bless you" (Gen 12:2). The fourth promise was the promise of the great name: "I will make your name great" (Gen 12:1). The fifth promise was the promise of mediating blessings to other people: "In you all the families of the earth shall be blessed" (Gen 12:3).[4] When God called Abraham to leave his country, God promised him that he and his descendants would become a great nation (Gen 12:1–3). According to Walter Brueggemann, "the promise is God's power and will to create a new future sharply discontinuous with the past and the present. The promise is God's resolve to form a new community wrought only by miracle and reliant only on God's faithfulness."[5]

The promise that Abraham and his descendants would become a great nation contains, implicit in it, another promise, the promise that God would give him the land of Canaan, since a great nation cannot come into being without a land of its own. God's promise to Abraham also implies that God would give Abraham an heir, a son who would carry his name and eventually inherit the land as the fulfillment of the divine promise, "God will do what God says God will do; God will be faithful to God's own promises."[6] But how could God's promise to Abraham that he would become a great nation be accomplished when his wife Sarah was barren?[7] Sarah's barrenness was a stumbling block to the fulfillment of the promise. How could an old man and an old woman be fruitful and become a source of blessings to many? Abraham trusted God's promise and took God at his word: "I will bless you"; "You shall become a great nation." God's promise was enough for Abraham. He believed and

3. Fretheim, *Suffering of God*, 34.
4. Grüneberg, *Abraham, Blessing and the Nations*, 66.
5. Brueggemann, *Genesis*, 106.
6. Fretheim, *Suffering of God*, 36.
7. Biddle, "'Endangered Ancestress,'" 599–611.

in believing he was blessed. And in being blessed Abraham's descendants became a great nation and his descendants received the promised land.

GOD'S COVENANT WITH ABRAHAM

A few years after his call, Abraham had some misgivings about God's promises. He feared that God would not fulfill his promise. God appears to Abraham to reassure him: "Do not be afraid, Abram" (Gen 15:1). Abraham's despondency was evident, since he did not have a son to inherit the land. For ten years Abraham had been following God and yet, he remained childless. Abraham said to God: "You have given me no offspring, and so a slave born in my house is to be my heir" (Gen 15:3). Abraham had lost hope of becoming the father of a son. He had followed the customs of his country of birth and adopted a slave to become his heir. But God once again reassured Abraham that he would fulfill his promise: "This man shall not be your heir; no one but your very own issue shall be your heir" (Gen 15:4). But, there was another doubt in Abraham's mind, his doubt about the possession of the land. Abraham asked the Lord: "O Lord GOD, how am I to know that I shall possess [the land]?" (Gen 15:8). In light of the presence of the Canaanites in the land, the fulfillment of the promise was almost an impossibility. Once again, God answered Abraham and renewed the promise that his descendants would receive the land: "The LORD said to Abram, 'Know this for certain . . . I am the LORD who brought you from Ur of the Chaldeans, to give you this land to possess'" (Gen 15:3; 15:7). God reaffirmed his promise to Abraham by saying that his descendants would be as numerous as the stars in heaven.

To confirm to Abraham that his promise would be fulfilled, that there would be a future for Abraham in the land of promise, God renewed the promise of a son by establishing a covenant with Abraham: "On that day the LORD made a covenant with Abram, saying, 'To your descendants I give this land, from the river of Egypt to the great river, the river Euphrates'" (Gen 15:18). A covenant is an agreement enacted between two people in which one or both parties of the covenant make promises to perform a certain action. The Hebrew word *berith*, which in English is translated by the word "covenant," comes from a root which means "to cut," that is, the act of cutting or dividing of animals used in the covenant ceremony into two parts. As an act of establishing a covenant, the contracting parties pass between the two halves, thus ratifying the covenant.

The ritual, in which God passed between the two halves of the sacrificed animals, represents God's unqualified intent to do what he had promised to Abraham. In the ancient Near East, the passing between the two halves of the sacrificed animals meant the invocation of a curse. In one of his oracles, the prophet Jeremiah makes a passing reference to this ritual: "And the men who transgressed my covenant and did not keep the terms of the covenant which they made before me, I will make like the calf which they cut in two and passed between its parts" (Jer 34:18). In his covenant with Abraham, God is the only one who walks between the slain animals, signifying that God's promise to give Abraham a son and the land of Canaan was binding on God as an eternal promise. Like the covenant with Noah, God's covenant with Abraham is also an everlasting covenant: "I will establish my covenant between me and you, and your offspring after you throughout their generations, for an everlasting covenant, to be God to you and to your offspring after you" (Gen 17:7).

THE ELECTION OF ISRAEL

The election of Israel is a given fact in the theology of the Old Testament, but scholars differ on when it took place. Some scholars speak of two election traditions in the Bible, one in the time of Abraham and another in the time of Moses. The election of Israel took place when God called Abraham and told him to go to the land of Canaan. However, the full implication of that election happened with Israel's redemption from Egypt and the promulgation of the covenant at Sinai. God's promise to Abraham was the basis for the election of Israel to be God's people. Israel became a nation after it was delivered from Egypt and established a covenant with God at Sinai. The study of Israel's election must begin with two questions. The first question is one of definition: What is the meaning of election? The second question is one of purpose: Why did God choose Israel to be his special people?

The word "election" comes from the Hebrew word *bāḥar* which means "to choose," "to elect." However, although the word *bāḥar* does not appear in the call of Abraham, the concept of divine election pervades the whole Old Testament. The idea of divine election is emphasized in the book of Deuteronomy: "For you are a people holy to the LORD your

God; the LORD your God has chosen you out of all the peoples on earth to be his people, his treasured possession" (Deut 7:6). Although the basic concept of election is expressed by the word *bāḥar*, other words are also used to convey the idea that Israel was set apart as God's special people. The terminology of election includes the word *bāḥar*, "to choose"; *qārā'*, "to call"; *yāda'*, "to know"; and *bādal*, "to separate." Amos uses the word *yādaʿ* to express Israel's election: "You only have I known of all the families of the earth" (Amos 3:2). The expressions "treasured possession" and "the people of the Lord" also convey the idea of election.

The second question, "why did Yahweh choose Israel?" is answered by Deut 7:7–8: " It was not because you were more in number than any other people that the LORD set his love upon you and chose you, for you were the fewest of all peoples; but it is because the LORD loves you, and is keeping the oath which he swore to your fathers, that the LORD has brought you out with a mighty hand, and redeemed you from the house of bondage, from the hand of Pharaoh king of Egypt." The choice of Israel to be a special people, at its most basic meaning, testifies to the fact of unmerited grace. Yahweh did not choose Israel because they were worthy of being chosen. In fact, Yahweh chose a people who were slaves in Egypt, redeemed them and established a special relationship with them. The point that the writer of Deuteronomy was trying to convey to the new generation of Israelites was that it was because of God's faithful love (*ḥesed*) and because of the promise he had made to Abraham that he, in his sovereignty, elected Israel to be his special people and his special possession. God told Israel on Mount Sinai: "Out of all the nations you will be my own special possession" (Exod 19:5).

Thus, it was at Sinai that Israel became God's special people. God had established a covenant with Abraham, choosing him to be the father of a great and mighty nation. Now, as the people understood their mission in the world and their place in the redemptive work of God, the people accepted their call and destiny as the elected nation of God: "And all the people answered together and said, 'All that the LORD has spoken we will do'" (Exod 19:8). Israel became a special nation not because they were great and mighty, but because of the sovereign grace of the God who had delivered them from Egyptian bondage. The election of Israel does not mean that God has rejected the other nations. To the contrary, the election of Israel is a call to service to God and to the other nations. T. C. Vriezen, in his book *An Outline of Old Testament Theology*, wrote:

> The truth of Israel's election is untruth if it is rationally understood to mean that *for that reason* God has rejected the nations of the world, that *for that reason* Israel is of more importance to God than those other nations, for Israel was only elected in order to serve God in the task of leading those other nations to God. In Israel God seeks the world. . . . For in His mercy He has called Israel to the service of His Kingdom among the nations of the earth.[8]

God chose Israel to become a paradigm to the nations. Israel was to be an example of what it means to be a people who live according to God's laws and teachings.[9] God saw fit to take a people who were slaves in a foreign land, a people rejected by society, with no laws, organization, or government in order to demonstrate his power and salvation to the world. Israel was not only small in number, but they were also hard-hearted, stiff-necked, and a stubborn people, and yet, God chose these people to be his own people. The election of Israel, therefore, is a great demonstration of God's electing love. God's love is absolutely free and unconditional, and this love was bestowed on one nation out of the many nations of the world. If there was some hidden potential in Israel, the Bible does not specify it. What is clear is that Israel was chosen to be God's people by divine sovereignty and by the kind of love that only God can demonstrate.

God's love and God's grace is the focus that permeates the concept of election in the Old Testament. The recipient of this love and grace is called to service to others. God's love is never conditional. However, as in all relationships, there must be a sense of responsibility and fidelity, and Israel was no exception. God established a relationship with Israel on Mount Sinai, on the day that he chose the descendants of Abraham to be his special possession. Yahweh gave himself to Israel and in return the people of Israel were to give themselves to him. Deut 4:40 states, "Therefore you shall keep his statutes and his commandments, which I command you this day, that it may go well with you, and with your children after you, and that you may prolong your days in the land which the LORD your God gives you for ever." The election of Israel is one of the most important concepts for understanding God's relationship with his chosen nation. The election of Israel explains the destiny of Israel as

---

8. Vriezen, *Outline of Old Testament Theology*, 76.

9. Brueggemann, "Israel as YHWH's Partner," 19–56. In describing Israel's role in the world, Brueggemann says that "Israel is said to have as part of its vocation and destiny a role in the well-being of the world" (35).

God's special people in the world and required of the nation an exclusive relationship, a relationship that God has maintained throughout the ages, despite Israel's rebellion and disobedience.

ISRAEL'S MISSION IN THE WORLD

"You have seen what I did to the Egyptians, and how I bore you on eagles' wings and brought you to myself. Now therefore, if you obey my voice and keep my covenant, you shall be my treasured possession out of all the peoples. Indeed, the whole earth is mine, but you shall be for me a priestly kingdom and a holy nation" (Exod 19:4–6). These words of Yahweh appear at the beginning of the Sinai pericope, within the context of the theophany in which Yahweh reveals himself to the Israelites on Mount Sinai after the people left Egypt. The theophany on Sinai was the climax of Israel's journey out of Egypt. These words of Exod 19:4–6 encapsulate God's purpose for Israel as it begins to live as the people of God in the world. Yahweh had redeemed the Israelites from bondage, brought them to the mountain on which he had appeared to Moses and now he was providing Israel with an understanding of what he expected from them as a redeemed people. After redeeming Israel from Egypt, Yahweh was about to establish a special relationship with the nation. Because of God's mighty act of redemption, Israel would become God's treasured possession among the nations and would carry out God's mission in the world as a priestly kingdom in order to proclaim God's glory and mediate God's blessings to all families of the earth.

By becoming a holy nation at the service of a holy God, Israel would demonstrate to the nations what it means to serve the true God. In the text cited above, verse 4 describes Israel's redemption from Egypt. Israel's redemption serves as the basis for all that follows. By redeeming Israel from Egypt, Yahweh became her savior and protector. Verses 5 and 6 detail what God expected from Israel and the nature of the relationship God was establishing with the nation. These verses are pivotal for the proper understanding of the existence of Israel and its mission in the world. This text also provides the proper understanding of Israel's future in the promised land. This declaration that Moses was to present to the people of Israel had special significance because it expressed a new perspective in the relationship that began with the call of Abraham. These words clarify the unique identity of Israel as the people of God.

The history of Israel as God's special people in the world begins here. Israel's destiny as a special people will be based on the degree of fidelity with which Israel adheres to its vocation as the people of God. The words of Yahweh to Israel are a reaffirmation of the promise God made to Abraham and of the covenant God established with him. In clarifying Israel's mission in the world, God was confirming the promises he made to Abraham. Israel was to have a special mission to the nations. The universal mission which Israel received at Sinai was a reformulation of what God told Abraham in Gen 12:1–3. In Gen 12:1–3 God shows his love for all the nations; in Exod 19:4–6, God shows his special love for a particular people. The establishment of God's relationship with Israel began with the proclamation of God's mighty acts of behalf of Israel (v. 4); it follows with the declaration of the conditions that will be the basis for this new relationship (vv. 5–6), and concludes with the response of the people and their commitment to God's demands (vv. 7–8).

The three terms in Exod 19:4–6, "treasured possession," "kingdom of priests," and "holy nation" are key terms which help clarify the scope of Israel's mission in the world. These three terms are integrally related, for one cannot exist without the other two. The three terms are to be interpreted in relation to each other. The first term, "treasured possession," defines Israel's relationship with God. The Hebrew word *segullāh* means "personal property." This means that Israel was God's personal possession: "For the LORD has chosen Jacob for himself, Israel as his own possession" (Ps 135:4). The second term, "a kingdom of priests" means that Israel was consecrated to the service of God. Since the priest was an intermediary between God and the people, Israel was to be God's representative to the nations. Israel was also to stand before God on behalf of the nations. Israel's mission was to bring God's light to the nations and to bring the nations closer to God. The third term "a holy nation" expresses Israel's special calling. Israel was set apart to become a holy people in the service of a holy God.

The election of Israel to be God's special people must be understood in relation to God's purpose to redeem the world. Before Israel, God was reconciling the world alone. Israel was redeemed to become God's own people and to become agents of reconciliation. Because of its intimate relationship with God, Israel became a "holy nation." Israel's mission in the world was to be a kingdom of priests. Yahweh made Israel his special nation to serve as his instrument in bringing redemption to all the nations of the world. God was working through Israel in order to make peace between the world and himself. Israel was called to be a witness to the world (Isa 19:20; 43:10; 55:4). Because God is the creator of the whole world, God has a special concern for the nations of the world. All the nations of the world need to experience his redemptive power in the same way Israel experienced God's redemption from Egypt. God's purpose for all the nations of the world is for them to participate together with Israel in the blessings of salvation. When the nations join Israel in the worship of God, then the prophetic vision will become a reality: "And the foreigners who join themselves to the LORD, to minister to him, to love the name of the LORD, and to be his servants . . . these I will bring to my holy mountain, and make them joyful in my house of prayer; their burnt offerings and their sacrifices will be accepted on my altar; for my house shall be called a house of prayer for all peoples" (Isa 56:6–7).

THE UNIQUENESS OF ISRAEL

The election of Israel to be God's special possession took place when he called Abraham to leave his country to go to a land that eventually would belong to him and to his descendants. The election of Israel as God's people was reaffirmed with the establishment of a covenant between God and Israel on Mount Sinai. It was at that time that Israel received instructions about its mission as the people of God. The mission of Israel in the world is expressed succinctly in Exod 19:5–6: "Now therefore, if you will obey my voice and keep my covenant, you shall be my own possession among all peoples; for all the earth is mine, and you shall be to me a kingdom of priests and a holy nation."

These words of God to Israel describe three different aspects of Israel's mission. First, as the elect people of God, Israel has a special relationship with God because of their call and deliverance from Egypt. This relationship is expressed by the demands of the covenant. The covenant is a document that places the people of Israel under legal obligation to obey the demands which the covenant imposed upon them. Second, as the special people of God, Israel was called to be a kingdom of priests. Third, as God's special possession, Israel was called to be a paradigm to the other nations of the world.

The covenant between God and Israel was a suzerainty covenant, the type of covenant which required Israel to obey God's demands. If Israel would obey God's voice and keep his covenant, then Israel would become God's special possession among all nations. This requirement to obey the demands of the covenant came as a result of Israel's decision to be God's people and to carry out God's mission in the world. The people responded to God's demands with a commitment to obedience: "All that the LORD has spoken we will do" (Exod 19:8). Israel's decision to follow God was a response to his love and grace.

Thus, when the people of Israel agreed to obey God's law, their decision was a response to what God had done by calling Abraham and by redeeming them from their slavery in Egypt. This commitment to obedience was the foundation of the election of Israel and the basis for their mission in the world. Israel was called to be an obedient people. Israel's mission and destiny as God's people in the world required them to obey God's laws. Israel was to be different from all the other nations because Israel was chosen by the Lord to receive the promises he had made to the patriarchs (Deut 7:6–9). God redeemed the people from their bondage in Egypt in order to bind Israel exclusively to himself so that the nation could carry out God's redemptive work in the world. In addition to its legal responsibility to obey the demands of the covenant, Israel was also called to be a kingdom of priests. The mission of Israel as a kingdom of priests was to teach and instruct the nations about the nature of the true God. The author of the book of Malachi describes the ministry of the priests as follows: "For the lips of a priest should preserve knowledge of sacred things, and people should seek instruction from him because he is the messenger of the LORD" (Mal 2:7 NET).

In its mission to teach the nations, Israel had several religious distinctives that served as the basis for its message. First, Israel's religion was to be focused on the worship of one God and one God only: "You shall have no other gods before me" (Exod 20:3). However this commandment was understood, the worship of the God of Israel excluded the worship of other gods. Second, the religion of Israel was to be aniconic: "You shall not make for yourself a graven image, or any likeness of anything that is in heaven above, or that is in the earth beneath, or that is in the water under the earth; you shall not bow down to them or serve them" (Exod 20:4–5).[10] Aniconism made Israel's religion different from the other religions of the ancient Near East since most of them made graphic representations of their many gods, either as human beings, animals, or objects of nature. The worship of Yahweh without the use of images "was the

---

10. Feder, "Aniconic Tradition," 251–74.

essential constitutive feature not only of ancient Israel's religious practice but also of its political identity, ostensibly differentiating it from every other people and nation."[11] Third, Israel should remember that God had entered its history to deliver them from Egyptian slavery. The memory of their deliverance became the basis for the treatment of the members of the covenant community (Deut 16:12). Finally, Israel had a special history to tell the nations. Never before in the history of other nations had a God chosen to reveal himself in the way God revealed himself to Israel on Mount Sinai. This great act of salvation was also part of the message Israel was to teach to the nations.

Israel's understanding of God, their religious practices, and their humane laws were to serve as a paradigm to the nations of the world. Just as the priests instructed the nation of their religious, legal, and moral responsibility to God, so Israel was to teach the nations. The function of the priest in Israel was to be a minister of God and to lead the people in the worship of God. Thus, if Israel was to be a kingdom of priests, then the people as a whole were to serve God and minister to those nations around them and to all nations of the world. As a people selected to be a special possession of God, Israel had a legal responsibility to respond in obedience to the demands of the covenant, a spiritual requirement to be a kingdom of priests, and an ethical responsibility to be a holy nation.

Israel, as a people of God, was called to be a holy nation: "And the LORD said to Moses, 'Say to all the congregation of the people of Israel, You shall be holy; for I the LORD your God am holy'" (Lev 19:1). As the people of God, Israel was called to be a paradigm to the rest of the world in respect to ethical living. Israel's call to holiness required ethical living. The laws Israel received at Sinai could be enforced by various penalties. However, the spiritual element of Israel's call, to be a kingdom of priests, could only be enforced by ethical living. The holiness to which Israel was called required total submission to the will of God and a participation in the very nature of God. Israel was to be more than a mere representative of God to the nations. They were to reflect the deepest spiritual and ethical qualities of God himself. Thus, as the people of God, Israel's mission was threefold: legal in responsibility, spiritual in practice, and holy in nature.

The election of Israel to be God's people and its mission to the nations made Israel a unique nation with a unique destiny. It is within the

---

11. McBride, "Essence of Orthodoxy," 133.

context of Israel's election and mission that the work of the prophets and the religious contribution of Israel to the world must be understood.

THE FAILURE OF ISRAEL

The failure of Israel to fulfill its mission and to be God's special people in the world was because the nation failed to conquer the Canaanites as they were commanded by God. Once Israel settled in the land, they adopted many of the religious practices of the Canaanites and they worshiped other gods in violation of the covenant they had established with Yahweh on Mount Sinai. Throughout its history, from the time of the judges until the deportation of Judah to Babylon, the prophets condemned the religious syncretism in Judah and Israel. Syncretism is the process by which the practices and beliefs of one religion are incorporated into another religion. The result of this union of different and, at times, opposing religious practices is a change in the fundamental nature of the religion that absorbed the foreign religious elements.

The greatest challenge Israel faced in maintaining its relationship with Yahweh and keeping the demands of the covenant was its encounter with Canaanite culture and Canaanite religion. After the death of Joshua and his generation, "another generation grew up after them, who did not know the LORD or the work that he had done for Israel" (Judg 2:10). What set apart this new generation of Israelites is that they departed from the ways of Yahweh and were not as faithful to God as the people in Joshua's generation had been. Of this new generation, the writer of Judges wrote: "The Israelites did what was evil in the sight of the LORD and worshiped the Baals; and they abandoned the LORD, the God of their ancestors, who had brought them out of the land of Egypt; they followed other gods, from among the gods of the peoples who were all around them, and bowed down to them; and they provoked the LORD to anger. They abandoned the LORD, and worshiped Baal and the Astartes" (Judg 2:10–13).

With the establishment of the monarchy in Israel, the problem of religious syncretism continued. The monarchy introduced foreign elements into the social and religious life of Israel in order to accommodate the needs of a large number of foreigners. The remnant of the Canaanite population continued to live in Jerusalem. David made an attempt to assimilate Canaanite cultic tradition that existed side-by-side with traditional Yahweh worship.

David centralized the worship of Yahweh in Jerusalem and promoted the worship of Yahweh as the God of Israel. Solomon's reign, however, departed from the worship of Yahweh as the sole God of Israel. In his effort to enlarge his kingdom, Solomon made concessions to foreign religious practices that made a profound impact on the life of the nation. In order to cement relationships with other nations, Solomon established political alliances which were sealed with marriages to women who were not Israelites. Solomon's wives did not abandon their native gods but brought their religious practices with them to Solomon's court. In an effort to please his foreign wives, Solomon promoted their religious traditions by building temples for their gods on the mountain east of Jerusalem. The writer of Kings said: "For Solomon went after Ashtoreth the goddess of the Sidonians, and after Milcom the abomination of the Ammonites. Then Solomon built a high place for Chemosh the abomination of Moab, and for Molech the abomination of the Ammonites, on the mountain east of Jerusalem" (1 Kgs 11:5, 7).

When the united monarchy divided after the death of Solomon, Jeroboam became king of the ten tribes that formed the Northern Kingdom. Jeroboam established two centers of worship, one at Dan, the northernmost city in the Northern Kingdom, and the other at Bethel on the southern border with Judah. He also built two golden calves or bulls to serve as the symbol of the worship of Yahweh. There is much controversy about the symbolism of the calves or bulls placed in Dan and Bethel since the bull was the symbol of El and Baal, the fertility god of the Canaanites. Many scholars today argue that the bulls were pedestals on which the invisible Yahweh was supposed to stand. In some Semitic religions the gods were represented as standing on the backs of animals. However, since Yahweh's presence in the temple was invisible, the people of Israel eventually began to worship the symbols as if they were gods.

The worship of Yahweh in the form of a bull opened the doors for the influence of Canaanite culture and religion to enter the life of the Northern Kingdom. Whatever intentions Jeroboam might have had, the commingling of Yahweh worship with Baal symbolism was disastrous for Israel's faith and produced severe criticism from the prophets of Yahweh. Hosea was the first prophet who openly criticized the worship of the calf. In Hos 8:5–6 the prophet criticizes the worship of the calf on behalf of Yahweh: "I have spurned your calf, O Samaria. My anger burns against them. How long will they be incapable of innocence? For it is from Israel; a craftsman made it; it is not God. The calf of Samaria shall be broken to pieces."

In the end, the Deuteronomic Historian has a stern condemnation of the Northern Kingdom: The people of Israel had sinned against Yahweh.

> They despised his statutes and his covenant that he made with their fathers and the warnings that he gave them. They went after false idols and became false, and they followed the nations that were around them, concerning whom the Lord had commanded them that they should not do like them. And they abandoned all the commandments of the Lord their God, and made for themselves metal images of two calves; and they made an Asherah and worshiped all the host of heaven and served Baal. And they burned their sons and their daughters as offerings and used divination and omens and sold themselves to do evil in the sight of the LORD, provoking him to anger. Therefore the LORD was very angry with Israel and removed them out of his sight. (2 Kgs 17:15–18)

Yet, the Lord gave the people an opportunity to change their ways. He warned Israel through the ministry of the prophets, but the people were unwilling to listen. As a result, the Northern Kingdom was conquered by Assyria and taken into exile in 722 BCE.

In the Southern Kingdom, the people of Judah continued the syncretism that Solomon had established. The extent of the depravity in the religious life of Judah can be seen in the message of the prophet Zephaniah, a prophet who preached a few years before the reforms of Josiah. In the seventh century, at the time Zephaniah was ministering in Jerusalem, Judah was facing a time of religious apostasy. Zephaniah preached to a people who had rejected the demands of the covenant. The people of Judah had become indifferent to their religious practices and had neglected the worship of Yahweh to follow other gods. They had become complacent in their religious duties, driven by the syncretism present in their society and by the excessive religious tolerance introduced by their political and religious leaders.

THE RELIGIOUS REFORMS OF JOSIAH

Manasseh, king of Judah, introduced astral worship and other pagan practices in the temple. Because Judah had been an Assyrian vassal for several decades, the gods of Assyria had become a part of the religious life of the people for as long as that generation could remember. The people who turned away from following Yahweh were probably those who were born during the reign of Manasseh. Those who from their youth had never submitted to Yahweh were being called to faithfulness and repentance. Many of these people were born after the religious reforms of Hezekiah. With the syncretism introduced by Manasseh, these people were not committed to follow Yahweh or to keep his laws. The religious persecution under Manasseh (2 Kgs 22:16) drove the prophets underground, probably after Isaiah's ministry ended in 687 BCE. No prophet arose in Judah until Zephaniah appeared at the beginning of the reign of Josiah.

Zephaniah's message was very critical of the political and religious leadership of the nation who lived in Jerusalem. He said: "The officials within it are roaring lions; its judges are evening wolves that leave nothing until the morning. Its prophets are reckless, faithless persons; its priests have profaned what is sacred, they have done violence to the law" (Zeph 3:3–4). The most severe criticism Zephaniah uttered against the people and their leaders, indeed, against the whole nation, is found in Zeph 2:1, where he called them a "shameless nation." The word used here for "nation" is *gôy*, a word generally used to designate pagan nations. The interpretation that *gôy* in this context is used derogatorily is based on the meaning of the word *kāsap* in verse 1. Although the meaning of the word in this context is not very clear, the two words are translated "shameless nation" (NRSV), "shameful nation" (NIV), "undesirable nation" (HCSB), and "a nation not worthy to be loved" (Douay-Rheims). With these words, Zephaniah accused the people of Judah of behaving like the gentiles. Zephaniah accused the people worshiping in the temple of practicing pagan rituals alien to Yahwism. The people were serving both Yahweh and idols. This is the reason Yahweh announced a severe judgment upon their pagan practices.

Josiah, king of Judah, tried to reverse the apostasy of Judah and bring the nation to abide by the demands of the covenant. The religious reform of Josiah was an attempt to renew the worship of God according to the teachings of Moses as it was understood in the seventh century BCE. These reforms included the centralization of the worship in Jerusalem.

The worship of Yahweh outside of Jerusalem was abolished and the Solomonic temple in Jerusalem became the only approved house of worship in Israel (2 Kgs 23:8). The reform made an attempt to eliminate Baal worship from the religious life of Israel. The reform decreed the elimination of the religious vessels and images dedicated to Baal and Asherah (23:4, 6). The reform also made an attempt at abolishing the hideous practice of child sacrifice. The practice of child sacrifice, a ritual that was common in the cult of Molech, the god of the Ammonites, was forbidden and the Topheth, the place in the Kidron Valley where these sacrifices were offered, was defiled (2 Kgs 23:10). This prohibition was reinforced by the legislation of Deut 12:31; 18:10. The reform of Josiah made an attempt to eliminate one of the most popular aspects of the religion of the Canaanites: the practice of sacred prostitution. Josiah destroyed the houses dedicated to sacred prostitution in the temple of the Lord in Jerusalem (2 Kgs 23:7). The prohibition against sacred prostitution was reinforced by the legislation of Deut 23:18.

The reform of Josiah was a revival of Mosaic faith and teaching as it was understood in the seventh century BCE. The reforms were based on the teachings of the book of Deuteronomy. The characteristic theme of Deuteronomy was love. Yahweh's gracious love had been manifested in the mighty acts of God on behalf of Israel (Deut 6:20–23). For this reason, Israel should respond to this divine love by loving God and by loving the fellow members of the covenant community. Israel must follow God in fear and in obedience. Because Yahweh is a jealous God, he will not tolerate the worship of other gods (Deut 6:10–15). Israel had been separated (elected) from all other nations for special service to Yahweh. As a separate people, Israel had a mission to the nations. As God's people, Israel must express God's concern for people. Yahweh's activities on behalf of the oppressed should motivate Israel to act in the same way. Yahweh is the defender of the weak, the orphan, the widow, and the resident alien, so also should Israel be. Thus, the book of Deuteronomy calls Israel to renew the covenant with Yahweh and to decide to live by the demands of this covenant.

Because of the rebellion of Israel, Yahweh called Jeremiah to proclaim a message of repentance to the people in Judah. Jeremiah was the last hope for a people who had abandoned their destiny. Jeremiah was a prophet of God who lived at the end of the seventh century and the first part of the sixth century BCE. Jeremiah lived at a very difficult time in the life of Judah. Jeremiah was called to preach a message of repentance to a people who had abandoned the true God to serve idols made with human hands. Jeremiah called Israel to return to the traditions of the past and be faithful to the covenant the nation had established with God at Sinai. In the end, Jeremiah failed to bring the people back to God and, as a result, Judah was conquered by Babylon and taken into exile.

THE FALL OF JERUSALEM

In the book of Jeremiah, Nebuchadnezzar is introduced as God's instrument to bring divine judgment on Judah.[12] In the past, God had sent his servants the prophets to warn the people to repent of their evil ways, but they refused (Jer 25:4). Now, God is sending his "servant" Nebuchadnezzar to punish Judah for their wickedness.[13] Jeremiah designated Nebuchadnezzar the "servant" of God as a way to present Babylon's king as the individual God appointed to have dominion over the nations and the one who would act as the instrument of God's justice (Jer 25:8–11). Because Nebuchadnezzar was acting as God's agent, Jeremiah declared to the people that rebellion against Nebuchadnezzar was rebellion against God.

The picture that Jeremiah paints of Nebuchadnezzar reflects the prophet's understanding of God's work. Jeremiah understood that Yahweh had given Nebuchadnezzar the power and the authority to subjugate kingdoms and nations. As the instrument of God's judgment, Nebuchadnezzar was God's chosen agent, God's servant who brought judgment over God's rebellious people. Jeremiah portrayed Nebuchadnezzar as the servant of the God of Israel—a chosen individual who had the responsibility of performing a designated function in Yahweh's behalf.

The fall of Jerusalem, the destruction of the temple, and the deportation of the people of Judah to exile in Babylon did not come suddenly, without a warning. Prophets like Jeremiah, Ezekiel, and others had been warning the people of Judah that unless they repented and turned to God, the curses of the covenant would be invoked upon the nation and the people would be removed from the land which they had received as their inheritance.

---

12. Overholt, "King Nebuchadnezzar," 39–48.

13. Smelik, "My Servant Nebuchadnezzar," 109–34. In the book of Jeremiah, Yahweh referred to "my servant" Nebuchadnezzar three times (Jer 25:9; 27:6; 43:10).

THE NEED FOR A NEW BEGINNING

Contrary to popular perception people have about the Old Testament, the whole Old Testament, from Genesis to Malachi, is a book of good news. Many people think that only the New Testament is good news, but there is good news everywhere in the Bible. Take for instance, the words of the prophet Nahum, probably one of the most difficult books of the Bible from which to teach and preach. In the midst of a book that pronounces a message of judgment against the brutalities of Assyria, we find these words: "Behold, upon the mountains, the feet of him who brings good news, who publishes peace" (Nah 1:15). In the book of Proverbs, that wisdom book compiled to teach everyone how to live a godly life, the words of the wise man emphasize good news: "As cold waters to a thirsty soul, so is good news from a far country" (Prov 25:25). And again: "The light of the eyes rejoices the heart, and good news refreshes the bones" (Prov 15:30). When Yahweh delivered Israel from the hands of their enemies, two men who despoiled the camp of the Arameans said: "This day is a day of good news" (2 Kgs 7:9).

The whole Old Testament is a book of good news. Paul says that Yahweh is a proclaimer of good news. Paul wrote, "Now the Scripture saw in advance that God would justify the gentiles by faith and told the good news ahead of time to Abraham, saying, All the nations will be blessed through you" (Gal 3:8 HCSB). Israel was called to become a blessing to the nations and proclaim the good news of God's love to the whole world. When God called Abraham, God told him that through him all the nations on earth would be blessed. And when Abraham showed his obedience to God, God told him: "And through your descendants all the nations of the earth will be blessed—all because you have obeyed me" (Gen 22:18).

It was to help those who were living in the valley of deep darkness that Yahweh called Israel. Yahweh made them a holy nation and a kingdom of priests to proclaim the good news to those who lived in darkness. Israel was brought out of Egypt to establish an alternative community,[14] to be a nation which would set an example to all the other nations of what it means to be a nation under God. In order for Israel to fulfill its mission in the world, Yahweh gave them a good covenant and good laws. Through the covenant given at Sinai, Yahweh established a special

---

14. On the concept of Israel as an alternative community, see Brueggemann, *Prophetic Imagination*.

relationship with Israel. Yahweh said: "I will be your God and you will be my special people." At Sinai, Israel agreed to be God's people: "The people all answered as one: Everything that the LORD has spoken we will do" (Exod 19:8).

Moses told the people of Israel that because of their disobedience they would be scattered among the nations. In Deut 28:64–65 Moses said to Israel: "And the LORD will scatter you among all nations, from one end of the earth to the other.... There among those nations you will find no peace or place to rest. And the LORD will cause your heart to tremble, your eyesight to fail, and your soul to despair." The refusal of Israel to proclaim the good news is clearly expressed in the story of Jonah. Israel is Jonah, a nation in revolt.[15] When Yahweh called Jonah, Yahweh told Jonah, "Go to Nineveh." In Nineveh Jonah learned that if God was willing to forgive the people of Nineveh, a city that was the archetype of pagan wickedness, God could forgive and save any nation that called upon his name. Jonah's torment over Nineveh's repentance mirrors Israel's reluctance to fulfill its mission in the world. As Hans Walter Wolff wrote:

> For God's compassion came as no surprise to [Jonah]: the theology of the confession of faith quoted in [4:2b] showed him that nothing else was expected. The way in which Jonah deals with Israel's experience of Yahweh's mercy is frightening and chilling. For him this confession of faith, with its consequences for the hostile Gentile world, completely calls in question Israel's beliefs and her ministry in the world.[16]

Psalm 137 has caused many uneasy feelings among believers and nonbelievers alike because in this song the psalmist reflects on his bitter experience in being taken into exile. The psalm also expresses the pain and suffering the deported people suffered as a result of being taken from their land. Because of the memories of that humiliating experience, the psalmist vents his anger on the people of Babylon. In Ps 137, the psalmist reminds his readers, that when he wrote his song, Israel was by the rivers of Babylon. Israel was in exile in Babylon, scattered among the nations. But God had a purpose for sending Israel to Babylon.

In exile Israel had an opportunity to share God's love with the gentiles. The nations were waiting for Israel to proclaim the glories of this amazing God. But Israel was restless: "By the rivers of Babylon—there

---

15. Wolff, "Jonah: The Reluctant Messenger," 8–19.
16. Wolff, *Obadiah and Jonah*, 176.

we sat down and there we wept when we remembered Zion. On the willows there we hung up our harps" (Ps 137:1–2). The Babylonians came and begged Israel to tell them about their God: "Sing us one of the songs of Zion" (Ps 137:3). But Israel's response was only despair: "How could we sing the LORD's song in a foreign land?" (Ps 137:4). What a missed opportunity! The people of Israel who were in exile in Babylon missed an opportunity to talk about the God who lived in Jerusalem; they missed an opportunity to sing one of those beautiful songs of Zion. So, they hung up their harps on the willows. The reason for Israel's despair was because they could only sing songs of Zion in Jerusalem. Then, instead of blessing the Babylonians, they cursed them: "O daughter Babylon, you devastator! Blessed shall they be who pay you back what you have done to us! Blessed shall they be who take your little ones and dash them against the rock" (Ps 137:8–9).

The psalmist's prayer is a witness against Israel that they never carried out their mission in the world. John Bright said that Israel never became a missionary religion. He wrote: "No more ringing challenge to Israel to take up her world mission, could be imagined than the little book of Jonah. Let Israel cease trying to run away from her destiny; let her take up her task of proclaiming the true God to the nations, however distasteful that may be, for God cares for foreigners also."[17] The curse the psalmist placed upon Babylon is a reversal of Israel's mission in the world. Israel was called to be a blessing to the nations, not to curse them.

Israel went to exile in Babylon because it failed to be Yahweh's special people in the world. Because Israel was Yahweh's special agent of reconciliation in the world, the failure of Israel became the failure of Yahweh. Israel was called to be a blessing to all people but, because of their disobedience and their failure to be God's people in the world, Israel became an astonishment among the nations, an object of scorn and ridicule among all the peoples among whom they lived (Deut 28:37). But Yahweh's plan was to reconcile humanity unto himself. Because of the failure of Israel to be a light unto the nations, Yahweh will begin his work of reconciliation again, this time through a restored Israel.

---

17. Bright, *Kingdom of God*, 161.

22

God Reconciling the World Through Restored Israel

THE EXILE OF JUDAH BROUGHT drastic changes to the fabric of Judahite society.[1] As a result of the exile, the history of Israel took a different turn. The political and religious structures that existed in Judah prior to the exile were no more and the lives of those who went to Babylon changed radically. Life in exile changed the people so much that they would never be quite the same again.

THE EXILE OF JUDAH

From a human perspective, the transformation of the political and religious life of Judah could have been considered the end of the political and religious existence of the nation. And yet, the vitality of Israel's faith and the presence of Yahweh with his oppressed people give evidence that the history of Judah did not come to an end with the destruction of the temple and the burning of Jerusalem, nor with the murder of men, women, and children, and not even with the removal of the people from their ancestral land.

Instead, the exile can be seen as the dawn of a new beginning for Israel. Although the exile caused the end of the monarchy and the cessation of religious life in the temple, the exile also became a time of purification, a time of restoration, and a time when Israel paid "double for all her sins"

1. Klein, *Israel in Exile*.

(Isa 40:2). As Routledge puts is, "The exile was the death from which the true nation of Israel could be reborn; it was a refining that would bring forth a chastened, faithful remnant."[2] But the exile was also a time when Israel would once again recognize Yahweh's faithfulness to his people and experience the great deliverance Yahweh would again reveal to Israel.

The exile had a broad impact on the religious and social life of Israel. It was during Israel's exile in Babylon that the nation's vitality was supremely tested. The people of Judah were rooted out of their homeland, separated from their cultural values, dispossessed of their religious moorings, taken into captivity, and yet, they were able to maintain their religious and ethnic identity.

However, the transition was not easy. At the beginning of their exile, there was a reevaluation of the nation's identity. The destruction of the temple and the deportation of the people forced the nation to look again at their relationship with Yahweh. There was a crisis of credibility in Israel's God. Many people questioned Yahweh's commitment to his people and his power to deliver the nation from the hands of Babylon.

THE PROMISE OF A NEW COVENANT

The promise of the new covenant in Jer 31:31–34 has been a topic of discussion among Old Testament scholars. Scholars disagree on whether the oracle was written by Jeremiah himself, by one of his disciples, or by the people who composed the Deuteronomic History. Another item of debate is whether the promise of the new covenant was addressed to Israel only or if it was a reference to the new covenant in Christ. In this chapter, I will argue that the oracle was written by Jeremiah and that it finds fulfillment both in Israel and in Christ.

The oracle about the new covenant is included in a section of the book of Jeremiah commonly known as "The Book of Consolation." These oracles display Jeremiah's hope for the future. Jeremiah sees beyond the rebellious nature of preexilic Israel to a bright future in which Yahweh will restore the nation and reestablish the relationship that was broken by the violation of the covenant. The promise of a new covenant was another demonstration of the redemptive love of God and his faithfulness to the promises he made to the ancestors of Israel. Yahweh's promise to Israel contains several important elements.

---

2. Routledge, *Old Testament Theology*, 277.

The Time

The time for the establishment of the new covenant is in the future: "The days are surely coming" (Jer 31:31). The time here is left undetermined, however, since the oracle refers to Israel, Jeremiah was looking at a time after the seventy years of exile (Jer 25:11–12).

The Recipients

Jeremiah says that the new covenant will be established with all Israel, that is, with "the house of Israel and the house of Judah" (Jer 31:31).

The Newness of the Covenant

The new covenant will be different from the one God made with Israel at Sinai: "It will not be like the covenant that I made with their ancestors" (Jer 31:32). The new covenant will not be a set of rules. Rather, it will be a disposition of the heart.

The Reason for the New Covenant

Yahweh promised a new covenant because Israel was not faithful to the demands of the Sinai covenant, "a covenant that they broke" (Jer 31:32). The history of Israel gives evidence to Israel's disloyalty to Yahweh. Israel's disloyalty can be described as idolatry, injustice, and many other violations of the demand of the covenant. Through its disobedience to the demands of the covenant, Israel rejected the special relationship it had established with Yahweh at Sinai and failed to fulfill its mission of being God's agent of reconciliation.

The Consequences of Breaking the Covenant

Israel's violation of the demands of the covenant was a rejection of Yahweh as their God: "though I was their husband" (Jer 31:32). The word "husband" in Hebrew is a verb: "I had married them" (Jer 31:32 HCSB). Israel constantly failed to abide by the demands of the covenant. Thus, a new covenant became necessary because Israel failed to keep the relationship established at Sinai.

THE CHARACTERISTICS OF THE NEW COVENANT

First, the new covenant presupposes a radical change in the people. The old covenant was written on tablets of stone: "When God finished speaking with Moses on Mount Sinai, he gave him the two tablets of the covenant, tablets of stone, written with the finger of God" (Exod 31:18). The new covenant will be written on the people's heart: "I will put my law within them, and I will write it on their hearts." In Hebrew psychology, the heart was the seat of human will. This means that the law of God must be internalized, that is, God's teaching must touch the whole life of an individual. God's teaching must affect both the mind and the will of the one who follows God.

Second, the new covenant will establish a new relationship between God and people. Because of obedience to God's Torah, those who obey become God's people: "I will be their God, and they shall be my people." In the Old Testament this language is used several times to indicate a relationship that is established by covenant.

Third, there will be no need for human mediators: "No longer shall they teach one another, or say to each other, 'Know the LORD.'" The lack of proper instruction during the old covenant would come to an end because this is what led the people to abandon the law of God. "My people are destroyed for lack of knowledge; because you have rejected knowledge, I reject you from being a priest to me. And since you have forgotten the law of your God, I also will forget your children" (Hos 4:6).

Under the traditions of the old covenant, the priests were the teachers of the law: "True instruction was in his mouth, and no wrong was found on his lips. He walked with me in integrity and uprightness, and he turned many from iniquity. For the lips of a priest should guard knowledge, and people should seek instruction from his mouth, for he is the messenger of the LORD of hosts. But you have turned aside from the way; you have caused many to stumble by your instruction; you have corrupted the covenant of Levi, says the LORD of hosts" (Mal 2:6–8).

Fourth, under the new covenant people will seek Yahweh: "they shall all know me, from the least of them to the greatest" (Jer 31:34). People will desire to know God's will and God's word. This desire to know more about God is the blessing of the new covenant. The Hebrew word "to know" means a personal, intimate knowledge of God. This intimate knowledge comes out of a deep and personal relationship that involves the will and the emotions of the people involved in the relationship.

Fifth, the whole community will enjoy the benefits of the new covenant. Since the new covenant is based on the grace of God and his love for Israel, Israel will be transformed and will learn how to live in relationship with God. Israel will live in a new relationship with God in which the sins of the past are forgiven: "I will forgive their iniquity, and remember their sin no more" (Jer 31:34).

THE FULFILLMENT OF GOD'S PROMISE

Although the promise of the new covenant is quoted in the book of Hebrews, scholars have problems in interpreting how this promise was fulfilled. Was this promise of the new covenant fulfilled with Israel or with the Church? According to Walter Brueggemann, those who advocate that the prophecy was fulfilled in the New Testament and that the church supersedes Israel, ignore the plain teaching of the text. Such a reading of the text, Brueggemann argues, "could hardly be expected or cogent in the midst of these several promissory oracles which anticipate the reconstitution of the Israelite community."[3]

Moreover, Brueggemann has problems with the manner the author of the book of Hebrews appropriates the oracle about the new covenant. Writing about the Jewish-Christian problem concerning the fulfillment of the promise of the new covenant, Brueggemann wrote: "The matter is not easily adjudicated, because the supersessionist case is given scriptural warrant in the book of Hebrews. My own inclination is to say that in our time and place the reading of Hebrews is a distorted reading."[4] I disagree with Brueggemann. I do not believe that the reading in Hebrews "is a distorted reading." In what follows, I offer a brief perspective of how I see the fulfillment of Jeremiah's oracle.

The Promise and Israel

First, the promise of a new covenant was given to Israel. The promise was given to "the house of Israel and the house of Judah." Again, the promise was given to Israel. Israel's failure in carrying out God's mission in the world would not derail God's purpose for Israel and for the world.

---

3. Brueggemann, *Commentary on Jeremiah*, 292.
4. Brueggemann, *Commentary on Jeremiah*, 292.

Second, according to Jeremiah's hope expressed in his promise of a new covenant, God would select a group of people, a restored Israel with whom he would establish the promise of this new covenant. The new covenant was promised to restored Israel, the remnant of Israel which returned from exile.

Third, the promise of the new covenant was given to a community that would be refined by the cruel experience of the exile. This new community was coming back to the promised land with a renewed vision of its mission in the world. This new community, in the language of Deutero-Isaiah, is the community who will follow the example of the Servant and be a light to the nations (Isa 42:6).

Fourth, the postexilic community failed to accomplish God's mission in the world. The vision of Deutero-Isaiah for Israel, a vision expressed in the four Servant Songs, never became a reality: "I will give you as a light to the nations, that my salvation may reach to the end of the earth" (Isa 49:6). Israel failed to bring God's light to the nations and his salvation never went beyond the borders of the Holy Land.

The disobedience of Israel is clearly presented by Paul:

> So that you may not claim to be wiser than you are, brothers and sisters, I want you to understand this mystery: a hardening has come upon part of Israel, until the full number of the Gentiles has come in. And so, all Israel will be saved; as it is written, "Out of Zion will come the Deliverer; he will banish ungodliness from Jacob." "And this is my covenant with them, when I take away their sins." As regards the gospel they are enemies of God for your sake; but as regards election they are beloved, for the sake of their ancestors; for the gifts and the calling of God are irrevocable. (Rom 11:25–29)

The Promise and the Church

The failure of Israel to accomplish God's mission in the world is the reason the early church saw that the fullness of the promise of the new covenant found fulfillment in Christ. During his last night with the disciples, after the supper, Jesus took the cup and said: "This cup that is poured out for you is the new covenant in my blood" (Luke 22:20). The twelve disciples are representatives of the new Israel; they represent the house of Israel and the house of Judah. Israel is still God's people, for as Paul said, "as regards election they are [still] beloved" since the call of God is "irrevocable." Israel is the tree; Christians, like "wild olive shoots," were grafted into the tree "to share the rich root of the olive tree" (Rom 11:17).

Therefore, when Christians speak of Jeremiah's promise of a new covenant, Christians are not promoting supersessionism, that is, they are not saying that the Jewish people have been rejected by God and no longer have a place in God's work in redeeming the world. Such a reading of Jeremiah's words is refuted by both Old and New Testaments. According to the Gospels, Jesus is establishing a new covenant with Israel, a renewed Israel.[5]

THE END OF THE EXILE

The people of Judah experienced an unprecedented suffering as the result of the destruction of the temple and of the city of Jerusalem. The book of Lamentations portrays Jerusalem as a lonely widow appealing for sympathy and comfort from anyone, especially from Yahweh. The writer of Lamentations vividly emphasized the horrors of the devastation caused by the Babylonians and the helplessness of the population of Judah by speaking on behalf of the people and lamenting that there was no comforter for the people and the nation.

According to the writer of Lamentations, this lack of a comforter was evidence that Yahweh did not care for his people: "She weeps bitterly in the night, with tears on her cheeks; among all her lovers she has no one to comfort her" (Lam 1:2). "For these things I weep; my eyes flow with tears; for a comforter is far from me" (Lam 1:16). "Zion stretches out her hands, but there is no one to comfort her" (Lam 1:17).

It is clear that the use of the word "comforter" in the first two chapters of Lamentations means a helper, either human or divine. In Lam 2:13 a voice addresses the personified city and laments his inability to help the hurt of Jerusalem and wonders who can heal her wound, a wound that is "as deep as the sea" (Lam 2:13). The absence of a comforter for the wounded city and the belief that Yahweh had abandoned and forsaken his people heightened the sense of hopelessness, more so as the prayers of the people went unanswered. At the time when Israel was agonizing the most, at the moment of the people's deepest despair, two significant

---

5. In chapter 23 I will discuss how God accomplishes his work of reconciliation with a renewed Israel.

events took place that changed the despair of the people into a hope for the future.

The first event was the release of Jehoiachin, the former king of Judah, from a Babylonian prison, thirty-seven years after his deportation. According to the conclusion of the book of Kings (2 Kgs 25:27–30), in the thirty-seventh year of his exile (560 BCE), Jehoiachin was set free by Evil-merodach, King of Babylon, and was given preference and a position of honor above the other kings who were vassals and captives in Babylon. The news that their anointed one, their messiah, was alive and out of prison brought great joy to the people in exile. This event gave the exiles the assurance that there was hope for the future.

The second event was the call of a prophet to announce to the people that the exile was over: "Comfort, comfort my people, says your God. Speak tenderly to Jerusalem, and proclaim to her that her hard service has been completed, that her sin has been paid for, that she has received from the LORD's hand double for all her sins" (Isa 40:1–2). This unnamed prophet, popularly known as Deutero-Isaiah, came preaching a message of comfort. The message that was to bring comfort to Israel was a message of hope, a message that God had come to bring an end to the people's suffering because he had forgiven their sins and now would deliver them from their exile.

The prophet's use of the word "comfort" was a direct response to the cry of the people in the book of Lamentations. In Lam 2:13, the writer asked who could help, heal, and comfort the suffering people. Now, the prophet proclaims that Yahweh was the comforter of his people: "Shout for joy, O heavens; rejoice, O earth; burst into song, O mountains! For the LORD comforts his people and will have compassion on his afflicted ones" (Isa 49:13).

The Old Testament pictures Yahweh as the one who comforts Israel (Pss 23:4; 86:17; Isa 40:1–2; 51:3). Deutero-Isaiah used the imagery of Yahweh as the comforter of Israel to emphasize that Yahweh has heard Israel's appeal for a comforter and to bring the good news that their exile was coming to an end: "For the LORD will comfort Zion; he will comfort all her waste places" (Isa 51:3). "Break forth together into singing, you ruins of Jerusalem; for the LORD has comforted his people, he has redeemed Jerusalem" (Isa 52:9).

The texts in Deutero-Isaiah where the word "comfort" is used have two things in common. First, the one who comforts is Yahweh and the one who is comforted is Israel. Second, the prophet uses the word "comfort" to express Yahweh's action in helping the people and restoring them to their homeland. Thus, the use of the word "comfort" in Deutero-Isaiah is a response to the lack of comfort in the book of Lamentations. The double use of the word "comfort" in Isa 40:1 expresses Yahweh's urgency in liberating the people from their oppression. Yahweh's urgency in delivering the exiles reflects his concern for the spiritual well-being of his people. After more than five decades in exile, many people were turning away from God and little by little they allowed their faith to grow cold, gradually accepting the culture and the religion of their captors. Thus, this threat to Israel's faith led to the urgency of the prophet's message. Yahweh's urgency may also reflect his desire to renew Israel's work of reconciliation in the world.

The purpose of the use of the word "comfort" in the message of Deutero-Isaiah was to turn the lamentation of the people into a hope for the future. The coming of Yahweh to liberate his people was a source of hope. It was also the beginning of his intervention in the events of history to redeem his people, as he had done in Egypt, to bring them back to their land, and to continue his work of reconciliation of the world through Israel.

Deutero-Isaiah's message of hope and the assurance that Yahweh would deliver his people was spoken with authority because the invitation to the people to find comfort in Yahweh was accompanied by an exhortation to prepare the way for the Lord (Isa 40:3).

THE CALL OF DEUTERO-ISAIAH

The call of Deutero-Isaiah is found in Isa 40:1–11. Yahweh called the prophet and sent him with a message of comfort to the people. His message must be understood in the despair of the exile. The despair of Israel is expressed in the book of Lamentations: "She [Jerusalem] weeps bitterly in the night, with tears on her cheeks; among all her lovers she has no one to comfort her" (Lam 1:2). "Zion stretches out her hands, but there is no one to comfort her" (Lam 1:17). Five times the poet says in Lamentations that there is no one to comfort the people of Judah,[6] no one, that is, until Deutero-Isaiah came proclaiming a message of hope and comfort: "Comfort, O comfort my people, says your God. Speak tenderly to Jerusalem, and cry to her that she has served her term, that her penalty

---

6. Lam 1:2, 9, 17, 21; 2:13.

is paid, that she has received from the LORD's hand double for all her sins" (Isa 40:1–2). Her term of service is the exile. Jerusalem had received a severe punishment because of her sins. Such a proclamation could only be made after the fall of Jerusalem. Deutero-Isaiah comes proclaiming the end of exile and the people's return to their homeland.

The end of exile is only possible because of Yahweh's faithful promise. Yahweh told the prophet: "Proclaim!" And he asked: "What shall I proclaim?" (Isa 40:6 TNK). And the response from Yahweh affirms God's faithfulness to his promises: "All people are grass, their constancy is like the flower of the field. The grass withers, the flower fades; but the word of our God will stand forever" (Isa 40:6–8). The constancy of the people does not last; it is like the flower of the field that withers and dies. Only the word of God, his promises to save and deliver his people, stands forever.

The message of Deutero-Isaiah is a message that God has come to redeem his people from their exile: "You who bring good tidings to Zion, go up on a high mountain. You who bring good tidings to Jerusalem, lift up your voice with a shout, lift it up, do not be afraid; say to the towns of Judah, 'Here is your God'" (Isa 40:9 NIV). Deutero-Isaiah is a herald of good news. The people who are now living in the darkness of exile are promised the light of a new day. Deutero-Isaiah proclaims a message of consolation to a hopeless and despairing people. The people have suffered severely for their sins, but that now is in the past.

THE MESSAGE OF DEUTERO-ISAIAH

Deutero-Isaiah was called and sent to proclaim two great messages of hope to the people in exile. The first message was that the physical hardship imposed upon Israel and enforced by the exile was now coming to an end. The second message was that the iniquity of the nation had been pardoned. To the prophet, the change in Israel's fortune and the restoration of the nation was based on divine mercy and divine forgiveness. It is here that Israel could see once again Yahweh's commitment to his people. It was Yahweh's *ḥesed*, his faithful love, a love based on a covenantal relationship that moved Yahweh to forgive his rebellious people. It was because of that unfailing love that Israel's time of servitude to alien masters had come to an end.

The expression "my people" in Isa 40:1 is significant in the context of the exile. When Israel was rebellious and serving other gods, Yahweh said that Israel was "not my people (Hos 1:9). When Yahweh was angry because Israel's heart was hardened, Israel was "this people" (Isa 6:9). Now that Yahweh has forgiven Israel, they are again "my people." The expression "my people" comes out of covenant language: "I will be their God, and they shall be my people" (Jer 31:33). At Sinai, Israel became Yahweh's special people united with Yahweh by a covenant of grace. Thus, the words "my people" express God's desire that the covenant relationship that once bound Israel to God be restored. The exile came because of Israel's violation of the covenant, and as a result, Israel had to suffer under the heavy hands of the Babylonians. Now, Deutero-Isaiah's message of hope and comfort revealed that, notwithstanding the overwhelming tragedy that fell upon the nation, Israel was still God's people and they were still the object of his love and part of his redemptive purpose for the nations.

The prophet was commanded to speak tenderly to the heart of Jerusalem. This expression is used to identify Yahweh's love for Israel as a husband speaks tenderly ("speaks to the heart") to his wife (Judg 19:3). This metaphor appears again in Isa 54:4-8: "Do not be afraid; you will not suffer shame. Do not fear disgrace; you will not be humiliated. You will forget the shame of your youth and remember no more the reproach of your widowhood. For your Maker is your husband—the LORD Almighty is his name—the Holy One of Israel is your Redeemer; he is called the God of all the earth. The LORD will call you back as if you were a wife deserted and distressed in spirit—a wife who married young, only to be rejected, says your God. For a brief moment I abandoned you, but with deep compassion I will bring you back. In a surge of anger I hid my face from you for a moment, but with everlasting kindness I will have compassion on you, says the LORD your Redeemer."

Several themes that appear in the book of Lamentations, in the cry of distress of the lonely widow, appear again in this text of Deutero-Isaiah which is part of the message of hope and restoration that the prophet was preaching to Israel. Israel had suffered shame, had been disgraced and humiliated. The prophet now proclaims that Israel would forget the shame it suffered, would remember no more the reproach of its widowhood, for Yahweh was her husband, the one calling back the abandoned wife who was deserted, distressed in spirit, and rejected. But that rejection was only for a brief moment: "For a brief moment I abandoned you, but with deep compassion I will bring you back" (Isa 54:7).

Deutero-Isaiah's message to Israel was that her "time of service" was over. This message of hope proclaimed by the prophet to a group of people who had lost their hope, reminded them of the time when their ancestors served as slaves in Egypt. In Babylon, most people were not put to forced labor as they had labored in Egypt, but Israel's hard service in Babylon may be a reference to the humiliations the people suffered in exile. Israel's time of service may be also a symbolic reference to the more than fifty years the people lived in the land of alien gods.

The message of comfort proclaimed by Deutero-Isaiah was a summons to a people who had lost hope for the future. The community's crisis of faith and loss of hope was expressed in Ezekiel's vision of the valley of dry bones. When Yahweh explained to Ezekiel the meaning of the dry bones, Yahweh said: "Son of man, these bones are the whole house of Israel. They say, 'Our bones are dried up and our hope is gone'" (Ezek 37:11).

The crisis of faith was also expressed in the complaints of the people in which they expressed their doubt in Yahweh's power to save them.[7] "Why do you say, Jacob, Why do you say, Israel, 'The LORD is not aware of what is happening to me, My God is not concerned with my vindication'" (Isa 40:27 NET). "Zion said, 'The LORD has forsaken me, the Lord has forgotten me'" (Isa 49:14). To counteract the despondency of the people and their hopelessness, the prophet announced that Yahweh had forgiven the nation and that announcement became a great source of hope for Israel. The people would soon return to their native land because Israel was still the object of Yahweh's great love.

THE NEW EXODUS

After almost seventy years in exile, Yahweh comes to "speak to the heart of Jerusalem" (Isa 40:2) and through the prophet, he speaks a message of grace and deliverance: "In overflowing wrath for a moment I hid my face from you, but with everlasting love I will have compassion on you, says the LORD, your Redeemer" (Isa 54:8). In exile, Israel had been purified: "See, I have refined you, but not like silver; I have tested you in the furnace of adversity" (Isa 48:10). As Yahweh had brought Israel "out of the iron furnace, out of Egypt" (Deut 4:20), now he will bring Israel out of the Babylonian "furnace of adversity." The exile was "the furnace of

---

7. Watts, "Consolation or Confrontation?," 31–59.

adversity" that gave Israel another opportunity to do God's work in the world, but again, Israel's salvation came not because Israel changed, but because of God's faithfulness to his promises.

One of the central motifs in the message of Deutero-Isaiah is that the liberation of Israel will be a new exodus. Eric Zenger says that the prophet is proclaiming a "new" exodus God.[8] This God of the new exodus "will end Israel's suffering without the use of war and destruction." According to Zenger, the reason the liberation of Israel will be without violence is because Yahweh wants "to wean Israel away from all ideas of a strong God who destroys the other; he wants Israel to discover that he is a loving God who wants to bestow new life." By emphasizing that the "new exodus" will be without violence, Zenger says, "God opposes the pictures of JHWH the Warrior and of a new Exodus that would annihilate enemies."[9]

The message of redemption that Deutero-Isaiah is to speak to the people in Babylon is a message of liberation. Israel will once again be redeemed from their heavy time of service in the same way Israel was redeemed from the house of bondage in Egypt, "Thus says the LORD, who makes a way in the sea, a path in the mighty waters, who brings out chariot and horse, army and warrior; they lie down, they cannot rise, they are extinguished, quenched like a wick" (Isa 43:16–17).

The exodus from Egypt was the most important event in the history of Israel. The exodus from Egypt was the time when Israel was born as a nation and received its mission to be God's people in the world. Deutero-Isaiah declares that the liberation of Israel from their exile in Babylon will be a new exodus,[10] a new beginning for Israel as a nation. After their return from exile, Yahweh will establish a new relationship with Israel. Yahweh's new relationship with Israel is a renewal of Israel's mission, a mission that involves the redemption of the nations.

RESTORATION OF ISRAEL'S MISSION

A unique feature of the message of Deutero-Isaiah is found in the four texts commonly known as the "Servant Songs."[11] These four texts are Isa

8. Zenger, "God of Exodus," 26.
9. Zenger, "God of Exodus," 27–28.
10. Anderson, "Exodus Typology," 177–95.
11. Rowley, "Servant Mission," 259–72.

42:1–4; 49:1–6; 50:4–9, and 52:13—53:12. When studying these texts, two main issues arise. The first issue of debate is the identification of the Servant: Who is the Servant? The other issue is about the role of the Servant within the historical context of Deutero-Isaiah.

The Hebrew word for servant is '*ebed*, a word that appears often throughout the Hebrew Bible. The word is applied to many individuals, including the patriarchs, prophets, kings, and even slaves. The way Deutero-Isaiah uses the word "Servant" in these four songs, implies that the prophet uses the Servant Songs to describe the mission of Israel in the world.

Over the years, scholars have presented several proposals concerning the identification of the Servant. One proposal used for identifying the Servant is the collective interpretation. Many scholars believe that the Servant is Israel or a pious remnant within the nation. This identification is supported by Yahweh's words to the Servant: "You are my servant, Israel, in whom I will be glorified" (Isa 49:3). "The Hebrew word for 'servant' appears 40 times in the Book of Isaiah. Of these 40 times, 7 clearly specify Israel as the servant: 41:8; 44:1–2, 21 (twice); 45:4; 48:20."[12]

The second proposal for identifying the Servant is the individual interpretation. When the four songs are evaluated in context, the language used to describe the Servant and his mission is strongly individual. The songs speak about the call, the education, the suffering, the death, and the eventual triumph of an individual who accomplishes his work by the power of Yahweh. As an individual, the Servant has been identified with Moses, Job, Jeremiah, Josiah, Deutero-Isaiah, and Jehoiachin. Most Christians believe the Servant to be an individual and interpret the songs from a messianic perspective and apply them to Jesus and his ministry.

The third proposal for understanding the songs is by using the concept of corporate personality. This view says that the Servant represents both the nation and an individual. Thus, the individual, maybe Deutero-Isaiah himself, represents the whole nation. In this view, Israel, represented by an individual, would have a mission to Israel. His mission was to call Israel to its vocation as the people of God with a message to the nations: "I will give you as a light to the nations, that my salvation may reach to the end of the earth" (Isa 49:6).

The first Servant Song introduces the Servant, "Here is my servant, whom I uphold, my chosen, in whom my soul delights; I have put my

---

12. Mariottini, "Israel as God's Servants," 59.

spirit upon him; he will bring forth justice to the nations" (Isa 42:1). According to Blenkinsopp, Yahweh is addressing an audience in the gentile world. Blenkinsopp writes, "The purpose of the address is to recommend an individual whom he has chosen, whom he supports, who is endowed with the divine spirit, and whose mission is to establish law and order among the nations, but without the violence and brutality generally associated with this task"[13] (see postscript).

The second Servant Song (Isa 49:1–6) deals with the commission of the Servant. The text can be divided into three sections: "The Call of the Servant" (Isa 49:1); "The Preparation of the Servant" (Isa 49:2–3); and "The Commission of the Servant" (Isa 49:4–6). In the Songs, the Servant has no name, but in Isa 49:3 he is identified with Israel: "And [Yahweh] said to me, 'You are my servant, Israel, in whom I will be glorified.'" In another passage, Isaiah identifies the Servant as an offspring of Abraham, "But you, Israel, my servant, Jacob, whom I have chosen, the offspring of Abraham, my friend" (Isa 41:8). The identification of the Servant as an offspring of Abraham means that the Servant carried on the mission of Abraham to be a blessing to "all the families of the earth" (Gen 12:3).

The Servant begins by addressing the nations: "Listen to me, O coastlands, pay attention, you peoples from far away" (49:1). The Servant will do his work by the words of his mouth, that is, his teaching (49:2). The Servant says that Yahweh commissioned him to be a light to the nations: "I will give you as a light to the nations" (49:6). The same commission was given to the Servant at the time of his call:[14] "I have given you as a covenant to the people, a light to the nations" (Isa 42:6). The Servant will be God's agent for the salvation of the world: "I will give you as a light to the nations, that my salvation may reach to the end of the earth" (49:6).

In the Old Testament, light is associated with salvation: "Yahweh is my light and my salvation" (Ps 27:1 NJB). As a light to the nations, the Servant's light will shine among people who live in darkness: "The people who walked in darkness have seen a great light; those who lived in a land of deep darkness—on them light has shined" (Isa 9:2). When the light of the Servant shines, God's good news of reconciliation will reach to the end of the earth.

The mission of the Servant is reaffirmed in the New Testament. When Jesus was presented in the temple, Simeon took the child in his

---

13. Blenkinsopp, "Second Isaiah-Prophet of Universalism," 88.
14. Lindsey, "Isaiah's Songs of the Servant," 12–31.

arms and, citing the commission of the Servant in Isa 49:6, said, "My eyes have seen your salvation, which you have prepared for all people to see. He is a light that will reveal salvation to the nations and bring glory to your people Israel" (Luke 2:30–32 GWN). To Simeon, Jesus is the light promised by God. As Barrett wrote, "The arrival of Jesus ushers in a new phase of redemptive history as He is a revelation. As light, He reveals before all to see that the Gentiles are the object of the redemptive plan, sharing an equal part in salvation."[15]

When Paul and Barnabas came to Antioch, they went to the synagogue to share the gospel to the Jews and to the gentiles who were converts to Judaism. When some of the Jews revolted against Paul and Barnabas, they said to them, "the Lord has commanded us, saying, 'I have set you to be a light for the Gentiles, so that you may bring salvation to the ends of the earth'" (Act 13:47). In response to the opposition by the Jews in Antioch, Paul cites Isa 49:6 to validate his proclamation of salvation in Christ. The reason Paul cites the commission of the Servant was to emphasize that God's desire was to bring salvation to all people. Barrett wrote, "Only if Isa 49:6 is a prophecy dealing with both the arrival of the Messiah and God's saving program for the spread of the gospel to all the world does Paul's use of the passage make sense."[16]

THE FAILURE OF ISRAEL

The message of Deutero-Isaiah and the commission given to the Servant indicate that God intended that restored Israel would again take up its mission and be a witness to the nations. Israel was to experience a new exodus, a new beginning. This new beginning would also include a new covenant and a renewed relationship between God and Israel. Once again, Yahweh will be the God of Israel and Israel will be the people of God (Jer 31:33). Upon its return to Jerusalem, the people of Israel were to carry out the mission of the Servant and become a light to the nations. John Bright wrote, "the Servant mission is always laid before Israel as her calling and destiny."[17]

The fourth Servant Song (Isa 52:13—53:12) speaks about the suffering of the Servant. He was despised and rejected by many (Isa 53:3).

---

15. Barrett, "Luke's Contribution to the Light Motif," 36.
16. Barrett, "Luke's Contribution to the Light Motif," 37.
17. Bright, *Kingdom of God*, 151.

He was oppressed and afflicted (Isa 53:7), but he was willing to suffer in order to accomplish his mission: "I gave my back to those who struck me, and my cheeks to those who pulled out the beard; I did not hide my face from insult and spitting" (Isa 50:6). The Servant endured pain and suffering in the hands of his enemies, but he rejected violence: "he had done no violence" (Isa 53:9). The work of the Servant would not be accomplished with sword and violence, but with and through suffering. By renouncing violence and accepting suffering, the Servant "becomes a witness to the power of reconciliation and love that can change the world."[18] The Servant had to endure pain and suffering, but it was through suffering that Yahweh's plan for humanity would be accomplished (Isa 53:10).

In order for restored Israel to become a light to the nations, Israel had to proclaim a message of inclusion. Israel had to invite the nations to accept Yahweh as the only God: "Turn to me and be saved, all the ends of the earth! For I am God, and there is no other. By myself I have sworn, from my mouth has gone forth in righteousness a word that shall not return: 'To me every knee shall bow, every tongue shall swear'" (Isa 45:22–23). Israel had to invite the nations to make pilgrimage to Jerusalem to worship God: "In days to come . . . Many peoples shall come and say, 'Come, let us go up to the mountain of the LORD, to the house of the God of Jacob; that he may teach us his ways and that we may walk in his paths.' For out of Zion shall go forth instruction, and the word of the LORD from Jerusalem" (Isa 2:2–3). Israel should invite the nations to pray in the temple:

> As for foreigners who adhere to Yahweh to serve him, to love Yahweh's name and become his servants, all who observe the Sabbath, not profaning it, and cling to my covenant: these I shall lead to my holy mountain and make them joyful in my house of prayer. Their burnt offerings and sacrifices will be accepted on my altar, for my house will be called a house of prayer for all peoples. (Isa 56:6–7 NJB)

Israel should include "the participation of foreigners in the temple service and their rights to minister before YHWH as priests and Levites."[19] This was the prophetic hope for Israel. Yahweh said,

> I am coming to gather every nation and every language. They will come to witness my glory. I shall give them a sign and send

---

18. Zenger, "God of Exodus," 28.
19. Weyde, "Is God a Violent God?," 298.

> some of their survivors to the nations, . . . to the distant coasts and islands that have never heard of me or seen my glory. They will proclaim my glory to the nations, and from all the nations they will bring all your brothers as an offering to Yahweh, Yahweh says, like Israelites bringing offerings in clean vessels to Yahweh's house. And some of them I shall make into priests and Levites, Yahweh says. (Isa 66:18–21 NJB)

This prophetic vision for restored Israel never became a reality. Two reasons contributed to the failure of Israel to carry out the mission of the Servant and become a light to the nations: the difficulties faced by the people who returned from Babylon and the failure of Israel to proclaim the knowledge of Yahweh among the nations.

The difficulties faced by the people who returned from Babylon were many. After Cyrus allowed the people to return to their homeland, those who returned under Sheshbazzar were only a small minority of the people in exile. Approximately one thousand Jews returned to Judah with Sheshbazzar; most of the people remained in Babylon (Ezra 1:1–11). A few years later, about fifty thousand people returned with Zerubbabel (Ezra 2:64–65). Jerusalem was in ruins. The first returnees laid the foundation of the temple after they arrived, but because of the poor economic conditions of the community, it took twenty years to finish building the temple. The people who returned were extremely poor and they had to face many hardships. Some people had to pledge their fields, their vineyards, and their houses in order to get grain during the famine. Others had to borrow money on their fields and vineyards to pay the king's tax (Neh 5:2–4).

The small community who returned from Babylon struggled to survive. They were discouraged by the opposition of people who disliked the returnees. Some people were so discouraged that they began to doubt God: "Where is the God of justice?" (Mal 2:17). "It is vain to serve God. What do we profit by keeping his command or by going about as mourners before the LORD of hosts?" (Mal 3:14). The people who returned from Babylon motivated by the preaching of Deutero-Isaiah did not have the strength or the enthusiasm to carry on their vocation as the people of God by being a light to the nations.

Israel did not accomplish the mission of the Servant because of its failure to proclaim the knowledge of Yahweh among the nations. Bright said, "Judaism certainly did make disciples. But Judaism never properly became a missionary religion. On the contrary, it tended to draw ever more tightly into itself."[20] Israel welcomed proselytes, but they were not active in recruiting them. John Bright wrote, "While there must have been many a devoted Jew who labored to win converts for his God, there is no evidence that Judaism as a religion made any concentrated attempt to do so. It would probably be accurate to say that while proselytes were accepted and welcome, they were rarely sought."[21]

Scot McKnight has written a detailed study of Jewish missionary activity in the Second Temple period.[22] McKnight explores the evidence of Jewish missionary activity during the Second Temple period and Jewish attitudes toward proselytism. McKnight's exploration is broad and comprehensive. He begins his study by examining the apocryphal and pseudepigraphical literature. He then proceeds by examining the Dead Sea Scrolls, Philo, Josephus, and many rabbinic writings. He also examines Greco-Roman authors and Jewish historians. McKnight supplements his research by commenting on inscription and epigraphical data. He concludes by examining the New Testament in order to determine whether the missionary zeal of Christianity was derived from Second Temple Judaism.

In order to truly ascertain whether Judaism was "the first great missionary religion of the Mediterranean world," McKnight studied Judaism attitudes toward gentiles, Judaism attitudes toward proselytes, the methods of proselyting, the requirements for proselytes, and levels of adherence to Judaism. McKnight concludes his book by studying Jewish missionary activity in the New Testament. Was Judaism in the Second Temple period a missionary religion? The answer McKnight gives to this question is based on his definition of "a missionary religion." McKnight defines a missionary religion as

> a religion that self-consciously defines itself as a religion, one aspect of whose "self-definition" is a mission to the rest of the world, or at least a large portion of the world. This religion at the same time practices its mission through behavior that intends to evangelize nonmembers so that these nonmembers will convert to the religion.[23]

---

20. Bright, *Kingdom of God*, 153.
21. Bright, *Kingdom of God*, 161.
22. McKnight, *Light Among the Nations*.
23. McKnight, *Light Among the Nations*, 4–5.

After reviewing the pertinent literature on Jewish missionary activity in the Second Temple period and using the two criteria that define a missionary religion, McKnight concludes that Judaism in the Second Temple period was not a missionary religion.

THE NEED FOR A NEW BEGINNING

With the failure of restored Israel to become a light to the nation in order that Yahweh's salvation might reach the remotest parts of earth (Isa 49:6), Yahweh was failing to reconcile the world unto himself. Since God had chosen Israel to become his agent of reconciliation in the world, the failure of Israel became the failure of Yahweh.

After the first human beings sinned and rebelled against him, Yahweh did not allow them to die in their sinful condition. Rather, he expelled them from the garden he had prepared for them. Yahweh also devised a plan to redeem fallen humanity and restore their broken relationship. But, as the years and centuries passed by, Yahweh saw how evil humans had become on the earth and that inclination of their minds and the thoughts of their hearts were always of evil only (Gen 6:5). As a result, Yahweh regretted having made human beings on earth and his heart was filled with pain. Confronted with the wickedness of human beings and the lawlessness and violence of their actions, with a broken heart (Gen 6:6 GWN), Yahweh sends his judgment upon the earth. His attempt at beginning again with Noah failed. Human rebellion at the Tower of Babel and the dispersion of humanity into nations required a different approach to reach them. God's work of reconciling the world by himself was not sufficient. So, God called Abraham and through him, God called Israel to become his agents of reconciliation in the world.

Yahweh commanded Abraham to be a blessing so that through him, all the families of the earth would be blessed (Gen 12:3). Israel came into being through the descendants of Abraham. God had great hopes for Israel. He redeemed Israel from their oppressive situation in Egypt to become his *segullāh*, God's personal possession. He made them a kingdom of priests and a holy nation (Exod 19:6). Israel was set apart to continue God's work of reconciliation in the world. God established a covenant with Israel which required Israel to be different from the other nations. But Israel was a great disappointment in God's purpose for the world. Soon after they entered the land of Canaan, instead of rejecting the gods of Canaan, Israel worshiped their gods: "The Israelites then did what is evil in Yahweh's eyes and served the Baals" (Judg 2:11 NJB). This disappointment continued through the history of the nation. In desperation Yahweh said, "My people are determined to turn from me" (Hos 11:7 NIV). "Ephraim, how could I part with you? Israel, how could I give you up? My heart within me is overwhelmed, fever grips my inmost being" (Hos 11:8 NJB). In dealing with Judah, Yahweh said,

> Who will find me a wayfarer's shelter in the desert, for me to quit my people, and leave them far behind? For all of them are adulterers, a conspiracy of traitors. They bend their tongues like a bow; not truth but falsehood holds sway in the land; yes, they go from crime to crime, but me they do not know, Yahweh declares. (Jer 9:1–2 NJB)

Yahweh wanted to quit his people and leave them far behind. Instead of leaving them, he sent them into exile. Yahweh sent his people into exile to refine them and to test them in the furnace of adversity (Isa 48:10). The purpose of the exile was to restore Israel and renew their mission of reconciliation. In Babylon, Yahweh renewed Israel's mission: "I will give you as a light to the nations, that my salvation may reach to the end of the earth" (Isa 49:6). But once against Israel failed; they never became a light to the nations and they never brought Yahweh's salvation to the farthest part of the earth.

Twice Israel failed to accomplish its mission in the world. Once again, the failure of Israel, Yahweh's agent, is the failure of Yahweh. In his nature, Yahweh is a God merciful and gracious and as a God who abounds in steadfast love and faithfulness (Exod 34:6). It is for this reason that Yahweh desires to reestablish his relationship with sinful humanity, because he has "no pleasure in the death of anyone" (Ezek 18:32). So, in order to save sinful humanity, Yahweh developed a new and radical approach in his work of reconciliation. Yahweh decided to empty himself, take human flesh, and become a human being (Phil 2:7). And when Yahweh became flesh, he lived among his people (John 1:14). The manner by which God is reconciling the word today is, as Soulen said, through Jesus Christ, "in whom God is revealed as YHWH the Father, Son, and Holy Spirit."[24] Yahweh's decision to become a human being will culminate with the death of Yahweh, the Warrior God of Israel, on the cross.

---

24. Soulen, "YHWH the Triune God," 48.

23

God Reconciling the World Through Renewed Israel

THE OLD TESTAMENT IS THE story of God's work of saving human beings from their sins and rebellion. Abraham was called by Yahweh to be his agent in the work of redemption. Abraham's mission was to be a blessing to the whole world: "in you all the families of the earth shall be blessed" (Gen 12:3). But Abraham was a latecomer in God's work of reconciliation. When Yahweh called Abraham, human beings had been in the world for thousands of years. What was Yahweh doing before Abraham?

BEFORE ABRAHAM

Before Abraham, Yahweh was at work trying to reestablish and renew the relationship between himself and humanity that had been broken because of sin.[1] The word "sin" appears only once in Gen 1–11, but the devastation caused by the sinful actions of human beings brought cataclysmic consequences to the created order.[2]

---

1. As Terence Fretheim, "Self-Limiting God," 184 puts it, "in the larger creational context in which the flood story is embedded, God is the subject of a remarkable string of activities that are all too commonly reserved for the chosen community (by the chosen community!): God elects, reveals, saves from danger and death, and makes promises. And this is long before Abraham!"

2. The Hebrew word *ḥāṭā'* is translated as "sin" in Gen 4:7. Sin is personified as an animal of prey or as a demon lying outside Cain's door ready to attack. The Hebrew word *'āwōn* is translated as "punishment" in Gen 4:13. The word is generally

After the man and the woman rebelled against Yahweh, Yahweh was actively working to restore the broken relationship, although the text does not say how God was planning to restore the relationship. Traditional evangelical interpretation sees Gen 3:15 as a promise for the coming Messiah who would do the work of reconciliation. However, such an interpretation leaves the pre-Abrahamic population without someone who could act on their behalf. If Gen 3:15 is a Messianic promise, that promise would not be fulfilled for thousands of years. In this period before Abraham, it is Yahweh himself who is doing the work of reconciliation. Yahweh is a "God with a mission."[3] In Gen 1–11 we meet a "God who refused to forsake his rebellious creation, who refused to give up, who was and is determined to redeem and restore fallen creation to his original design for it."[4]

The biblical text presents a God who is highly involved with human beings. Yahweh walks with (Gen 3:8) and talks to the man (Gen 3:9) and to the woman (Gen 3:13). Yahweh talks to Cain, he talks to Noah, and he comes down to observe what the builders of the tower were doing (Gen 11:7). As a result of God's work of reconciliation, the biblical writer says that "people began to call on the name of Yahweh" (Gen 4:26 HCSB). Although scholars are not agreed with the meaning of this statement, this statement implies that during the generation of Enosh, people began worshiping God. Most translations translate the Hebrew verb in an impersonal way, "people began to invoke the name of the LORD." However, the NJB makes the verb personal by making Enosh the subject of the verb, "This man [Enosh] was the first to invoke the name Yahweh." However the text is translated, the biblical writer is saying that the worship of Yahweh began at this time. Another person who also had a personal relationship with Yahweh was Enoch: "Enoch walked with God; then he was no more, because God took him" (Gen 5:24). Before there was an Israel, Yahweh was manifesting himself to people and people were worshiping Yahweh. Yahweh is not the God of Israel alone; Yahweh is the God of the whole world.

Before Cain killed his brother, Yahweh tried to help him control his anger (Gen 4:6), but Yahweh was not successful. Cain invited his

---

translated as "iniquity." Cain's punishment is the consequence of his iniquity. Kitz, "Demons in the Hebrew Bible," 447–64, however does not believe that the word *rōbēṣ* in Gen 4:7 refers to a demon.

3. Wright, *Mission of God*, 62.
4. Taber, "Missiology and the Bible," 232.

brother to the field and killed him (Gen 4:8). Yahweh becomes involved with Noah because of human violence and human wickedness. Because of the sinful actions of human beings, the good creation became corrupt before God and the earth was filled with violence, wickedness, and evil. The flood destroyed what Yahweh had created. The story of Noah and his family becomes a new beginning for the world and for humanity. The command that God gave to Adam, "Be fruitful and multiply, and fill the earth" (Gen 1:28), was given to Noah: "God blessed Noah and his sons, and said to them, 'Be fruitful and multiply, and fill the earth'" (Gen 9:1).

But human beings once again rebelled against Yahweh. They decided to build a city and a tower (Gen 11:4) and remain in the land of Shinar, the place where they had settled (Gen 11:2). By remaining in one place, the people were rejecting the divine command to multiply and fill the earth (Gen 11:4). In order to compel humans to fill the earth, "Yahweh scattered them all over the world" (Gen 11:8).

The Primeval History (Gen 1–11) ends with humanity divided into nations. These nations had grown in size and were spread all over the earth. Yahweh had worked by himself to reconciled humanity unto himself. However, with the increase of the number of nations and the large number of people in the world, Yahweh decided that a new approach was needed to redeem humanity and restore the broken relationship. According to Brueggemann, the end of the Primeval History is an ending waiting for a beginning, He writes, "Thus far, the creation has turned out quite against the dreams of the creator. . . . creation has not been responsive to God's purposes."[5] God's new beginning is the creation of a special people. God brought Abraham from serving other gods (Josh 24:2) and began preparing him to become the father of a nation called Israel. Israel will become God's agent in the work of reconciliation.

GOD RECONCILING THE WORLD THROUGH ISRAEL

The Primeval History in Gen 1–11 ends with the scattering of the nations. Three times the biblical text emphasizes that the nations were scattered abroad over the face of all the earth (Gen 11:4, 8, 9). The effort to build a tower that would reach the heavens (Gen 11:1–9) was a demonstration of human ingenuity, but it was also an evidence of human pride and human arrogance. The Primeval History dealt with the human race as a whole

---

5. Brueggemann, *Genesis*, 96.

and shows a humanity in rebellion against the creator. By their rebellion, human beings reject God's purpose for their lives and refuse to live the life God intended them to enjoy. God's desire was to bless men and women as they lived in fellowship with him. The call of Abraham in Gen 12 marks a new beginning in God's quest to bring salvation to rebellious humanity and to bless them. Abraham "stands at a new beginning, at the place where the divine purpose is inaugurated anew in the world, where Yahweh is taking the initiative for a nation and, indeed, for the world of nations."[6]

God called Abraham and gave him a destiny. Abraham was called to be a blessing to "all the families of the earth" (Gen 12:3). God made several promises to Abraham, promises that would provide the means by which Abraham could be a blessing to the nations. Among the promises God gave to Abraham was the promise of a son and the promise of a land. The birth of a son would lead to the birth of a nation. This nation to be called Israel would become God's agent in the world through whom God's purposes for the nations would be accomplished. God made a covenant with Abraham in which he bound himself to fulfill his promises.

The relationship between God and Israel began with the call of Abraham and continued with Israel's redemption from their oppression in Egypt. After Yahweh brought Israel to Mount Sinai, God made a covenant with Israel which would establish the reason for their liberation and clarify Israel's mission in the world. The basis for Israel's mission in the world was what Yahweh had done for them in bringing them out of Egypt. Israel was redeemed from being slaves to Pharaoh to be servants of Yahweh, to serve as his agents of reconciliation to all nations. This was Yahweh's charge to Abraham, to be a blessing to the nations, and this was the mission and the calling of Israel, to be a priestly kingdom and a holy nation (Exod 19:6).[7] However, the success of Israel's mission in the world had one condition. Israel had to live by the demands of the covenant: "if you obey my voice and keep my covenant, you shall be my treasured possession out of all the peoples" (Exod 19:5).

The success of Israel's mission in the world was contingent on Israel abiding by the demands of the covenant. The history of Israel shows that Israel failed to accomplish its mission because of disobedience and rebellion. The message proclaimed by the prophets gives evidence that

---

6. Muilenburg, "Abraham and the Nations," 390.

7. On the conditions of Israel's calling and the implications of Israel's mission in the world, see Block, "Privilege of Calling," 387–405.

Israel abandoned Yahweh to serve other gods. They made images and bowed down to them. They introduced foreign religious practices into the worship of God and led the people astray. As a result, the curses of the covenant were invoked against Israel. However, Israel was not deprived of a warning of the coming judgment. According to the Chronicler, "The LORD God of their fathers had sent word to them through His messengers daily without fail, for He had pity on His people and His dwelling-place" (2 Chr 36:15 TNK). According to Brueggemann, "The whole history of prophecy is an act of mercy. In this usage, however, mercy is not rescue but warning, to deter Jerusalem from its self-destructive action. Israel, however, refused and resisted, until God's wrath arose and there was 'no remedy.'"[8] Israel went into exile because of its rebellion against Yahweh. Israel failed to accomplish its mission; and as a result, Israel did not become a blessing to the nations, rather they became a reproach and a byword, an object of ridicule and an offense to all the kingdoms of the earth (Jer 24:9).

GOD RECONCILING THE WORLD THROUGH RESTORED ISRAEL

After the fall of Jerusalem, the people of Judah were deported to Babylon and scattered throughout the empire. The exile had a radical impact on the life and religion of Israel. As a result, the structures of Israelite society and their religious practices were radically changed. However, Israel was still a people bound to Yahweh by covenant. Yahweh was still committed to fulfill the promises he had made to Abraham that through him and his descendants, all the families of the earth would be blessed.

In exile, many nations ceased to exist while others lost their ethnic identity. Israel did not cease to exist, and it did not lose its identity as the people of Yahweh. Instead, the exile became the dawn of a new beginning. The call of Deutero-Isaiah brought hopes of restoration to the people in exile. His proclamation of the end of exile and his announcement of a new exodus was a reaffirmation of Yahweh's faithfulness to the covenant and of his steadfast love for Israel.

The restoration of Israel would begin with the return of Israel to Jerusalem. Deutero-Isaiah proclaims a message of comfort to a hopeless people and announces that Israel's time of service has ended, that her

---

8. Brueggemann, "At the Mercy of Babylon," 11.

iniquity has been pardoned, and that she has received from the LORD's hand double for all her sins (Isa 40:1–2). The proclamation of the prophet is a call to renew. It is also an invitation to a new beginning, a beginning that will remind the people of their redemption from Egypt. The end of Israel's exile is good news to the nations: "Declare this with cries of joy, proclaim it, carry it to the remotest parts of earth, say, 'Yahweh has redeemed his servant Jacob'" (Isa 48:20 NJB).

The restoration of Israel would also include a restoration of its mission in the world. Deutero-Isaiah announces that Yahweh is renewing the mission of Israel: "You are my servant, Israel, in whom I will be glorified" (Isa 49:3). The Servant is "the offspring of Abraham," Yahweh's friend (Isa 41:8). The mission of restored Israel is to be "a light to the nations" (Isa 49:6). Paul says, "This is God's ultimate purpose: Israel is destined to be a light unto the nations."[9] Israel was commissioned to be the light of the world so that Yahweh's "salvation may reach to the ends of the earth" (Isa 49:6). If after the people return to their homeland and if they are faithful to their call and their mission, then nations shall come to Israel's light (Isa 60:3). When that happens, many people will come to know Yahweh. Then, they will say, 'Let's go to the house of the God of Jacob" (Isa 2:3) and the nation will acknowledge that "The LORD is the true God! The LORD is the true God!" (1 Kgs 18:39 NET).

But Israel never became a light to the nations.[10] After Israel returned from Babylon, they remained under Persian control until their defeat by Alexander in 336 BCE. Ezra and Nehemiah tried to reform the social and religious life of the restored community. The covenant renewal ceremony was a day of confession and mourning (Neh 7:73—9:37). Nehemiah came to Jerusalem to rebuild the wall of the city. However, the leaders of the postexilic community were never able to bring the vision of Deutero-Isaiah to become a reality. With the rise of the Greeks and their efforts at Hellenization, the people of Israel faced a crisis of culture in which many people were attracted to Greek culture. When Antiochus Epiphanes tried to enforce Hellenism upon the Jewish Community, the Jews revolted under the Maccabees.

The pressures faced by the Jewish community under the Persians, the Greeks, and the Romans did not allow the postexilic community to become the nation of the Servant, a unique community elected by

---

9. Paul, *Isaiah 40–66*, 327.

10. McKnight, *Light Among the Nations*. See also Bird, *Crossing Over Sea and Land*.

Yahweh to become the light to the nations, a people through whom God's blessings would be bestowed to all in the name of Yahweh. The people who were a nation of priests were unable, or maybe unwilling, to become the servants of Yahweh, the bright light shining upon people who were walking in darkness (Isa 9:2).

Once again Israel failed in carrying out the mission they had received from Yahweh. Israel's redemptive mission to the nations had to wait for another day, a day when Yahweh would raise Israel again, a people who would be willing to become coworkers with God in the work of redemption of sinful humanity.

THE EMBODIMENT OF GOD IN THE OLD TESTAMENT

The act of God becoming a human being and having personal contact with other human beings (John 1:14 NLT) is a unique event in the history of Christianity.[11] However, the Old Testament gives witness to the embodiment of God.[12] There are two passages in the book of Genesis where God appears to the patriarchs in the form of a man (*'iš*). Esther Hamori calls these manifestations of God the "*'iš* theophany". The first manifestation of God in the form of a man was to Abraham: "Yahweh appeared to [Abraham]. . . . He looked up, and there he saw three men standing near him" (Gen 18:1–2 NJB). In this manifestation, Yahweh was accompanied by two other men, who later on leave to go to Sodom. After the men left, "Yahweh remained in Abraham's presence" (Gen 18:22 NJB). The majority of interpreters believe that the word *' iš* should be understood metaphorically. However, the word should be taken literally because when the men come to Abraham's tent, Abraham invited the men to his tent, he washed their feet, invited them to rest, and then he prepared a meal for them. Hamori says that the "*' iš* language in this text should be taken as literally as the language in other theophany texts."[13] The second appearance of God in the form of a man was to Jacob. The man wrestled with Jacob (Gen 32:23–33) all night until daybreak. When the man could not prevail against Jacob, the man changed Jacob's name to Israel. Then the

---

11. Clines, "God in Human Form," 24, says that "God's becoming man in Jesus Christ is of course a unique event . . . because nowhere else in human history has a human life expressed in its totality the reality of God."

12. Hamori, *When Gods Were Men*.

13. Hamori, *When Gods Were Men*, 10.

man explained the reason for the new name, "because you have fought with God and with men and have prevailed" (Gen 32:28 NET). The fact that the man says that Jacob fought with God indicates that the man with whom Jacob fought was God.[14] Jacob called the name of that place Peniel, and said "For I have seen God face to face" (Gen 32:30).

THE EMBODIMENT OF GOD IN THE NEW TESTAMENT

The people of Israel believed that there was only one God and his name was Yahweh, "I am Yahweh, that is my name" (Isa 42:8 NJB). Yahweh said about his name, "This is my name forever, the name by which I am to be remembered from generation to generation" (Exod 3:15 NIV). Although the people of Israel worshiped foreign gods, the prophets proclaimed that there is only one God: "I am Yahweh, and there is no other, there is no other God except me" (Isa 45:5 NJB). The basic confession of faith in Israel was the *Shema*, "Hear, O Israel! Our God is Yahweh, Yahweh alone."[15]

Hamori says that the Christian concept of incarnation is a natural outgrowth of the Israelite belief in the embodiment of God: "It is a picture of anthropomorphic realism to its fullest extent, encompassing the entire lifetime of a named character."[16] However, most traditions in Judaism have rejected the Christian doctrine of incarnation. Early Jewish writers viewed the Christian faith as unreasonable and the idea of the presence of God within the womb of a woman as illogical and outrageous.[17] Jewish incarnational theology declares that "God enters the world of humanity, that he appears at certain places and dwells in them which thereby become holy."[18] In Jewish thinking, God is present in God's Name, in the people of Israel, in the Torah, in the Tabernacle, and in the temple.

Wyschogrod, however, says that incarnation cannot be ruled out a priori. He writes that

---

14. Hamori, *When Gods Were Men*, 23.

15. In his study of the *Shema*, McBride, "Yoke of the Kingdom," 291, said that "no statement in the Hebrew Bible has provoked more discussion with less agreement than this one. McBride said (p. 274) that by New Testament times the text of the *Shema* had become "a living expression of allegiance to God's eternal kingdom." The translation of the words of the *Shema* is taken from McBride's translation. His article lists how English translation differ in the translation of the *Shema*.

16. Hamori, "Divine Embodiment in the Hebrew Bible," 181.

17. Goshen-Gottstein, "Judaisms and Incarnational Theologies," 220–21.

18. Wyschogrod, "Jewish Perspective on Incarnation," 204.

> the Jewish objection to an incarnational theology cannot be based on a priori grounds, as if something in the nature of the Jewish concept of God made his appearance in the form of humanity a rational impossibility. Very often, Jewish opposition to the incarnation is based on just such grounds without realization of the implications of such a posture. If we can determine a priori that God could not appear in the form of a man or, to put it in more Docetistic terms, that there could not be a being who is both fully God and fully human, then we are substituting a philosophical scheme for the sovereignty [sic] of God.[19]

The writers of the New Testament identify Jesus with the God of the Old Testament. Paul uses embodiment language when he refers to the humanity of God. Paul said that Christ who, being in the form of God, took the form of a servant, became as human beings are and became in every way like a human being (Phil 2:5–7 NJB).[20] John uses the language of incarnation to describe how God revealed himself in Christ: "In the beginning was the Word, and the Word was with God, and the Word was God.... And the Word became flesh and lived among us.... No one has ever seen God. It is God the only Son, who is close to the Father's heart, who has made him known" (John 1:1, 14, 18 NRSV). If the God whom Jesus revealed in the Gospels, if the God about whom Paul writes, if the God of the New Testament is the God of Israel, then Yahweh is the Triune God that the church proclaims.[21]

Goshen-Gottstein, writing from a Jewish perspective, seeks to understand the language of incarnation. He asks, what does it mean for a Christian to say that the incarnation took place? He presents four claims that Christians make when speaking about the incarnation.

First, the incarnation reveals God's love. Goshen-Gottstein writes that the

> underlying the theological statement that God took human form is a more fundamental statement of a relational nature: God loves. Because God loves, says the Christian, God sent God's son.... The incarnation for the Christian is the supreme expression of God's care for us, a care that finds expression

---

19. Wyschogrod, "Jewish Perspective on Incarnation," 204.

20. Clines, "God in Human Form," 24, says that the anthropomorphic language of the Old Testament, that is, the presentation of God in human terms "is part of the divine movement towards revealing himself in human form."

21. Soulen, "YHWH the Triune God," 25–54. Soulen speaks about the eternal identity of YHWH as Father, Son, and Holy Spirit (50).

through what might be taken to be the highest form of love, self-sacrifice.[22]

Second, the incarnation reveals the humility of God. Goshen-Gottstein writes, "For God to take human form is clearly an act of descent and limitation. . . . God's humility and love extend to the point that God is willing to suffer on our behalf."[23]

Third, the incarnation reveals the presence and closeness of God. Goshen-Gottstein writes, "God is present to us in the most real and concrete manner, as real as the contact with any human. . . . For the Christian, Jesus is not simply a sage, prophet, priest, wise man, miracle worker, etc. Jesus is—whatever that might mean—God."[24]

Fourth, the incarnation reveals God's care for the world. Goshen-Gottstein writes, "The incarnation is not only a statement about God. It is also a statement concerning the world and concerning human nature." Theologians have "related the incarnation to the meaning of existence and creation and, more particularly, to the value of humanity. . . . That God incarnates in human form says something about human life, indicating its enormous value, to the point that God can take human form for Godself."[25]

Notwithstanding these affirmations and claims by Christians, Goshen-Gottstein says that Judaism cannot accept the reality of the incarnation because of its concern in preserving the "boundaries between the human and God." He writes,

> In the various attempts I have made to explore the possibility of a shared language around the incarnation, one difference seems to remain. The Christian can point to Jesus and, with all the power of this idea, say, "*Ecce Deus*." The Jew does not seem to cross that line. The constellations of thought I have explored, as well as the thoughts of previous scholars, do not permit one to point to a human being and say that the person is God. One might say that the person is divine, but one would never say that the person is God. This, it seems to me, is a chasm over which it is hard to build a bridge.[26]

---

22. Goshen-Gottstein, "Judaisms and Incarnational Theologies," 223–24.
23. Goshen-Gottstein, "Judaisms and Incarnational Theologies," 224.
24. Goshen-Gottstein, "Judaisms and Incarnational Theologies," 224.
25. Goshen-Gottstein, "Judaisms and Incarnational Theologies," 224–25.
26. Goshen-Gottstein, "Judaisms and Incarnational Theologies," 242–43.

JESUS IS YAHWEH IN HUMAN FORM

Jason Staples says that the double use of the word "Lord" (κύριε κύριε) in Matt 7:21, 22; 25:11; and Luke 6:46 reflects the use of the divine names *yhwh ʾădōnāy* and *ʾădōnāy yhwh* in the Hebrew Bible. One example is found in the book of Psalms: "But You, Yahweh my Lord (*yhwh ʾădōnāy*), deal kindly with me because of Your name; deliver me because of the goodness of Your faithful love" (Ps 109:21 HCSB). The Greek version translates *yhwh ʾădōnāy* as κύριε κύριε (Ps 108:21). Another example is found in the book of Ezekiel: "The Lord Yahweh says this: I shall take the Israelites from the nations where they have gone. I shall gather them together from everywhere and bring them home to their own soil" (Ezek 37:21 NJB). The Septuagint translates *ʾădōnāy yhwh* as κύριος κύριος. Staples concludes that "the double κύριος formula outside the Gospels always serves as a distinctive way to represent the Tetragrammaton and that its use in Matthew and Luke is therefore best understood as a way to represent Jesus as applying the name of the God of Israel to himself."[27] Staples also says that the "blurring between the name of God and the name of Jesus is reminiscent of the Christ hymn of Phil 2, in which Jesus is "given the name above every other name" and that name is Yahweh.[28]

In his study of Christ in the Gospel of Mark, Geddert writes, "Mark's Gospel implies in numerous ways that Jesus is God, indeed is the embodiment of Yhwh."[29] He says that although there is no explicit Yahweh Christology in Mark, Geddert cites four key texts that reveal an implicit Yahweh Christology in Mark. In Mark 10:18 Jesus says that "No one is good but God alone." Geddert says that Jesus is not denying that he is good, he is implying that he is God. According to Geddert, "In Mark, Jesus is what only God can be, does what only God can do, and claims the allegiance that belongs only to the one true God."[30] In Mark 2:5 Jesus said to a paralyzed man, "your sins are forgiven." The teachers of the law accused Jesus of blasphemy because only God can forgive sins.[31]

In Mark 4:35–41 Jesus calmed the storm after the disciples asked Jesus for help. Geddert says that since God is the only one who has the power to command the wind and the waves, the disciples "did in fact cry

---

27. Staples, "'Lord, Lord': Jesus as YHWH," 19.
28. Staples, "'Lord, Lord': Jesus as YHWH," 15.
29. Geddert, "Implied Yhwh Christology," 325.
30. Geddert, "Implied Yhwh Christology," 329.
31. Geddert, "Implied Yhwh Christology," 329.

out to *Yhwh—by calling on Jesus' help.*"³² In Mark 6:45–52 the disciples "were utterly astounded" when they saw Jesus "walking on the sea (Mark 6:49). Geddert says, "What the disciples did not grasp was that Jesus was doing for them what Yhwh did in the OT when the people of God needed reassurances of God's presence."³³ The reason the disciples were utterly astounded is because it is Yahweh who walks on the sea: "He alone spreads out the sky and walks on the waves in the sea" (Job 9:8). To calm the disciples' fear, Jesus said, "Take heart, I am" (ἐγώ εἰμι Mark 6:50), the same "I AM" (ἐγώ εἰμι) of Exod 3:14. Geddert concludes that these four key texts and several others support the claim "that Mark is hinting at the true hidden identity of Jesus: He is Yhwh, bodily present on earth in the person of Jesus."³⁴

John Ronning, in his article "When YHWH Became Flesh and Dwelt Among Us," says that "when John says 'the Word became flesh' (1:14), he means for us to understand that YHWH became flesh, and that much of John's Gospel is taken up with showing us in the words and deeds of Jesus Christ, the words and deeds of YHWH in the Old Testament, who now accomplishes these words and deeds as a man."³⁵ Ronning bases his argument on the Targum's use of the title "Word" to refer to what Yahweh has said and done. John, however, uses the title "Word" to refer to God, Elohim, or Yahweh. He concludes that "'YHWH became flesh' is therefore an interpretation, or inference, of John 1:14, not a suggested translation."

To support the idea that John 1:14 should be understood as saying that Yahweh became flesh and dwelt among us, Ronning studies several texts in John's Gospel that shows that the words and deeds of Jesus Christ in the gospels, are the words and deeds of YHWH in the Old Testament. Among the many examples Ronning cites is Exod 33–34, a text dealing with the revelation of the glory of Yahweh to Moses on Mount Sinai.³⁶ Ronning points to a number of similarities between Exod 33–34 and John 1:14–18. John says that "God's unfailing love and faithfulness came through Jesus Christ" (John 1:17 NLT). Israel's credo says that Yahweh is "filled with unfailing love and faithfulness" (Exod 34:6 NLT).

---

32. Geddert, "Implied Yhwh Christology," 331.
33. Geddert, "Implied Yhwh Christology," 333.
34. Geddert, "Implied Yhwh Christology," 338.
35. Ronning, "When YHWH Became Flesh," 1.
36. Ronning, "When YHWH Became Flesh," 8.

THE FORMATION OF RENEWED ISRAEL

Jesus came into the world to embody God's work of reconciliation, as Paul said, "in Christ God was reconciling the world to himself" (2 Cor 5:19). The Greek word καταλλάσσω carries the idea of restoration of a relationship between individuals. In Christ, God was reestablishing a new relationship with human beings, a relationship which was broken because of the estrangement and alienation caused by sin and rebellion against the Creator. Beale says that Paul's view of reconciliation is based entirely on Isaiah's message of a new creation. He writes, "a general linkage is made between 'new creation' and 'reconciliation' in the sense that God's reconciliation of humanity in Christ has begun to reverse the alienation introduced at the Fall, and a return to the peaceful conditions of the original creation."[37]

Jesus As Israel

In order to bring salvation to the world and in order to be God's agent of reconciliation, Jesus had to establish a renewed Israel since all the families of the world had to be blessed through Abraham. This is the reason Matthew begins his genealogy by linking Jesus to Abraham and David, "An account of the genealogy of Jesus the Messiah, the son of David, the son of Abraham" (Matt 1:1). By beginning his genealogy with Abraham, Matthew identifies Jesus as a true Israelite and as the one who will fulfill Yahweh's promise to Abraham that through him all the families of the earth would be blessed. By identifying Jesus as the son of David, Matthew links Jesus to the Messianic hope of the Old Testament and the prophetic hope of a new David, "On that day, says the LORD of hosts, . . . [Israel] shall serve the LORD their God and David their king, whom I will raise up for them" (Jer 30:8–9). Kynes says that the many Old Testament references in Matt 1–2 is an introduction "to the history of Israel as a whole."[38] In order for Jesus to become "a light to the nations" so that God's salvation may reach to the end of the earth (Isa 49:6), Jesus had to fulfill the destiny of Israel and of the Servant: "You are my servant, Israel, in whom I will be glorified" (Isa 49:3). The Gospels make several references to the Old Testament, linking Jesus to Israel and to the Servant.

37. Beale, "Old Testament Background of Reconciliation," 554. See also Hafemann, "Paul's Use of the Old Testament," 246–57.

38. Kynes, *Christology of Solidarity*, 20.

Jesus's Return from Egypt

Matthew related the return of Jesus from Egypt with Israel's exodus from Egypt, "Out of Egypt I have called my son" (Matt 2:15). The exodus from Egypt is repeated and fulfilled in Jesus.[39] The reference to Egypt in Hos 11:1 is very significant. Scholars associate the return from Egypt with the second exodus in Isa 40–55. This association, however, may not be correct. The second exodus cannot begin until Jesus takes upon himself the mission of the Servant. The reference to the return from Egypt in Matthew is designed to identify Jesus with Israel. Both Israel and Jesus began their work of reconciliation after they left Egypt. Because Israel is Yahweh's firstborn son (Exod 4:22), Matthew puts "Jesus in the place of Israel as he assumes the filial relationship with God once predicated of the nation."[40] "This is my Son" (Matt 3:17). In addition, the reference to Egypt will serve as a background for Jesus being led into the wilderness and to the temptation narrative.

Jesus in the Wilderness

Jesus began his ministry after he was baptized by John in the Jordan River (Matts 3:13). When Jesus came up from the water, a voice from heaven said, "This is my Son, whom I love" (Matt 3:17 NIV). The words from heaven is an indirect reference to the call of the Servant in Isa 42:1. The full reference to the call of the Servant is found in Matt 12:8 "Here is my servant, whom I have chosen, my beloved, with whom my soul is well pleased." Jesus's baptism in the waters of the Jordan is reminiscent of the people of Israel going through the sea after they came out of Egypt (Exod 14:22). Paul associates baptism with the Israelites going through the sea. Paul said, "our ancestors were all under the cloud, and all passed through the sea, and all were baptized into Moses in the cloud and in the sea" (1 Cor 10:1–2).[41] Thus, when Jesus came out of Egypt, he went "through the sea" just like Israel did.

After Jesus went "through the sea," he was led by the Spirit into the wilderness. The parallels between the experience of Israel in the

---

39. Luz, *Matthew 1–7*, 121.

40. Luz, *Matthew 1–7*, 121.

41. Wright, "New Exodus, New Inheritance," 28 says that when "Paul speaks of baptism in Romans 6 he has in mind the crossing of the Red Sea at the Exodus."

wilderness and the experience of Jesus in the wilderness demonstrate that Jesus is reliving the experience of Israel. Where Israel failed, Jesus as the faithful Israelite does not fail. Jesus spent forty days and forty nights in the wilderness, symbolic of the forty years Israel spent in the wilderness where they were tested by Yahweh, "I will test them" (Exod 16:4). The testing of Jesus in the wilderness is also symbolic of the testing of Israel. However, where Israel disobeyed God, Jesus did not fail the test. In the wilderness Israel was hungry and they ate "bread from heaven." In the wilderness Jesus was hungry but he refused to eat by saying that "one does not live by bread alone" (Matt 4:4).

In the wilderness Jesus was tested when he was asked to throw himself down from the highest point of the temple and trust that God would deliver and protect him. Jesus answered, "Do not put the Lord your God to the test" (Matt 4:7). Jesus's unwillingness to put God to the test contrasts with Israel's attitude, for in the wilderness they tested Yahweh ten times and they did not obey his voice (Num 14:22). In the wilderness, the devil promised to give Jesus all the kingdoms of the world "if you will bow down and worship me" (Matt 4:9). Jesus responded by saying, "Worship the Lord your God, and serve only him" (Matt 4:10). Jesus's refusal to worship the devil contrasts with Israel's worship of the golden calf in the wilderness (Exod 32:1–6).

JESUS AS THE SERVANT OF YAHWEH

God's work of reconciliation would be accomplished in the world by restored Israel. Deutero-Isaiah speaks about the Servant of Yahweh who has a mission to the nations, "I will give you as a light to the nations, that my salvation may reach to the ends of the earth" (Isa 49:6). According to Goldingay, the Servant is "the embodiment of Israel." The Servant "acts as Israel only in order to enable Israel itself to be Israel."[42] The Servant has a mission to Israel. Yahweh called the Servant "to bring Jacob back to him" (Isa 49:5). Yahweh wants to restore Israel so that Israel can fulfill its mission in the world. But the mission of the Servant goes beyond restoring Israel; the Servant has a universal mission, "You will do more than restore the people of Israel to me. I will make you a light to the Gentiles, and you will bring my salvation to the ends of the earth" (Isa 49:6 NLT).

---

42. Goldingay, *Message of Isaiah 40–55*, 371.

The New Testament uses the Servant motif to identify Jesus and his mission in the world. Zechariah says that the birth of Jesus would be evidence that God "has remembered his holy covenant, the oath that he swore to our ancestor Abraham" (Luke 1:72–73). He said that Jesus would "give light to those who sit in darkness and in the shadow of death" (Luke 1:79). Simeon said that Jesus will be "a light for revelation to the Gentiles" (Luke 2:32). As the Servant, Jesus has a mission to Israel, to restore Israel in order for the nation to fulfill its destiny as the people of God and fulfil God's promise to Abraham, that his descendants would proclaim God's salvation to all nations, so that people might be blessed through them.

In her study of the Servant motif in Luke-Acts, Holly Beers says that Luke applies the Servant motif to Jesus as the ultimate fulfillment of the Servant mission to Israel. She also says that Jesus's disciples also embody aspects of the Servant's character and mission. The Servant is the human agent of the new exodus.[43] At his baptism, Jesus was anointed with the Spirit for his mission. At Pentecost, the disciples were anointed with the Spirit for their mission as servants. Jesus said, "I am the light of the world" (John 9:5). Jesus said to his disciples, "You are the light of the world" (Matt 5:14). Beers says that Jesus was "anointed with the Spirit as the servant at his baptism." As the Servant, Jesus was "baptized as/for Israel."[44] Jesus was anointed by the Spirit for his mission in the world.

After his resurrection, Jesus expands his mission to the gentiles: "Repentance and forgiveness of sins is to be proclaimed in his name to all nations, beginning from Jerusalem" (Luke 24:47). After the resurrection Jesus reaffirms the universality of his mission to his disciples, "But you will receive power when the Holy Spirit has come upon you; and you will be my witnesses in Jerusalem, in all Judea and Samaria, and to the ends of the earth" (Acts 1:8). There are several allusions to the mission of the Servant in Jesus's commission to his disciples. According to Isaiah, the people of Israel are witnesses and servants of God (Isa 43:10, 12; 44:8). The Servant's mission was to bring God's salvation "to the ends of the earth" (Isa 49:6).[45]

---

43. Beers, *Followers of Jesus as the 'Servant,'* 85.
44. Beers, *Followers of Jesus as the 'Servant,'* 102.
45. Moore, "'To the End of the Earth,'" 389–99.

THE FORMATION OF THE NEW ISRAEL

The Servant Songs in Isa 40–55 commissioned Israel to be a light to the nations, but instead of becoming a missionary nation, Israel failed in fulfilling its mission; it became involved with itself, trying to survive Hellenization, rather than establishing an outreach to the gentile world. Israel failed to carry out the mission Yahweh assigned to the Servant. Jesus took upon himself to fulfill the mission of the Servant by forming a new Israel and by delegating the mission of the Servant to his disciples.

The view that Jesus was forming a new Israel does not mean this view represents supersessionism. Rather, it is a reaffirmation of the promise that Yahweh made to Abraham that, in him and through Israel, all the nations shall be blessed. The Hebrew name of Jesus is Yeshua. The name means "Yahweh saves." Jesus came to save Israel. When the angel appeared to Joseph, the angel said, "She will bear a son, and you are to name him Jesus, for he will save his people from their sins" (Matt 1:21). By his people, Matthew means Israel, "As it does through the Gospel of Matthew, 'people' (λάος) here means the OT people of God, Israel."[46]

After the forty days in the wilderness, Jesus called twelve men[47] to become representatives of the twelve tribes of Israel. In the Gospels, the twelve "stand representatively for renewed Israel, being prepared for its mission to the whole world."[48] McKnight says that the selection of the twelve evokes the theme of covenant renewal and eschatological restoration, "the choice of twelve was symbolic but had only one motive: to inaugurate the restoration and reunification of the twelve tribes as promised in ancient Jewish traditions."[49]

Jesus came to restore the mission of the Servant to a "Renewed Israel." Jesus sent his disciples on a mission to the people of Israel announcing the presence of the kingdom of God, a reference to the renewal of the people.[50] Jesus told his disciples, "Go nowhere among the Gentiles, and enter no town of the Samaritans, but go rather to the lost sheep of the house of Israel. As you go, proclaim the good news" (Matt 10:5–7). Jesus's mission was to Israel. McKnight says that "Jesus had no mission to

---

46. Luz, *Matthew 1–7*, 95.

47. The names of the twelve disciples are listed in Mark 3:16–19 ; Matt 10:2–4; Luke 6:14–16; and Acts 1:13.

48. Geddert, "Implied Yhwh Christology," 335.

49. McKnight, "Jesus and the Twelve," 212.

50. Horsley, *Jesus and Magic*, 111.

the Gentiles; his mission was directed toward Israel because his mission was about the restoration of Israel as it realized its covenant expectations and hopes."[51]

The New Testament shows that many of the early Christians were Jews (Israelites): "The word of God continued to spread; the number of the disciples increased greatly in Jerusalem, and a great many of the priests became obedient to the faith" (Acts 6:7). This group of Jewish believers in Christ is "Renewed Israel." When the Jews failed to reach out to the gentiles and there was a parting of the ways,[52] God grafted gentiles into Renewed Israel: "But if some of the branches were broken off, and you, a wild olive shoot, were grafted in their place to share the rich root of the olive tree, do not boast over the branches. If you do boast, remember that it is not you that support the root, but the root that supports you" (Rom 11:17–18). Paul says that Israel's "rejection [of the Messiah] is the reconciliation of the world" (Rom 11:15). McKnight says that "Israel's rejection means gentile inclusion, and gentile inclusion means eventual Israelite fullness—peace now by including gentiles, and peace later by including all Israel."[53] The tree is Israel. Gentiles have been grafted into the tree. As Paul said, "For not all Israelites truly belong to Israel" (Rom 9:6). This means that in Christ God is reconciling the world unto himself through this Renewed Israel, "the Israel of God" (Gal 6:16).[54] Paul says

51. McKnight, "Jesus and the Twelve," 224.
52. Dunn, *Partings of the Ways*.
53. McKnight, *Reading Romans Backward*, 82–83.
54. Second Isaiah is popularly known as a prophet of universalism. The universalism of Deutero-Isaiah is expressed in his openness to include gentiles into the worship of Yahweh. During Israel's exile in Babylon, some people feared that they would be extinct as a nation. In his discussion of Isa 44:1–5, Blenkinsopp, *Isaiah* 40–55, 233, says that the words "Fear not" in Isaiah 44:2 reveal the people's fear of national extinction, a fear expressed by the metaphors of "thirsty land" and "dry ground." Yahweh promises that Israel will not cease to exist. The renewal of Israel will occur when Yahweh pours his spirit on the descendants of Israel and bestows his blessing upon future Israelites. According to Blenkinsopp, the reference to blessing "inevitably brings to mind the demographic blessing pronounced over Abraham." Deutero-Isaiah mentions several people who will worship Yahweh (Isa 44:5), people whom Blenkinsopp calls "the future people of Israel." According to Blenkinsopp, these "future people of Israel" are proselytes, "the foreigners who join themselves to the LORD, to minister to him, to love the name of the LORD, and to be his servants" (Isaiah 56:6). According to the prophet, this group of people, the "future people of Israel," adopted for themselves "the name of Israel" (Isaiah 44:5). The disciples whom Jesus called to become the new Israel together with the foreigners who join themselves to Yahweh, to minister to him, to love his name, and to be his servants are the renewed Israel, "the Israel of God." See

that Christ died on the cross "that he might create in himself one new humanity in place of the two [Jews and Gentiles], thus making peace, and might reconcile both groups to God in one body through the cross" (Eph 2:13–16). James Dunn says that "the Israel of God's purpose" consists of Jews and gentiles. Drawing from Paul's statement in Eph 2:15, Dunn says that Jews and gentiles "have been recreated in the Israelite of God's purpose."[55]

---

also Blenkinsopp, "Second Isaiah-Prophet of Universalism," 83–103.

55. Dunn, *Partings of the Ways*, 148–49. On the "Israel of God," see Torrance, "Israel of God," 66–77.

24

The Warrior God and His Death on the Cross

RECONCILIATION IS COSTLY TO GOD. "God was in Christ, reconciling the world unto himself" (2 Cor 5:19), but in order to accomplish reconciliation between God and humans, God in human form had to die on the cross. As Paul writes, "For in him [Christ] the complete being of God, by God's own choice, came to dwell. Through him God chose to reconcile the whole universe to himself, making peace through the shedding of his blood upon the cross" (Col 1:19–20 NEB).

THE THEOLOGY OF RECONCILIATION

The Hebrew word for reconciliation is *kāpar*.[1] The basic meaning of the word is "to make an atonement." The people of Israel were required to make atonement wherever a person had unintentionally sinned against Yahweh, "When anyone sins unintentionally in any of the LORD's commandments about things not to be done, and does any one of them" (Lev 4:2). The animal for the atonement sacrifice must be offered on the altar which is "before the LORD" (Lev 4:6). The purpose of the atonement

---

1. Two other Hebrew words are translated "reconcile" in our English Bibles. The word *rāṣâ* is translated "reconcile" in 1 Sam 29:4 in the NRSV and the KJV. The Hebrew word means "be pleased with, be favorable, to find favor." The NIV translated the word as "regain [his master's] favor." The word *ḥāṭā'* is translated "reconciliation" in 2 Chr 29:24 in the KJV. However, the word is derived from a Hebrew word which means "sin." The NRSV translates the word as "made a sin offering."

was "to reestablish a destroyed relationship with God."[2] The shedding of the blood was an important element in the ritual of atonement: "For the life of the flesh is in the blood; and I have given it to you for making atonement for your lives on the altar; for, as life, it is the blood that makes atonement" (Lev 17:11).

Atonement is an act of God. The psalmist said, "When all manner of sins overwhelm me, you atone our iniquities" (Ps 65:3). Yahweh atones for the people's sins because he is a God merciful and gracious (Exod 34:6). When the psalmist was remembering the sins of Israel in the wilderness, he said, "He was compassionate; He atoned for their guilt and did not destroy them" (Ps 78:38). In these two psalms, most English Bibles translate *kāpar* as "forgive." Reconciliation is what God does in order to restore the fellowship between himself and humanity, a relationship that was broken because of human rebellion.

THE HUMILIATION OF GOD

The biblical text shows that Yahweh has been in the work of reconciliation since the time the first pair rebelled against him. However, because of human rebellion, his work of reconciliation did not accomplish what Yahweh wanted to accomplish. Cain killed his brother notwithstanding Yahweh's effort to help him (Gen 4:6–7). Lamech killed a man in an act of vengeance because the man hit him (Gen 4:23).[3] In the days of Noah, the earth was full of violence and human wickedness; no one turned to God except Noah and his family. After the flood, humans once again rebelled against God by building a tower in defiance of God's command to fill the earth. God had to punish them by confusing their language and by scattering them throughout the earth (Gen 11:7–8).

God's work of reconciliation had some success. In the days of Seth "people began to worship the LORD" (Gen 4:26 NET). After the flood, the nations grew in number and were spread over the earth (Gen 10:32). The work of reconciliation became more difficult. In order to reach the nations and bring them to himself, Yahweh called Abraham and promised him that people all over the earth would be blessed through him

---

2. Maass, "*kpr* to atone," 810.
3. Lamech mentions "a man" and "a young man." The text does not say whether these are two people, or a father and a son, or whether they are the same person.

(Gen 12:3). Abraham would become the father of a nation which would become Yahweh's agents of reconciliation in the world.

Israel was to become God's special people in the world. God redeemed Israel from their oppressive situation in Egypt and brought them to Mount Sinai to establish a covenant with them and to clarify Israel's mission in the world. Yahweh said:

> You have seen what I did to the Egyptians, and how I bore you on eagles' wings and brought you to myself. Now therefore, if you obey my voice and keep my covenant, you shall be my treasured possession out of all the peoples. Indeed, the whole earth is mine, but you shall be for me a priestly kingdom and a holy nation. (Exod 19:4–6)

The success of Israel as God's special people depended on Israel's obedience, "if you obey my voice and keep my covenant." When God established his covenant with Israel, God gave them commandments and laws by which Israel would show the nations they were a special nation; they were the people of Yahweh. Among the commandments Yahweh gave to Israel, two were crucial in distinguishing Israel from the other nations. Yahweh said, "you shall have no other gods before me (Exod 20:3). Israel was to repudiate all other gods and serve Yahweh only. The second command was about idols. Yahweh said, "You shall not make for yourself an idol, . . . You shall not bow down to them or worship them" (Exod 20:4–5). Israel would be the only nation in the ancient Near East that would worship a god without the use of images. The worship of other gods was a rejection of Yahweh. Yahweh gave the people the reason for this prohibition, "for I the LORD your God am a jealous God, punishing children for the iniquity of parents, to the third and the fourth generation of those who reject me" (Exod 20:5).

Israel turned out to be a big disappointment as God's partners in the work of reconciliation. While Israel was still at Mount Sinai, the people built a golden calf. They worshiped the image by sacrificing burnt offerings and by presenting fellowship offerings to it. They dishonored Yahweh by eating and drinking and indulging in a festival dedicated to the image (Exod 32:6). Yahweh was angry at Israel. He told Moses to leave him alone so that his wrath might burn hot against them and that he might consume them (Exod 32:10). In the wilderness, Israel tested Yahweh ten times by rebelling against him and by not obeying him (Num 14:22). As a demonstration of their disloyalty against Yahweh, while they were still in the wilderness, "the people began to have sexual relations with the women of Moab." They sacrificed, ate, and bowed down to their gods. There, "Israel yoked itself to the Baal of Peor" (Num 25:1–3). Once again, Yahweh was angry and disappointed with his people.

The failure of Israel continued after they entered the promised land. From the days of the judges and throughout the period of the united and the divided monarchy the people rebelled against Yahweh by worshiping Baal and Asherah, by sacrificing in the high places, by burning their children to Molech, by practicing augury, and by promoting sexual depravity. Several times God's expressed his frustration with the people's unfaithfulness, "Why have they provoked me to anger with their images, with their foreign idols?" (Jer 8:19). "Why then has this people turned away in perpetual backsliding?" (Jer 8:5). These "why" questions "seem to imply a genuine loss on God's part as to what might explain the faithlessness of the people."[4] So disappointed was Yahweh with Israel that he wept and wanted to abandon them, "O that my head were a spring of water, and my eyes a fountain of tears, so that I might weep day and night for the slain of my poor people! O that I had in the desert a traveler's lodging place, that I might leave my people and go away from them! For they are all adulterers, a band of traitors" (Jer 9:1–2).

Over the years Yahweh warned both Israel and Judah through his servants the prophets. Yahweh called his people to repent, "Turn from your evil ways and keep my commandments and my statutes, in accordance with all the law that I commanded your ancestors." The people rejected the prophets's call to repentance, "They would not listen but were stubborn, as their ancestors had been" (2 Kgs 17:13–14). Because of the stubbornness of the people, Yahweh sent Israel and Judah into exile.

Before the people went into exile, Yahweh took Ezekiel in a vision to the temple in Jerusalem where he showed the prophet all the abominations the people were committing that provoked him to anger (Ezek 8:17–18). In the temple there was the idol that provoked God's anger. Carved on the walls of the temple were engravings of reptile and repulsive animals. Women were weeping for Tammuz, and the men were worshiping the rising sun. These abominations provoked Yahweh to anger. Yahweh's words to the prophet reveal "YHWH's frustration with a

---

4. Fretheim, *Suffering of God*, 56.

population that purportedly has turned to foreign worship and corrupted the temple."⁵

The people's violation of the sanctity of the temple prompted Yahweh to leave the temple, the place in which Yahweh chose to put his name and live among his people (Deut 12:5). Yahweh abandoned the temple by stages. First, Yahweh went from the holy place to the threshold of the temple (Ezek 9:3); from the threshold of the temple he went to the entrance of the east gate of the temple (Ezek 10:18–19); from the east gate of the temple, Yahweh went over the city to the mount of Olives, the mountain on the east side of the city (Ezek 11:23). From there Yahweh went into exile with his people. In exile the people would be deprived of the temple. Yahweh promised that for a brief period of time, as long as they were in Babylon, he would be a sanctuary for the people (Ezek 11:16).

The exile was a reversal of the exodus from Egypt. But in exile, Yahweh promises a new exodus in which the people would return to their land and renew their mission in the world, "You are my servant, Israel, in whom I will be glorified. . . . I will give you as a light to the nations, that my salvation may reach to the end of the earth" (Isa 49:3, 6). The liberation of Israel would be through Cyrus of whom Yahweh said, "He is my shepherd, and he shall carry out all my purpose" (Isa 44:28). However, a group of "spiritually obtuse" people complained against Yahweh for selecting the Persian king Cyrus as his servant and as his anointed one to become his chosen instrument for the deliverance of Israel. Blenkinsopp summarizes the prophet's argument, "Yahveh cannot be called to account for choosing Cyrus."⁶

To Deutero-Isaiah, the restoration of Israel and its return to its native land would be the salvation of Israel and of the nations. The failure of Israel to become a light to the nations and to be God's agents of reconciliation thwarted God's plan of bringing his message of salvation to all peoples and to all nations. According to Deutero-Isaiah, that is God's desire for all nations, "Turn to me and be saved, all the ends of the earth! For I am God, and there is no other" (Isa 45:22). There was an urgency; the nations wanted God: "My righteousness is near. My salvation is on the way. I will bring justice to people. The coastlands put their hope in me, and they wait eagerly for me" (Isa 51:5 GWN). Although Israel failed, God would still accomplish his purpose: "My purpose shall stand, and I

---

5. Sweeney, *Reading Ezekiel*, 59.
6. Blenkinsopp, *Isaiah 40–55*, 250–55.

will fulfill my intention" (Isa 46:10). "I have spoken, and I will bring it to pass; I have planned, and I will do it" (Isa 46:11). "I will do it." Because of the failure of Israel, God made a decision to do the work himself. He made a decision that only God could make: God decided to live among humans and select a group of special people who would carry out his work of reconciliation.[7]

THE HUMILIATION OF CHRIST

One of the most important Christological declarations in the New Testament is Paul's statement in Phil 2:5–11 about the humiliation and the exaltation of Jesus. This text has received much attention by New Testament scholars and some of the conclusions about the meaning of the text continue to be debated. Paul says that Jesus "was in the form of God." According to McClain, "to say that Christ Jesus was 'existing in the form of God' is to affirm that He was very God manifesting Himself in some external form through which he could be known."[8] The statement that Jesus "did not regard equality with God as something to be exploited" is a reference to Jesus's divine nature.

The humiliation of Jesus was self-imposed; he "emptied himself." The humiliation of Jesus is reflected in the statement that although he was in the form of God, he humbled himself by taking the form of a slave. Some translations use the word "servant" (KJV, NIV) to identify Jesus with the Servant in Isa 40–55. Other translations use the word "slave" (NRSV, NJB) to reflect the social world of the New Testament. Slaves had the lowest legal rank in the Roman world. The word "slave" was "a term of extreme abasement."[9]

---

7. McKnight, *King Jesus Gospel*, 35, summarizes the reason God's redemptive wok in the world was not successful and the reason God sent his Son: "God chose one person, Abraham, and then through him one people, Israel, and then later the Church, to be God's priests and rulers in this world on God's behalf. What Adam was to do in the garden—that is, to govern this world redemptively on God's behalf—is the mission God gives to Israel. Like Adam, Israel failed, and so did its kings. So God sent his Son to do what Adam and Israel and the kings did not (and evidently could not) do and to rescue everyone from their sins and systemic evil."

8. McClain, "Doctrine of the Kenosis," 90.

9. Hellerman et al., *Philippians*, 115.

Paul says that he who had the form of God assumed human form.[10] He who created all things (John 1:3) assumed a human body and became a man. Paul also emphasizes the embodiment of God, "And without controversy great is the mystery of godliness: God was manifest in the flesh" (1 Tim 3:16 KJV).[11] According to Paul, God in the person of Jesus became a man in order to identify with humans. As a human being, Jesus humbled himself and became obedient to the point of death, death on a cross.

Jesus was publicly humiliated: he was forsaken and ridiculed by the crowd, people spat in his face, some struck him on the head, and others slapped him. He was flogged, nailed on the cross, and endured execution on the cross as a criminal. In the Roman world, crucifixion was a "ritual designed publicly to shame the crucified individual and all who would associate with him."[12] The disciples of Christ carried the stigma of being the followers of a crucified God.

Because of Jesus's humiliation, God "also highly exalted him and gave him the name that is above every name so that at the name of Jesus every knee should bend, in heaven and on earth and under the earth, and every tongue should confess that Jesus Christ is Lord, to the glory of God the Father" (Phil 2:9–11). The Greek word κύριος, "Lord," is used in the Greek translation of the Old Testament (Septuagint) for the divine name Yahweh. Paul says that every knee shall bow before Jesus and that every tongue shall confess that he is Lord, thus identifying Jesus with what Isaiah said about Yahweh: "To me every knee shall bow, every tongue shall swear" (Isa 45:23). What God began in Eden, his work of reconciliation, finds its highest point in the death of Jesus on the cross. Since reconciliation requires atonement, on the cross God was in Christ, "reconciling the world to himself" (2 Cor 5:19).

The reason Jesus took the form of a slave and became human can be explained from Jesus's parable of the wicked tenants (Matt 21:33–44). The parable is based on the Song of the Vineyard in which the prophet Isaiah describes Yahweh's disappointment with the house of Israel and the people of Judah (Isa 5:1–7). In the song, Isaiah says that Yahweh planted a vineyard, cared for it, and in the end, the vineyard produced undesirable wild grapes. Yahweh's statement, "What more was there to

---

10. Barth, *Humanity of God*, 49, says that "It is when we look at Jesus Christ that we know decisively that God's deity does not exclude, but includes His *humanity.*"

11. The Greek text reads "Who"; other ancient texts read "God."

12. Hellerman et al., *Philippians*, 117.

do for my vineyard that I have not done in it?" (Isa 5:4), reflects Yahweh's frustration with the failure of his people.

In Jesus's parable, the landowner sends his servants to the tenants to collect his fruit, but the tenants seized his servants and mistreated them. Finally, the landowner sent his son to them but instead of respecting the son, the tenants "took him and threw him out of the vineyard and killed him" (Matt 21:39). The mistreatment of the servants is a reference to Israel's rejection of the prophets. J. Lyle Story says that the abuse and rejection of the prophets and the shameful murder of the son "all portray the tragic and bitter history of the people of God."[13]

The difference between the Song of the Vineyard in Isaiah and the parable of the wicked tenants in Matthew is that Isaiah said that the owner of the vineyard (Yahweh) expected good fruit, but the vineyard produced sour grapes. In Matthew, the tenants refused to give the fruit of the vineyard to the owner of the vineyard. For this reason, Jesus said to the religious leaders of Jerusalem that the kingdom of God will be taken from them "and given to a people who will produce its fruit" (Matt 21:43).

A popular interpretation of Jesus's statement is that the kingdom will be taken away from the Jewish people and given to the church. However, David Turner says that a better understanding of Jesus's words is that "the kingdom is to be taken away from the disobedient religious leaders and given to the twelve disciples who will lead Jesus's church."[14] The twelve disciples, the renewed Israel, will carry the message of reconciliation, first to the Jews in Jerusalem, then to those in all Judea and Samaria, and finally to all nations of the world (Acts 1:8).

THE NEW COVENANT

In Jer 31:31–34 God promised to make a new covenant[15] with the house of Israel and the house of Judah because they had violated the covenant by their rebellion against God and by their worshiping other gods. According to Jeremiah, the new covenant would be different from the one

---

13. Story, "Hope in the Midst of Tragedy," 191.

14. Turner, *Matthew*, 516.

15. The expression "new covenant" appears in Jer 31:31; Luke 22:20; 1 Cor 11:25; 2 Cor 3:6; Heb 8:8, 13; 9:15; 12:24.

God established with Israel on Mount Sinai.[16] The uniqueness of this new covenant is that it is not a renewal or an expansion of the Mosaic covenant. Lundbom says that the new covenant announced by Jeremiah, although having some "admitted continuity with the Sinai covenant, it will still be a genuinely new covenant, one that marks a new beginning in the divine-human relationship."[17] Jeremiah emphasizes four distinctive aspects of the new covenant.

First, the new covenant is unique because the law of God, his *torah*, will be written in the human heart: "I will put my law within them, and I will write it on their hearts" (v. 33). Jeremiah says that the human heart is deceitful, corrupt, and depraved (Jer 17:9). However, God promises to remove the evil heart and give the people who will live under the new covenant, a new heart and a new spirit, a heart of compassion, a heart that will be ready to respond to God's word and enable them to live by his laws, and obey his commandments (Ezek 11:19; 36:26–27). Second, the new covenant will establish a new relationship between the people and God: "I will be their God, and they shall be my people" (v. 33). Third, the new covenant will allow people to know the true character of God, "they shall all know me" (v. 34). The people of Israel rebelled against God because they did not know him (Hos 4:6). Fourth, the new covenant is grounded on divine grace, "I will forgive their iniquity" (v. 34; see Exod 34:6–7).

When Jesus met with his disciples to celebrate the Passover, he told them about his coming death. Jesus uses this occasion to associate the Passover meal with the covenant-making ceremony. He interprets his ministry and his death as the fulfillment of Jeremiah's prophecy of the new covenant. Jesus "took a loaf of bread, and when he had given thanks, he broke it and gave it to them, saying, 'This is my body, which is given for you'" (Luke 22:19). Then he took the cup and said to them, "This cup that is poured out for you is the new covenant in my blood" (Luke 22:20). The shedding of blood was used in the ratification of the covenant between God and Israel, "Moses took the blood and dashed it on the people, and said, 'See the blood of the covenant that the LORD has made with you'" (Exod 24:8). By associating the shedding of his blood with the new covenant, Jesus is telling his disciples that the ratification of the new covenant will be done by his own death. The author of the book of

---

16. The author of the book of Hebrews calls the Mosaic covenant "the first covenant" (Heb 9:15).

17. Lundbom, *Jeremiah 21–36*, 466.

Hebrews says that Jesus is the mediator of the new covenant (Heb 9:15). He is also the guarantor of the covenant (Heb 7:22). The new covenant is a better covenant because it "has been enacted through better promises" (Heb 8:6).

George Law,[18] adopting the groundbreaking studies of George Mendenhall[19] and Dennis McCarthy[20] dealing with covenants in Israel and the ancient Near East, says that the form of the covenant God established on Mount Sinai is used by Matthew in his presentation of the Sermon on the Mount. According to Mendenhall, in the ancient world covenants regulated relationships between individuals, social groups, and political units. Covenants generally included oaths which bound the parties to the covenant and stipulations which detailed the expected behavior of those united by the covenant.[21] William Shea finds the form of the covenant in the letters to the seven churches in Rev 2–3.[22] Law applies the covenant formulary used by Mendenhall in his study of Hittite suzerainty treaties in his analysis of the Sermon on the Mount. According to Law, this is the form Matthew uses to introduce Jesus's sermon: (1) Preamble: (5:1–2); (2) Prologue: [Beatitudes]—benefits of the law-code (5:3–16); (3) Covenant Stipulations (5:17—7:12); (a) General–Christ's Ten Commandments (5:17—6:34); (b) Specific (7:1–12); (4) Covenant Sanctions (7:13–23); (5) Epilogue: Personal Ratification (7:24–27).

At the beginning of the Sermon on the Mount, Jesus "went up the mountain" (Matt 5:1)[23] to give his disciples what would be the expectation for his followers in the future. The content of the Sermon on the Mount is what Paul probably meant when he referred to "the law of Christ" (Gal 6:2). Glen Stassen called the teaching of Christ on the Sermon on the Mount "Kingdom Ethics."[24]

---

18. Law, "Form of the New Covenant in Matthew," 17–32.
19. Mendenhall, *Law and Covenant in Israel*.
20. McCarthy, *Treaty and Covenant*.
21. Mendenhall, "Covenant," 1714–23.
22. Shea, "Covenant Form," 71–84.
23. When Yahweh established his covenant with Israel, Moses went up the mountain to receive the commandments from God (Exod 19:3).
24. Stassen and Gushee, *Kingdom Ethics*; see also Gushee and Norred, "Kingdom of God," 3–16.

THE ETHICS OF THE KINGDOM

The teaching of Jesus in the Sermon on the Mount gives Christians ethical principles to conduct their lives and build character worthy of citizens of the kingdom of God.[25] The teachings of Jesus are based on the teachings of the law and the prophets. "There is an essential continuity of the teaching and mission of Jesus with the redemptive ethical intent of the Hebrew Bible."[26]

Jesus did not come to abolish the law; he came to fulfill it. Jesus said, "Do not think that I have come to abolish the law or the prophets; I have come not to abolish but to fulfill. For truly I tell you, until heaven and earth pass away, not one letter, not one stroke of a letter, will pass from the law until all is accomplished" (Matt 5:17–18). Barth says that Jesus Christ "is in His Person the covenant in its fulness."[27] Jesus did not come to abolish the law and the prophets because their goal was to help the people of Israel to love God and to love one another. Jesus's teaching was focused on love for God and love for others. Twice more Jesus said that his teaching was based on the law and the prophets. The so-called Golden Rule, "In everything do to others as you would have them do to you" (Matt 7:12), is based on the teachings of the law and the prophets. When Jesus was asked which commandment in the law was greatest, he responded, "You shall love the Lord your God with all your heart, and with all your soul, and with all your mind. This is the greatest and first commandment. And a second is like it: 'You shall love your neighbor as yourself.' On these two commandments hang all the law and the prophets" (Matt 22:37–40).

The commandment to love God comes from the *Shema*, a text that commands Israel to worship only one God: "Hear, O Israel: The LORD is our God, the LORD alone. You shall love the LORD your God with all your heart, and with all your soul, and with all your might" (Deut 6:4–5). The commandment to love God with all the strength "implies the devotion of the will to the fulfilment of the purposes of God."[28] The commandment to love your neighbor comes from Lev 19:18: "you shall love

---

25. According to Lohfink, "Unmasking of Violence in Israel," 106, "Hope for the world lies in a Christian community that lives in accord with the Sermon on the Mount."

26. Turner, *Matthew*, 157.

27. Barth, *Humanity of God*, 47.

28. Spencer, "Christian Moral Ideal," 304.

your neighbor as yourself" (Lev 19:18). These two great commandments are taken from the Torah, the law God gave to Israel on Mount Sinai. The teaching of Moses and the teachings of the prophets can be summarized in these two commandments.

The Sermon on the Mount

The Sermon on the Mount and the teachings of Jesus must be focused on his statement that he did not come to abolish the law and the prophets but to fulfill it.[29] Jesus said, "For truly I tell you, until heaven and earth pass away, not one letter, not one stroke of a letter, will pass from the law until all is accomplished" (Matt 5:18). Jesus did not come to abolish the law; he interpreted the law and gave new meaning to old laws. As the Lord of the law, Jesus has the authority to provide an interpretation that will become the guideline for those who will follow him.

Jesus also proclaimed a message about a new and better righteousness. "Jesus instructs his disciples more concretely on how to emulate divine graciousness and righteousness in situations of conflict. Jesus's guide for righteous living is the Torah."[30] Jesus said, "For I tell you, unless your righteousness exceeds that of the scribes and Pharisees, you will never enter the kingdom of heaven" (Matt 5:20). Jesus said that his disciples must be faithful in observing God's commandments, "So whoever sets aside any command that seems unimportant and teaches others to do the same will be unimportant in the kingdom of heaven. But whoever does and teaches what the commands say will be called great in the kingdom of heaven" (Matt 5:19 GWN). Although the new community live under the ethics of the kingdom, Jesus's disciples should not disregard or neglect the law.

Jesus said that the righteousness of his disciples should exceed the righteousness of the Scribes and Pharisees. The Scribes and Pharisees were faithful observants of the law, but their righteousness was superficial because in their observance of the law they neglected the "more important matters of the law–justice, mercy and faithfulness" (Matt 23:23 NIV).

Jesus taught his disciples that they are heirs to the mission of the Servant. The Servant received the commission to be "a light to the nations"

---

29. McKnight, *Sermon on the Mount*.
30. Reid, "Which God Is With Us?," 381.

(Isa 49:6). Jesus said to his disciples, "You are the light of the world" (Matt 5:14). As followers of Jesus, the disciples were called to become a missionary community: "Let your light shine before others, so that they may see your good works and give glory to your Father in heaven" (Matt 5:16).

Jesus and Violence[31]

In his interpretation of the law, six times Jesus says, "You have heard that it was said" . . . "But I say to you." In his interpretation of the law, Jesus corrects what the religious leaders were saying about the law with what the law actually says. Gardner says that when Jesus said, "But I say to you," "he is not simply giving his commentary on the law. He is placing his word on a par with God's word, claiming divine authority to redefine the law's demands."[32] Jesus interprets the prohibition about murder (Matt 5:21–22); he interprets the prohibition about adultery (Matt 5:27–28), he interprets the law about divorce (Matt 5:31–32), he interprets the prohibition against false oaths (Matt 5:33–34), he interprets the law about revenge (Matt 5:38–39), and he interprets the law about loving and hating one's enemy (Matt 5:43–44). In these six interpretations of the law, "Jesus defines God's will in radical and surprising ways, fulfilling the law by going beyond the law."[33]

Jesus's teaching about murder (Matt 5:21–22). Addressing the prohibition against murder in the Ten Commandments (Exod 20:13; Deut 5:17), Jesus said that anger and abusive language is equal to murder and makes one liable for judgment. Jesus condemns violence and anger as a violation of God's will.

Jesus's teaching about revenge (Matt 5:38–39). Jesus interprets the *lex taliones*, the law of retaliation, a law that demands an eye for an eye and a tooth for a tooth (Exod 21:23–25; Lev 24:19–20; Deut 19:21). The *lex taliones* limits the extent of revenge in case of offence or personal injury. A person who was injured cannot punish the other person who committed

---

31. For a nonviolent and peacemaking perspective on the Sermon on the Mount see Stassen, "Fourteen Triads of the Sermon on the Mount," 267–308; Schlabach, "'Manual' for Escaping Our Vicious Cycles," 86–91.

32. Gardner, *Matthew*, 105.

33. Gardner, *Matthew*, 102.

the crime more than the crime itself. Instead of revenge, Jesus teaches his disciples not to retaliate against the evil person. Instead of using violence, the disciple should not resist the evildoer.

Jesus's teaching about loving and hating one's enemy (Matt 5:43–44). On the law about love and hate, Jesus said, "You have heard that it was said, 'You shall love your neighbor and hate your enemy'" (Matt 5:43). Jesus was referring to Lev 19:18 which says, "you shall love your neighbor as yourself." Leviticus commands the people not to hate a member of the community: "You shall not hate in your heart anyone of your kin" (Lev 19:17); however, nowhere in the law is found a command to hate one's enemy. Instead of hate, Jesus commanded his disciple to love their enemies and pray for those who persecute them.

THE WORK OF CHRIST

Jesus called a group of people to renew the mission of Israel in the world. His twelve disciples represented a renewed Israel. Their mission was to call Israel to be faithful to its destiny. They were to take upon themselves the mission of the Servant: "I will give you as a light to the nations, that my salvation may reach to the end of the earth" (Isa 49:6). Jesus took upon himself the mission and destiny of the Servant: "I am the light of the world" (John 8:12). Jesus transferred the mission of the Servant to his disciples: "You are the light of the world" (Matt 5:14). The Servant had a mission to Israel. His mission was "to bring Jacob back to him, so that Israel might be gathered to him" (Isa 49:5). This is the reason Jesus commanded his disciples to begin his work with Israel: "Go nowhere among the Gentiles, and enter no town of the Samaritans, but go rather to the lost sheep of the house of Israel (Matt 10:5–6).

Jesus taught his disciples how to live as citizens of the kingdom of God. The ethics of the kingdom demanded a more spiritual approach to everyday living. Jesus called for a radical obedience to a righteous living. His disciples must be the salt of the earth and the light of the world. They should live their lives in such a way that their light would "shine before others, so that they may see your good works and give glory to your Father in heaven" (Matt 5:13–16). According to Bright, it is in light of the teachings of Christ that kingdom ethics should be understood. Bright writes, "Jesus did not present his ethical teachings as a program which he expected the secular order either of his day or ours to carry out."[34]

It is for this reason that the non-Christian world cannot live by the ethics of the kingdom. For them, "the message about the cross is foolishness to those who are perishing" (1 Cor 1:18). On the other hand, followers of Christ must be obedient to the teachings of Christ and be willing to take up their cross to follow him (Matt 16:24).

After Jesus finished teaching his disciples, he prepared for his death. Before his death, Jesus prepared to establish the new covenant with the new Israel. Jesus summoned his disciples to prepare the Passover meal. Jesus used the same procedures used for the ratification of the covenant on Mount Sinai (Exod 24:1–11). The ratification of the covenant on Mount Sinai had the following elements: twelve pillars, representing the twelve tribes of Israel, a sacrifice, the sprinkling of the blood, and a covenant meal. When Moses sprinkled the blood on the people, he said, "See the blood of the covenant that the LORD has made with you." The Lord's Supper was the ratification of the new covenant with the new Israel. Jesus said to his disciples, "This cup that is poured out for you is the new covenant in my blood" (Luke 22:20). The early Christians recognized that Jesus had established the new covenant with his disciples (1 Cor 11:25; 2 Cor 3:4–6; Heb 8:6–13).

Jesus died as "the Lamb of God who takes away the sin of the world" (John 1:29). In the Old Testament, the separation between God and an individual was breached through the presentation of a sin offering. In the Day of Atonement, the high priest made atonement for the whole nation. The biblical view of reconciliation is the restoration of the fellowship between God and humanity which was lost because of the sin and the rebellion of human beings.

The basic Hebrew word for reconciliation is *kāpar*, "to make atonement." When the people of Israel sin, Yahweh makes atonement for his people: "Forgive, O LORD, thy people Israel, whom thou hast redeemed, and set not the guilt of innocent blood in the midst of thy people Israel; but let the guilt of blood be forgiven them" (Deut 21:8 RSV). The word "forgive" in Hebrew is *kāpar*. The verb is an imperative second-person singular; it is Yahweh who makes atonement for the people. In Lev 10:17 it is Yahweh who gives the sin offering to the people to remove the sin of the congregation: "Why did you not eat the sin offering in the sacred

---

34. Bright, *Kingdom of God*, 221.

area? For it is most holy, and God has given it to you that you may remove the guilt of the congregation, to make atonement on their behalf before the LORD." The death of Christ was not a sacrifice to pacify an angry God. Christ's death was God's gift of love to humanity. Out of love, God gave his son as an atonement for sin, "God so loved the world that he gave his only Son" (John 3:16). Thus, "in Christ God was reconciling the world to himself" (2 Cor 5:19).

THE CRUCIFIXION OF THE WARRIOR GOD

The Divine Warrior ideology is found throughout the New Testament.[35] Soulen says that "the church has always affirmed that the Triune God is YHWH, and that YHWH is the Triune God."[36] If the God of the Old Testament is revealing himself in Jesus, then this revelation "encompassed every facet of the Hebrew concept of God, including the imagery of the Lord as a Divine Warrior."[37] The use of the Divine Warrior imagery in the intertestamental period, the eschatological hope in Yahweh's victory against Israel's enemies, and the strong messianic speculation of the first century contributed to the "identification of Jesus of Nazareth as the Divine Warrior" in the New Testament."[38]

The story of Jesus walking on water (Matt 14:22–33) recalls the Old Testament tradition of Yahweh, the divine warrior's power over the water of chaos. According to Job 9:8, Yahweh is the one who "stretches out the heavens by himself and walks on the waves of the sea." Angel sees in the confession of Jesus as the "Son of God" in Matt 14:33 and the use of ἐγώ εἰμι in Matt 14:27 the disciples' recognition "that Jesus is God the divine warrior who conquers the forces of chaos."[39]

Angel calls attention to the disciples' confession—"Truly you are the Son of God" (Matt 14:33)—and the declaration of the centurion at the cross—"Truly this was the Son of God" (Matt 27:54). The implication of both statements is that Matthew is declaring "that in his crucifixion Jesus

---

35. Longman, "Divine Warrior," 290–307; Stevens, "Jesus as the Divine Warrior," 326–29; Stevens, "Why Must the Son of Man Suffer," 101–10; Duff, "March of the Divine Warrior," 55–71; Huie-Jolly, "Threats Answered by Enthronement," 191–217; Angel, "Crucifixus Vincens," 299–317.

36. Soulen, "YHWH the Triune God," 32.

37. Stevens, "Jesus as the Divine Warrior," 328.

38. Stevens, "Jesus as the Divine Warrior," 327.

39. Angel, "Crucifixus Vincens," 310.

is the divine warrior, the conqueror of the forces of chaos, and the rescuer of the disciples."[40] Thus, on the cross, Jesus, the Divine Warrior, conquers the forces of chaos and evil.

Angel also says that Matthew uses his narrative of the crucifixion to make an important declaration, "that Jesus on the cross won the victory over the principalities and powers (Col 2:15). Thus, the cross is to be understood not as the place of defeat but rather as the place of victory, for on it Jesus as the divine warrior defeated the powers of evil. The crucified conquers."[41]

Only Matthew mentions that at the time of Jesus death the earth shook and the rocks were split (Matt 27:51). Angel links these details to the divine warrior motif in the Old Testament. Earthquakes appear in theophanies of the divine warrior in the Old Testament (Pss 18:7; 46:3; Nah 1:5). Rock splitting is also associated with the theophany of the divine warrior (Nah 1:6). Angel concludes that "at the moment of Jesus's death, Matthew describes a series of portents, some of which draw on the theophany of the divine warrior."[42] Angel believes that the inclusion of the theophany of the divine warrior on the cross and that through his death the divine warrior conquers evil are two important themes in Matthew's crucifixion narrative.[43]

With his death on the cross, Jesus, the Divine Warrior, transforms the divine warrior ideology of the Old Testament.[44] In the Old Testament the forces of chaos and evil were generally identified with animals, such as serpents, dragons, sea monsters, and other creatures.[45] These forces of chaos and evil were also identified with the enemies of Israel. It was Yahweh the Warrior God who cut the sea monster into pieces; it was he who pierced the dragon (Isa 51:9–10). Jeremiah compares Babylon with a dragon (Jer 51:34). Ezekiel identifies Pharaoh with "the great dragon that lies in the midst of his rivers" (Ezek 29:3). Rahab is identified as Egypt (Ps 87:4). Isaiah also identifies Egypt with Rahab, "For Egypt's help

---

40. Angel, "Crucifixus Vincens," 313.
41. Angel, "Crucifixus Vincens," 313.
42. Angel, "Crucifixus Vincens," 314.
43. Angel, "Crucifixus Vincens," 315.
44. Holloway, "Ethical Dilemma of Holy War," 67, said that in the New Testament, "the motif of God the Warrior comes to its ultimate expression in the triumph over evil through the cross and resurrection of Christ."
45. According to Heiser, "Chaos," 83, "In the Hebrew Bible the concept of chaos refers broadly to cosmic disorder—conditions contrary to God's design for all things."

is worthless and empty, therefore I have called her, 'Rahab who sits still'" (Isa 30:7). The enemies of Israel are portrayed as the waters of chaos (Isa 17:13).

When Jesus died on the cross, Israel was under Roman domination, "He suffered under Pontius Pilate." The Romans used crucifixion to punish political enemies of Rome and common criminals. Before his death Jesus was flogged and stripped of his clothes. People spat upon him and struck him on the head. His death on the cross was slow and painful. Although Jesus suffered the humiliation of the cross, Jesus never identified the Romans as his enemies. As Angel puts it,

> Matthew has Jesus defeat the cosmic forces of chaos and evil, which are not identified with any particular historical enemy. The battle of Jesus the divine warrior on the cross is not against a particular historical enemy but against the spiritual forces of chaos and evil. In this way, Matthew has developed and transformed the meaning of the myth from its traditional sense of the defeat of the historical and political enemies of Israel to the defeat of the spiritual and cosmic forces.[46]

The cross marks a new beginning in God's work of reconciliation. In the past, God worked with agents who used violence on his behalf in order to accomplish his work in the world. Israel wanted to be like the nations (1 Sam 8:5) even though God told them that they should be different from the other nations (Deut 26:19). The establishment of the monarchy in Israel was a rejection of Yahweh as their king.[47] Yahweh said to Samuel, "Listen to the voice of the people in all that they say to you; for they have not rejected you, but they have rejected me from being king over them" (1 Sam 8:7). With the establishment of the monarchy in Israel, the kingdom of God became the kingdom of David. As John Bright puts it, the kingdom of God was made equal to the kingdom of Israel, "the citizens of the Davidic state."[48] On the cross, the kingdom of Israel became again the kingdom of God.

---

46. Angel, "Crucifixus Vincens," 316.

47. Mendenhall, "Monarchy," 155–70, calls the monarchy "the paganization of Israel."

48. Bright, *Kingdom of God*, 39, 45.

THE RENEWAL OF ISRAEL'S MISSION

Beginning with the cross, the work of God in the world would be accomplished without violence. Jesus told his disciples, "All authority in heaven and on earth has been given to me. Go therefore and make disciples of all nations, baptizing them in the name of the Father and of the Son and of the Holy Spirit, and teaching them to obey everything that I have commanded you. And remember, I am with you always, to the end of the age" (Matt 28:18–20).

When the new people of God carry out their ministry of reconciliation, then the earth "will be filled with the knowledge of the glory of the LORD, as the waters cover the sea" (Hab 2:14). When the Lord establishes "a new heaven and a new earth" (Rev 21:1), then violence in the world will end because the nations "shall beat their swords into plowshares, and their spears into pruning hooks; nation shall not lift up sword against nation, neither shall they learn war any more" (Isa 2:4).

When the earth is "full of the knowledge of the LORD as the waters cover the sea" (Isa 11:9) then there will be no violence in the animal world,

> The wolf shall live with the lamb, the leopard shall lie down with the kid, the calf and the lion and the fatling together, and a little child shall lead them. The cow and the bear shall graze, their young shall lie down together; and the lion shall eat straw like the ox. The nursing child shall play over the hole of the asp, and the weaned child shall put its hand on the adder's den. They will not hurt or destroy on all my holy mountain. (Isa 11:6–9)

But unfortunately, we do not live in that kind of world yet. Christians must refrain from using violence in a violent world, but those who do not live by the ethics of the kingdom will have no compulsion using violence. We live in a violent world. Until the world is "full of the knowledge of the LORD," we shall "hear of wars and rumors of wars." War will take place in this world, for as Jesus said, "this must take place" (Matt 24:6). Before nations turn "their swords into plowshares" they will prepare for war and beat their plowshares into swords, and their pruning hooks into spears (Joel 3:9–10).

THE RENUNCIATION OF VIOLENCE

Our modern world is filled with violence. Christians everywhere deplore and reject violence. Much violence in the world is done in the name of God or under the guise of religion. To many Christians divine violence is an embarrassment and, at times, a situation that leads to despair and to the rejection of God. However, one must realize that there was human violence in the world before there was divine violence.

Human violence entered into the world after Adam and Eve rebelled against God. God created a world that was "very good" (Gen 1:31). Soon, the goodness of creation was affected by the violent murder of Abel.[49] Cain was very angry at God and in his anger, Cain killed his brother. God did not act violently at the violence of Cain. Rather, God put a mark on Cain and he lived the rest of his life under God's protection. Lamech killed a man for striking him (Gen 4:23). This violent act was not met with divine violence since the text does not say how Yahweh reacted to this brutal act. In the midst of God's work of redeeming the world, human wickedness and evil had affected every human being (Gen 6:5) and violence had become universal (Gen 6:11).

The time when Noah lived is the first occasion where we encounter divine violence in the Bible. Other occasions for divine violence were the destruction of Sodom and Gomorrah, during the exodus of Israel from Egypt, at the occasion of the apostasy of Israel with the golden calf, the conquest of Canaan, and several others. But on each occasion, there was a justification for the use of divine violence. All the violent acts of God in the Hebrew Bible are in response to the violation of the moral order set by God at the time of creation.

Take the case of God and the Egyptians. Before divine violence was used, God gave Pharaoh an opportunity to avoid violence. God sent Moses and Aaron to Pharaoh with a message, "Thus says the LORD, the God of Israel, 'Let my people go.'" If Pharaoh had allowed the people to leave Egypt there would be no violence. But Pharaoh refused. He said to Moses, "I will not let Israel go" (Exod 5:1–2). God could accept Pharaoh's decision and let Israel suffer as slaves in Egypt. Or he could act and deliver the people. The decision to deliver Israel would involve violence. Divine violence happened because of human intransigence.

When Pharaoh took his army with him and his hundreds of chariots to pursue the people of Israel to kill them or to bring them back to Egypt

---

49. Dietrich, "Mark of Cain," 3, calls Gen 4 "the primeval history of violence."

(Exod 14:6–7), Yahweh had only two choices: to do nothing and let the people be killed by Pharaoh and his army or act on behalf of Israel and deliver the people from the threat posed by Pharaoh's army. The decision to act required violence. Israel could not defend itself; Yahweh acted as a warrior to defend Israel (Exod 15:3).

Throughout the history of Israel God had to act violently to defend his honor and holiness, to defend Israel from the hand of their enemies, or to punish Israel for their rebellion and apostasy. The work of God is reconciliation. However, because Israel failed to accomplish God's work in the world, Yahweh had to use his "alien work" in order to discipline his rebellious people.

When God became a man, God decided to renounce violence in doing his work of reconciliation. On the cross, God renounced violence because the Warrior God died on the cross. The cross was the beginning of a new way of reconciling the world. In Christ, "God was reconciling the world unto himself" (2 Cor 5:19). In his work of reconciliation, God selected a special group of people and entrusted to them the message of reconciliation.

His disciples would do the work of reconciliation according to kingdom ethics. Renewed Israel are not to be the disciples of Moses, but rather they are disciples of Christ. They should go to the nations in peace and avoid violence. As disciples of Christ, they would encounter violence and persecution, but they should not meet violence with violence. Jesus said, "When they persecute you in one town, flee to the next" (Matt 10:23).

God renounced violence in doing his work of reconciliation, but God is not renouncing violence in judging evildoers and human violence. As Reimer said, "God is love but not a pacifist."[50] Tremper Longman says that the Divine Warrior image is found throughout the book of Revelation. He says that the book of Revelation describes Christ's second coming by

> employing military imagery strongly reminiscent of Divine Warrior passages in the OT. As a matter of fact, one finds a description of Christ the Divine Warrior which on the one hand connects him with Yahweh the Divine Warrior in the OT and, on the other hand, contrasts him and sets him in opposition to the satanic warrior, the unholy warrior of Revelation 13.[51]

---

50. Reimer, "God Is Love but Not a Pacifist," 486.
51. Longman, "Divine Warrior," 298.

In his work of reconciliation God will always act as "a God merciful and gracious, slow to anger, and abounding in steadfast love and faithfulness, keeping steadfast love for the thousandth generation, forgiving iniquity and transgression and sin" (Exod 34:6–7). In his work of judging evil and violence, God acts as a God who by no means clears the guilty (Exod 34:7).

In conclusion, Reimer's statement that "God is love but not a pacifist" is relevant to understanding divine violence. Reimer is an Anabaptist and a pacifist. He has the correct understanding of the God of the Old Testament. In the conclusion of his article, he articulates his view of God and violence. He writes,

> God is not arbitrary—God is just, righteous, good, and loving, but in ways that are not fully transparent. . . . God's revelation through the Son in Jesus Christ is a revelation of this mystery—the mystery that despite the reality of violence and evil in the world there is a movement of divine redemption and reconciliation in the cosmos. . . . The loving God is amid death and violence in ways that are not clear to us. The non-violent way of the cross, mediated to us in Jesus the Christ, reveals the hidden purposes of God. . . . God's means of achieving the ultimate reconciliation of all things are not immediately evident to us. God cannot be subjected to our interpretation of the non-violent way of Jesus. Our commitment to the way of the cross (reconciliation) is not premised on God's pacifism or non-pacifism. It is precisely because God has the prerogative to give and take life that we do not have that right. Vengeance we leave up to God.[52]

---

52. Reimer, "God Is Love but Not a Pacifist," 492.

Postscript

THE TEXT OF THE OLD Testament contains many acts of violence, both human and divine. As for human violence, Walter Dietrich said that "As shocking and fascinating as the OT texts on violence are, they realistically portray humanity's attitudes, fate, and actions."[1] Reimer said that people who take a pacifist position "have never quite gotten at the root, irrationality, and tenacity of evil and violence" in the world.[2] According to the biblical text, violence first appears in the Old Testament when Cain violently killed his brother. Violence came into the world against the will of God. God did not use violence to deal with Cain's violence. Rather, God put a mark of protection on him. As for divine violence, the Old Testament also presents a realistic way in which God acts when dealing with violence. The first act of divine violence only occurred after "the earth was filled with violence" (Gen 6:11). Divine violence came in response to human violence: "Violence is restrained by violence."[3] Dietrich writes, "It would be no help to anyone if the Bible painted a picture of a cozy, violent-free world or set forth a God who was far removed from the violent realities of the earth and humanity. To present a holy and healed world would be no help against violence."[4]

In his study of the characterization of God in the book of Hosea, Brueggemann writes, "The outcome of Hosea's characterization is a God who is a *recovering agent of violence* who has deep violence in the marrow of personhood, a memory of violence, a memory of violence regretted, and many lapses back into violence . . . but a resolve to be a spouse of

---

1. Dietrich, "Mark of Cain," 5.
2. Reimer, "God Is Love but Not a Pacifist," 488.
3. Lohfink, "Unmasking of Violence," 103.
4. Dietrich, "Mark of Cain," 5.

generosity and a parent of compassion."⁵ Brueggemann then talks about the problem of the image of God as a recovering agent of violence. He writes, "As is in all such recovery programs, the process is always continuing and never completed."⁶

The Old Testament presents two different views of God; both views are described in a creedal statement that reveals the true nature and character of Yahweh. The first view of Yahweh is that of a God who is merciful and gracious. Yahweh identifies himself with this merciful and gracious God: "The LORD, the LORD, a God merciful and gracious, slow to anger, and abounding in steadfast love and faithfulness, keeping steadfast love for the thousandth generation, forgiving iniquity and transgression and sin" (Exod 34:6–7).

This is the most important aspect of the character of God in the Bible. Yahweh is always a merciful and gracious God. He is always slow to anger and ready to forgive. He is always a God of love who keeps and shows his love to everyone in the world. God only uses violence as a last resort, when he is provoked to anger.

The other view of God that is seen throughout the Old Testament is of a God who is a righteous judge who visits people to demand an account of their violence and their wickedness. Yahweh identifies himself with that God: "The LORD, the LORD, a God . . . [who] by no means clearing the guilty, but visiting the iniquity of the parents upon the children and the children's children, to the third and the fourth generation" (Exod 34:7).

Ezekiel says that Yahweh has no pleasure when he acts as a judge, rather, he wants people to repent so that they might live. When he acts as a judge, he acts because of the people's unwillingness to repent, "Therefore I will judge you, O house of Israel, all of you according to your ways, says the Lord GOD. Repent and turn from all your transgressions; otherwise iniquity will be your ruin" (Ezek 18:30).

The view of God as a righteous judge who brings justice upon evildoers, who visits people who commit wickedness, and who uses violence to restrain human violence is problematic to many people because they believe that the God revealed by Christ on the cross is a loving God who abhors violence. Those who struggle with the violent God of the Old Testament ask whether this is the same God revealed in the New Testament.

---

5. Brueggemann, "Recovering God of Hosea," 19.
6. Brueggemann, "Recovering God of Hosea," 20.

The Old Testament shows that the people of Israel believed that the immeasurable love and mercy of God was a reality in their lives even in the midst of pain and suffering: "The steadfast love of the LORD never ceases, his mercies never come to an end" (Lam 3:22). They also experienced the hiddenness of God because of his anger: "Do not hide your face from me. Do not turn your servant away in anger, you who have been my help. Do not cast me off, do not forsake me, O God of my salvation" (Ps 27:9). Israel also experienced divine wrath, "When God heard, he was full of wrath, and he utterly rejected Israel" (Ps 78:59).

Divine violence and divine wrath pose an ethical dilemma for Christians who want to live according to the teachings of Jesus. How do we justify so much violence and so much anger in a God who is also known as a God of love, "God is love" (1 John 4:16). One way to explain divine violence in the Old Testament is by suggesting that the imagery of a violent God reflects the fallen and culturally conditioned view of the biblical text and does not reflect the true character and nature of God. Boyd believes that "the manner in which the conception of Yahweh as a violent divine warrior parallels the common warrior conception of other gods in the ANE indicates that this conception in the OT reflects a culturally conditioned aspect of the ancient Hebraic conception of God."[7]

Another way of interpreting texts containing divine violence is by saying that Old Testament characters misunderstood what God had commanded them to do. If Yahweh told them to enter the land of Canaan and conquer the kings and soldiers of Canaanite cities (Josh 6:2), the people believed that they were free to commit violent acts against the cities' inhabitants, including killing women and children. This view puts in doubt the credibility of biblical characters in conveying God's will and demands to the community.

Another way of dealing with divine violence is by differentiating between the God of the text and the true God. According to this view, the God of the text is the violent God while the true God is the God of love and peace revealed by Christ on the cross. This view comes close to Marcionism. The only way to know God is by what the biblical text says about him. The biblical God is a God known through revelation. Even the God of the New Testament is a God of the text. To separate God from the biblical text is to create a god according to one's own imagination.

---

7. Boyd, *Crucifixion of the Warrior God*, 302–3n67.

Divine violence is found throughout the Old Testament and it cannot be explained away. The history of Israel can serve as an example for understanding why God, at times, acts violently: "The God of the OT did not succeed in definitively dissociating himself from violence. Yet we find there a continuing and powerful advance toward overcoming violence."[8] In the midst of their oppression of the poor, the widows, and the orphans, confronted with their rebellion and disobedience against God, when challenged to abandon their sins, wickedness, and the worship of other gods, Israel refused to listen to the prophets to turn from their evil ways (2 Kgs 17:13). The people would not listen because they were stubborn (2 Kgs 17:14). God offered them mercy and grace; they rejected God's *ḥesed* which was offered to them.

By rejecting God's offer of forgiveness, Israel had to face the consequences of their evil actions, of their violence, and of their oppression of the vulnerable people in Israelite society. Yahweh commanded Israel not to abuse the widow or the orphan and when they did there would be consequences: "when they cry out to me, I will surely heed their cry; my wrath will burn" (Exod 22:22–24).

God is a righteous God. Only God has the right to judge and to punish those who commit evil and violence. The problem is that today we refrain from talking about sin and its consequences. We refrain from believing that evil and violent people need to be accountable for their actions. In Rom 13 Paul says that civil authorities have the right "to carry out the death sentence." According to Paul, the government "is God's servant, an avenger to execute God's anger on anyone who does what is wrong" (Rom 13:1–4 GWN). Christians may oppose the death penalty as inhumane and as a violation of kingdom ethics; but civil authorities have the right to carry out the death sentence. Paul said that people who do what is right should not be afraid of the government, but those who do evil should. The Bible says that God as a righteous judge does not let the guilty go unpunished (Exod 34:7). Violence begets violence and in certain situations divine judgment requires violence.

In our society today it is difficult to make a distinction between good and evil. The moral values of our society allow people to do things that a century ago were not allowed in society. Morals change with time and what was considered morally acceptable by one generation becomes unacceptable to another.

---

8. Villar, "Does the Bible Portray a Violent God?," 207.

God is in the work of reconciliation. God is "not willing that any should perish, but that all should come to repentance" (2 Pet 3:9 KJV). He desires to reconcile humanity to himself without violence and without judgment. If divine judgment comes it is because of people's refusal to accept God's call to repentance. Those who choose to commit evil and to act violently will become recipients of the wrath of God for "the wrath of God is revealed from heaven against all ungodliness and wickedness of those who by their wickedness suppress the truth" (Rom 1:18). Or, as Paul said, "by your hard and impenitent heart you are storing up wrath for yourself on the day of wrath, when God's righteous judgment will be revealed" (Rom 2:5).

Chief Joseph of the Nez Perce, an indigenous tribe who lived in the Pacific Northwest, was known in his community as "Thunder Traveling to the Loftier Mountain Heights." When he surrendered to the US Army on October 5, 1877, he gave what is known as the "I will fight no more forever" surrender speech:

> Tell General Howard I know his heart. What he told me before, I have it in my heart. I am tired of fighting. Our Chiefs are killed; Looking Glass is dead, Ta Hool Shute is dead. The old men are all dead. It is the young men who say yes or no. He who led on the young men is dead. It is cold, and we have no blankets; the little children are freezing to death. My people, some of them, have run away to the hills, and have no blankets, no food. No one knows where they are—perhaps freezing to death. I want to have time to look for my children, and see how many of them I can find. Maybe I shall find them among the dead. Hear me, my Chiefs! I am tired; my heart is sick and sad. From where the sun now stands I will fight no more forever.[9]

Chief Joseph was tired of fighting; he realized that violence did not produce peace for his people. As a result, many had died and many more were about to die. His heart was sick and sad. He renounced violence by saying that "I will fight no more forever."

Because of human wickedness and human violence, God's heart "was filled with pain" (Gen 6:6). In his work of redeeming the world, the use of divine violence did not accomplish the intent God had for his creation. When Jerusalem was about to fall into the hands of the Babylonians, Yahweh, the Divine Warrior decided to fight once again. Yahweh said to Zedekiah, king of Judah, "I myself will fight against you with

---

9. "Chief Joseph," para. 2.

outstretched hand and mighty arm, in anger, in fury, and in great wrath. And I will strike down the inhabitants of this city, both human beings and animals" (Jer 21:5–6).

Instead of fighting for Israel as he had done before, the Divine Warrior was fighting against his own people. As a result, many people died and many went into exile, but Israel did not change. The cross changed the way God works in the world. "On the cross, God suffers and is changed. God does this so that his experience may change us and bring us back into relationship with him. . . . Because of that change our judge is not blindfolded Justice with a scale and a sword, but one wearing a robe dipped in blood."[10] On the cross, Yahweh, the Divine Warrior of the Old Testament, stopped being an agent of violence. On the cross the Divine Warrior, to a certain extent said, "I will fight no more forever." Because of the death of Christ on the cross, God's work of reconciliation would be accomplished without violence.

Christians must renounce violence as they work as agents of reconciliation. The work of reconciliation will be accomplished by the people of God without the use of the sword. As Paul said,

> never avenge yourselves, but leave room for the wrath of God; for it is written, "Vengeance is mine, I will repay, says the Lord." No, "if your enemies are hungry, feed them; if they are thirsty, give them something to drink; for by doing this you will heap burning coals on their heads." Do not be overcome by evil, but overcome evil with good. (Rom 12:19–21)

This is the reason the death of the Warrior God on the cross makes a difference in how God's work of reconciliation is accomplished in the world. In the past God worked with a people who lived in a violent world and had to use violence to survive and defend themselves. And God used violence to help them survive and defend themselves. Looking back from the perspective of the cross, the violent acts in the Old Testament, both human and divine, do not meet the ethical standards set by Jesus's teaching. The cross marks the end of violence in the work of reconciliation.

---

10. Carson, "Suffering God and Cross," 331.

Bibliography

Ackerman, Susan. "The Queen Mother and the Cult in Ancient Israel." *Journal of Biblical Literature* 112 (1993) 385–401.
Ahlström, Gösta. "King Jehu: A Prophet's Mistake." In *Scripture in History and Theology: Essays in Honor of J. Coert Rylaarsdam*, edited by Arthur L. Merrill and Thomas W. Overhold, 47–69. Pittsburgh: Pickwick, 1977.
Aichele, George. "Jesus' Violence." In *Violence, Utopia, and the Kingdom of God: Fantasy and Ideology in the Bible*, edited by George Aichele and Tina Pippin, 72–91. New York: Routledge, 1998.
Albertz, Rainer. *A History of Israelite Religion in the Old Testament Period*. Louisville: Westminster John Knox, 1994.
Allen, Leonard. "Archaeology of Ai and the Accuracy of Joshua 7:1—8:29." *Restoration Quarterly* 20 (1977) 41–52.
Andersen, Francis I., and David N. Freedman. *Amos: A New Translation With Introduction and Commentary*. The Yale Anchor Bible 24A. New Haven: Yale University Press, 2008.
Anderson, Bernhard W. "Exodus Typology in Second Isaiah." In *Israel's Prophetic Heritage: Essays in Honor of James Muilenburg*, edited by Bernhard W. Anderson and Walter J. Harrelson, 177–95. New York: Harper, 1962.
———. *Understanding the Old Testament*. 4th ed. Englewood Cliffs: Prentice Hall, 1986.
Anderson, Elizabeth. "If God Is Dead, Is Everything Permitted." In *The Portable Atheist: Essential Readings for the Nonbeliever*, edited by Christopher Hitchens, 333–48. Philadelphia: Da Capo, 2007.
André, G. "*pāqad*." In *Theological Dictionary of the Old Testament*, edited by G. J. Botterweck et al., 12:50–63. Grand Rapids, MI: Eerdmans, 2003.
Andreasen, Niels-Erik A. "The Role of the Queen Mother in Israelite Society." *The Catholic Biblical Quarterly* 45 (1983) 179–94.
Angel, Andrew R. "Crucifixus Vincens: The 'Son of God' as Divine Warrior in Matthew." *The Catholic Biblical Quarterly* 73 (2011) 299–317.
Assmann, Jan. *The Invention of Religion: Faith and Covenant in the Book of Exodus*. Princeton: Princeton University Press, 2018.
———. *Moses the Egyptian: The Memory of Egypt in Western Monotheism*. Cambridge: Harvard University Press, 1977.
"Atomic Bombings of Hiroshima and Nagasaki." https://en.wikipedia.org/wiki/Atomic_bombings_of_Hiroshima_and_Nagasaki.

Azuelos, Yaacov. "The 'Angel Sent from Before the Lord' in Targum Joshua 5,14." *Biblica* 96 (2015) 161–78.

Bailey, Wilma. "Thoughts on Eric A. Seibert's *Disturbing Divine Behavior*." *Direction* 40 (2011) 163–67.

Barrett, Charles. "Luke's Contribution to the Light Motif in Scripture as It Relates to the Prophetic Ministry of Christ and His Disciples." *Puritan Reformed Journal* 5 (2013) 29–40.

Barth, Karl. *The Humanity of God*. Atlanta: John Knox, 1960.

Bartlett, John R. "Sihon and Og, Kings of the Amorites." *Vetus Testamentum* (1970) 257–77.

Barton, John. "The Dark Side of God in the Old Testament." In *Ethical and Unethical in the Old Testament: God and Humans Dialogue*, edited by Katharine J. Dell, 122–34. New York: T. & T. Clark, 2010.

Baruchi-Unna, Amitai. "Jehuites, Ahabites, and Omrides: Blood Kinship and Bloodshed." *Journal for the Study of the Old Testament* 42 (2017) 3–21.

Beal, Lissa M. Wray. *Joshua*. The Story of God Bible Commentary. Grand Rapids, MI: Zondervan, 2019.

Beale, G. K. "The Old Testament Background of Reconciliation in 2 Corinthians 5–7 and Its Bearing on the Literary Problem of 2 Corinthians 6.14—7.1." *New Testament Studies* 35 (1989) 550–81.

Beers, Holly. *The Followers of Jesus as the 'Servant': Luke's Model from Isaiah for the Disciples in Luke–Acts*. London: Bloomsbury T. & T. Clark, 2015.

Belousek, Darrin W. Snyder. "Nonviolent God: Critical Analysis of a Contemporary Argument." *The Conrad Grebel Review* 29 (2011) 49–70.

Ben-Barak, Zafrira. "The Status and Right of the *Gĕbîrâ*." *Journal of Biblical Literature* 110 (1991) 23–34.

Ben Zvi, Ehud. "The Dialogue Between Abraham and Yhwh in Gen. 18.23–32: A Historical-Critical Analysis." *Journal for the Study of the Old Testament* 53 (1992) 27–46.

Berges, Ulrich. "The Violence of God in the Book of Lamentations." In *One Text, a Thousand Methods: Studies in Memory of Sjef van Tilborg*, edited by Patrick C. Counet and Ulrich Berges, 21–44. Leiden: Brill, 2005.

Berlejung, Angelika. "Sin and Punishment: The Ethics of Divine Justice and Retribution in Ancient Near Eastern and Old Testament Texts." *Interpretation* 69 (2015) 272–87.

Berlin, Adele. *Lamentations*. Old Testament Library. Louisville: Westminster John Knox, 2002.

Biddle, Mark E. "The 'Endangered Ancestress' and Blessing for the Nations." *Journal of Biblical Literature* 109 (1990) 599–611.

Bird, Michael F. *Crossing Over Sea and Land: Jewish Missionary Activity in the Second Temple Period*. Peabody, MA: Hendrickson, 2010.

Bleibtreu, Erika. "Grisly Assyrian Record of Torture and Death." *Biblical Archaeology Review* 17 (January–February 1991) 52–61, 75.

Blenkinsopp, Joseph. *Isaiah 40–55: A New Translation with Introduction and Commentary*. Anchor Bible 19A. New York: Doubleday, 2002.

———. "Judah's Covenant with Death (Isaiah XXVIII 14–22)." *Vetus Testamentum* 50 (2000) 472–83.

———. "Second Isaiah-Prophet of Universalism." *Journal for the Study of the Old Testament* 41 (1988) 83–103.

Bloch-Smith, Elizabeth. "The Impact of Siege Warfare on Biblical Conceptualizations of YHWH." *Journal of Biblical Literature* 137 (2018) 19–28.

Block, Daniel I. "How Can We Bless Yhwh? Wrestling with Divine Violence in Deuteronomy." In *Wrestling with the Violence of God: Soundings in the Old Testament*, edited by M. Daniel Carroll R. and J. Blair Wilgus, 31–50. Winona Lake, IN: Eisenbrauns, 2015.

———. "The Privilege of Calling: The Mosaic Paradigm for Missions (Deut. 26:16–19)." *Bibliotheca Sacra* 162 (2005) 387–405.

Boase, Elizabeth. "The Characterisation of God in Lamentations." *Australian Biblical Review* 56 (2008) 32–44.

Borowski, Oded. "The Identity of the Biblical *sir' â*." In *The Word of the Lord Shall Go Forth: Essays in Honor of David Noel Freedman in Celebration of His Sixtieth Birthday*, edited by Carol L. Meyers and M. O'Conner, 315–19. Winona Lake, IN: Eisenbrauns, 1983.

Bosman, Hendrik. "The Function of (Maternal) Cannibalism in the Book of Lamentations (2:20 & 4:10)." *Scriptura* 110 (2012) 152–65.

Bosworth, David A. "The Tears of God in the Book of Jeremiah." *Biblica* 94 (2013) 24–46.

Bowman, Richard. "Review of *The Violence of Scripture: Overcoming the Old Testament's Troubling Legacy*." *Interpretation* 68 (2014) 211.

Boyd, Gregory A. *Crucifixion of the Warrior God: Interpreting the Old Testament's Violent Portraits of God in Light of the Cross*. Minneapolis: Fortress, 2017.

Braaten, Carl E. *Christian Dogmatics*. Minneapolis: Fortress, 1984.

Brettler, Marc Zvi. "God, Merciful and Compassionate?" In *Encountering God: God Merciful and Gracious*, edited by Lawrence A. Hoffman, 21–26. Woodstock: Jewish Lights, 2016.

———. "The Hebrew Bible and the Early History of Israel." In *The Cambridge Guide to Jewish History, Religion, and Culture*, edited by Judith R. Baskin and Kenneth Seeskin, 6–33. Cambridge: Cambridge University Press, 2010.

Bridge, Edward J. "An Audacious Request: Abraham's Dialogue with God in Genesis 18." *Journal for the Study of the Old Testament* 40 (2016) 281–96.

Bright, John. *A History of Israel*. 3rd ed. Philadelphia: Westminster, 1981.

———. *The Kingdom of God*. Nashville: Abingdon, 1953.

Brueggemann, Walter. "At the Mercy of Babylon: A Subversive Rereading of the Empire." *Journal of Biblical Literature* 110 (1991) 3–22.

———. *A Commentary on Jeremiah: Exile and Homecoming*. Grand Rapids, MI: Eerdmans, 1998.

———. *Divine Presence Amid Violence: Contextualizing the Book of Joshua*. Eugene, OR: Cascade, 2009.

———. "'Exodus' in the Plural (Amos 9:7)." In *Many Voices, One God: Being Faithful in a Pluralistic World*, edited by Walter Brueggemann and George W. Stroup, 15–34. Louisville: Westminster John Knox, 1998.

———. *Genesis*. Interpretation. Atlanta: John Knox, 1982.

———. "Israel as YHWH's Partner." In *An Unsettling God: The Heart of the Hebrew Bible*, 19–56. Minneapolis: Fortress, 2009.

———. *Jeremiah 1–25: To Pluck Up, To Tear Down*. Grand Rapids, MI: Eerdmans, 1988.

———. *The Prophetic Imagination*. Philadelphia: Fortress, 1978.
———. "The Recovering God of Hosea." *Horizons in Biblical Theology* 30 (2008) 5–20.
———. *Revelation and Reason*. Philadelphia: Westminster, 1946.
———. "Revelation and Violence: A Study in Contextualization." In *A Social Reading of the Old Testament: Prophetic Approaches to Israel's Communal Life*, edited by Patrick D. Miller, 285–318. Minneapolis: Fortress, 1994.
———. *A Social Reading of the Old Testament: Prophetic Approaches to Israel's Communal Life*, edited by Patrick D. Miller, 285–318. Minneapolis: Fortress, 1994.
———. *Theology of the Old Testament: Testimony, Dispute, Advocacy*. Minneapolis: Fortress, 1997.
———. "Warrior God." *Christian Century* 130.26 (2013) 30–31.
Brunner, Emil. "The Problem of the 'Divine Attributes.'" In *The Christian Doctrine of God*, 1:241–47. Philadelphia: The Westminster, 1950.
Busch, Eberhard. "God's Reconciliation of the World in Christ." *Communio Viatorum* 47 (2005) 150–57.
Callaway, Joseph. "Excavating Ai (Et-Tell): 1964–1972." *Biblical Archaeologist* 39 (1976) 18–30.
Carroll R., M. Daniel. "'I Will Send Fire': Reflections on the Violence of God in Amos." In *Wrestling with the Violence of God: Soundings in the Old Testament*, edited by M. Daniel Carroll R. and J. Blair Wilgus, 113–32. Winona Lake, IN: Eisenbrauns, 2015.
Carroll R., M. Daniel, and J. Blair Wilgus. *Wrestling with the Violence of God: Soundings in the Old Testament*. Winona Lake, IN: Eisenbrauns, 2015.
Carson, Jordan. "The Suffering God and Cross in Open Theism: Theodicy or Atonement? *Perspectives in Religious Studies* 37 (2010) 323–37.
Carvalho, Corrine. "The Beauty of the Bloody God: The Divine Warrior in Prophetic Literature." In *Aesthetics of Violence in the Prophets*, edited by C. Franke and J. M. O'Brien, 131–52. London: T. & T. Clark, 2010.
Chan, Michael J., and Brent A. Strawn. *What Kind of God? Collected Essays of Terence E. Fretheim*. Winona Lake, IN: Eisenbrauns, 2015.
Chapman, Stephen B. "Martial Memory, Peaceable Vision: Divine War in the Old Testament." In *Holy War in the Bible: Christian Morality and an Old Testament Problem*, edited by Paul Copan et al., 47–67. Downers Grove: IVP Academic, 2013.
Childs, Brevard S. *Isaiah: A Commentary*. Old Testament Library. Louisville: Westminster John Knox, 2001.
"Chief Joseph." http://www.historyplace.com/speeches/joseph.htm.
Chisholm, Robert B., Jr. "'The Bloodshed of Jezreel': Harmonizing Hosea 1:4 and 2 Kings 10:30." *Bibliotheca Sacra* 176 (2019) 429–43.
Claassens, L Juliana M. "Calling the Keeners: The Image of the Wailing Woman as Symbol of Survival in a Traumatized World." *Journal of Feminist Studies in Religion* 26 (2010) 63–77.
Clark, Gordon. *The Word "Hesed" in the Hebrew Bible*. Journal for the Study of the Old Testament Supplement Series 157. Sheffield: Sheffield Academic Press, 1993.
Clarke, Terrance A. "Complete v. Incomplete Conquest: A Re-examination of Three Passages in Joshua." *Tyndale Bulletin* 61 (2010) 89–104.
Clines, David J. A. "God in Human Form: A Theme in Biblical Theology." *Christian Brethren Research Fellowship Journal* 24 (1973) 24–40.

Cogan, Mordechai. "'Ripping Open Pregnant Women' in Light of an Assyrian Analogue." *Journal of the American Oriental Society* 103 (1983) 755–57.
Collins, John J. *Does the Bible Justify Violence?* Minneapolis: Fortress, 2004.
———. *What Are Biblical Values? What the Bible Says on Key Ethical Issues.* New Haven: Yale University Press, 2019.
Copan, Paul. *Is God a Moral Monster? Making Sense of the Old Testament God.* Grand Rapids, MI: Baker, 2011.
———. "Yahweh Wars and the Canaanites: Divinely Mandates Genocide or Corporate Capital Punishment? Responses To Critics." *Philosophia Christi* 11 (2009) 73–90.
Copan, Paul, and Matthew Flannagan. *Did God Really Command Genocide? Coming to Terms with the Justice of God.* Grand Rapids, MI: Baker, 2014.
Copan, Paul, et al. *Holy War in the Bible: Christian Morality and an Old Testament Problem.* Downers Grove: IVP Academic, 2013.
Cotter, David W. *Genesis.* Berit Olam. Collegeville: Liturgical, 2003.
Cowles, C. S. "The Case for Radical Discontinuity." In *Show Them No Mercy: 4 Views on God and Canaanite Genocide*, edited by C. S. Cowles et al., 13–44. Grand Rapids, MI: Zondervan, 2003.
———. "A Response to Eugene H. Merrill." In *Show Them No Mercy: 4 Views on God and Canaanite Genocide*, edited by C. S. Cowles et al., 97–101. Grand Rapids, MI: Zondervan, 2003.
———. "A Response to Tremper Longman III." In *Show Them No Mercy: 4 Views on God and Canaanite Genocide*, edited by C. S. Cowles et al., 191–95. Grand Rapids, MI: Zondervan, 2003.
Cowles, C. S., et al. *Show Them No Mercy: 4 Views on God and Canaanite Genocide.* Grand Rapids, MI: Zondervan, 2003.
Craigie, Peter C. *The Book of Deuteronomy.* Grand Rapids, MI: Eerdmans, 1976.
———. *The Problem of War in the Old Testament.* Grand Rapids, MI: Eerdmans, 1978.
———. "Yahweh Is a Man of Wars." *Scottish Journal of Theology* 22 (1969) 183–88.
Creach, Jerome F. D. *Violence in Scripture.* Louisville: Westminster John Knox, 2013.
Crenshaw, James L. "Popular Questioning of the Justice of God in Ancient Israel." *Zeitschrift für die alttestamentliche Wissenschaft* 82 (1970) 380–95.
Crüsemann, Frank. *The Torah: Theology and Social History of Old Testament Law.* Minneapolis: Fortress, 1996.
Davidson, A. B. *The Theology of the Old Testament.* New York: Scribner's, 1904.
Dawkins, Richard. *The God Delusion.* Boston: Houghton Mifflin, 2006.
Day, John. "Canaan, Religion of." In *The Anchor Yale Bible Dictionary*, 1:831–36. New York: Doubleday, 1992.
———. *Molech: A God of Human Sacrifice in the Old Testament.* Cambridge: Cambridge University Press, 1989.
Day, Peggy L. "'Until I Come and Take You Away to a Land Like Your Own': A Gendered Look at Siege Warfare and Mass Deportation." In *Women in Antiquity: Real Women Across the Ancient World*, edited by Stephanie Lynn Budin and Jean MacIntosh Turfa, 521–32. New York: Routledge, 2016
Dearman, J. Andrew. *The Book of Hosea.* New International Commentary on the Old Testament. Grand Rapids, MI: Eerdmans, 2010.
———. "The Topheth in Jerusalem: Archaeology and Cultural Profile." *Journal of Northwest Semitic Languages* 22 (1996) 59–71.
De Backer, Fabrice. "Cruelty and Military Refinements." *Res Antiquae* 6 (2009) 13–50.

deClaisse-Walford, Nancy L., et al. *The Book of Psalms*. New International Commentary on the Old Testament. Grand Rapids, MI: Eerdmans, 2014.

de Lafayette, Maximillien. *And as Written in the Bible God Is Against Women for Perpetuity*. New York: Times Square, 2017.

Dell, Katharine J. "Amos and the Earthquake: Judgment as Natural Disaster." In *Aspects of Amos: Exegesis and Interpretation*, edited by A. C. Hagedorn and A. Mein, 1–14. London: T. & T. Clark, 2011.

Dietrich, Walter. "The Mark of Cain: Violence and Overcoming Violence in the Hebrew Bible." *Theology Digest* 52 (2005) 3–11.

Dozeman, Thomas B. *Exodus*. Eerdmans Critical Commentary. Grand Rapids, MI: Eerdmans, 2009.

———. "Inner-Biblical Interpretation of Yahweh's Gracious and Compassionate Character." *Journal of Biblical Literature* 108 (1989) 207–23.

———. *Joshua 1–12: A New Translation with Introduction and Commentary*. The Yale Anchor Bible 6A. New Haven: Yale University Press, 2015.

Dubovsky, Peter. "Ripping Open Pregnant Arab Women: Reliefs in Room L of Ashurbanipal's North Palace." *Orientalia* 78 (2009) 394–419.

Duff, Paul Brooks. "The March of the Divine Warrior and the Advent of the Greco-Roman King: Mark's Account of Jesus' Entry into Jerusalem." *Journal of Biblical Literature* 111 (1992) 55–71.

Duke, Rodney K. "'Visiting the Guilt of the Fathers on the Children': Is God Immoral?" *The Evangelical Quarterly* 87 (2015) 347–65.

Dunn, James D. G. *The Partings of the Ways: Between Christianity and Judaism and Their Significance for the Character of Christianity*. London: SCM, 1991.

Earl, Douglas S. *The Joshua Delusion? Rethinking Genocide in the Bible*. Eugene, OR: Cascade, 2010.

Edelman, Diana. "Are the Kings of the Amorites 'Swept Away' in Joshua XXIV 12?" *Vetus Testamentum* 41 (1991) 279–86.

Eichrodt, Walther. *Theology of the Old Testament*. Vol. 2. The Old Testament Library. Philadelphia: The Westminster, 1967.

Ellington, Scott. "Who Shall Lead Them Out? An Exploration of God Openness in Exodus 32:7–14." *Journal of Pentecostal Theology* 14 (2005) 41–60.

Emery, A. C. "Ḥērem." *Dictionary of the Old Testament: Pentateuch*, edited by T. Desmond Alexander and David W. Baker, 383–87. Downers Grove: InterVarsity, 2003.

Ephal, I. *The City Besieged: Siege and Its Manifestations in the Ancient Near East*. Boston: Brill, 2009.

Esau, Ken. "Disturbing Scholarly Behavior: Seibert's Solution to the Problem of the Old Testament God." *Direction* 40 (2011) 168–78.

Feder, Yitzhaq. "The Aniconic Tradition, Deuteronomy 4, and the Politics of Israelite Identity." *Journal of Biblical Literature* 132 (2013) 251–74.

Fernández, Andrés. "El castigo de los hijos por los pecados de los padres." *Estudios Eclesiasticos* 2 (1923) 419–26.

Fishbane, Michael. "Revelation and Tradition: Aspects of Inner-Biblical Exegesis." *Journal of Biblical Literature* 99 (1980) 343–61.

Freedman, David Noel. "God Compassionate and Gracious." *Western Watch* 6 (1958) 6–24.

Fretheim, Terence E. "The Authority of the Bible and Imag(in)ing God." In *The Bible as Word of God In a Postmodern Age*, edited by Terence E. Fretheim and Karlfried Froehlich, 21–32. Eugene, OR: Wipf & Stock, 1998.

———. "The Character of God in Jeremiah." In *Character and Scripture: Moral Formation, Community, and Biblical Interpretation*, edited by William P. Brown, 212–30. Grand Rapids, MI: Eerdmans, 2002.

———. "Divine Dependence upon the Human: An Old Testament Perspective." *Ex Auditu* 13 (1997) 1–13.

———. "Divine Judgment and the Warming of the World: An Old Testament Perspective." In *God, Evil, and Suffering: Essays in Honor of Paul R. Sponheim*, edited by Terence E. Fretheim and Curtis L. Thompson, 21–32. St. Paul: Luther Seminary, 2000.

———. *Exodus*. Interpretation. Louisville: John Knox, 1991.

———. *First and Second Kings*. Louisville: Westminster John Knox, 1999.

———. "God and Violence in the Old Testament." *Word & World* 24 (2004) 18–28.

———. *God and World in the Old Testament: A Relational Theology of Creation*. Nashville: Abingdon, 2005.

———. *God So Enters into Relationships That . . . A Biblical View*. Minneapolis: Fortress, 2020.

———. "'I Was Only a Little Angry': Divine Violence in the Prophets." *Interpretation* 58 (2004) 365–75.

———. *Jeremiah*. Macon, GA: Smyth & Helwys, 2002.

———. "Jonah and Theodicy." *Zeitschrift für die alttestamentliche Wissenschaft* 90 (1978) 227–37.

———. "Prayer in the Old Testament: Creating Space in the World for God." In *A Primer on Prayer*, edited by Paul R. Sponheim, 51–62. Philadelphia: Fortress, 1988.

———. "The Repentance of God: A Key to Evaluating Old Testament God-Talk." *Horizon in Biblical Theology* 10 (1988) 47–70.

———. "The Self-Limiting God of the Old Testament and Issues of Violence." In *Raising Up a Faithful Exegete: Essays in Honor of Richard D. Nelson*, edited by K. L. Noll and Brooks Schramm, 179–91. Winona Lake, IN: Eisenbrauns, 2010.

———. "Some Reflections on Brueggemann's God." In *God in the Fray: A Tribute to Walter Brueggemann*, edited by Tod Linafelt and Timothy K. Beal, 24–37. Minneapolis: Fortress, 1998.

———. *The Suffering of God: An Old Testament Perspective*. Philadelphia: Fortress, 1984.

———. "Theological Reflections on the Wrath of God in the Old Testament." *Horizons in Biblical Theology* 24 (2002) 1–25.

———. "To Say Something—About God, Evil, and Suffering." *Word & World* 19 (1999) 339, 346–50.

———. "Violence and the God of the Old Testament." In *Encountering Violence in the Bible*, edited by Markus Zehnder and Hallvard Hagelia, 108–27. Sheffield: Sheffield Phoenix, 2013.

Fritz, Volkmar. *1 & 2 Kings*. Continental Commentary. Minneapolis, Fortress, 2003.

Frymer-Kensky, Tikva. *Reading the Women of the Bible: A New Interpretation of Their Stories*. New York: Schocken, 2002.

Gangel, Kenneth. *Joshua*. Holman Old Testament Commentary. Nashville: B&H, 2002.

Gardner, Richard B. *Matthew.* Believers Church Bible Commentary. Scottdale: Herald Press, 1991.

Garroway, Kristine. "2 Kings 6:24–30: A Case of Unintentional Elimination Killing." *Journal of Biblical Literature* 137 (2018) 53–70.

Geddert, Timothy J. "The Implied Yhwh Christology of Mark's Gospel: Mark's Challenge to the Reader to 'Connect the Dots.'" *Bulletin for Biblical Research* 25 (2015) 325–40.

Gelston, Anthony. "Wars of Israel." *Scottish Journal of Theology* 17 (1964) 325–31.

Gerstenberger, E. S., and W. Schrage. *Suffering.* Nashville: Abingdon, 1977.

Gesenius, F. W. *Gesenius' Hebrew Grammar.* Edited by E. Kautzsch and A. E. Cowley. Oxford: Oxford University Press, 1956.

Goldingay, John. *Biblical Theology: The God of the Christian Scriptures.* Downers Grove: IVP Academic, 2016.

———. "Covenant, OT and NT." In *The New Interpreter's Dictionary of the Bible*, edited by Katharine Doob Sakenfeld, 1:767–78. Nashville: Abingdon, 2006.

———. *The Message of Isaiah 40–55: A Literary-Theological Commentary.* London: T. & T. Clark 2005.

———. *Old Testament Theology.* 3 vols. Downers Grove: InterVarsity, 2003.

Goshen-Gottstein, Alon. "Judaisms and Incarnational Theologies: Mapping Out the Parameters of Dialogue." *Journal of Ecumenical Studies* 39 (2002) 219–47.

Gottwald, Norman K. *The Hebrew Bible: A Socio-Literary Introduction.* Philadelphia: Fortress, 1985.

Gray, John. "Social Aspects of Canaanite Religion." *Vetus Testamentum Supplement* 15 (1966) 170–92.

Greengus, Samuel. *Laws in the Bible and in Early Rabbinic Collections.* Eugene, OR: Cascade, 2011.

Grüneberg, Keith N. *Abraham, Blessing and the Nations: A Philological and Exegetical Study of Genesis 12:3 in Its Narrative Context.* Berlin: De Gruyter, 2003.

Guenther, Allen R. *Hosea, Amos.* Believers Church Bible Commentary. Scottdale: Herald, 1998.

Guillemette, Nil. "Did Yahweh Promote Genocide?" *Landas* 9 (1995) 3–36.

Gushee, David P., and Codi D. Norred. "The Kingdom of God, Hope and Christian Ethics." *Studies in Christian Ethics* 31 (2018) 3–16.

Haag, H. "*chāmās.*" In *Theological Dictionary of the Old Testament*, edited by G. J. Botterweck et al., 4:478–84. Grand Rapids, MI: Eerdmans, 1974.

Hafemann, Scott J. "Paul's Use of the Old Testament in 2 Corinthians." *Interpretation* 52 (1998) 246–57.

Hagedorn, A. C., and A. Mein, eds. *Aspects of Amos: Exegesis and Interpretation.* London: T. & T. Clark, 2011.

Hallman, Joseph M. "The Mutability of God: Tertullian to Lactantius." *Theological Studies* 42 (1981) 373–93.

Halpern, Baruch. "'The Excremental Vision': The Doomed Priests of Doom in Isaiah 28." *Hebrew Annual Review* 10 (1986) 109–21.

Hamori, Esther J. "Divine Embodiment in the Hebrew Bible and Some Implications for Jewish and Christian Incarnational Theologies." In *Bodies, Embodiment, and Theology of the Hebrew Bible*, edited by S. Tamar Kamionkowski and Wonil Kim, 161–83. New York: T. & T. Clark, 2010.

———. *When Gods Were Men: The Embodied God in Biblical and Near Eastern Literature*. Berlin: De Gruyter, 2008.

Harris, J. G. "The Laments of Habakkuk's Prophecy." *Evangelical Quarterly* 45 (1973) 21–29.

Hartung, John. "Chastity, Fidelity and Conquest: Biblical Rules for Women and War." In *The Oxford Handbook of Evolutionary Perspectives on Violence, Homicide, and War*, edited by Todd K. Shackelford and Viviana A. Weekes-Shackelford, 77–90. Oxford: Oxford University Press, 2012.

Hawk, L. Daniel. *Joshua*. Berit Olam. Collegeville: Liturgical, 2000.

———. *The Violence of the Biblical God*. Grand Rapids, MI: Eerdmans, 2019.

Heiser, M. S. "Chaos." *Dictionary of the Old Testament Prophets*, edited by Mark J. Boda and J. Gordon McConville, 83–86. Downers Grove: IVP Academic, 2012.

Hellerman, Joseph H., et al. *Philippians*. Exegetical Guide to the Greek New Testament. Nashville: B&H Academic, 2015.

Hengel, Martin. *The Cross of the Son of God*. London: SCM, 1981.

Hens-Piazza, Gina. "Forms of Violence and the Violence of Forms: Two Cannibal Mothers before a King (2 Kings 6:24–33)." *Journal of Feminist Studies in Religion* 14 (1998) 91–104.

Herzog, Chaim, and Mordechai Gichon. *Battles of the Bible*. New York: Barnes & Noble, 1997.

Heschel, Abraham J. *The Prophets*. Two Volumes in One. Peabody: Prince, 2000.

Heyed, David. "Divine Creation and Human Procreation: Reflections on Genesis in the Light of Genesis." In *Contingent Future Persons*, edited by Nick Fotion and Jan C. Heller, 57–70. Boston: Kluwer, 1997.

Hillers, Delbert R. "Analyzing the Abominable: Our Understanding of Canaanite Religion." *Jewish Quarterly Review* 75 (1985) 253–69.

———. "History and Poetry in Lamentations." *Currents in Theology and Mission* 10 (1983) 155–61.

Hoffman, Lawrence A. *Encountering God: God Merciful and Gracious*. Woodstock: Jewish Lights Publishing, 2016.

Holland, T. A. "Jericho (Place)." In *The Anchor Yale Bible Dictionary*, edited by Daniel Noel Freedman, 3:723–40. New York: Doubleday, 1992.

Holloway, Jeph. "The Ethical Dilemma of Holy War." *Southwestern Journal of Theology* 41 (1998) 44–69.

Honeyman, A. M. "An Unnoticed Euphemism in Isaiah IX 19–20?" *Vetus Testamentum* 1 (1951) 221–23.

Horn, Siegfried H. "The Babylonian Chronicle and the Ancient Calendar of the Kingdom of Judah." *Andrews University Seminary Studies* 5 (1967) 12–27.

Horsley, Richard A. *Jesus and Magic: Freeing the Gospel Stories from Modern Misconceptions*. Eugene, OR: Wipf & Stock, 2014.

Hossfeld, Frank-Lothar, and Erich Zenger. *Psalm 2: A Commentary on Psalms 51–100*. Hermeneia. Minneapolis: Fortress, 2005.

Huffmon, H. B. "The Israel of God." *Interpretation* 23 (1969) 66–77.

Huie-Jolly, Mary R. "Threats Answered by Enthronement: Death/resurrection and the Divine Warrior Myth in John 5:17–29, Psalm 2 and Daniel 7." In *Early Christian Interpretation of the Scriptures of Israel: Investigations and Proposals*, edited by Craig A. Evans and James A. Sanders, 191–217. Sheffield: Sheffield Academic, 1997.

Irvin-Erickson, Douglas. *Raphaël Lemkin and the Concept of Genocide*. Philadelphia: University of Pennsylvania Press, 2017.

Irvine, Stuart A. "The Threat of Jezreel (Hosea 1:4–5)." *The Catholic Biblical Quarterly* 57 (1995) 494–503.

Janzen, Waldemar. "The First Commandments of the Decalogue and the Battle Against Idolatry in the Old Testament." *Vision* 12 (2011) 14–24.

Japhet, Sara. *I & II Chronicles*. Old Testament Library. Louisville: Westminster John Knox, 1993.

Jaruzelska, Izabela. "Les prophètes face aux usurpations dans le royaume du nord." *Vetus Testamentum* 54 (2004) 165–87.

———. "Prophets and *coups d'état* in the Kingdom of Israel." *Poznańskie Studia Teologiczne* 12 (2002) 19–31.

Jensen, Joseph. "Yahweh's Plan in Isaiah and in the Rest of the Old Testament." *The Catholic Biblical Quarterly* 48 (1986) 443–55.

Johnson, Aubrey R. *The One and the Many in the Israelite Conception of God*. Cardiff: University of Wales Press, 1961.

Johnstone, William. *Exodus 20–40*. Smyth & Helwys Bible Commentary. Macon, GA: Smyth & Helwys, 2014.

Jones, Clay. "We Don't Hate Sin So We Don't Understand What Happened to the Canaanites: An Addendum to 'Divine Genocide' Arguments." *Philosophia Christi* 11 (2009) 53–72.

Jones, Gwilym H. "Holy War or Yahweh War?" *Vetus Testamentum* 25 (1975) 642–58.

Jørstad, Mari. "The Ground That Opened Its Mouth: The Ground's Response to Human Violence in Genesis 4." *Journal of Biblical Literature* 135 (2016) 705–15.

Josephus, Flavius. *The Works of Josephus*. Translated by William Whiston. Peabody: Hendrickson, 1987.

Kang, S. I. "In Search of the Origins of Israelite Aniconism." *Acta Theologica* 38 (2018) 84–98.

Kass, Leon. *The Beginning of Wisdom: Reading Genesis*. New York: Free Press, 2003.

Keener, Craig S., and John H. Walton. *Cultural Backgrounds Study Bible*. Grand Rapids, MI: Zondervan, 2019.

Kelley, Page H. "Prayers of Troubled Saints." *Review & Expositor* 81 (1984) 377–83.

Kern, Paul B. *Ancient Siege Warfare*. Bloomington: Indiana University Press, 1999.

Kessler, Rainer. "The Crimes of the Nations in Amos 1–2." *Acta Theologica* 26 (2018) 206–20.

Kidner, Derek. *Genesis*. Tyndale Old Testament Commentary. Downers Grove: InterVarsity, 1967.

King, Andrew. "Did Jehu Destroy Baal from Israel? A Contextual Reading of Jehu's Revolt." *Bulletin for Biblical Research* 27 (2017) 309–32.

Kinzer, Todd A. "The Strange and Foreign Work of Yahweh: An Emphasis on Divine Mercy in Isaiah 28:20–22." PhD diss., Dallas Theological Seminary, 2017.

Kitchen, K. A. *On the Reliability of the Old Testament*. Grand Rapids, MI: Eerdmans, 2003.

Kitz, Anne Marie. "Demons in the Hebrew Bible and the Ancient Near East." *Journal of Biblical Literature* 135 (2016) 447–64.

Klein, Ralph. *Israel in Exile: A Theological Interpretation*. Philadelphia: Fortress, 1979.

Kline, Meredith G. "Divine Kingship and Genesis 6:1–4." In *The Essential Writings of Meredith G. Kline*, 63–78. Peabody: Hendrickson, 2017.

———. "The Intrusion and the Decalogue." *Westminster Theological Journal* 16 (1953) 1–22.

Knierim, R. "ḥṭ' to miss." *Theological Lexicon of the Old Testament*, edited by Ernst Jenni and Claus Westermann, 542–48. Peabody: Hendrickson, 1997.

Korsch, Dietrich. "Das Kreuz Christi und das Heil der Menschen." *Luther* 84 (2013) 159–67.

Krašovec, Jože. "The Source of Hope in the Book of Lamentations." *Vetus Testamentum* 42 (1992) 223–30.

Kritsky, Gene. "The Insects and Other Arthropods of the Bible, the New Revised Version." *American Entomologist* 43 (1997) 183–88.

Kruger, Paul A. "Mothers and their Children as Victims in War: Amos 1:13 against the Background of the Ancient Near East." *Old Testament Essays* 29 (2016) 100–115.

Kuyper, Lester J. "Suffering and the Repentance of God." *Scottish Journal of Theology* 22 (1969) 257–77.

Kynes, William L. *A Christology of Solidarity: Jesus as the Representative of His People in Matthew*. Langham: University Press of America, 1991.

LaCocque, André. *Daniel*. Atlanta: John Knox, 1979.

Lamb, David T. *God Behaving Badly: Is the God of the Old Testament Angry, Sexist and Racist?* Downers Grove: InterVarsity, 2011.

Lane, Nathan C. *The Compassionate, but Punishing God: A Canonical Analysis of Exodus 34:6-7*. Eugene, OR: Pickwick, 2010.

Laney, J. Carl. "God's Self-Revelation in Exodus 34:6–8." *Bibliotheca Sacra* 158 (2001) 36–51.

Lang, Bernhard. "The Number Ten and the Iniquity of the Fathers: A New Interpretation of the Decalogue." *Zeitschrift für die alttestamentliche Wissenschaft* 118 (2006) 218–38.

Lanner, Laurel. "Cannibal Mothers and Me: A Mother's Reading of 2 Kings 6.24—7.20." *Journal for the Study of the Old Testament* 24 (1999) 107–16.

Lasine, Stuart. "Jehoram and the Cannibal Mothers (2 Kings 6:24–33): Solomon's Judgment in an Inverted World." *Journal for the Study of the Old Testament* 16 (1991) 27–53.

Law, George R. "The Form of the New Covenant in Matthew." *American Theological Inquiry* 5 (2012) 17–32.

Levine, Baruch A. *Numbers 1–20: A New Translation with Introduction and Commentary*. Anchor Bible 4A. New York: Doubleday, 1993.

Levinson, Bernard M. "The Reworking of the Principle of Transgenerational Punishment: Four Case Studies." In *Legal Revision and Religious Renewal in Ancient Israel*, 57–88. Cambridge: Cambridge University Press, 2008.

Limburg, James. *Hosea-Micah*. Interpretation. Louisville: Westminster John Knox, 2011.

Linafelt, Tod, and Timothy K. Beal, eds. *God in the Fray: A Tribute To Walter Brueggemann*. Minneapolis: Fortress, 1998.

Lindars, Barnabas. "Ezekiel and Individual Responsibility." *Vetus Testamentum* 15 (1965) 452–67.

Lindsey, F. Duane. "Isaiah's Songs of the Servant Part I: The Call of the Servant in Isaiah 42:1–9." *Bibliotheca Sacra* 139 (1982) 12–31.

Littrell, Amie D. "The Origin of the Divine Punishment Limit to the Third and Fourth Generation (Exod 34:6–7)." *Biblical Research* 60 (2015) 7–14.

Lloyd, Gareth Jones. "Sacred Violence: The Dark Side of God." *Journal of Beliefs and Values* 20 (1999) 184–99.

Lockwood, Jeffrey A. "Insects as Weapons of War, Terror, and Torture." *Annual Review of Entomology* 57 (2012) 205–27.

Lohfink, Norbert. "The Unmasking of Violence in Israel." *Theology Digest* 27 (1979) 103–6.

Long, Philips V. *Israel's Past in Present Research: Essays on Ancient Israelite Historiography.* Winona Lake, IN: Eisenbrauns, 1999.

Longman, Tremper, III. "The Divine Warrior: The New Testament Use of an Old Testament Motif." *Westminster Theological Journal* 44 (1982) 290–307.

———. *God Is a Warrior.* Grand Rapids, MI: Zondervan, 1995.

Lundbom, Jack R. *Deuteronomy: A Commentary.* Grand Rapids, MI: Eerdmans, 2013.

———. *Jeremiah 1–20: A New Translation with Introduction and Commentary.* Anchor Bible 21A. New York: Doubleday, 1999.

———. *Jeremiah 21–36: A New Translation with Introduction and Commentary.* Anchor Bible 21B. New York: Doubleday, 2004.

Luz, Ulrich. *Matthew 1–7: A Commentary.* Hermeneia. Minneapolis: Fortress, 2007.

Maass, F. "*kpr* to atone." *Theological Lexicon of the Old Testament*, edited by Ernst Jenni and Claus Westermann, 805–17. Peabody: Hendrickson, 1997.

Macdonald, Nathan. "Listening to Abraham—Listening to Yhwh: Divine Justice and Mercy in Genesis 18:16–33." *The Catholic Biblical Quarterly* 66 (2004) 25–43.

MacDonald, Neil B. "YHWH and Jesus in One Self-same Divine Self: Christological Monotheism as an Experiment in Objective Soteriology." *American Theological Inquiry* 6 (2013) 23–36.

Machinist, Peter. "Assyria and Its Image in the First Isaiah." *Journal of the American Oriental Society* 103 (1983) 719–37.

Mariottini, Claude F. "The Egyptian Army," *Biblical Illustrator* 25 (1998) 46–49.

———. "Israel as God's Servants." *Biblical Illustrator* 35 (2009) 56–60.

———. "Jehu: His Leadership and Legacy." *Biblical Illustrator* 30 (2003) 51–55.

———. "Swords: Their Development and Use." *Biblical Illustrator* 37 (Fall 2010): 51–54.

Maré, Leonard P. "Creation Theology in Psalm 139." *Old Testament Essays* 23 (2010) 693–707.

Mastnjak, Nathan. "Judah's Covenant with Assyria in Isaiah 28." *Vetus Testamentum* 64 (2014) 465–83.

Matthews, Victor H. "Taking Calculated Risks: The Story of the Cannibal Mothers (2 Kings 6:24—7:20)." *Biblical Theology Bulletin* 43 (2013) 4–13.

May, Herbert G. "An Interpretation of the Names of Hosea's Children." *Journal of Biblical Literature* 55 (1936) 285–91.

McBride, S. Dean, Jr. "The Essence of Orthodoxy: Deuteronomy 5:6–10 and Exodus 20:2–6." *Interpretation* 60 (2006): 133–50.

———. "Yoke of the Kingdom: An Exposition of Deuteronomy 6:4–5." *Interpretation* 27 (1973) 273–306.

McCarthy, Dennis J. *Treaty and Covenant: A Study in Form in the Ancient Oriental Documents and in the Old Testament.* Rome: Pontifical Biblical Institute, 1963.

McClain, Alva J. "The Doctrine of the Kenosis in Philippians 2:5–8." *Master's Seminary Journal* 9 (1998) 85–96.

McKane, William. *A Critical and Exegetical Commentary on Jeremiah.* Vol. 2. Edinburgh: T. & T. Clark, 1996.

McKnight, Scot. "Jesus and the Twelve." *Bulletin for Biblical Research* 11 (2001) 203–31.
———. *The King Jesus Gospel: The Original Good News Revisited.* Grand Rapids, MI: Zondervan, 2016.
———. *The Letter to the Colossians.* The New International Commentary of the New Testament. Grand Rapids, MI: Eerdmans, 2018.
———. *A Light Among the Nations: Jewish Missionary Activity in the Second Temple Period.* Minneapolis: Fortress, 1991.
———. *Reading Romans Backward: A Gospel of Peace in the Midst of Empire.* Waco: Baylor University Press, 2019.
———. *Sermon on the Mount.* Story of God Bible Commentary. Grand Rapids, MI: Zondervan, 2013.
Mendenhall, George E. "Covenant." In *Interpreter's Dictionary of the Bible*, edited by Katharine Doob Sakenfeld, 1:714–23. Nashville: Abingdon, 1962.
———. "The Incident at Beth Baal Peor." In *The Tenth Generation: The Origin of the Biblical Tradition*, 105–21. Baltimore: Johns Hopkins University Press, 1973.
———. *Law and Covenant in Israel and the Ancient Near East.* Pittsburgh: Biblical Colloquium, 1955.
———. "The Monarchy." *Interpretation* 29 (1975) 155–70.
———. "The 'Vengeance' of Yahweh." In *The Tenth Generation: The Origin of the Biblical Tradition*, 69–104. Baltimore: Johns Hopkins University Press, 1973.
Meyers, Carol. *Exodus.* Cambridge: Cambridge University Press, 2005.
Milgrom, Jacob. "The Nature and Extent of Idolatry in Eighth-Seventh Century Judah." *Hebrew Union College Annual* 69 (1998) 1–13.
———. *Numbers.* The JPS Torah Commentary. New York: Jewish Publication Society, 1990.
———. "Religious Conversion and the Revolt Model for the Formation of Israel." *Journal of Biblical Literature* 101 (1982) 169–76.
Miller, Patrick D. *The Divine Warrior in Early Israel.* Cambridge: Harvard University Press, 1973.
———. "God the Warrior: A Problem in Biblical Interpretation and Apologetics." *Interpretation* 19 (1965) 39–46.
———. *The Ten Commandments.* Louisville: Westminster John Knox, 2009.
———. *They Cried to the Lord: The Form and Theology of Biblical Prayer.* Minneapolis: Fortress, 1994.
Mills, Mary. "Divine Violence in the Book of Amos." In *The Aesthetics of Violence in the Prophets*, edited by Julia M. O'Brien and Chris Franke, 153–79. New York: T. & T. Clark, 2010.
Mintz, Alan. "The Rhetoric of Lamentations and the Representation of Catastrophe." *Prooftexts* 2 (1982) 1–17.
Moberly, R. W. L. "Did the Serpent Get It Right?" *The Journal of Theological Studies* 39 (1988) 1–27.
———. "'God Is Not a Human That He Should Repent': (Numbers 23:19 and 1 Samuel 15:29)." In *God in the Fray: A Tribute To Walter Brueggemann*, edited by Tod Linafelt and Timothy K. Beal, 112–23. Minneapolis: Fortress, 1998.
Moltmann, Jürgen. *The Crucified God: The Cross of Christ as the Foundation and Criticism of Christian Theology.* Minneapolis: Fortress, 1993.
Moore, Alan Mintz. "The Rhetoric of Lamentations and the Representation of Catastrophe." *Prooftexts* 2 (1982) 1–17.

Moore, Michael S. "Human Suffering in Lamentations." *Revue Biblique* 90 (1983) 534–55.

———. "Jehu's Coronation and Purge of Israel." *Vetus Testamentum* 53 (2003) 97–114.

Moore, Thomas S. "'To the End of the Earth': The Geographical and Ethnic Universalism of Acts 1:8 in Light of Isaianic Influence on Luke." *Journal of the Evangelical Theological Society* 40 (1997) 389–99.

Moran, William L. "The Ancient Near Eastern Background of the Love of God in Deuteronomy." *The Catholic Biblical Quarterly* 25 (1963) 77–87.

Morson, Gary Saul, and Morton Schapiro. *Minds Wide Shut: How the New Fundamentalisms Divide Us*. Princeton: Princeton University Press, 2021.

Muffs, Yochanan. "Who Will Stand in the Breach? A Study of Prophetic Intercession." In *Love and Joy: Law, Language and Religion in Ancient Israel*, 9–48. New York: The Jewish Theological Seminary of America, 1992.

Muilenburg, James. "Abraham and the Nations: Blessing and World History." *Interpretation* 19 (1965) 387–98.

Muis, Jan. "Human Rights and Divine Justice." *HTS Theological Studies* 70 (January 2014) 1–8.

Nelson, Richard D. *Deuteronomy*. Old Testament Library. Louisville: Westminster John Knox, 2002.

———. *Joshua*. Old Testament Library. Louisville: Westminster John Knox, 1997.

Newsome, Carol A. *Daniel*. Old Testament Library. Louisville: Westminster John Knox, 2014.

Neufeld, Edward. "Insects as Warfare Agents in the Ancient Near East (Ex. 23:28; Deut. 7:20; Josh. 24:12; Isa. 7:18–20)." *Orientalia* 49 (1980) 30–57.

Niehaus, Jeffrey J. "Joshua and Ancient Near Eastern Warfare." *Journal of the Evangelical Theological Society* 31 (1988) 37–50.

Nogalski, James D. *The Book of the Twelve: Hosea-Jonah*. Macon, GA: Smith & Helwys, 2011.

Noon, Theodore W. "The Idea of Individualism in Jeremiah and Ezekiel." *The Methodist Quarterly Review* 75 (1922) 659–65.

Nysse, Richard. "The Dark Side of God: Considerations for Preaching and Teaching." *Word & World* 17 (1997) 437–46.

O'Brien, Julia M., and Chris Franke. *The Aesthetics of Violence in the Prophets*. New York: T. & T. Clark, 2010.

O'Connor, Kathleen M. "Reclaiming Jeremiah's Violence." In *The Aesthetics of Violence in the Prophets*, edited by Julia M. O'Brien and Chris Franke, 37–49. New York: T. & T. Clark, 2010.

———. "The Tears of God and Divine Character in Jeremiah 2–9." In *God in the Fray: A Tribute to Walter Brueggemann*, edited by Tod Linafelt and Timothy K. Beal, 172–85. Minneapolis: Fortress, 1998.

Oded, Bustenay. "The Table of Nations (Genesis 10): A Socio-cultural Approach." *Zeitschrift für die alttestamentliche Wissenschaft* 98 (1986) 14–31.

Oei, Amos Winarto. "The Impassible God Who 'Cried.'" *Themelios* 41 (2016) 238–47.

Olmstead, A. T. *History of Assyria*. Chicago: The University of Chicago Press, 1951.

Olyan, Saul M. "2 Kings 9:31—Jehu as Zimri." *Harvard Theological Review* 78 (1985) 203–7.

Overholt, Thomas W. "King Nebuchadnezzar in the Jeremiah Tradition." *The Catholic Biblical Quarterly* 30 (1968) 39–48.

Parunak, H. Van Dyke. "Semantic Survey of *nḥm*." *Biblica* 56 (1975) 512–32.
Patrick, Dale. "How Should the Biblical Theologian Go about Constructing a Theological Model: A Debate with Terence Fretheim." *Encounter* 47 (1986) 361–69.
Paul, Shalom M. *Amos*. Hermeneia. Minneapolis: Fortress, 1991.
———. *Isaiah 40–66*. Eerdmans Critical Commentary. Grand Rapids, MI: Eerdmans, 2012.
Payne, J. Barton. *The Theology of the Older Testament*. Grand Rapids, MI: Zondervan, 1962.
Penchansky, David. *What Rough Beast? Images of God in the Hebrew Bible*. Louisville: Westminster John Knox, 1999.
Petersen, David L. *Haggai and Zechariah 1–8: A Commentary*. Louisville: Westminster John Knox, 1984.
Peterson, Brian N. "The Sin of Sodom Revisited: Reading Genesis 19 in Light of Torah." *Journal of the Evangelical Theological Society* 59 (2016) 17–31.
Phetsanghane, Souksamay K. "What Is the צִרְעָה of Exodus 23:28, Deuteronomy 7:20, and Joshua 24:12?" *Wisconsin Lutheran Quarterly* 113 (2016) 175–94.
Piper, Otto A. "Vengeance and the Moral Order." *Theology Today* 5 (1948) 221–34.
Pomeroy, Richard M. *Paul Tillich: A Theology for the 21st Century*. Lincoln: Universe, 2002.
Pomeroy, Trevor. "'As Commander of the Army of the LORD I Have Now Come': Joshua 5:13—6:27 as War Narrative in Context." MA thesis: Memorial University of Newfoundland, 2014.
Pressler, Carolyn. *Numbers*. Abingdon Old Testament Commentaries. Nashville: Abingdon, 2017.
Preuss, Horst Dietrich. *Old Testament Theology*. 2 vols. The Old Testament Library. Edinburgh: T. & T. Clark, 1995.
Pritchard, James B. *Ancient Near Eastern Texts Relating to the Old Testament*. Princeton: Princeton University Press, 1969.
Quine, Cat. "The Host of Heaven and the Divine Army: A Reassessment." *Journal of Biblical Literature* 138 (2019) 741–55.
Rad, Gerhard von. *Holy War in Ancient Israel*. Grand Rapids, MI: Eerdmans, 1991.
———. *Old Testament Theology*. 2 vols. Edinburgh: Oliver and Boyd, 1962, 1965.
Reid, Barbara E. "Violent Endings in Matthew's Parables and Christian Nonviolence." *The Catholic Biblical Quarterly* 66 (2004) 237–55.
———. "Which God Is With Us?" *Interpretation* 64 (2010) 380–89.
Reimer, A. James. "God Is Love but Not a Pacifist." In *Mennonites and Classical Theology: Dogmatic Foundations for Christian Ethics*, 486–92. Kitchener, Ontario: Pandora, 2001.
Richard, Lucien. *What Are They Saying About the Theology of Suffering*. New York: Paulist, 1992.
Richardson, Neil. "Moses, Joshua and the Violence of God." In *Who on Earth is God? Making Sense of God in the Bible*, 47–72. London: Bloomsbury T. & T. Clark, 2014.
Roberts, J. J. M. "The Motif of the Weeping God in Jeremiah and Its Background in the Lament Tradition of the Ancient Near East." In *The Bible and the Ancient Near East: Collected Essays*, 132–42. Winona Lake, IN: Eisenbrauns, 2002.
Robinson, H. Wheeler. *Suffering: Human and Divine*. New York: Macmillan, 1939.
Römer, Thomas. *Dark God: Cruelty, Sex, and Violence in the Old Testament*. New York: Paulist, 2013.

———. "Joshua's Encounter With the Commander of YHWH's Army (Josh 5:13–15): Literary Construction or Reflection of a Royal Ritual?" In *Warfare, Ritual, and Symbol in Biblical and Modern Contexts*, edited by Brad E. Kelle et al., 49–63. Atlanta: Society of Biblical Literature, 2014.

Ronning, John. "When YHWH Became Flesh and Dwelt Among Us: John 1:14 as Programmatic for John's Gospel." Unpublished paper delivered at the ETS annual meeting in Toronto, November 2002.

Routledge, Robin. *Old Testament Theology*. Downers Grove: IVP Academic, 2008.

Rowley, H. H. "The Servant Mission: The Servant Songs and Evangelism." *Interpretation* 8 (1954) 259–72.

Rowley, Matthew. "The Epistemology of Sacralized Violence in the Exodus and Conquest." *Journal of the Evangelical Theological Society* 57 (2014) 63–83.

Sakenfeld, Katharine D. "The Problem of Divine Forgiveness in Numbers 14." *The Catholic Biblical Quarterly* 37 (1975) 317–30.

Sarna, Nahum. *Genesis*. The JPS Torah Commentary. New York: Jewish Publication Society, 1989.

———. *Understanding Genesis*. New York, Schocken, 1966.

Scalise, Pamela J. "The Way of Weeping: Reading the Path of Grief in Jeremiah." *Word & World* 22 (2002) 415–22.

Scharbert, Josef. "Formgeschichte und Exegese von Ex 34,6f und seiner Parallelen." *Biblica* 38 (1957) 130–50.

Schlabach, Gerald W. "A 'Manual' for Escaping Our Vicious Cycles." *Journal of Moral Theology* 7 (2018) 86–91.

Schmitt, Rüdiger. "'And Jacob Set Up a Pillar at Her Grave . . .': Material Memorial and the Landmarks in the Old Testament." In *The Land of Israel in Bible, History, and Theology: Studies in Honour of Ed Noort*, edited by J. van Ruiten and J. C. de Vos, 389–403. Leiden: Brill, 2009.

Schroeder, Gerald L. *God According to God: A Physicist Proves We've Been Wrong About God All Along*. New York: HarperOne, 2009.

Schulte, Hannelis. "The End of the Omride Dynasty: Social-Ethical Observations on the Subject of Power and Violence." *Semeia* 66 (1994) 133–48.

Schwager, Raymond. *Must There Be Scapegoats?* San Francisco: Harper & Row, 1987.

Seibert, Eric A. *Disturbing Divine Behavior: Troubling Old Testament Images of God*. Minneapolis: Fortress, 2009.

———. "Recent Research on Divine Violence in the Old Testament: (With Special Attention to Christian Theological Perspectives)." *Currents in Biblical Research* 15 (2016) 8–40.

———. *The Violence of Scripture: Overcoming the Old Testament's Troubling Legacy*. Minneapolis: Fortress, 2012.

Shea, William. "The Covenant Form of the Letters to the Seven Churches." *Andrews University Seminary Studies* 21 (1983) 71–84.

Simian-Yofre, Horacio "'el raḥûm." In *Theological Dictionary of the Old Testament*, edited by G. J. Botterweck et al., 13:449. Rev. ed. Grand Rapids, MI: Eerdmans, 2004.

Skinner, John. *Genesis*. The International Critical Commentary. New York: Scribner's, 1910.

Smelik, Klaas A. D. "My Servant Nebuchadnezzar: The Use of the Epithet 'My Servant' for the Babylonian King Nebuchadnezzar in the Book of Jeremiah." *Vetus Testamentum* 64 (2014) 109–34.
Smith, D. A. "The Sin of Jehu." *Journal for Semitics* 10 (1998–2001) 112–30.
Smith, Gary V. *Amos*. Mentor Commentaries. Fearn, UK: Mentor, 1998.
Smith, Morton. "A Note on Burning Babies." *Journal of the American Oriental Society* 95 (1975) 477–79.
Smoak, Jeremy D. "Assyrian Siege Warfare Imagery and the Background of a Biblical Curse." In *Writing and Reading War: Rhetoric, Gender, and Ethics in Biblical and Modern Contexts*, edited by Brad E. Kelle and Frank R. Ames, 83–91. Atlanta: Society of Biblical Literature, 2008.
Soggin, J. Alberto. *Joshua: A Commentary*. Old Testament Library. Philadelphia: Westminster, 1972.
———. "The Negation in Joshua 5,14 (Emphatic Lamed)." In *Old Testament and Oriental Studies*, 219–20. Rome: Biblical Institute, 1975.
Soulen, R. Kendall. "YHWH the Triune God." *Modern Theology* 15 (1999) 25–54.
Sparks, Kent. "Gospel as Conquest: Mosaic Typology in Matthew 28:16–20." *The Catholic Biblical Quarterly* 68 (2006) 651–63.
Spencer, Frederick A. M. "The Christian Moral Ideal: Its Nature and Validity." *Modern Churchman* 20 (1930) 304–15.
Sperling, S. David. "Blood, Avenger of." In *The Anchor Yale Bible Dictionary*, edited by David Noel Freedman, 1:763. New York: Doubleday, 1992.
Stager, Lawrence E. "Child Sacrifice at Carthage." *Biblical Archaeology Review* 10 (1984) 31–51.
Staples, Jason A. "'Lord, Lord': Jesus as YHWH in Matthew and Luke." *New Testament Studies* 64 (2018) 1–19.
Stassen, Glen H. "The Fourteen Triads of the Sermon on the Mount (Matthew 5:21—7:12)." *Journal of Biblical Literature* 122 (2003) 267–308.
Stassen, Glen H., and David P. Gushee. *Kingdom Ethics: Following Jesus in Contemporary Context*. Downers Grove: InterVarsity, 2014.
Stendebach, F. J. "šalōm." In *Theological Dictionary of the Old Testament*, edited by G. J. Botterweck et al., 15:13–49. Grand Rapids, MI: Eerdmans, 2006.
Stevens, Bruce. "Jesus as the Divine Warrior." *The Expository Times* 94 (1983) 326–29.
———. "Why Must the Son of Man Suffer: The Divine Warrior in the Gospel of Mark." *Biblische Zeitschrift* 31 (1987) 101–10.
Story, J. Lyle. "Hope in the Midst of Tragedy (Isa 5:1–7; 27:2–6; Matt 21:33–46 par.)." *Horizons in Biblical Theology* 31 (2009) 178–95.
Strong, John T. "Israel as a Testimony to Yhwh's Power: The Priests' Definition of Israel." In *Constituting the Community: Studies on the Polity of Ancient Israel in Honor of S. Dean McBride*, edited by John T. Strong and Steven S. Tuell, 89–106. Winona Lake, IN: Eisenbrauns, 2005.
Sundberg, Walter. "'Evil' after 9/11: The Alien Work of God." *Word & World* 24 (2004) 204, 206.
Swart, I., and C. W. Van Dam. "ḥms." In *New International Dictionary of Old Testament Theology and Exegesis*, 2:177–80. Grand Rapids, MI: Zondervan, 1997.
Sweeney, Marvin A. *I & II Kings*. Old Testament Library. Louisville: Westminster John Knox, 2007.

———. *Reading Ezekiel: A Literary and Theological Commentary*. Macon, GA: Smyth & Helwys, 2013.

Taber, Charles R. "Missiology and the Bible." *Missiology* 11 (1983) 229–45.

Terrien, Samuel. *The Elusive Presence*. San Francisco: Harper & Row, 1978.

Tertullian, *Against Marcion*. Edinburgh: T. & T. Clark, 1868.

Thompson, J. A. *The Book of Jeremiah*. New International Commentary on the Old Testament. Grand Rapids, MI: Eerdmans, 1980.

Tietmeyer, Lena-Sofia. "When God Changes His Mind: A Theological Exploration of Jonah 3:9–10 and 4:2." In *Gamla testamentets teologi och tolkningar*, edited by Birger Olsson and James Starr, 125–46. Skellefteå, Sweden: Artos, 2018.

Tigay, Jeffrey H. *Deuteronomy*. The JPS Torah Commentary. Philadelphia: The Jewish Publication Society, 1996.

Torrance, T. F. "The Israel of God: Israel and the Incarnation." *Interpretation* 10 (1956) 305–20.

Trible, Phyllis. *God and the Rhetoric of Sexuality*. Overtures to Biblical Theology. Philadelphia: Fortress, 1978.

Trimm, Charlie. "Recent Research on Warfare in the Old Testament." *Currents in Biblical Research* 10 (2012) 171–216.

———. *YHWH Fights for Them!: The Divine Warrior in the Exodus Narrative*. Piscataway: Gorgias, 2014.

Tucker, Gene M. "Isaiah." *The Oxford Study Bible*. New York: Oxford University Press, 1992.

Turner, David L. *Matthew*. Baker Exegetical Commentary on the New Testament. Grand Rapids, MI: Baker, 2008.

Via, Dan O. *Divine Justice, Divine Judgment: Rethinking the Judgment of Nations*. Minneapolis: Fortress, 2007.

Villar, Evaristo. "Does the Bible Portray a Violent God?" *Theology Digest* 30 (1982) 203–7.

Volf, Miroslav. "Divine Violence?" *Christian Century*, October 13, 1999.

Volz, Paul. *Das Dämonische in Jahwe*. Tübingen: Mohr, 1924.

Vriezen, T. C. *An Outline of Old Testament Theology*. Oxford: Basil Blackwell, 1958.

Walker, Alyssa. "Jonah's Genocidal and Suicidal Attitude—and God's Rebuke." *Kairos: Evangelical Journal of Theology* 9 (2015) 7–29.

Walton, John H., and J. Harvey Walton. *The Lost World of the Israelite Conquest: Covenant, Retribution, and the Fate of the Canaanites*. Downers Grove: IVP Academic, 2017.

Walzer, Michael. "The Idea of Holy War in Ancient Israel." *Journal of Religious Ethics* 20 (1992) 215–28.

Watts, Rikki E. "Consolation or Confrontation? Isaiah 40–55 and the Delay of the New Exodus." *Tyndale Bulletin* 41 (1990) 31–59.

Weaver, J. Denny. "The Peace Church as Worship of God." *The Mennonite* 13 (July 2010) 17–22.

Webb, William J., and Gordon K. Oeste. *Bloody, Brutal, and Barbaric: Wrestling with Troubling War Texts*. Downers Grove: IVP Academic, 2019.

Weinfeld, Moshe. *Deuteronomy 1–11: A New Translation with Introduction and Commentary*. Anchor Bible 5. New York: Doubleday, 1991.

———. "Divine Intervention and War in the Ancient Near East." In *History, Historiography, and Interpretation: Studies in Biblical and Cuneiform Literatures*, edited by H. Tadmor and M. Weinfeld, 121–47. Leiden: Brill, 1984.

———. *The Promise of the Land: The Inheritance of the Land of Canaan by the Israelites*. Berkeley: University of California Press, 1993.

Wenham, Gordon J. "The Deuteronomic Theology of the Book of Joshua." *Journal of Biblical Literature* 90 (1971) 140–48.

———. *Genesis 1–15*. Word Bible Commentary 1. Waco: Word, 1987.

Wénin, André. "Dieu qui visite la faute des pères sur les fils" (Ex 20,5): En marge d'un livre récent de B. M. Levinson." *Revue Théologique de Louvain* 38 (2007) 67–77.

Westermann, Claus. *Genesis 1–11*. Continental Commentary. Minneapolis: Fortress, 1994.

Weyde, Karl W. "Is God a Violent God?" *Theologisk Tidsskrift* 6 (2017) 280–300.

Whybray, R. N. "The Immorality of God: Reflections on Some Passages in Genesis, Job, Exodus and Numbers." *Journal for the Study of the Old Testament* 12 (1996) 89–120.

———. "'Shall Not the Judge of All the Earth Do What is Just?' God's Oppression of the Innocent in the Old Testament." In *Shall Not the Judge of All The Earth Do What is Right?: Studies on the Nature of God in Tribute to James L. Crenshaw*, edited by David Penchansky and Paul L. Redditt, 1–19. Winona Lake, IN: Eisenbrauns, 2000.

Widmer, Michael. *Standing in the Breach: An Old Testament Theology and Spirituality of Intercessory Prayer*. Winona Lake, IN: Eisenbrauns, 2015.

Wolff, Hans Walter. "Jonah: The Reluctant Messenger in a Threatened World." *Currents in Theology and Mission* 3 (1976) 8–19.

———. *Obadiah and Jonah*. Minneapolis: Augsburg, 1986.

Wright, Christopher J. H. *The Mission of God: Unlocking the Bible's Grand Narrative*. Downers Grove: IVP Academic, 2006.

Wright, G. Ernest. "Divine Name and the Divine Nature." *Perspective* 12 (1971) 177–85.

Wright, N. T. "New Exodus, New Inheritance: The Narrative Substructure of Romans 3–8." In *Romans and the People of God: Essays in Honor of Gordon D. Fee on the Occasion of His 65th Birthday*, edited by S. K. Soderlund and N. T. Wright, 26–35. Grand Rapids, MI: Eerdmans, 1999.

Wyschogrod, Michael. "A Jewish Perspective on Incarnation." *Modern Theology* 12 (1996) 195–209.

Yee, Gale A. "Jezebel (Person)." *The Anchor Yale Bible Dictionary*, edited by David Noel Freedman, 3:848–49. New York: Doubleday, 1992.

Younger, K. Lawson, Jr. "Some Recent Discussion on the Herem." In *Far From Minimal: Celebrating the Work and Influence of Philip R. Davis*, edited by D. Burns and J. W. Rogerson, 505–22. New York: Bloomsbury T. & T. Clark, 2014.

Zaehner, Robert Charles. *Our Savage God: The Perverse Use of Eastern Thought*. Glasgow: Collins, 1974.

Zehnder, Markus. "The Annihilation of the Canaanites: Reassessing the Brutality of the Biblical Witnesses." In *Encountering Violence in the Bible*, edited by Markus Zehnder and Hallvard Hamelia, 263–90.Sheffield: Sheffield Phoenix, 2013.

Zehnder, Markus, and Hallvard Hagelia. *Encountering Violence in the Bible*. Sheffield: Sheffield Phoenix, 2013.

Zenger, Eric. "The God of Exodus in the Message of the Prophets as Seen in Isaiah." In *Exodus—A Lasting Paradigm*, edited by Bas van Iersel and Anton Weiler, 22–33. Edinburgh: T. & T. Clark, 1987.

Zorn, Jeffrey R. "War and Its Effects on Civilians in Ancient Israel and Its Neighbors." In *The Other Face of the Battle: The Impact of War on Civilians in the Ancient Near East*, edited by Davide Nadali and Jordi Vidal, 79–100. Münster: Ugarit-Verlag, 2014.

Index of Authors

Ackerman, Susan, 212n5
Ahlström, Gösta, 224n30
Aichele, George, 44, 44n16
Albertz, Rainer, 150, 151n8
Allen, Leonard, 256n48
Andersen, Francis I., 158n7
Anderson, Bernhard, 154n15, 322n10
Anderson, Elizabeth, 172, 173n3
André, G., 104, 104n6
Andreasen, Niels-Erik A., 212n5
Angel, Andrew R., 365n35, 365n39, 366, 366nn40–43, 367, 367n46
Assmann, Jan, 17, 17n3, 49n1, 106, 106nn13–14, 119, 119n13, 242, 242n2
Azuelos, Yaacov, 235n33

Bailey, Wilma, 249, 249n20
Barrett, Charles, 325, 325nn15–16
Barth, Karl, 76, 76n26, 356n10, 360, 360n27
Bartlett, John R., 230n19
Barton, John, 15n29
Baruchi-Unna, Amitai, 215n7
Beal, Lissa M. Wray, 230, 230n18
Beale, G. K., 343, 343n37
Beers, Holly, 346, 346nn43–44
Belousek, Darrin W. Snyder, 18, 19n4, 23, 23n20, 24, 24n21–24, 44, 44nn17–18, 45, 45n19, 47, 47n27, 102, 103n3
Ben-Barak, Zafrira, 212n5
Ben Zvi, Ehud, 203n21
Berges, Ulrich, 30, 30n39, 46n23, 46n26

Berlejung, Angelika, 50n5, 51, 51n11, 145n15
Berlin, Adele, xvn10, 180, 180n3, 187, 187n21
Biddle, Mark E., 291n7
Bird, Michael F., 336n10
Bleibtreu, Erika, 162n20
Blenkinsopp, Joseph, 148n1, 324, 324n13, 348–349n54, 354, 354n6
Bloch-Smith, Elizabeth, 22n16, 181, 181n7, 182, 182n8, 185n18
Block, Daniel I., 258, 258n56, 334n7
Boase, Elizabeth, 94n22
Borowski, Oded, 230, 230n15
Bosman, Hendrik, 186, 186n19
Bosworth, David A., 68, 69n2, 72, 73, 73n11, 74, 74nn17–18, 74n20
Bowman, Richard, 151, 151n10
Boyd, Gregory A., x, xn2, 8, 8nn9–11, 9, 9n12, 12, 12n22, 13, 14, 14nn25–26, 19, 19n5, 22, 23, 23n18, 33, 35, 41, 43,44, 45, 45nn21–22, 46, 46n26, 48, 84, 84n2, 91, 92, 92n14, 103, 103n5, 129, 129n1, 151, 151nn11–12, 152n13, 161, 161nn14–17, 172, 172n7, 173n8, 178, 181, 181nn4–5, 183, 184, 184n14, 184n16, 195, 199, 199nn8–10, 200, 200nn13–15, 201, 201n16, 219, 219nn17–19, 220, 226, 226nn1–2, 227, 227nn3–6, 228, 228n7, 228n9, 229, 229n10, 231, 232, 232n21, 233, 233nn23–26, 234, 234nn27–28, 238, 241, 243,

(*Boyd, Gregory continued*)
243n8, 244n9, 255, 255n45, 374, 374n7
Braaten, Carl E., 54, 54n20
Brettler, Marc Zvi, 4n3, 92, 92nn15–16, 104, 105n8
Bridge, Edward J., 204n23
Bright, John, 149, 149n4, 218n13, 219, 219n15, 309, 309n17, 325, 325n17, 327, 328, 328nn20–21, 363, 364n34, 367, 367n48
Brueggemann, Walter, 9n12, 19, 53, 53n15, 54, 54nn17–18, 55n22, 61, 71, 71n9, 73, 73n15, 74, 75, 75nn21–23, 86n3, 101, 101n2, 205, 205n26, 244n10, 249n22, 260, 260n61, 261, 261nn62–63, 262, 262nn64–66, 263, 263n68, 291, 291n5, 295n9, 307n14, 314, 314nn3–4, 333, 333n5, 335, 335n8, 372, 373, 373nn5–6
Brunner, Emil, 12, 12n20, 13, 13n23, 76, 76n27
Busch, Eberhard, 32nn43–44

Callaway, Joseph, 256, 256n49
Carroll R., M. Daniel, 9n12, 157n6
Carson, Jordan, 377n10
Carvalho, Corrine, 35n1
Chapman, Stephen B., 252, 252n28
Childs, Brevard S., 53n14
Chisholm, Robert B. Jr., 220n20
Clark, Gordon, 89, 89n11
Clarke, Terrance A. 259, 259n59
Claassens, L Juliana M., 70n4
Clines, David J. A., 337n11, 339n20
Cogan, Mordechai, 176, 176n21, 177, 177n22, 178, 178n24
Collins, John J., x, xn3, 9n12
Copan, Paul, 8n11, 9n12, 243n3
Cotter, David W., 279n10
Cowles, C. S., 4, 4nn4–6, 5, 5n7, 7, 8n11, 9, 9n12, 12, 13, 43, 48, 160, 160n11, 243, 243nn5–6
Craigie, Peter C., x, xn4, 245, 245n11, 248n19, 264n72
Creach, Jerome F. D., 8n11, 9n12, 219, 219n17

Crenshaw, James L., 3, 3n2, 203, 204n22
Crüsemann, Frank, 248, 248nn16–18

Davidson, A. B., 53n16
Dawkins, Richard, 12, 12n21, 19, 243, 243n4
Day, John, 192n27, 246, 246n14
Day, Peggy L., 171, 171n2
Dearman, J. Andrew, 171n1, 192n26
De Backer, Fabrice, 174, 174n10, 175n16
deClaisse-Walford, Nancy L., 150n7
de Lafayette, Maximillien, 172, 172n4
Dell, Katherine J., 26n26
Dietrich, Walter, 19, 19n8, 28n35, 369n49, 372, 372n1, 372n5
Dozeman, Thomas B., 123, 165, 239, 240, 249, 250
Dubovsky, Peter, 175, 175n15, 175n17, 176n20
Duff, Paul Brooks, 365n35
Duke, Rodney K., 92, 93n19, 109, 109n18, 127, 127n29, 197, 198n3
Dunn, James D. G., 348n52, 349, 349n55

Earl, Douglas S., 232, 232n22, 234
Eichrodt, Walther, 235, 235nn36–37
Edelman, Diana, 230n19
Ellington, Scott, 123n22, 124, 124nn25–26
Emery, A. C., 254n40
Ephal, I., 180n2
Esau, Ken, 33n46

Feder, Yitzhaq, 299n10
Fernández, Andrés, 119n15
Fishbane, Michael, 110, 110n19, 111n20
Flannagan, Matthew, 9n12
Freedman, David Noel, 90, 90n13, 123n21, 130, 130n2, 158n7
Fretheim, Terence E., v, xiii, 9, 9n13, 10n14, 10n16, 19n9, 20, 20n12, 21n14, 26, 26n27, 29, 29n37, 30, 30n40, 34, 34n47, 37, 37n5, 39, 39n7, 41n12, 44, 44n15, 50,

50nn7–8, 52, 52nn12–13, 55n21, 56n24, 59, 59n6, 64, 64n11, 65, 65n12, 69n3, 70, 71n6, 71n8, 72, 72n10, 75n25, 77n30, 79, 79n31, 80n33, 97nn25–26, 123, 124, 124nn23–24, 125, 125nn27–28, 135, 135n9, 139, 139nn1–2, 140, 140n5, 145, 145n15, 146, 146n16, 165, 165n26, 166, 166n28, 168, 170, 170n33, 179, 179n25, 189, 189n24, 191n25, 195, 196n31, 197, 197n2, 198, 198n4, 198n6, 206, 206n29, 208, 208n33, 218n14, 282n14, 284, 284n17, 290, 291n3, 291n6, 331n1, 353n4
Fritz, Volkmar, 183, 183n12
Frymer-Kensky, Tikva, 180, 180n1

Gangel, Kenneth, 235, 235n31
Gardner, Richard B., 362, 362nn32–33
Garroway, Kristine, 183n13
Geddert, Timothy J., 341, 341nn29–31, 342, 342nn32–34, 347n48
Gelston, Anthony, 252n29
Gerstenberger, E. S., 61, 61n8, 63, 63n9
Gesenius, F. W., 272, 272n2
Goldingay, John, ix, 4n3, 30, 31n41, 55n23, 89, 89n12, 279, 279n11, 282, 282n15, 285n19, 345, 345n42
Goshen-Gottstein, Alon., 338n17, 339, 340, 340nn22–26
Gottwald, Norman K., 217n11
Gray, John, 245n12
Greengus, Samuel, 112n22
Grüneberg, Keith N., 291n4
Guenther, Allen R., 223n25
Gushee, David P., 359n24

Hafemann, Scott J., 343n37
Hagelia, Hallvard, 9n12
Hallman, Joseph M., 205n27
Halpern, Baruch, 151, 151n9
Hamori, Esther J., 337, 337nn12–13, 338, 338n14, 338n16
Harris, J. G., 21n13

Hartung, John, 172, 172n6
Hawk, L. Daniel, 206, 207n30, 240n51, 241, 241n53, 266, 266nn76–77
Heiser, M. S., 366n45
Hellerman, Joseph H., 355n9, 356n12
Hengel, Martin, 39, 39n10
Hens-Piazza, Gina, 183n13
Heschel, Abraham J., 57n1, 58n4, 64, 64n10, 66n13, 70, 70n5, 71, 71n7, 74, 74n19, 79n32, 81, 81nn34–35, 81n38
Heyed, David, 284, 284n18
Hillers, Delbert R., 187n22, 245, 245n12
Holland, T. A., 256n46
Holloway, Jeph, 366n44
Honeyman, A. M., 183, 183n11
Horn, Siegfried H., 185n17
Horsley, Richard A., 347n50
Hossfeld, Frank-Lothar, 16n2
Huie-Jolly, Mary R., 365n35

Irvin-Erickson, Douglas, 258n57
Irvine, Stuart A., 222n14

Janzen, Waldemar, 114n3, 119n14
Japhet, Sara, 251n24
Jaruzelska, Izabela, 210n2, 215n8, 224n32, 225, 225n33
Jensen, Joseph, 42n14
Johnson, Aubrey R., 235, 235n34
Johnstone, William, 106n12
Jones, Clay, 81, 81n37, 257n53
Jones, Gwilym H., 252, 252n31
Jørstad, Mari, 274, 274n6
Josephus, Flavius, 177, 178, 178n23, 328

Kang, S. I., 106, 106n15
Kass, Leon, 277, 277n9
Keener, Craig S., 184n15
Kelley, Page H., 155, 155n16
Kern, Paul B., 174n13
Kessler, Rainer, 158n8, 159n10
Kidner, Derek, 277, 277n8, 286, 286n21
King, Andrew, 216n10

Kinzer, Todd A., 152, 152n14
Kitchen, K. A., 259, 259n58
Kitz, Anne Marie, 332n2
Klein, Ralph, 310n1
Kline, Meredith G., 264, 264nn71–73, 280, 280n12
Knierim, R., 51, 51n9–10
Krašovec, Jože, 96n24
Kritsky, Gene, 230, 230nn16–17
Kruger, Paul A., 174n11, 175n18
Kuyper, Lester J., 57n2, 75n25, 76, 76n28
Kynes, William L., 343, 343n38

LaCocque, André, 235n30
Lamb, David T., 8n11, 9n12
Lane, Nathan C., 92n17
Laney, J. Carl, 29n38
Lang, Bernhard, 120n17
Lanner, Laurel, 183n13
Lasine, Stuart, 183n13
Law, George R, 359, 359n18
Levine, Baruch A., 140, 140n4
Levinson, Bernard M., 117, 117nn8–10, 118, 118n12
Limburg, James, 221n22, 223n26
Lindars, Barnabas, 14. 14nn27–28, 93, 93n21, 120, 120n18, 254n38
Lindsey, F. Duane, 324n14
Littrell, Amie D., 101n1, 103, 103n4
Lloyd, Gareth Jones, 15n29
Lockwood, Jeffrey A., 229, 229n12, 230n13
Lohfink, Norbert, 360n25, 372n3
Long, Philips V., 149, 149n5
Longman, Tremper III, 35n1, 242n5, 365n35, 370, 370n51
Lundbom, Jack R., 73, 73n13, 111, 111n21, 114, 114n4, 193, 193n29, 194, 194n30, 358, 358n17
Luz, Ulrich, 344nn39–40, 347n46

Maass, F. 351n2
Macdonald, Nathan, 199n12
MacDonald, Neil B., 13, 13n24, 39, 39n6, 39n9, 39n10
Machinist, Peter, 181n7

Mariottini, Claude F., x, 36n2, 210n1, 236n40, 323n12
Maré, Leonard P., 50n2, 50n4
Mastnjak, Nathan, 149n2
Matthews, Victor H., 183n13
May, Herbert G., 221n23
McBride, S. Dean Jr., 300n11, 338n15
McCarthy, Dennis J., 359, 359n20
McClain, Alva J., 355, 355n8
McKnight, Scot, xiin8, 95, 95n23, 328, 328nn23–23, 329, 336n10, 347, 347n49, 348, 348n51, 348n53, 355n7, 361n29
Mendenhall, George E., 27, 27nn31–33, 28n34, 247n15, 359, 359n19, 359n21, 367n47
Meyers, Carol, 119, 119n16
Milgrom, Jacob, 115n7, 140, 140n7, 255n43, 263, 264n70
Miller, Patrick D., 35n1, 37, 37nn3–4, 114, 155n5, 237, 237n42, 239, 239n45, 275, 276n7
Mills, Mary, 157n6
Mintz, Alan, 186n20
Moberly, R. W. L., 75n25, 272n1
Moltmann, Jürgen, 58, 58n3
Moore, Alan Mintz, 186n20
Moore, Michael S., 186n20, 216n9
Moore, Thomas S., 346n45
Moran, William L., 105, 105n9
Muffs, Yochanan, 132, 132nn5–6, 133, 133n7, 134, 134n8, 141nn9–10, 142, 142n12
Muilenburg, James, 334n6
Muis, Jan, 157n4

Nelson, Richard D., 228n8, 237, 237n41, 249, 249n21
Newsome, Carol A., 235n29
Neufeld, Edward, 229, 229n11, 230, 230n14
Niehaus, Jeffrey J., 263, 263n67
Nogalski, James D., 164, 164n24
Norred, Codi D., 359n24
Nysse, Richard, 15n29

O'Connor, Kathleen M., 73, 73n16, 74, 75, 75n24, 188, 189n23

Oded, Bustenay, 286n20
Oeste, Gordon K., x, xn2, 252n30
Olmstead, A. T., 174, 174n9, 175, 175n19
Olyan, Saul M., 217n12
Overholt, Thomas W., 306n12

Parunak, H. Van Dyke, 76n29
Patrick, Dale, 10, 10n15, 41, 41n12
Paul, Shalom M., 157n5, 336, 336n9
Payne, J. Barton, 235, 235n32
Penchansky, David, 19, 19n
Petersen, David L., 32n42
Peterson, Brian N. 81, 81n36, 201, 201n17
Phetsanghane, Souksamay K., 231, 231n20
Piper, Otto A., 50, 50n6
Pomeroy, Richard M., 172n5
Pomeroy, Trevor, 239n49
Pressler, Carolyn, 140, 140n6, 141n8
Preuss, Horst Dietrich, 105, 105n10, 166n17, 236, 236n38
Pritchard, James B., xiv

Quine, Cat, 37n3

Reid, Barbara E., 361n30
Reimer, A. James, 45, 45n20, 46, 46nn24–25, 370, 370n50, 371, 371n52, 372, 372n2
Richard, Lucien, 61, 61n7
Roberts, J. J. M., 68n1
Robinson, H. Wheeler, 59, 59n5
Römer, Thomas, 239, 239nn46–47, 253, 253n33
Ronning, John, 39n8, 342, 342nn35–36
Routledge, Robin, 105n11, 235, 235n35, 311, 311n2
Rowley, H. H., 322n11
Rowley, Matthew, 265nn74–75

Sakenfeld, Katharine D., 92, 92n18, 139, 140n3, 142, 143n13, 144, 144n14
Sarna, Nahum, 208, 208n34, 283, 283n16

Scalise, Pamela J., 68n1
Scharbert, Josef, 141, 142n11
Schlabach, Gerald W., 362n31
Schmitt, Rüdiger, 120n19
Schrage, 61, 61n8, 63, 63n9
Schroeder, Gerald L., 10, 10n17, 11, 11n18
Schulte, Hannelis, 219, 219n16, 223, 224, 224nn27–29, 224n31, 225, 225n34
Schwager, Raymond, 19, 19n11
Seibert, Eric A., 5, 5n8, 6, 7, 8n11, 9, 9n12, 12, 13, 23, 33, 33n46, 43, 44, 45, 46n26, 48, 151, 160, 160n12, 161n13, 161n19, 172, 199, 199n7, 243, 243n7, 249n20
Shea, William, 359, 359n22
Simian-Yofre, Horacio, 87n8
Skinner, John, 273, 273n4
Smelik, Klaas A. D., 306n13
Smith, D. A., 221n21
Smith, Morton, 193n28
Smoak, Jeremy D., 182, 182n9
Soggin, J. Alberto, 237, 238, 238nn43–44
Soulen, R. Kendall, 330, 330n24, 339n21, 365, 365n36
Spencer, Frederick A. M., 360n28
Sperling, S. David, 25, 26n25
Staples, Jason A., 39n8, 341, 341nn27–28
Stassen, Glen H., 359, 359n24, 362n31
Stendebach, F. J., 16n1
Stevens, Bruce, 365n35, 365nn37–38
Story, J. Lyle, 357n13
Strong, John T., 281n13, 287n22, 289, 289n1
Sundberg, Walter, 149, 150, 150n6
Sweeney, Marvin A., 215n6, 354n5

Taber, Charles R., 332n4
Terrien, Samuel, 66, 67, 67nn14–15
Thompson, J. A., 73, 73n14
Tietmeyer, Lena-Sofia, 169n31
Tigay, Jeffrey H., 108, 108n16, 181, 181n6
Torrance, T. F., 349n55
Trible, Phyllis, 87, 87n9

Trimm, Charlie, 9n12, 35n1
Turner, David L., 357, 357n14, 360n26
Tucker, Gene M., 162, 162n21

Via, Dan O., 157n3
Villar, Evaristo, 375n8
Volf, Miroslav, 83, 83n1
Volz, Paul, 57n1
Von Rad, Gerhard, 42n13, 113, 113n1, 115, 115n6, 118, 118n11, 149, 149n3, 169, 169n32, 198, 198n5, 203, 203n20, 236, 236n39, 253, 253n32
Vriezen, T. C., 294, 295n8

Walker, Alyssa, 163, 163n23, 168, 168n29, 169n30, 209, 209n35
Walton, John H., 184n15, 253, 253nn35–36, 254n37, 256, 256n50, 257, 257n54, 258n55
Walton, J. Harvey, 253, 253nn35–36, 254n37, 256, 256n50, 257, 257n54, 258n55
Walzer, Michael, 242, 242n1
Watts, Rikki E., 321n7
Weaver, J. Denny, 23, 23n19
Webb, William J., x, xn2, 252n30
Weinfeld, Moshe, 108, 108n17, 253n34, 260n60
Wenham, Gordon J., 240n52, 273, 273n3

Wénin, André, 93, 93n20
Westermann, Claus, 273, 273n5
Weyde, Karl W., 22, 22n15, 23n17, 29, 29n36, 32n45, 326n19
Whybray, R. N., 3, 3n1, 19, 19nn6–7, 54, 54n19, 199, 199n11, 204, 204nn24–25
Widmer, Michael, 130, 130nn3–4, 202, 202nn18–19, 207, 207n31, 208, 208n32
Wilgus, J. Blair, 9n12
Wolff, Hans Walter, 308, 308nn15–16
Wright, Christopher J. H., 332n3
Wright, G. Ernest, 87n6
Wright, N. T., 344n41
Wyschogrod, Michael, 114n2, 338, 338n18, 339n19

Yee, Gale A., 212n4
Younger, K. Lawson Jr., 254, 254n39

Zaehner, Robert Charles, 156, 156nn1–2
Zehnder, Markus.
Zehnder, Markus, 9n12, 251, 251n25, 252, 252nn26–27, 255n42
Zenger, Erich, 16, 16n2,
Zenger, Eric, 322, 322nn8–9, 326n18
Zorn, Jeffrey R., 182, 183n10, 256, 256n47, 257nn51–52

Index of Subjects

Aaron, 85, 118, 121, 138, 369
Abel, 28, 274, 275, 276, 277, 279, 284, 287, 369
Abraham, 6, 7, 17, 21, 28, 30, 38, 40, 60, 80, 84, 124, 136, 139, 140, 142, 152, 155, 198, 199, 200, 201, 202, 203, 204, 205, 206, 207, 208, 214, 242, 244, 245, 248, 250, 255, 257, 264, 271, 286, 287, 288, 289, 290, 291, 292, 293, 294, 295, 296, 297, 298, 299, 307, 324, 329, 331, 332, 333, 334, 335, 336, 337, 343, 346, 347, 348n54, 351, 352, 355n7
Abraham Lincoln, 149
Absalom, 120
abusive, 19, 362
accommodation, accommodate, 40, 41, 213, 232, 301
Adam, 271, 272, 273, 274, 275, 279, 283, 286, 333, 355n7, 369
adultery, 81, 201, 362
agape, 24, 89
agents, 10, 12, 25, 31, 50, 52, 53, 55, 96, 129, 130, 179, 189, 190, 193, 195, 200, 225, 228, 229, 230, 265, 266, 297, 329, 334, 352, 354, 367, 377
Ahab., 133, 210, 211, 211n3, 212, 213, 215, 215n7, 216, 216n9, 217, 218, 220, 220n20, 221, 222, 223, 224, 225
Ahaz, 173, 178, 179, 192
Ahaziah, 217, 218
Ai, 256

alien, 7, 66, 154, 304, 305, 319, 321
alien work, 80, 148, 149, 150, 151, 152, 153, 155, 203, 370
alienation, 66, 288, 343
altar, 24, 25, 104, 204, 213, 214, 246, 247, 255, 298, 326, 350, 351
Amalek, Amalekites, 6, 22, 40, 138, 161n19, 162n19
Ammon, Ammonites, 40, 159, 176, 179, 192, 244, 302, 305
Amorites, 17, 18, 138, 229, 230, 231, 243, 246, 250, 257, 260, 261, 263, 264
Amos, 18, 104, 157, 157n3, 158, 159, 160, 176, 224, 244, 294
Anabaptists, 23, 24, 33, 33n46, 44, 45, 47, 48, 371
Ancient Near East, ix, 48, 101, 119, 158, 159, 171, 176, 178, 181, 239n49, 243, 248, 293, 299, 352, 359
angel, angelic, 130, 227, 234, 235, 250, 251, 280, 281, 347
Angel of the Lord , 235, 236
anger, angry, xv, xvii, 12, 14, 18, 19, 25, 29, 30, 31, 32, 51, 53n14, 57, 59, 62, 64, 65, 71, 75, 77, 78, 79, 80, 81, 82, 86, 86n4, 88, 93, 94, 114, 116, 119, 122, 123, 126, 131, 132, 133, 135, 141, 146, 150, 152, 154, 162, 165, 166, 168, 169, 177, 179, 183, 186, 187, 192, 195, 198, 203, 205, 246, 247, 274, 278, 284, 291, 301, 302, 303, 308, 320, 331,

(*anger, angry continued*)
332, 353, 362, 369, 371, 373, 374, 375, 377
aniconic, aniconism, 106, 119, 299
annihilate, annihilation, xv, 19, 152, 155, 160, 243, 250, 251, 252, 253, 255, 258, 322
anoint, anointed, anointing, 176, 210, 214, 215, 216, 216n9, 219, 224, 224n30, 225, 317, 346, 354
anthropomorphic, anthropomorphism, 69n3, 282, 338, 339n20
Antiochus Epiphanes, 336
apocryphal, 190, 247, 280, 328
apostasy, 61, 68, 77, 84, 88, 105, 106, 128, 140, 142, 143, 154, 179, 189, 208, 247n15, 255n43, 264, 303, 304, 369, 370
Aram, Arameans, 116, 146, 158, 159, 178, 183, 183n13, 214, 236, 307
ark of the covenant, 67, 231, 232
army, 18, 20, 21, 22, 27, 36, 37, 40, 41, 74, 152, 158, 171, 173, 177, 178, 182, 184, 185, 195, 211, 215, 216, 224, 226, 227, 228, 229, 231, 232, 233, 234, 235, 236, 237, 238, 239, 240, 241, 243, 249, 250, 251, 254, 256, 257, 258, 259, 260, 261, 262, 263, 264, 266, 322, 369, 370, 376
Ashdod, 158, 182
Asherah, 116, 212, 212n5, 213, 263, 303, 305, 353
asherah pole, 213, 247
Assyria, Assyrians, 18, 53, 53n14, 116, 121, 146, 148, 149, 152, 153, 154, 155, 158, 159, 162, 162n20163, 164, 165, 166, 167, 168, 170, 171, 171, 172, 173, 174, 175, 176, 177, 178, 179, 180, 181, 182, 184, 189, 198, 215, 215n7, 217, 220, 221n21, 228n8, 236, 239, 251, 257, 263, 266, 303 304, 307
Astarte, 246n13, 301
asylum, 25, 26
Athaliah, 211, 211n3, 217
atheists, xv, 6, 11
atone, atonement, 51, 129, 130, 192, 350, 351, 356, 364, 365

atrocity, atrocities, 40, 55, 155, 159, 163, 164, 171, 175, 177, 178, 179, 195, 220, 241, 257
authority, 27, 76, 91, 157, 219, 239n49, 284, 306, 318, 319, 362, 368
authority of Scriptures, 4, 5
avenger of blood, 25, 26, 277

Baal, 108, 116, 194, 210, 212, 213, 214, 216, 218, 219, 220, 225, 246, 247, 263, 301, 302, 303, 305, 330, 353
Baal Melqart, 212
Baal Peor, 247, 247n15, 353
babies, 172, 174, 199
Babylon, Babylonians, 18, 20, 21, 25, 28, 31, 32, 52n13, 69, 74, 84, 94, 109, 116, 117, 146, 159, 160, 181, 184, 185, 185n17, 186, 187, 188, 189, 190, 191, 193, 194, 195, 196, 198, 236, 257, 262, 266, 301, 306, 308, 309, 310, 311, 316, 317, 320, 321, 322, 327, 330, 335, 336, 348, 354, 366, 376
Balaam, 236
Baruch, 78, 190
belief, 33n46, 46, 60, 108, 119, 135, 192, 301, 308, 316, 338
Bethel, 104, 223, 302
Bible, ix, x, xi, xv, 3, 4, 4n3, 5, 6, 7, 10, 11, 12, 19, 23, 24, 33, 38, 44, 48, 49, 52, 58, 59, 72, 74, 75, 78, 88, 89, 91, 103, 104, 106, 120, 152, 156, 160, 172, 181, 192, 215n7, 225, 227, 230, 236, 237, 242, 245, 250, 253, 257, 260, 275, 277, 278, 281, 290, 293, 295, 307, 350n1, 351, 369, 372, 373, 375
bigamy, 278, 279, 119
blessing, 28, 72, 168, 202, 255n44, 291, 296, 298, 307, 309, 313, 324, 329, 331, 334, 335, 337, 348n54
blessings and curses, 55, 121
blood, bloody, ix, x, 25, 26, 53, 66, 112, 126, 188, 194, 216, 216n9, 217, 219, 220, 221, 222, 224, 225,

INDEX OF SUBJECTS

243, 247, 248, 275, 276, 277, 284, 315, 350, 351, 358, 364, 377
bloodshed, 84, 129, 210, 215, 220n20, 222, 225
breach, 105, 107, 125, 126, 171, 364
brother, 28, 128, 129, 158, 257, 274, 275, 276, 277, 278, 286, 315, 327, 332, 333, 351, 369, 379
brutality, 20, 26, 31, 40, 85, 160, 162, 163, 176, 179, 210, 218, 219, 220, 221, 244, 257, 258, 265, 266, 324
bull, 85, 121, 162, 302
burnt offering, 85, 192, 194, 298, 326, 352

Cain, 28, 274, 275, 276, 277, 278, 279, 280, 286, 331, 332, 332n2, 351, 369, 372
Caleb, 138, 144, 145
calf, calves, 4361, 77, 85, 88, 116, 120, 121, 122, 128, 129, 130, 131, 132, 135, 137, 140, 142, 145, 155, 208, 223, 246, 293, 302, 303, 345, 352, 368, 369
Calvin, John, 41
Canaan , 6, 17, 18, 23, 30, 40, 41, 43, 48, 86, 121, 124, 137, 138, 139, 140, 142, 144, 226, 227, 228, 229, 230, 231, 233, 241, 242, 243, 244, 245, 246, 247, 248, 249, 250, 252, 254, 255, 255n43, 256, 257, 258, 259, 260, 261, 264, 265, 266, 287, 290, 291, 293, 329, 330, 369, 374
Canaanite army, 27, 261
Canaanite nations, 5, 260, 263
Canaanite population, 18, 260, 263, 301
Canaanite religion, 245, 245n12, 246, 247, 301, 305
Canaanites, xv, 4, 5, 6, 17, 18, 23, 27, 30, 40, 41, 57, 81, 85, 138, 140, 142, 160, 161, 213, 227, 228, 229, 231, 236, 241, 242, 243, 244, 235, 246, 247, 248, 250, 251, 254, 255, 255n43, 257, 258, 259, 260, 261, 262, 263, 264, 266, 287, 292, 301, 302

cannibal mothers, 12, 57, 180, 181, 184, 186, 187, 191, 195
cannibal, cannibalism, xv, 57, 171, 180, 181, 183, 184, 187, 187n22, 190, 193, 194
chaos, 30, 58, 285, 365, 366, 366n45, 367
chariots, 35, 53, 149, 153, 163, 190, 211, 217, 249, 250, 260, 261, 262, 264, 369
Chief Joseph, 376
child sacrifice, 81, 192, 193, 194, 195, 245, 246, 246n13, 305
children, xv, xvn10, xvi, 3, 5, 8, 11, 12, 14, 15, 18, 20, 22, 36, 43, 64, 65, 70, 71, 71, 85, 86, 91, 92, 93, 101, 102, 103, 104, 107, 109, 110, 111, 112, 116, 117, 118, 119, 120, 121, 122, 123, 126, 128, 131, 134, 136, 141, 142, 144, 145, 146, 153, 156, 160, 164, 167, 172, 173, 174, 174n12, 175, 176, 180, 181, 182, 183, 184, 185, 187, 188, 191, 192, 194, 195, 196, 198, 199, 202, 203, 205, 212, 221, 223, 240, 241, 242, 246, 248, 257, 260, 295, 310, 313, 352, 353, 373, 374, 376
Christ, see Jesus
Christian, Christians, xvi, 4, 5, 6, 7, 10, 11, 12, 19, 32, 33, 37, 40, 41, 42, 47n26, 48, 57, 73, 74, 92, 102, 151 183, 184, 195, 234, 265, 266, 282, 314, 316, 323, 338, 339, 340, 348, 360, 364, 368, 369, 374, 375, 377
Christianity, 32, 328, 337
Christology, 341
Christophany, 235
Chronicler, 22, 251, 335
church, ix, xi, xv, xvi, 23, 44, 45, 57, 57n2, 75n25, 314, 315, 339, 355n7, 357, 359, 365
city, cities, xv, 6, 18, 20, 21, 25, 29, 40, 53, 70, 80, 84, 96, 126, 150, 154, 155, 156, 163, 164, 165, 166, 167, 168, 170, 171, 172, 175, 177, 180, 180n2, 181, 182, 184, 185, 186, 187, 188, 191, 194, 195, 197,

(*city, cities continued*)
   197n1, 198, 199, 200, 201, 202, 204, 204n23, 205, 206, 207, 208, 212, 218, 220, 227, 232, 240, 241, 244, 253, 254n41, 256, 256n48, 257, 259, 261, 262, 263, 264, 266, 302, 308, 316, 333, 336, 354, 374, 377
colonialism, 266
command, commanded, xv, 3, 4, 5, 6, 7, 8, 9, 36, 37, 42, 43, 49, 51, 70, 71, 108, 110, 111, 112, 113, 114, 121, 122, 123, 129, 160, 161, 163, 164, 181, 193, 194, 210, 215, 216, 216n9, 217, 225, 226, 232, 239, 241, 243, 248, 258, 262, 263, 264, 271, 273, 283, 286, 287, 295, 320, 325, 327, 329, 333, 341, 351, 352, 360, 361, 363, 368, 374, 375
commandments, 3, 42, 58, 85, 102, 104, 107, 108, 109, 110, 111, 113, 114n3, 115, 116, 117, 118, 123, 223, 246, 247, 299, 301, 303, 350, 352, 253, 358, 359n23, 360, 361
commitment, 46, 89, 151, 218, 282, 297, 299, 311, 319, 371
Commander of the army, 22, 41, 211, 227, 231, 232, 233, 234, 235, 236, 237, 238, 239, 239n49, 240, 240n52, 241
community, 22, 23, 48, 61, 69, 70, 92, 109, 110, 111, 115, 116, 121, 129, 135, 137, 142, 143, 146, 157, 186, 207, 212, 215, 224, 286, 291, 300, 305, 307, 314, 315, 321, 327, 331, 336, 360, 361, 362, 363, 374, 376
compassion, compassionate, 14, 18, 30, 32, 39, 57, 59, 60, 61, 63, 68, 72, 79, 80, 86, 87, 88, 90, 92, 140, 152, 155, 162, 166, 167, 168, 169, 187, 273, 274, 308, 317, 320, 321, 351, 358, 373
congregation, 138, 300, 364
conquer, 5, 6, 17, 18, 20, 22, 41, 84, 158, 159, 162, 163, 167, 168, 173, 177, 179, 182, 228, 233, 241, 244, 248, 249, 250, 255, 256, 258, 259, 260, 261, 262, 301, 303, 306, 365, 366, 374
conquest, 5, 17, 18, 22, 23, 41, 53, 116, 146, 158, 161, 173, 178, 181, 226, 227, 229, 231, 233, 234, 237, 240, 241, 242, 243, 248, 249, 251, 252, 253, 254, 255, 258, 259, 260, 261, 263, 264, 265, 266, 369
corruption, 281
covenant, 24, 27, 30, 49, 50, 60, 61, 66, 67, 76, 77, 85, 89, 93, 104, 105, 106, 107, 108, 109, 110, 111, 112, 113, 114, 115
covenant, Abraham, 17, 60
covenant, Sinai, 60, 106, 107
creation, 20, 27, 32, 49, 50, 50n5, 51, 52, 54, 58, 60, 64, 67, 68, 76, 79, 81, 82, 157, 200, 208, 271, 274, 275, 278, 281, 282, 283, 284, 285, 286, 290, 291, 333, 340, 343, 360, 369, 376
creation, fallen, 13, 332
creation theology, 49
creational purpose, 20
Creator, 11, 27, 49, 50, 51, 54, 55, 58, 66, 76, 159, 160, 189, 271, 279, 284, 298, 333, 334, 343
crime, 26, 51, 111, 112, 152, 163, 164, 195, 198, 275, 276, 277, 330, 363
criminal, 111, 356, 367
cross, x, xv, xvi, 8, 9, 12, 13, 21, 23, 32, 35, 38, 45, 59, 82, 83, 84, 108, 161, 181, 200, 208, 226, 233, 234, 243, 244, 330, 349, 350, 356, 364, 365, 366, 367, 368, 370, 371, 374
crucified, 23, 39, 84, 356, 366
crucifixion, 9, 32, 35, 37, 356, 365, 366, 367
Cruciform interpretation, x, 23, 41, 183, 200, 226, 232
cruel, 23, 25, 84, 127, 156, 159, 162, 176, 220, 225, 315
cruelty, 29, 31, 57, 134, 158, 159, 162, 174, 177, 178, 179, 189, 226
cry, 60, 63, 70, 71, 72, 75, 84, 138, 139, 165, 186, 187, 202, 221n21, 275, 276, 277, 317, 318, 320, 341, 375

cry for help, 17, 64, 84, 188, 197, 201, 202
cult, cultic, 23, 106, 108, 150, 192, 212, 212n5, 248, 253, 302, 305
cultural, 32, 40, 48, 161, 184, 195, 209, 225, 229, 234, 244, 311
cultural context, 5, 8, 32, 40
culture, ix, 33, 47, 48, 109, 209, 246, 271, 279, 301, 302, 318, 336
curse, curses, 28, 55, 107, 121, 130, 184, 188, 189, 190, 219, 275, 283, 293, 306, 309, 335
Cyrus, 50n3, 52n13, 327, 354

Damascus, 158, 176, 214
Dan, 223, 260, 302
Daniel, 109
dark, darkness, 15, 47n26, 70, 149, 152, 155, 172, 198, 203, 307, 319, 324, 337, 346
David, 22, 42, 43, 44, 149, 236, 249, 264, 301, 302, 343, 367
Day of Atonement, 364
death, xvi, 8, 9, 19, 23, 24, 28, 36, 39, 42, 43, 45, 52, 55, 66, 70, 75, 79, 83, 85, 93, 95, 96, 111, 112, 114, 120, 129, 130, 134, 135, 137, 139, 141, 143, 145, 146, 148, 149, 155, 164, 167, 169, 173, 174, 182, 185, 187, 199, 203, 206, 208, 210, 211, 214, 217, 222, 227, 228, 233, 247, 254, 255, 265, 272, 273, 275, 284, 301, 302, 311, 323, 330, 331, 346, 350, 356, 358, 364, 365, 366, 367, 371, 375, 376, 377
debt, 212, 224
Decalogue, 85, 93, 107, 108, 109, 110, 113, 114n3, 117, 119, 123, 264
demon, demonic, 3, 57, 247, 331n2, 332n2
deportation, 158, 171, 173, 174, 184, 185, 301, 306, 311, 317
depravity, 31, 303, 353
descendants, 6, 7, 17, 30, 55, 102, 104124, 138, 139, 142, 202, 218, 220, 244, 244, 255n44, 257, 264, 279, 280, 283, 284, 286, 288, 290, 291, 292, 295, 298, 307, 329, 335, 346, 348
Deutero-Isaiah, 36, 315, 317, 318, 319, 320, 321, 322, 323, 325, 327, 335, 336, 345, 348, 354
Deuteronomic, 107, 108, 110, 111, 112, 114, 117, 118, 146, 193, 214
Deuteronomic History, 93, 107, 303, 311
Deuteronomist, 111, 115, 239
Deuteronomy, 105, 107, 108, 109, 110, 111, 113, 114, 115, 115n7, 117, 118, 190, 229, 255n43, 293, 294, 305
disciples, xv, xvi, 5, 8, 43, 102, 311, 315, 327, 341, 342, 346, 347, 347n47, 348, 348n54, 356, 357, 358, 359, 361, 362, 363, 364, 365, 366, 368, 370
disembowelment, 172, 175, 176, 178
disobedience, disobedient, 28, 51, 58, 59, 92, 95, 121, 188, 190, 296, 308, 309, 312, 315, 334, 357, 375
divine anger, 30, 81, 88, 114, 126, 198
divine anguish, 31
divine attributes, 109, 110, 140, 141
divine behavior, 5, 6, 7, 172
divine character, 85, 86, 86n5
divine humiliation, 67
divine imperium, 27
divine justice, xvi, 3, 29, 76, 92, 101, 111, 119, 123, 130, 141, 156, 157, 158, 160, 188, 190
divine lament, 65, 71
divine mercy, 78, 89, 111, 119, 202, 276, 277, 319
divine name, 4n3, 11n19, 36, 38, 152, 341, 356
divine nature, 9, 87, 355
divine pain, 76
divine pathos, 63, 64, 67, 68, 73, 74
divine plan, 41, 142, 150
divine punishment, 28, 93, 120, 132, 135, 144, 176
divine repentance, 79, 125
divine righteousness, 66
divine self-abasement, 66, 67
divine suffering, 61, 62, 64, 65, 79, 125

divine violence, xi, xvi, xvii, 3, 8,
   8n11, 9, 9n12, 10, 12, 13, 15, 16,
   19, 20, 25, 26, 27, 28, 32, 33, 35,
   37, 38, 39, 40, 41, 42, 43, 44, 45,
   46, 47, 48, 56, 57, 63, 65, 68, 81,
   83, 84, 85, 94, 101, 151, 265, 267,
   282, 369, 371, 372, 374, 375, 376
Divine Warrior, xvii, 22, 35, 37, 228,
   239, 250, 365, 366, 367, 370, 374,
   376, 377
drought, 26

earthquakes, 26, 366
Ecclesiastes, 133, 265
Eden, 13, 271, 288, 356
Edom, Edomites, 158, 159, 160, 252
Egypt, 7, 17, 18, 35, 36, 40, 41, 52n13,
   60, 64, 85, 106, 107, 121, 122,
   131, 138, 139, 141, 142, 143, 144,
   149, 149n2, 153, 168, 202, 227,
   228, 228n8, 230, 240, 244, 245,
   251, 261, 292, 293, 294, 296, 298,
   299, 301, 307, 318, 321, 322, 329,
   334, 336, 344, 352, 354, 366, 369
Egyptians, 18, 22, 36, 37, 64, 85, 140,
   142, 168, 230, 251, 294, 296, 300,
   352, 369
election, 242, 293, 294, 295, 297, 298,
   299, 300, 301, 315, 316
Elijah, 133, 210, 213, 214, 215, 217,
   218, 219, 220, 224
Elisha, 176, 210, 212, 214, 215, 216,
   219, 220, 223, 224, 225
Elohim, 236, 342
embodiment, 13, 38, 68, 73, 337, 338,
   339, 341, 345, 356
enemy, enemies, x, xv, xvi, 3, 4, 4, 6, 8,
   21, 22, 23, 27, 28, 37, 41, 43, 45,
   62, 67, 70, 71, 96, 135, 139, 145,
   150, 158, 159, 163, 168, 171, 172,
   174, 175, 176, 178, 179, 181, 186,
   188, 190, 193, 205, 229, 230, 236,
   237, 238, 241, 250, 253, 259, 260,
   261, 262, 265, 307, 315, 322, 326,
   362, 363, 365, 366, 367, 370, 377
Enoch, 279, 280, 332
Enosh, 332

Ephraim, 63, 65, 148, 177, 183, 260,
   330
equality, 355
eschatological, 149, 347, 365
eternal , xii, 75, 90, 134, 293, 338n15,
   339n21
Ethbaal, 211, 212
ethics, 43, 45, 46, 48, 84, 265, 266,
   359, 360, 361, 363, 364, 368, 370,
   375
Euphrates River, 17, 177, 290, 292
evil, 3, 6, 8, 12, 28, 29, 30, 31, 37, 46,
   50, 51, 52, 53, 54, 57, 59, 66, 74,
   76, 77, 78, 79, 81, 82, 88, 101,
   104, 108, 114, 116, 129, 133, 134,
   149, 150, 155, 165, 166, 167, 169,
   170, 172, 176, 200, 203, 205, 208,
   209, 247, 258, 263, 265, 266, 271,
   272, 273, 274, 280, 281, 283, 284,
   287, 301, 303, 306, 329, 330, 333,
   353, 355n7, 358, 363, 366, 367,
   369, 371, 372, 375, 376, 377
exegesis , 37, 86, 234
exile, 14, 15, 28, 52n13, 63, 70, 96,
   108, 109, 116, 117, 125, 146, 158,
   159, 167, 184, 185, 188, 303, 306,
   308, 309, 310, 311, 312, 315, 316,
   317, 318, 319, 320, 321, 322, 327,
   330, 335, 336, 348n54, 353, 354,
   377
Exodus, book of, xii, 36, 109, 229, 231
exodus (from Egypt), 18, 60, 143, 322,
   344, 354, 369
exodus, new, 321, 322, 325, 335, 346,
   354
extermination, xv, 85, 161, 252, 258
Ezekiel, 14, 31, 95, 103, 111, 117, 125,
   126, 134, 137, 146, 159n9, 169,
   184, 189, 197, 198, 201, 306, 321,
   341, 353, 366, 373
Ezra, 109, 336

failure, 59, 60, 109, 140, 188, 273, 301,
   309, 314, 315, 325, 327, 329, 330,
   353, 354, 355, 357
faith, 6, 44, 62, 105, 139, 195, 267,
   288, 302, 305, 307, 308, 310, 318,
   321, 338, 348

faithful, 16, 49, 51, 57, 61, 66, 90, 97, 104, 107, 108, 110, 111, 118, 126, 152, 157, 161, 218, 233, 244, 245, 291, 294, 301, 306, 311, 312, 319, 336, 341, 345, 361, 363
faithfulness, xvi, xvii, 12, 14, 65, 66, 86, 89, 90, 93, 94, 96, 97, 121, 127, 131, 132, 139, 141, 144, 145, 146, 152, 154, 168, 188, 203, 241, 245, 274, 291, 304, 311, 319, 322, 330, 335, 342, 361, 371, 373
family, families, 6, 25, 26, 55, 103, 108, 114, 120, 126, 127, 185, 210, 211, 215n7, 217, 218, 220, 222, 223, 225, 227, 233, 242, 258, 274, 279, 281, 283, 288, 290, 291, 294, 296, 324, 329, 331, 333, 334, 335, 343, 351
famine, 20, 71, 171, 180, 180n2, 182, 183, 184, 327
father, fathers, 11, 13, 14, 15, 38, 39, 46, 64, 92, 93, 102, 103, 104, 107, 108, 109, 110, 111, 112, 116, 117, 118, 120, 134, 141, 143, 144, 145, 146, 188, 198, 247, 248, 278, 287, 290, 291, 292, 294, 303, 330, 333, 335, 339, 339n21, 351n3, 352, 356, 362, 363, 368
fear, ix, 28, 37, 174, 178, 200, 230, 255n43, 261, 263, 277, 286, 292, 305, 320, 342, 348n54
fear of Yahweh, 87n7
fetus, 162, 173, 175, 178, 179, 181
fire, 19, 36, 62, 105, 125, 176, 183, 186, 191, 192, 193, 194, 198, 199, 201, 214, 236, 255, 261, 262
firstborn, 85, 192, 222, 228, 344
flesh, 26, 133, 183, 184, 190, 191, 193, 194, 248, 282, 283, 285, 330, 339, 342, 351, 356
flood, xv, 18, 28, 31, 37, 55, 76, 79, 96, 199, 250, 265, 274, 280, 281, 282, 283, 284, 285, 286, 287, 289, 290, 331, 333, 351
foreign nations, 157, 157n3, 158, 164
forgive, xvi, 6, 51, 57, 66, 78, 86, 91, 95, 96, 128, 130, 131, 132, 133, 140, 141, 142, 143, 144, 155, 161n19, 192, 195, 203, 204, 205, 206, 207, 208, 222, 278, 308, 314, 317, 319, 320, 321, 341, 351, 358, 364, 373
forgiveness, 87, 95, 123, 132, 133, 134, 142, 143, 207, 276, 319, 346, 375
forty, x, 40, 96, 113, 116, 137, 144, 145, 146, 164, 206, 218, 249, 245, 247
free will, 54, 55, 95, 274
freedom, God's, 60, 102
freedom, human, 9, 20, 51, 54, 55, 76, 274
fulfillment, 41, 42, 291, 292, 311, 314, 315, 346, 358
furnace, 321, 330
future, 20, 34, 78, 79, 80, 104, 119, 123, 125, 131, 135, 149, 168, 265, 283, 284, 288, 291, 292, 296, 311, 312, 317, 318, 321, 348n54, 359

Gaza, 158
generation, ix, 11, 14, 22, 65, 79, 82, 85, 86, 90, 91, 93, 94, 97, 101, 102 103, 104, 105, 108, 109, 110, 111, 115, 117, 118, 119, 120, 122, 123, 127, 128, 131, 132, 136, 141, 142, 143, 144, 145, 146, 152, 155, 168, 205, 220, 223, 244, 245, 247, 249, 257, 274, 279, 280, 293, 294, 301, 304, 332, 338, 352, 371, 373, 375
genocide, xv, 5, 57, 160, 161, 167, 168, 181, 226, 243, 249, 251, 252, 258, 259, 263
gentiles, 288, 304, 307, 308, 315, 324, 325, 328, 345, 346, 347, 348, 349, 363
Gibeon, Gibeonites, 148, 151, 222, 256, 261
Gideon, 24, 236, 247
Gilead, 158, 159, 176, 178, 216
Gilgal, 232, 238
glory, 67, 70, 86, 96, 131, 142, 143, 296, 325, 326, 342, 356, 362, 363, 368
God, crucified, x, 84, 356
God as Redeemer, 58, 320, 321

INDEX OF SUBJECTS

God of the New Testament, xi, xii, xvi, 5, 6, 7, 8, 44, 47, 339, 374
God of the Old Testament, ix, xi, xii, xv, xvi, 3, 4, 5, 6, 7, 8, 9, 10, 11, 12, 13, 15, 19, 21, 23, 29, 33, 35, 38, 41, 43, 45, 46, 47, 57, 58, 59, 60, 61, 63, 73, 75, 81, 82, 83, 92, 94, 121, 126, 156, 167, 181, 243, 278, 339, 365, 371, 373
God, acts of, xv, 20, 26, 27, 45, 172, 195, 305, 369
God, anger, 29, 30, 64, 75, 146, 196, 353, 375
God, anguish, 31, 62, 63, 69, 71, 140, 221
God, attributes of, 65, 76, 109, 110, 140, 141
God, changed mind, 21, 62, 78, 85, 86, 124, 128, 142, 165, 166, 167, 169, 205
God, character of, xii, xvi, 4, 5, 7, 8, 11, 13, 19, 30, 31, 43, 45, 50, 60, 65, 69, 71, 73, 83, 84, 85, 87, 88, 89, 90, 91, 93, 94, 95, 97, 101, 102, 121, 128, 136, 152, 167, 184, 208, 226, 234, 273, 278, 282, 358, 373
God, compassion of, 14, 18, 30, 39, 57, 59, 79, 80, 86, 87, 140, 152, 162, 166, 167, 168, 169, 273, 274, 308
God, grace of, 28, 55, 119, 124, 132, 167, 273, 274, 279, 280, 282, 286, 287, 295, 314
God, gracious, xvi, xvii, 7, 12, 13, 14, 17, 18, 29, 30, 31, 65, 79, 81, 85, 86, 88, 91, 92, 94, 96, 97, 105, 114, 126, 131, 132, 141, 146, 152, 154, 155, 162, 165, 168, 169, 192, 198, 203, 204, 208, 245, 246, 273, 274, 278, 288, 305, 330, 351, 371, 373
God, heart of, 31, 39, 63, 75, 76, 221, 233, 234, 282, 376
God, immorality of, 93, 204
God, jealous, 8, 62, 85, 93, 102, 105, 106, 107, 114, 115, 122, 223, 246, 305, 352
God, judgment of, ix, 30, 50, 66, 78, 80, 81, 92, 150, 151, 157, 197, 203, 219, 220, 282, 286, 306
God, kingdom of, 266, 347, 357, 360, 363, 367
God, knowledge of, 11, 84, 313
God, love of, 18, 60, 66, 67, 69, 90, 123, 156, 295, 307, 308, 311, 339
God, merciful, xvi, xvii, 7, 12, 13, 14, 17, 18, 29, 31, 39, 51, 57, 65, 79, 80, 81, 83, 85, 86, 87, 88, 91 92, 94, 96, 101, 114, 126, 131, 132, 140, 141, 146, 152, 154, 155, 156, 166, 167, 168, 169, 192, 196, 198, 203, 204, 208, 246, 274, 276, 278, 288, 330, 351, 371, 373
God, mercy of, 132, 169, 206, 207, 208, 276, 374
God, nature, xvi, 4, 20, 24, 30, 77, 87, 152, 278, 300, 374
God, nonviolent, xvi, 7, 23, 24, 37, 43, 44, 45, 47, 83, 160, 181
God, power, 60, 291
God, regret, 31, 63, 77, 329
God, relational, 9, 10, 55, 56, 339
God, repentance, xii, 75, 75n25, 77, 78, 124, 125, 165
God, savage, xv, 19, 156, 160
God, slow to anger, xvi, xvii, 12, 14, 18, 29, 65, 79, 86, 86n4, 88, 93, 94, 126, 131, 132, 141, 146, 152, 154, 168, 169, 192, 195, 198, 203, 246, 274, 278, 371, 373
God, sovereignty of, 27, 42, 50, 265, 271, 289, 294, 295
God, tears, xvii, 58, 66, 68, 69, 70, 71, 72, 73, 74, 75, 353
God, violence, 44, 65, 127, 189, 225
God, weeping, 58, 68, 69, 70, 72, 73, 74, 80
God, what kind of, xi, xiii, 14, 65, 83, 86, 87, 96, 97, 160, 203, 206
God, will of, 43, 56, 79, 81, 168, 196, 207, 278, 300, 313, 362, 372, 374
God's actions, 7, 96, 102, 135
God's heart, 39, 62, 63, 66, 68, 71, 75, 76, 77, 79, 80, 96, 200, 221, 233, 234, 245, 282, 329, 330, 339, 376

gods, foreign, 194, 338
golden calf, 61, 77, 85, 88, 120, 121, 122, 128, 129, 130, 132, 135, 137, 140, 142, 145, 155, 208, 246, 345, 352, 369
Goliath, 22, 249
Gomer, 221, 222
gospel, 7, 13, 38, 39, 44, 46, 48, 288, 315, 316, 325, 339, 341, 342, 343, 347
Greek, Greeks, 57, 58, 69, 76, 159, 253, 266, 336, 341, 343, 356
guilty, 11, 14, 29, 30, 33, 65, 66, 81, 86, 91, 92, 93, 95, 101, 109, 110, 114, 116, 118, 125, 128, 129, 130, 131, 132, 133, 134, 135, 136, 137, 141, 144, 145, 146, 164, 166, 168, 192, 195, 196, 203, 204, 207, 208, 371, 373, 375

Habakkuk, 21, 84
hand of Yahweh, 145, 260
Haran, 118
hate, 93, 102, 103, 104, 105, 107, 108, 109, 110, 118, 120, 123, 201, 248, 363
Hazael, 176, 214, 216, 220
Hazor, 40, 178, 254n41, 260, 261, 262
heart, 16, 28, 31, 39, 55, 62, 66, 71, 75, 76, 79, 80, 81, 95, 114, 115, 161, 174, 202, 208, 217, 221, 223, 227, 244, 258, 281, 283, 307, 308, 312, 313, 320, 321, 329, 342, 358, 360, 363, 376
heart, new, 52, 358
Hebrew, 26, 29, 36, 47, 52, 69, 72, 87, 88, 89, 90, 91, 103, 104, 105, 111, 117, 118, 132, 143, 154, 165, 202, 204, 208, 222, 229, 234, 237, 238, 247, 248, 249, 250, 251, 253, 257, 272, 281, 292, 293, 297, 312, 313, 323, 331n2, 332, 347, 350, 350n1, 364, 365
Hebrew Bible, 5, 10, 16, 26, 27, 51, 73n12, 76, 78, 88, 89, 93, 113, 113n2, 157, 197n1, 289, 323, 338n, 341, 360, 366n45, 369
Hellenism, 336

ḥērem, 161, 243, 253, 254, 254n41, 255, 255n43, 258, 262
hermeneutics, x, 243,
ḥesed, 16, 61, 89, 90, 126, 141, 143, 294, 319, 375
Hezekiah, 148, 304
high priest, 212, 364
Hiroshima, 40
holiness, 105, 134, 300, 370
holy, 129, 232, 239, 248, 252, 254, 284, 293, 296, 297, 298, 300, 315, 326, 338, 346, 365, 368, 372
holy nation, 296, 297, 298, 300, 307, 329, 334, 352
Holy One, 41, 62, 77, 149, 153, 320
holy place, 219, 276, 354
Holy Spirit, 4n3, 330, 339n21, 346, 368
holy war, 37, 149, 239, 242, 252, 253
hope, xvii, 28, 29, 64, 79, 96, 97, 164, 165, 168, 169, 191, 209, 233, 292, 305, 311, 315, 316, 317, 318, 319, 320, 321, 326, 329, 335, 343, 348, 354, 357, 360, 365
Horeb, 214
hornets, 41, 227, 228, 229, 230, 231
horses, 53, 149, 153, 217, 222, 224, 249, 250, 261, 262
Hosea, 63, 162, 171, 172, 173, 174, 177, 178, 219, 220, 220n20, 221, 222, 224, 225, 247n15, 302, 372
human sacrifice, 192, 193

idol, 85, 102, 106, 107, 114, 115n7, 116, 122, 223, 246, 247, 255, 303, 304, 306, 352, 353
idolatry, 46n23, 81, 85, 106, 107, 109, 110, 113, 114, 114n2, 115, 115n7, 116, 117, 120, 121, 122, 123, 124, 125, 129, 223, 247, 254, 290, 312
image of God, 11, 27, 54, 280, 284, 373
immutability, 10
impassibility, 57, 57n2, 58, 73, 74
incarnation, 338, 339, 340
indifference, 81
inherit, inheritance, 17, 18, 30, 139, 140, 184, 243, 255, 291, 292, 306

iniquity, xvi, 11, 14, 30, 51, 52, 53, 65, 66, 71, 85, 86, 91, 93, 95, 101, 102, 103, 107, 109, 117, 118, 122, 125, 126, 128, 129, 131, 132, 135, 136, 141, 145, 146, 152, 155, 168, 188, 189, 191, 192, 195, 203, 204, 207, 208, 223, 257, 258, 264, 274, 278, 313, 314, 319, 332, 336, 351, 352, 358, 371, 373
injustice, 58, 65, 80, 82, 114n2, 117, 157, 157n3, 164, 186, 189, 202, 203, 204, 208, 312
innocent, 9, 15, 19, 22, 25, 66, 109, 166, 119, 127, 145, 146, 156, 188, 189, 194, 196, 198, 199, 203, 204, 207, 208, 241, 247, 248, 277, 364
insects, 228, 228n8, 229, 230
inspiration, 5
intercession, 137, 146, 203, 207
intercessor, 123, 142, 169
intercessory prayer, 87
intergenerational punishment, 11, 13, 91, 92, 93, 101, 102, 103, 105, 106, 118, 119, 120, 121, 127, 132, 145, 146, 223
intergenerational punishment statement, 11, 14, 15, 91, 93, 101, 107, 110, 117, 119, 128, 136, 143
interpretation, 4, 33, 37, 41, 44, 45, 47, 48, 57, 72, 75, 110, 117, 118, 165, 200, 203, 208, 220, 221, 225, 226, 234, 258, 273, 280, 304, 323, 332, 342, 357, 361, 362, 371
Isaac, 6, 60, 201, 214, 245, 255n44, 290
Isaiah, 41, 63, 133, 148, 149, 150, 152, 153, 154, 155, 159, 162, 168, 178, 179, 183, 201. 203, 228n8, 276, 277, 304
Ithamar, 118

Jacob, 50n3, 60, 105, 245, 255n44, 290, 297, 315, 321, 324, 326, 336, 337, 338, 345, 363
Jehoiachin, 184, 185, 317, 323
Jehoiakim, 78, 184
Jehu, 210, 211, 214, 215, 215n7, 216, 216n9, 217, 218, 218n14, 219, 220, 220n20, 221, 221n21, 222, 223, 224, 224n30, 225
Jeremiah, 25, 28, 31, 63, 66, 68, 69, 70, 71, 72, 73, 75, 78, 93, 111, 156, 184, 188, 191, 193, 194, 198, 207, 284, 293, 305, 306, 311, 312, 314, 315, 316, 323, 357, 358, 366
Jericho, 227, 231, 232, 233, 234, 237, 238, 239, 240, 241, 253, 254, 256, 262
Jeroboam I, 42, 43, 223, 302
Jeroboam II, 167
Jerusalem, 20, 25, 31, 42, 51, 66, 70, 94, 96, 103, 109, 117, 125, 149, 150, 151, 152, 154, 155, 159, 180, 184, 185, 186, 187, 188, 189, 190, 191, 193, 194, 195, 198, 204, 207, 217, 301, 302, 303, 304, 305, 306, 309, 310, 316, 317, 318, 319, 320, 321, 325, 326, 327, 335, 336, 346, 348, 353, 357, 376
Jesus Christ, ix, x, xi, xv, xvi, 4, 5, 6, 7, 8, 9, 12, 13, 19, 21, 23, 24, 32, 33n46, 37, 38, 39, 39n8, 43, 44, 45, 46, 47, 48, 55, 58, 59, 75, 81, 82, 83, 84, 102, 134, 135, 136, 137, 143, 151, 161, 181, 196, 235, 265, 311, 315, 316, 323, 324, 325, 330, 337, 337n11, 339, 340, 341, 342, 343, 341, 343, 344, 345, 346, 347, 348, 349, 350, 355, 356, 357, 358, 359, 360, 361, 362, 363, 364, 365, 366, 367, 368, 370, 371, 373, 374, 377
Jewish, ix, 10, 38, 39, 103, 134, 136, 137, 258, 314, 316, 328, 329, 336, 338, 339, 347, 348, 357
Jews, ix, 38, 247, 258, 325, 327, 336, 348, 349, 357
Jezebel, 211, 211n3, 212, 213, 214, 216, 217, 218, 222, 223, 224
Jezreel, 210, 217, 218, 219, 220, 220n20, 221, 221n21, 222, 223, 224, 225
Job, 54, 323
Joel, 39, 159
John, 13, 339, 342

INDEX OF SUBJECTS 415

Jonah, 84, 126, 132, 145, 161, 162, 163, 164, 165, 166, 167, 168, 169, 308, 309
Joram, 217
Jordan River, 138, 220, 231, 344
Josephus, 177, 178, 328
Joshua, 4, 5, 6, 18, 27, 41, 44, 84, 138, 144, 145, 226, 227, 230, 231, 232, 234, 235, 236, 237, 238, 240, 240n52, 241, 243, 247, 249, 250, 256, 258, 259, 260, 261, 262, 263, 264, 266, 290, 301
Josiah, 115n7, 117, 303, 304, 395, 323
Judah, 21, 25, 26, 28, 31, 42, 65, 68, 69, 70, 75, 78, 79, 84, 94, 95, 96, 112, 115n7, 117, 125, 146, 147, 148, 149, 149n2, 150, 153, 154, 155, 157n3, 159, 162, 163, 173, 178, 180, 181, 183, 184, 185, 187, 188, 189, 190, 191, 192, 193, 194, 195, 210, 211, 217, 218, 222, 224, 225, 301, 302, 303, 304, 305, 306, 310, 311, 312, 314, 315, 316, 317, 318, 319, 327, 330, 335, 353, 356, 357, 376
Judaism, 325, 327, 328, 329, 338, 340
judge, 5, 8, 33, 49, 52, 53, 76, 80, 95, 101, 156, 195, 197, 204, 205, 265, 373, 375
judgment, ix, xvii, 3, 5, 7, 19, 20, 21, 25, 26, 28, 29, 30, 31, 32, 34, 42, 50, 52, 52n13, 53, 55, 66, 67, 70, 71, 72, 73, 77, 78, 79, 80, 81, 87, 9295, 96, 104, 108, 109, 110, 119, 122, 125, 130, 135, 130, 140, 143, 144, 145, 146, 148, 149, 150, 151, 152, 153, 154, 155, 157, 158, 160, 163, 164, 166, 167, 168, 169, 177, 179, 183, 187, 188, 189, 190, 191, 192, 193, 194, 197, 198, 199, 200, 201, 203, 204, 205, 206, 207, 208, 209, 211, 219, 220, 221, 223, 245, 251, 264, 265, 276, 281, 282, 284, 286, 287, 289, 290, 304. 306, 307, 329, 335, 362, 375, 376

king, 27, 40, 42, 49, 52n13, 53n14, 77, 78, 108, 109, 112, 120, 121, 133, 146, 148, 150, 158, 159, 160, 162, 163, 165, 173, 176, 177, 178, 179, 181, 184, 185, 187, 189, 190, 191, 192, 193, 194, 210, 211, 212, 214, 215, 216, 217, 218, 219, 221, 224, 229, 230, 231, 240, 241, 251, 252, 256, 257n52, 259, 261, 262, 264, 266, 280, 294, 302, 304, 306, 317, 323, 327, 343, 354, 367, 374, 376
kingdom of God , 266, 347, 357, 360, 363, 367
kingdom of priests, 297, 298, 299, 300, 307, 329

Lamech, 278, 279, 280, 351, 351n3, 369
Lamentation, 34, 94n22, 96n24, 180, 185, 186, 187, 188, 316, 317, 318, 320
lamentation, 69, 70, 179, 318
land of Canaan, 6, 17, 18, 23, 30, 40, 41, 43, 48, 86, 121, 124, 137, 139, 142, 144, 226, 227, 228, 229, 231, 233, 242, 244, 245, 248, 249, 250, 252, 254, 255, 256, 257, 259, 290, 291, 293, 329, 374
law, 25, 49, 50, 58, 77, 108, 111, 112, 113, 123, 132, 157, 158, 160, 190, 201, 208, 223, 255n43, 264, 295, 299, 300, 304, 307, 313, 324, 341, 352, 353, 358, 359, 360, 361, 362, 363
Levites, 128, 129, 326, 327
Lex taliones, 362
Lo-ammi, 222
Lord of Hosts, 36, 69, 93, 154, 168, 183, 194, 313, 327, 343
Lo-ruhamah, 221, 222
Lot, 197n1, 201, 204, 244
love, xvii, 12, 14, 16, 18, 60, 65, 66, 79, 82, 86, 86n4, 88, 89, 90, 93, 94, 94n22, 96, 97, 102, 118, 119n14, 121, 123, 126, 131, 132, 141, 142, 146, 152, 154, 155, 168, 169, 203, 223, 246, 274, 330, 335, 371, 373, 374
loyalty, 62, 89, 104, 110, 111, 176, 218, 245, 312

Luther, Martin, 150

Malachi, 105, 299, 307
man of war, 22, 23, 36
Marcion, Marcionites, ix, xi, 7, 46, 47, 81, 205, 374
marriage, 211, 212, 221, 255n43, 278, 279, 280, 281, 302
mask, 12, 126, 150
Menahem, 177, 178
Mennonites, 46
Mesha, 192
Messiah, 317, 325, 332, 343, 348
Micah, 192
Michael, 234, 235
Midian, Midianites, 40, 236
miracles, 38, 291, 340
mission, 28, 50n3, 53n14, 106, 179, 217, 220, 244, 289, 290, 294, 296, 297, 298, 299, 300, 301, 305, 307, 308, 309, 312, 314, 315, 322, 323, 324, 325, 326, 327, 328, 329, 330, 331, 332, 334, 334n7, 335, 336, 337, 344, 345, 346, 347, 348, 352, 354, 355n7, 360, 361, 363, 368
missionary, 212, 233, 309, 327, 328, 329, 347, 362
Moab, Moabites, 40, 80, 160, 192, 302, 353
monarchy, 42, 254, 260, 278, 301, 302, 310, 353, 367, 367n47
monogamy, 278, 279
monotheism, 17
moral, x, 6, 19, 23, 38, 45, 51, 59, 76, 86, 91, 123, 134, 157, 157n3, 172180, 188, 208, 219, 243, 248, 249, 279, 300, 375
moral law, 49, 50, 160, 208
moral order, 18, 27, 50, 51, 95, 157, 199, 208, 280, 369
Moses, xvi, 4, 5, 8, 13, 14, 17, 21, 44, 61, 62, 65, 77, 78, 83, 84, 85, 86, 87, 88, 89, 90, 91, 92, 94, 97, 101, 109, 110, 112, 121, 122, 123, 124, 125, 126, 128, 129, 130, 131, 132, 136, 137, 138, 139, 140, 141, 142, 143, 144, 145, 146, 152, 153, 154, 155, 161, 162, 169, 190, 208, 227, 228, 231, 235, 236, 243, 244, 246, 251, 256, 257, 258, 261, 264, 274, 293, 296, 300, 304, 308, 313, 323, 342, 344, 352, 358, 359, 361, 364, 369, 370
Mount Carmel, 213
Mount Sinai, xvi, 8, 1, 14, 18, 60, 61, 77, 84, 85, 86, 91, 94, 101, 106, 107, 109, 119, 11, 128, 129, 136, 138, 140, 152, 153, 154, 169, 214, 236, 250, 293, 294, 295, 296, 297, 298, 300, 301, 306, 307, 312, 320, 334, 342, 352, 358, 359, 361, 364
mourning, 69, 70, 80, 165, 187, 336

Nagasaki, 40
Nahum, 93, 163, 168, 307
Nebuchadnezzar, 160, 184, 185, 185n17, 189, 191, 195, 306, 306n13
Nehemiah, 108, 336
Nephilim, 138, 281
New Covenant, 311, 312, 313, 314, 315, 316, 325, 357, 357n15, 358, 359, 364
New creation, 283, 343
Noah, 68, 79, 274, 280, 281, 282, 283, 284, 285, 286, 287, 289, 293, 329, 332, 333, 351, 369
nonviolence, nonviolent, xv, xvi, 7, 8, 19, 23, 24, 33, 33n46, 38, 41, 43, 44, 45, 48, 102, 194, 229, 362n31
nonviolent conquest, 23, 41, 226, 227, 228, 229, 231
nonviolent God, xvi, 7, 23, 24, 37, 43, 44, 45, 47, 81, 83, 160, 181
Northern Kingdom, 42, 108, 116, 117, 147, 148, 149, 162, 163, 167, 168, 171, 174, 177, 179, 198, 210 182, 212, 213, 215, 224, 225, 302, 303

obedience, 33, 42, 119, 121, 123, 221, 299, 300, 305, 307, 313, 352, 363
Og, 40, 230
Omri, Omrides, 133, 210, 211, 211n3, 212, 214, 215, 215n7, 219, 220, 221, 221n21, 222, 223, 224, 225

oppression, 81, 85, 198, 201, 202, 224, 281, 318, 334, 375
oracles, xv, 18, 32, 74, 104, 148, 152, 157, 157n3, 158, 163, 164, 173, 176, 177, 179, 216, 217, 224, 276, 293, 311, 312, 314
outcry, 80, 164, 202, 303

pacifism, 21, 45, 265, 371
pacifist, 33, 41, 44, 45, 46, 48, 370, 371, 372
pain, 31, 58, 59, 61, 62, 63, 64, 65, 66, 68, 75, 76, 77, 79, 94, 96, 170, 173, 180, 185, 186, 187, 221, 229, 257, 282, 308, 326, 329, 374, 376
parable, xv, 221, 356, 357
paradox, 72, 101, 130, 203
Passover, 232, 358, 364
pathos, 63, 64, 67, 68, 71, 73, 74, 75
Paul, xvi, 38, 39, 47, 101, 134, 135, 137, 255, 265, 288, 307, 315, 325, 339, 343, 344, 348, 349, 350, 355, 356, 359, 375, 376, 377
peace, ix, 4, 16, 17, 19, 21, 23, 24, 31, 38, 40, 42, 45, 63, 71, 134, 151, 163, 217, 256, 261, 265, 266, 298, 307, 308, 348, 349, 350, 370, 374, 376
Persia, 52n13, 266, 336, 354
Pharaoh, 22, 35, 36, 153, 228, 251, 261, 294, 334, 366, 369, 370
Pharisees, 361
Philistines, 22, 40, 67, 138, 158, 211, 244, 250
plague, 26, 85, 131, 135, 139, 144, 210, 228, 229, 251
plowshares, 24, 196, 368
polygamy, 278, 279, 280
poor, 58, 74, 81, 185, 188, 198, 201, 212, 216, 224, 249, 327, 353, 375
postexilic, 108, 109, 167, 247, 315, 336
prayer, 21, 58, 72, 85, 86, 87, 94, 109, 124, 125, 126, 130, 142, 143, 144, 145, 146, 155, 169, 203, 204, 205, 206, 207, 213, 214, 275, 276, 277, 298, 309, 316, 326
pregnant women, 159, 162, 171, 172, 173, 175, 176, 177, 178

priest, 37, 108, 109, 118, 149, 188, 194, 212, 218, 219, 231, 240, 254, 289, 297, 298, 299, 300, 304, 307, 313, 326, 327, 329, 334, 337, 340, 348, 355n7, 364
Primeval History, 271, 286, 287, 288, 289, 333, 369n49
prisoners, 158, 159, 162, 164, 171, 174
promise, promises, 6, 7, 12, 17, 22, 24, 28, 29, 30, 66, 92, 116, 122, 124, 126, 138, 139, 140, 144, 146, 150, 158, 159, 160, 202, 220, 223, 227, 228, 229, 230, 242, 244, 245, 246, 248, 250, 255, 255n44, 264, 283, 285, 287, 287n23, 289, 290, 291, 292, 293, 294, 296, 297, 299, 311, 312, 314, 315, 316, 319, 322, 325, 331, 332, 334, 335, 343, 345, 346, 347, 348n54, 351, 353, 354, 357, 358, 359
promised land, 22, 142, 227, 228, 292, 296, 315, 353
prophecy, 314, 325, 335, 358
prophet, 14, 21, 24, 36, 39, 52n13, 63, 64, 66, 68, 69, 70, 71, 72, 73, 74, 79, 84, 93, 126, 133, 134, 148, 149, 150, 154, 156, 157, 159, 163, 164, 167, 168, 171, 176, 184, 185, 187, 188, 189, 191, 205, 205n28, 210, 212, 213, 214, 215, 216, 219, 221, 224, 225, 284, 298, 301, 302, 303, 304, 306, 317, 318, 319, 320, 321, 323, 334, 338, 340, 348n54, 353, 357, 360, 361, 375
providence, 46, 289
pruning hooks, 24, 196, 368
psalmist, 36, 49, 51, 67, 94, 125, 126, 133, 150, 157, 203, 205, 247, 308, 309, 351
punish, xvii, 21, 27, 28, 55, 66, 69, 79, 80, 85, 92, 93, 102, 103, 104, 197, 120, 126, 129, 130, 150, 153, 154, 162, 167, 169, 173, 176, 177, 179, 182, 189, 191, 193, 195, 205, 207, 220n20, 221, 222, 236, 306, 351, 362, 367, 370, 375
punishment, 3, 11, 13, 14, 15, 19, 20, 26, 28, 31, 51, 62, 66, 69, 77, 78,

(punishment continued)
85, 91, 92, 93, 101, 102, 103, 104, 105, 106, 107, 108, 109, 110, 111, 112, 115, 116, 117, 118, 119, 120, 121, 122, 123, 125, 127, 128, 130, 131, 132, 133, 134, 135, 136, 137, 139, 142, 143, 144, 145, 146, 157, 158, 159, 163, 165, 167, 176, 177, 186, 188, 189, 205, 209, 223, 273, 275, 276, 277, 284, 319, 331n2

punishment, delayed, 132, 133, 134

radical discontinuity, 4
Rahab, 227, 231, 233
Rahab (chaos monster), 366, 367
rainbow, 285, 290
Ras Shamra, 245
rebellion, xvi, 14, 21, 28, 31, 33, 34, 51, 52, 56, 58, 59, 61, 62, 64, 65, 67, 68, 74, 75, 77, 91, 126, 129, 130, 138, 139, 141, 144, 153, 154, 176, 188, 189, 191, 192, 198, 210, 249, 271, 282, 286, 287, 290, 296, 305, 306, 329, 331, 334, 335, 343, 351, 357, 364, 370, 375
reconcile, 4, 6, 41, 123, 156, 274, 287, 288, 309, 329, 333, 349, 350, 376
reconciliation, xvi, 32, 38, 47, 83, 91, 130, 287, 288, 289, 290, 291, 297, 309, 312, 316n5, 318, 324, 326, 329, 330, 331, 332, 333, 334, 343, 344, 345, 348, 350, 351, 352, 354, 355, 356, 357, 364, 367, 368, 370, 371, 376, 377
reconciling, xvi, 3, 13, 17, 32, 38, 39, 47, 53, 55, 83, 196, 271, 287, 289, 290, 297, 310, 329, 330, 331, 333, 335, 343, 348, 350, 356, 365, 370
redemption, 7, 24, 50, 53, 271, 290, 293, 296, 297, 298, 322, 331, 334, 336, 337, 371
Rehoboam, 42
relational theology, 9, 10
Remnant, 42, 104, 282, 301, 311, 315, 323
Renewed Israel, 316, 316n5, 330, 331, 343, 347, 348, 348n54, 357, 368, 370

repent, 52, 53, 65, 66, 70, 72, 77, 78, 79, 95, 96, 124, 126, 134, 137, 154, 161n19, 168, 169, 188, 191, 192, 193, 194, 195, 223, 306, 353, 373
repentance, xii, 51, 75, 75n25, 78, 79, 95, 123, 124, 125, 126, 130, 133, 134, 135, 146, 154, 164, 165, 167, 168, 169, 304, 305, 308, 346, 353, 376
repentant, 7
Restored Israel, 309, 310, 315, 325, 326, 327, 329, 335, 336, 345
Retribution, 33n46, 93, 103, 108, 117, 118, 158, 220, 277
Revelation, 13, 83, 370
revelation, ix, xvi, 4, 8, 12, 13, 14, 18, 37, 46, 60, 72, 75, 76, 83, 84, 85, 86, 89, 91, 92, 97, 101, 109, 110, 128, 136, 154, 161, 169, 181, 184, 213, 227, 233, 234, 237, 239, 246, 290, 325, 342, 246, 365, 371, 374
righteous, 5, 21, 30, 53, 80, 96, 97, 129, 132, 145, 160, 188, 197, 198, 199, 200, 203, 204, 205, 206, 207, 208, 276, 277, 283, 361, 363, 371, 376
righteous God, 30, 123, 160, 167, 375
righteousness, 5, 16, 53, 66, 88, 97, 123, 129, 156, 157, 158, 188, 202, 204, 205, 244, 257, 276, 326, 354, 361

Sabbath, 326
sacrifice, 10, 59, 81, 122, 144, 192, 193, 194, 195, 213, 245, 246, 247, 254, 276, 293, 298, 305, 326, 340, 350, 353, 364, 365
salvation, 3, 16, 20, 32, 36, 42, 43, 52n13, 71, 79, 125, 150, 154, 158, 168, 169, 206, 290, 295, 298, 300, 315, 322, 323, 324, 325, 329, 330, 334, 336, 343, 345, 346, 354, 363, 374
Samaria, 42, 149, 162, 163, 171, 172, 173, 174, 177, 178, 179, 183, 184, 198, 212, 213, 218, 224, 302, 346, 357

INDEX OF SUBJECTS

Samuel, 42, 278, 367
Saul, 42, 77, 222, 250
savior, 17, 38, 58, 134, 296
Second Commandment, 85, 96, 102, 105, 106, 107, 108, 112, 114, 115, 122, 123, 129, 223
self-abasement, 66, 67
Sennacherib, 148
Septuagint, 69, 74, 103, 193, 237, 272, 341, 356
Sermon on the Mount, x, xv, 48, 359, 360, 360n25, 361, 362n31
serpent, 272, 366
servant, 24, 42, 50n3, 53, 129, 164, 165, 178, 184, 185, 189, 191, 195, 204, 205, 214, 215, 216, 216n9, 232, 239, 248, 284, 298, 306, 306n13, 323, 324, 326, 334, 336, 337, 339, 344, 346, 348n54, 353, 354, 355, 357, 374, 375
Servant, 315, 322, 323, 324, 325, 326, 327, 336, 343, 344, 345, 346, 347, 355, 361, 363
Servant Songs, 315, 322, 323, 347
Seth, 279, 280, 351
Shema, 338, 338n15, 360
Sheol, 149
shepherd, 71, 144, 274, 354
Shiloh, 67,
siege, 66, 96, 117, 171, 174, 177, 178, 180, 180n2, 181, 182, 183, 184, 185, 186, 190, 191, 193, 195, 257
siege warfare, 171, 177, 181, 182
Sihon, 40, 229, 230, 231, 256
sin, sins, xvi, 8, 11, 14, 15, 18, 26, 28, 29, 30, 31, 33, 34, 38, 45, 50, 51, 52, 52n13, 53, 58, 61, 62, 65, 66, 77, 78, 79, 81, 86, 87, 91, 92, 93, 95, 96, 102, 103, 104, 109, 110, 111, 112, 113, 114, 115, 116, 117, 120, 123, 124, 125, 126, 128, 129, 130, 131, 132, 133, 134, 135, 136, 137, 141, 144, 145, 146, 147, 152, 153, 155, 162, 164, 167, 168, 176, 188, 189, 190, 191, 192, 195, 197, 198, 199, 201, 202, 203, 204, 208, 217, 221, 221n21, 223, 227, 233, 257, 258, 265, 271, 274, 275, 276, 278, 279, 280, 282, 286, 288, 289, 310, 314, 315, 317, 319, 331, 331n2, 336, 341, 343, 346, 347, 350, 350n1, 351, 355n7, 364, 365, 371, 373, 375
sinner, sinner, ix, xv, 4, 7, 8, 51, 52, 95, 114, 118, 132, 133, 135, 137, 143, 167, 201, 206, 271, 276, 277
slaves, slavery, 36, 64, 107, 138, 158, 159, 159n9, 173, 187, 202, 224, 245, 249, 256, 264, 292, 294, 295, 299, 300, 321, 323, 334, 355, 356, 369
Sodom, xv, 18, 20, 21, 38, 80, 81, 84, 85, 96, 152, 155, 164, 197, 197n1, 198, 199, 200, 201, 202, 203, 204, 205, 206, 207, 208, 265, 337, 369
soldiers, 36, 53, 172, 173, 174, 178, 179, 219, 229, 231, 240, 241, 248, 249, 250, 251, 262, 374
Solomon, 42, 51, 114, 204, 210, 247, 264, 302, 303, 305
Son of God, 134, 365
Song of the Vineyard, 64, 356, 357
sons of God, 280, 281
Southern Kingdom, 93, 108, 117, 148, 149, 198, 210, 303
sovereignty, 27, 42, 50, 265, 271, 289, 294, 295
spear, 22, 24, 53, 196, 250, 368
spies, 136, 137, 138, 141, 145, 146, 231
suffering, xvii, 3, 10, 17, 19, 21, 31, 34, 37, 57, 58, 59, 60, 61, 62, 63, 64, 65, 66, 67, 73, 75, 77, 79, 80, 85, 94, 96, 109, 116, 117, 125, 173, 180, 181, 185, 186, 187, 202, 208, 223, 230, 257, 308, 316, 317, 322, 323, 325, 326, 374
Suffering Servant, 59
sword, 22, 24, 25, 27, 29, 40, 53, 71, 95, 109, 128, 129, 138, 150, 154, 159, 162, 166, 172, 176, 177, 182, 196, 214, 215, 222, 224, 226, 228, 229, 231, 232, 234, 236, 237, 240, 241, 249, 250, 256, 262, 326, 368, 377
synagogue, 325
syncretism, 247, 301, 303, 304

Syro-Ephraimite War, 171, 173

tabernacle, 48, 338
Table of Nations, 285, 286
Tammuz, 353
tears, xvii, 58, 66, 68, 69, 70, 71, 72, 73, 74, 75, 188, 316, 317, 318, 353
temple, 26, 51, 66, 78, 150, 184, 188, 193, 194, 204, 219, 245, 265, 302, 304, 305, 306, 310, 311, 316, 324, 326, 327, 328, 329, 338, 345, 353, 354
temptation, 46, 273, 344
Ten Commandments, 113, 145, 359, 362
Terah, 118, 287, 290
Terebinth, 24
Tetragrammaton, 341
Textual God, 23, 24
Theophany, 238, 239, 240, 296, 337, 366
Tiglath-pileser I, 175, 176
Tiglath-pileser III, 162, 171, 173, 177, 178, 181
Topheth, 191, 192, 193, 194, 195, 305
Torah, 81, 201, 313, 338, 358, 361
Tower of Babel, 286, 287, 290, 329
transgenerational, 110, 111, 117, 118
treasured possession, 294, 296, 297, 334, 352
tribe, 114, 137, 177, 183, 255, 302, 347, 364, 376
Tyre, 158, 159, 211, 212, 216

Ugarit, 245, 246, 263
unfaithfulness, 65, 69, 75, 116, 139, 198, 353
universal, 31, 42, 81, 157, 158, 202, 208, 236, 274, 289, 297, 324, 345, 346, 369
universalism, 49, 348n54

vengeance, 3, 24, 26, 27, 28, 33n46, 101, 102, 266, 276, 277, 279, 351, 371, 377
victim, victims, 25, 157n3, 159, 159n, 160, 163, 174, 182, 196, 281
victory, 21, 22, 28, 36, 37, 174, 176, 192, 213, 214, 229, 237, 252, 253, 265, 366

vindictive, 12, 19, 125, 126
vision, ix, x, 64, 239n49, 240n52, 298, 315, 321, 327, 336, 353

war, ix, x, 5, 6, 17, 18, 19, 20, 21, 22, 23, 25, 26, 29, 36, 37, 40, 45, 53, 115n7, 116, 138, 146, 149, 158, 159, 162, 164, 171, 173, 174, 175, 176, 177, 178, 180, 181, 182, 183, 184, 191, 194, 196, 216, 220, 222, 225, 229, 232, 233, 234, 236, 237, 239, 240, 241, 242, 243, 248, 249, 250, 252, 253, 255, 256, 257, 258, 259, 260, 261, 262, 263, 264, 265, 266, 281, 322, 368
warfare, x, 18, 20, 171, 174, 176, 177, 181, 182, 227, 228, 229, 230, 239, 243, 249, 252, 254, 257, 263, 265
warrior, x, xvi, xvii, 5, 13, 16, 21, 22, 36, 37, 40, 63, 71, 228, 233, 237, 239, 240, 241, 243, 249, 251, 281, 285, 322, 365, 366, 367, 370, 374
Warrior God, 4, 8, 9, 12, 13, 16, 17, 19, 21, 22, 33, 35, 36, 37, 38, 47, 53, 82, 83, 126, 253, 266, 267, 322, 330, 350, 365, 366, 370, 377
weapons, 18, 36, 190, 198, 229, 230, 236, 249, 261, 262
weep, weeping, 58, 68, 69, 70, 71, 72, 73, 74, 80, 151, 159, 176, 186, 316, 318, 353, 358
wicked, 5, 19, 21, 43, 66, 95, 96, 116, 132, 134, 145, 155, 161n19, 163, 166n27, 167, 169, 195, 197, 198, 199, 200, 201, 203, 204, 205, 206, 208, 258, 276, 356, 357
wickedness, 14, 15, 18, 25, 28, 31, 45, 52, 53, 55, 78, 79, 80, 95, 129, 163, 164, 167, 168, 191, 202, 203, 205, 206, 207, 208, 244, 245, 257, 265, 266, 281, 306, 308, 329333, 351, 369, 373, 375, 376
widow, 66, 114n, 186, 187,l 188, 305, 316, 320, 375
wilderness, 69, 75, 76, 77, 115, 116, 138, 142, 143, 144, 145, 146, 155, 214, 247, 247n15, 249, 344, 345, 347, 351, 352

wisdom, x, 11, 114, 162, 307
Wisdom of Solomon, 114, 247
witness, 23, 24, 161, 180, 215, 233, 289, 298, 309, 325, 326, 337, 346, 353
woman, women, xv, xvi, 3, 5, 6, 8, 9, 10, 18, 20, 22, 36, 43, 51, 53, 69, 70, 71, 87, 114, 116, 121, 146, 156, 159, 160, 162, 164, 167, 171, 172, 173, 174, 175, 176, 177, 178, 179, 189, 181, 182, 183, 184, 185, 187, 191, 196, 198, 205, 227, 231, 233, 241, 248, 257, 257n52, 260, 271, 272, 273, 278, 279, 280, 281, 284, 291, 302, 310, 332, 334, 338, 353, 374
womb, 87, 162, 172, 173, 174, 176, 178, 181, 190, 284, 338
worship, 22, 43, 48, 62, 77, 78, 85, 88, 94, 102, 105, 106, 107, 113, 114, 114n, 115, 116, 119, 121, 122, 128 129, 130, 132, 135, 137, 145, 168, 208, 210, 212, 213, 216, 218, 219, 220, 223, 225, 232, 246, 247, 248, 263, 279, 290, 298, 299, 300, 301, 302, 303, 304, 305, 326, 330, 332, 335, 338, 345, 348, 351, 352, 353, 354, 357, 360, 375
wrath, divine, 50, 123, 124, 130, 139, 374
wrath, God of, xvi, 30, 50n, 61, 102, 119n14, 124, 151, 205, 206, 266, 335, 376, 377

Yahweh War, 252

Zechariah, 346
Zedekiah, 185, 191, 376
Zephaniah, 36, 164, 303, 304
Zion, 150, 186, 188, 309, 315, 316, 317, 318, 319, 321, 326

Index of Scriptures

GENESIS

1–11	55, 271, 274, 289, 331, 332, 333
1–2	278
1:26–28	54
1:28	286, 333
1:31	287, 369
2:5	275
2:16–17	28, 51, 271
2:17	272
2:24	279
3:3	272
3:4–5	272
3:6	272
3:8	332
3:9	332
3:13	332
3:15	332
3:21	275
3:22	54, 272, 273
4	274
4:2	274
4:6–7	351
4:6	332
4:7	331n, 332n
4:8	333
4:10–12	275
4:12	28
4:13–14	28, 275
4:13	331n
4:15	276
4:19–24	278
4:23	351, 369
4:26	248, 279, 332, 351
5:24	280, 332
6–8	31
6–7	17
6:1–4	280, 280n, 281
6:2	281
6:3	192
6:4	281, 369n
6:5–6	79
6:5–7	290
6:5	28, 81, 265, 281, 285, 329, 369
6:6	31, 62, 63, 68, 76, 77, 282, 329, 376
6:7	282
6:11–13	26
6:11	26, 79, 265, 281, 369, 372
6:13	26
8:21	28, 55, 283, 285
8:22	285
9:1	283, 333
9:5	275
9:6	280, 284
9:9–10	283
9:9	283
9:11	283, 287
9:12–13	285
9:15	282
9:16	285
9:19	286
9:21	248
10	285
10:32	287, 351
11:1–9	333
11:2	333
11:4	286, 290, 333

(Genesis continued)

11:5	286
11:7–8	351
11:7	286, 332
11:8	333
11:9	290, 333
11:10–26	287
11:27–32	287
11:28	118, 12, 334
12:1–3	28, 291, 297
12:1–2	255n
12:1	242, 291
12:2	140, 291
12:3	287, 291, 324, 329, 331, 334, 352
12:6	242, 287
13:13	201
13:15	255n
14:1	40
14:8	197n
14:13	257
14:15	40
15:1	292
15:3	292
15:4	292
15:7	292
15:8	292
15:16	30, 255n, 257, 258
15:18–21	17
15:18–20	255n
15:18	292
17:7	293
17:8	255n
18:1–2	59, 337
18:17–19	202
18:17	199
18:18	287n
18:20–21	203
18:20	164, 202, 265
18:21	80, 200
18:22	337
18:23–33	84
18:23	200, 204
18:24	205
18:25	21, 52, 198, 204, 205
18:26	21, 205
18:32	206
19:4–5	201
19:4	202
19:13	164
19:15	207
19:23	197n
19:24	201
20:7	205n
22:17	255n
22:18	287n, 307
26:3–4	255n
26:4	287n
28:13–14	255n
28:14	287n
32:23–33	337
32:28	338
32:30	338
35:12	255n

EXODUS

2:24–25	60
3:3–4	236
3:7–8	18, 64
3:7	60
3:9	202
3:14	13, 342
3:15	338
4:14	146
4:22	344
5:1–2	369
7:4	240
9:3	139, 251
9:15	251
9:23–24	251
12:41	240
13:17	138
14:6–7	370
14:7	36
14:17	261
14:22	344
15:1–21	22
15:1–3	52n
15:3	16, 17, 35, 36, 370
16:4	345
17:16	22
19:3	359n
19:4–6	296, 352
19:5–6	290, 298
19:5	49, 294, 334

19:6	329, 334	32:27–28	129
19:8	66, 294, 299, 308	32:28	96, 134
20	105	32:29	129
20:1–17	107	32:30	130
20:3	299, 352	32:32	130
20:4–6	102, 103, 123, 223	32:34	95, 104, 114, 115, 116, 117, 129, 130, 135, 137, 195
20:4–5	85, 106, 299, 352		
20:5–6	86n	33—34	342
20:5	14, 15, 91, 92, 93, 103, 105, 107, 109, 110, 111, 115, 117, 118, 119n, 122, 145, 146, 246, 352	33:5	131
		33:13	131
		33:14	131
		33:17–19	131
20:6	119n	33:19	86, 86n, 274
20:8–11	107	34	105, 141
20:12	107	34:6–16	247
20:13	362	34:6–7	xii, xvi, 14, 15, 29, 65, 84, 86, 91, 92, 94, 105, 107, 114, 132, 140, 141, 141n, 152, 162, 168, 169, 192, 203, 274, 358, 371, 373
20:17	107		
21:13	25		
21:14	25		
21:23–25	362		
22:20	254	34:6	12, 16, 18, 29, 31, 57, 79, 82, 86n, 88n, 153, 198, 246, 330, 342, 351
22:22–24	375		
22:27	86n		
23:20	227	34:7	11, 14, 30, 51, 65, 82, 91, 95, 101, 107, 108, 110, 111, 116, 128, 136, 137, 142, 143, 145, 146, 164, 195, 203, 204, 207, 208, 371, 373, 375
23:22	260		
23:23	251		
23:28	227, 228, 229		
23:31	250		
23:33	247		
24:1–11	364	34:10	154
24:8	358	34:14	62, 105, 115, 137
31:18	313		
32—34	77, 88, 121		

LEVITICUS

32	61, 121, 142
32:1–14	84
32:1–6	246, 345
32:4	121, 131
32:6	96, 352
32:7–10	122
32:8	85
32:9–14	146
32:10	21, 61, 77, 89, 122, 123, 139, 142, 274, 352
32:11	122, 124, 124
32:12	21
32:14	21, 62, 78, 85, 86, 96, 124
32:19	122
32:26–28	128

4:2	350
4:6	350
10:17	364
17:11	351
18:24–25	227
18:24	250
19:1	300
19:17	363
19:18	360, 361, 363
21:7	248n
21:14	248n
22:13	8n
24:19–20	362
26:25	27

(Leviticus continued)

26:27–29	191
26:29	181
27:21	254
27:29	254

NUMBERS

3:4	118
11:10	88
11:33	139
13—14	137
13:1	137
13:26	138
13:28–33	138
14	136, 137, 139, 141, 143
14:2–5	138
14:9	138
14:10–11	138
14:11	139, 140, 144
14:12	139, 140, 142, 144
14:13–14	140
14:17–19	141
14:18–19	15, 91, 92, 107
14:18	86n, 88n, 105, 108, 110, 141, 144, 146
14:19	141
14:20–23	142, 143
14:22–24	144
14:22	66, 77, 115, 345, 352
14:23	144
14:27	139
14:28–30	116
14:30–32	144
14:33	116, 144
14:37	144
21:14	36, 252
21:21–23	40
21:22–25	231
21:33–34	40
21:33–35	231
22:23	236
25:1–3	353
25:3	247
25:4	88
30:10	248n

DEUTERONOMY

1:39	142
2:9	244
2:10	244
2:14–16	249
2:20–21	244
2:21	250
2:22	244
2:24–28	256
2:30	256
4:7	62
4:13	113
4:20	321
4:23	114
4:24	105
4:25	59
4:31	86n
4:40	295
5:6–21	107
5:6–10	107
5:8–10	114
5:9–10	10, 15, 86n, 91, 92, 107
5:9	93, 107, 109, 111
5:10	118
5:12–15	107
5:16	107
5:17	362
5:21	107
6:4–5	360
6:10–15	305
6:16	66, 143
6:19	250, 251
6:20–23	305
7:1	250, 263n
7:2	5, 254
7:5	255
7:6–9	299
7:6	294
7:7–8	245, 294
7:9–10	86n, 108, 110, 118
7:9	104, 108, 111, 245
7:10	118, 245
7:11	111
7:16	254
7:20	228, 229
7:23	250
8:19	114, 115
8:20	250

9:3	250	5:13–14	236, 237
9:4–7	241	5:13	238
9:4	257	5:14	235, 236, 237, 238, 238n, 240
9:5	245	5:15	239
9:11	113	6	253
9:14	139	6:1–27	240
11:31	250	6:1–5	239
12:5	354	6:2–5	239, 239n, 240, 241
12:29	250	6:2	241, 262, 374
12:31	305	6:3	249
13:1–18	214	6:17	227, 233, 256
13:1–5	214	6:19	254
16:12	300	6:21	254n
16:21	213	8:18	249
18:10	193, 305	8:25	256
18:12	257	8:26	254n
19:12	26	9—10	261
19:21	362	9:15	256
20:1	262	10:11	151
20:3–4	37	10:20	259
20:16–17	243, 255	10:28	254n
20:17	264	10:40–43	258
21:8	364	10:40	258
23:18	305	11:1–3	261
24:16	111, 112	11:4	250, 261
25:6	120	11:6	261
25:18	40	11:11	254n, 262
26:19	367	11:16–23	258
27—28	121	11:16	258
28:37	309	11:18	259
28:47–57	188	11:19	256
28:49–53	190	11:20	258
28:64–65	308	13:1	260
29:19	114	15:63	260
29:23	197n	16:10	260
30:19	55	17:8	177
32:35	24, 101	17:12	260
32:39	265	17:16	260
		21:43–45	258
		21:43–44	260
		22:17	247n
		23:4–5	260

JOSHUA

1—12	259
5:8	232
5:13—6:27	238, 239
5:10–12	232
5:13—6:5	239
5:13–15	41, 227, 231, 232, 233, 234, 239, 239n, 241n

24:2	290, 333
24:12	228, 229, 230, 231
24:19	105

JUDGES

1:27–35	260
2:10–13	301
2:10–11	247
2:10	301
2:11	330
2:12	30, 59
2:18	62
2:20	30
3:1	249
3:5–7	263
4:15	250
4:2–3	264
5:20–21	250
6:11–18	236
6:24	24
6:25	247
19:3	320

1 SAMUEL

1:3	36, 37
4:1–11	67
8:5	367
8:7	367
12:14–15	42
13:13–14	42
13:22	250
15:3	6
15:11	77
17:6	249
17:45	22, 240
17:47	22
17:51	22
18:17	252
25:28	22
29:4	350n

2 SAMUEL

5:20	151
8:18	249
18:18	120
21:1	222
23:8–39	249
23:3	17
24:6–7	264

1 KINGS

2:31	222
8:32	204
8:46	51, 129
9:20–21	264
11:5	302
11:7	302
11:38	43
12:28–30	223
16:8–22	211
16:9	211
16:11–12	211
16:12–13	211
16:16	211
16:21–22	211
16:24	212
16:30	133
16:31	211
16:32	213
16:33	213
17:1	213
18	213
18:4	213
18:19	212
18:20–40	213
18:36	214
18:37	214
18:39	213, 336
18:40	214
19:3	214
19:8	214
19:9	214
19:10	214
19:11	214
19:15–17	215
19:16	215
21:1	222
21:2	222
21:17–19	215
21:22	30
21:23	218
21:27–29	133
21:28–29	215

2 KINGS

3:26–27	192

4:1–7	224	17:14	375
4:1	212	17:15–18	303
4:38–42	224	17:19	117
6:5	224	18:11–12	189
6:24–33	183	19:35	251
6:24–31	180	21:6	192
7:9	307	21:15	30
8:11–12	176	22:16	304
8:12	159n 174n	23:7	305
8:18	211, 211n	23:8	305
8:26	211n	23:10	305
9—10	219, 220n	24:8	184
9:1–13	216	24:11	184
9:1–10	216	24:12–16	185
9:1–3	216	25:1–2	185
9:2	215	25:3	180
9:6	216	25:5–7	185
9:11–13	216	25:27–30	317
9:14	215		
9:17–24	217		
9:20	215		

1 CHRONICLES

3:16	184
21:16	236

9:25–26	215		
9:27–29	217		
9:27	217		
9:36–37	218		
9:42–43	224		
10:11	218		

2 CHRONICLES

10:12–14	218	8:46	129
10:13	212	21:6	211n
10:16	218	22:2	211n
10:28	216, 219	29:24	350n
10:30	220	30:9	86n, 94
10:31	223	32:21	251
10:32	220	36:15	335
14:5–6	112		
14:6	112		
14:25	167		

EZRA

15:12	223	1:1–11	327
15:16	159, 175n, 177	2:64–65	327
15:29	178	9:70	109
16:3	192		
16:6	252		
16:7	178		

NEHEMIAH

16:9	158	1:5	86n
17:6	163	5:2–4	327
17:9–18	116	7:73—9:37	336
17:13–14	353	9:17	86n, 88n
17:13	375	9:29	58

INDEX OF SCRIPTURES

(Nehemiah continued)

9:31–32	86n
9:33–34	109

JOB

9:8	342, 365

PSALMS

7:12	95
11:5	25
18:7	366
23:4	317
23:6	95
24:8	36
27:1	324
27:9	374
29:11	16, 24
30	150
30:5	30
33:4	90
33:5	49, 157
35:27	24
37:28	204
46:3	366
46:10	49
47:8	49
50:6	49
59:5	36
65:3	351
78:38	30, 86n, 126, 351
78:40–41	77
78:59	374
78:59–61	67
79:5	62
85:8	16
85:10	16
86:5	86n
86:15	86n, 88n
86:17	317
87:4	366
94:1	27
96:13	203, 205
99:4	101
99:8	86n, 133
102:27	17
103:6	204
103:8	86n, 88n, 106, 247
106:7	66
106:21	17
106:23	125
106:28	247n
108:21	341
109:21	341
111:4	86n
112:4	87n
116:5	86n
135:4	297
137	308
137:1–2	309
137:3	309
137:4	309
137:8–9	309
137:9	174n
143:2	51
145:8	86n, 88n

PROVERBS

15:8	276
15:30	307
21:31	253
25:25	307

ECCLESIASTES

3:8	265
7:20	129
8:11	133

ISAIAH

1:2–9	64
1:15	276
2:1–4	25
2:2–3	326
2:3	336
2:4	368
5:1–7	64, 356
5:4	64, 357
6:9	320
7:4	178
7:7	178
7:14	62

7:15	56	42:6	315, 324
7:18	228n	42:8	4, 338
9:2	324, 337	42:13–14	63
9:19–21	183	42:13	36
10:5	53n, 162, 179	43:10	298, 346
10:7	179	43:12	346
10:12	179	43:16–17	322
10:13	162	44:1–5	348n
11:6–9	368	44:1–2	323
11:9	368	44:2	348n
13:16	174n	44:5	348n
14:24	41	44:8	346
15:5	80	44:21	323
16:9	80	44:28	354
16:11	80	45:1–8	52n
17:13	367	45:4	50n, 323
19:18–25	251	45:5	338
19:20	298	45:22–23	326
19:23	168	45:22	354
19:24–25	168	45:23	356
20:1	158	46:10	355
23:1	159	46:11	355
23:8–9	159	47:1–15	52n
	28, 148	47:6	32
28:1–6	148	48:9	30, 86n, 133
28:7–22	149	48:10	321, 330
28:21	80, 148, 150, 151, 152, 154, 155, 203	48:20	323, 336
		49:1–6	323, 324
30:1–3	153	49:1	324
30:7	367	49:2–3	324
30:15–16	153	49:3	323, 324, 336, 343, 354
30:18	153, 154, 155	49:4–6	324
31:1	149, 153	49:5	345, 363
31:5–6	154	49:6	315, 323, 325, 329, 330, 336, 343, 345, 346, 354, 362, 363
31:8	154		
40—55	344, 347, 355		
40:1–11	318	49:13	317
40:1–2	317, 319, 336	49:14	321
40:1	318, 319	49:26	58
40:2	311, 321	50:4–9	323
40:3	318	50:6	326
40:6–8	319	51:3	317
40:6	319	51:5	354
40:9	319	51:9–10	366
40:27	321	51:12–13	201
41:8	290n, 323, 324, 336	51:12	200
42:1–4	323	51:13	200
42:1	324, 344	52:9	317

(Isaiah continued)		9:1–3	73n, 74
52:13—53:12	323, 325	9:1–2	330, 353
53:3	325	9:1	72
53:7	326	9:2–9	73
53:9	326	9:3–6	73
53:10	24, 326	9:5	192
54:4–8	320	9:10	69
54:7–8	32, 86n	9:17–18	69
54:7	30, 320	9:20–22	70
54:8	321	9:24	157
54:10	24	11:14	72
55:4	298	11:23	104
55:8	135	13:16	70
56:6–7	298, 326	13:17	70
56:6	348n	14:7	71
59:2	52	14:8	71
60:3	336	14:9	71
61:8	101	14:11–12	71
63:7	86n	14:13	71
63:9	63	14:17	71, 72
65:16	90	16:5	72
66:4	56	17:9	358
66:18–21	327	17:10	80, 95
		18:7–8	169
		19:1–5	194
JEREMIAH		19:9	181, 193, 194
		19:15	194
1:5	284	21:5–6	377
2:5	64	22:24	184
4:27	28	24:9	335
5:1	207	25:4	306
5:3	95	25:6–7	xvii
5:15–17	29	25:8–11	306
5:18	29	25:9	189, 306n
6:10	53	25:11–12	312
6:23	25	25:12	189
7:5–7	188	25:14	80
7:5–6	66	26:3	79
7:18	30, 198	27:1–6	159
7:31	193	27:6	306n
7:32	193	30:8–9	343
8:5	65, 353	30:24	82
8:12	104	31:3	66
8:18—9:3	73	31:20	69
8:18–21	73	31:31–34	311, 357
8:18—9:1	73	31:31	312, 357n
8:19	30, 353	31:32	66, 312
8:22—9:2	73, 73n	31:33	320, 325
8:23	92n		

31:34	313, 314	11:19	358
32:18	86n, 93	11:23	354
34:18	293	12:19	25
36:1–7	78	16:42	30
36:3	78	16:49–50	201
36:7	78	18	14, 103
36:31	191	18:1–4	117
38:17–18	191	18:2	14
42:10	31	18:4	126, 134, 137, 143, 144, 146, 197
43:10	306n	18:20	52, 129, 137
48:38	80	18:21	95
50:25	198	18:23	43, 95, 167, 206
51:34	366	18:24	137
		18:29–32	52
		18:30	95, 373
		18:32	43, 66, 167, 206, 330

LAMENTATIONS

1:1	187	22:30–31	125
1:2	316, 318, 318n	23:24	190, 191
1:5–6	188	23:25	189, 195
1:9	318n	24:14	95
1:12	187	27:13	159n
1:16	316	29:3	366
1:17	316, 318, 318n	33:11	155, 169
1:21	318n	36:26–27	358
2:6	26	37:11	321
2:11–12	186	37:21	341
2:13	316, 317, 318n	44:22	248n
2:20	180, 187		
3:18–25	96		
3:22–23	94	## DANIEL	
3:22	374		
4:4	180	8:11	234, 235
4:9	180	9:4	86n
4:10	187	9:16	109
4:11	186	10:13	234
4:13	188	10:21	234
		12:1	234

EZEKIEL

HOSEA

3:20	129	1:4–5	221
5:13	62	1:4	219, 220n, 225
7:8–11	25	1:6–7	222
7:23–24	25	1:7	224
8:17–18	353	1:8–9	222
8:17	25	1:9	320
9:3	354	2:23	63
10:18–19	354	4:6	313, 358
11:16	354		

(Hosea continued)

6:4	65
8:5–6	302
9:10	247n
10:14	174n
11:1–9	59
11:1	344
11:7	330
11:8–9	146
11:8	63, 330
11:9	62
13:16	162, 172, 173, 174n, 175n, 177, 181
14:1	223

JOEL

2:13	59, 86n, 88n, 146
3:5	39
3:6	159
3:9–10	368

AMOS

1—2	157n, 159n
1:3	50, 158
1:5	158
1:6	158
1:8	158
1:9	158
1:13	159, 175n, 177
2:1	160
3:2	55, 294
3:7	205
3:14	104
9:7	244

JONAH

1:2	163
3	162n, 169
3:4	164
3:5–9	165
3:7–10	155
3:10	77, 165, 167
4:1	165, 166
4:2	86n, 88n, 126, 162, 166, 166n, 169, 308
4:11	167

MICAH

6:3	65
6:6–7	192
7:18	51 86n

NAHUM

1:1	163
1:2–3	86n
1:3	93, 168
1:5	366
1:6	366
1:15	163, 307
2:13	163
3:1–3	53
3:1	126, 163
3:10	174n

HABAKKUK

1:1–6	21
1:2	84
1:6	25, 84, 201
1:7	25
1:9	200, 201
1:13	129
2:8	84
2:14	368

ZEPHANIAH

2:1	304
2:13	164
3:3–4	304
3:17	36

ZECHARIAH

1:14	31
1:15	31, 189, 195

MALACHI

1:2–3	105
2:6–8	313
2:7	299
2:17	327
3:6	17
3:14	327

New Testament

MATTHEW

1—2	343
1:1	343
1:21	347
2:15	344
3:13	344
3:17	344
4:4	345
4:7	345
4:9	345
4:10	345
5:1–2	359
5:1	359
5:3–16	359
5:17—7:12	359
5:13–16	363
5:14	346, 362, 363
5:16	362
5:17—6:34	359
5:17–18	360
5:18	361
5:19	361
5:20	361
5:21–22	362
5:27–28	362
5:31–32	362
5:33–34	362
5:38–39	362
5:43–44	362, 363
5:43	363
5:44	265
7:1–12	359
7:12	360
7:13–23	359
7:21	341
7:22	341
7:24–27	359
10:2–4	347n
10:5–6	363
10:5–7	347
10:23	370
12:8	344
12:35	266
14:22–33	365
14:27	365
14:33	365
16:24	364
21:33–44	356
21:39	357
21:43	357
22:37–40	360
23:23	361
24:6	265, 368
25:11	341
27:54	365
27:51	366
28:18–20	368

MARK

2:5	341
3:16–19	347n
4:35–41	341
6:45–52	342
6:49	342
6:50	342
10:18	341

LUKE

1:72–73	346
1:79	346
2:30–32	325
2:32	346
4:12	143
6:14–16	347n
6:46	341
22:19	358
22:20	315, 357n, 358, 364
24:47	346

JOHN

1:1	13, 38, 339
1:3	356
1:14–18	342
1:14	13, 38, 39n, 330, 337, 339, 342
1:17	342
1:18	339
1:29	364
3:16–18	134
3:16	365
8:12	363
8:24	135, 136
8:58	13, 38, 136
9:2	102
9:3	102
9:5	346
10:30–33	38
10:30	13
15:13	61
20:28	38

ACTS

1:8	346, 357
1:13	347n
6:7	348
13:16–19	255

ROMANS

1:18	376
2:5	376
6:23	8, 114, 134, 135, 137, 167
9:6	348
10:13	39
11:15	348
11:17–18	348
11:17	316
11:25–29	315
12:18	265
12:20	266
12:19–21	377
12:19	24, 33n, 102, 266
12:21	266
13	375
13:1–4	375
13:4	284

GALATIANS

3:8	288
6:2	359
6:16	348

EPHESIANS

2:13–16	349
2:15	349
4:5–6	47

PHILIPPIANS

	2, 341
2:5–11	355
2:5–7	339
2:7	330
2:9–11	356

1 TIMOTHY

3:16	356

TITUS

2:13	38

HEBREWS

4:15	59
5:8	59
7:22	359
8:6–13	364
8:6	359
8:8	357n
8:13	357n
9:15	357n, 358n, 359
12:24	357n
13:8	47

1 PETER

3:19–20	280

2 PETER

1:1	38, 134
2:4–9	209
2:4–6	280
3:8	272
3:9	8, 273, 376

1 JOHN

4:16	374

REVELATION

	2—3, 359
	13, 370
21:1	368

Apocrypha

WISDOM OF SOLOMON

12:3–7	248
14:27	114

BARUCH

2:1–3	190

www.ingramcontent.com/pod-product-compliance
Lightning Source LLC
Chambersburg PA
CBHW071223290426
44108CB00013B/1272